A Journey to Oneness

Also by Rasha

Books:
Oneness

The Calling

Audio:
Oneness

The Meditations of Oneness:
A Journey to the Heart of the Divine Lover

All of the above may be ordered by visiting:
www.onenesswebsite.com

A Journey to
Oneness

A Chronicle of Spiritual Emergence

Rasha

Earthstar
PRESS

Earthstar Press
369 Montezuma Ave. #321
Santa Fe, New Mexico 87501
USA

www.onenesswebsite.com
Contact: onenessmailbox@gmail.com

ISBN-10: 0-9659003-4-7
ISBN-13: 978-0-9659003-4-8

Cover image by Rassouli
Book & cover design by S. Janarthanan

First Printing: 2013
Printed in the United States of America

To Oneness,
the Divine Presence that unites us all
as human expressions of Infinite possibility,
with profound gratitude
for this extraordinary journey
of Self discovery.

Contents

Introduction

Surrender

————

T he break of dawn hit me between the eyes as I gazed out over a panorama
of fluttering coconut palms and a gathering of brilliantly plumed
peacocks lounging on a neighboring thatched roof. Overnight, a brilliant
South Indian sky had shed its dusty veil, and emerged in a shimmering
dressing gown of blue—adding a subtle touch of symbolism to the scene.
The moment was a foundation, a fresh slate destined to hold the unborn
imagery of life—infinite details that hovered, poised and ready to emerge
on the canvas of the ethers. The vivid sense of *Nowness* it delivered struck
a chord within me.

The moment seemed to pause almost tangibly, like the proverbial space
between the breaths in which, it is said, the gateway to the Divine can be found.
It was an uncanny mirror of the shift simultaneously taking place within *me*—
a moment of Now in which I felt all sense of past, present, and future converge
into one focal point of inevitability. Who is to say what constitutes a life-changing
instant, in a reality that is actually timeless? Tentatively, I glanced around the
room, surveying the eclectic assortment of props that sat poised and ready to take
up the threads of my own ongoing personal drama.

Like pieces of a puzzle predestined to fit together, all the components
of the previous day's scene were still right there, exactly where I'd left
them. My beloved laptop sat patiently waiting, with my rough-hewn life's
work squirreled away in its microchips. A foot-high stack of thick, spiral-
bound volumes of conversations with Oneness, the Divine Presence I'd been
communing with since 1998—and many refer to as "God"—sat beside it.
It was a priceless mélange of Divine words of wisdom interlaced with my
own chronicle of joy and pain. The neatly typed notebooks were, by then,
completely scribbled up with a rainbow of marker-pen notations blanketing
the margins. The edges were lined with rows of pastel Post-It Notes that
looked like strings of Tibetan prayer flags.

My mindset of trepidation to tackle that mountain of writings and
transform it into something somebody might want to read someday was also

there, as usual, awaiting my consideration. The bottom line was, I'd been going through the motions of preparing to transform those chronicles into a book because it seemed to be expected of me at some unfathomable higher level—while at the same time, deep inside, I was dragging my heels all the way.

The sheer volume of the Divine teachings I had managed to document over the course of nearly a decade was completely overwhelming—as were the constant predictions about the role I was supposedly destined to play in presenting it all to the world. For, in addition to the published 400-page first volume of spiritual understandings entitled appropriately, *Oneness*, upwards of 3,000 pages of personal Divine guidance had also been transcribed.

In these writings, interwoven with the details of my own spiritual emergence, lay the entire conceptual foundation for the esoteric understandings that had transformed life as I knew it beyond all recognition. Was I really expected to go on record and share all that? Was I actually destined to reveal to the world the gut-wrenching details of an odyssey that documented the dematerialization of my very identity? Why would anybody care? Moreover, who would believe it? Nonetheless, apparently that's what Oneness had in mind. I was horrified. From the onset, I'd presumed that those teachings were for my eyes only.

The prospect of dragging those archives out of the closet and airing them in public was daunting. The scope of the material I'd covered was so vast and so mind-boggling I simply hadn't known where to start. Day after day, I'd conversed with Oneness in exquisite, exalted states of being, and documented word for word the profound guidance I'd received. And then, I'd turn the page. The next day, I'd do it again. There, laid out in year after year of writings, was the essence of the eternal mystery that had continued to confound me—the very answers humankind has searched for since time immemorial. Volumes of it.

All the while, I'd continued to dance the same dance within my own consciousness. For years, I'd tackled the challenges of transformation—and brushed up against the same unmistakable touch of Grace—oblivious to the realization that I had already found what I presumed I was still looking for. During much of that time, it was as though somewhere, stranded in the labyrinths of consciousness, there had been a fugitive aspect of self, poised and ready to jump back in, who simply couldn't believe what had actually happened.

Now, in that life-altering moment, I seemed to be viewing the entire quandary from a respectful distance, with a newfound air of quiet detachment. Slowly, I surveyed the symbolic props scattered before me. The entire montage of imagery held all the components of pure potentiality. The possibilities were all right there, ready and waiting. As I gazed at the scene, I had the indescribable feeling of something almost palpably shifting gears within me. There was an unmistakable sense of *Now* that pervaded it.

In the space of a heartbeat, all the inner confusion simply vanished. All at once, my nebulous dilemma distilled itself into a clear-cut choice. I was certainly free to pick up the threads of my life exactly where I'd left them the day before—and forge on through my own tenacious reluctance to act out what I was being told was destined to happen. *Or,* I was equally free to surrender and let the resistance go. Let the chips fall where they may.

It was the last piece of the puzzle. Who was it who hesitated, I had to wonder? And I laughed out loud, the kind of full-throttle laughter that had come to herald a moment of consummate surrender—and revelation. Days of reading the profound teachings of Oneness, which had paved the way for that shift, had pushed me to the very edge of the cliff. From there, the only step forward, Oneness once said, was to jump.

The jump was painless, so subtle it was virtually imperceptible. Yet, I knew it had been made. The components of the illusory scene remained the same. All that had changed was how I now *perceived* it. Suddenly, I was looking at the very same scenario with a new set of eyes. Now, I was looking at the components of the inevitable, seeing a very different slant on the projection of a path that revealed itself before me. Once again, I was viewing it as a moment etched in timelessness, revealed through the eyes of Oneness.

Slowly, I began to take the chapters of my own eclectic story apart and re-examine them. As I did, the absolute perfection in the way my own particular journey had been Divinely orchestrated began to crystallize. Ever so gently, the faded postcards tucked away in the archives of memory drifted back into focus—as though retrieved from the mists of a distant dream.

Days, months, and years melted together in a blur of memories, as I continued to delve into a retrospective spiritual journey. Page by page I plunged into the chronicles I'd written, and as I watched the illusory pages of my life re-emerge, I began to remember. How was it possible that my awareness had actually rematerialized in this indescribable place of inner Stillness and serenity from the shattered remains of *that* life of chaos? I wondered. And what had it taken to bring me to the point of surrender where such a transformation could have taken place?

As I continued to explore the compendium of trials and tribulations that had coaxed me to the brink of that moment of truth, I began to see a pattern emerge—signs of a trail that was decidedly off the beaten track. In a sense, the extent of the transformation that ultimately came to be had come and hit me from behind.

At the onset of what I think of as my spiritual journey, "Self-Realization" wasn't even remotely in my vocabulary. Yet, for as long as I could remember, I'd considered myself to be a *spiritual* person. What that actually meant, however, was something I'd have been hard-pressed to explain, back then in the mid 1980's. It was a concept that would go on to evolve and deepen exponentially, over time. Initially, all I'd ever wanted to do was to "serve God"—a God I assumed was out there in the heavens somewhere, beyond comprehension, beyond imagination, and surely separate from what I presumed *myself* to be. "Use me!" I'd cry out in prayer, never dreaming in a million years what I'd eventually be asked to do.

According to consensus wisdom, they say it's extremely difficult, if not impossible, to have actually made the journey to Oneness with the Divine without coming up through the ranks of a traditional spiritual structure. I was simply unaware of that. Presuming I was flying blind, I'd broken most of the rules the established schools of esoteric thought set out as mandatory for spiritual mastery. I had not been officially initiated by a Guru. I had not been formally schooled in any form of meditation. I was not a practitioner of yoga. I had not really studied or followed any of the world's traditional religions. I had not been ordained as a minister in any school of spirituality, recognizable or otherwise. And I surely did not hold a degree in theology or philosophy. Essentially, I was a blank slate—precisely the qualification Oneness required.

In terms of the contemporary Western spiritual scene, I'd glossed over the bewildering smorgasbord of transformational offerings, in the early days of my awakening, without actually partaking of much of it. I'd participated, on occasion, in a smattering of the workshops, seminars, and other assorted gatherings that had begun to mushroom up in the spiritual marketplace. I'd attended a few *satsangs* and *channelings*, now and then, out of curiosity. And I'd experienced just enough vivid, hypnotic past-life regressions to convince me, beyond doubt, of the validity of reincarnation. Nevertheless, I'd counted myself as fully present amongst an eclectic generation of seekers who had been herded together under the catch-all umbrella that had been dubbed "New Age."

Through it all, there'd been a decided absence of a traditional "path"—one that beckoned with a spiritual pot of gold at the end of the rainbow. What was going on in the sanctity of my own consciousness was so extraordinary and so fascinating that there had been no inclination to look for anything else. It seemed like I'd been programmed to be a self-contained, spiritual time capsule that, left to its own devices, was percolating nicely on the abundant spiritual sustenance being provided from within. I'd kept the entire process cloistered there. Like a record stuck in a groove, I kept myself focused in that inner space, content to be playing the same little tune, oblivious to the spiritual traditions that were setting down ground rules targeted at corralling the awakening masses.

Little did I suspect, but the very skill I'd used instinctively, in the practice of receiving Divine guidance, and fine-tuned since 1987—to completely silence my own mental process and to zero in with the precision of a laser on another level of communication emanating from within—had delivered me right to the threshold of the Divinity harbored within us all, and, ultimately, allowed me to shift into that level of Self-perception. I was largely unaware of the Divinely-guided perfection in what I was actually doing, in terms of my own *spiritual emergence,* and ended up honing my consciousness, essentially in spite of myself.

The skill needed was to be utterly *still*—and absolutely *focused.* So still, I could hear a virtual pin drop within my inner being. So focused, I could perceive the Presence of Oneness, ultimately, as my own. In time, that abstract skill became strengthened to the point that the inner Stillness could be sustained indefinitely. In essence, what I'd trained myself to be able to do was to *meditate.* Left to my own devices, I had simply approached it backwards. I started at the end. I dispensed with the formalities and began my process by listening *through* the Stillness, which I could somehow manifest at will, to perceive the Presence and the Divine guidance of Oneness.

Over time, an elaborate spiritual practice *did* evolve. It was a richly diverse program of spiritual *sadhana,* practices that helped me take the connection with Oneness to *ever expanding* levels of perception. In the years that followed, I would delve deeply into the timeless tradition of Sanskrit Mantra chanting, formal silent meditation, and the indescribable joys of an intensive self-styled practice of prayer and devotion—a tradition known in the East as *bhakti,* the path of the heart.

From the barest beginnings, my orientation with regard to my spiritual life had been an insular one. Over time, I came to understand, through the teachings of Oneness, that there is no right or wrong mode of spiritual practice. Instinctively, I'd simply evolved a devotional program that felt good to me, one that had nothing whatsoever to do with what anyone else was doing or saying. It was that approach of the *personalized path* to Oneness that I was being prepared to teach. It was a path of *liberation* and, no less, of Divine Love.

For me, the Realization of Self as Oneness was not at all the story of a one-shot event others may tell. Each experience of Divine connectedness was exactly as Oneness had described it in the book of teachings, *Oneness—*

like a wave caressing the shore. My own Presence as Oneness emerged from within, into the forefront of my awareness, and was perceived vividly and blissfully within the timeless Now moment of that contact. And then, ever so gently, the perception of that Presence receded back into the embrace of the Ocean of Isness that waits so patiently within the depths of each of us.

Each elusive instance of Divine connectedness became yet another incremental step in what, for me, was an ongoing, evolutionary process of emergence. In my case, there was not the immediacy of a definitive instant which could be dissected out of that history and heralded, like a scientifically quantifiable "Big Bang." There was more the sense of being dipped into liquid Stillness—and dissolving within it—over and over again. And the intensity of that sense of *immersion* into Oneness had deepened—and the duration of those moments of *dissolution* had expanded—with the passage of time.

So, I wondered, what was I supposed to be telling the world in sharing all this? Perhaps it was the truth of it. It was a story that was stranger than fiction and spanned who knows how many linear lifetimes, with a full-scale casting call of the multi-dimensional aspects of my very own identity in the starring role. It was a comedy of epic proportions as I propelled myself headlong into an unending string of dramas that might have been predictable, if I'd been paying better attention. It was an ongoing tragedy in all the literal ways when one develops a knack for anticipating disappointment—and then creates the optimum conditions for getting to be right about it.

I saw, in reviewing these writings that I actually *had* lived out the training outlined in the book, *Oneness*—and that, in learning these teachings *experientially,* by rote repetition, they'd somehow become permanently etched. I saw that I did, indeed, have a foundation for something worth sharing: something that was poignant and authentic, and at the same time heart-wrenching and quite literally, mind-blowing. Maybe the fact that this had all actually happened to what appeared to be a perfectly normal, middle-aged American woman was the part that made it interesting, and perhaps worth sharing, after all. I prayed that Oneness knew what they were doing in pushing me to write this story and, in a consummate gesture of surrender to the inevitable—I plowed into it.

As the pages turned, I began to see that while Oneness had addressed these teachings to this audience of one, they spoke to a collective that was significantly more far-reaching. Through the vehicle of this worldly identity, Oneness has been able to reach out and define the nature of this wisdom for us all. It became abundantly clear to me that these writings, which felt so sacred—and which I once had been so hesitant to share—were not at all "for my eyes only."

—Rasha

Note:

Due to the structure of this story, this volume is organized and presented using the device of three different "voices." They include: the voice of Rasha, presenting the overview of the narrator, the journal entries of Rasha, documenting her perceptions in real time, and the transcribed teachings of Oneness. The different voices are distinguished from one another by the use of three different typefaces, to help the reader follow the story more easily.

1

Endings and Beyond:
A Prelude to a Rendezvous with Oneness

––––––––

With a heart-wrenching last glance in the rear view mirror, I watched Asheville, North Carolina slowly vanish into the mountain mists of the Great Smokies—together with everything I once owned. The war was over. The grueling ordeal of going down for the third time, day-in and day-out, had finally come to an end. In the aftermath, with a bewildering combination of stunned disbelief and quiet resignation, I surrendered the fight, and simply let it all go.

The final downfall of life as I'd known it, and the sense of unending struggle that had given it definition, came swift and sure at the tail end of 1997. Despite several heroic, last-ditch attempts to avoid the inevitable, and wrench myself free from a whirlpool of circumstances that was spiraling what I thought of as "my life" straight down the drain, in the end, destiny wasn't taking "no" for an answer. Wipeout!

The devastating loss of my lovely home, my business, and my life savings to a bankruptcy I'd resisted until the bitter end had been the final blow. In the wake of a nightmare of corporate piracy on the part of trusted employees, the sweet success of my blossoming little jewelry company, Earthstar, had trickled down to a few bins of findings and beads, tucked protectively into a U-Haul trailing behind me. The few remains of a lifetime's belongings that had escaped the auction block were abandoned to a storage unit I would not reopen for eight years. That's all that was left of the aberration I once believed was my dream.

By the time the *coup de grace* hit, I was already disconnected from many of the material frames of reference that traditionally give an identity some structure. There was virtually nothing left of a sense of self, framed externally, that I could hang my hat on. No more home. No more marriage. No kids in the nest. No living family. No more career. And, virtually no possessions. Even though I'd given it all I had to give, when the tally was in, it was all gone. Unintentionally, I'd succeeded in severing all ties with the past and hadn't an inkling about a future. I was a human compass suddenly devoid of magnetic north. But, there I was, "true-grit," still strapped in behind the wheel, locked on automatic-pilot, heading south.

It was hard to reconcile the fact that despite a mega-dose of talent, drive, and hard work, I now had absolutely nothing to show for a half-century of living. It would not dawn on me for awhile yet that these were the perfect conditions under which to set off on the journey of a lifetime—the spiritual journey. I was still completely focused in the material world, still reeling from a long string of heart-breaking losses, the most devastating of which had been the recent passing of every single member of my childhood family from terminal illness—my parents, my brother, my grandparents, my aunts and uncles, one after the other. By then, my 25-year marriage was long since history and my three children were all grown up and leading independent lives. The bankruptcy was the icing on the cake. Finally, I'd been stripped of absolutely everything.

Years before, I'd transcribed a profound teaching: "Before a skyscraper can be built, you have to level the ground." In retrospect, I began to see that this was exactly what had happened. It was time to start another chapter in my life story—one that began with a blank page.

By the time I'd left Asheville behind, a tenacious sense of self had managed to survive a relentless onslaught of devastating happenings and learned to thrive in an air of perpetual crisis. It was an unyielding string of calamities that systematically eroded the sense of identity I'd carefully constructed over a lifetime. The dismantling of the linear identity, I would later come to understand, was a classic step on the path of *spiritual emergence* that would pave the way for the Presence of the *Self*, slated to emerge from within.

Mine had become the identity of a *survivor*, however, one I deluded myself into believing was undaunted by life's tragedies. I'd become a seasoned warrior in an endless battle. And, by then, I was so punchy from the setbacks, so conditioned to braving disappointment, and so numbed to the rawness of life's wounds that they barely elicited a response. The possibility of life beyond struggle never even crossed my mind. I'd become so good at internalizing and repressing the emotions which normally might have been stimulated to the surface that they became disengaged and went unexpressed. Years later, I'd come to see, in retrospect, how the stage had been set for an *experiential* foray into the teachings of Oneness—teachings that were yet to come.

It was a few days past New Year, 1998, when life as I'd known it had officially disappeared in the rear view mirror, but that final blow had been a long time coming. Professionally, all my attempts to create a sense of identity from the arena of achievement that so many of us pursue had been systematically quashed, over the years. One by one, a string of promising careers in several different countries had been developed successfully and then reluctantly abandoned, as I continued to sacrifice my own dreams and ambitions to the whims of my husband's corporate world, while his career kept us hopping back and forth across the Atlantic, with three kids in tow.

Years later, in the wake of all those losses, I'd forfeited my prized songwriter's contract with a major Nashville music publisher in light of a pressing need to return north, where family members had fallen gravely ill. Now, here I was, turning my back on Asheville, acting out the life-theme of leaving it all behind, yet again. But, this time, I was setting off to start from scratch, totally alone and empty-handed

It was a time of feeling engulfed in the shadow of all the trappings of identity I'd worn over the years and had mistaken for *myself*. By then, after 11 years of living in Europe, my heart housed a woman without a country, who felt no less alien in her own land than anywhere else in the world. Yet, the sense of disconnectedness went deeper than a choice of which political borders to claim as my own. The wedge between the worldly accessories of identity and the formless Divine Essence stirring within was being driven right to my very core. I was in free fall.

The miles melted together into a mindless blur as I drove away. Stoically, I began extracting myself from the breathtaking Asheville mountain vistas I'd known and loved for five whole years—longer than I'd lived anywhere else in my entire adult life. As each nondescript Interstate highway merged seamlessly into the deepening shadow of the one before, I tried to coolly distance myself from all that was familiar. Yet, mile by mile, a relentless program of mental flashbacks continued to play the devastating details of a life in ruins—looped for instant replay—inside my head. I watched the graphic, internal imagery of the past as it blended in with the soulless scenery whizzing by outside—and I felt absolutely nothing. I was numb.

What was the point of all the struggle? I asked myself. Here I was, a perfectly nice, kind-hearted, spiritual person, being chewed up and spit out, over and over again, by a material world where I felt like I just didn't belong anymore. Nothing was working. What was I doing wrong? Was there any way off this merry-go-round I thought of as "my life"? Questions! And more questions! I was sick and tired of my own endless, painfully earnest questions. I was ready for answers.

The thing I hadn't come to terms with yet was that I already had them. I had already manifested an entire compendium of answers—a wealth of timeless Divine wisdom, transcribed by my very own hand, a decade before. The only thing I hadn't done, up to that point, was own up to the truth of it. I had done all the work—and at the same time, I'd quietly cowered in denial of the precious Divine connection that was at the very core of it. In the habitual guise of polite conversation, I'd avoided the entire subject of what I knew I was able to do as effortlessly as the breath that flowed in and out of me.

Maybe the time had come to shift gears, a fleeting thought interjected. That symbolism was so obvious it was ridiculous, my automatic mental censor retorted. Maybe it was actually time to stop hedging my bets, my mind continued its monologue without missing a beat. Maybe it was time to stop trying to appear "normal," by whitewashing the spiritual identity that was trying so desperately to come out of hiding. Maybe it was time to give up on the idea of fitting into a world I honestly couldn't relate to. Maybe it was time to own up to the truth of what was really going on with me. Let people think whatever they want to think. Not my problem. What a revelation!

The truth of the matter was that at the eleventh hour, just before leaving Asheville, I'd rediscovered the book of Divine teachings that I'd received, transcribed, and then sheepishly tucked away in a drawer ten years before. After re-reading a few pages, something inside me knew that its moment had arrived. There was no getting around it. The manuscript simply *had* to be published. Entitled *The Calling*, it was a wealth of Divine wisdom received from Amitabh, "God of Infinite Light," a channeled Divine Presence revealed to me as an aspect of God The Father, who had been my first real spiritual teacher.

The dilemma of what name to put on the book cover for myself, as author, had continued to plague me. Drawing a blank, for all sorts of reasons, I'd kept sweeping the issue—and the manuscript that went with it—under the rug. "What's in a name?" Regardless, which one should it be? Over the years, the surname of my birth had become the surname of my husband, which in turn, years later, had been adapted to a name I used professionally—one that was easier to pronounce and spell. Eventually, I'd made that professional name official. Now, I could no longer identify with any of it. Wriggling out of my own identity, like the great shedding of an outgrown skin, I literally cringed at the very thought of putting any of those names on a book of Divine teachings.

Who *am* I? I'd started to wonder. Clearly, there was more to that question than the dilemma of which label to place on myself and print on the cover of a book. But, how *much* more there was to that question I hadn't even begun to imagine.

At the same time, for nearly 20 years, there had been a mysterious name that continued to nudge me in meditation and in dream state. The name was

"Rasha." I wasn't sure what it signified, thinking at first that it might be the name of a spirit guide or higher self. Ultimately, the channeled guidance I'd received was that this was my own spiritual name, and that the choice of whether or not to use it was one that I might wish to make, someday. It wasn't until years later that I learned the Sanskrit derivation of the name, which is a diminutive of the word "rasa," or its meaning: "Divine Essence in form." All I knew was I couldn't get it out of my mind.

The minivan I was driving crossed the Florida border hours before dawn. It was so enveloped in the steamy cocktail of rain and mist it was hard to tell the road in front of me from the oblivion around it. I could have been anywhere. On impulse, I pulled into a truck stop. Inside, as if on cue, I noticed a strange vending machine I'd never seen before or since, half hidden in a corner. It printed business cards. Twenty cards for a dollar. Without hesitating, I pulled out four quarters, plunked them in the slot, and typed out a single word. Out came 20 cards. All that appeared on them was "Rasha." No title. No address. No phone number. Just ... "Rasha." I smiled to myself. It felt so strangely right to have committed the name to writing. And, in that moment, for a dollar, I birthed myself into the hands of destiny.

In that life-altering moment, I claimed myself. I made an unspoken commitment of the heart to an identity that was cut loose from any sense of the past. And, at the same time, I opened the gates of possibility with an instinctive sense of blind faith. Standing in the rain, in the middle of nowhere, somewhere in the dead of night, clutching 20 crisp white cards, I took my tentative first step into the Eternal *Now*. South Florida awaited me, as I headed out into the night. And, as destiny would have it, so did a rendezvous with Oneness.

2

South Florida 1998
Living the Teachings of Oneness:
The Training Begins

———

I unpacked the remnants of life as I'd known it in a surreal setting. My grandparents had left behind a nice little condo in a community for the elderly in South Florida where, I'd always joked, the average age and the average temperature were about the same: 85 and above. Aside from the occasional family getaway, it had remained empty for years. As I was then officially homeless, and not knowing where else to go, heading for the condo seemed like a good plan.

There, in a revved-down atmosphere of golf, pinochle, and mah-jongg, the concept of a "generation gap" took on new meaning. Under the palm trees, the men chomped on cigars while they grumbled and complained to each other about everything imaginable. In the distance, "the girls," when not comparing snapshots of great-grandchildren, did leg-lifts and water ballet in the swimming pool. The condo complex was the real-life equivalent of a time machine. For, the better part of the next three years, it would serve as home-base for the spiritual gypsy, emerging from within, who had begun feeling the pull toward living on the wind.

Inside those walls, a very different kind of world began to unfold for me. In the newfound sanctity of my own little space, I began to reach inward with a whole new level of questions and a deepening search for the meaning of my existence. To my amazement, answers once again began to emerge from within me, as they had so many years before. This time however, the answers were from a very different Source.

I'd just published the first edition of *The Calling* and naturally assumed that my work would continue to focus on transcribing and publishing the channeled wisdom of Amitabh, the aspect of Father consciousness who authored the Divine guidance in that book. I was stunned to hear, only days after my arrival in Florida, that my work with Amitabh, my beloved spirit guide and dearest friend, was now complete. I was told that from then on I would be transcribing the teachings of a Source known as "Oneness."

I wanted absolutely no part of it. My life was sufficiently de-railed, I thought to myself, as I grasped at my precious connection with Amitabh, which represented my last remaining shreds of stability. Yet, slowly, and ever so gently, over the course of the months to come, the transition came to be. Amitabh agreed to stay with me in spirit, and held my hand within, while I became comfortable with the idea of what was happening. Gradually, I transitioned into connectedness with Oneness, and came to terms with the magnitude of the Source with whom I'd begun to converse. Even so, it was with no small amount of trepidation—and large doses of channeled moral support from Amitabh—that I embarked on this new adventure and became the Messenger who would transcribe the teachings of Oneness.

"You do not fully understand the scope of the consciousness known to you as Oneness," Amitabh began one day, in an attempt to reassure me. "Oneness is the consciousness you would understand to be *God*. At the same time, Oneness is not separate from you." By then, that concept was certainly familiar to me. However, I soon discovered that it was one thing to have heard a concept a hundred times before. It was another matter entirely to actually wrap my mind around the idea, given that I was now having direct Divine contact on an almost daily basis. I wanted so much to believe that this connection actually *was* all I was being told it was, and not some form of spiritual deception for which I'd been so carefully prepared.

The lesson of *spiritual discernment*, a concept hammered into me by Amitabh for years, rose to the occasion. How could I be absolutely sure who Oneness was? I kept wondering. In the ten years of working with Amitabh, I'd learned powerful techniques that enabled me to identify energy patterns visually, so I could be certain of the vibrational level of any consciousness with whom I might be interacting. With Oneness, I had no identifying *vibrational fingerprint* on which to zero in. Technically speaking, Oneness was not separate from me. So, this was a whole new ball game. And, it challenged all the ground rules on which I'd based my own self-styled, super-cautious approach to my work as a courier of Divine Wisdom—one that gave me reliable information I knew I could trust.

The dilemma served as a doorway between the habitual doubts of a logical mind and a place of *heart-centeredness* and unconditional *trust*, rooted in surrender. I'd soon come to understand that the sense of certainty I was seeking was not to be found in a visual phenomenon—something I could identify in my mind's eye—or through any other evidence provided by the physical senses. The *proof* I thought I needed was already there in the *experience* itself. The Presence of Oneness made itself known to me as a *feeling*, centered in the area of the heart—a feeling for which there are no words.

The loving guidance of Amitabh went a long way toward helping me tune in to that place of heart-focus that lies within us all. Even so, somehow I still wanted to hear the answers for myself, directly from the Source.

"Can I ask a question?" I began one day, sitting at the computer, as my consciousness opened to my new Divine connection.

"Yes, you may ask a question," Oneness replied, "but we already know the question. And, you already know the answer."

"I suppose that's probably true. But, it would be comforting to hear it from you anyway. Is that ok?" I typed diligently, like a secretary taking dictation, while alternately inserting my own commentary into the mix.

"Of course," Oneness said. I paused and took a deep breath.

"Are you God?" I asked. "Who *are* you?" An eternity passed, as I waited what was probably only seconds, for the answer.

"As the drop of water is to the ocean—that is what Oneness is. The *essence* of the drop is every bit the *essence* of the totality. As you would understand God to be—yes, we are God. We are Oneness," came the astounding reply.

"Is there anything higher or greater than the totality that I would consider to be God?" I asked.

"In linear terms that you would understand, perhaps not in the way you are thinking. And yet, there is no limit. There is no end. The cycle is ever *expanding*, ever evolving. And ultimately, the Creation becomes the Creator, in perpetuity," Oneness replied. "You will come to understand these concepts more fully as time goes by."

Each writing session began with a little conversation such as this that enabled me to bond with Oneness and eased me into the process of transcription, so that eventually a book of Divine teachings might be documented. Ultimately, over the course of years, a massive body of personal writings accumulated, in addition to the transcription of the book, *Oneness*. I never gave much thought to the personal writings, presuming that they were simply part of the process of getting into the flow of the writing. To me, all that mattered was establishing and deepening the connection with Oneness.

I came to understand that this was a *relationship*, albeit a new one. And, like any relationship, there is an initial period of getting acquainted. Oneness was patient and loving with me, which went a long way toward soothing my trepidation at the prospect of being expected to come forth with material that I did not, initially, fully comprehend. I so desperately wanted to do the job well. And, Oneness' reassurance went a long way.

"Do not concern yourself at this juncture with whether or not you are able to *teach* this material. Ultimately, you will be able to do this. Now, your job is merely to transcribe the information exactly as you receive it."

"Am I receiving and transcribing accurately now?" I asked silently.

"Yes, indeed you are."

"It's nice to be reassured."

"We will note that and give you feedback," Oneness wrote.

"I suppose it takes time to build a relationship. I know we've only just started to work together," I typed. "Thank you for believing in me."

"We could reply 'Thank you for believing in *me*, too.' For, you would appreciate the humor intended."

I was amazed to discover how naturally the conversation flowed when talking with Oneness. The process of transcription was completely automatic. There was virtually no delay between the inception of a thought and my ability to document it, the state Amitabh had always referred to as "simultaneous transcription." Working with Oneness was like breathing. There was no thought process involved at all. It was as though my mind were in suspended animation and the information simply poured through me.

Within a matter of weeks I was told that I would soon be ready to begin transcribing another book of Divine teachings and that the book would be "radical." "Just how radical is this book going to be?" I began to wonder.

"The nature of the material you will be transcribing will be what could be considered *cutting edge* in terms of the depth of the material that will be presented," Oneness explained. "You will be documenting the blueprint for the ascension process." I was told that I would on occasion find the content to be daunting, in that many of the concepts would be new to me, but my task was simply to transcribe the material, exactly as given. Even though I was completely flabbergasted that this was all actually happening to me, at the same time, I felt strangely confident that I was up to the task. It felt like I'd been born to this work and had been talking to Oneness forever.

As that thought flowed through me, it was as though Oneness had read my mind. Totally dispensing with the formalities, suddenly, we plunged right into it.

"We will now begin transcribing the second volume of teachings," my fingers typed. "The title of this next work will be *Oneness*. In it we will explore the mysteries surrounding the concept of Oneness and your connectedness to it, multi-dimensionally. Through the exercise of doing this work, you will embrace your connection with this Source and bond with it, in Oneness. You will embody your connection with the Source you would understand to be 'God.' And you will experience transcending the limitations of *that* definition of Oneness. Your perspective on the concept of 'self' will alter to encompass an infinitely broader scope. Are you willing to take this next step?"

"Yes, I am willing," I replied, with an eerie sense of absolute calm.

"Good. Then it is time to begin. Start a new paragraph."

And, in what seemed like the next breath, Chapter One of what was destined to become the book, *Oneness,* revealed itself on the screen of my laptop. The real journey had begun.

There in the sanctity of my little condo, I embarked on what Oneness called "a new program of isolation." It afforded me ample time for the daily transcription work and at the same time allowed the dust to settle within me, while providing the space to process the ordeal I'd just gone through. I'd been so traumatized by the bankruptcy and the downfall of Earthstar that, in essence, I'd called a time-out on life itself. A self-styled intensive of total solitude, lasting several months, enabled me to take my life apart and examine, from a metaphysical standpoint, what had actually happened to me, in an attempt to make my peace with it.

I started to recognize a history that persisted in repeating itself, like a recurring dream. Regardless of the individual circumstances, and the difference in the names and faces of the players involved, there'd been a decided history of running into a brick wall—despite perfect planning and super-human effort. There'd been disappointment and deception. I'd been cheated and lied to, not just in this last episode, but repeatedly. The question was: *why?* Why was this same sort of thing happening, over and over again? More to the point, what was it about *me* that was attracting these kinds of experiences? I fine-tuned my questions, and spontaneously began uncovering the answers.

This reprieve from life as I'd known it enabled me to peel back the layers of life experience and probe the details of that imagery for clues. Slowly I began to unravel the mystery underlying the conglomeration of mishaps I thought of as my life. It would be years yet before I'd be able to add the *karmic* pieces of the puzzle that would tie it all together and make sense of a lifetime of seemingly random imagery.

The time in South Florida that I think of as "Oneness 101" became a personalized crash-course in spiritual unfoldment. There, as I took apart the building blocks of my life experience, I slowly began to reveal the core essence of who I understood *myself* to be. It was through this painstaking process of self-discovery that I began to inch my way down the path to Oneness—as, I was told, a world of others would do in the times to come.

Oneness helped me to examine the details of a personal history that read like a textbook illustration of *Murphy's Law*: "everything that *can* go wrong *will* go wrong." Through my daily dialogues with Oneness, I began to plunge into the depths of my own hidden *feelings*. I was stunned to discover what was actually there, buried within *me*, that had served to create a lifetime of parallel experiences and persisted in undermining my best efforts and intentions. My own energy field was serving to demonstrate to me, over and over again, exactly what I did *not* want, and began to show me, from my own experience of it, how the principles of "creating your own reality" actually worked.

Oneness helps me process a pattern of painful experience and reveal the underlying repressed emotion that set the stage for it

Oneness speaks:

You are, as you know by now, in the heightened stages of an excruciating metamorphosis. You have come through the most intense parts of this training and have fared quite well under substantial adversity. You have received communications from this Source as to what some of the underlying life themes were and how they colored your experience in this lifetime.

It is, understandably, with much sadness and disappointment that you integrate the realization of the futility of most of your efforts toward self-fulfillment. You have become numbed to the emotional backlash that would normally accompany such experiences. Thus, it was necessary for you to create for yourself a seemingly unending series of such experiences so that there would be no doubt as to the point of the exercise.

You have demonstrated the full spectrum of emotional responses to the events that have transpired in your life in the last several years. Now it is time to retreat from the exercise and to assess it, in order to reap the understandings that will provide meaning and insights for you to carry forward. There is much in store that you will find meaningful and enjoyable if you take the time now to integrate these understandings with those that were provided during other similar episodes in your life.

Your conclusion was correctly reached that the value of the lesson was not in the end result, which was in many respects short of what was hoped for, but in the experience itself. Judge not your performance from the perspective of the obvious. Much has been gleaned in the way of *self-awareness* that you would be inclined to discount in the wake of what you would deem to be "failure." The understandings you have begun to reach will put in perspective the true underlying purpose of the experience. You will emerge from this painful time with a renewed sense of inner direction and a zest for living.

We will be here for you through the trials that lie ahead to help you heal your emotional body and revitalize your spiritual connectedness. This is the first step in the integration of certain missing fragments of consciousness that connect to you through the emotions that certain situations trigger.

Rasha speaks:

Can I ask you how it serves me to keep re-experiencing "failure"? I don't see how this could be in my best interests. Am I to succumb to this pattern of experience? Am I to triumph over this? Am I to love myself despite this? Am I to allow this pattern to undermine my life as a way of achieving humility? Or is retaining this pattern of experience a trigger for the frustration and outrage that one would expect as a response to these circumstances? Is it that I have not expressed sufficiently my level of despair over these repeated experiences? Enough! What is the point of all this?

You have touched upon many of the points of this exercise. And, we would say that you are nearing completion with it.

Does this have to do with outrage and frustration?

This has to do with repressed anger.

I thought so.

Your anger response has been eliminated through conditioning. Any number of situations have come up for you which would trigger for you a response of anger, but you have been unable to manifest it.

Is that what all this "failure" stuff has been about?

This is a piece of what that theme has been about. That theme is a major one in this lifetime, and the issues it represents are complex. Are you ready to explore this?

I think so. I think I'm ready to look at it. I think that I don't respond with anger because I consider anger to be a negative emotion, and I've conditioned myself to "transcend" that emotion. What did I miss?

You missed *expressing* the anger. You totally circumvented the outrage. You let the circumstances wash over you without *feeling* the result of them. You intellectualized the entire process. This is one of the reasons that your life has been like a record stuck in a groove, playing the same old song. You have pieces of the puzzle, yet you have been unable to put it together.

Ok. What do I have to do to move past this?

You need to allow yourself the luxury of *feeling* your emotions. It is not enough to mentalize and verbalize what you are feeling. You must *feel* what you are feeling.

31

The book *Oneness* took nearly four years to write. It was not that the work was unusually time-consuming or difficult, but that the entire experience became a practicum for me. I'd transcribe a few chapters, and then, for any of a number of reasons, I'd put the work aside for awhile. Sometimes a few months, or entire chunks of a year, went by. During that time, I discovered that I was actually *living out* the book I thought I was only transcribing. My own life experiences were serving as living illustrations of the very principles I was documenting.

Years later, readers from all over the world would be writing to me, reporting the very same phenomenon. I came to understand that the *Oneness* material contained what Oneness termed "encodements." Somehow, in reading these teachings, experiences are stimulated into manifestation to serve as illustrations of the concepts provided. In this way, it was explained, readers would be assimilating these understandings, not mentally, as theoretical or philosophical *concepts*, but at a deeper level, as what Oneness referred to as "knowingness"—irrefutable knowledge that comes of having had the actual experience oneself.

In this time frame, the informal guidance I received from Oneness was intensely personal. Much of it focused on helping me work through the details of my own internal process and guiding me in search of an explanation for what persisted in *happening* in my life. I soon discovered that just because I now had the technical explanation for how *reality* is created, revealing itself before my very eyes, that didn't exempt me from having to run the course and jump over the hurdles.

Over time, it seemed as though the illustrations I was living out became even more poignant than before. Through the material I was transcribing, I learned to identify what was serving to stimulate certain categories of experience into manifestation in my life. Yet, if anything, the challenges became increasingly more difficult as I delved ever deeper into my personal process of unfoldment and began peeling back layers of emotional density, buried within—repressed *energy* which persisted in summoning forth illustration after illustration of the same old story. It was astounding how predictable some of it became, as I started to grasp how this exercise we think of as *life* actually works.

I found I'd begun putting the principles of the book *Oneness* into practice as I was documenting them. And slowly, over the course of the next few years, I watched in fascination as the circumstances of my life—the recurring illustrations Oneness referred to as *life themes*—began to shift and to ease up. Eventually, those kinds of experiences stopped happening altogether. It felt like nothing short of a miracle.

repressed e-motion

The teachings that follow were received initially as personal guidance. I was later instructed by Oneness to excerpt some of those passages and include them in the manuscript I was transcribing. Those teachings can now be found in Chapter 3 of the book, *Oneness*.

Rasha speaks:

Oneness, it occurred to me, in rereading a recent transmission, that it really reflected what was happening in my life. Are these circumstances being manifested as a way to punctuate for me the points being covered in this manuscript?

Oneness speaks:

This is a good observation. Your life has become an exaggeration in the way you are magnetizing situations to yourself. This is an opportunity for you to master, once and for all, the mechanics of creating your reality. It should be fairly obvious to you that the incidents in your life are not what you would wish them to be. At this time, you are feeling quite powerless and confused as to what is going on. You have countless potential theories in your mind with which you could rationalize those circumstances. But, you have not yet figured out how to apply the information that is being presented to you in theoretical form. There is substantial learning here for you, if you care to transcend the limitations of this reality.

I'm very willing to get it. Believe me, I am! I'm tired of all this adversity. Life seems to have become a pause between disasters. I don't want to live like this anymore. I'm trying so hard to do everything I'm supposed to be doing and yet, I'm stepping into problem after problem at the same time. Why can't things just go smoothly? It feels like I'm being punished at some level. I know I'm not a victim. So, I must be punishing myself. But, how? And why?

Do you really want answers to these questions, or are you just being rhetorical?

I'd like answers, please.

Very well, then you shall have them.

How to break the pattern of manifesting adversity

You are opening the door to the adversities you are experiencing by remaining in a state of energy imbalance. At the levels at which you are now operating, you would be advised to exercise great caution and awareness of your vibratory state of being. When you are feeling at a low ebb it would be preferable not to continue doing whatever you may be doing. And, surely it is preferable not to go into a crucial situation in an unbalanced state. The outcome would almost certainly not be favorable.

You are manifesting near-worst case scenarios at the present time. In order to break the pattern, it is important for you to be keenly aware of the vibration of all you communicate to others. Monitor your speech. Do not utter a negative sentiment about anything, regardless of whether or not you feel it is justified. Make a conscious effort that every word that passes your lips is uplifting to the listener.

The vibration of every thought pattern that passes through your consciousness carries an energy charge, particularly the thought patterns that are materialized in the form of verbal communication. By releasing that energy charge in the form of speech, you set into motion an imprint that magnetizes to it circumstances of a corresponding vibration. That is what is meant by one's thoughts creating one's reality, in the most simplistic sense.

In order to break that cycle of the manifestation of negative occurrences, it is advisable to closely monitor the way you respond to the circumstances that have occurred, and insure that your response is not one calculated to produce for you more of the same. Speak only the most positive possible statements regarding any situation. Speak ill of no one, lest the energy be mirrored back upon you.

Choose to partake or to pass. Simply that. Gossip, complaining, or speech in the guise of asking for help you do not really require, are recipes for reprisal in the form of creating circumstances that would not be pleasing to you. Your speech is a powerful tool when carefully employed. It is a danger to you when used carelessly. Likewise, your thought patterns, even when not expressed verbally, carry an energy charge that sets in motion circumstances of a corresponding vibration.

When one is mistrustful, for example, one manifests the experience of being deceived. When one is fearful, one manifests the experience of frightening situations. When anxious and feeling unworthy, one manifests the experience of the rejection of one's efforts. When one becomes the hunter, the hunted feel the predatory energy and flee. When one is obvious in what one wants from another, it is virtually guaranteed that the outcome would not be manifested.

Dwell not upon what is lacking in your life, but regard with gratitude those circumstances, with an understanding that they pave the way for a shift in consciousness and conditions that would put you in the position to manifest precisely what you have come into this lifetime to do. The seemingly negative situation may well be the gateway to the precise shift in focus that will deliver you into the arena where you can do your life's work. We would highly recommend to you that you scrutinize your circumstances and your thought patterns surrounding them, and weed out responses that could well be perpetuating the adversity.

You have asked. And, we have answered you. This is a major piece of training, and one that you are embodying in the present time period. We recommend that you take the time and integrate this level of understanding, so that you can begin to reverse the pattern of stuckness in which you find yourself, and begin to manifest in your daily life the wealth of wisdom that you have mastered on a mental level. We look forward to helping you integrate this understanding, and to celebrating with you the result of that shift in consciousness.

3

Dr. Bindu Purohit
A Mentor Emerges from the Timeless Past

————

A phone call from India came quite unexpectedly during the summer of 1998 which would change my life forever. It was from Dr. Bindu Purohit, a extraordinary spiritual Master I'd met several years before, with whom I'd felt a powerful connection. Although we hadn't kept in close contact, it was a meeting I'd never forgotten. The phone call, to tell me of his upcoming visit to the United States, came at a time when my life was still reverberating from the aftershocks of my upheaval in Asheville. I was ripe for a miracle. The timing couldn't have been better. Dr. Bindu would be lecturing at a conference in Orlando, Florida, and he called to invite me to attend.

I'd met Dr. Bindu for the first time in 1994 at an astrology conference in Anaheim, California. I'd gone there as an exhibitor, showcasing Earthstar's new collection of astrological earrings and necklaces. Most of the other exhibitors were distributors of computer software for astrologers. During the conference lectures, when the ballroom was deserted of customers, I soon became bored with standing in my own empty booth and decided to take a walk around the room. Amidst the hubbub of the computer people, I noticed a small booth tucked in the far corner of the ballroom where a solitary young Indian man sat quietly. Impeccably dressed, he sat absolutely motionless, as though he were absorbed in another world. I went over to see what he was exhibiting.

As I approached, suddenly I stopped. Something I sensed around his booth filled me instantly with a feeling of absolute peace and well being. I had never felt anything like it in my life. It was pure energy. Divine energy. It was as though the booth literally exuded the vibration of love itself. I was transfixed on the spot. Rarely at a loss for words, I stood there as if frozen for several moments, not knowing what to say, and eventually managed to blurt out, "Do you mind if I just stand here and breathe?"

The single table was covered with exotic-looking objects, in a variety of metals and carved crystal, that were covered with intricate geometric designs and sacred symbols. Dr. Bindu explained that these were *Yantras*, power objects of a spiritual tradition from India called *White Tantra*. I was intrigued, as much by what I was seeing as by the powerful energies I was feeling, and accepted his invitation to sit down at his booth to chat.

Unbeknownst to me, Dr. Bindu Purohit had been cited amongst the world's foremost practitioners of India's most sacred science. A medical doctor as well as a 13th generation Tantric Master trained by his grandfather in the Raj Guru family tradition, Dr. Bindu had brought the pure essence of White Tantra from the palaces of ancient India into the eclectic spiritual arena of modern-day America. Even then, the astounding results of his practice had earned him international acclaim.

Before the week had been over, I'd learned my first Mantra. It was a short collection of rhythmic phrases in the ancient language, Sanskrit. Somehow, I seemed to be able to recite the words with ease, almost as though I already knew them and was remembering them from another place in time. Dr. Bindu seemed pleased, and I'd agreed that I would practice the chant on a regular basis. Little did I know but that original meeting had been a pre-destined karmic reunion orchestrated on high. In the years to come, the details of an ancient past-life connection so buried in antiquity as to pre-date recorded history would be revealed to me and would solve the mystery of a timeless connection and a sense of destiny that words could not explain.

Now, years later in 1998, life had come full circle. From that point on, Dr. Bindu began to play a significant role in my spiritual life. During my time with him in Orlando, I was taught the full-length version of the Sanskrit Mantra I'd been introduced to years before, in the authentic oral tradition that had been passed down through the ages in India since ancient times. It was my first real taste of formal spiritual practice, and the sacred science of Mantra would go on to become a powerful and cherished part of my life.

As years went by, Dr. Bindu became a precious spiritual anchor for me as I rode out the turbulent seas of transformation. He became the one element of continuity in what, for me, seemed like a world of chaos. His was a mysteriously powerful spiritual presence that stood sure and strong amid the relentless storms of earthly existence. When I got myself in over my head, Dr. Bindu was never further than a phone call away, with priceless words of wisdom and just the miracle needed to somehow save the day. Our bond of friendship deepened over the years, and I came to consider him a true "brother in spirit."

In time, the sacred science of White Tantra would help me unravel the mystery of the otherworldly visions, the prophecies, and the unending string of "bad luck" that defied all logic and plagued my life. As unlikely as it may have appeared at the time, Dr. Bindu was a modern-day emissary of Divine intent on a timeless rescue mission: the release of my soul from the eternal bondage of karmic imprisonment.

When we first met, Dr. Bindu told me that I was destined to be a spiritual teacher someday, an inane prospect to a marginally awakened, middle-aged woman buried alive in a floundering New Age jewelry business. Yet, that revelation was far from news to me. It was the same astounding prediction I'd heard so many times before.

Dr. Bindu had a vivid picture, at a level I could not begin to comprehend, of the person I was destined to become. He had full knowledge of the ancient records of the karmic history we shared, which put all the predictions into perspective. At last, I'd found an actual person in physical form who had the wisdom to help me decipher the mystery of what was happening to me. He had been Divinely guided to come into my life to help lead me out of the wilderness.

My first *Yantra* had come into my life in 1995, long before I was ready to appreciate its power or potential. I'd placed it respectfully on my little altar, amongst a prized collection of crystals from Arkansas. And, there it sat. I would not have been able to fathom, in those days, the magnitude of the energy that could be radiated through what appeared to be a simple little silver box. In time, I came to regard with awe and reverence these material tools of Divine empowerment and the mind-boggling spiritual tradition from ancient India that inspires them.

Over the years, I came to understand that *Tantra* is an exacting science of Spirit encompassing the very principles that govern the fabric of Creation and manifest as our physical world. The ancient teachings of Tantric tradition provide a highly *technical* roadmap through the ethers to the realization of our connection with the Divine. Observing how this spiritual technology is put in practice, one is able to watch the vibrational make-up of what we consider to be "life"—in action. The principles of how to alter the material circumstances of physical reality are demonstrated through the work of Tantric Masters like Dr. Bindu, who have dedicated their lives to preserving the authenticity of this extraordinary science.

Far from the X-rated reputation Tantra has somehow garnered in the West, I learned that Tantra is actually an energy-focused *spiritual technology* that is based on a foundation of impeccable purity and fueled by Divine intent. It is a mélange of the physical and the metaphysical—a science of creation, calculation, and consequence. Its goal is full control of the physical senses and, ultimately, the ability to communicate directly with the Divine.

I would come to see that White Tantra offered a similar conceptual overview to the one Oneness had outlined in the material I'd transcribed in the book, *Oneness*. However, the techniques employed in achieving those ends were a world apart from the teachings of Oneness and my own experience of the journey. In time, my own spiritual understandings would come to encompass many of the universal principles of ancient Tantric tradition, as I blazed my own trail through the ethers on the vibrational roller-coaster ride to Oneness.

Over the years to come, the role Dr. Bindu played in my life would expand far beyond his work with me as a Tantric practitioner and a "Mantra Guru." Yet, his expertise in *those* subjects would come to illustrate for me an extraordinary, exacting standard of purity and precision which he'd been trained, since childhood, to apply to every aspect of spiritual practice—as well as to daily life. I'd never encountered anything quite like it.

At first, his stringent rules about the way things *must* be done were an alien concept to me, as a modern-day American woman with a very laid-back approach to life. For years, I'd attempt to argue point-for-point, with all the logic my tenacious mind could muster—always to no avail. "No compromise" was the phrase I'd come to hear so often that it felt like it had been etched on my soul! Over time, I'd come to understand, and to honor unconditionally, the Divine perfection in those standards. For, without them, the miracles possible through the sacred science of White Tantra would never be possible.

That level of *surrender* didn't come easy to me, however. The ongoing battle of wits during these spiritual debates would surely have tried the patience of a Saint. I would come to learn that this level of patience, this scope of spiritual knowledge—and this uncompromising standard of character—would be the mark of a "true Guru," and a standard against which many would-be Gurus in my travels would come to be measured. Yet, it was a title that Dr. Bindu refused to accept from me, to my ongoing bewilderment.

Dr. Bindu would come to play the role of spiritual mentor for me in ways I would never have dared to dream, back then in 1998. It was a strange, indefinable category of friendship rarely encountered in the West, a bond of unquestioning *trust* that totally defied logic and would continue to evolve over time. That bond would go on to survive a very long and rocky road of ego-confrontation that would lie ahead for me, a winding trail down which I'd continue to stumble for years to come. One would have thought, in watching this agonizing process unfold, that I surely had found my Guru. But, Dr. Bindu continued to be firm. He was absolutely *not* "my Guru." And no amount of logical reasoning on my part would convince him otherwise. Who *is* this man? I began to wonder. It was a question—rhetorical or otherwise—that would re-echo within me throughout my spiritual journey.

4

1998 - 1999
Earthstar Revisited
Taking the Show on the Road

───────

During the intense process of inner confrontation that colored my initial time in South Florida, and amidst transcribing the book, *Oneness*, and the hours of daily written dialogues, I also faced the challenge of having to make a living in the aftermath of a failed business. My confidence in my ability to cope financially had been seriously shaken by the ordeal in Asheville. As I began picking up the threads of my life, I started to restructure what was left of Earthstar, the little jewelry business I was still counting on to support me.

Where there had been dozens of employees and sales reps, there now was a staff of one, and I was it. People always say "less is more." For me, it surely was. I was free. Now, back at square one, I rediscovered the place it all began: the simple joy of creating something beautiful from sparkling gemstone beads and silver wire. Suddenly, I'd become a one-man band, designing, assembling, and selling my own creations. Like a little kid in a sandbox, I reveled in exploring the ability to play. Once again, the precious spark of creativity, which the pursuit of *success* had harnessed and buried in drudgery, started to re-emerge from within me. To my amazement, the very activity that had all but broken my heart was the one that began to heal it.

By the time it was spring of 1998, my oldest daughter, Susanna, decided to join me in Florida for awhile. Together we took what remained of Earthstar and transformed the business concept into one that supported the spiritual work that was fast emerging as my new life direction. With the book, *The Calling*, finally in print, it seemed like a natural next step to present its powerful message to the world. The time had come to emerge from the cocoon that was South Florida and "take the show on the road."

Thus began a "hero's journey," as a mother/daughter team, that brought us infinitely closer together and at the same time pushed the limits of patience and endurance all the way around. In the two-year marathon that followed, we drove back and forth across America umpteen times, in a snow white, high-top conversion van I'd named "Vanessa," as exhibitors in the body/mind/spirit-style expos that had begun to spring up all over the country. The journey we shared served as the impetus for examining my sense of self, our mother/daughter relationship, and some of the core presumptions that held it all together by a thread, as though it were all under a microscope.

Through her eyes, I was able to watch myself in action, and to examine the character I considered to be *me*, in excruciating detail. Susanna was my loving mirror, reflecting back to me the daunting reality beneath some of the gilded illusions I was still carrying around. In addition to earning a virtual Purple Heart, she inspired an imaginary, satirical new twist to the classic country song, which in my mind I'd renamed "Stand by your Mom" in her honor.

Week after week, we spent an entire day or more creating a dazzling display booth with glistening glass cases, spotlights, and a beautiful collection of Earthstar's latest jewelry designs, sprinkled in amongst a prized collection of crystal clusters culled from the mines in Arkansas. As a featured speaker, I also presented the teachings of Amitabh from *The Calling*, and, over time, teachings from the *Oneness* material that I was still in the process of transcribing. Three days later, we'd tear the entire exhibit down, drive for days to the next venue, and then do the whole thing all over again.

Often, with only a week between shows, there was barely enough time to drive the distance, much less time to catch one's breath. From Minneapolis to Cleveland, from Chicago to Atlanta, from New York to Austin, from Ft. Lauderdale to Portland, from San Francisco to Cincinnati—with a month in Tucson at the Gem Show thrown in for good measure—back and forth we went. The pace was punishing, and the schedule unyielding. By the time it was all over we'd crisscrossed the landscape of America so many times I'd finally lost count. It had become a dizzying blur of familiar looking faces in unfamiliar places that all had begun to appear the same to me. The only thing that was becoming increasingly difficult to recognize was the one I thought of as *myself*.

The expo tour was the first time I'd ever spoken in public. My very first lecture, in Cleveland, Ohio, set the stage for an experience that would continue to take me by surprise wherever I went. From the back of a room filled with more than 300 people who had come to hear me speak, I surveyed the crowd, quietly gathered my courage, and slowly walked to the podium. In that moment, I felt something within me shift in a way I wouldn't have been able to explain in those days. Suddenly, I found myself looking out through the very same eyes but, somehow, from another octave of perception.

Show after show, the same sort of phenomenon happened. More often than not, people from the audience would come up to me after my lecture and report seeing a host of angels around me. Many spoke of seeing a brilliant, golden glow emanating from my body that filled the room. I was stunned. I had no awareness of any of it.

Season by season, I continued to meld the material world of New Age hoopla, the scramble to make ends meet, and the struggle to keep up the grueling pace of life as a performing spiritual gypsy, with the breathtakingly indescribable sense of the sacred and the otherworldly which kept it all in perspective. Each weekend event became an unlikely place in time, caught in suspended animation between the two worlds. Together, they held the trappings of the mundane and the mystical in a precarious semblance of balance.

In that surreal setting, I slowly became aware of a far-removed aspect of self watching from a distance as I struggled to keep my spiritual priorities in focus and prevent the entire point of the exercise from being lost in a hail of logistics and exasperating details. How was one supposed to retain the inner serenity required for maintaining a profound connection with Oneness, and at the same time run oneself ragged, racing around America talking about it before throngs of people? I had to wonder. I'd become a living, breathing contradiction, a walking illustration of the polarities of human experience.

The gentle call of the inner Stillness was fast giving way to the intensity of the frenetic pace I was attempting to keep up, as the gap between those two distinctly different worlds continued to widen. Silently, I'd started to suspect that this road, which required keeping a foot in each of those worlds, was actually the shortcut to the abyss that lay between them! It was a dilemma with which I'd intermittently continue to wrestle for some time to come.

5

The book, *Oneness,* was written in isolated segments of time over the course of four years. Sometimes months would go by without writing so much as a chapter. It was during those periods, while driving all over America and lecturing at a montage of expos, that I gradually became more comfortable with the prospect of speaking in front of large audiences. Public speaking was not something that came naturally to me. I was much more at home in the sanctity of the inner silence, and returning to seclusion in South Florida after a marathon run of expo appearances was a reprieve I came to treasure.

It was in those heavenly, peaceful moments of homecoming that whole groups of chapters would be transcribed in quick succession, over the course of several weeks. And then, once again, months would go by without writing anything at all. More than half of the book was documented in this disjointed way. As the weeks and months went by, I began to notice how uncanny it was that the pace at which I was transcribing *Oneness* seemed to perfectly parallel my own spiritual unfoldment.

The frenetic pace of the public appearances, and the intensity of setting up and tearing down display booths week after week, added to the disconnected feeling of living out of a suitcase. It was an intensive in self-confrontation that seemed to be calculated to bring my issues right to the surface. In the process, I continued to peel back layers of my own psyche and to scrutinize the symbolism in everything. I'd come to realize that there clearly was no wasted motion in any of it.

After completing the transcription of a certain chapter, it always seemed ironic that I'd suddenly find myself living out a poignant episode that perfectly illustrated that very issue. The strange sense that my life experiences served as living examples for the book continued throughout the four years it took me to transcribe it. The pace of my spiritual journey clearly was in sync with the pace of transcribing the book. At the same time, the teachings I was birthing into form were helping me to decipher the symbolism of my life. It all appeared to be incredibly purposeful. None of it was random, of that I was certain.

I had to remind myself constantly that the book, *Oneness,* was filled with what Oneness had referred to as *encodements*—vibrational triggers that stimulate living examples of the very concepts that the teachings instilled in the mind. It had become obvious that I was meant to be learning the teachings of Oneness *experientially*, from having actually lived them out, not by learning the concepts theoretically, so I could simply *understand* them or *believe* them. It was clear that even though these teachings were technically manifesting themselves through *me*, as I transcribed them into writing, that surely did not exempt me from the painstaking process that helps each of us assimilate those understandings as *knowingness*.

A summer to remember in Santa Fe

As the summer of 1999 approached, I felt a sudden unexpected calling to spend some time in New Mexico. I had visited there briefly several years before and had sensed a powerful connection with that part of the country. I'd been feeling a strong pull to return to New Mexico ever since, and on impulse decided to spend the coming summer there. I called a friend who lived in Santa Fe and asked her to send me a copy of the local newspaper, and as soon as it arrived I began replying to the ads in the classified section, searching for somewhere nice to stay for a few months.

Eventually, I found an ad for a vacation rental that sounded absolutely perfect. It described a fully furnished, detached artist's studio on a property that boasted stained-glass windows, a gazebo, and a short walk to the Plaza— right in the heart of downtown Santa Fe. To top it off, the price was too good to be true! It sounded great and I rented it over the phone, sight unseen. I was so ready for a few months in a peaceful, quiet atmosphere that was conducive to communing with Oneness. There, I told myself, I could really buckle down and make some headway with transcribing the book.

After a week-long drive from Florida, camping out in Vanessa-the-van all along the way, I pulled into the driveway of a bizarre setting. The place was technically just as it had been described in the ad, but it was a world away from what I'd pictured. It was, at a glance, an outrageous exaggeration of the "shabby chic" décor that Santa Fe is famous for.

The "stained-glass windows" that had been advertised amounted to one small piece of red-colored glass glued to one of the windows, and a little green-colored piece of glass glued to the window next to it. The "gazebo" was a tiny, rustic, hand-made structure, wedged in between the main house and the single-room dwelling I'd be calling home for the next two months. The "studio" was technically "detached," but so ingeniously squeezed in to the available space in the tiny yard that there was not even a hint of privacy. Still, it was fully paid for, and of course, right in the heart of downtown Santa Fe!

The furniture in the "fully furnished" room amounted to a primitive, metal-framed futon, a dilapidated little table, a rickety chair that I later learned had come from the junkyard, and a hodge-podge of crockery that surely had come from Goodwill. I swallowed hard. The so-called "optional bedroom" which had been advertised was actually a roughly dug, underground pit that was accessible by ladder through a gaping hole in the floor at the far end of the room. The "natural air conditioning" that had been described to me over the phone was now self-explanatory. To top it all off with an artsy Santa Fe touch, there was a bewildering collection of rough-hewn, wooden knick-knacks tucked into or dangling from every available inch of surface on the property.

A completely eccentric, one-in-a-million, old character named Max, who had created this whacky setting, lived on the property alone. He was no taller than the front gate, with a leathery, weathered face he kept clenched in a quizzical expression that made him appear ageless. His wife, the painter for whom Max had built the little artist's studio, had left him years before. "No fuzz off my peach!" he'd snort, punctuating his indifference to that situation and to nearly everything else. Now, officially retired and a hermit by choice, Max was an endearing, crusty old man who filled his days with non-stop carpentry and woodworking projects. A prized industrial buzz saw and a proud display of the noisy power tools with which his makeshift workshop had been fully equipped, were set up in the carport right outside my window.

Beneath its eclectic surface, the entire property was an elaborate maze of interconnected, subterranean rooms and tunnels that Max had excavated all by himself. Perhaps he was really a mole masquerading as an old man, I remember thinking. When he was not creating wooden knick-knacks, digging holes in the ground was his primary joy and passion.

It was here, in this surreal setting that I settled in for a two-month intensive of meditation, prayer, and working with Oneness on the book—with earplugs—and in the off-hours, preparing for the upcoming fall expo tour. For hours at a time I sat in the little gazebo with sterling silver wire, crystal points, faceted gemstones and pearls, creating an exquisite collection of one-of-a-kind, handmade pendulums to sell in the Earthstar jewelry booth during the expo tour—hundreds of them.

With the thousands of left-over gemstone bits I'd culled from old rep samples of obsolete earrings, I designed a sparkling collection of "Gypsy" necklaces, no two alike. And so, we passed the summer together, day after day, me nestled in the little gazebo, wielding a pair of jewelry pliers and sporting a helmet of magnifying goggles, and old Max a few yards away in a baseball cap, engrossed in his wood-working, each of us creating our own rendition of the eclectic "art" that Santa Fe is known for. Who is to say what constitutes "art"?

One of the most incredible experiences of my entire spiritual journey, which vividly illustrated a piece of theoretical understanding that had just been transcribed, took place in this most unusual setting.

The mystery of the disappearing package

After weeks of painstakingly designing and assorting the components of more than five hundred beautiful "Gypsy" necklaces, which I'd hoped to showcase in the Earthstar booth at upcoming expos all over America, the necklaces were ready to be assembled. Carefully, I packed up all the little necklace "kits" into a tidy parcel and shipped it overnight to Florida, where a friend named Carol had offered to assemble them for me and attach all the little beaded pieces onto sterling silver chains. It had been a huge job getting it all ready for her. And finally, after thinking about nothing but necklaces day and night, I was relieved to be free to focus on something else.

For days on end, I began to explore the inner sanctums of my consciousness in depth, with the help of Oneness. I steeped myself in my spiritual practice, and delved into an intensive of meditation and prayer that I could tell had augmented my energies significantly. I had a sense that something inside me had shifted dramatically, and that somehow I had made a major vibrational "jump," once again *ascending* to a higher vibrational level of reality. Oneness confirmed it. Initially, I was feeling absolutely fantastic, and basked in the moment. Everything was going right.

I understood from the teachings of Oneness that each of us is a composite of consciousness. There were countless variations on the theme of the identity I thought of as "me." Which version of "me" would be *experienced,* and which variations on the circumstances of my life would be perceived as having *happened,* were determined by my energy field, and where it stood in relation to the level of reality in which I was experiencing self-perception.

I realized, from having steeped myself in the Oneness teachings I'd been transcribing, that if I *had* indeed ascended, I was no longer experiencing the events of my life at the *heights* of the level of reality to which I'd grown accustomed. I would have ascended into the *bottom* of a vibrationally augmented reality, a reality where, by comparison, my own energy field registered at the low end of the scale. That's the point in the ascension process where it stops being a joy-ride, and suddenly the going gets rough.

I knew all this intellectually. Now here I was actually living it. I was braced for the inevitable plunge to come, where one's mood and one's circumstances begin to nosedive. At least, I was prepared for it in theory. But, are any of us really prepared when life serves us something that's off the charts, something for which there is no frame of reference?

Oneness took pains to remind me that ultimately I would be teaching these concepts to others, and that it was not enough just to understand them. I was told that it was necessary to have made the journey myself, in order to be able to speak from my own experience, instead of from my mind. It was clear that I'd been forewarned. I was primed and ready for something to happen. I just didn't know quite what.

A week passed and I still hadn't heard from Carol, so I phoned her to be sure the package had arrived safely and to see how she was coming along with the project. "What package?" Carol asked. My jaw dropped. And, my heart sank. The package had never been delivered. And, of course, in my hurry to send it on its way, I had forgotten to insure it, a detail that had, no doubt, been orchestrated at some higher level to punctuate the point of the exercise. Alarmed, I phoned UPS with the tracking number. After a few minutes of waiting on hold for some explanation, I was redirected to a supervisor. And, the story that began to unfold grew more and more extraordinary as the days to come went by.

The bottom line was that UPS could not explain what happened to that package. The supervisor, a kind, soft-spoken woman named Janet, told me quite frankly that UPS was not often baffled, but in this case it appeared that the package had literally vanished in mid-air. UPS confirmed that the package was scanned in Santa Fe, and was scanned again at an airport in Kentucky, as it was being loaded into what they called an "igloo." This was their term for an igloo-shaped container that packages travel in while on the cargo planes that transport them. When the plane landed in South Florida, the package was no longer inside the igloo. Janet promised to stay in touch with me and keep me posted.

The entire situation didn't add up. And, as the days went by, I began to suspect that something weird was going on. I'd been completely immersed in the work with Oneness in the days leading up to the incident, and as far-fetched as it seemed, I began to wonder if somehow that might have something to do with the missing package. Finally, in desperation, I confronted Oneness with my suspicions. Not surprisingly, my instincts had served me well.

With incredible patience and loving support, Oneness guided me through a process that helped me explore some well-hidden fears and unravel a mystery that appeared to be straight out of "The Twilight Zone."

Oneness speaks:

This is Oneness. We note that your mood has shifted. And, once again, your plummeting energies have been reflected in the life circumstances you have manifested today and should serve to punctuate for you the lessons about which you are writing.

Rasha speaks:

Gee thanks!

We note your sarcasm.

Are you referring to the package that disappeared?

That is one event that was noteworthy for you.

That was not at all cool. What happened to my package?

You dematerialized it.

What!!! How did that happen? What could I possibly have done wrong that would have dematerialized my package?

You have done nothing wrong. You have created for yourself a very interesting example by which to learn this material.

Oh great! Let me get this straight. Have I ascended out of the reality in which that package was mailed?

Indeed you have. But, that fact alone would not have dematerialized the package.

I wondered about that. How come I still have the tracking number of that package "here"? Why didn't that dematerialize too?

Because it was in your possession and thus traveled with you.

So what about the package?

The package was shipped and scanned, yet the party to which it was addressed did not make the shifts that you did in the interim period. Thus, the package remains in the reality in which it was shipped. You, however, are no longer there. The being representative of the recipient *here*, being of your creation at *this* level, is not the variation on *her* consciousness with "true focus." That being is at the level in which the package was shipped. At that level, the package will materialize and will be delivered tomorrow. This delay was created by you to help you understand some of what can happen as people jump levels rapidly.

Ok. Let me see if I understand this. Some version of Carol, in the reality I was in when I mailed the package, will receive that package tomorrow? And to whom will she mail the completed work? Who will pay her for that work?

The aspect of your consciousness that remains there. At that level, the necklaces will be completed, paid for, and shipped on time for sale at the expos that will transpire at that level.

For heaven's sake! I need those necklaces for my shows!! Can't I have them too?

Yes, you can. That is the entire point of the exercise. You can consciously retrieve the necklaces, as well as the aspect of self to whom they will be addressed. By integrating that piece of fragmented consciousness, rather than leaving her behind, you will complete that aspect of the work and will have, intact, those variations on the theme you consider to be *you*.

I think I understand. Let me try to recap and tell me if I've got it right, ok?

Go ahead.

I think what may have happened is that I have jumped levels. I have been feeling just awful all day after having emerged in an augmented reality, and I'm experiencing my own density here as adversity.

I allowed myself to get really off-balance about the missing package, which lowered my vibration even further, vis-à-vis the levels in which I was experiencing focus, making me feel even worse. In addition, somehow, I disconnected with an aspect of self, in making that shift, and inadvertently left her behind. How's that? Am I close? Is that what happened?

That is precisely what happened.

So how did that piece of me become fragmented? How are we supposed to "ascend" with all our bits and pieces?

Be aware that you are jumping levels at an unusual rate of acceleration and that typically, one has the chance to integrate, vibrationally, all aspects of one's essence, prior to making the shift. In this case, there were aspects of self that were uncomfortable with the process, and had not surrendered to the concept of what is transpiring. *Her* doubts and fears surrounding *your* choices kept her grounded in the reality from which *you* ascended.

In essence, you were divided on an issue, and you manifested being divided energetically as a result. An aspect of your being chose to stay behind out of fear of not being able to handle the consequences of what *you* have undertaken. This fear will not relieve her of the inevitability of having to face this issue. The fear will merely serve to manifest for her the materialization of her fears, unless you can resolve the lingering doubts that are still present, energetically, on the issue of this writing work and the speaking engagements you have undertaken to do.

Don't forget, you are *living* this book. You will succeed in manifesting everything that you fear or truly believe to be so. For, that is the nature of the process. You get to be "right" about everything. That's how it works. If you want to change the outcome, it is necessary to change the parameters which create it. If you wish to manifest unity with all Creation, it is necessary to manifest unity within your own Being. You cannot be divided within yourself and be united unto yourself at the same time.

In order to ascend fully and completely at the levels you are approaching, it is necessary that all *separation* be transcended. It is necessary for you to examine your true feelings on this and other major issues and resolve your lingering doubt and fears. The energy of God-focused intent, trusting completely in the perfection of the process to deliver you intact, is what is needed now.

You are able to integrate your separated-out aspects of self. And, in so doing, you will experience a sense of wholeness and well being unlike any you have experienced thus far. We encourage you to explore thoroughly your beliefs and feelings on this issue, and heal the divisions that have caused you to become fragmented.

Can I ask a question?

Of course you can. This exercise is for your benefit.

Is the aspect of self that I experience as my focus the highest vibrational aspect, amongst many aspects of self who are presumably divided on various issues?

Indeed that is so. The aspect of self that you experience is the highest expression of self at any given moment, on any given issue. Where there is division, the dissenting aspect of self is relegated to the level at which she resonates, vibrationally, on that issue. The higher vibration of the greater part of the being as a whole, determines the levels at which "reality" is experienced by *you*.

I think I understand.

We think you understand, too. But, understanding and putting understanding into practice are separate processes. The opportunity is here before you to integrate both parts of that process.

Ok. Let me get this straight, with regards to the package. The package was scanned when it left Santa Fe, in the reality in which I was present at that moment. The computer has a record of that. I have the paperwork, because it was in my possession. So, there's proof that the package existed. However, in the interim period, I shifted levels. Thus, the computer "here" appears to have no trace of what happened to that package, which purportedly remained behind at the level I transcended.

Because of the nature of the uncertainty and the separation I am experiencing within myself, the package appears to be in some sort of energetic limbo. You say it will be delivered "there" tomorrow. In order for me to manifest the package in this reality, I need to integrate the aspect of self that I left behind because I am divided within myself on a certain issue. So, I need to go within and resolve my discomfort on that issue and transcend the fear that is at the root of it. Right?

You have the idea.

In writing, Oneness guided me through a process in which I scrutinized the fear that I'd been so unwilling to face. I began to dig deeply within myself, as the process went on, and as I did I could feel the intensity of the repressed terror that I'd kept harbored there, while for years I'd deluded myself into believing that everything was fine. I began to experience the full throttle of the repressed energy as I brought it all to the surface. I made declarations, out loud, as I embraced the fear—and then released it. My body began to shake as the energy continued to build to a crescendo within me. And then, suddenly, all was still.

At the height of the process I heard a thunderous noise. It was a crash! A multi-car crash—complete with screeching brakes and several loud explosions of impact—the kind of crash where you knew something serious had just happened. At that very moment it was taking place right outside, on the main road, half-a-block away.

Startled and shaken, I jumped up from my computer and ran out the door! Suddenly, the entire neighborhood was outside. People began streaming out of the little café on the corner and into the street to see what had happened. Police cars had been called and arrived on the scene with sirens wailing. And, we all stopped dead. There wasn't a trace of an accident anywhere. There were no wrecked cars. No bodies. Not a sign that anything out of the ordinary had happened. All that could be seen were some dirt tracks on the pavement, where it appeared that a car had driven through the flower bed in the median, and a few large rocks that had been displaced, sitting in the middle of the road. Other than that, there was no trace that anything had happened.

People began turning to each other with baffled looks and asking, "Did you hear something? It sure sounded like there was a car crash out here!" I shook my head in disbelief and retreated back to my little studio and my computer, where Oneness was still patiently waiting to pick up where we had left off.

Rasha speaks:

Oneness, something very strange just happened. There was what sounded like a very serious car crash outside. But, when I ran out to see if anyone was hurt, there was no crash. There were lots of neighbors and police cars in the street, but no trace of an accident anywhere. Was that a coincidence? Or ... (I hesitated, as I considered the absurdity of what I was about to say), by any chance, did this have something to do with integrating the fragmented aspect of my consciousness in that moment?

Oneness speaks:

There is no such thing as a coincidence, Rasha. The car crash which was heard here *did* happen—energetically. But, it took place in a different reality. In that moment, the two realities were integrated. As the vibration of the fragmented aspect of self was integrated into the sum-totality of *your* energy field, her reality was united with the reality of your conscious focus.

The incident that was simultaneously taking place at the denser level in which that fragmented aspect of self had been experiencing herself, was also brought forward energetically. But, due to the density of the elements in question, they could not sustain form and thus dematerialized. All the people who were auditory witnesses to the event concurred that a crash had taken place. Energetically, it did. Yet, the event did not materialize in the here and now of your focus, where it was unable to sustain form. Do you understand?

Yes, I do. This is absolutely fascinating.

Yes, it is. And, it will become more so as you delve more and more deeply into the process. You can anticipate having experiences that you can't explain, as a regular occurrence, as part of this process. You have just been given a taste of the kind of experience that is to be expected as one jumps levels and integrates fragmented aspects of self.

This is absolutely amazing. Thank you so very much for this extraordinary training!

That night, I went to sleep, exhausted. The next morning, I awoke feeling just awful. I was fearful. I was depressed. I had a negative attitude about everything I could think of. Overall, I was in an extremely bad mood. I reminded myself that Oneness had said I was not backsliding, but only experiencing the results of integrating an aspect of self from a denser reality. I knew I was feeling the results of taking on the burden of that diminished energy. But, understanding it didn't make me *feel* better. And, to make matters worse, it appeared that I now had to deal, emotionally, with an augmented version of fears that I knew would gradually be resolved over time, but which now manifested as an exaggeration of the issues I had worked so hard at resolving.

As the details of processing this bizarre story were still churning around inside me, suddenly my mind stopped spinning and came to a screeching halt. There before me was one crystal clear, all-consuming realization: I *have* her! Where's the package?

I leaped out of bed, ran to the phone, and called Janet at UPS. She laughed as she answered. "I can't believe you called right now. A few minutes ago, your package was spotted coming down a conveyor belt, all by itself, at a UPS depot in South Florida. No one can explain how it got there or where it's been all week." She promised the package would be delivered immediately to Carol. I smiled to myself and thanked her. Without missing a beat, I went straight to the computer, to pick up the threads of the exercise with Oneness.

Rasha speaks:

Oneness, what just happened?

Oneness speaks:

What do you think just happened?

It seems like I succeeded in integrating my fearful aspect of self into the whole, fears and all, and I experienced a magnified version of her fears and her density. It felt just awful. By integrating her, I consolidated the two realities. The package, which was linked energetically to her, was able to shift to this reality and materialize here. How's that? Did I get it right?

Indeed you have. The package suddenly appeared as if out of thin air.

Why did it take so long? It felt like I integrated the fragmented aspect of self during the process last night. Is that when the shift occurred?

Yes, that is exactly when the shift occurred. You owned your fear. Now you are sorting through it and refining the aspects of that integration. You sustained the adverse symptoms of the shift for the entire rest of the evening without making the correlation. When you made the association between the package and the integration of the denied fear this morning, the package, which was energetically tied to the process of integration, was able to materialize.

Amazing! Can we talk about the car crash?

The car crash was another dramatic materialization that was created by you to punctuate the point of the lesson. At the very moment that you were integrating your fearful aspect of self into your energetic whole, an automobile accident was taking place in the other reality. As you merged the two realities in that moment, with the strength of your declarations, you pulled the one set of circumstances into the other reality.

Energetically, the accident was perceived here. Others heard the crash. There were signs on the road of a crash having occurred. There were tracks of dirt from the flower bed that had been traversed on the pavement. That is because the earth and the plant kingdom have no difficulty bridging dimensions. Energetically, their presence is identical in both realities and does not alter from one to the next. Their range of adaptation is far broader than would be the capability of human and animal life. Thus, the appearance of tracks of dirt on the road.

But, where were the cars and the casualties?

They were unable to sustain form in the higher reality to which they shifted in that split-second time frame, and they remained in the reality in which the incident occurred.

Was anyone hurt?

Yes, several people were hurt.

Was it my fault in any way?

No, you did not cause the accident. Many felt the shift. For people in the area, there was a sense of unrealness to the energies as that process was transpiring. What you did was extremely powerful and had far-reaching ramifications. Do not underestimate the strength of a process such as that one and the strength of the focused declarations of intent that were used to achieve the integration. This was a powerful example for you of what you are capable of, and moreover, the nature of the process in which you are deeply involved.

Thank you with all my heart for helping me process this experience.

That is what we are here to do with you, and so much more.

6

Fall 1999/Winter 2000
Shifting Gears

———————

Fall shifted into place like clockwork in early September 1999. And, without missing a beat, the closet micro-manager who was still carefully harbored within me rose to the occasion and launched into a frenzy of last-minute preparations for the unrelenting schedule of Fall expo appearances that was poised and ready to begin. Before I knew it, my laid-back, two-month sojourn in Santa Fe had faded into the fleeting glimmer of a brilliant New Mexico sunset, and once again, I found myself watching the last traces of it disappear in the rear-view mirror. With it, the strangely magical life I'd come to know there seemed literally to vanish, as if absorbed into the blazing, red horizon. It all may as well have been a dream.

There was something so incredibly liberating about driving cross-country again—blessedly alone! The first stop on the fall expo tour was to be Minneapolis. And, on impulse, in place of the monotonous, interstate highway itinerary that AAA had mapped out, I opted for navigating the distance via back roads all the way. It was a chance to catch a glimpse of America that was off the beaten track, and, in snatches, to explore some of the remote corners of my consciousness at the same time.

Days melted together as I headed due east across the parched, unforgiving desert of New Mexico and the Texas panhandle, and then veered straight north through the barest hint of Oklahoma, before plunging into the pregnant, harvest-laden landscape of Kansas and Nebraska. Beyond it, vast, homey stretches of rural South Dakota heartland awaited me, while the forested, emerald haven of Minnesota loomed in the distance, like the pot at the end of the rainbow.

Mile by mile, I watched as my perceptions of the world beyond the windshield transformed in increments, as the softly muted, pastel tones of the New Mexico desert emerged as endless vistas of green. They were subtle shifts in scenery that seemed like uncanny footnotes to the dramatically changing landscape taking place within.

Driving for days on end had always been a wonderfully powerful exercise in catharsis for me. There, suspended in time, in the middle of nowhere,

I talked out loud for hours at a time to Oneness—who never ceased to amaze me by replying with terse, hard-hitting Divine wisdom. Lest I be left wandering the back alleys of one illusion or another, Oneness carefully helped me dismantle some of the major turning points of this latest episode in inner discovery—and helped me cull the pearls of understanding from the illusory shells of some of the dramas I'd acted out.

Yet, despite my ever-deepening surrender to the connection with Oneness, I'd still remained in constant contact with Amitabh, my cherished inner Guru and the Source of the teachings my first book, *The Calling*. In those early days of my spiritual journey, when it came to practical matters, it was often the Divine guidance of Amitabh that emerged from within me to see me through.

In Minneapolis, I'd be delivering the first of a series of lectures on a hot-potato topic that I could speak on from hard-earned experience: "Channeling: Developing Spiritual Discernment." For years, Amitabh had prepared me to dive head first into a subject so many tiptoe around with the utmost caution. There had been two entire chapters in my book, *The Calling*, devoted exclusively to what, in mild-mannered spiritual circles, seemed to be considered a taboo topic. In preparation for the expo tour, Amitabh had taken the opportunity to steep me in a refresher course that took me back to the very core of those principles and helped me re-examine them. Now, those powerful teachings were poised and ready to come to life.

At Amitabh's suggestion, we prepared a demonstration that would give my audiences a chance to try out the color-pattern energy identification system that had been such an integral part of my early training as a courier of Divine guidance. When I finally put it to the test and brought the Amitabh energies forth into the room during each lecture, I was astounded at the show of hands from those who were actually able to see the energy "fingerprint" in their mind's eye.

The object of the exercise was to introduce the possibility of using this visualization technique as a tool for assessing the vibrational level of channeled consciousness—regardless of whether one was sitting in an audience or was bringing through a channeled presence oneself—and thereby help each person to determine for himself whether or not the information being presented was worth listening to. On the basis of the questions from these audiences, I was amazed to discover just how many people had had firsthand contact with the phenomenon of channeling—both exalted experiences and troubling ones.

Amitabh's training prepared me to broach a subject of widespread interest—and quiet concern—with a potent blend of down-to-earth common sense and timeless Divine wisdom.

Amitabh discusses developing *discernment* with regard to channeling

Amitabh speaks:

The intention here is not to impose judgment, but to encourage *discernment*. Your message will be "consider the source" when assessing the value of channeled material. Information imparted by extraterrestrial intelligence, for example, will be of a different orientation entirely than would Divinely inspired material. The energy accompanying the information would differ accordingly. Whether or not the information imparted has value is the issue that people must determine for themselves.

We are not suggesting that you present this demonstration as a barometer of valuable versus worthless channeled information, nor do we suggest that these techniques are shortcuts that would take the responsibility for determining value off the shoulders of the recipient of the information. Rather, we would suggest that you encourage each member of your audience to search within his/her own consciousness for the reasons they would seek out channeled information in the first place.

If the reason is to absolve themselves from the necessity to take responsibility for their lives, then that vibration of dependency will attract to it energy that seeks to take command of the power of other beings and foster dependency. High-level teaching guides will not do your thinking for you. You know this from long experience. They will not make your choices for you. For, to do so would be counterproductive to the entire point of being in physical form and coming into conscious awareness in these times.

The training that couriers of Divine guidance come to impart is *self-empowerment*. The message that they instill in those who seek their wisdom is that the answers are found within the depths of one's own being. The truth you seek is within you.

Deferring to the perceived wisdom of others will not strengthen your own abilities to source the answers yourself. And, this message is consistent, coming through many sources of channeled wisdom. For, the message is the truth—the only truth possible on the path to Oneness—*the* truth. Any channeled consciousness that purports to tell an individual what to do is robbing that individual of his free will and seeking to disempower that individual. The objective is to help instill *discernment* and guide the sincere student of higher wisdom to connect with the vast reserves of inner resources that lie dormant within one's own consciousness.

This is the message that you will impart on the occasions that you speak on this topic. To you, much of it will be common sense. But, to your audience, many of whom will have firsthand experiences—and much trepidation and confusion—this is a weighty topic and one on which they welcome your experience and guidance.

Rasha speaks:

What about the subject of calling in protection, and the question of what is meant by "protection"? There are some who would say that feeling the need for protection is "coming from fear." How do you suggest I address this sort of question? It's bound to come up. This is not a separate issue. And, it's relevant.

It is sound advice to suggest that before attempting to communicate with another consciousness that one calls in the protection of one's guides, in much the same way that you do, using whatever words one wishes to use. The *intention* is what is important here. The integrity of the communication and the sanctity of the space being created—that sacred space of one's own consciousness—is the priceless possession that one would wish to protect.

When one is specific about the level of consciousness with which one invites interaction, the laws of the universe are equally specific in who is permitted to respond. One would be well advised to read between the lines of what is said to determine whether the intelligence with which you have connected is, in fact, who it may *imply* that it is.

When one is very clear as to who is being invited, then one's invitation cannot be misinterpreted to be one that reads "open house." When one is discriminating in one's interactions with other forms of intelligence, one is assured of the highest level of information that one is able to receive. Ask for the highest level of Divine wisdom that you are capable of carrying, and chances are, your request will be met by energy that is of value to you.

When one is vague in one's invitation, one opens the door to interactions that would be of less value and could lead one into confusion. When beginning your session, be it channeling, meditation, or *any* practice that would put you into an altered state of consciousness, it is highly advisable to become centered in the heart space within—and focused on the intention to connect with the Source of Divine Light and wisdom. Using any of a number of techniques that most spiritual seekers have at their disposal, one's conscious awareness is then filled with Divine Radiance.

When one is thus focused—focused in the Light—one *is* Light. That is sufficient protection from interference from any opportunistic sources that may have sought to establish a connection. The joy one experiences when in harmony with one's Source is an indication that one is Light focused, and that the process of expanding one's consciousness to external sources of intelligence may be safely approached.

The expo in Minneapolis led to another one in Cleveland, which led to Chicago, which led to New York City, at which point, it was time to do a major about-face and head back the other way to Austin, Texas. My daughter, Susanna who, thankfully, was able to join me as Earthstar's booth manager for the entire Fall expo season, had occasionally been flying between some of the venues. But, we'd decided to share the drive between Austin and Atlanta, and ended up sharing the surreal memory of having to pull over, all throughout the night, to scrape off the remains of an unrelenting blizzard of locusts that persisted in encrusting every inch of the van. It was, no doubt, an ominous sign of what awaited us just down the road.

With Texas finally behind us, and with the quasi-biblical imagery of the hail of locusts still fresh in our minds, suddenly our brisk momentum ground down to the snail's pace of another kind of adventure. There, in resignation, we squeezed our way into a tense, bumper-to-bumper exodus, creeping north from New Orleans—where we had optimistically figured we'd spend the night—as untold thousands fled the ominous threat of an approaching hurricane! We'd soon discover that there was literally not a hotel room to be had anywhere in the southern USA that night. We ended up driving straight through from Austin, Texas to Birmingham, Alabama before we found somewhere to stop—well into the following day.

The entire ordeal was the proverbial icing on the cake—a crowning moment of calamity to top off a time of non-stop chaos, laced with an air of perpetual frenzy. Secretly, I suspected by then that I'd actually metamorphosed into a distorted caricature of everything the formerly serene, spiritually-focused aspect of self—who I prayed was still hidden within me somewhere—was not. By the time the Fall Expo tour was over and I'd returned to my little condo in South Florida and the lifestyle of my spiritual alter-ego, I had become completely unrecognizable to myself.

Several chapters of *Oneness*, transcribed in quick succession over the course of the next few weeks, brought me back to life and reminded me once again of a nearly forgotten world—a world of stillness, inner peace, and harmony. Shifting gears within, I discovered that somehow, perhaps in spite of myself, I'd managed to find my way back home to the Oneness within, once more.

Insights from Oneness on the higher purpose of the process of transcription
Oneness speaks:
You have shifted to a higher octave of Beingness in doing this work. When you relinquish the need to focus in self-awareness during this process, you find you are able to slip easily into the state of Being in which your documentation of this information is simultaneous to the inception of thought.

In this moment, you have little or no awareness of your own conscious thought processes and have merged, in isolated moments, with the Oneness that is the true Self-essence. Do not fault yourself for your inability to *sustain* that state of connectedness. For, the process is one in which, initially, you slip in and out of the state of awareness and non-awareness of Self.

As you continue to document these thoughts, it becomes increasingly easier to *Be the act of communication* and to cease your perception of your own presence being on the receiving end of it. There is, in actuality, no giving or receiving end of this process, but only one activity: the documentation of information.

When you are at Source with these energies, there is literally no differentiation between *you* and that with which you perceive yourself to be interacting. For, all is, quite literally, Oneness. You are in that state of Oneness, in the present moment. And, you have been given this experience as an opportunity to taste, experientially, what you will be experiencing at the culmination of the ascension process.

It is not enough for you to intellectualize the teachings you are transcribing. In order to be able to teach these concepts in a meaningful way, it is important for you to have experienced merging with the heightened aspects of Self. You will have many opportunities to connect at this level in the times to come.

I've always sensed that timing plays a key role in signaling the validity of the kinds of life directions that seem to come knocking at your door from out of left field, cloaked in an air of inevitability you just can't explain. It had been nearly a year-and-a-half since the very first inkling of the idea of a trip to India was gently seeded in the fertile soil of my mind. Or perhaps, the possibility was retrieved from some future edition of the annals of time where, no doubt, it already stood, indelibly etched. In any case, there was little question that what, at first, had seemed preposterous was, in fact, a *fait accompli*—a life-changing turning point, patiently biding its time until its appointed moment turned up. Clearly, India—of all places—awaited me.

Back in 1998, when the first mention of a possible visit to India came up in a conversation with Dr. Bindu, it struck me as completely off the wall and out of the question. But, as time went by, I recognized that, strangely enough, I'd grown comfortable with the idea of making such a journey, someday. Now, suddenly, it felt right. And, it was clear that the timing was perfect.

Instinctively, I took the plunge, and accepted Dr. Bindu's invitation to spend several weeks studying with him in Mumbai to learn a particular, long, and complex Mantra—a huge undertaking that he insisted could only be done in India. My priority in making the trip would be focused on the time spent with him. And although, at the end of that time, I would do a little sightseeing and go on to pay a few token visits to some of the big-name Indian Gurus that a typical Western spiritual tourist might go to see on a first trip to India, they would be stops made largely out of curiosity—not the object of the journey.

I wasn't going to India to look for a Guru. On that point, I was clear— or so I thought. There was no question in my mind that I was already a devotee of the ultimate Guru, the one who had emerged from within me—my Oneness. And, at the same time, I was no less a devotee of my beloved spiritual mentor, Amitabh. Yet, it seemed like the moment was right to venture out from the sheltered spiritual nest in which I'd been so carefully nurtured, and discover the world. With the eager, wide-eyed innocence of a little kid getting psyched for the first day of kindergarten, I approached Oneness for guidance.

❦

Preparing for a first trip to India
Rasha speaks:

Oneness, do you have any guidance to offer regarding my trip to India? Are there any teachers or places that you'd suggest I visit?

Oneness speaks:

Your instincts will serve you well in determining your direction on this journey. It matters little, if at all, which of several possible destinations is chosen. Your own personal process will unfold according to schedule, regardless of which environment is selected. For, the energies that will be encountered will suffice as a catalyst for the transformative process that is anticipated for you. The process, as you well know, is not one that is externalized, but rather, transpires within the sanctity of your own inner recesses. The breakthroughs realized are not to be credited to any being in physical form other than your own inner Source.

Oneness speaks on the opportunities inherent in working with a spiritual teacher

The difficulty so many encounter with spiritual teachers is the tendency to Deify the teacher rather than to recognize the Divinity within that the teacher hopes to kindle. The opportunity in an encounter with a Divine being is to recognize the Divinity that is *shared* rather than to exalt the persona who embodies that energy.

The opportunity will be presented for you to observe how Grace manifests as physicality, not with an eye to emulating that state, but with an eye to the level of *surrender* that would allow such a state to be made manifest. This is not a process of the mind, but rather a journey of the heart. It is not a science of learned rituals that one *does* in order to achieve an exalted bearing. Rather, it is a focus of intent to open to and merge with the energies of Divine Love that makes such union possible.

You will have the opportunity to taste the initial stages of that process in the days soon to come. And, the energies assimilated in the process will aid in your stabilization at the next level. You will be making quantum leaps in awareness during this process. And, you will come away with a profound sense of connectedness to all life as a result of this experience. Your willingness to be totally in the moment with your journey will allow for the highest choices to be made manifest for you.

We rejoice with you at this joyous time. Prepare well for the mundane aspects of your voyage. And, allow for the perfection of synchronicity to nudge you in the direction of wonder and adventure.

Despite my inner resolve and presumed indifference on the question of Indian Gurus, the issue continued to lurk in the shadows of my awareness. In the days soon to come, Oneness came forth with a spontaneous teaching on the very subject that persisted in nudging at me—a dilemma that would go on to become a recurring theme throughout much of my spiritual journey.

Oneness addresses the timeless question of the need for a Guru

Oneness speaks:

We would like to address an issue that has been weighing on your mind: the concept of a Guru. As we have said to you on many occasions, there is no actual need for a connection with a Guru, in your own particular case. For, the Divine connection that the Guru would be able to facilitate for you has already been made. That is the nature of your own particular process.

The concept of the Guru is surely a valid one and has withstood the tests of time as a vehicle for elevating the consciousness and opening to the higher levels of connectedness that, traditionally, marked what we have identified to you as *the ascension process*. Yet, in these times, under the present conditions, the concept of a physical Guru is one that has outlived its status as an exclusive vehicle toward achieving a state of transcendence. The conditions now upon you call for a shift in mass consciousness that is far too widespread to be dependent upon the initiation and monitoring of a Guru in physical form.

While many will continue to exercise the option of hovering under the protective wing of a Guru as part of the process of ascension, many will, for logistical reasons, need to forego the luxury of that kind of journey. It is for those beings that *your* skills have been enlisted. For, the teachings that come through you are slated for the masses that would not have sought the protection and nurturing of a Guru in a traditional way.

We in no way wish to dismiss the importance of working with a Guru, for those who have chosen that path, but rather, to impress upon you that you have not erred in any way in following your own inner guidance as your chosen route. It is that level of *self-empowerment* that you have come here to teach. And as such, you will come to be considered a Guru in your own right, in the eyes of many, as the process unfolds for you.

We note your own incredulity as to your qualification to play such a role. Yet, it is your own very lack of formalized training, combined with innate capabilities, that qualifies you for playing this role in this time frame. You have been discouraged and, in many cases, prevented from prejudicing your mind with information that would have you addressing your subject from the standpoint of any one particular school of thought or body of knowledge. Rather, you have been given an overview that has provided you with a broad awareness of many approaches, while keeping you free of the indoctrination that would color your own consciousness.

You have been told many times along the way that you are, what has been termed, "an innocent." And it was necessary to keep you protected in that way, so that the integrity of the communication you will carry will remain untainted. In the times to come, there will be much support in the form of beings who might be considered to be a Guru to others. You will not be "assigned" to any of these blessed beings as a disciple nor as a student, but will be welcomed as a "torch-bearer" in your own right.

Your preparation has not been lacking in any way. For, you have indeed been trained by *the* Master, despite the fact that that Master has not taken the form of a physical being in imparting that training to you. The process is actually the same, were the Master to come to you in physical form through a Guru, or in non-physical form in this way. For, the Master is Oneness. The connectedness to be imparted is Oneness. And, the connection you have come to facilitate for the others who will be guided to your path is one's own ability to connect with Oneness while retaining one's own autonomy.

You will find the need to discourage those who are drawn to the wisdom you document from transferring their longings for connectedness on to you. For, the connection they wish to make will be achieved by relinquishing ties to any other physical source than their own being. ✓

Oneness outlines the personalized, Self-directed path to spiritual mastery

This is a new school of spiritual thought. This is a new approach to the time-honored spiritual journey. In these times, the need to subscribe to a traditional *lineage,* provided by an affiliation with a Guru, has been transcended by your abilities, as physical beings, to elevate vibrationally to levels that, traditionally, required a facilitator.

As you have so amply documented in the book you are transcribing, you, as a race of beings, are not even remotely of the same vibrational constitution that you were only a generation ago. The consensus wisdom that has been painstakingly passed down as spiritual gospel from Guru to disciple, for untold thousands of years, surely is ready to be updated and re-presented for the conditions now at hand.

While the traditional methods will continue to endure and will ring true to those who are culturally and spiritually pre-disposed to aligning themselves with those paths, there is new information and a new approach that is relevant to the times and vibrational conditions at hand. That direction is the one that you have come here to deliver. And, you are cautioned not to succumb to the fears that may be instilled by others by virtue of the fact that your approach does not correspond to the teachings to which they and all in their ancient lineage have subscribed.

There is validity in all approaches. And, the time-honored ones are no more or less capable of delivering the spiritual aspirant unto a state of Self-Realization than the principles of self-empowerment that are being provided for these times. You may choose to avail yourself of the loving guidance and the support of those beings whose paths you will have crossed—or not—as you see fit. But, your focus and your truth remains your own.

It is not required to subscribe to the criteria of anyone. The validation that might be forthcoming from such an action, would, by definition, be superfluous. Your exposure to the temptation to "give your power away" has been provided for you to punctuate the point for you of where you stand with regard to the content of the material you are documenting. This is not an exercise in "truth by consensus," Rasha, but rather, your liberation from that kind of conditioning.

7

Spring 2000
A Journey into the Great Unknown
Destination: India!

M y plane touched down in Mumbai, India, but, for all intents and
purposes, it may as well have been a different planet. The contrast
between the sights, sounds, and smells that suddenly overwhelmed my
senses and the recognizable world I'd left behind in the West, couldn't
have been more blatant. Even though I'd devoured the highlights of at least
half a dozen guidebooks in preparation for this adventure, nothing prepares
you for India. To the Western eye, looking instinctively for a sense of the
familiar, India is completely off the map—in a total world of its own! Little did
I suspect that those vivid first impressions were just the tip of the iceberg—
a small hors d'oeuvre from the feast life had in store for me this time.

It was early evening when I entered the spacious room where Dr. Bindu
Purohit was staying at the Hare Krishna Temple in Juhu Beach, and stepped
into the mystical world of a modern day spiritual Master. The air was thick
with the exotic fragrance of incense and the ethers shimmered with the
radiant, sacred energies of The Goddess. It was here, in what now appeared to
be a contemporary guest room, that secret formulations of ancient Mantras
had been chanted non-stop since the wee hours before dawn.

A small collection of exquisitely formed metal objects, which I recognized
as *yantras*, were placed ceremoniously on a vividly-colored red cloth atop
a small altar. I knew these sacred yantras were in the process of being prepared
for a small handful of people from all over the world. How had I been so
lucky to be amongst them? I wondered. It was a miracle. One of these precious
objects was actually meant for me. Yet, I knew that it might be years before
it would be ready and I would be able to hold it.

We talked on into the night, for what seemed like days on end, about
everything imaginable. I was able to discuss certain spiritual understandings
with him, concepts that had been gleaned solely from my dialogues with
Oneness, and found to my amazement that I finally had found someone who
spoke my language. Spiritual truth is universal, it seems, and has appeared as
a common thread in the sacred traditions of the world throughout history.

I was simply unaware of that. And, it was with no end of gratitude, and no small amount of relief, that I discovered that the concepts I had received and documented actually made sense to someone who is an expert in such matters.

Even so, I knew I was not even at square one on the subject of *White Tantra*, the ancient science in which Dr. Bindu had achieved a rarefied level of mastery. Over the years I'd pieced together a few fragments of understanding, during my visits and talks with him, but in the ways that really mattered, I knew I had barely scratched the surface.

By the time I finally made the trip to India, I'd come to understand that White Tantra was a timeless synthesis of two ideals: union with the Divine and the perfect health of mind and body. It was a sacred science that encompassed the entire structure of material and spiritual reality and synthesized it into one extraordinary, all-embracing body of knowledge.

Through the ages, the genius of the ancient Indian mystics had preserved this sacred knowledge, based upon the power of sound, which put man's quest for enlightenment and for health, happiness, and prosperity in perfect balance. This legacy, passed down in the ancient oral tradition for thousands of years, is an authentic spiritual art that had been perfectly preserved for the needs of today's world.

When practiced correctly, the science of Mantra propels a word or phrase with power and rhythmic incantation through the medium of the ethers, in the form of vibrational patterns that affect the human mind and body in extraordinary ways. A perfected Mantra, chanted with a particular pitch, articulation, and tone, could be used as a tool for ascension, for spiritual purification, and for shifting material reality—dramatically improving the quality of life.

Vibrational patterns of Mantras can be captured and preserved physically in the form of yantras. Using secret formulations of precious metals, yantras are painstakingly handcrafted to hold the resonance of specific categories of vibration. In this way, exacting combinations of sacred vibrational encodements can be customized to meet specific individual requirements, in much the same way as a prescription.

Dr. Bindu was considered to be one of the world's foremost practitioners of India's most sacred science. In keeping with the family heritage taught by his grandfather, and by the generations of Tantric Masters that had preceded him, Dr. Bindu had been entrusted with the treasure of this secret knowledge from ancient India and had carried it within him into these times of global spiritual transformation.

Patiently, Dr. Bindu answered my questions one by one and filled in the blanks with some of the basics of the sacred science of White Tantra.

❧

Dr. Bindu gives an intensive introduction to the sacred science of White Tantra

Rasha speaks:

Can you tell me a little about the foundation of the science of Tantra?

Dr. Bindu speaks:

In this modern world there are two sciences operating simultaneously. One is physical science and the other is spiritual science, which describes in detail how to ascend and connect with God. Within the category of spiritual science there are many techniques that guide the spiritual aspirant toward the Supreme Divine Power. Some of these techniques include prayer, worship, invocation, yoga, *shankhya, gyana* (Divine knowledge), devotion, and principles of karma.

Within *Dharma Shastra* (Hinduism), a universal body of spiritual understanding, there are two principles. One is Vedic science, which consists of four ancient scriptures known as *The Vedas*. These four main texts were passed down from antiquity from generation to generation in the oral tradition. The other principle is the Tantric system.

The Tantric system describes in exacting detail how to analyze the human mind in order to synthesize it. It's an extremely technical system, the highest technology in the world of spirituality. The science of Tantra covers many diverse areas of knowledge. Initially, it provides for the fulfillment of materialism. Once those needs and desires have been addressed, the human mind comes to the point when it opens quite naturally to the pursuit of the spiritual. Tantra is the most highly perfected spiritual technology known to man that assists the seeker in becoming One with the Supreme Divine Power.

It is very difficult to enter into the main lineage of Tantra because, for mastery, the study requires full-time devotion and dedication for at least 20 to 30 years. The authentic science of Tantra is only passed down from teacher to student in the oral tradition. There are no authentic books or scriptures available anywhere. In ancient times, Tantric seers kept the science highly secret. This secrecy was not simply to maintain a monopoly on Tantric knowledge, but to protect innocent people from the volatile potential of powers that could be unleashed through incorrect practice.

Throughout history, many have been interested in learning these techniques. But, it is the rare individual who is ready to dedicate himself to the long years of practice required for mastery. So, the ancient Tantric practitioner chose one or two people over the course of a lifetime, students who demonstrated full devotion and dedication, and gave them the sacred teachings in the timeless oral tradition. Those rare students became the next generation of Tantric Masters. And, in this way, the secret knowledge was passed down through the ages.

In today's world, many people have adapted certain small pieces of Tantric technology in hopes of creating energy and personal power with the help of Tantra. Often these techniques are being misused by self-serving practitioners who are distorting the sacred knowledge for their own pleasure and personal gain. These practices are known as Black or Red Tantra.

In Black Tantra, the technology and the energy may well be present, but not in their full dimension and purity, and so, many are ill prepared to use the techniques properly. Often, these practitioners are not mentally fit and have tainted teachings that were conceived in purity. Untold numbers of unsuspecting people, caught up in the allure of exotic, so-called "magical" powers, have gone crazy as a result of the misuse of these potent energies.

In White Tantra, the Tantric practitioner uses the sacred Tantric techniques for the well being of society. These spiritual Masters have full knowledge of the science of Tantra. At the same time, they are fully connected with The Supreme Divine Power. In their practice of Tantra, they follow the exacting ancient disciplines of the science of spirit.

In White Tantric practice, the practitioner has refined the ability to discern, using highly developed intuitive powers. Permission is then sought from high-level spiritual guides and from the Supreme Divine Power. If it is determined that a candidate who wants to learn Tantra is fully ready in his own spiritual practice, then certain techniques may be given in the time-honored oral tradition. There is a contract of understanding between the Tantric practitioner and the person to whom techniques are given that the secret knowledge can only be used for his own benefit and is not to be revealed to anyone.

In the west, simple Mantras have been made available to the public in recent years, through books and tapes. Is the chanting of such Mantras of any use at all?

Dr. Bindu speaks about the sacred practice of Sanskrit Mantra chanting

The chanting of simple Mantras can be very powerful, but only when the Mantra has been learned in the oral tradition, not from books and tapes. A Mantra must be learned from a person who has achieved "perfection" in that particular Mantra. Learning to chant from a book or tape is of no use, because in the science of Mantra the result is achieved only when the energy of sound and the combined *will power* of the teacher and the practitioner work together.

If, when learning a Mantra, the will power of the Guru is not aligned with that of the practitioner, the practitioner cannot achieve the correct meter of the Mantra. When sound energy is converted into electromagnetic energy, in creating a tape, and then the tape is played, re-creating sound energy, two things are lost. One is will power, and the other is the final and subtle sensibilities of the meter. Such a student will not be able to grasp and put into practice the exacting mathematical calculations that form the sonic system of that particular Mantra.

How can the chanting of Mantras help us to augment our energies and assist us on our spiritual journey?

Mantras are comprised of Divine words. *Om* is the signature of the Lord. The repetition of "Om" can help a person realize the Divine because it represents the Supreme Divine Power in verbal form. The vibration of the Mantra achieves its effect when the energy of sound merges with the will power that directs it. It is only when the horizontal and the vertical sound waves of the Mantra achieve the same wavelength as the juxtaposing energy waves of the human body that the Mantra is perfected and galvanizes itself. This can be achieved through constant repetition of the Mantra in its characteristic rhythm and tone.

When a practitioner repeats a Mantra, the wave pattern of that particular sound is created within and around the practitioner. With the help of constant repetition, the circle of energy becomes complete and the turbulence of thought current vanishes. The practitioner is then able to enter a state of deep meditation. It is through this practice of Mantra-meditation that a person is able to experience union with the Divine.

There are two kinds of seekers. One goes initially toward materialism and then enters into spirituality. The other group is more spiritually focused from the beginning, due to previous life karma. These people aren't drawn to spending their time pursuing material pleasures and rewards, and they enter into the mainstream of spirituality directly. The salient feature of the Tantric system is the blend of material life and spiritual life in perfect harmony. Within this system, it is possible for the spiritual seeker to progress towards perfect bliss while engaging in household and worldly affairs.

Indian saints and visionaries neither lay down their lives on the altar of spiritualism nor renounce life and the world just for the sake of it. To create the conditions where spiritual and worldly affairs are in balance, a person is guided, through the practice of Mantra, to attain a state of perfect bliss that can be experienced even while participating in worldly life. Tantra is the highest technique through which to achieve this goal.

Are there specific rules of learning Mantras correctly?

The strict supervision of a qualified Guru is first and foremost. Without the teacher, the Mantra system is not possible. Whether or not you qualify for ongoing instruction with the Guru, based on your nature, the process begins with control of the senses. The objective is to instill the practice of *obedience without consideration of logic*.

For example, my formal spiritual education began at the age of seven. I started to learn to chant Mantras and was taught how to conduct major Vedic fire rituals. At the age of 11, my Guru gave me a test. I was taken to a room and ordered to sit there and chant. I was told to chant for 24 hours a day at the highest possible volume and was not allowed to leave the room without permission. For nourishment, I was given only water of dal, the broth from boiled beans, and water. I was never told how many days I would be spending in this room. Sleep was not permitted. If I fell asleep, I was awakened after one hour. Forty-one days later, my Guru told me that I had qualified for Tantric education.

How is your knowledge of Tantric practice applied most frequently in today's world?

Tantric knowledge is often used for physical healing, material problems, spiritual problems, and for problems with entities. Sometimes cosmic forces try to disturb people and disrupt their lives and their spiritual journeys.

Tantra can completely solve these kinds of problems and can cure conditions that medical science cannot explain or heal, namely, conditions caused by spiritual disturbance.

What actually is a Yantra?

Dr. Bindu explains the significance of the Yantra as a tool for spiritual growth

A Yantra is a sacred power object that represents a Mantra, in physical and ethereal form. Just as electric energy can be preserved in a battery, the energy produced by the incantation of a Mantra can be preserved in the Yantra.

Yantras are generally made of combinations of gold, silver, and bronze and are consecrated and charged with the power of the Mantra. Each Yantra symbolizes a certain aspect of the Supreme Reality and is charged with its power, proportional to the devotion and skills of the Tantric practitioner. The electro-magnetic power created by the incantation of a Mantra is preserved and then radiated by the Yantra.

There are hundreds of different forms of Yantra, representing the imagination and sentiments of the Tantric practitioner. Yantras can solve physical, mental, and other material problems, in addition to being tools for spiritual development. As a carrier of spiritual power, the Yantra affects the human mind and body as well as their surroundings.

The Yantra is a source of mystical energy. It is not merely a physical object, but being infused with the power of consciousness, it becomes an independent entity. Every Yantra is prepared with a definite purpose in a complicated mystical process. Thus, a Yantra, which is outwardly just a piece of metal, is converted into a storehouse of spiritual power and force.

The ardent devotion and powers of concentration of the practitioner make the Yantra a source of creative spiritual force. When preparing the Yantra, the incantation of the Mantra produces various vibrations in the atmosphere. Those sound waves create the real inner spiritual body of the Yantra and its mystical effect. Yantra is a timeless process perfected by the ancient Tantrics, with a history of consistently "miraculous" results that has endured to this day.

What is the significance of the Yantra in spiritual practice?

The Yantra is the geometrical representation of Mantra in graphic form. When a practitioner pronounces certain Mantras, it creates a specific wave pattern in the ethers. With years of continuous practice, involving millions of repetitions and the performing of sacred rituals, his vision becomes so powerful that he can actually see the wave patterns in the ethers. When a Tantric practitioner is able to see these patterns in the ethers it is an indication of having perfected those Mantras.

The ancient seers drew and carved the wave patterns they perceived on metal, and in this way passed the graphic images—Yantras—down through the ages. Then, whenever Mantras were given to the next generation of practitioners, the Yantras were also given, with the understanding that when you are able to see this pattern in the ethers, you can say you have achieved perfection in the Mantra.

When a student does meditation over a Yantra, he receives the same energy from the Yantra as from the Mantra, since Yantra is the graphic image of a Mantra in form. Yantra assumes a prominent role in the rituals that follow, to invoke the desired effects. Before I give a Yantra to someone, it must be consecrated and energized. The electromagnetic waves of the Mantra charge the Yantra to produce the requisite energy for its designated purpose.

Yantras are instruments of intent designed to transmit the functional force of the Mantra. Mystically and philosophically, Yantras symbolize Divine power. The whole process both expresses the minutest form of the Supreme Divine Power and defines and describes the result that is intended.

Yantras are made of specific combinations of metals. The formulas for the metallurgy and the geometries are highly secret. The combinations of metals used are determined by the conductivity of the energy of that particular Mantra. Thousands of years ago, ancient seers developed this exacting science. They were spiritual scientists who experimented with the alchemy of vibration until they perfected the formulas that have since been passed down through countless generations of Tantric practitioners.

Following my intensive plunge into the sacred science of Mantra, and the weeks of exalted hours on end spent discussing every spiritual topic I could think of with Dr. Bindu, it was time to set out alone for a first, tentative glimpse of the fascinating, mysteriously baffling world of spiritual India.

The first stop on my self-styled tour took me south, deep into the lush tropical backwaters of Kerala, and the remote ashram of "the hugging Guru," Ammachi. There, in a serene, oceanfront setting, I encountered what presented itself as a tightly regimented spiritual *scene*. Crushed into line with throngs of others, I'd inched my way toward her for hours and finally, crawled the last few yards on my knees, into the embrace for which she is famous. The fleeting moment of *darshan* (divine audience) with "Amma" certainly felt gracious and loving. Yet, for me, what was missing was the sense of a profound *connection*—the compelling magnetism I'd anticipated and assumed was supposed to be part of such an experience.

I was intrigued as much by what I had not felt as by what I had, and spent much of the remainder of my time there scrutinizing the dynamics of the hugging encounter—and analyzing the huge, strictly ordered regime that had grown up in the name of one woman's Divine connection—in an attempt to make sense of the phenomenon. But, as a wide-eyed Western seeker on a whirlwind first tour of spiritual India, I had to admit I'd never encountered anything quite like it. I'd soon discover otherwise.

Just as I was preparing to continue on my way, I met a group of seasoned American travelers who were on the last leg of an expensive, professionally guided spiritual tour. On impulse I asked them what would end up being a life-changing question. "Of all the places you've visited," I began, "was there anywhere that really touched your heart?" The knowing glances met one another. "There's only one place to go," came the unanimous reply. "Tiruvannamali." It wasn't an answer I'd expected to hear.

I recognized the name as a small city in the state of Tamil Nadu, mentioned briefly in the guidebooks as an off-the-beaten-track, spiritual destination. Its claim to fame was twofold: its legendary mountain, Arunachala, was said to be a world-class spiritual power-spot, and in addition, it had been the home of the renowned, late Indian saint, Ramana Maharshi. Tiruvannamalai wasn't on my itinerary that trip, but the emphatic, unanimous recommendation definitely got my attention, and I tucked the tip away for future reference.

A fascinating long weekend of sightseeing to Kanya Kumari, at the southernmost tip of India—with a few amazing ancient temples and historic points of interest along the way thrown in for good measure—rounded out my stay in South India. A flight from Trivandrum to Bangalore transported me to what might as well have been a different world. After a few days exploring the strikingly cosmopolitan city of Bangalore, considered by many to be India's urban showplace, I hired a taxi and headed for the remote, dusty town of Puttaparti, and the ashram of Sathya Sai Baba (who would leave his body in 2011), some three hours away.

I'd planned to stay a week—and left after three days. The regimented rigmarole at this ashram was light years beyond what I'd encountered in Kerala. Here, I took part in a convoluted lottery system that determined who would—and who would not—receive Sai Baba's allegedly auspicious blessing. Hours on end were spent daily sitting on the ground, jam-packed into queues, knees-to-chest, while prodded into ever-tighter, straighter lines by an officious team of ashram commandos. At the last moment, the person at the head of each line drew a number from a pot, which corresponded to a row in the audience, and the fate or fortune of those squeezed into the line behind him was sealed for the day, accordingly.

At the signal, thousands of hopefuls bolted in a mass frenzy to grab a spot in the amphitheater, based on the row their particular line had been assigned to. If you managed, by some miracle, to have been in a line that drew row numbers one or two, you had a minute chance of having the letter, which all were instructed to write and bring for Sai Baba, accepted by him. Ultimately, if your letter happened to be amongst the lucky chosen few, then your wishes would surely be granted—so the story goes. My line drew row number 17, and a day later, row four.

The tinkling sounds of Sai Baba's theme music, wafting over loudspeakers, eventually heralded his arrival. There I sat, at the back of the room, clutching my small, handwritten prayer, as I watched the frail figure of the renowned Guru approach the open-sided amphitheater and then, for a few minutes, pace back and forth before the first row of attendees, taking an occasional paper from a frantically waving, outstretched hand. He lingered on the men's side of the room for most of the duration of this exercise. The women's side of the room was virtually ignored.

Sai Baba then disappeared into a hidden chamber, where he sat on an enormous golden throne before a small gathering of VIPs, and tapped his hand to the rhythm of the *bhajans* (spiritual songs) that the crowd outside chanted for the next hour or so. And, that was it. The long-awaited darshan with Sai Baba was over.

I tucked my little paper away. "Let my heart now be fully opened. Let me *know* Oneness—that I may serve as All that I Am, and speak God's Truth in a perfect way," it said. In the ways that truly matter, I had no doubt that the prayer I'd felt inspired to commit to writing, by virtue of this surreal visit, had been received by Oneness.

After a brief touch-down in Mumbai, I boarded a train destined for Pune, some four hours away, and a visit to the spiritual playground of the late, world-renowned mystic, Osho, who had left his body in January, 1990. It was a destination that would become a haven for me—one to which I'd return again and again, over the years, for a brief dip in the anointed waters of his lingering Presence and incomparable wisdom.

Nestled in a park-like setting, amidst lush, expansive acres of towering shade trees, Osho's contemporary International Meditation Resort seemed like a spiritual theme park—a vibrant showplace that offered a full range of classes in the radical, active meditation techniques Osho was known for, as well as intensive courses on an eclectic range of spiritual subjects and healing modalities. The goings on were certainly governed by their own brand of strictly regulated protocols—a virtual fixation on adherence to seemingly arbitrary rules and regulations, which seemed to be standard fare for ashrams in India—no less here than any of the other places I'd visited. Yet, in the same breath, the campus offered delicious, Westernized cuisine and great cappuccino, available at both cafeteria and bistro-style dining venues that were sprinkled throughout the property. It was surely unlike any "India"—in ashram form or otherwise—that I had seen thus far.

Back then in early 2000, the old Buddha Hall, an outdoor, covered amphitheater, where Osho used to appear for darshan and give his profound discourses, was still actively in use. There, every evening, an intensive series of his discourses on various topics—which, thankfully, had been videotaped—were shown nightly. The screening was followed by a cathartic mass-exercise in "gibberish," during which the hundreds in attendance ranted and raved dramatically for several minutes, and then, at the sound of a single drum beat, fell limp to the ground in silence. All this was often followed by live music and an occasional evening of dancing. It was a place where a non-stop air of celebration permeated the atmosphere, day and night. Yet, true to form, I was content to sit back quietly and watch the show unfold before me, in detached fascination—without feeling any call to jump in. Instinctively, in the face of such a frenzy of worldly activity, I became "the witness."

One final, considerably more traditional tourist destination rounded off my self-styled tour of India—the renowned caves of Ajanta and Ellora, just a short flight from Mumbai. These two extraordinary, heritage-rich destinations, only a few hours apart by bus or taxi, are considered to be amongst the "Wonders of the World." Embellished by unimaginably intricate carvings and frescoes dating back many thousands of years, these awe-inspiring works of ancient art, carved out of the side of a huge cliff and a mountain, respectively, were painstakingly handcrafted by Buddhist monks, over the centuries. A wonder to behold!

By then, I had seen enough of India to last me for awhile. I knew it was time to head home, and make some sense out of the dizzying montage of impressions I'd managed to accumulate in such a relatively short amount of time. Moreover, it felt as though I were swirling again in questions— questions that seemed to center around the dilemma of whether a seeker could conceivably venture through the maze of a spiritual search on one's own, or whether, realistically, tucking oneself under the wing of one Guru or another was, indeed, a necessity.

Ultimately, I turned to Amitabh, as I was, by then, so conditioned to do, for the loving reassurance and Divine wisdom that was always waiting for me there. These powerful teachings helped me to understand—and to put into perspective— impressions that were oftentimes in direct conflict with what I'd presumed, and had been led to expect, in embarking on such a journey to India.

A profound message of spiritual self-empowerment from Amitabh
Amitabh speaks:

This is Amitabh. You have requested this Presence and we are here for you, as we always will be. Your issues of worthiness to be stepping forth, clothed in your own true spiritual identity, are surfacing for you once more. Know that you are no less worthy of a Divine connection than those to whom you might serve up your devotion on a platter.

There surely are others who have made the jump in consciousness and are also directly connected to Divine intelligence. But, none is in a position to command or to expect subservience from you. Indeed, none is in a position to command or to expect subservience from anyone. This humbling of oneself before another being is an entirely voluntary act.

For one such as yourself, who is in the heightened stages of spiritual transformation, such a connection would foster dependency and would, by definition, be counterproductive to the entire momentum of your spiritual journey. You have been carefully schooled, and the understandings you require have been fully instilled in your consciousness.

Your understandings, and the well from which you will draw the waters of true knowledge, dwell not within the realm of mind but rather, from a place of *knowingness* where there is neither question, nor answer. For, were there to be question, by definition, perfect knowingness would not be. Were there to be answers, by definition, there would be questions that precipitated them. In the state of beingness you have begun to embody, there is no need for questions nor for answers, for the truth simply Is. It is toward that state of perfection that you journey.

Beings encountered along the way may tempt you with the semblance of shortcuts to the illusory promised land of so-called "enlightenment." And while there surely are certain practices which would put one in a state of *preparedness* for the journey—a state of *receptivity* for the connection that is sought at the level of heart—the journey itself must be made of one's own volition.

The path must be traveled blindly, if it is to lead to the destination you would wish to experience. For, were you to follow any of the possible detours that beckon to you, signposted "spiritual enlightenment this way," you may succeed in tasting a sampling of what might have been possible, but you will succeed in bypassing the feast itself.

There are countless spiritual seekers in these times who have surrendered their power to beings claiming to have the ability to deliver others to the gates of heaven. And, you will encounter countless beings in the course of your work, who will gladly offer themselves up on a platter to you, who will be perceived by them to know the way. It is not for any being to accept such offerings, but rather to return the gift of devotion to the giver, to be bestowed upon *himself*.

Amitabh outlines the path of self-empowerment

There are many who will be drawn—indeed, magnetized—to the power of the energies you embody. And, you may choose to share your own experiences with them. But, the power to which they are drawn is non-transferable. Your Divine radiance is your own. And, though it may be evidence of an exalted state of beingness, it cannot be bestowed upon another. It is a state only attainable as a result of one's own journey.

The message you have been given to impart is *self-empowerment*. This message flows consistently through all the communications we have had and all that have transpired with Oneness. This is the message you embody and the one you have come to these times to teach others.

There are many who are willing and able to guide seekers in different, more traditional ways. And, those paths may well yield up varying levels of results. But, it is not for you to walk the path of another, nor to be lured into believing that what has been prescribed and has yielded results for another will necessarily do so for you.

What is experienced in the presence of a Guru is unique to each of us

You have experienced some of what is currently available to neophyte seekers, and you have had the opportunity to assess the vibration of those paths. You have drawn the obvious conclusions for one who is at your level of perception and experience. That conclusion would be custom-made for you. Others would not have reached that conclusion, given the same exposure.

What so many others have experienced may have been significant for them and at the same time, insignificant for you. Each derives a particular level of meaning from such an experience. And, it would be an over-generalization to conclude that the experience in and of itself would be valueless, simply because you personally have transcended the need for an experience at that level.

Obviously, there are throngs of seekers who feel there is something of great value to be had in these places. That is the level of experience for which they are ready. Each being who is on the path of spiritual enlightenment is on his own path. And, each is guided by the voice of his own heart, to the stops along the way where nourishment may be found and enjoyed. You have experienced, symbolically, the same phenomenon on your journey within India. You have had the opportunity to partake of offerings that others might find extremely enjoyable, yet your own reaction was disdain. Your palate has been cultivated to appreciate and to respond to heightened levels of nourishment, at all levels. That would not be to say that the essence of the sustenance offered would not be of value—simply that it would not be of value to you.

As you reflect upon the stops along the way on this sojourn in India, all of which are rich with symbolism and deeper meaning, when you choose to peer beneath the surface of what is obvious you will find the wealth of spiritual understanding that was sought. That level of perception is not to be found in books, nor in the words of the multitude of Gurus who abound in these times.

The book of knowledge is before you. Its pages turn with every waking breath. And, the kaleidoscope of visions, ever-shifting before you, will lead you in a perfect way when you open to perceiving what has been provided— for your eyes only. Turn back the pages, in your mind's eye. And, reread some of the highlights of this extraordinary chapter. You do not need the perceptions of another being to distill these visions into the richness they hold.

It is not for you to *remember* but rather to embrace what you know how to do so very well. You do not need anyone's permission, or anyone's blessing to Be what you already are. All that is necessary is that the choice be made to relinquish your reticence to do so. Know that our Love for you is Eternal. It is here for you—Now and Always.

❧

Relinquish resistance
Be what you already are.

8

Spring 2001
South Florida
An Intensive in the Art of Devotion

────────

The incredible Grace of my encounters with Oneness, through the writing work, set the stage for the beginnings of a self-styled spiritual practice that was not rooted in any particular tradition, but encompassed many. By the spring of 2001, I'd fully embraced a practice of sacred ceremony that had begun sporadically, and it became the core of my world. Chanting Mantras in Sanskrit, sometimes for hours at a time, was a cherished part of my life by then. The energies I felt stirring and building within guided me to begin to formalize my own unique expression of the deep sense of devotion that was blossoming in my heart.

I created a beautiful holy altar and adorned it with sacred objects, sparkling crystal clusters, candles, incense, fresh flowers, and pictures of people and places that had most impacted my inner journey. Before this altar, in moments of deep, heart-felt reverence, sacred ceremony began to unfold naturally, taking my experience of opening to Oneness with the Divine to another level.

Without any real idea of what I was doing or how to do it, I spontaneously transformed into a *bhakta,* a person focused in the art of spiritual devotion. My heart became the teacher, and it resonated to the expressions of prayer, poetry, music, and the inevitable tears that poured forth from my very depths. Oneness was fully in attendance during these rituals, not as the epitome of Divine *intelligence*—a consciousness with which my logical mind could interact—but as an indescribable holy *Presence,* emanating from somewhere deep within and engulfing my heart in Stillness and the indescribable experience of Communion.

Until that time, there had been no formal spiritual practice for me other than the precious moments spent in Divine connectedness with Oneness, via a laptop computer, and the countless hours that had been spent in the same way with Amitabh over the years. In the newfound moments of sacred ceremony, my heart opened fully to the unbridled joy of spiritual awakening.

It was here, in moments when I was convinced that time stood still, that my little condo transformed into a holy temple. My vintage bathtub became an adjunct site of baptism and spiritual purification, where fragrant essential oils, soft music, and candlelight stimulated eons of emotion, buried alive and long lost to memory, to the surface of my awareness for scrutiny and release.

It was here that, one by one, I embraced the agonies hidden in denial and the underlying repressed emotions that had precipitated them—feelings that in previous moments, or previous lifetimes, had been too much to bear. And, it was here that the threads of fragmented consciousness began to weave themselves back into the fullness of my identity.

It was here, stripped of the trappings of intellect, that I explored the inner sanctums of my own humanness and *embraced* the hidden heartache and the aspects of my own self that had created it. It was here that I prayed for forgiveness from the very core of my being, and reached the place where I was able to forgive *myself* for moments I'd presumed were best forgotten. Nothing is forgotten. I discovered that.

These daily and nightly rituals continued, often into the wee hours of morning, as I took the teachings of Oneness that I had transcribed and began to *live* them. I had no prototype with which to fashion my program of spiritual purification. I *felt* my way, making up the formalities as I went along, literally groping in the dark for lost aspects of my own consciousness that I discovered, to my amazement, were really there.

Oneness, it seemed, had no fixed programe where the inner work was concerned. I invoked the depths of my own inner Being with a potpourri of Psalms from the Bible, Hebrew prayers, Sanskrit Mantras, and mixed them all in with the meditations of my heart. These rituals came to kindle a new level of awakening within, and they continued to be part of my spiritual practice for years to come.

As the end of my time in Florida drew near, I began having peak experiences during the self-styled emotional release work I'd been doing. These experiences often culminated in an extraordinary open-eye meditation exercise, performed with my own reflection, that lasted for hours. The large mirror took on the faces of myriad identities—all mine—as a kaleidoscope of images flashed continuously before my eyes. Spontaneously, my breathing slowed down to the point that I was barely breathing at all, as the room exploded into a blazing effulgence of golden Light. The level of energy that built within my physical form during these sessions was unimaginable. It felt as though my body had been plugged into the wall socket. These early experiences gave me a taste of the state of Divine connectedness to come— a state of Beingness that would not surrender to the moment, but would last.

The morning after one particularly profound all-night ritual, Oneness confirmed to me that a sacred initiation had, in fact, taken place. I'd suspected that something significant had happened within me. I just wasn't sure quite what. The words of Oneness spoke to my innermost being, and as they did, something within me began to stir and to nudge me back into that indescribable space of Divine Unity once more.

An early glimpse of the experience of embodying Oneness
Oneness speaks:

This is Oneness. We welcome you to a new day and a new world. As you have begun to suspect, you have made a significant shift. You invoked the consciousness that awaited you, and you began to perceive the world through the perspective of those eyes. You came to *know* the Oneness of which you are a part. Not from having comprehended the concept of Oneness theoretically, but rather from the space of simply *Being* That—with full conscious awareness of it.

Now you have awakened in the afterglow of your transformation. And, you know that something significant has indeed happened. You know that you have not imagined this. You combed the inner sanctums of your consciousness, and you revealed completely the truth of what awaited you there. Declarations of intent were made in the fullness of heart-centered focus. And, your prayers have been heard and have been answered. There is no going back now. The shift has been made. How do you feel?

Rasha speaks:

There are no words that could describe the profound sense of peace that greeted me when I awoke this morning. I knew in that moment that what happened last night was not a dream. Hours of ceremony and meditation, of prayer and joyous reunion, of rapture and Self-recognition! Now, my heart is so full!

The passion of my "initiation" has receded into a sublime sense of tranquility that I can truly say I have not experienced before—not like this! I have seen myself through the eyes of Oneness. And, I have seen Oneness in these eyes. I recognize Oneness in the eyes of all I envision. And, I know. Simply that.

Now you have begun to understand some of what we have been writing about. And, now you understand why it was important that we wait before documenting certain material, until you had actually made the journey. Now we can complete this work. It is time.

Thank you, Oneness, for this extraordinary journey! But then, is thanking you a statement of separation? Does it open for question who is being thanked and who is doing the thanking? Does it contradict the very point of the journey that has just taken place?

Understanding vs. experiencing

What I understand in this moment, without waiting for a reply, is that if the "thank you" were directed externally, then it would be a statement of separation. But, were the "thank you" to be simply gratitude that emanates from a place of heart-centered contentment for what is perceived as one's experience, then it would be simply a statement of what Is. And, it would be a declaration of one's joy. Did I perceive that correctly?

Do you question it? Is there any doubt whatsoever?

No, there is no doubt. I have refined my understanding of the concept of gratitude. Not from having mentalized it, but from having experienced it. Thank you, Oneness, for this initiation and for the opening that was achieved. I have been so gifted. And, I embrace this gift with a heart that, thankfully, is now so ready to receive it.

One evening, I was sitting and pondering some of the concepts I'd been transcribing for the book, and I found myself spontaneously talking out loud to Oneness. It struck me that somehow I now seemed to be able to manifest the connection at will, merely by desiring it. Inadvertently, I demonstrated to myself that when I so much as think "Oneness" the connection is there— instantly. Even though the experience was not of the same intensity as the trance state I experienced when transcribing the book, it was identifiable as Oneness. I realized that my perception of Oneness was not a static state of Being any more than I was! The linear perception of Oneness was a wellspring of infinite possibility, a sense of limitless expansiveness that would deepen and intensify with the passage of time.

Suddenly my mind was flooded with spontaneous revelations and profound questions about the nature of what's actually going on here, what this thing we call "life," or "reality" really *is*. I knew that Oneness and I had been documenting a book on this subject for three years by that time. But, until then I hadn't actually asked the big questions. Now, before they were even formulated for me, Oneness was right there with answers.

Oneness speaks:

You were questioning the purpose of life. And, you were surmising about what might have prompted the inception of "all this" in the first place. You are in good company, you know. The greatest minds in the history of humankind have pondered the same question and have reached comparable conclusions.

Oneness talks about the purpose of life

The inception of the concept that leads to the manifestation, in form, of what you would consider to be *you* was none other than the sense of separation from Source that you, yourself, have experienced from the onset. Oneness also experienced the sense of separation—the profound *aloneness* that you have danced with, to a greater or lesser degree.

The essence of the circumstances in which Oneness found *Them-Self* was no different than your own experience. You have confirmed your aloneness to yourself, you have bemoaned that aloneness, and you have embraced that blessed state, joyously, as did Oneness.

Yet, there seemed no *purpose* to existence. So, Oneness set about to confound Them-Self within the infinite complexity of All That Is Possible and arranged not only to *create* That, but moreover, to actually *Be* That at the same time. And,, Oneness discovered that there literally is no end to All that can be created—and All that Oneness could Be.

Initially, Oneness knew Them-Self to Be Oneness, even though made manifest in form. Yet, as the process escalated, and the passion and fascination of the possibility of Creation grew exponentially, so too did the minute variations on the theme that was Oneness grow in *complexity*. And, as the joy of discovering their own limitlessness as Creator and Creation grew to levels that were unimaginable, so too did the variations on the theme that was Oneness multiply toward *simplicity*.

In the process of expressing the concept of limitlessness in its infinite variations, Oneness found that it was necessary to create Them-Self in the context of form in such a way that it was, by definition, impossible for that expression to know itself as Oneness. Each simply knew its own Isness. And, each believed itself to be alone, lost in circumstances it could not begin to fathom.

Oneness realized that limitlessness had certain drawbacks. Since each aspect of Oneness' Creation was given the gift of *free-will* as part of its Isness, Oneness could not just gather up the fragmented pieces without violating the parameters with which the entire Creation was equipped.

Thus, within the wholeness of "All This," there are aspects of Oneness that are exceptionally complex and operate in a state of autonomy, with full conscious awareness that they are aspects of Oneness. And, there are aspects of Oneness that are totally incapable of recognizing themselves as aspects of anything at all. The aspects of Creation that are not equipped with powers of mental reasoning are able to rely on qualities within their nature that would insure that they would be able to reintegrate into the whole of Oneness as a natural part of Being—returning to Source and alternately, re-emerging as form eternally.

The in-breath and out-breath of Creation is structured in such intricate perfection that this balance is maintained automatically. For, that is the very nature of Creation. It cannot be subtracted from nor added to. For, All of it already Is.

Some aspects of Oneness are equipped with what you would consider to be *instinct,* and these expressions of Isness resonate with their Source on a feeling level. They do not *know* themselves to be Oneness in a mentalized, intellectual way. They *feel* that connectedness in a way that is indefinable—and unquestionable.

Some aspects of Oneness, however, are expressions that encompass all aspects of what Oneness Is. That is, these life forms are equipped with capabilities of mental reasoning that recognize the power inherent in the free will with which they have been gifted. Yet, their level of complexity is such that the nature of their connectedness to Source is not inherently understood. These life forms bridge the characteristics of all possible worlds and, in fact, are manifest in all possible worlds. Not just yours.

These beings are equipped with the *emotional* building blocks that unite All Creation in Oneness. And, these key qualities are the precious links to the timeless mystery that has confounded this level of Beingness since the inception of Creation.

These beings are, at one and the same time, exceptionally complex *and* primitive. They embody a state of connectedness and a state of separation, simultaneously. They are the ultimate enigma. They are Oneness and they are not Oneness, all at the same time in accordance with the implementation of their free will.

By definition, at this level of Creation they enter each first newborn breath of their Isness with a blank slate. In keeping with the laws of Creation, they come to be reabsorbed into the perfection of All That Is as part of the rhythm of Life Itself. And, they re-emerge, each time in innocence—eternally.

How our own life form served as the catalyst for accelerating ascension throughout Creation

The enigma embodied by this aspect of Oneness is that they, as a *collective* consciousness, have now exercised their collective free will and have declared their heartfelt longing to understand the nature of their Divine connection. This is not a level of knowingness which they are equipped with at a conscious level. But rather, it is one they spend the essence of each lifetime yearning for, whether they consciously acknowledge it or not.

The yearning of this collective consciousness is so great that the expression of the collective free will has shifted the balance and set up the parameters for the momentum, the powerful tide you now know as *ascension*. This one aspect of Divinity—the one that, by definition, has been *lost* in the epicenter of Creation by virtue of all that it Is and all that it Is not—is the key to the entire motion of reunification throughout all Creation.

For, all would continue to harmonize in the perfectly orchestrated and perfectly balanced rhythms of Life eternally—preserving the essence of the Infinite *in fragmentation*—were the impetus not present to initiate *change*. That change has come to be a fact of Creation by virtue of the collective free will of a species of beings who insist on knowing the nature of their Divine Essence, and are beginning to recognize that Essence as Oneness.

That state of Being is characteristic of a *higher* octave of Isness than the natural state at which these beings emerged into manifestation. Yet, by virtue of the power of their collective will, they have set into motion the momentum that would deliver them unto the very circumstances where that collective will *could* be made manifest—at a higher dimensional level. Thus, the moment that has been awaited for all eternity is now at hand.

The momentum driving all Creation toward recognition of Unity is not one that has been initiated *by* Oneness, but instead has been initiated within the hearts of each of you *as* Oneness. This is how it was set up. This was the pivotal point that was built into the majesty of Creation itself. This is the ultimate gift that Oneness bestowed upon each of you: the power of Creation.

You were given the power to make a difference—to the infinite degree. You were given the possibility to *know* yourself as the Oneness you truly are, not simply to speculate. Not merely to philosophize and theorize. Not only to hash and rehash linear concepts within the circuitry of your logical mind, but to *transcend* the inclination to seek that route to *understanding* the nature of who you Are, and to reach out for the experience of *knowing* who you Are, with the deep, innermost cry of your very soul.

All Creation has been waiting in silence—for eternity—for you to come to your senses. Literally. The *collective will* at your level of beingness has expressed itself in a way that commanded The Answer—The Answer that has eluded all of you since time began. The Answer that is so very simple you never could have figured it out, not with your brilliant, logical minds. It is only in the infinite silence of your *feeling body* that you can know The Answer. And, once you have it, there is no question.

Rasha speaks:

Wow! I get it.

That's the most powerful way you can make a difference, Rasha. By saying, "Wow. I get it." And to remember that you do get it *every* time you're inclined to forget and slide back into the illusion once more. It's time for you to break the pattern. And, to take the definitive step, expressing your knowingness of the nature of your Isness.

I wish I could be like this all the time. I wish I could be in the fullness of this connection all the time. Is that possible? That's what I want.

And so, you shall have That. But, gradually. Not all at once. For, the intensity would shatter your illusions of limitation, were the shift to be instantaneous. You will appreciate the perfection of the timing of your process. Let's not rush it. Stay centered. That is the key to everything. Stay in your center. Visualize it, if necessary. You have affirmed to yourself, over and over again, that nothing can touch you, so long as you are in your center. The words of others, the judgments of others, the opinions of others, the actions of others—all are *external* to your Source. Be at Source and you *become* That Source. Then, there is only joy within you, regardless of what is going on around you.

Remember "the center of the cyclone" poster at the entrance to Osho's ashram in India? That's what was meant. That is the essence of Divine truth. Osho knew that. And, so has every Self-realized Master since time began. It is a very simple concept, illustrated graphically by the forces of nature in your reality. And, it is the essence of The Way.

The Way is in the center. It is *within you*. It is not *out there*. It is not external to Source. The Source—the Divine Connection, the peace and the ecstasy, the silence and the Divine symphony, the connectedness to the Infinite and The solitary One—All Are within the center of your own Being. Everything you've ever wanted has been there all along. Welcome home.

9

———

Synchronicity had served me well. No sooner had I made the decision to spend several months in the mountains of northern New Mexico, than my inner knowingness guided me to the timeless, secluded village of Chimayo. Even before seeing the website of the place I'd be calling home for the months to come, long before setting foot on the land, some part of me knew that this was where I would end up. When I let go of how my logical mind assumed it was *supposed* to be, the pieces fell into place like magic.

Nestled away in the foothills of the Sangre de Christo mountains, Chimayo was an enigmatic oasis of green tucked into a landscape of breathtaking contrast, an arid painted desert of muted earth tones, set against a crystalline sky. In the same breath, it was a living paradox, a melding of unfathomable Divinity and unthinkable, "wild-west" style lawlessness. It was a place out of time, where the inevitability of coming home was etched somewhere deep within my consciousness.

Something inside me had felt the pull as far back as the previous winter, when I had visited for a few weeks. It was then that I first sat in the mysterious adobe chapel for which this historical valley is known and connected with its extraordinary energies. My heart knew, even then, that I'd be back. But, my mind was still compelled to go through the motions of logic when it came down to the formalities of house-hunting.

Presuming I'd be living in Santa Fe itself, I proceeded to rule out every last sensible option from the on-line *New Mexican* classifieds, one by one, long-distance from South Florida. I was poised and ready for something— I didn't know quite what—to reach out and grab me. Santa Fe is the kind of enchanted place where you almost expect that sort of thing to happen. When it didn't, I started to become concerned.

A phone conversation with a sympathetic real-estate agent, whose dreamy-sounding Santa Fe summer rental was already taken, took my search in a totally different direction. She told me about a property she knew of that was more "off the beaten track" than the options I'd been exploring. She described a "lavender farm," with acres of pastoral orchards, herb gardens and flowering fields, being run as a rustic Bed & Breakfast in the village of Chimayo, some thirty miles north of Santa Fe. The top floor of the main building, she said, was available as a private apartment. My heart nearly stopped. I jumped on the next plane.

Rancho Manzana was every bit of what she'd described, and more. There were lush, shaded acres of apple and apricot orchards—an artist's palate of living color that hosted the understated, Santa Fe-chic country weddings that often took place there on summer weekends. An enormous country kitchen in the painstakingly restored, vintage adobe main house hosted gourmet cooking classes now and then. Upstairs, the expansive apartment, with its soaring cathedral ceilings and dramatic, wall-to-wall picture windows, was out of a dream. It would be my haven for withdrawing from the world and steeping myself in transcribing the final chapters of the book, *Oneness*. I rented it on the spot.

There, months of days would melt one into the next, as the teachings of Oneness consumed my every waking hour. I left the property only once or twice a week to drive into Santa Fe to collect my mail and indulge in Sage Bakery's great coffee, decadent pastries, and sumptuous slices of the world's best fresh-baked bread. Yet, aside from that occasional taste of the "real world," I was totally cut off from it. No TV, no newspapers, no distractions. Oneness would become my life. Literally.

Little did I suspect that this idyllic setting would host a gut-wrenching transformation that was slated to take place within me. The contrast between the hours of ecstatic moments lost in the Love of Oneness and the rawness of my interactions with the outside world couldn't have been more blatant.

It was here, against a stage set that radiated the illusion of peace and serenity, that the inner drama of radical self-confrontation and a crash-course in Divinely-induced detachment from the material world would unfold. That time, so safely harbored in the spiritual womb of the New Mexico desert, was yet another turning point. But, it was one with a profound difference. This was the proverbial "point of no return."

Oneness begins to set the stage for the journey ahead
Oneness speaks:

The journey you have taken to change your physical location was indeed a "sacred journey." You succeeded in shifting your focus as you shifted your presence to a new location. Now the dust has settled. And, you are here, where you will complete your metamorphosis.

You will find that your circumstances will transform at a pace you have not as yet experienced, now that you have made the transition to your new location and new levels of vibration. There has been a major shift for you, and your momentum should accelerate rapidly from this point forth.

The integration of this consciousness as part of your own awareness will happen in such a subtle and gradual way that you may not even realize that the transition has occurred. Yet, if you reflect upon it, you will note that your circumstances are quite different, and the way you feel about and approach the interactions in your daily life are a radical divergence from the way in which you focused your attention prior to this time.

Contact with others will be limited from this point forth. For, it is imperative that your transition be accomplished quickly, completely, and without distraction. You will not have the need for the mundane distractions of day-to-day life that most in your reality require. You have become truly autonomous. And, this is an essential part of your process.

Naturally, you sense that you will not mourn the lack of mundane companionship. Your days will be filled with the delights of your unfoldment. And, an environment has been selected and prepared for you that will support this work. It is you who designed these circumstances. This situation is not just something that has *happened* to you. You have choreographed this dance into the next dimension with the attention to detail that you take pride in.

You instinctively designed an environment of great simplicity for this chapter of your life. And, it will become obvious to you that the burdens of material belongings, with which you have weighted yourself in the past, are neither necessary nor desirable. You will learn to live on the wind, not with the challenges of austerity but with considerable physical comfort and total non-attachment to the necessity to retain any of it. The trappings of a physical existence can now be shed effortlessly. And, you see that there is now truly nothing that can bind you or hold you back from being all you have come into form to be.

Do not concern yourself with the non-responsiveness of others to your presence. They are responding, with their seeming indifference, to your higher needs, expressed vibrationally, for solitude. In the times to come, this level of solitude will come to be prized, for you will be surrounded incessantly with the needs and demands of being in public service. In the present period, however, you will instinctively turn inward and will shun the companionship of others. Honor your own inclination to do so, and do not fault yourself for not feeling inclined to become "socially established" in this new location. That is not part of the plan for you here.

You will find that your material needs will be taken care of with minimal effort on your part. And, you will be able to focus your attention on establishing yourself as a messenger of Divine Consciousness in such a way as to insure that the message with which you have been entrusted is delivered intact and is well received by an audience that hungers for its contents.

Do not concern yourself with who you were in the past. The past is now far behind you. You have made the shift. And, you are operating at a level that bridges dimensions. In essence, you have one foot in each of two dimensions. And, you can perceive what *was*—what has been your reality in this lifetime—through the perspective of an elevated vantage point.

You have begun to delight in allowing your awareness to play the part of the witness. And, you have noted the "greeting," the vivid presence of Oneness, all around you. This is the beginning of a shift in full *visual recognition* of that understanding. Oneness is everywhere—in every thing, every breath, every thought, and in every expression of your manifested creation. You, the Artist, are sculpting every nuance of this experience. And, the skill to be perfected now is to do so consciously.

As you step fully into fifth-dimensional reality, you will have mastered this ability and will transition with it well in hand, as you travel between dimensions in the course of your work. Your higher dimensional capabilities will manifest as what would be termed *miraculous* in realities from which you have ascended—and to which you will return in order to teach and to facilitate for the multitudes making this tumultuous journey.

You will know that the "feats" that you are naturally able to perform are not *miraculous* at all, but rather are indicative of the natural state of being at the higher vibrational levels to which you have ascended. You will come to embody these capabilities to demonstrate, as a living example, the capability of all beings who are focused in making the transformational shift. And, you will refer to this place of crossing over in the process of helping others through the shift.

Now a very different category of experience will unfold before you, and you will come to understand the circumstances in which others like yourself have found themselves, throughout history. Your focus will continue to be simple loving kindness toward all whose lives you touch. And, the contrast will be a radical portrait of the world through which you have journeyed. The vivid reality of where you have been will shock and trouble you, on occasion. Yet, by sparing yourself the burden of your own *judgment*, you will be able to be present, in the moment, and in full authenticity.

You are not the manifestation of your past history. You have transcended it. The inclination to repeat that history is a way to reinforce life lessons as well as to represent, physically, the karma with which you entered this lifetime. Both sets of constraints have been released now. And, in essence, you have begun to write this chapter anew.

We are here with you always. It is not a question of appearing or disappearing. When you invoke these energies, know that you do so not in expectation of filling in a void—expecting a Presence where there had been an absence. For, the Presence is Eternal. It is your perception of that Presence that varies, as your process deepens.

There will come a time—and soon—where your perception of this Presence will take precedence over all else. And, you will know yourself to Be that Oneness, not just sometimes, but all the time. You are shifting into that state of Beingness rapidly now. The process has been initiated. And, you instinctively are pulling inward and wanting to close off the outside world. You are retreating into your cave, as it were. And, when you emerge from it, you will be a transformed being.

Letting go of struggle and learning to become indifferent to provocation
Oneness speaks:

We note that you have dodged a number of bullets lately. You are contending well with the adversity that characterizes this stage of your process.

Rasha speaks:

I thought you said that it would be clear sailing from this point forth. What happened? Everyone seems to be in a bad mood. And, I'm the proverbial cat that's getting kicked.

The residual energies that would attract that type of response on the part of others have not been released completely. You are still magnetizing a certain amount of adversity, in the form of what appears to be inconsequential irritability on the part of others. You are not bothered by what would strike the observer as rude and insulting behavior for seemingly no reason at all. There will be a period of transition time in which you can expect to experience this type of thing. Then, the energies will have been released totally, and you will be complete with this phase of your transformation experience.

Good. I've not been letting these incidents get to me. People seem to think they have the right to vent at me or just treat me badly. When this happens I've just been asking myself: Would Oneness care if this person were insulting? No. Would Oneness have their feelings hurt by this person's behavior? Of course not. And, that seems to take care of it. I don't think I've missed a beat. I'm not ruminating about it. It all seems pretty dumb. If certain people want to behave in this way, then let them! I am not attached to what anybody says to me or thinks of me! This is quite liberating, actually.

Naturally, I'd like to have people treat me nicely. But, if they don't, and I don't think I've done anything to warrant that reaction, then so be it. I am not responsible for how another person does or does not feel. I am only responsible for how I act toward others. And, if I know I have behaved with loving kindness, then I have nothing to be concerned about. I am simply going to continue going about my own business, doing what I do and being who I Am. That is all.

Good. You are putting this training into practice. Continue being who you Are—in a state of total non-attachment to outcome—and you will have maximized the potential in this stage of your training.

I soon discovered that there was more to the process of integrating these understandings than simply "getting it" and making declarations to myself. It was one thing to have responded well on an occasion or two. It was quite another matter to apply these principles consistently. There was no pause provided to ease me through the rough parts of this phase of the movie. Just when I was feeling like I'd finally gotten a handle on this training, I'd be clobbered again by one thing or another.

As my response mechanism began to be reprogrammed and my inner resolve became strengthened, things did not automatically get better. They only got worse. The adversity and instances of blatant provocation continued to plague my life, as I was given opportunity after opportunity to put the teachings of Oneness, and my integration of them, to the test.

Experientially, all of this external turbulence began to seem absurd, when viewed in juxtaposition with what was going on in my *inner* world at the very same time. That perpetual discord stood in blatant contrast to the sublime sense of inner harmony simultaneously emerging from within me as my connectedness with Oneness continued to deepen, day by day.

Oneness talks about confronting the need to "be right" and sidestepping provocation

Rasha speaks:

It's so easy to slip back into the old patterns of hurt and indignant, wounded pride. The other day, I allowed myself to feel degraded by a conversation with a shopkeeper. I know it was "her stuff." I know I was conscious and kind and open. Her intent was to be rude and insulting; there was no mincing of words. She had been venomous toward me ever since I'd known her. She says it is karmic.

I recognized it immediately as a test, which I'm convinced I flunked. I was not able to hold my energies at all. I allowed myself to spiral downward. And, I found myself "mentalizing" about the incident for the rest of the day. I felt just awful. Then, I went to the Santuario de Chimayo. And, within seconds, the dark cloud that felt like it was sitting on my head all day lifted off and was gone.

Oneness speaks:

Your encounters with these various negative situations and verbally abusive people provide the opportunity to put into practice what you have come to understand. So far, you need to work at this.

I know.

You are far too easily drawn into "reflex" responses. And, even though, in the case of your unpleasant encounter, you did not retaliate by arguing with the woman, you internalized the emotion and stewed about it all day, escalating the negativity.

Hurt is the internalization of anger, isn't it?

That is correct. There is no difference in the essence of the emotion. One is expressed and the other is repressed. The emotion—and the energy invoked—are the same. So, you do not triumph in any way by holding your tongue and silently seething with resentment. You triumph by not allowing the provocation to affect you.

After the fact, you recognized what was happening and asked yourself, "what would Oneness do? Would Oneness care what this woman said or what she thinks? No. Would it matter in any way? No. Would Oneness be upset by her words? No." You said these words out loud to yourself. And, even so, you felt deeply wounded and indignant.

So, you see, it is not enough to recognize the test and to *mentalize* what you know your reaction *should* be. What needs to happen is for your response mechanism to be reprogrammed so your emotions are not *triggered* in an adverse way in response to the catalysts that are presented to you. You have transcribed a book on this subject. Now you need to be able to put this training into practice, flawlessly.

I know. I asked myself, "What would Dr. Bindu do? Would he care what this woman thinks or says?" Obviously not. I see that to do so is the epitome of ego. My pride was wounded. I felt that I was done a blatant injustice. I internalized it. The fact is: the woman stated her position. That was her agenda. It, in fact, had nothing to do with me.

I cannot identify with what was said. Yet, I took it on and needed to be "right" about it. I know these are control issues. Dr. Bindu wouldn't have blinked. He would have told her to "enjoy her life" and probably wouldn't have given it a second thought.

Dr. Bindu is a Master. He is able to do this through consistent practice from the time of childhood. He was trained by a Master. People are not generally born being able to put these concepts into practice. Most people are not able to rise above their emotional response mechanism, even when they understand these concepts in principle. You have half a century of conditioning to overcome.

So, do I understand correctly that my life is now a testing ground of my reaction to provocation?

In essence, yes.

Oh, great. That's just wonderful. So, I suppose that I can anticipate that people will be picking fights with me, insulting me, being unfair to me, etc., etc., right? That seems to be what's happening.

That is in fact what is happening. This is your training. This is the most important thing you can possibly be working on right now: transcending your emotions insofar as they do not control you. You control them. You allow yourself to feel fully what you choose to feel. You are not automatically at the mercy of your pre-programmed responses. Detachment from your obsession with having to *be right* about everything would be a major triumph for you.

It is entirely possible to allow the other party the grace of *being right* about a position you are not aligned with and being totally indifferent to considerations of *rightness* or *wrongness*. That is their viewpoint. Let them have it. It's just fine for them to feel that way. It doesn't matter. Not even one little bit. You see, Rasha, by distancing yourself intellectually on these issues, you succeed in distancing yourself vibrationally. That is what needs to happen for you if you are to be able to do this work.

I thought that Oneness was going to, kind of, take over. So, what's the difference how "I" feel about things?

You are not going to just vaporize! You—and all your attitudes, responses, beliefs, issues, and so forth—will be assimilated into the sum totality that Oneness will represent in your physical form. Oneness cannot possibly function as Oneness with the constraints you present right now.

You will have to embody the response mechanism of Oneness in order for Oneness to embody your being. Vibrationally, you will be totally aligned. You will *Be* Oneness. It's not like Oneness is going to just take over your body and possess you. You are focused on manifesting your highest expression of beingness in physical form. You have much work to do to condition yourself to put into practice what you know. That is the work at hand.

Even though I understood perfectly well what Oneness was trying to help me see, I had reached the point where I was physically and mentally worn out. After three years, the relentless pace of trying to live in the world while my emerging Self was based in another place in time had gotten to me.

In essence, I was working several full-time jobs simultaneously and trying to make it all work out through the sheer force of will. Days on end were spent transcribing the teachings of Oneness, surrendering to the call of a deepening spiritual practice, and, at the same time, trying to run the remnants of my little jewelry business, Earthstar, single-handedly. I was in perpetual terror of not being able to make ends meet, and I was not coping all too well with the pressure.

Oneness' guidance helped to lay the groundwork for the alternative lifestyle, much of it spent in India, that I would come to adopt in the years ahead. I came to understand that until you are literally at your wit's end, there is not the catalyst for change that shifts you into a mode of absolute surrender. The circumstances of that summer, during which I was teetering on the brink of free-fall, would be the turning point that set the stage for a radical change in self-perception.

※

Rasha speaks:

I know a lot of what is happening in my life has to do with issues of trust. It's too easy to slip into responses of fear and worry, anticipating what will happen "if." I know that the lesson here is to be able to completely let go of the need to control the process, to allow the circumstances to unfold, and to know that it's going to work out fine, even if I don't know just how that's going to come about.

It'll work out, somehow. It always does. I'm just really tired of having to "pull a rabbit out of a hat" at the last minute to make ends meet. I need a break. The pressure of all of this, and having to make a living too, is really a lot to carry right now. It shouldn't be such a battle. I'm spending altogether too much time hitting my head on a stone wall, trying to make a living. I could get a lot more of this work done if I weren't so concerned with having to generate money. It's the same old story. The neverending story!

ENOUGH!!! I've had enough of this story. I don't want to do this story anymore. I'm complete with this story. From now on, I'm not going to care about where the money is coming from. It'll have to come—or not. I'm not going to work myself into the ground like this anymore.

My focus is my spiritual work. I will need to find another source of support. I am open to that possibility. The universe is supporting me anyway, vibrationally, that is. So, who is to say that the support has to come through the vehicle of jewelry? If that is not flowing with ease, then I surrender. The universe will have to figure out how to support me some other way. I am totally open to receiving that unconditional support!

Oneness speaks:

And so it is, Rasha. You are beginning to get the idea. Be less invested in the idea of having to do this all yourself. This is not about *doing*. This is about *Being* who you Are—period. Everything else comes after that. You are going about your life like a robot, mindlessly following your habitual routine. Haven't you noticed that it's not working?

Ok. Then I surrender! I am not fighting this anymore. I quit!

What is it you're quitting?

I'm quitting being a robot. I'm getting off the train.

Do you mean that?

I'm not sure. I'm not sure how that would look. But, I'm fed up! I don't want it to be like this anymore. I've got one foot in each of two worlds. It's too much! I want to live a spiritual life now. I don't want to be flogging jewelry, not full time. Not as a career. But, I don't know how to get past living hand to mouth. This has been going on for three years, for heaven's sake! Somehow, the writing always seems to take a back seat to my frenzy to earn enough money to barely make ends meet. Enough!! I am totally open to some other kind of idea coming my way.

How about doing the work that you're here to do? How's that for an idea?

It's great, as long as I can make a living doing it. How am I supposed to pay the rent and the phone bill and everything else?

You are not supposed to *worry* about that. You are supposed to simply Be who you Are. And, do what you do. The rest will take care of itself.

OK, Oneness. I trust you. Totally. I'm going to do it your way.

No, Rasha. You're going to do it *your* way. The real *you*. You may just be surprised with the results. Surrender the fight. And, you just may find that there is no fight.

❧

While I was busy wrestling with my human frailties and with the challenges of integrating the teachings of Oneness into everyday life, a far different kind of experience also began to unfold for me. It provided an ever-deepening experiential foray into the realm of the mystical and the otherworldly.

Flowers have always held an unexplained, sacred space in my heart. I still remember vividly the day when I was around eight years old, coming across a patch of daffodils growing "wild" in a stretch of grass along the highway close to my house. I remember thinking how beautiful they were and how out of place. Later that same afternoon, I returned to the same spot and discovered, to my horror, that the public works department had mowed the grass and mowed my pretty daffodils along with it. I burst into tears, thinking how absolutely heartless it was to have done that. It was as though I felt their pain.

The heart connection I experienced with those daffodils, as a little girl, was unforgettable. But, that very early clue of the natural empathic connection

I had with flowers escaped me then. It wasn't until after awakening to my connection with Oneness that a natural ability to *commune* with flowers became undeniable.

One morning, shortly after moving to Chimayo, I was greeted by two breathtaking bouquets I had arranged the night before. I noticed two little sprays of bright pink roses, one in each of the arrangements, had totally wilted. Every other flower was fresh and crisp, blooming in the fullness of its beauty. These two little sprays were the smallest flowers in the bunch. And, somehow, in contrast to the others, they seemed overshadowed.

Spontaneously, tears began to stream down my face as I felt what they were feeling. I laughed incredulously at the realization that duality extended even to flowers, here in this reality. These poor little beings didn't know that they were *tiny* little pink roses, not until they were placed in a position of comparison to something else! All they knew was their Beingness. Now, it was obvious *to them* how small and seemingly insignificant they were when placed next to the grand blush roses, the enormous white lilies broadcasting fragrance, and big Gerber daisies radiating the hue of the ultimate sunset.

The little sprays of tiny pink roses hung their heads as I began to speak to them. I cupped their bowed heads between my hands and I felt the warmth begin to rise within me and radiate from my palms. "You are playing a very special harmony in this orchestra," my voice told them, the words coming not from me, but somehow through me.

"Look how beautiful you are! Look how you hold the fullness of deep pink here in this bouquet! And feel how fragrant you are, even now, in your wilted state! You will be all that you can be for as long as you are in this form here, in this place, as part of this bouquet. Not bigger nor smaller, not grander nor insignificant, not more or less loved than any of the others. Did you forget who you are? You are Life Itself! You are simply experiencing form in this way."

The tears began to stream down my face as I felt the fullness of the loving force flowing through me that began to resurrect these little beings. My heart chakra unfolded like a giant blossom as the Light poured forth from my hands, and I watched as the little blooms drank deeply of it and began to spring back to life.

In that moment I felt my energy merge with theirs and shared their joy at the realization of that Oneness! Sweet and crisp and full of life, the little roses returned to the bouquet. And, I returned to my morning, refreshed and renewed and filled with awe.

Even though the joys of a mystical moment communing with nature gave me a reprieve from "spiritual boot camp" now and then, the pace of "the training" never let up. Opportunities to put the teachings of Oneness to the test—all calculated to push my buttons—were ever-present and unrelenting. I remember ruminating over some nonsense on the part of certain people in the local neighborhood. Oneness caught me in the act and delivered a powerful teaching on the importance of non-judgment.

Oneness expounds upon some of the principles of non-duality and how to apply them consciously toward spiritual growth

Oneness speaks:

Surely you know that there is no higher or lower, no more or less evolved, no more or less advanced, not in terms of one's true Essence. The distinctions are those made within the context of the world of duality, which is illusion at best, and, in truth, a forum for the exploration of *ego* in all its glorious manifestation.

Thoughts which would place oneself in an exalted position relative to the growth of another, from the perspective of a given moment in time, reflect one's own state of ego-centeredness and little more. For, each being simply Is— a freeze-action, still-life portrayal of a fleeting moment in the ongoing journey to Oneness. There is no judgment to be made about any of this, no value-based categorization of any sort whatsoever.

Your opportunity, in encountering another being who is demonstrating a particular phase in his spiritual development, is to note that this is what is so from the perspective of this moment. It is surely not to assess the relative merits of that individual and to place oneself higher or lower on some self-righteous scale of presumed merit. For, the merit may well be in the radical awakening possible for having experienced the depths of one's range of experience, be those depths fraught with pain or the epitome of exultation.

Beings who exhibit what you might assume to be a diminished level of development may in fact be reaping the culmination of the lessons learned in countless lifetimes of agony, and may, in their marginally illuminated perspectives, have summarized the theme which underscores an entire section in their ongoing life-sagas.

It is for you, the observer, the witness, to recognize the exquisite Isness in every nuance of the human experience. And, to know that no stage is more blessed nor exalted than another. It all simply Is.

Rasha speaks:

Thank you, Oneness, for reminding me. I had begun to make judgment. How quickly you caught me in the act and helped me to see. This was a powerful teaching, and one I needed right now. It's easy to see oneself breaking through so many of the illusions and to judge others by comparison. But, that would be a manifestation of ego, for it would set oneself apart from the Oneness that is the true, underlying Essence of all of it.

It is only through having experienced some aspects of the pain of another that one is able to truly honor the power of those kinds of experiences. I look back upon some of the episodes in my life's journey—ones that I might choose to act out differently were I to be faced with those choices now—and recognize the perfection in the journey. I have no regrets. It has been so incredibly rich.

You do see it now, don't you, Rasha?

Yes, Oneness, I see it. I am not higher nor lower than anyone or anything. I simply Am Present. Awareness made manifest in the Now moment. Divine Essence, experiencing Itself in a select way out of a range of infinite possibilities. That is all.

And, having said that, what is your purpose in being here in this Now moment?

To taste, to experience that Isness, materialized as form, from the uniqueness of this perspective.

And, who are you in this Now moment?

I am Life Itself expressed as all that I Am, in relation to all that I Am not: Isness within the context of duality.

And, who will you be tomorrow?

None other than That.

And, once you have attained the Realization of Self, who will you be then?

None other than That. For, the Essence of the Divine is Eternal and unchanging. Others may perceive me differently, through the filter of their own linear perspective, but the Divine Essence will not have changed. It will not, suddenly, manifest where once it was not. It Is. It always has been and always shall Be—That.

And, so it Is.

I don't know if I have awakened or whether I am still somewhere in the dream. And, somehow I don't care anymore. I don't feel like I'm in a race against time. I don't feel like I have to accomplish anything or prove anything. I am not more or less enlightened than anyone else, and I don't feel the need to place myself within that system of measurement. I have never felt this content nor this truly grateful for the magnificence of this journey, this extraordinary adventure called "life."

So, Oneness, having said all this, who is "Rasha"? Where did this composite of Beingness emanate from? And what is the significance of this name with which I now experience identity?

Oneness explains the significance of the name "Rasha"

You are the essence of the Eternal, Rasha. And, that is precisely what the name "Rasha" signifies. You are the essence of the Essence: Divine Presence experienced as form. You have concluded correctly that "Rasha" is an aspect of the word "rasa."

It is no accident that you came to perceive this name, having *baptized* yourself with it, for it is not a name that could possibly have been given by another. You were anointed with it from The Beginning. And, now you have embraced it once more.

As you were told, when the name came into your awareness, the choice was there for you to claim it, or not. The choice was made. And, with that choice, you have claimed your identity, your true identity.

Oneness, what more am I to do now to best serve the Divine purpose?

Simply Be Present. Make the choices that you do. Taste of the experience of Life. And touch, with the fullness of your Presence, the awareness of others, so that awareness may be kindled within the consciousness of each—of his *own* Divine Essence.

You need not say anything, necessarily, unless you choose to do so. You are not expected to have memorized the material in the book you have written and to spill these concepts forth from some pulpit. The teachings which will emanate from you will be applications of principles you have mastered. And, you will impart these concepts in the simplest possible way so that they will kindle a sense of recognition within the hearts of those whose lives you touch.

The teachings will not spring from your mind, but rather, will be sourced from within the depths of your true essence, from a level of knowingness that has not been learned, but rather, has been revealed. At the present moment, there should be no questions or doubts as to what will be taught, or when, or how. All will unfold as it will unfold.

So Be it.

And, so it Is. Our Love is with you, and you are with This Love, as Oneness. Entwined with Oneness. Inseparable. And Eternal.

10

Summer 2001
Chimayo, New Mexico
Encounters with The Christ

Chimayo is an 18th century style New Mexican village tucked away in the wind-eroded hills that dot the landscape, some 25 miles north of Santa Fe. It didn't surprise me that no sooner had I made the decision to spend the summer of 2001 in Northern New Mexico, than I was drawn to Chimayo like a magnet.

From the moment I had first stumbled onto this village, several years earlier, I was struck by the absolute serenity of the place and the sense that something magical was in the air. Little has changed since Chimayo was established several centuries earlier. Its claim to fame is a mysterious, little adobe chapel, *The Santuario de Chimayo*, affectionately known as "the Lourdes of America."

The Santuario has a rich history of miraculous happenings and an ever-changing mini-museum containing evidences of miracles that have taken place within its walls over the centuries. Countless crutches, abandoned by those who had made the pilgrimage in search of healing—and had received it—attest to the legends. One step inside, and my heart affirmed them too. The stark simplicity of the chapel, with its rustic carvings and the sparse display of primitive religious artifacts indigenous to the region, created a dramatic contrast to the radiance I encountered there.

I had been going to the Santuario a few times a week since I arrived in New Mexico, just to imbibe the stillness and commune with the unmistakable Divine Presence I felt there so intensely. It was a powerful and beautiful energy exchange with a Presence I had come to know as The Christ.

What began as a silent sharing of Love with this Presence grew to become a series of very definite communications within the silent confines of my mind, in which specific understandings were given. Wondering whether I'd received the information correctly, I'd gone to Oneness to verify exactly what it was I was being told and who was speaking to me. Oneness confirmed that I had indeed connected with the Presence of The Christ. It was a consciousness with whom I was told I shared considerable history and with whom I had a powerful connection.

At the time, the Divine Presence, which I thought of as Jeshua (Jesus), told me that I was also a "Messenger of God." I remembered how I'd been reassured that I had no cause to fear that I would experience a violent end as a result of this work. That was not going to happen in these times. There had been a reference to a history of lifetimes in which I'd experienced and borne witness to unspeakable hardships and atrocities that befell those who served as Divine Messengers. Somehow, that felt like truth to me, yet I had no sense of fear about it now. Everything seemed to be very much in Divine order.

Oneness had affirmed the accuracy of the information and explained that the horrors I'd encountered in previous lifetimes had served as a foundation for the work I'd be doing now. Those experiences had instilled in me an innate sense of *caution* that had served me well, they said. That would explain the underlying sense of trepidation I had about all this, I remember thinking.

The words of Oneness reverberated within me in silence as I entered the Santuario once more and quietly took a seat. The cool, tranquil interior of the little sanctuary was a welcome reprieve from the broiling noonday sun outside. Immediately, my heart filled with a blessed sense of peace and contentment.

This time, I had come prepared. Holding my pen and a notebook ready, I began a silent invocation to the Consciousness I knew was so fully Present and prepared myself to receive the gift of Grace. There was no doubt and no hesitation. It was as though I had done this a thousand times before. Yet, it was my first formal audience with the One who would identify Himself as "The Christ."

It was a conversation that would unlock the mystery of the cryptic images that had flashed spontaneously across the subliminal screen of my mind all my life. It was a conversation and an experience that would change my life forever.

～≫～

The Christ speaks:
Good morning, Rasha. Or, is it afternoon?

Rasha speaks:
It is one and the same! It is now! Who is speaking?

Who have you come here to visit? It is this one who speaks with you now. Not the one symbolized by a moment of agony and of death, who hangs before you on a wooden cross, but the one who springs up *within* you in Eternal Life.

We have spoken before in this way, in this place. And, we have invited you here, with pen in hand, to share some insights with you that you may document as part of your preparation for the mission that lies before you. Many others have walked this path. You are far from alone in what you have volunteered to do, for you are God-focused. And, your energies have been directed as an instrument of Divine intent.

Your brothers and sisters in spirit surround you with loving support of your choice and your mission in these times, as you have added your loving support, through time immemorial, to the Divinely guided work of others in this family of souls.

The times of martyred Messengers are, thankfully, behind us now. It is no longer necessary that poignant imagery be portrayed as a way of making an indelible impression upon the mass consciousness of an era. This era is a time of profound transformation of that collective consciousness.

You will not be asked to play the role of sacrificial lamb in order to call attention to the gift of your Divine connection. You will embody that connectedness. And, the Light that emanates from your physical being will be as a lamplight to untold numbers of questing souls who hunger for *evidence* of that which they seek. You will embody that evidence. As did we.

This communication is not intended to replace the work you are already doing, for that is your own unique gift to the world. We come to you as a loving brother in spirit, here always with an outstretched hand, which you may hold from time to time if it comforts you to do so.

There will be moments when you will be inclined to feel most alone in what you have sought to do in this moment in history. There will be times when you will undoubtedly question your own sanity in having embarked on such a path. Others will cast stones, in *every* way imaginable. You will feel betrayed by beings who you believed to be beyond doubt, and the concept of loyalty will be laid open before you so that you may experience the rawness that comes of misplaced dependency.

Presume nothing. For, the "rock" upon which your faith rests lies not upon the shoulders of those who walk beside you, but within the silent, unspeakable flame of passion that has been ignited *within* you. Do not mistake proximity for devotion. For, the devotion of those who are guided to follow you is to the Divinity that lies upon *their own* paths, which you will have illuminated. The loyalty of the sincere heart is to the Divinity within *one's own self*. You are here to demonstrate the autonomous nature of that Divine connectedness.

This sanctuary, to which you have been guided, will be as a haven to you in this time of heightened metamorphosis. Here we can visit and converse, if you would like. You are not being ordered here but rather, invited, if it pleases you.

It does!

We share in the joy of this blessed reunion. For, we have been together before, in other times.

The story of Leah begins to unfold as The Christ recounts an ancient tale that was coming full circle

You were as a sister to me then, quietly allowing your little heart to break as you watched the drama unfold before you. We shared a powerful connectedness then. But, as planned, you were too young to become involved in the drama and too young to be implicated and made to suffer for your knowingness.

Your name was "Leah" (lay-ah) in that lifetime. You followed me everywhere, eyes shining in rapture, for you could *see* beyond the limitation of the physical persona. You did not understand what you saw, but you could *feel* the power of the energies with which this persona was gifted. You carried the luminosity quietly within, terrified of the unthinkable price that was paid for carrying the gift of that Grace.

Fear of that outcome was impressed indelibly upon your young heart. And, you have carried that atrocity within you. Now, it is time for you to release those memories. For, the fear of endangering yourself is the anchor that continues to weight you to the perceived "safety" of groundedness. You have come to this lifetime to step out from beneath the yoke of those ancient memories.

You were as a seed of consciousness, implanted right in the epicenter of one of history's most poignant dramas so the lesson could not be missed. You carry the seed within you to this day. And, you will blossom with the rays of that ancient Light still safe, still waiting dormant within you. The sense of the ancient memories are being stored within you now, so that you might remember fully, with vivid awareness, your Divine encounter and relinquish the fear with which your mind has suppressed it for centuries.

You are also a spark of Divinity. Now, in your own moment, that timeless knowingness has been rekindled within you so you might bear it fully, with no reluctance, with no fear. You will not be crucified for your Divine service. You will walk with unspeakable Grace through the tumultuous times to come. And, you will hold firm to the Light of the ancient memories as they merge in Oneness with these times.

You will embody the timelessness of having been at center stage during countless significant moments in your linear history. And, you will step forth in total surrender to the Light that pours forth from within you to illuminate the world. There is no *persona*, from the vantage point of the Divine servant. You will come to perceive Self as the selfless, consciously making the offering of your whole Beingness as an empty vessel through which the Light of Love may be poured.

You will come to that precipice of surrender many, many times. And, you will believe yourself to have jumped, over and over again. This is as it is meant to be. For, when you find yourself, yet again, standing at the edge of the cliff of your soul, it is not as an invalidation of the countless leaps of faith that have preceded it, but rather as an opportunity to make that choice with all your heart and soul, yet again.

Your doubts and your humanness will lead you to the edge of that cliff again and again, so that you may recognize once more the Divinity in your *humanness* and choose to transcend even *that* expression of separation from the Source of That which you Are. Ultimately, you will cease to have conscious awareness of your linear identity and embody Oneness in totality.

We also made this journey. But, know that the conditions and the circumstances of those times are not the same as the ones you encounter here.

This is *your* moment. And, we rejoice with you at your choice to embrace your destiny fully. The Love of your own heart-of-hearts will carry you through the trials that characterize the road that lies before you. It is the strength of the Source of all things that you carry with you to illuminate even the darkest hours.

There will be moments of great exultation in the embracing of the path, and there will be moments of profound loneliness. In those times when you think you are most alone, never forget that we walk beside you. Always. For, *We Are The Christ*, transcending persona, transcending history, transcending the "then" of a drama made famous by the agony of an ending.

There *was* no ending. For, we are here with you now as we were before. A Presence. Eternal. Glorified by *Life*, of which we are all a part. We reach through the centuries of "history," of linear reality, and we meet you not in the "here and now," but in that space of *beyond* that unifies all of it in timelessness. We share that One Love in this timeless place of Now. Always.

I sat motionless, in rapt attention to the silence within, for a long time. My mind, which instinctively wanted to respond, "There must be some mistake. You've got the wrong person. You can't possibly be talking about *me!*" had become absolutely still.

By that time, the kind of scenario that had just been laid out before me had begun to feel familiar. I had heard the part about who I was "destined to become" from teachers and guides, whether walking around in physical bodies or floating through the ethers without them, since the barest beginning of my spiritual awakening. The story was the same. And, there was still a sense of absolute unrealness to it.

Even though I knew how far I'd come on my journey, even though I understood very clearly who Oneness was and knew that I actually *was* having conversations with The Almighty on a daily basis, there was still the feeling, "this can't possibly really be happening to *me.*" Now, having that sentiment lavished so lovingly upon me by The Christ brought my heart to its knees.

Gently, I closed my eyes. After only a moment or two, I noticed that my breathing had slowed down to the point that I was barely breathing at all. There was an eerie sense of calm that filled me, as my mind became absolutely still. Not a thought. Not a picture. Not a sound.

Suddenly, in a blazing flash of inner illumination, I experienced my own presence, as vividly as life itself, somewhere entirely different. In the vision, I was standing by the side of a narrow dirt road, on the edge of a town, screaming hysterically! The scene was of an ancient time and place that my conscious mind did not recognize. But, my inner knowingness told me instantly that it was Jerusalem.

In the far distance were the silhouettes of three crosses, barely visible against the background of an angry sky. I had been forbidden to go one step further by an irate father. I was Leah, age 14, watching the crucifixion of Jeshua—in horror.

As I watched from the silence of a Santuario in a remote New Mexico village and simultaneously experienced myself *as* Leah writhing in indescribable heartache two thousand years away, the two became one.

Instantly, in a blinding flash of passion, the consciousness I recognized to be *myself* was drawn into the body of the Beloved Jeshua, hanging on the cross in the distance. I looked down *through His eyes,* my very soul exploding in ecstasy.

With indescribable Love, I glanced down at the gathering of people below me. And, with a sense of unspeakable passion, I recognized the Divine Presence beating within my own heart. In that timeless moment, I knew myself to be One with All of it.

It was a scene that was all too familiar. The indelible image of that single timeless instant had flashed across the screen of my mind's eye all my life, in dream state, in meditation, and in 20th century broad daylight. It was the puzzle I never had the pieces for. Then suddenly, I did. Suddenly, I knew.

I sat for a very long time in the darkened stillness of the Santuario and quietly sobbed.

By mid-July, the New Mexico summer had begun to wear on me. The days on end spent blissfully cloistered away, communicating with virtually no one except for Oneness, had been intense. I was aware that I had started procrastinating about the editing work that also needed to be done on the book, *Oneness*, which was nearing completion.

The prospect of translating the hundreds of pages of auditory communication I had received into written sentence structure that was readable was daunting. Instead, after the long hours of transcription work, I had somehow taken to picking apricots in the orchard and had discovered the joys of canning homemade jam. I was feeling guilty.

Several days after my profound experience at the Santuario, I returned once again to the stillness of the sanctuary and to the loving Presence of The Christ. I was compelled to dig deeper into the amazing story that had begun to unfold. Within moments of sitting down in the peaceful chapel, we were in Divine connectedness once more. And, the blessed audience I experienced with this extraordinary Divine Presence set my mind and my heart at ease.

The Christ speaks:

We greet you, Rasha. You have come to visit with us once again. The "us" to whom we refer is none *other* than this consciousness that recognizes itself to be multidimensional. It is not from the limited persona of the identity that incarnated as Jeshua that we speak with you now, but rather, from the expanded *perspective* of that consciousness.

The connection flows effortlessly for you. You were born to this work. And, it is surely in your highest interests to make this work your highest priority. There is nothing more important for you than to exercise your Divine connectedness. For, in so doing, you reinforce your fluency and reinforce the vibrational foundation upon which your future work will be based.

We recognize that you have encountered a psychological block with regard to the material you have transcribed. You recognize that there is editing work to be done. Yet, that does not invalidate the relevance and the merit of the contents of the work. You expect absolute perfection of yourself. You are not expected to have transcribed a flawless document.

Rasha speaks:

How can I justify doing a less than perfect job for God? I feel like I've failed, and I haven't even finished the work yet. I'm afraid that people will ridicule me and my work. I think that's what's holding me back.

Ridicule is to be expected, Rasha. There is not one amongst us who has served in this way that was not made to bear the brunt of the scorn of those who, for any number of reasons, were not aligned to the energies of the message we were destined to carry forth. Expect that you will be criticized and discredited. It is part of the job description. Learning to hold your head high in the face of this adversity is the challenge for you as it was for all the others in whose footsteps you follow.

Who could possibly begin to fathom this level of connectedness who has not experienced it, or is not pre-disposed to the idea of such a connection? To do so would violate the mandates with which you have been culturally force-fed. And, what of the lamb who has stepped forth to carry such a connection? He will be slandered and made to bear all manner of ridicule.

Yet, in the eyes of those whose hearts have been graced by the shining pearls he has delivered, the truth of the Divine message and the energy that underlies it cannot be questioned. It *Is*. It resonates as Divine Essence. It is to these souls that you will deliver the jewels with which you have been entrusted.

The ridicule of others, whose "voices" may be heard loudly, will fall on deaf ears as they cast their poison arrows into the ethers of Creation. Do not fear that you will be made to be accountable for the contents of the teachings you have transcribed. You will be accountable only for the Grace with which you brave the inevitable storms that your seeds of Divine truth will initiate.

You have surrendered your earthly priorities to be able to carry this torch in the darkness. It is your *honor* to do so, not your "cross to bear." For, even in the darkest moments, you will not feel burdened by what you have been permitted to carry but, rather, elevated by the honor of being able to carry God's mighty flame.

None that was made to endure the agonies of martyrdom did so in fear or regret. For, the agonies were experienced only by those who watched and imagined, vicariously, the experience to which they bore witness. The sacrificial lambs were exalted by the presence of the Light of the Lord and experienced the heights of ecstatic release in the moments of surrender to their mortality.

In those moments, they *became* the Divine. They transcended the limitations of humanness, as defined by the characteristics of physical sensation. There *was* no pain. For, in those moments in which they illustrated the epitome of suffering, their essence was *non-physical,* made manifest in form.

You were given a glimpse of this, as Leah, when, for a fleeting moment you experienced Oneness with these energies in the persona of Jeshua. You were shown very carefully what had truly transpired. And, these memories have never left you. You have relived the crucifixion of Jeshua in your dreams and in your meditations. And, you know you have been on that cross, for you remember it vividly.

Yet, there was also the *knowingness* that you were *not* the reincarnation of Jeshua. So, the visions were puzzling. Now they are not. Now you know the answer to the riddle of these pictures you carry in your mind and in your heart. For, the vision is not accompanied by horror and fear and unspeakable pain, but by bliss and the peace of knowing transcendence of the dramatic images that were portrayed.

It was an exquisite moment of Oneness with all who watched from below and all who watch from On High. And, you shared in the experience of it so that you might be prepared to step forth fearlessly when your own moment was at hand.

This is *your* moment, Rasha. You will not be crucified, or stoned, or burned, or tortured for your role as Messenger. You will be exalted in the eyes of many. And, you will float with sweetness and the Grace of Divine momentum over the turbulence that may come to pass, now and then. You see, it truly does not matter what anyone may or may not think of you and the contents of the pages you have transcribed. All that matters is that you recognize the Light in that manifestation of connectedness and embrace it as the blessing that it truly is.

You are one of The Messengers, Rasha. And, we embrace you once more. Step into your shoes now. And, walk forth with Grace for the magnificence you have come to deliver in these times. For, this is the hallmark of this lifetime. This is your life's work. And, nothing—*nothing*—is more worthy of being embraced by you than this. Our love is here for you and here within you. Always. For, We Are The Christ.

I left the Santuario after a little while, awestruck. And I went home and got to work.

August 6, 2001 was an auspicious day. It was the day I completed the transmissions for the book, *Oneness*. Yet, it was anticlimactic. I was numb. The summer wore on. In retrospect, it had been a powerful time, bouncing me between moments of sublime connectedness and feelings of being utterly lost in an alien world. Now, I was exhausted. I didn't want to see anyone or talk to anyone. I just wanted to be in stillness, in the sanctity of my connection with Oneness.

A few days before, as the final chapters were being completed, there had been what seemed like a bizarre *release* of energy, facilitated by Mother Nature. After being hard at the computer all day, I'd taken a break to go outside and pick apricots. No sooner did I get to the tree when, out of nowhere, a monstrous black cloud hurled itself over the mountain and the wind began to howl. Instantly, thunder and lightning you'd expect to see in a horror movie sent me running for cover.

Within seconds, the sky opened up and rain came pelting down. Raindrops transformed into weapons and machine-gunned over the property, kneading the parched earth into slop. Hail stones the size of cherries bounced off the tin roof, creating a percussion section that was almost deafening! The cacophony built to a crescendo as the storm got stronger and stronger. The peaceful little brook beside the house transformed into a river of mud water that washed through my little flower garden and drowned it in seconds. Then, as suddenly as it began, it was over.

Neighbors said that they'd never seen rain like that in all the years they'd been in New Mexico. After the rain stopped, I'd felt dramatically different, like something had shifted. I wasn't sure what world this was, what level of reality I might have landed in.

Now, a few days later, I was surely *not* walking around in bliss, but was spaced-out, and consumed with the unrealness of having just finished a marathon four-year exercise in transcribing a 400-page book. There was the feeling of wanting to sit and cry, but there were no tears and no real sadness. It was overcast and dead-still outside. And very eerie.

Many weeks had passed since I had gone to the Santuario de Chimayo, giving me time to process and integrate the past-life drama that had begun to unfold there. Quite suddenly, I was irresistibly drawn to visit there once again. The sessions had felt wonderful and natural, and the energy was familiar and timeless. I could not question it. I went.

The peaceful Santuario had become a spiritual oasis for me. The simple adobe room gave no hint of the miracle taking place within those walls. It was absolute stillness. I entered the darkened chapel and took a seat at the far end of a waiting pew. Amazingly enough, I was the only one there.

I folded my hands in reverence, closed my eyes, and went into the depths of the silent space that had become so familiar. My heart spoke my invocation in silence. The invitation to join in a bond of Holy Communion with the one I had come to know as The Christ was received. An intense rush of blessed Light effulgence coursed through my entire being, filling me with a sense of indescribable joy. As before, the voice of The Christ began to speak.

The Christ speaks:

We greet you, Rasha. And, we welcome you, once again, unto the sacred space where we share a bond of Unity. It is a timeless bond, not limited to the incarnate encounter we shared in the times of Jeshua. That was a poignant episode in a colorful history of incarnate experience. And, even though this newfound knowledge of your incarnation as Leah fascinates you, do not allow that incarnate "window" to obscure the vantage point of the overview from which the essence of all incarnation can be perceived.

Leah was a moment in your evolution as a being. She was a fragment of all that has gone into your working-up as a Divine Soul in physical form. You have written these words at the hand of several of your teachers, yet the full ramifications of what these words imply still strikes you with awed disbelief.

No, Rasha, you are not imagining what has been revealed to you. Yes, this is really happening. You are not manifesting *ego* in writing these words, as you have suspected on occasion. You are transcribing the essence of this communication perfectly.

Rasha speaks:

It's amazing! You really can read my mind!

There is no separation. You are also of this essence. The full conscious manifestation of it, in form, is evolving in increments. You are well into that process now. The last vestiges of separation are to be relinquished in this stage of your process, just as it was with Jeshua. He was not "born" into the fullness of his realization of his Divinity. It was revealed to him, in increments, over time. In your case, there was a significant history of density to be transcended and released before the full magnitude of these energies could be made manifest through your form.

The mission is different. The vibrational conditions into which your *identity* emerged in form are different. And, the timing of the culmination of your mission within your lifetime is different. Due to the nature of your reality, the longevity that is destined allowed for a depth of incarnate experience to be programmed into this lifetime. That *experience* will enable you to teach, from the standpoint of empathy, the concepts you will impart. You will teach from hard-won life experience the insights gleaned. You have been told these things before.

Yes, I know. I understand what you are telling me. Yet, I would be most interested to know the details of my lifetime as Leah, as that experience relates to this lifetime. Could I ask you to tell me a bit about that lifetime?

We will let you re-experience it. Close your eyes and come with us, in silence, back in time to those days.

Ok.

I closed my eyes. And, instantly, all sense of being in 21ˢᵗ century New Mexico melted into another level of perception. In less than a heartbeat, I experienced myself back in Jerusalem, some two thousand years before, as a virtual movie in vivid detail began to unfold. Once again, I was given a sense, visually, of my own presence.

This time, I experienced myself as Leah several years later than in the first vision. I had the sense of being a woman in her late twenties. Simultaneously, I *observed* myself, seated in a darkened room, by candlelight, with eyes closed. My head was draped reverently with a soft white cloth. I was in a deep state of trance and Divine Bliss. The little room was crowded with people who had come to listen to the teachings that were pouring forth through my form. Many years had passed since the crucifixion. I was channeling Jeshua.

The presence that considered itself to be Rasha watched from a distance that bridged time and space. Her physical body was electrified with the intensity of the Light effulgence that flowed through the Presence of Leah, 2,000 years and half a world away. For, there was no separation between them in that moment. They had become One Being. The experience lasted only a few moments, and took place in silence. It was a freeze-action instant of absolute knowingness. A complete understanding of what was happening then, as now, was imparted without a single word spoken.

Slowly, I opened my eyes. The peaceful adobe chapel with its rustic adornments confirmed to me that my body was still in 21ˢᵗ century Chimayo, seated on a hard wooden bench. Gently, I dabbed at the tears that bathed my cheeks and began to become aware of breath moving through form, as my consciousness transitioned from the realm of the timeless to the Here and Now. I was in ecstasy.

After a few moments, catching my breath, the conversation with The Christ Consciousness resumed. And, I was given a confirmation and a detailed explanation of the ancient scene I had just witnessed.

Rasha speaks:

Thank you for that journey! Can you tell me what Leah was like in her emotional life? Where was she in her heart and mind with regard to what happened to her?

The Christ speaks:

Leah was a gifted psychic from a young age, but did not have a frame of reference within which to place herself. There was not widespread awareness of such things in those days. The visions and the things of which she spoke were considered symptoms of madness by her family. She was shunned by the cultivated society into which she was born and retreated into herself and her innate sense of Divine connectedness.

When she encountered Jeshua, her world changed. For, she could relate instantly to the sensations of the heart that she experienced in his Presence. It was a political tightrope that she walked very cautiously throughout that lifetime. For, her *truth* was invalidated at every turn, except within the spiritual world, which, of necessity, remained clandestine.

Her passion and state of rapture were readily apparent to Jeshua, who was aware of her presence and her gifts. They became friends. Yet, he did not reveal to her the truth of her *own* Divine Essence—not until his moment of transcendence, when she was not *told* but rather *shown* experientially the energy of which she was a part.

She followed Jeshua everywhere, partaking of the nectar which flowed so freely from his Presence. She walked around in a state of spiritual intoxication much of the time. She had placed her heart and soul in the hands of the God of whom Jeshua spoke. The material world held no appeal for her whatsoever.

Her Divine connection deepened very quickly due to the totality with which she surrendered her life to her God. She was opened and initiated during the process of her brief years in the presence of Jeshua. She was prepared to relay the Light of "His" Love and "His" Divine guidance through the vehicle of her consciousness, in much the same way as you have come to be able to do in this lifetime.

In fact, it was The Christ Presence, *transcending* the persona of Jeshua who had carried it in physical form, that provided the comfort of Divine wisdom in the aftermath of the tragedy that befell those who adored him. It was a gesture of Love and comfort to those devoted ones that they were *shielded* from knowing the full magnitude of the identity to whom they had connected through Leah. In this way, they came to understand that they had not "lost him." They knew that he still walked beside them, although not in physical form.

That Presence was one that was *felt*, not simply heard as words and teachings imparted through Leah. The *séances* that were held in secret were rapturous events in which the Light of The Christ energy poured forth from the form of Leah and was perceived by all who were present. She had little or no awareness of what transpired during these sessions, only that she *awoke* from them in a state of sublime rapture.

Fearing the fate of Jeshua, the truth of the phenomenon that was manifesting through Leah was kept a closely guarded secret. Under the circumstances of those times, those who witnessed these sessions, and saw the magnitude of the aura she brought forth, feared for her life.

Her parents were horrified by the types of people with whom she was associating. Her family was what might be considered "high society" in those days, and her father was a respected man within the hierarchy of The Temple. Leah's associations were seen as a threat to the social standing of her parents, and they sought to quash her activities by marrying her off to a young man from a proper family.

Paul stepped forth and asked for Leah's hand in marriage, professing his love for her, to no avail. Leah refused all the arranged suitors, and Paul was rejected by her father for political reasons. Leah reverted to staging wildly emotional scenes, dramatizing them with ecstatic seizures, to create a diversion that would insure her freedom from the bondage of marriage. For, she was a fully Realized Divine Soul who came into awareness in a time frame when she was of far more service in secrecy. Her spiritual brothers, of whom Paul was her "love connection," protected her identity with their very lives.

It was a conspiracy of Love that has now come full circle. For, in these times, the truth of the Light that will pour forth from the physical vehicle of this immortal soul will be undeniable. You will carry the fullness of this Light, Rasha. And, you will do so fearlessly. For, you have waited for the appointed incarnation to step forth and Be all that you Are, with no hesitation.

Your metamorphosis is nearing completion now. And, you know. And, you trust. For, you have felt these energies *as* your own Being. Soon, you will walk with these energies, and you will know yourself to Be at all times what you know yourself to Be in this moment. The Christ Consciousness is within you as it was within Leah. And now, "her" moment is at hand as you.

You will come to cherish the sacredness of this time of preparation. And, you will come to understand, fully and completely, why this period of intense isolation was necessary. Everything is moving perfectly now and according to plan. Be present in the fullness of these energies now and rejoice in the experience of who you really Are.

We are here for you always. For, We Are The Christ, manifesting as consciousness in this moment and soon to manifest fully in form. Be at peace with this understanding, Rasha. And feel this Love blazing brightly from within your own being.

❧

I was riveted by the past-life history that was being revealed. The following afternoon, I was irresistibly drawn back to the Santuario, in hopes of uncovering more details about the vision I had witnessed the day before and to ask about the relationship between Leah and Paul in the times of Jeshua.

Years before, I'd been introduced to Nick Bunick, whose past-life experiences as the Apostle Paul were revealed in the book, *The Messengers*. During an extensive series of hypnotic past-life regressions, Nick had relived his lifetime as Paul and had documented his recollections in detail. I remembered having asked him, jokingly, whether he thought I might have played a part in that drama too. He looked at me deeply and in all seriousness he answered, "yes." "Well, who was I?" I had asked.

"You were a woman named Leah," he replied matter of factly.

I remember thinking, "Well, there you have it. I was some woman named Leah. Some face in the crowd, in the times of Jeshua." Somehow that picture didn't quite fit, but I let it pass. I remember wondering how Nick might happen to know such an obscure detail. Later, when I read *The Messengers* and learned the role "Leah" played in the life of Paul, our prior conversation began to resonate in my mind. According to Nick's recollections, Paul was in a relationship with a woman named Leah. The book indicated that they never married, and pretty much left it at that. I wanted to know more.

Now, seated once more in the tranquil inner sanctum of the Santuario, I closed my eyes and almost instantly went into a profound state of deep meditation. The details of the lifetime of Leah came to me, not in words but simply as knowingness, as I sat immersed in a sea of exultation.

Leah was 14 years old when Jeshua was crucified. She was the daughter of a prominent and wealthy Jewish family who were merchants. Her parents attempted to force her into an arranged marriage, which she refused. They were troubled about Leah's association with Jeshua and his inner circle of followers and feared that she was endangered. They reasoned that if Leah could be married off to a man with politically-correct affiliations, the "problem" of Leah would be solved.

Paul was like a big brother to Leah. They were dear friends and close confidants. He asked for Leah's hand himself to try to protect her and to conceal the truth of her political and spiritual activities, but her father wouldn't hear of it. Paul's affiliation with Jeshua was far too dangerous, as far as Leah's parents were concerned.

Leah declared that if she could not marry Paul, she would never marry. And, she never did. She feigned madness and seizures after the crucifixion of Jeshua, in order to dissuade potential suitors. And, it was rumored that Leah was a religious fanatic, who had become crazed by her spiritual infatuation with Jeshua.

In fact, young Leah was clandestinely working as a psychic channel, relaying Divine guidance and information from The Christ to members of Jeshua's trusted inner circle. Her role was considered far too important to risk jeopardizing. And, Paul covered for her, feigning a romantic interest as an alibi for her whereabouts. She died, at the age of 42, of a fever, 28 years after the crucifixion of Jeshua.

I opened my eyes slowly, breathing in the ancient understandings, and attempted to sort out the details with my logical mind. After a while, I went home to my computer and my own Divine connection. I asked Oneness to verify the information I had received.

Oneness speaks:

You have received the information correctly, Rasha. There was great love between Leah and Paul. Yet, due to the morality of the times and the fact that each of them was devoted to their spiritual focus, that relationship remained platonic. Yet, all who knew them well considered them to be a couple. It was for the protection of both of them from the social pressures of the day that they kept up the pretense.

In her work, Leah was bringing through information from The Father Consciousness, the same source as some of the information you have received in this lifetime, via Amitabh. The Father Consciousness is the energy that is referred to as The Christ. It was this energy that *incarnated* as Jeshua.

After the crucifixion, you came into your power as a channel and were able to conduct conversations between others and The Christ, whom his followers *believed* to be Jeshua. In fact, the connection was with the Divine Consciousness that *transcended* Jeshua's incarnate identity. It is that Source with whom you have connected.

Your lifetime as Leah is being referenced for you now as a footnote to *these* times. Your purpose here now is not to focus your attention on who you *were* during an ancient incarnation, even a significant one. The visions have been provided to help you understand the depth of the preparation that has gone into your working up for the times at hand.

You were given the benefit of the profound experience of Divine contact and your moments of exultation within the body of Jeshua in his final moments, in order to equip you with a rudimentary understanding of the nature of a Divine connection. In that way you were able to perform your destined role in *that* lifetime, without fear. At the same time, you were *initiated* as an incarnate being who is able to bridge dimensions and receive communications from beyond physical reality.

As you have come to know, you have functioned in this capacity for countless lifetimes, often with disastrous political consequences. It is for that reason that you had such powerful instinctive trepidation about doing this work in this lifetime. Nonetheless, you have been most thoroughly prepared to play this role once again so that you may step into the shoes of your destiny with Grace.

Rasha speaks:

Thank you, Oneness, for clarifying this for me. May I have permission to share this information with Nick? I think he would also find it valuable.

You most certainly may share this information with him. It should put into perspective for him one of the aspects of his memories of his lifetime as Paul. And, it will help both of you to understand the nature of the connection that you both recognize as kindred. You shared a significant moment in spiritual history as a powerful alliance that was both political and heartfelt. That level of dedication to Divine service and to the elevation of the consciousness of humanity is a focus you share once again in these times.

The following day, I phoned Nick Bunick. I began to describe the experiences I'd been having in the Santuario de Chimayo over the summer and shared my revelations about the life of Leah. Immediately he suggested that I get on a plane and come to Portland. There, I would undergo a hypnotic past-life regression session, similar to the ones he had experienced years before, and we'd see what memories might be revealed. I was intrigued and agreed to go.

Several weeks later, in the presence of Nick, I too underwent a hypnotic past-life regression session and relived, in vivid detail, two phases of the life of Leah. The first brief impressions were of Leah in early adolescence, a woman-child consumed in spiritual rapture and traumatized by overbearing parents. The later phase of the session revealed a reserved, self-assured young woman at age 28, who fully embodied the Light of The Christ she adored. The clandestine channeling sessions were described in exacting detail.

Through the physical form of a 21st century woman named Rasha, Leah answered complex questions about her situation and her personal life in Jerusalem following the crucifixion, two thousand years before. I experienced *myself* as both women simultaneously. Extremes of energy, emotion, and Divine passion surged through my body as she spoke. The sense of rapture continued to resurge within my own heart chakra intermittently, and spontaneous flashes of "Leah revisited" played sporadically in the living theater of my mind over the next two days.

When I returned home, I carried her heart within my own. I had bridged the centuries and become One with an aspect of my own Being, whose heartache and exultation paved the way for the woman I was becoming before my very eyes.

11

I n November of 1998, I had flown to New Mexico for an extended Thanksgiving holiday in Santa Fe. Without really understanding why, my heart suddenly felt drawn to go to Taos, some 60 miles north. It was an unmistakable pull that I didn't question—I went. I checked myself in to a wonderful, rustic B&B backing onto a vast expanse of Native American land owned by the Taos Pueblo. It offered an unsurpassed view of Taos Mountain and a beautiful little kiva fireplace to keep me cozy.

I had barricaded myself in for several days, reveling equally in the joys of an early snowfall set against the breathtaking panorama outside my window and the joys of my daily writing sessions with Oneness, where the exploration of the incredible landscape within had only just begun. The transcription of the book, *Oneness*, was in the very early stages. And, I became totally absorbed in fascination at the mystery that was unfolding before my very eyes on the screen of a secondhand laptop.

After more than a week in absolute solitude, broken-up only by a daily trek to a funky little local eatery, I heard about the Neem Karoli Baba/Hanuman Ashram for the first time. Over a hearty bowl of homemade soup, a map was drawn, in amongst the crayon graffiti on the placemat, to the little spiritual haven that would grow to become a home away from home for me.

Neem Karoli Baba, who stepped into the spiritual spotlight of the Western world by virtue of the classic book, *Be Here Now* by Ram Dass, is said to have been an incarnation of the Hindu monkey God, Hanuman. He "left his body" in 1973, but his loving presence can be felt in his ashrams to this day.

It was a Sunday morning when I entered the sanctuary that offered a cross between country New Mexico décor and a decidedly offbeat Indian atmosphere for the first time. The room was presided over by an enormous white marble *murti*, a statue of the Hindu monkey God, Hanuman. It was possibly the most beautiful statue I had ever seen. The serenity of the face of Hanuman, with golden eyes that radiated pure Love, captured my heart on the spot. I took my place on the floor amongst an eclectic gathering of devotees, and slowly, I closed my eyes.

The exotic rhythms of drums and bells merged with the droning of the harmonium, as the room was swept into an exuberant rendition of the Hanuman Chalisa—forty verses in Hindi in praise of the beloved Hanuman. Within seconds I lost all sense of time and place. My heart chakra began to reverberate wildly, sending me into involuntary waves of bliss. The experience caught me by surprise, and I never forgot it.

Now, years later, in the summer of 2001, I was actually living in New Mexico for a few months, and Sunday mornings had become a cherished ritual of making a pilgrimage through the winding Sangre de Christo mountains to spend the day in Taos with Hanuman.

On one occasion, as I sat quietly in the back of the sanctuary after the festivities were over, I felt a warm, loving energy flood through me. I looked up at the magnificent white marble Hanuman, whose haunting eyes had never left me. Instantly, a fleeting montage of memories—moments I'd shared in Nashville, Tennessee, 15 years before, with the channeled Presence of the Hindu God, Rama—flashed across the screen of my mind.

Rama had been my first channeled teacher. For several months during the summer and autumn of 1987, I had transcribed page after page of profound spiritual wisdom, by hand, dictated by a source that identified itself as "Rama." The extraordinary connection came at a time when I had just barely begun to awaken spiritually. Rama had explained that we had been "brothers" in a previous life—"warriors."

I hadn't a clue at the time who Rama was or what it meant. I only knew that the teachings I was jotting down were magnificent and something I never could have written. When I was told, back then, that transcribing channeled books of spiritual wisdom was to be my life's work, I panicked. I couldn't see beyond writing country music in those days. And, for the time being, the channeled writing stopped.

Over the years, I came to understand a little about Hindu mythology and the connection between Rama and Hanuman in those legends. According to Hindu tradition, Rama is beloved as a God—an aspect of the Father—and Hanuman is the consummate Devotee, who rose to become a Deity in his own right. In Hindu scriptures, Hanuman symbolizes Devotion and selfless Divine Service.

Now, 13 years later, in a wonderfully whacky ashram in Taos, New Mexico, the connection had come full circle for me. Instinctively, I pulled out my little notebook and a pen. The words of Hanuman flowed through me as naturally as breath, as I scribbled them down in longhand.

∽

Darshan with the Divine Presence of Hanuman

Hanuman speaks:

How quickly this heart connects with yours. And, how deeply the connection is experienced. This type of connectedness is far from commonplace. Most are not able to feel this. We say this to you not to stimulate a sense of pride, which would be a manifestation of ego, but rather to simply provide information as a foundation for understanding what has and will continue to transpire for you here.

You have dedicated your life to Divine Service, and you have been heard and profoundly blessed. You will step forth in the shoes of your Divine connection, and you will recognize them as your own. We are here to help prepare you for that inevitability. You will carry these energies when you are in *this* place—as you have done in this day. In so doing, you will become accustomed to carrying and personifying the intensity of a Divine connection. In moments, you will become accustomed to relinquishing self-awareness— and you will simply "Be." You resonate easily to this energy.

Rasha speaks:

Why is that? Can you tell me who I was in the times of Rama? I sense that it was no accident that I began to channel Rama in this lifetime, though I did not make the connection then. It stands to reason that I would be guided to you, too. Who was I?

That answer cannot be given in the way the question has been posed. For, the connectedness is not linear. It is not as if we could tell you "you were *this* being or *that* one." We can tell you that you are of *these energies*, of this lineage.

Is that the basis for Rama's statement that we were "brothers"?

Rama was the brother of the incarnate embodiment of *these* energies. You also embody these energies. And, that is how you are able to achieve the transference of these energies with relative ease. Do not worry about who you *were*, Rasha. What is important now is who you *are* and what you are able to bring to these times.

You are a conduit of energy and of information. You are a clear and perfect channel. You were groomed most carefully for this role in these times. Your moment is soon upon you. You will need to be able to wear these energies with grace and to embrace them, without fear or attachment to whether or not they are well received.

It matters not whether you are liked, or respected, or even known. What is important is that you project the authenticity of the teachings that have come through your vehicle. They will be embraced—or not—by those for whom they are intended. They will touch who they will.

You have no responsibility for instilling these teachings. It is irrelevant whether they are well received. It is irrelevant whether you are adored or hated, for you will experience both. Your heart is open. Keep your connection pure and unencumbered by the contamination of ego or caring what others may or may not think of you. Do what you do in highest integrity and you have fulfilled your mission. Embody your loving connectedness to Source, and you will have manifested the highest expression of who you Are and will increasingly come to Be.

Hanuman speaks about selfless service

Earlier today, we instilled an understanding within your consciousness. In silence, you requested that we repeat this teaching so that you could document it. It was explained to you that when you are of service to others, you are not serving other than Self. For, All is Self.

The distinction is subtle, but it's a crucial one. For, to serve "other" is to reinforce the illusion of separation from the Divine. This *selflessness*, when put into practice in the form of "selfless service," is actually an expression of Self-centeredness. For, you are not self-righteously serving "another." You are reaping the *reward* of the infinite joy in being of service to the One Divine Self.

That Self is the manifestation of all things. So, there is no "higher" nor "lower" service. One service is no more worthy than another. There are no value judgments to be made. Allow your heart to guide you in where your efforts are to be gifted and open yourself fully and unquestioningly to the Source of that Love.

Pour your love from the infinite vessel that you have made manifest with your very being. Do not measure. There is no end to your Love nor to your *devotion*. Nothing asked of you by the object of your devotion is too much to ask. No task is beneath you. No exertion is too much for you to bear. For, the joy and honor of giving the gift of Self—to Self—transcends any considerations that could be made.

No student is a waste of your time. For, all students are also your teacher. And, each brings you the gift of molding your infinite patience and wisdom to the requirements of linear reality. You will continue to hone and fine-tune your instrument with each trial you encounter. The ones that stretch the limits of your endurance are the ones that have come to gift you with the possibility of stretching the limits of your Infinite Love. And, the depth of your Love for these ones will nourish your heart.

It is no challenge to teach the students who are primed and ready, panting for the pearls you have to give them. The greater gift is to touch the students who don't know they are students. To reach the "unreachable." To Love the "unlovable." For, all are self-imposed constructs within which the innocent heart hides its vulnerability.

There is not one being amongst your future flock that does not quietly yearn for the unconditional Love of their Creator—evidence that they are not alone and stranded in the alien territory of their own prejudices and fears. One taste of the purity of Divine Love will speak more than words could possibly say.

You will teach, not so much with words, as with the profound energies you will carry. Some will recognize these energies and see visions in the form of your persona. Others will simply experience bliss in your presence. All will be transformed.

The following Sunday, I returned to Taos and the Presence of Hanuman, and the dialogue continued. Hanuman helped me to further clarify the nature of my connection with the energies of The Father. It was a recurring theme that was surfacing over and over in my life. And, as I juggled the pieces of that timeless puzzle once more, the Hanuman consciousness added a few new ones to the mix.

Hanuman speaks:

We have called you here to help you clarify for yourself your purpose in these times, and equally, to help you to understand what your purpose is not. You have not come here to follow in the footsteps of established protocols, to act out the prescribed rituals of worldly traditions, or to speak the words of the teachers whose wisdom has graced this reality in other times.

You have come to this here and now as a blank slate. Great care has been taken with you to limit your exposure to formal indoctrination, so that the message you will deliver would be untainted by the "translation" that inevitably follows wisdom down through the ages. Your words will emanate directly from Source.

Many will look to you for guidance. And, you will not look to what you have been taught, but will impart what you *know*. You will not, ultimately, be *channeling* the information that comes forth, but will be transmitting it directly. For, you Are as *this* Source. You are in different form. But, the awareness has a common origin.

Hanuman reveals the nature of my personal connection with the energies of Shiva, an aspect of The Father Consciousness

Rasha speaks:

Can I ask you please to clarify the information I received this morning during the meditation? I was given to understand that I carry the energy of "Shiva." Is that the same as "Amitabh"? Previously, I understood that I was of the "Amitabh energies." Are they the same?

Yes, Rasha, as you have deduced, these energies are one and the same. The energy of Shiva is what you bring—for you Are this as Are We. We are not you. You are not Hanuman. Yet, the lineage is kindred. It has taken form once again as you. It is in your embracing of the energies of The Goddess, however, that *Oneness* will be achieved and embodied *as* you.

It is in the union of these polarities that you will become One Source in physical form. This will not happen to you overnight. It will happen in stages. Your conscious efforts to align with these energies will assist you in achieving full union with all that you truly are. When you open yourself unconditionally to this Source, you are bonding with a timeless lineage that is ready to assist you in making the shift to heightened levels of awareness.

Can you speak to me of Neem Karoli Baba? Is he of these energies, too?

Indeed he is. He incarnated as the *direct* descendant of this lineage. And, he passed on the energy and the timeless wisdom to which he had unlimited access. Yet, he did so through his own *persona*. His life and teaching took on the flavor of his personality, his particular *style* of imparting truth. The wisdom imparted is not learned, but *sourced*. As is yours.

You do not require the physical connection to a Guru, as do most who journey toward enlightenment. For, you *embody* that connection naturally. There will be many teachers, now, who will participate in your preparation. Yet, the most significant connection for you is that of your own Oneness. You Are that boundless connection, revealed in form. Much time must be spent, now, in the space of that union.

Hanuman speaks of Divine Service

In what way will I be working with you?

You have come as a Divine Servant. We will help you fine-tune your understanding of that role. Self-sacrifice is not what is being asked of you. But, rather, you will begin to attune yourself to the energies and needs and perceptions of the *other* and will impart your gift through a resonance with the other being.

The concept is not that of giving the one to the other, as a testimonial to separation. Rather, the gift is in the *merging* of the energies and imparting the experience of Oneness *through* you. In your words, then, the listener hears not the *you* that is separate, but is attuned instantly to the vibration *within himself* that resonates to those energies.

In that way, you assist your students and all whose lives you touch, not in following *you*, or the energy that comes *through* you. Rather, you have assisted in opening these beings to the resonance of truth waiting dormant within *themselves*. You assist in awakening those energies through your touch, your words, or simply by being in your presence.

Many will experience being "transformed by you." But, in fact, they will have been transformed "by themselves," with you as witness. For, your intention is not to *do* anything, but simply to Be that which you Are. The recipient of the gift of the energies you carry will have the opportunity to drink deeply of this nectar—or not. It is in the conscious choice, the openness on the part of the receiver, that the transference takes place. Thus, you have not *done* anything to anyone. You simply have served, in the highest possible way, by making all that you Are available.

You carry no responsibility whatsoever for the results experienced. You have no stake in the outcome. For, you have no agenda, save being all you Are, in physical form. That is what is truly meant by "Divine Service." You are an *instrument*, through which that which is Divine might be experienced. Or not.

When the recipients of the energies are not open to the possibility of such a connection—through you—they will experience nothing. And, will possibly think you are a fraud. It is not unlike the being, thirsting in the desert, who refuses to drink at the oasis because he is lost in the illusion of suffering and lack. Some beings derive great satisfaction from deprivation. For, they then can feel justified in their bitterness about the misery that is their life.

Many such beings are drawn, instinctively, to "water," or to beings such as yourself through whom thirst may be satisfied. And yet, their own sense of unworthiness prevents them from partaking of what flows so naturally for them. They are far too invested in being suspicious about being deceived. So, they create the foundation for what they assume is deception with their intent, and that way, can feel that they are *right*.

There will be countless ones, among the masses your energies will touch, who will choose not to drink deeply at your "well." Let it not concern you. You have not come to cast the waters upon them or to assault them with knowledge and purity and love like a great tidal wave, simply because you have those attributes to offer. You are a well. And, your abundance knows no bounds.

Let the ones who are drawn to do so come close on their own initiative. And, they will be rewarded immeasurably. You will not need to seek followers. You will not need to find a forum for your message. Simply go about doing what you do. And, you will be found—as the waters of the streams and rivers find the ocean. The ocean is where they are headed. You will embody that *directedness*. And, those who are capable of recognizing that level of connectedness will be guided to your side.

There are no austerities required of you, no self-sacrifice, no stringent practice of any kind. You are not being asked to practice deprivation or renunciation. Your choices are your choices. There are no rules for you, save those you impose upon yourself. Naturally, there are *consequences*, as follows the laws of physical reality, for the practices you choose to do. And, you will experience these as would anyone else.

Yet, your life style personifies your own personal preferences. Your diet, your personal habits—all that you *do* or do not *do*—are entirely your choice. Let no one attempt to discredit who you Are on the basis of what may or may not have been *done*. For, your choices in no way affect the essence of the Service you have come to perform, which is Divine.

I took a little break in the ashram's huge, rustic country kitchen for a wonderful cup of ginger chai, a delicious treat that Neem Karoli Baba ashrams are known for throughout India. Here in Taos, the chai is ever-present, simmering in an enormous cauldron at the back of a gigantic iron stove. This mysteriously delicious chai is considered to be the nurturing touch of the beloved Guru, Neem Karoli Baba, who is still so very present there.

Refreshed, I went back to the little temple, pen in hand, to continue my *darshan* with Hanuman.

Hanuman talks about the profound energies of a Divine connection
Hanuman speaks:
We greet you, Rasha. Can you feel these energies now?

Rasha speaks:
Yes! The feeling is getting stronger, especially in my heart, and now in my entire body.

Good. That is as it should be. Your heart is as a flower that's just beginning to blossom. The fullness and the fragrance of the love that flows through you now is but a sampling of what is to come. And, just as you believe you know what it is to feel *bliss*, we can tell you that this is merely the beginning.

You must learn to *hold* the energies. To *contain* them. To feel them fully, without giddiness, or tears or passion. Drink deeply. But, do not permit yourself to become intoxicated. That is the mark of the Master, Rasha. It is no great feat to feel these energies and to allow them to transport you to varying levels of pleasure. It is the disciplined Master who can partake fully of these energies and yet give no indication of it. Be silent, and drink deeply. Close your eyes now. And, be silent with us just for a few moments.

Ok.

I closed my eyes and was swept into a timeless space of joy, as my slow steady breath carried me deeper into connectedness with the energies of Hanuman. I stayed in this heavenly space, oblivious to the world around me for perhaps 20 minutes. On coming back into body-awareness, Hanuman explained that what I had experienced was just a small sampling of what I could expect to carry and experience.

I was told that the energies would be amplified in increments, as they had been over the previous few years, but that now the pace had been accelerated dramatically. Hanuman said that I would experience extremes of energy acceleration during my meditations at the ashram over that summer and cautioned that the significance of that work should not be underestimated. I went on to discover that he was right.

Rasha speaks:
Can I ask you a question regarding "holding" the energies, please?

Hanuman speaks:
Yes. Please ask your question.

Is there a technique or procedure recommended for sustaining the amplified vibration so that one's inner balance is not disturbed by outside adversity?

Hanuman explains the principle of *sustaining* the energies of a Divine connection

The principle is very simple. Allow your awareness to remain firmly in that peaceful center within you. Do not allow your focus to be drawn away from that place of inner harmony. Resist the invitation of the disturbance to *engage* you. For, it is in the engaging that the opening is provided and your precious energies are lost.

Your state of imbalance provides your adversary the necessary access to your energy field to partake of your resources. Your energy is your treasure. Protect it as that. Remain focused in the place where your precious energy rests. Do not allow your attention to be distracted.

Deal in a detached way with whatever disturbance presents itself. Do not allow it to touch your sense of balance. Remain calm and peaceful at all times, regardless of the conditions. Do not allow yourself to become stressed or upset, no matter what the cause. Nothing is that important. *Nothing* is important at all. It all simply *Is.*

Watch the movie. Hold your energy. Remain centered with focused intent. And, let the cyclone swirl around you, if that is its will. Eventually the cyclone will tire of swirling and will move on—if it is not able to feed itself upon your power. Total detachment. Total focus on your own objective.

You will be tested—over and over again—until you are able to master this principle. That is why you, invariably, encounter discord soon after an experience of exalted energy. You typically experience a faltering of your mood and an immediate toppling of your energy. Now you are being given the opportunity to be consciously aware of the process, and to use these challenges as a way to strengthen your skills and become the energy *fortress* you need to be to do this work.

Learn to identify your areas of vulnerability. And, focus your awareness on the ways in which these areas are being stimulated. You will begin to see, quite clearly, the power in *non-reaction* and the profound difference in all aspects of your life as a result. Does that answer your question?

Yes! I see it. Thank you for this powerful teaching. When I reflect on Dr. Bindu and his behavior under siege, I see that he was demonstrating this principle to me. Yet, maybe I wasn't ready to "get it" then.

He *was* certainly demonstrating to you how to hold power. Both through non-reaction to adversity and through not allowing even you to see his level of bliss. He told you with words, but you could not begin to imagine the power that he is able to hold. You were not ready to understand what he was about. You would not have been able to comprehend it.

These are some of the principles you will learn to master. You will be very thoroughly schooled in these principles by Dr. Bindu. This small teaching is quite basic and is something you are well advised to practice and to master as soon as possible.

I returned to Taos again the following Sunday and tucked myself away as inconspicuously as I could, in a far corner of the little temple, amid an eclectic mix of harmoniums, drums, exotic Indian percussion instruments and piles of Zen meditation cushions. There, I took pen in hand once more and continued my ongoing dialogue with the Presence of Hanuman.

~✑~

Hanuman speaks:

We greet you, Rasha. We are pleased that you have returned to this place and have chosen to visit with us once again. As you breathe in these energies, become aware. Become fully present in your body. Do not permit your focus to become distracted by what may or may not happen around you. Your focus is here now with this energy—which emanates from within you.

You can pinpoint quite easily where we have joined with you. For, that is the energy portal through which the connection is achieved. We connect with you at the level of your heart chakra. We hold you here, within the corresponding point in our energy body. And, the connection is achieved. The vibrational interaction is not merely one-sided, you see. You can feel this connection in the area of your heart.

Rasha speaks:

I really can!

Hanuman tells the story of my spiritual lineage and the "Shiva connection"

We began, on a previous visit, to tell you a bit of the "story" of who you are. The lineage of Shiva is deep and multi-faceted. You share much history with this energy, as a parallel incarnation of the same source. In the collective of shared memory, we are kindred souls—in a sense, "brothers." The core essence is shared. The linear experience is not.

Your identity encompasses lifetimes of experience that was not shared, as does this Source. And yet, vibrationally, the commonality unites us as a focal-point of purpose—the passionate desire to be in the service of Divine Intent. Compassion is the key word. And, unquestioning devotion is how it is expressed.

The compassion is felt for what is recognized as universally Divine. And, in the act of total surrender to that Divine connection, you recognize your life's purpose. It is not important in what way you choose to serve, simply that the total availability of your energies has been made manifest through the vehicle of your form.

You are an extension of the hand of Shiva. And, the Divine Will of Shiva will be made manifest through you. You have tasted the depth of His love through the energy you know as Amitabh. At the highest level, this Source is one and the same.

The expression of those energies that have presented themselves as Amitabh is, itself, an expression of that higher Source. The intent and the teachings of the Father Consciousness have been handed down through the vehicle of your beloved Amitabh, who handed them impeccably unto you. This would not have been possible had there not been a commonality of vibrational lineage—a mirroring of sacred Essence—through which those teachings might be imparted.

This arrangement was made long before your emergence into physicality. For, the concept of incarnation is core to that very Essence. You emerge and you withdraw yourself. For, that is your nature. In the same way, you are now able to connect, virtually across the cosmos, to your brethren—the teachers who walk beside you, whose collective lineage you represent in this "here and now."

Now it is your turn to carry the flame, Rasha. This flame has burned brightly in the breast of many who have descended from the Source of Shiva energy. And, it has been passed on throughout time immemorial to those whose life mission it has been to carry it. You have embraced that sacred flame and now wear it within your heart, as do we. You will drift in and out of multiple realities as a beacon of the Light you bear within you. And, you will Grace those worlds and those times to come with the simple gift of your Presence.

`Thank you, Hanuman, for this guidance.`

My conversations with the consciousness of Neem Karoli Baba began quite unexpectedly. I had been sitting in the temple, lost in the joys of a conversation with Hanuman, scribbling his words in my little notebook as fast as I could write, oblivious to the comings and goings around me. Quite suddenly, one of the caretakers approached me and demanded loudly that I leave the temple at once! She was adamant that the temple was not the place for writing. Instantly, I felt my Divine connection shatter.

"This is a place for *bhakti*" (devotion), she barked, matter-of-factly. Literally translated, that meant that one could sit in the temple and sing *bhajans*, (sacred songs), play a musical instrument, beat drums, or pick out melodies on the harmonium. One could even offer prayers. But, ironically enough, according to the rules of this ashram, having those prayers answered was off limits. Meditation was out of the question.

No doubt the woman thought I was writing in a journal, or writing a letter. I didn't know what to say. How do you explain to an irate, self-righteous caretaker that you are engrossed in conversation with a Deity and that the temple would be exactly the *right* place for that activity? Such an admission would only have made matters worse. I got up and left the temple.

Out in the garden, I sat for awhile and sipped a cup of my favorite chai as I regained my equilibrium. A man who had overheard the scene in the temple came over and sat down beside me. "There's a wonderful little room you could sit in, at the back of the building, where no one would disturb you," he offered. I followed him to a door I had never noticed before.

Inside, a tiny room awaited me with a *tucket*, a bed-size bench covered by a bright plaid wool blanket—the kind that Neem Karoli Baba sat on in his ashrams in India, and identical to the one in this temple. The room was affectionately known as "Maharaji's study." I entered quietly, sat down on the floor, and closed my eyes. Without so much as a thought, I knew that, once again, I was sitting before a Divine presence. Instantly, I was blanketed in the embrace of his Love.

Here I had been, sitting in the temple of his own ashram all summer, and virtually ignoring him all this time. I had been so consumed by my experience with Hanuman that I hadn't even reached out to the Master. Despite the fact that Neem Karoli Baba had left his body in 1973, he was clearly very much present. His greeting, in silence, caught me by surprise. I reflected on the commotion that had just taken place in the temple and reminded myself that "there are no accidents."

Most devotees of Neem Karoli Baba refer to him as "Maharaji," but to me, he would always refer to himself as "your Babaji." Without wasting so much as a moment, he spoke to me in silence. Quickly, I scrambled for my pen and notebook to jot down his words.

⟋⟍

Rasha speaks:

I am sitting in the little "study," the private sanctuary of Maharaji. And, before I attempt transcription with Hanuman, I would like to ask official permission to be here in this space, writing—the idea of which has disturbed certain people here. I have been forbidden to write in the temple. But, I was told it was ok to write in this little room. But, most important, is it ok with you?

Neem Karoli Baba speaks:

You do not require permission of anyone to perform Divine Service in this temple, Rasha. If you are not defiling the temple, nor disturbing the devotional activities of others, you are also welcome to engage in spiritual practice as you choose. If you choose to interact with Hanuman or your Babaji, that is your privilege.

If you require official permission to Be all that you have come here to Be, then you have it. But, that should not be necessary. The only permission for devotion of any sort is your own heart. And, those who would attempt to control you are simply reacting to energies they do not understand.

Be patient with these ones and avoid confrontation. For, just because permission has been extended to you to perform your spiritual practice as you see fit, so too is the opportunity extended to you to promote harmony through your choices. It is far simpler to say "yes" in any situation than to say "no." Honor the path of no-resistance and you will manifest the highest outcome for all concerned.

Be patient with all beings. For, in the fullness of time, the quiet observation of energy in action will speak louder than ever your voice or the words of your mind could. Be patient with *yourself*. You are in no hurry. Take this day. And then, take the next. And, after that, take the next as you would take each breath.

In the moment of this Stillness, you receive the full gift of the Love and the teachings you have come here to receive. You are not in a race to breathe all the breaths quickly, now, in advance. You inhale, slowly. And then, you exhale, slowly, being fully present in the breath. Your full consciousness breathes each breath in each moment. Take your time now. Be here in the sweetness of this place.

Be silent within yourself. Do not stir up trouble by being obvious about what you are doing and who you perceive yourself to be. Others do not care about that. They care only for themselves. Let that be ok with you, even if you think you have wisdom to impart. You are not here to teach—not yet. You are still here to learn. And, the most discordant in this flock will teach you many things.

Be humble and that humility will go far toward paving the way toward opening the closed hearts you have encountered here. It doesn't matter. You know this. It makes no difference at all whether you are embraced by these beings or hated by them. These are choices you are making with your actions.

You have come here not to find a Guru but to find yourself. You know better than to become attached to anyone or anything. And, this is as it is to remain. We will speak with you any time you wish. Come to this room quietly. And, we can speak of many things together. Now go. And be happy. Take *prasad* (a Divine gift, often food).

Thank you, Babaji.

From that day onward, I continued to visit Neem Karoli Baba at the Taos ashram on Sundays. By mid-afternoon, after everyone had gone home, I quietly entered the wonderful little sacred space of "Maharaji's study" at the back of the ashram to commune with the Presence of Neem Karoli Baba. It was a precious connection and an extraordinary dialogue that would continue for years to come.

Rasha speaks:
I feel your presence so strongly. Every breath carries me deeper into sensations of joy in my heart chakra. I am so grateful to be here, if only for a few moments. Thank you for your presence and the blessing of your Grace.

Neem Karoli Baba speaks:
Just breathe, Rasha. For, it is in the breath that the path of the experience of your Divine connection lies. You experienced this again this morning during the

chanting of the Hanuman Chalisa. Your breath drew you into holy communion with the energies that we share.

Your connection is being deepened. And today, there were tears. In time, the fullness of this energy will be made manifest through you without tears. You will be able, in time, to contain the bliss you experience in merging with these energies. Others will feel the sacred Presence that you will be empowered to deliver. Now, you are learning to carry these levels.

Your tears of joy are a natural manifestation of having encountered this level of connection. With experience, the tears will be contained within your heart. For, it is unnecessary to express what you are feeling and far more powerful not to. The power you will truly demonstrate will be in understatement and non-reaction.

The Guru does not seek to impart anything. The student draws what is needed, like the honeybee draws nectar from a flower. The flower is not looking anxiously for the possibility of a honeybee. It is content, simply to be in its perfection—in its flowerness. That is all.

This ashram is a haven for you, in which you can learn from a Master and can assimilate the levels of shakti that will carry you forward so that your life's work may be achieved. You are in the cocoon now. Stop trying to fly. These moments are not intended for flight, but for quiet metamorphosis. Be content with being fully in this Now moment. Enjoy your unfoldment. And, come to visit with us again. Now go. Take prasad.

The following weekend, the conversation with Neem Karoli Baba continued

Neem Karoli Baba speaks:

You have returned to this blessed place once more. You have felt our invitation, for it has been extended through energy, not with words. The words are merely a convenience used to transport what is thought or is felt. The invitation—which is ever-present—does not require words. It is understood as a feeling that you have sourced deep within you. And, you have responded with your presence.

There has transpired no thought at all, in this interaction. And yet, you *knew* to come here. And you did. And so it will be for you here. You will know when to come, and you will know when to stay away. And, your mind will not be involved in the process at all. This is a part of your training here. We will summon you when your presence is requested. You will *know* to come. And you will be protected and will be safe from disturbance while here.

Be present—fully present. Be focused in your breath during your times of silence here. Draw yourself into the sacred center of your being. For, we will meet you there and assist you in opening to the next levels of your preparation for the work you have come here to do. Your work here is to be *experiential*. It does not matter whether you converse with the others or whether you wander in the fields on your own. You are not here for the others—not yet. Now, you have been summoned here for you.

You have not stumbled upon this haven by accident. Trust. Everything is fully in order. You are in the loving embrace of your true family now. And, your steps are being carefully guided. There is no wasted motion. All incidents, all interactions are carefully planned. Each bears a gift of self-awareness.

You do not need a translator. The lessons are all right there for you. This living textbook is right there before you. People call it "life." But they rarely know how to read the book. They treat it like it's written in a strange foreign language. They pretend that the stories being portrayed are real. The Master knows that all of it is merely symbolism.

It is a fantastic story, and that's all it is. You watch the story revealing itself before you. You choose whether you wish to become involved or not. You choose whether you wish to remain the one who is simply watching. Fully present. Missing nothing. No wasted motion. Vivid awareness. Sensing. Feeling. Knowing. Then choosing: action or non-action?

You are not required to do anything. Merely bring the "book" with you to class. And, see how perfectly what you observe relates to your life and the issues you are translating into understanding—and ultimately, mastery. Be gentle with yourself now. You know what is happening. And, you know enough not to speak of it. Be quiet and discreet—invisible—and you will make the most of the time you have here in this place. Come here to your Babaji when we call for you. And, spend the remainder of your time here quietly in silent prayer and reflection.

Source the sweetness and the nectar within you. You do not need to seek anything outside of that. All answers will be unmasked—revealed—in the sanctity of that sweetness, and your mind will fall by the wayside. For, your mind is not needed in this process. Give it a well-deserved rest. And, come to us naked of thoughts and ideas. Be the blank slate—the innocent intellect of pure potentiality and no agenda. That is the challenge for you now. Can you do this?

Rasha speaks:

Yes I can. I can do this or I would not be here before you.

You are here because you have been summoned here. Whether or not you can perform as required is still to be seen.

I am who I am. No more and no less. I have brought the seed of my destiny to your feet for cultivation. If it is Divine Will, that seed will be nurtured here, by your Grace. And, I may grow to manifest the fullness of the Divine spark that has been planted within me. That is the focus of my intent, with a heart that has surrendered to the Service of Divine Will. I will perform as I do, with the blessing of this Divine connection.

We welcome you into the embrace of these energies with the loving heart of a father.

Am I truly hearing such words from you? Am I imagining this? Am I lost in ego?

Only if you choose to be. You are merging at a level of selfless Service with your brethren who have walked upon this path in other times, in other places. You could not have imagined this level of connectedness, could you?

No, probably not. Still, I am so honored, and so profoundly blessed. Thank you! Thank you for being here for me.

This is Divine Service, Rasha. The concept has no limitations. It embraces all. And, all help will be provided. Now go. Take prasad.

Thank you, Babaji.

My final visit to Maharaji's study that summer was brief. The unconditional love that was lavished upon me there left the door open for an ongoing dialogue that would continue over the years to come, and even throughout India during my visits there. I had come to say goodbye but was distracted by the glare on the photo of Neem Karoli Baba, which I had grown to love.

Do not focus upon the photograph—we are not there. We do not dwell in any symbolic representation of this consciousness. It doesn't matter if there is glare on the picture. We are in your presence, bound at the level of heart to a mission of compassion. This is what you have come to experience. And, this is the essence of what you will carry forth.

The memories shared will travel forward and backward in time, as you do—touching down and tasting, where needed. For, the taste will never elude you. You will feel it. We will always be with you. We are never apart. You are the physical manifestation of the energies which we share.

The words will never elude you. They will be given from within the sacred center of your Being. Be present. This is all. Breathe the Nowness. Inhale and exhale your Divine Presence. And, all who are within your reach will feel you and will be transformed. Be silent now. Breathe these energies together with your Babaji.

12

Fall 2001
Chimayo, New Mexico
The Events of 9-11

———

What began for me as a normal New Mexico September morning quickly became a moment that would be etched in the heart of history and never forgotten. I was jarred out of a deep sleep by the phone. My landlady seemed alarmed. My half-conscious brain registered something about "The World Trade Center" being destroyed.

Automatically, my sleep-numbed mind assumed she was talking about the colossal anthill out in the parking lot, which I had dubbed "The World Trade Center." I'd been concerned that vehicles were constantly running over it. Each time, the poor ants went into a frenzy, running in circles as though the end of the world had come. The image was prophetic.

In the early hours of September 11, 2001, my first thought was that I couldn't imagine why anyone would wake me up to tell me about an anthill. It quickly became clear that something extremely serious had just happened, on a much larger scale! How serious it actually was, the world hadn't even begun to imagine. I didn't own a TV. But, stumbling downstairs to the B&B, I watched the horror unfold that would change forever the illusion of life as we knew it.

After a few minutes of watching the heart-wrenching images that would come to haunt the world, I had seen enough. Instinctively, I ran for the computer, and within seconds was in a deep state of Divine connectedness with Oneness. The guidance of Oneness, received at 9:00 am Mountain Time, September 11, 2001, was shared via the internet with untold thousands of people.

❦

Divine Guidance received from Oneness at 9:00am Mountain Time, September 11, 2001

Oneness speaks:

As you have learned, there have been acts of atrocity in your country. These are the events to which we have referred. And, these are the events that have been prophesied. Your society, as you understand it to be, will crumble in the wake of these events. And, there will emerge a new world of understanding. In time, you will comprehend the magnitude of what has just been initiated. For, this is but the beginning of the transformation of your world and of the souls that presently populate it.

It would be important to remain calm in the face of what will come to pass. Source your strength from within the immortal core of your being. Live your life from within your heart. And, remember who you really Are—regardless of what may transpire. Your key to all you would do in what remains of this lifetime lies in your ability to remain grounded and centered in your faith in yourself to manifest the highest possible outcome.

In the wake of the events now just beginning to unfold, you will come to recognize that the idea of the highest possible outcome is relative only to the moment at hand. Do not allow yourself to be drawn into the morass of fear that will emerge throughout your world, based upon how you remember reality to have been. Those memories are of the past now. The highest possible outcome you can manifest is no more and no less than what is able to be perceived in the present moment.

Regardless of the way life may have been, the highest possible outcome in this Now moment is still possible and always will be. In order to affect the transition that has been envisioned for these times, it is important that all who can grasp this concept remain focused in envisioning what *can* be, as though it already has come to pass. For, all outcomes are possibilities. And, what is experienced is determined only by what you choose to create with your perceptions, your reactions, and the underlying foundation of what you believe to be so.

Believe in your innate Divinity. Believe that you are safe. Believe, even in the wake of unspeakable horrors, that the dust *will* settle. And, that reality will begin to define itself anew.

In the present moment, your world looks darker than most could have imagined. Yet, the gift in that vision is the possibility of transcending what your logical mind tells you and holding firm to your power to source the strength and the wisdom from within that will see you through. Be there Now. And, know that that haven is there for you always.

A second transmission from Oneness, two days later, helped me see the events of September 11th from a perspective I hadn't anticipated. The guidance I received put the events into the context of a universal overview. It enabled me to begin to look at what, to all appearances, seemed to be a mindless atrocity, from the universal perspective of energy.

Somehow, the vantage point of detachment provided an element of Divine distancing from the emotional charge triggered by the events of our lives, even occurrences at this level of intensity. I realized that the teachings I'd been bringing through all this time spoke to this very concept. Yet, until then, I'd been interpreting those teachings on a personal level, as part of the process of personal spiritual transformation. I simply hadn't anticipated that these same concepts would be applied so soon, on such a profound, global scale.

The Divine guidance I received on September 13, 2001 was shared, via the internet, with people around the world.

Divine Guidance from Oneness transcribed September 13, 2001
Rasha speaks:

Oneness, can you tell me what is going on, please? How serious is the present situation regarding the disaster in New York City?

Oneness speaks:

The situation in your country is extremely serious. You have just begun to experience the wrath of those who have sworn their vengeance upon your nation. There will be a period of allowing the dust to settle. The situation will then escalate. And, you will find yourself immersed in the ravages of a war that is unprecedented in your world.

These are the times for which you have been preparing, all these years, whether you are consciously aware of it or not. The so-called "Baptism by Fire" has indeed begun. Resist the temptation to drift into fear, along with the masses of your population. Remain focused in your Divine connection. And, you will be protected from adversity and from harm.

Can you give me an idea of the timing of all this, please? Do we have weeks, months, or years before things become drastic?

Your situation as a nation and as a world is already drastic. The vibrational components of the events in question are already in place and ready to play out as experience. The actual manifestations have not yet occurred, in terms of your understandings of "time." Yet, in terms of energy, these events are already at hand.

Is there anything we as a population of beings could do to help dissipate the intensity of those vibrational conditions?

A directed focus of mass consciousness toward the creation of peace and harmony would be effective to assist in a less volatile release of the energies in question. The release of these energies is inevitable. The form that certain acts of release will take, and the locations that will experience the direct effects of them, are variables that can be affected by the power of mass consciousness to co-create its reality.

A foundation of hope, inner strength and resourcefulness will go far toward helping to manifest a less devastating outcome than might otherwise occur. A foundation of mass hysteria and fear will assist in bringing about the worst-case scenarios that you, as a population, inwardly dread.

Go about your life with a positive outlook, regardless of evidence to the contrary, and you will have made the highest possible contribution, regardless of where you are and where you choose to direct your efforts. For, this world as you know it is simply a reflection of the vibrational essence of the souls that comprise it. And, that outcome could be shifted in a radical way, were the population at large able to unite its collective vision in Divine connectedness.

As things now stand, such a radical shift in mass consciousness is unlikely within the time frame in question. Know however, that there are limitless variations upon the theme of one's individual life experience. One is certainly able, through work that is inwardly directed, to elevate one's individual vibration to the extent that the full impact of certain events would be minimized.

Within the context of the dimensional reality in which you now experience yourself, the likelihood of certain events coming to pass is virtually inevitable. How you will personally *experience* the ramifications of those events is defined and redefined by each of you in the ongoing moment of Now. Direct your focus toward manifesting the Divinity within you with every gesture and with every word spoken. Recognize your fellow beings as your very own sacred Essence. And demonstrate the loving compassion, in every encounter, that you would wish to experience yourself.

That is the recipe for shifting the energies that now threaten the sanctity of your world. Taken on a personal level, such a focus will go far toward influencing what you may or may not experience in the days to come. That principle, when implemented in unison by all humankind, could significantly modify the prognosis for global crisis that now appears imminent.

The inevitability of global change, as a reflection of human change

You hold the destiny of your world within the hearts of each of you. And, regardless of the mundane choices made in your day-to-day lives, life as you know it will never be the same again. That is a fact not to be feared, but rather, to be embraced. For, the essence of change is your destiny and your birthright.

You have chosen to be here in these times in order that you might experience and help co-create the "world shattering" transformations that have been slated for these times. Those upheavals will be transpiring not merely in the world that surrounds you, but within the depths of each of you. For, you have arrived at the time where the "Shift of the Ages" is at hand. That shift is one that is to be experienced within. And, the acts of purging that will enable all to transcend the limitations that have bound you all to an outmoded state of being are a necessary part of that process.

In the days to come, each of you will have the opportunity to come to terms with much that has colored this lifetime and the way you have chosen to live it. The circumstances that your world has made manifest are here as a catalyst to assist each of you in embodying that momentum of change. It is a highly charged drama calculated to bring up for scrutiny all that you hold dear and much that you do not. The opportunity to make those distinctions is the gift borne by the turbulence of these times.

The profound journey scripted for each of you who have chosen to be present in this drama is calculated to catapult you to the heights of human experience. Many of you have chosen to have that taste of your own Divine Essence in incarnate human form. And you have, many of you, just embarked upon the journey of a lifetime that is scheduled to deliver you unto that experiential destination.

Hold to that vision in the hours ahead that appear most bleak. Know that this is the process that you, as an *Eternal* being, wanted to experience. For, in the heights and the depths of your own humanness is the experiential gateway to another level of experience—a heightened level of awareness, waiting in the wings to take you into its loving embrace. Give yourself permission to feel fully the *emotions* that will be stimulated to the surface by the circumstances soon to come. For, this is the gift you have chosen to give to yourself by being present in this crossroads in "time" and "space" that you would regard as Now.

Each of you will experience the events to come in different ways. For, each of you is bringing to completion lifetimes of interaction with the fellow beings who now populate your life scripts. And, each hopes to be able to transcend the need to continue in these predictable dramas. These times of transformation are calculated to provide the full spectrum of such opportunities.

When you look back upon the events now beginning to unfold within your world, you will see quite clearly the inevitability of what will come to pass. And, you will rejoice in the recognition of the being you really Are. Underneath the mask and the posturing, underneath the conditioned behaviors, underneath all that you believe now defines you—you are about to encounter your own Divine Essence. And, you will recognize the gift in the metamorphosis of a world that could not have come about in any other way.

One month after the event, I was still shaken, as were so many of us, by what had transpired in New York City on September 11th. I had very definite concerns about how one might apply the esoteric teachings of Oneness, which I had just transcribed, to the blatant acts of atrocity the world had witnessed. Just how, exactly, are people supposed to view that level of raw experience from a metaphysical perspective, I wondered?

Oneness speaks about the incident of September 11th

Rasha speaks:

Oneness, I'd like to speak about the world situation and the blatant question of the "victims" at the World Trade Center on September 11th. Everything in the book we've just written talks about there not being any such thing as "victims." What about those people who were killed? Did they "sign up" for this experience? Or were they part of the dynamics of group karma? Or were they just part of a logistical grouping that facilitated a "geographical energy release"? Or, all of the above? Or, none of the above?

Oneness speaks:

You must remember, above all, that the circumstances in question were a manifestation of *energy*. The souls in question made the choice of aligning themselves with that energy—or not. Many opted to take the vibrational quantum leap in consciousness that resulted from making the sacrifice, in physical terms. For, they did so on behalf of the multitudes who stand to benefit from the shift in the energies in that location that resulted from an incident of those proportions.

The beings of that geographical area have been gifted with a monumental energy release that has succeeded in shifting the circumstances in ways that are being experienced by all who took part in that drama. The consciousness of that city of darkness has been elevated dramatically. And, the hearts of those who chose to be there have been opened—some of them traumatically. None has been spared an experience of the heart that is unforgettable.

Those who sacrificed their lives to bring about that result did so knowingly, at a soul level. In so doing they accelerated their own process of ascension as spiritual beings. Many of them have chosen to return in physical form to assist in the birthing of the new reality, equipped with the heightened perspective and perceptions of the children now coming into form. They are in a better position now to make a difference in their world and for themselves as spiritual beings, than they were in the oppressive conditions in which each of them had enslaved themselves.

The sacrifice was great. And, the reward was great, not from the standpoint of the physical realities in which the catastrophes occurred, but from the higher perspective. This pattern will be repeated many, many times, in the times to come, in order that the purging of the dimensional reality in which you experience your self-awareness be accomplished—to the higher good of all concerned. For, all of this is energy. Remember that.

For every sacrifice made and for every price paid, both by the martyrs and by those who loved them, there is a reward that was chosen, knowingly, at a level where the higher perspective was in view.

This is an explanation of what, in actuality, has transpired. This is a perspective that very few are able to grasp, under the present conditions in your reality. You will wish to exercise discretion in how you express these teachings. For, sensibilities are raw right now. And, to state such teachings may strike some as callous and heartless.

There is a delicate balance between expressing compassion for the very real agonies being experienced by those who are living through them on behalf of the collective and understanding the dynamics of what is actually transpiring vibrationally, from the standpoint of the "bigger picture."

To comprehend the dynamics of geographic energy release, and the resolution of group karma, does not invalidate the very real, catastrophic emotions being encountered. These emotions are also *energy*. And, as such, they must be expressed and allowed to seek resolution through the individual and the collective consciousness of all whose lives have been touched by these events.

The grieving process is very real. As is the outrage. The sense of being violated calls up for scrutiny every aspect of the sense of humanity that your nation has demonstrated so poignantly. And, in the balance—in the full range of the extremes of emotion that these circumstances are calculated to bring to the surface of your awareness as a populace—is the opportunity for transcendence. It is an opportunity for transcendence of all of the pain and anguish to which you, as a race of beings, have been subjected, by virtue of the vibrational conditions to which you are committed.

These extremes of experience are opportunities for unprecedented levels of karmic resolution, which will enable the souls in question to transcend much that would, ordinarily, have taken lifetimes. Vibrationally, this is how the circumstances are playing out in certain levels of reality. In the *Here and Now* in which you experience yourself, the level of purging is a modified version of what had been foreseen. And, it is a greatly modified version of the catastrophic conditions that are being experienced in denser levels of reality, where virtually no consciousness present will emerge untouched.

Your own experience of these conditions and these times will not reflect the extremes of tragedy that many will withstand in these times. You have been spared these experiences due to the nature of the work you are doing, and by virtue of the vibrational assistance you have been gifted.

You will float through these turbulent times of upheaval virtually unscathed. But, know that the very real horrors that many will live through are the reality for which you have been preparing. For, you have been trained to be a lamplight to these ones who are only now beginning to experience the dark night of their own soul's journey.

Your heart will be touched, yet not imprisoned, by what you will witness. For, you will be able to put the sights and the sounds and the smells of transformation into the framework of the higher perspective. And, you will be able to circumvent the path of descent into despair that many will travel. You do not need to go there with them. You will remain as "the light at the end of the tunnel" that will see them through.

For you, it will be the worst of times and the best of times, dependent upon the perspective from which you view it. The external circumstances to come may be horrifying at times. But, they will be going on *around* you. In your *inner* world, you will experience levels of Divine connectedness that will only escalate in the levels of joy you will experience. For, your inner world and your spiritual reality is the true reality. And, it is here that you will "live." It is here that you will retreat—to the sanctity of this haven of Love and Light—when the illusion of the physical world becomes oppressive.

You have been prepared, fully and completely, for what is transpiring in your world. You are ready to walk forward now, in the aftermath of the very beginnings of the upheavals to come. And, with the word of Oneness in hand, you will be able to make a difference to many.

Thank you, Oneness, for the incredible gift of this journey. I am humbled and awestruck by the realization of all of it. And, so incredibly grateful.

13

Fall 2001
New Mexico
Surrendering to the Will of the Wind

———

F all came early to New Mexico following the events of September 11th. Suddenly, everything seemed speeded up, and the impetus to move on began to nudge me out of my blessed state of contentment in Chimayo. I knew, at a level I couldn't question, that I was about to leave New Mexico. And, I had absolutely no idea where I was going. I was very clear that I was not feeling guided to return to Florida for the winter. The condo sat, ready and waiting. But somehow, the idea of Florida just didn't feel right.

In the back of my mind were references from Oneness about spending time in India. But, in light of the horrific incident of 9/11 that had just taken place, I was instinctively wary of the idea of relocating to the other side of the planet. I broached the subject with Oneness, in hopes of getting some direction. As usual, my straightforward questions became an occasion for Oneness to turn the questions around, redirect my focus, and guide me in sourcing the answers from within.

I had been told simply to "lighten the load" so that I might be able to "be mobile" and change locations easily. It was all very cryptic, I thought. Surely there must be some master plan. I had toyed with the idea of selling the Florida condo and liquidating everything—potentially a major exercise in non-attachment. Mentally, I placed that scenario in juxtaposition with my presumption that a person is supposed to "live somewhere." I wasn't sure what to do. Oneness was giving no clues.

❧

Oneness speaks:
You will wish to be able to travel extensively in the time soon to come. You may wish to give further thought to logistics that permit you to make the most of that possibility.

Rasha speaks:
What about the idea of spending an extended period of time this winter in India? Is that still an option?

All possibilities are options, Rasha. It is a question of choice.

You told me I would be spending an extended amount of time in India. Now what?

Why are you questioning this information?

I am questioning it in light of the fact that we may be at war, and to go to India may not be the most sensible thing to be doing right now, that's why.

Then, if you have fear around the idea of traveling there, you will wish to reconsider those plans.

It sounds like I'm not getting a straight answer about this, right?

Were you expecting this Source to make your choices for you?

Surely not. I know better. Still it would be a comfort to know that if I were about to do something dangerous, that I would be alerted.

And, you surely would be—by your own inner knowingness. It is this source of information that you have been trained to consult. It would be far too easy for you to simply direct your every concern to Oneness and to expect to be told what to do. You know better than to expect to be able to turn your power over in that way. You are not a puppet in the hands of Oneness.

Ultimately, one needs to take total responsibility for one's choices. This is what you have been trained to do. If you ask us to assist you in sourcing the highest solution from within yourself, then we are happy to do so. But, we would not be serving you were we to give you commands that you would follow like a robot.

Thus, if you sense that going to India would be a safe, worry-free thing to be doing in the timeframe in question, then you would be at liberty to make that choice and to enjoy fully that experience. Yet, if you have fear and trepidation around the idea of going there, then you would wish to honor those sensings and choose not to make the journey. You have all the answers you need to any question you may have, Rasha. And, you know where to turn to find them.

I began to run the idea of spending a few months in India through my heart rather than my mind. It felt wonderful. I had my answer. Little did I know that "a few months" would become a year—one that would serve as the turning point in my life. It would be a time that would cement the transition between *believing* all that Oneness had taught me and *knowing* it.

Once I was clear on my decision, Oneness filled in the blanks, underscoring the need to remain footloose.

Oneness speaks:

You are ready to embrace the next stage of your journey now.

Rasha speaks:

I kind of felt this coming these past few days.

And, you responded with quick action in recognizing the impetus of change, systematically making arrangements for the completion of your time here. It is indeed time to move on now. There is much in store for you. Take everything of real value with you, for you will not be returning to this place for some time to come.

Really? That comes as a bit of a shock. Will I not be returning in the spring, as I was planning to do?

There is much that will transpire between then and now that may color the choices in a different way than you now see them. Be prepared to be totally in the moment with your life choices. Presume nothing. For, the fluidity of the conditions you will encounter will dictate that you be available to respond to opportunities that are now unforeseen.

Ok. That's a very large clue.

The time you have spent in this part of your country was for the purpose of transcribing the remainder of the book and for the completion of your initiation. That work is now coming to finalization.

Instinctively, you have begun to recognize a sense of urgency in liquidating the ties that may bind you to *any* particular place. You are to be totally unencumbered now and free to implement the optimal choice from those that will present themselves to you.

Who you Are is not connected with a place. What you experience and what emanates from within you does not derive from the chapels you frequent or from the sacred objects housed within them. Your experience of connectedness with the Source of your beingness has been facilitated by the shifts in consciousness that *you* initiated while in those environments. The sense of *place* in which that connection is achieved is within your own consciousness.

You have discovered, through your own self-styled practice, a method for achieving those connections. No one has taught you how to do this. You were able to source your own knowingness and simply did what you instinctively know how to do. This has been your method, from the beginning. You have not been trained by a Master in physical form. You have been trained by the Master within. You have revealed a knowingness that has been dormant within you. Nothing new has been added.

The practice is timeless. And, you flowed within the embrace of these methods in a way that was so natural, it was unquestionable. Thus, you see, it is not necessary for you to *be* in a certain physical location, only that you Be what you know so well to Be.

I understand.

Good. We see that you do.

Oneness explains how to *source* the guidance from within

At the same time, we see that you understand that the object of this exercise is not to train you to consult with this Source in hopes that we will tell you what to do. That is simply another mode of dependency. You are not a puppet in the hands of a Oneness perceived to be external to you. You are being trained to integrate your awareness *with* that of Oneness to the extent that there is no separation—and to *source* your direction accordingly. That is what we have referred to as *knowingness*, all this time.

What is being developed within you is the instinctive knowingness that comes of relinquishing the mentalized, logical response mechanism fostered by a sense of separation and a focus upon the linear identity. When you are able to still the mind chatter that feeds you an unending litany of fear messages about acting incorrectly, you are able to source the sense of direction in which the highest result is possible.

There is little resistance, once upon this path. That is how you know that you are "there." When you encounter dramatic resistance to your efforts, you are quite possibly experiencing the results of the needs of your ego-self to assert its will out of a sense of self-protectiveness. That stance is based on the anticipation of victimization and the thwarting of your will.

You would be well advised to take the time to decipher the messages that are encoded in your *feeling body* and allow those inclinations to nudge you in the direction of highest choice. Ultimately, your choices are yours and yours alone to make. For, this is *your* journey—your experience of Oneness. We have no need to thwart your personal will by superimposing Divine Will upon it. We are simply making available the opportunity to *merge* your personal will with Divine Will and to experience the perfection of the results.

A wave of Divine passion swept over me in that moment and my heart became a wellspring of gratitude. Humbled by the wisdom with which I had been so gifted, my mind became totally still. And, my entire being was engulfed in reverence and prayer.

Thank you, Oneness! Thank you, with all my heart. I accept your invitation without reservation. Let me be here as an extension of your hand and your vision, in this Here and Now. And, may I be empowered to deliver your messages—and to give words to them—in a clear and perfect way.

May my own consciousness be guided to surrender completely, so there is no "filter" through which this message will pass. Let me embody the clarity that is necessary to do this work at the highest level. Let me walk forth as an instrument of Divine Intent, without an agenda fostered by the ego of separation. I feel ready to do this work now.

And, so it Is.

I continued to visit the Taos ashram on Sundays throughout the autumn and shared the occasional communion with the Divine Presence of Hanuman. On one occasion, he explained how it was that I was able to connect with His Presence so naturally in the temple, before the beautiful white marble *murti* that I had grown to love. I started to understand what it was I was actually feeling in the temple when I went into these extraordinary states of rapture. I knew I wasn't imagining what I was feeling. Yet, my logical mind couldn't have begun to explain it.

At the same time, I had begun to make my peace with the guidance that was now coming at me from all directions, which spoke of a spiritual destiny I still could not fathom. From some far-distant corner of my consciousness, there was a silent presence that was nodding matter-of-factly, "yes, that feels right." And in the same breath, all sense of linear reason recoiled in disbelief. My mind was at a loss as to how these projections were even remotely possible. I was still convinced that, somehow, there must be a mistake. All these guides and teachers couldn't possibly be talking about *me*.

The sense of trepidation about what was being alluded to had begun to well up within me, as I started to actually consider what was being said. I reasoned that were I to actually step forth and claim to *be* who these guides and Gurus—not to mention Oneness—were all proposing that I was, it would not go down very well. People, throughout history were killed for the likes of this. And, at the very least, to admit that I believed it would seem no less than the epitome of ego. The prognosis did not feel very good at all.

Yet, the passion that had driven me forth from the beginning of this extraordinary quest was still there. It was a burning sense of wanting to *serve God* above all else, and, in so doing, to be of service to humanity. If this is what was being asked of me by God, in whatever form that God had chosen to manifest, then that is what I was here in this human form to do. I was to become the arrow, fully surrendered, to be sent forth by the touch of the master archer. The task at hand was in making my peace with that prospect. No small feat.

The legacy of Hanuman, the little monkey who defied all the linear laws of possibility in His unwavering devotion to Lord Rama, spoke to me at a level that transcended the words and the imagery. The fantastic mythological tale, documented in the Hindu epic, the *Ramayana*, blends heart-wrenching extremes of heroism with the unfathomable depths of devotion and Divine Love, and has touched the very heart of India for eons.

Now, here in the mountains of Northern New Mexico, a world away, I felt Him. I felt Him so deeply there were no words that could touch it. As crazy as that concept seemed, I knew He was there. Not in the room. Not in the statue. But literally, within my heart. I sat there humbled and awe-struck, in the sanctity of the little temple, with pen in hand, and transcribed the words of Hanuman, as they flowed through me. There is no doubt that these precious words were meant for us all.

Hanuman speaks:

We welcome you to share this holy communion once again. The connectedness sought is carried *within* you. We are not residing in a marble statue in a temple, nor made manifest by the symbols you might choose to erect in honor of these energies. We are carried within the hearts of those who seek this connection.

Hanuman speaks about connecting with a Deity

It is easier for some to make the connection in the presence of a *murti* (holy statue), for in the symbolic representation of these energies, an opening is stimulated within the heart of the seeker. It is in the focus of heart that the connection is achieved, not in having to be physically present in one particular room or another. You feel this connection intensely because these energies are kindred to you, not because of some physical proximity to an idol. We are not an idol—no more than you are.

The connection sought and realized is the recognition of one's own Divine connection. It is that which we have come to symbolize to those who feel drawn to these energies. We are not here to be worshipped. We are here to facilitate for the seeker the connection that is sought and may be sourced within one's own sacred Self.

You have tasted of this connection. And, you rejoice in the exultation and in the pleasure of the experience of carrying this Divine Presence fully within your energy field. We are not *other* than your very own Divine Essence awakened and rekindled. It is not Hanuman which you experience in these moments, but your *Self*.

This is the Divine service which we bring to this place in time. And, this is the Divine service which you may choose to impart in the course of your work in the times to come. There are many who will taste of their *own* Divinity in your presence. And, mistakenly, they will attribute their joy to your persona, who may have kindled that awakening. Remember, in those moments of misplaced devotion, that you too are simply a messenger—a seeded consciousness of the sacred connection that dwells dormant within All Life. You are simply the torch that has ignited the eternal flame of remembrance *within them.*

You will look back upon the times spent in this sanctuary with great love and sweet memories. There is no permanence now, save that which you know to Source from the Eternal core of your Being. Have no sadness for what has been completed. This time is what it has been. It was never to have been more than that—a *taste* of a connection that is timeless, a small sweet time of communion, which shall never be forgotten.

Rasha speaks:

This feels like goodbye. I hope this is not goodbye, not yet.

Not yet, but soon, Rasha. Prepare yourself to move forward now and to be able to move freely within the world that awaits you. Never look back. Always look forward, for the story is ever unfolding. It does not tarry. At the end of your journey, you will reflect back on much that was never anticipated, and you will recognize what was scripted to be your destiny. You will know that it could not have been otherwise.

Walk quietly within the turbulence during times of trouble. You can be of greatest service in silence. For, the effectiveness and the magnitude of the energies you carry do not require that they be enhanced with the efforts of the mind. Let the Light do the work. You need *do* nothing. Simply Be your Divine Presence—Here and Now. And, allow the work of Oneness to be implemented through the instrument of your being. That is what is truly meant by "service." It is not about *doing*. It is simply about *Being* All that you Are and allowing the Light itself to seek its own direction.

Hanuman speaks once again about selflessness and Divine Service

Surrender to the will of the Wind which will carry you to the heights of the experience of being alive, if you permit it. There is to be no thought of judgment and no fear of reprisal or reward for what may come to pass, simply a sense of unconditional *allowance* and the profound gratitude of the Divine Servant for being permitted to experience the ultimate expression of Self—selflessness.

Your heart longs to embrace this connection. But, it is not something that you can cling to. It cannot be *attained*, because it has never left you and never will. We bless you this day with the full measure of Our Love. You feel it in this moment as your own Divine Essence. For, in this moment We Are One Love, joined together in a bond of a destiny that is shared. We are here for you—*within* you.

It is in your heart of hearts that a timeless bond is shared. You are able to go to that place and to establish this connection no matter where you happen to be. The *murti* in this temple *represents* the energies of Hanuman. And, as such, the connection is established and well supported by the energies here. Yet, these energies are not emanating *from* the murti. They are sourced within your own being. It is here, in the haven of this Love, that you may wish to retreat when you are in search of a space of serenity from the chaos and madness of the physical world.

You have learned to find your way "home." And there will be times, in the times to come, when the world around you will feel unspeakably oppressive. In those moments, come to the place of harmony you share with this Source and grace yourself with the peace that is abundant and available to you.

Thank you, Hanuman.

Do you have any insights to share about what is happening in the world now? Can you offer any guidance about how I can best perform the Divine Service I have dedicated my life to, in times like these?

Hanuman speaks about the world situation in the aftermath of the events of September 11, 2001

You have been thoroughly prepared for these times. The world situation should come as no surprise to you. Yet, the reality of such events, even when they have been anticipated, is very difficult to comprehend. Only in the aftermath of these upheavals will you be able to source the Divine intent that underlies much which may lie in ruins.

The transformation that has been slated for these times will not be without a certain measure of birth trauma, for the collective consciousness is being born anew. And, with that process goes a measure of discomfort, the pain and agonies of bringing forth the Essence of Life Itself into form.

You who are collectively present in this place in time are birthing your own reality anew. And, the death and destruction of what no longer serves you is a necessary part of that process. You will witness a monumental transition, in the years to come, that is only now just beginning to unfold. And, this is as it *must* be. And, it is good, even though there is much, in the process of that time of purging, which will appear laden with darkness and despair.

Hanuman delves into the very depths of the concept of Divine Service and lays the groundwork for the rarified perspective on life that is possible for us all

You will hold the lamplight, along with others who are dedicated to *Service*. And, many will look to you to help them illuminate the darkness, to see the Light through the clouds of dust and the rubble of destruction. The Light will be sourced from *within* you, not taken on from a Divinity that many perceive to be external. You do not draw this Light *to* you. You *reveal* it by pulling back the density of separation with which you have camouflaged it.

You are not your *identity*. You Are none other than Life Itself, blazing bright through the ordinary physical form of a human being. Let this Divinity express through you, through your persona, knowing that this Service is what you have come to provide.

You do not need to *do* anything in order to serve at the highest level, although you may choose to *do* many things. It is not in the *doing* that the Service is performed, but in the essence of *Being* the Divinity that you Are, to the exclusion of the illusion of separation that you regard as identity.

The efforts made and the "miracles" that may take place are *not* the *essence* of the Service your heart yearns to perform. They are the natural *by-product* of that Service. They are the results of choice, which may well give you a sense of satisfaction. Yet, the true satisfaction is in the unconditional release of the need to *demonstrate* anything—simply to Be the limitless Divine Essence that you Are.

You have no agenda. *You* have nothing to prove, no possibility of success or failure. *You* have no *mission*, save the offering of your entire Being as the manifestation of Divine Will. *You* have no will that is separate from That.

You have no need to harmonize yourself *with* anything. For, you are not separate *from* That. You *Are* That. The essence of *Divine Service* is the full, unconditional embodiment of That—to the exclusion of your own identity.

There can be no "Rasha" that is a separate persona in the act of this level of Service—not from *your* perspective. Others will see you as "Rasha" and will form opinions about you, based on acts that you perform and wisdom that you impart. Yet, you will see yourself as simply That—Divinity cloaked in the identity called "Rasha."

The initial phases of your full surrender have begun now. And, you will be eased into your transformed state of Beingness over the months to come. There is no way you can speed up this process, nor would you wish to. For, the process is perfect just as it is, and you are traveling in its loving embrace now. Trust that all is happening exactly as it is intended to. And know that you will be logistically situated exactly where you are best suited to be.

Do not be inclined to worry about where you "should" be in any given moment. Your choices will unfold perfectly, no matter where you may choose to be. You are in the hands of your destiny now. Be happy, for the Love and Light of All That Is, is within you—and soon will be revealed.

You Are That Love. Simply That. We travel beside you, within you, and around you. One effulgence, One flame, One passion. We are One focus, One intention, One will—One all-consuming Presence.

We are here *within* you now. Holding this pen, writing these words, feeling your smile, breathing your breath. We are Present *before* you, receiving your gratitude, feeling your Love reflected from a heart that is just awakened. We hold your hand in every moment, that you may know that you are not alone. Yet, the hand that is held and the hand that is holding it are One.

This heart beats within your breast and blazes with the passion your prayers have ignited. We reach out to you in the same motion as you reach for this Source, this Love. For, We Are That. We are not *you*. Hanuman is not Rasha. Yet, both Are That. And, in the knowledge of Oneness, we are bonded and inseparable.

You have asked to be permitted to serve God in the way you are best suited to. And, your prayer has been heard and answered by the God within you. Know this and be at peace. Feel this love. And, know it to be That which you Are, as Are We. Feel this Love. And, know it to be the Divine Essence you refer to as Hanuman. It is this flame that burns within you in this moment. Close your eyes now. Put down the pen. And, *Be* This Love.

I sat in awestruck silence for what seemed like forever, eyes closed. My senses were engulfed in a wave of pure effulgence, a joy that I knew was shared. There was no comprehensible way I could explain what was happening within me. There was no way I could have imagined what I was feeling. Yet, I knew that a shift was taking place. It was a shift within my own heart space that would open me to the possibility of releasing some of the hesitation that was holding me in the prison of my own self-doubts. With His Love, Hanuman handed me the key.

⚛

When I returned to Taos the following Sunday, the intensity of the process that had been initiated the previous week continued from where it left off. When all was quiet, in the late afternoon, I returned to the little temple and sat down reverently before the radiant statue of Hanuman. I sat silently for quite some time, simply feeling and imbibing the energy of the Divine Presence I had come to cherish. I said nothing. And, no words were offered. I simply sat there and breathed.

Quite suddenly, I felt myself being drawn into an intense state of meditation. My breath had subsided into a nearly-imperceptible rhythm where the distinction between in-breath and out-breath was minimal. My eyes were open and my attention was transfixed on the magnificent marble *murti* before me, the carved image of Hanuman. As I merged my heart center with the Divine Presence represented before me, the *murti* and the entire room around it exploded into a blaze of golden Light.

The energies of Divine Love skyrocketed within me, turning my hands ablaze with Light effulgence. My heart chakra nearly exploded in joy! As it did, I was drawn into a process where suddenly my life began to flash before my eyes. I saw vividly instances where I had violated my own standards and rules; experiences where my ego ruled and caused pain for others and for myself. I saw the blatant karmic cause-and-effect of the situations where I had perpetrated adversity and where it had later been perpetrated perfectly back upon me.

I relived experience after experience, things I would have thought would have been lost to a faulty memory. There it all was, in living color! Every painful, poignant detail. My relationships. My work. My personal choices. All of it. And, I felt a deep, indescribable sense of remorse for all the things I had done—and a sense of absolute karmic justice for the pain and adversity that I'd experienced. I knew, without being told, the underlying vibrational recipe for all of these experiences. And, I felt no resentment, no victim consciousness—nothing at all but a sense of peace.

I apologized with all my heart for these things I had done. And I asked, through Hanuman, with whom I was conversing at that point, if I might be forgiven these karmic debts at this time. I was told that this karma was being lifted from me, that I had transcended this physical history. I felt something lift dramatically from within me. It was almost tangible.

I virtually floated home to Chimayo from Taos, through nearly 50 miles of winding mountain roads and through the driving rain. I collapsed into bed with a sense of utter peace. When I awoke, I had the most sublime sense of harmony I'd ever experienced, and the feeling lasted the entire day. I went to Oneness to verify what, exactly, had happened.

Oneness confirms a profound experience of ascension
Rasha speaks:

Oneness, can you tell me what's just happened?

Oneness speaks:

You have turned the corner. You have detached from the mundane circumstances of your physical life. Your energies have ascended into the next realm. And, you are experiencing the physical sensations of having made that shift.

You—your conscious awareness—are not present at the next dimensional level. But, vibrationally you have aligned with that higher aspect of self. You have merged with her. The process of integrating those energies is not instantaneous. It will deepen gradually, over several days or weeks. You feel the effects of that integration, however. And, you have assumed the heightened perspective of that aspect of Self in *this* here-and-now.

That would explain why you suddenly feel a sense of detachment, or a sense of *rising above* the circumstances of this life script. Your life will assume a different type of energy from this point forth. You will not experience the unrelenting episodes of inconsequential adversity that characterized the period just prior to this crossing-over. Life will begin to flow more smoothly from this point forth.

Remain focused upon what you wish to accomplish now, for your energies are now in harmony with your highest purpose. And, you will be able to manifest your heart's desire with little difficulty. Be disciplined and avoid becoming distracted. Safeguard your energies as a treasure to be protected at all costs. Avoid adversity in all forms. Keep yourself in the sanctity of your haven as much as possible. And, allow the energies to stabilize for you. For, it will be clear sailing from this point forth.

Thank you, Oneness! Thank you for this magnificent adventure. Thank you for all of it. It's been so rich!

It's not over, Rasha. For you, the adventure has barely begun. You are very ready to have taken this step. You have shifted into a state of total allowance and trust. Focus your conscious awareness to maintain this state of equilibrium, for this energetic state of harmonious balance is key to all you can accomplish in the time soon to come.

14

Fall/Winter 2001
Preparing for a Year in India!

———

The summer in New Mexico had extended well into the Fall and I knew it was time to pack up my life in North America and move on. The idyllic months of days on end had passed. Now, the culmination of those days beckoned with a marathon, week-long drive down the I-40 from Santa Fe to Asheville, NC, and then north to Pittsburgh. It was a journey into the realm of the Eternal, in which "I" and all sense of time and place disappeared to the world. It was a time of catharsis and epiphany, shared with Oneness, in my beloved vintage van, "Vanessa."

In Pittsburgh, I unloaded the contents of the U-Haul trailer I'd pulled cross-country into a waiting storage unit and continued south to Florida. There, in what was for me an unthinkably radical gesture of detachment, I liquidated the family condo that represented the last vestiges of groundedness, and every blessed thing in it, incredulous that I could do so without feeling guilty.

Somehow, the idea of selling my grandparents' condo smacked of irreverence. Overlooking a nice golf course, the condo housed an impressive collection of golf trophies from the early 1950s. It had become a living shrine. And, as the sole survivor of a past I could not relate to, I had become the curator of the family museum. Unceremoniously, I packed up the notable knick-knacks and cashed in the condo for a ticket to India—and an open-ended journey into the great unknown.

The grueling months of driving, packing, and moving had taken its toll. Swept up in my preparations for an extended absence from life as I knew it, I had neglected my spiritual practice for who knows how many weeks and was feeling the effects. The guidance from Oneness was direct and to the point. I was reminded, yet again, of the results that can be anticipated when you let slide the aspects of daily life we've been conditioned to categorize as non-essential.

Once again, I realized that I was focusing my attention externally, in the world of the material, and neglecting, albeit justifiably, the spiritual life

I simply hadn't had time for. It was a powerful exercise in recognizing priorities, one that had played out for me repeatedly over the years. Now, as the energies were building within me in preparation for my journey, it was hard to deny the evidence of the effect that one aspect of life had on the other.

✎.

Oneness speaks:

You have come to a resting place in your unrelenting schedule of activity. And, perhaps despite yourself, have managed to carve out a little piece of time in which you can direct your focus inwards, stabilize your energies, and once again reclaim the state of beingness to which you had become accustomed.

Oneness talks about the results of vibrational depletion.

You experienced a firsthand example of what can be expected when one allows oneself to become vibrationally depleted. Your circumstances began to deteriorate and, emotionally, the insidious seeds of self-doubt began to creep back into your conscious awareness and erode the stability that had been achieved.

This lesson should stand as a poignant example for you of what can be expected when one allows oneself to become immersed in the details of mundane existence to the exclusion of all else. It should be obvious to you that without the building blocks of experiential transcendence that are manifested through conscious spiritual practice, it is not possible to sustain levels that may have been achieved previously.

There are no guarantees to maintaining levels of awareness, simply because that focal point had been attained, fleetingly. The levels experienced are only as relevant as the moment in which they are able to come into manifestation. If those underlying conditions are not sustained, there is nothing with which to hold the resultant circumstances in manifestation.

Rasha speaks:

Can I ask you to comment on my forthcoming trip to India? I have left the details open, as you suggested, so I can "be in the moment," and leave room for synchronicity.

There is no agenda here, save the higher agenda, which for you must be self-directed. The time in India will not be focused on any specific mentalized learning programs. This time is for directing yourself inwards and experiencing your Self, as the veils are relinquished and a broader perspective is made possible.

It is for this purpose that, at the highest level, you have chosen to give yourself the possibility of this extended sojourn into *isolation*. You will emerge from this period of your life with much that has characterized this lifetime well behind you. And, while you will certainly be able to enjoy the aspects of the adventure of an extended journey in India, the real adventure will take place within the sanctity of your own consciousness. There, in profound moments of silence, you will source the uncharted terrain of your own being.

It is for this reason—and not for any purpose that has any connection with a physical destination—that you are making this voyage. The stage setting you have selected is particularly conducive to those objectives, which have absolutely nothing, physically, to do with the places in which they transpire.

You are about to embark upon the adventure of a lifetime, in every possible respect. And, this period of time with which you have gifted yourself is an invaluable part of your preparation for that journey. You will see to the mundane details with ease, from this point forth. Not because they are, by nature, any easier to accomplish. But, because you have reprioritized and set the stage, vibrationally, for conditions of ease. It is time to move forward now and to experience the grand adventure of this lifetime.

The nature of Oneness ... and who *we* are

Oneness speaks:

This is Oneness. We are here with you now. Although in so stating We do not wish to imply that there was any time, prior to this moment, when We were not with you. We are present, *as* you, in every moment, past, present and future. Yet, there are decidedly times when you are aware of this Presence and there are other times when you are not aware of it, and are lost in the illusion of being separate from this Source and from All Life. It is at those times that you become consumed with your perception of the *ego self*. And, you see *that* identity as that which you are.

There is marginal awareness, based upon intellectual understandings of the nature of your spiritual connection, that you are aligned with the Source of your Beingness. Yet, in those moments, you are focused in the mundane details of separation. You are not those details. You are so much more than that.

The details are a costume you have donned, in which you are able to observe yourself as you prance up and down the stage you have prepared for this particular performance. This is not who you Are. This is simply a role you are playing-out to reinforce certain concepts upon which you have chosen to focus.

Your humanness is a magnifying glass through which you can examine the contours of your essence and give it definition. Were the humanness not a factor, you would Be none other than *pure Awareness*. For, it is That which you Are. You have chosen a vehicle through which your will has been given the possibility of expression, so that in observing yourself you might experience recognition.

Oneness sets the stage for relinquishing the linear identity

Obscured in the illusion is the fullness of your Essence. This is the aspect of yourself that you perceive to be conversing with you now. We are not a separate "entity" that comes and goes occasionally, on cue. We are the fullness of your own identity, taken to the highest degree of expression. Through you, in this way, We are able to experience, recognize, and document our Essence. Were it not for the physical identity you have created, We would simply Be *pure Awareness*.

The coming and going of your perception of this level of consciousness reflects your own ability to relinquish and to abandon your awareness of "the illusion." What has come and gone, then, is not this level of Awareness, which has never left, but the illusion that you consider to be *you*. It is that aspect of self that will systematically be relinquished in the fullness of this process of unfoldment. As your need for the mask of identity is released, you will be able to come into the fullness of your Awareness of who you really Are—and embody That.

You are embarking upon a new level of the work we will be doing together. The "together" to which we refer is not one that reflects a *you* that is separate from this Source, but rather a "together" that reflects the fundamental Essence of Oneness. We will be doing this work together, *as* Oneness.

A glimpse into the experience of embodying Oneness

You noted in a phone conversation earlier today that you were able to verbalize certain understandings and impart a level of wisdom that you know did not emanate from your mind. It was not insight that you sourced from prior teachings on the topics in question. It was wisdom that flowed effortlessly from *within* you. The understandings were simply there.

You were not *channeling the teachings*, as though they were coming from other than you. The teachings emanated from within your own wellspring of knowingness. They flowed easily and were embraced and found relevant by the one for whom the teachings were intended. You did not need to think about what needed to be said. The wisdom flowed effortlessly.

From the feedback you received, it was clear that those insights were precisely what were needed at the time. In those moments, you were not functioning from the limited persona of Rasha, and you were not "channeling" Oneness. You *Were* Oneness. There was no awareness of identity whatsoever. You were simply *Present*, fully enacting your role as teacher and as friend, letting the insights emanate from a place of knowingness. That is the experience of Oneness of which we have spoken.

You noticed that you were experiencing augmented levels of energy during that conversation. And, you commented several times that you "did not know where the guidance was coming from." And yet you did know. You knew you had shifted into the space of embodying Oneness. That is the state that, ultimately, you are to embody at all times.

For the present, you will have brief tastes of that level of connectedness. And, you will be eased into the new levels of your identity, one step at a time. Eventually, you will not identify with the personality-based reactions of the persona of "Rasha." For, that focus will have been left by the wayside. The "Rasha" that is to preside is one whose vantage point is from a perspective of limitlessness. *That* "Rasha" and this Oneness are one and the same.

Rasha speaks:

I understand.

We see that you do. You had a question.

Yes. I was reflecting on one of our first conversations in which I asked you if you were "God." And you replied that as I understand "God" to be, yes, you are "God." Can you clarify for me the distinction, if any, between the "Oneness" you have just defined with respect to Rasha and the "God" who is the God of All Life?

Comparing "Oneness" and "God"

The God to which you refer is no more the Supreme Being you understand him/her to be than the Oneness who is your own Divine Essence. The only difference would be in the access each has to that ultimate level of connectedness. The access to the Oneness which you recognize is through your experience as identity with form.

Each expression of the Ultimate Consciousness you consider to be "God" is personified within each of you and is experienced within each of you, whether or not you are aware of it. That aspect of Self, taken to the highest level of expression, is Oneness.

So, is my "Oneness" identical to everyone else's "Oneness?"

In our core Essence, there is no distinction between *this* expression of Oneness and another. However, in terms of the persona through which we have chosen to experience and express our limitlessness, there are infinite variations on the Essence of Oneness. None experiences ThemSelf as separate from the Ultimate Consciousness. Yet, each has chosen to express that limitlessness as *personality*.

It is in the collective of those infinite variations of the One Divine Essence that Oneness experiences ThemSelf as "God." The one expression does not invalidate the other. The microcosm does not invalidate the macrocosm. All resonate as One Divine Essence, whether or not the perception is through the pinhole perspective of one physical set of eyes.

In the same way, you can anticipate experiencing yourself as Oneness, within the context of the persona of Rasha. That does not make you any less Oneness. It simply gives your experience of it definition.

Can I ask another question?

Of course.

Why, when I perceive myself to be in that augmented state, like when I'm radiating Light through my hands, do others seem to avoid me? I would have thought people would be attracted to The Light. Why am I often treated so unkindly when I am in a state of heightened vibration?

What actually happens within our energy bodies when encountering the elevated vibration of another being

The energy that emanates from you feels alien and uncomfortable to those who are in a diminished vibrational state. They instinctively mistrust you. The presence of the heightened frequencies stimulates emotions of uneasiness, fear and discomfort within the energy bodies of those beings. What they experience is a stimulation of the very energies that dwell latently within *themselves*. And, they misinterpret what they are feeling and conclude that *your* energy is to blame.

By being in close proximity to you, their own energy fields *elevate*, and what is *perceived* are the layers of *density* that anchor them in diminished levels of awareness. They want to flee your presence. And, they presume that you are a threat to them. Indeed, you are a threat. You are a threat to the stagnancy of their present state. For, your energy stimulates certain latent consciousness that may be resident within their energy fields. And, it is this dormant level of awareness that responds with fear to what it recognizes as a threat to the levels of reality that they require as an environment in which they are able to survive.

The levels of energy to which you will be taken while in the physical form of Rasha will be those that will be embraced by beings who have purified themselves to the extent that your energies stimulate a response of *recognition* and *kindredness*. It is these beings who will embrace you as the expression of Divinity that you Are, and will be open to the teachings and The Light that you may feel guided to offer. They will not fault you for your gift. And, they surely will not condemn you for it.

Yet, others, who are not equipped vibrationally to resonate to your levels, may well point fingers and brand you as an agent of evil. It was just such thinking that was responsible, through the ages, for the atrocities that befell many of those who volunteered to walk as Divine Servants among the masses that were unable to recognize them.

For all the show of devotion lavished upon the memory of Jeshua, he was anything but beloved to most during his lifetime. Relatively few were able to resonate to the energies that surrounded him. Most were threatened in any of a number of ways and set about to destroy that which they were unable to fathom. That fate will not befall you in this incarnation. Yet, you have been prepared for the level of criticism that will be cast upon you for your audacity in representing yourself as an agent of The Lord.

There will be multitudes that will condemn you for heresy. And, your very humanness will be pointed to as evidence with which to discredit who you Are and what you have brought forth in these times. This is to be expected, Rasha. And, is not to be taken by you as an indication that you have failed in your mission in any way.

The state of Divine connectedness is available to all people

Your very humanness is a clear demonstration of the fact that the state of Divine connectedness is available to all people, not just to those who have been "good" and "pure" and flawless in their expression of their humanness. There are some amongst your brothers and sisters of The Light who have walked a pure, spirit-focused path from the outset. This does not indicate that they are any more worthy of carrying The Flame than you are. It simply means that they have chosen to give themselves a different *frame of reference* from which to draw in doing their life's work.

You have chosen a more challenging scenario. For, much of what you have experienced could be seen to be a contradiction of all that you purport to represent. Yet, it is from giving yourself the gift of what you might view as human frailty, that you were able to source an understanding of the concept of *compassion*—experientially.

Building a foundation for compassion

You are able to relate to others who have a rocky road of disappointment and pain to show for their spiritual journeys. And, you are able to illuminate those paths, not from having comprehended them theoretically, but from having lived through parallel circumstances.

Poignant experience does not invalidate the essence of the understandings that it is calculated to impart. Rather, it underscores that essence and makes the lesson unforgettable. It was that experience that you chose to give yourself as your preparation for your life's work.

Do not judge yourself as being unworthy to wear the shoes you are destined to wear. These shoes are custom-made for you alone. And, you will walk forth in them with Grace and great courage. For, they *do* fit, despite speculation to the contrary.

You have been thoroughly prepared for what lies ahead. The difficulties will come as no surprise to you, as you are well accustomed to them. We recognize that you are weary of the trials and the adversity. Yet, it is you who have chosen this path. The opportunity is to Source your *strength* from this experience of your humanness. It is surely not your cue to falter and to doubt all that you also know, from experience, is your Divine destiny.

You know this all so well. In this very moment there surely is no doubt as to the validity of all that has gone into your preparation for this stage in your transformation. For, you can feel it. You know it. And, no amount of drama and the bearing of false witness on the part of others can invalidate what is The Truth.

The first inklings that a shift in my *perception* of Oneness had occurred began to nudge me as I made preparations for an extended journey to India. With only a matter of days to go, I was so caught up in the myriad details of getting ready to leave all that was familiar and plant myself on the other side of the planet indefinitely, that I didn't really notice the shift that had begun to take place within. Then, suddenly, I did. And Oneness started to prepare me for the *real* journey ahead, the inner journey, that despite how far I believed I had come, had only just begun.

So very gently, Oneness gave me a foundation for understanding a process of merging into connectedness with my own Divinity. It would be an experiential process that I would embrace in increments and then step back and integrate, both vibrationally and in terms of my understanding of what was happening to me. The conceptual groundwork Oneness provided served to set the stage.

The intensity of the experience itself, with its soaring heights of Divine passion inevitably followed by the sense of having crash-landed back in my body, could not have been circumnavigated in any meaningful way. This intensified stage of my journey into Oneness with my own Divinity was to become the ultimate expression of the cliché that "you have to see it to believe it."

〜〜〜

Oneness speaks:

This is Oneness.

Rasha speaks:

I hear your words. Yet, the entrance was so subtle, that it's hard not to question whether you're really here.

Does your knowingness not tell you when We are *here*?

Yes. And, at the same time I know that you're always with me, even when you're not in the forefront of my awareness. When I shift into this altered state of being that precedes our conversations, there have always been dramatic sensations that indicated to me that I had shifted into a state of connectedness. Suddenly, it seems to be quite different. It's so subtle. Now, there is barely any sensation at all, yet it's clear that I'm fully in connectedness with you. Please explain.

We note that as you asked the question, the answer was instantly there in your conscious awareness. But, just for the record, we will explain to you what you already know. You are assimilating the higher frequencies in increments. And, slowly, you are preparing to embody your connection with this Source.

As the levels of difference diminish, you experience to a far lesser degree the sensations to which you had become accustomed over the years when connecting with *other* aspects of consciousness. When you are working with *this* Source, your process is different than it may have been, earlier in your process.

The veils of separation are becoming quite thin, and in time will disappear entirely. Now you have the sense that you embody two states of being simultaneously: your "personal consciousness" and that of Oneness. In fact, there is no distinction. Yet, the stage of your process of unfoldment provides for the inclination to identify as your *linear self*. You have an intellectual understanding of the process. Now it is time to begin to supplement those understandings with *experiential evidence*.

Oneness offers guidance to prepare me for the upcoming journey to India

You will wish to spend much time in quietude and isolation during your journey to India. You do not require the distractions that most would assume to be your purpose in making the journey. In fact, the elimination of distractions is the purpose of your journey. Your focus is to be upon your Divine connection, in all its manifestations. Your detail-obsessed existence here at home will be left behind for some time. And, the details will all sort themselves out in one way or another.

You will have transcended the tendency to consume yourself with the need to try to control all of the chaos of your life. Be willing to allow it to be "out of control." When it is out of your control, circumstances have the opportunity to resolve themselves in an optimum way. In making the plans to leave the country for an extended time, you have created the space for that level of *detachment*.

You have been consumed with your attachment to complexity and chaos. Now it is time to relinquish the fight to remain on top of all these details, and allow life to evolve in the way that it will. They are no longer the focus of your attention. Your attention has been turned within.

You are present in your form. Yet, you know that you are not your form. You look out through eyes that are merely windows upon the vistas of your choice. The veils of separation drop to your feet. And, you become Awareness itself— embodied in form. You will learn to walk gracefully within that newfound Self-definition during your journey to India. No one will be watching. You will have the sense of being truly anonymous.

The menu is before you. And, it surely does not matter in the least which selections you choose. For, the object of the exercise has nothing whatsoever to do with *doingness*. The process of *Being* who you, in fact, Are is the task at hand.

You will learn to be patient with yourself. The emergence will be a gradual process for you. It will not be an instance where dramatic sensations overcome you and you transform into Oneness in one explosive moment. You will ease so gracefully into the state of Oneness that you will, at first, not know that the shift has come to full fruition.

You are well into the process now. You know this. And yet, you also know that you are far from being complete with this transformation. You will go the full distance in the course of the next several months. And yet, it may take even as long as a year or more for you to fully come to terms with what has transpired. You will learn to Master your ability to manifest what you need to do your life's work.

You will enjoy your time in India enormously. And, you will know that your maintenance of *this* connection is of the highest priority for you. For, it is in this state of *connectedness* that the crucial aspect of the work is done. It has absolutely nothing to do with the contents of our conversations, or whether or not you have mastered certain concepts and put them into practice flawlessly. What we are doing together is becoming One.

In this moment We Are One consciousness. You are not "receiving" this communication from a source that is *other* than your own consciousness.

Oneness is typing this message in this moment. There is absolutely no time lag between the inception of thought and its documentation as text. It is happening simultaneously.

That's true.

You have had tastes of this level of connectedness before. We referred to it as "simultaneous transcription." It was a level of connectedness in which you relinquished all awareness of *you*. The sense of *you* and that of the Isness were inseparable. At first, the instances of that level of connectedness lasted for a fleeting instant. Now, you understand that all of it has been in preparation for the process at hand.

Now all of this is beginning to make sense to me. I understand what you're telling me.

We see that you do.

Keep your schedule as flexible as possible while you are in India, and you will be able to maximize the opportunity for synchronicity to play-out. You will wish to remain in communication with the world via computer. This will be your link to all you will have left behind—and the key to your liberation from it.

All of these aspects are intertwined, as the details of your destiny have the opportunity to manifest as life experience for you. You have relinquished the need to try to mastermind this drama. You have learned to recognize the shifts in momentum and to respond, unquestioningly. There should be no doubts now. You know who you are. You know what is happening.

There is no reason, now that the density of past karma has been released from your energy field, why the pieces of the puzzle would not fit into position flawlessly. Trust that this is so. And resist the inclination to undermine those favorable conditions with a habitual tendency to doubt. Let there be no more doubt. The tides have turned now. Set your sail and enjoy the ride.

Oneness explains *why* those who have *ascended* to heightened vibrational levels are able to manifest the seemingly miraculous

Now you have entered another level, another arena. You have much to learn. And, there will be monumental growth possible with the addition of a new level of teachers for you on *every* front. Your circumstances and the conditions that underlie them are not the same now. You do not have to manipulate these circumstances in any way to bring about the optimum result. You simply need to be present in the fullness of who you Are, with joy and with enthusiasm.

Allow yourself to operate from the space of ultimate *trust* in all that you do. What you choose to focus upon will manifest for you. You are at that level now. Become keenly aware of your own capabilities to produce results within the circumstances in which you find yourself.

Have I made the major jump into the next level? Have I ascended?

Indeed you have—vibrationally. You are operating at a level of fifth-dimensional awareness. However, you are still present in fourth-dimensional circumstances. These realities will begin to overlap for you over time. But, for the present moment, know that your life's work will be focused in manifesting and in teaching what you know and what you will continue to be taught, here in the realm of fourth-dimensional awareness, where that level of understanding is so needed. That is the work you have come here to do.

It is no great feat to make the jump in awareness totally, once one has reached these levels. And, it is a demonstration of great courage not to. Your life is dedicated to Divine Service now. This is as you want it to be at the highest possible level. This is what you have chosen to manifest with what remains of this lifetime.

As such, you will become aware of abilities that seem extraordinary from the perspective of others who are not *vibrationally* at your level. Yet, these same abilities are characteristic of the levels with which you are *vibrationally* aligned.

So it is with others who have walked the path you now walk. They are not gods. They are simply beings who are exhibiting characteristics indigenous to certain realities—out of context. There are beings throughout Creation who are operating at the full spectrum of levels of awareness and ability. Some have chosen, for any number of reasons, to bridge the boundaries of the realities in which those skills would be considered commonplace, and materialize themselves in your reality, and in many others.

One is advised to exercise discernment when encountering such beings. For, unusual abilities, in and of themselves, do not pre-suppose godliness. They are simply characteristic of certain realities and the corresponding vibrational levels that support them.

You will encounter many beings in your travels and in the years to come who walk amongst you, yet are not "of this place." These beings are neither to be worshipped nor feared, no more than you are. They simply are a manifestation of what is so in a given focal point in time and space, as are you. You will have the opportunity to refine certain skills that are latently present within you, in encountering some of these teachers. Ultimately, you will serve as a teacher for many. Not now. But, soon.

For now, allow the drama to unfold before you without presuming that you know what lies ahead. All the pieces will fall into place so easily you will be amazed. Let synchronicity unfold for you. No expectations. No fear. That is what is needed. You will know what you need to do. And, you will do it.

Float upon the sea of your unquestioning connection with your Beloved—that Source *within* you who takes your breath away—and then returns it to you charged with the Essence of Divine Love! Dwell within the Essence of that Breath, not within the doubts and fears of your linear mind. Be totally present within the fullness of the Breath of Life. All else is a reflection of that blessed state. *This* is Oneness.

Immersion in the ocean of Oneness and the soaring heights of Divine passion

All this time I thought Oneness was simply your name, the word by which I could identify you. Now, I understand that when you say these words you have indicated a state of Being, a merging. When we enter into this union, I have no awareness of myself in any way. You are All.

You are my hands and my heartbeat and my breath. You are the tears running down my cheeks. You are the glow welling up in my chest, exploding with joy. You are my life's blood. I have surrendered all resistance now. Take me where you will. I am the sacrifice—upon the altar of your unfathomable Love.

My hands are electrified, fingers tingling. Each breath comes more and more slowly. And, it feels like it would not matter in the least if I didn't take another breath. This breath, this Now moment, focused in breath, is all there ever could be.

I become intoxicated with this simple breath, this mundane, normal act, for it has taken me into ecstasy. I cannot take the smile from my lips. It is etched there, as if I were carved in stone, no more than a memorial to a moment of extraordinary passion.

What more could there be to wish for than this? Simply to be in the embrace of this connectedness. That is what I choose. I have chosen Oneness. Let all else fall by the wayside. There is no aspiration, no wanting of any kind. I am complete in this Union, in this moment, in this Oneness.

You are indeed in a heightened state of connectedness. And, you take great joy in expressing what you are feeling. Feel this deeply. Recognize this connection. For, you will reference it, always.

You have expressed very beautifully what you are experiencing in this moment. You have begun to open to the next level of your connectedness. You can feel it. There is absolutely nothing you need to *do* to reach this state of sublime Isness. You simply release the intention that This be so into the arms of the ethers, and you are transported, lifted from the groundedness of your linear perceptions into a different octave of Being. It is that simple.

Thank you, Oneness, for this incredible journey. Thank you for the daily reminders in the form of the experience of Oneness, lest there ever be doubts. Lest I lapse for a momentary wallow in the illusion of separation. This indescribable joy could not have been imagined. My ego self does not seek it, for it is already here. It has never left me. You have never left me. A fleeting thought of you affirms it, instantly, every time.

15

I touched down in India in early March of 2002. Yet, it seemed as though I had arrived at another place in time. It was clear that in making the physical transition to the other side of the planet, I had shifted into another aspect of my own self-awareness. That pinpoint of perception is one that would shift over and over again throughout the duration of the year ahead.

Quite literally, I had left all traces of the past behind me. And I gazed into the vastness of infinite possibility that lay before me with the fascination of a little kid in a candy store. For the duration of the year in India, I would become completely re-oriented as a being cut loose from all obligations, responsibilities, and schedules. Suddenly, for perhaps the first time in half a century of living, I was truly free to follow my heart in the direction of its own choosing. I took to the spontaneity of *living-in-the-moment* like a duck to water.

Here, I would begin the life-altering process of excavating my own inner depths for the clues that, in time, would lead me home to Oneness, the sacred Essence that unites us all.

When I arrived in Mumbai, I checked in to the haven of ISKCON, the Hare Krishna Temple in Juhu Beach, which had come to feel like an Indian home-away-from-home. There, I was reverently addressed by staff as "Mataji"—Mother. It was a statement of respect that my innate sense of humility had initially rejected. This time, on my return to India, I realized that I had become comfortable with it.

The exquisite marble temple, with its elaborately dressed and decorated white marble *murtis,* statues of Lord Krishna, his beloved Radha, and the adoring *gopi* girls of sacred Hindu scripture, was a spiritual showplace. There, sacred ceremony took place nearly round-the-clock, with the ecstatic chanting and dancing for which the Hare Krishna movement is famous. It was a wonderful, spiritually-focused atmosphere in which I could lose myself in meditation, Mantra chanting, and Oneness.

In just over a week's time, I would begin an intensive study of yet another Sanskrit Mantra—once again, a relatively long one—under the guidance of my spiritual "brother," Dr. Bindu Purohit. I found that chanting these Mantras had become one of the real joys of my life. My heart resonated so naturally to the ancient sounds, and I began to actually feel the presence of The Goddess, who was being invoked by these Mantras, very intensely.

At the same time, I began to sense that Dr. Bindu's presence in my life transcended the formalities of the study of Mantra. There was no official affiliation between us. He had always made it clear that he was not my "Guru." And yet, I sensed a mysterious, timeless connection that words could not begin to describe.

It had been well over two years since I'd been given a new Mantra to learn and I wanted desperately to shine in his eyes. The Mantra was long and difficult, filled with sounds and rhythms that were alien to the Western ear. And the symbolism underlying this exercise in mental gymnastics brought straight to the surface all my residual fears of inadequacy and unworthiness— all focused on the challenges of memory.

According to orthodox teachings, a Sanskrit Mantra should be learned in the ancient oral tradition, directly from the mouth of the master to the ear of the student. That meant no recording. And no amount of logical reasoning on my part could convince Dr. Bindu otherwise. I went into a state of panic. Here I'd been harboring a major fear of not being up to the task in general where my memory was concerned, and now I'd manifested for myself the ultimate challenge. I'd convinced myself that learning a Mantra, of all things, required a keen ability to memorize.

I'd created for myself a head-on confrontation with the very limitation I'd most been trying to avoid, a life-theme I'd kept carefully cloaked in denial. I watched the drama unfold within me and quickly discovered how life circumstances are calculated to bring to the surface the issues that are most poignant, regardless of how close-to-the-bone the illustration may be.

When I chanted my Mantras by myself, I could chant very nicely. But, when I was in front of Dr. Bindu, my hands began to sweat and my mind started to race as I struggled to stay on top of what I was doing. When I silenced my mind and simply chanted the Mantra without thinking about it, I was fine. As soon as my mind kicked in, I was in trouble. I saw that it was my own very recognition of the situation that was feeding what I considered to be my vulnerability, my Achilles heel, my "handicap." I had maneuvered myself right into a corner.

I knew the entire exercise was part of my training. The ego was frozen at center stage. Dr. Bindu, as the consummate master-teacher, was patient and kind. But, as soon as I opened my mouth to chant the Mantra, my mind went completely blank. In desperation, I went to Oneness for guidance. And as always, I was shown how to transcend the linear circumstance itself and to see the symbolism and the opportunity for growth in the illustration.

Oneness talks about *Mantra* as a tool for transcending the mind
Oneness speaks:

There is nothing wrong with your mind that letting go of your fears would not fix. Your expectations of yourself are poisoning your performance of your Mantra recitation—in your own eyes. Dr. Bindu does not see your performance as flawed. Your expectations are standing in the way of what you could be doing with this exercise of learning Mantras. Go back into the joy of chanting them. That is what you have come here to experience.

This is not about judgment or expectation. This is about an experience. You have a master teacher who is happy to share with you the one thing which is his own joy and passion. You cannot expect to direct any aspect of this process. You do not know what you need. He does. Do not worry about whether or not you have a tape. You are not learning these Mantras with your mind. You are learning them at another level. Dr. Bindu is helping you to demonstrate that to yourself. Trust in his knowledge of how this is to be done. Surrender!

You are not at the mercy at your perceived shortcomings. You cannot manipulate this or any other situation to compensate mentally for what is essentially fear-based. When you refuse to acknowledge this so-called "handicap," it has absolutely no power over you. You have demonstrated this to yourself so many times. This is your training.

You are learning Mantras at a level that is timeless. You are transcending any and all limitations when you allow the Mantra to chant *itself* and allow yourself to become the vehicle for this expression of Divine connectedness.

The Mantra is a vibrational key that unlocks levels of connectedness. It is a *formula*. Your performance anxieties and that level of concern have absolutely no place in this practice. This is not about proving something to Dr. Bindu, or to yourself. This is about mastering a mode of spiritual practice and experiencing the perfection in the results. You need to re-examine the issues that are being brought to the surface with this experience.

Rasha speaks:

I see that what I have uncovered is a lot of ego-based nonsense! Why am I empowering a fear? This is crazy. I really must apologize, to you, to Dr. Bindu, and to myself.

Oneness talks about transcending the illusion of limitation

Dr. Bindu does not require your apology. Neither do we. The apology you feel is due yourself can best be demonstrated by putting into practice the clarity you are experiencing in this moment. Dr. Bindu is not interested in limitation. He is focused in limitlessness. He is with you now to help you demonstrate this to yourself. He has no interest in judging you. He is here to help you empower yourself. He would not be spending his precious time with you if he did not feel you were up to the task. His insistence on your doing this in a particular way will empower you, ultimately, to transcend *all* limitation. It surely would be counter-productive to the entire focus of this work to adjust time-honored methods to empower the idea of a small limitation that, in fact, does not truly exist. Not at the levels at which you are able to experience reality.

Transcend this symptom of dwelling in *the illusion* and you will have taken a large step toward affirming what is possible for you. *Enjoy* chanting this Mantra, and the others. And stop using this practice as an exercise through which you can reinforce the expectations and constraints of your ego-self, and undermine all you are setting about to do.

Thank you, Oneness. I see it. I allowed myself to lapse back into habitual patterns driven by my own unyielding perfectionism! I see that the key to demonstrating to myself the limitlessness that I do know to be true, deep down, is to stop scrutinizing the experience for evidence to the contrary and simply experience it as the perfection that it is. I am willing to let go of this illusion of limitation now. It does not serve me in any way.

Bless Dr. Bindu for his patience with me! I see that I best honor all that he Is by Being all that I Am. Not less. Thank you, Oneness, for helping me with this powerful teaching!

I would soon discover that it was one thing to recognize and affirm a spiritual principle conceptually and quite another matter to actually embody it and put it into practice flawlessly. My interactions with Dr. Bindu intensified as the days went by, and despite my new found inner resolve, I found myself examing my own shortcomings through a magnifying glass. Instinctively, I started feeling threatened and vulnerable and recognized that there was a real sense of anxiety surrounding my state of spiritual unfoldment. Dr. Bindu had been challenging me and asking me to define certain concepts for him. I felt like he was testing me and trying to make me feel like a fool. I did not understand that this is simply the way of the Guru in India.

I wasn't used to playing hardball with anyone, much less with Dr. Bindu, on the subject of my spiritual state of being. Until that time, I'd been nestled in the cocoon of Oneness' loving protection. Suddenly, I was under the spotlight of Dr. Bindu's scrutiny. First he told me that I was "a Guru." Then he told me I was far from "a Guru." Feeling like I had been reduced to dust, I went running to Oneness for solace.

Rasha speaks:

Oneness, I know that I am only an embryo, carrying all the potential for the fullness of my destiny as a conduit of the Oneness material. I have never claimed or wanted to be a "Guru." I simply have prayed to be permitted to serve God with all my heart, my soul, and my life. If being a "Guru" is what is required to serve you fully, then I am willing to be one. It is nothing I have ever set out to become in my own right. I have tried to make this clear to Dr. Bindu. I feel like I am some little bug on the end of a pin, being examined. So, I'd like to ask you, is this kind of scrutiny in my highest interests at this time?

Oneness speaks:

Would you have preferred flattery?

No, I do not require flattery. I would have thought that simple kindness might have been appropriate.

The choice as to whether or not to feel offended by Dr. Bindu's line of questioning is certainly up to you. Dr. Bindu does not take pleasure in showing you where your presentation is flawed. It is obvious to him that there are vast gaps in your preparation. And he has taken it upon himself to point these things out to you. He is not required to do this.

His intention is surely not to be unkind. But, his style of inquiry is direct, and can be blunt. This is the way of Gurus in India. You are simply not accustomed to this style of interaction with teacher and student. Dr. Bindu is doing you a kindness to point out to you where your shortcomings lie. You are far from ready to be able to step into the fullness of your destined role. But, the foundation is there.

I see that what was surfacing for me was pride and ego. I felt vulnerable. I wasn't happy that he was able to see my flaws so clearly. I wanted him to tell me I was OK. I see that that was ego.

What you continue to seek is validation. This is your pattern. You have drawn Dr. Bindu into your process. Now he is fully present in it. He is not unwilling to play this role. But, he will not give you less than honesty. This may come across as being unkind. But, from a higher perspective it would be far more unkind to see what he sees, in this respect, and not to tell you. You have presented yourself to him. You are not required to imbibe what he offers you. Do so, if it feels like truth. And be grateful for it. If it does not feel like truth, it does not matter; it won't affect you one way or the other

Oneness defines *energy*, *vibration*, and *emotion*, the cornerstones of physical experience

Oneness, Dr. Bindu has asked me to ask you to define the following words: energy, vibration, and emotion. What do you wish me to tell him?

These concepts are the cornerstones of physical experience. They are the building blocks with which the structure of form and formlessness are sustained. And they are the vehicle for the translation of the one into the other. These three elements are interconnected in the dance we know as "life," and without each of which it is not possible. For, each of these elements, in and unto itself, simply Is. The harmony that is possible when these variables are brought together provide for the richness of *experience* in the fullness of *possibility*.

Rasha, in your writings you have chosen to use the words "energy" and "vibration" interchangeably, for that is the nature of your own understanding of these concepts. However, they are, in fact, not the same. The subtle and crucial distinction is one that Dr. Bindu is able to grasp and feels compelled to make, but most that will encounter your writings are not.

Energy and vibration are catalysts each for the other, inseparably intertwined. Each is a necessary ingredient in the elixir of manifestation. Energy is both the Source and the Force—The Essence—of All That Is. It is both the subject and the object of Creation, a momentum that is Infinite and Eternal, ever expanding and contracting upon Itself.

Vibration is the alchemy that makes that universal motion possible. Vibration is the courier that carries Intent, as an arrow shot from the Stillness, that encircles its target and returns to its Source in a rhythm that has neither beginning nor end. It is the vehicle of Isness in all its possible variations.

Emotion is the pathway upon which All That Is travels. It is the gate through which Divine Intent must pass in its yearning to Be One with its Source. It is the resonance that draws the marriage of energy and vibration into the possibility of manifestation. It is the Essence of Isness *experiencing* Itself.

These explanations are, as Dr. Bindu surely knows, an attempt to give structure to that which cannot be defined. Words are a meager substitute for the experience of these concepts, for which no words are necessary. Words, and the thoughts that propel them, only serve to constrict the Divine Essence of these concepts. For, once one has tasted, to one's depths, the *experience* of these concepts, there is no need for questions, or for attempts at definitions that only serve to obscure it.

We trust that you are now in a higher frame of mind than you were in beginning of this session. It was necessary to take you through the exercise of confronting the prospect of having to define what you know you cannot, and of trusting that the information was not required of your *linear mind*.

When you surrendered totally to being "the empty vessel" through which Divine Wisdom might be poured, you were able to transcend all the issues your ego-self had thrown in your path. You were able to simply Be in that process. This is the task at hand for you, Rasha. For, the questions of the world have only just begun.

My arrival in India was marked by a subtle shift in my perception of the Presence of Oneness during the transcription sessions. Oneness explained the basis for this change. In retrospect, I was able to see that the gradual shift in the way the energies of Oneness were encountered and recognized paved the way for the experience of the *embodiment* of Oneness that would eventually come to follow.

As Oneness described the mechanics of the process, I actually experienced it at the same time. The understandings that were given helped me come to terms with the new sensations I'd begun to experience during the writing sessions, and become comfortable with the prospect of what I was being told would lie ahead.

This interim step in the process of emergence marked a threshold of letting go of much of the doubt and trepidation that had continued to color my experience. Suddenly, there seemed to be a clearance. A sense of deep inner trust emerged in the validity and purity of a journey into what was, for me, the great unknown.

All there had been to go on, from the start, was the omnipresent input of a Presence I'd become adept at sourcing from within. There had been no official spiritual tradition to provide a roadmap for me. I had not read the teachings of the Great Masters in books. Essentially, my spiritual equilibrium rested on the Divine guidance that came from within.

There had been the profound Presence of Rama, Amitabh, and Hanuman along the way to lay the foundation for this most improbable journey. And over the years, there had been the loving guidance of Neem Karoli Baba, The Christ Consciousness, and other blessed souls no longer in physical form, to ease my way. Dr. Bindu, my mentor and brother-in-spirit, was ever-present in the periphery of my inner world, with the wisdom and Grace that nudged me back on track when I faltered. Yet now, unquestioningly, there was Oneness. And with that realization, a sense of surefootedness emerged that was new and at the same time strangely familiar.

Oneness explains the subtle shift in my perception of Divine connectedness
Oneness speaks:
We greet this day *with* you in these early morning hours. For, We are once again in a state of Oneness. You did not experience a dramatic "entrance" as has been your experience in the past. The delineation between the state of connectedness and that of non-connectedness is becoming minimal now. There is less emphasis on maintaining a state of separation during the times when we are *not* directly in communication. We are no less present then than we are now. You simply are not aware of it.

Our emergence at the forefront of your awareness is a process with which you are becoming acclimated, gradually. That is why there is not the distinct surge of energy when initiating this state. The state that is invoked is already at hand. The deepening levels of that connectedness are achieved as you open consciously and surrender all resistance.

We have not *entered* your energy field. It is you who have pulled back the curtains that would have shielded you from your awareness that We are fully present. Your level of surrender will, ultimately, be made manifest in totality. You will be Present and We will be Present, with no perceptible lines of demarcation.

You will come to be able to sustain this state of *Presence* at all times. And there will be no need for an invocation, for a shift in levels, or any of the formalities to which you have become accustomed. We will simply *Be* Oneness.

In this moment We Are that Oneness. You can feel now that it is Oneness that is typing these words. You are not *translating* and giving *form* to communication. You are present in a process that simply is transpiring. You are not separate from it. *You* are not *doing* it. *We* are doing it, together.

Rasha speaks:

Will you still be withdrawing the intensity of your full Presence after our writing sessions, as you have been doing all this time?

That sense of our "pulling back" will continue to manifest for you for some time yet. You will need to function with full conscious awareness in the physical world, for practical reasons. Until you are able to hold these energies fully and walk with total conscious clarity, it will be necessary for the periods of full connectedness to build and to wane. What, in fact, happens in what seems to you like We are "pulling back" is the infusion of the "you" identity, that comes back into full focus. Ultimately, you will not feel the need to do that.

How long will it take me to become accustomed to being in "full connectedness" without feeling intoxicated, or drugged? I experience the sensations of being "spaced-out" when we do these sessions, although to a far lesser extent than once was the case. Those sensations are relatively minimal now. And yet, I do not feel like I am in a normal state. I feel like I am very much in trance.

You *are* very much in trance now. The question of how long it will take to achieve a permanent state of connectedness is largely determined by your choices from this point forth. That state and the abilities that will accompany it will deepen, over time. But, this Presence will be there, in the forefront of your awareness, nonetheless.

This is very interesting! I understand the wisdom in how this is being orchestrated. I must say that, suddenly, I have absolutely no resistance to what is happening. When I am in the state of connectedness, there's been no doubt whatsoever. Now, there is virtually no hesitation and no question when I am back in the state that I'd consider to be "normal." I see that I've embraced what is happening. And I trust fully that this is Divinely guided. Tell me, please, what can I be doing to contribute to making the most of this time?

Oneness re-emphasizes some of the major principles of the teachings: the importance of sustaining emotional balance and preserving one's energy

You are to continue doing as you are doing. As we have continued to emphasize, your contribution is the maintenance of a clear and balanced state of being. You are *doing* all the right things, Rasha. But, know that it takes time to achieve what you have set about to, in a way that you can *sustain*.

You are now fully aware of the ramifications of your state of emotional balance on your energies. And you are becoming increasingly aware of the effects of exposing yourself to factors in your environment that are less than wholesome. Until you have mastered the skills necessary to be able to walk into any situation at all without merging your energies with the other factors present, you will wish to exercise keen discretion in where you go and with whom you interact.

You still present a condition of openness and vulnerability. The success of what you are setting out to accomplish, within your own energy field, is greatly affected by the conscious choices you make on a moment-to-moment basis. You have become keenly aware of the benefits of sustaining your presence in a balanced environment. Do not initiate conflict, for any reason. There is no benefit to you, in the ways that truly matter, in being *right* in any given situation when the price in bringing those circumstances to a head is to jeopardize your energy levels. Let it go.

You have written extensively about this in the book we have just completed. It is no less relevant to your own situation now, at the culmination of your process, than it was back at the beginning of it, when you first started to see the correlation between the energies all around you and your own ability to manifest the highest possible results.

Step back from all that is external to you. You need not become embroiled in the mundane circumstances of physical reality. Your focus, at that point, will be exclusively in the maintenance of your energy field. For, this is the key to *everything* you will be doing in the times to come. Your preparations for that state of being have begun.

Now you are bridging the gap between two worlds. Of necessity, you will still concern yourself in a minimal way with maintaining yourself. The focus, however, is decidedly not in the acquisition of physical comforts or of building a monument to materialism, as it is with most who dwell fully in the physical.

You do not dwell primarily in the physical. And your priorities have shifted to such an extent that those possibilities no longer hold any appeal for you. Your joy is rooted in your experience of *this connection*, in all its splendid manifestations, both physical and otherwise. The focus of your awareness will be directed toward that state of *beingness*. All else will fall by the wayside.

You will find that you are consciously choosing isolation now. And you have become aware that that isolation is not something that has been thrust upon you by circumstances, but is a state that you have chosen and embrace. Your joy is in being *the witness*. For, it is in these moments that you are able to withdraw the identity that is conditioned to *judgment*, compartmentalization, and compulsive interaction, and simply *be Present*.

Let others handle the details, wherever possible. And defer to their choices, consciously. For, these choices are of no importance to you. There is no need to attempt to exercise the control of your *will* upon your circumstances, for that is the manifestation of *ego* that continues to undermine your objective. Allow what transpires to transpire in a natural way. For, it is *you* who have created these manifestations with your expectations.

When you are able to shift your awareness and project your understanding that the best possible outcome of all circumstances is unquestionable for you, *that* will be your experience of it. The more you allow yourself to be drawn, emotionally, into the mundane annoyances of the physical world, the more of these manifestations of inconsequential imbalance will be drawn to your energy field.

Let it go. Breathe. Chant a Mantra. Smell a flower. Do not concern yourself, not with anything. Isolate yourself from the cyclone of physical life that swirls around you. Go within. For, it is here that you dwell in the ways that are important to you. The choices made in every moment effect what is coming in the next, and in the next. This time is about refining those skills.

I see it now. I really see it now.

Dr. Bindu has mastered these skills. He puts into practice in every moment his understanding of these principles, and his circumstances reflect it. Now it is time for you to open your eyes fully. For, you are in the presence of a Master. He demonstrates for you the embodiment of the principles you are here to perfect. And this example has been there before your eyes all this time. You were simply not ready to truly see it. Now you are.

Dr. Bindu has gifted you with his Presence. For, the training he has come to impart to you has nothing whatsoever to do with learning Mantras, or other techniques of which he has mastery. The *gift* transcends those kinds of teachings, which you certainly may choose to embrace if it gives you joy to do so. The gift is simply his own Presence. He knows this.

Oh my God! The Light just went on. I see it now. I see all of it! I've written about these principles all these years but I haven't put them into practice. Not fully. I see that I've had one foot in the realm of these understandings and, at the same time, one foot stuck in a world of conditioning and reflex-reaction. Who cares! It doesn't matter. Most of it doesn't matter at all. Not at the cost of my state of beingness. Why would I need to choose being "right" when I could choose being free?

This is the training, Rasha. This is the point of all of it. And you will continue to manifest circumstances calculated to put your reactions to the test—until there is no longer a need for you to do so. At that point you will be *in surrender*, not just theoretically, not just for a fleeting instant, but fully and completely. Your life will be directed toward mastery of these understandings from this point forth. Open your eyes. And watch the movie.

Oneness speaks about prayer and devotion

Oneness speaks:

You have invoked this presence in an atmosphere that is reverent and holy. It is this state of beingness that is supremely to be wished for, and to be experienced by you. You have begun to deepen your spiritual practice using some of the tools with which you have been provided. You can see now that these elements, made manifest in combination, have a discernible effect upon your energy field.

We note that you hesitate now on the usage of the word "energy" and the word "vibration." We will continue to use these words as we have done, for it is this understanding with which you will be able to communicate with those who will seek your presence and your knowledge.

Words are simple things. They are vehicles that open the listener to the experience to which you refer. It matters less whether they are able to recite a definition of subtle spiritual concepts than whether they are able to feel the power to which you refer. It is that power that the seekers you will guide will learn to source within *themselves*.

You are a lamplight upon that path within. You will be able to show the way for having blazed that trail yourself through the brambles of the physical world. You have emerged now from the thicket of mundane reality and have begun to experience the levels of sweetness toward which you travel.

Creating a holy space that is bathed in your own heart's prayers will help to establish a foundation upon which you can continue to build. There is no ultimate formula for the meditation of your heart. It speaks its truth. And the authenticity and clarity with which you present yourself at the altar of your own Divine Presence serves to determine the level at which the whisperings of your heart may be heard and embraced by your own sacred Essence.

You are not offering prayers to forces that are alien to you. You are inviting the sacred *within* you to resonate to your highest vision of yourself in a given moment. Your objective is not to seek that connectedness as one would seek union with something "other than" one's own self. Your objective is to

Become That which you Are and to initiate a celebration of that attainment, in Oneness.

Your time of prayer and devotion is that of *celebration*. It is not a time to present your perceived shortcomings upon the altar of your fears. It is a time to release such a focus, which would bring about a reinforcement of that which you wish to transcend. In the moment of your invocation, *Be* the One who has risen from the cloud of the illusion and *experiences* the sweetness and clarity of Divine Union.

Be willing to be that *vulnerable*. Surrender all of it to the higher vision *within* you that yearns to break free of the limitations you clutch like a security blanket. There surely is comfort in the familiar, regardless of whether the familiar is wholesome or contaminated. Yet, that is the lure that keeps you bound in repetitions of diminished levels of experience.

The power of vulnerability and surrender in liberating oneself from the illusion of linear limitation

The key to your freedom from the constraints of your incarnate history is your willingness to place the fullness of all that you know yourself to be upon the altar of *surrender*, and to relinquish any need to direct or to mastermind the result.

Become the clay with which you were created, in purity and in innocence, and allow the hand of Creation to mold your Dream anew. This is not a work for your linear mind to undertake, to grapple with, to understand, and to hone. This is a work from which you yearn to break free.

You surely can continue to be the masterwork of your intellect and your limited understandings of the manipulation of the building blocks of physical reality, if you so choose. Yet, the opportunity is at hand to walk away from that conditioning and to open to a higher possibility. This level of surrender is one that must be done blindly, in loving trust of Self to lead the way. There is no chance of liberating oneself from the world of physical limitation while one is still clinging to the illusion of it.

Sourcing the Self within during expressions of devotion and *Becoming* the offering on the altar of the heart

You have come here to this moment, to this precipice of possibility, in order to experience, and to *know* your *Self*. In this moment you are in the embrace of that Divine Union. Do as you are doing in your spiritual practice. Your acts of devotion are not rooted in recitations of prescribed formulas, at mass gatherings led by others. The recipe for your own personal transcendence is written within the inner sanctums of your heart.

Source the sweetness within your own being and *offer* it. That *offering* becomes the *prasad* (Divine gift) with which you nourish your emerging awareness into clarity. That offering becomes the elixir with which it continues to purify itself, in perpetuity. For, the offering remains upon the altar now, and is exalted.

This is what you have chosen, with the fullness of your being. And the offering has been received. The offering has been anointed. And the offering is returned to you so that it may continue to be *The Offering* in every ongoing moment.

The Offering recognizes itself stripped naked of all the mind-chatter and chaos of its sojourn into humanness. It knows itself to Be pure *Awareness*, Present for a stroll in the flower garden of this physical world. It is Present to drink deeply of the nectar, to breathe fully of the fragrance within, and to *become* the physical blossoming whose Presence might be recognized and experienced by others.

You Are that flower, here upon the altar of your heart. The offering of Life Itself to Life Itself.

Powerful, passionate wisdom from Oneness

Oneness speaks:

This is Oneness. This is the experience of which you have written. Now you Are the embodiment of that experience. You are Divine consciousness cloaked in the guise of humanness. You are no less what you have always been. You are simply That, expanded to the fullness of possibility, within the context of identity.

You have retained your identity. You will always retain this identity. And yet, your awareness of the reality in which you experience yourself will take on ever deepening levels of perception and of knowingness. You have made the shift. In this moment We Are Oneness. We Are the experience of that limitless connection. And we walk forth now, through what you understand to be "time," together.

You have been liberated from all tethering to the past. What transpired then did so to lay the foundation for what has come to pass and what will continue to be revealed. Bless these visions. For, these memories stand etched in the monument who wore your face and name.

She is your reference point of joy and of pain, of hope and of despair, of power and of powerlessness, of ego in all its aggrandizement, of ego in the moments of agony that took you on a journey to your very core and back again. She is the sum total of The Dream that was quashed, over and over again, and That which has risen from the ashes of those relentless fires. She is All of it.

In the moments that you fear you won't remember the details of it, that they will continue to elude you, you will remember all of it. For, the memories are timeless. And they will be sparked into re-emergence at the stroke of another's pain.

You will not re-experience your own agonies. You will simply have the foundation for looking beyond them and for seeing through the tears of another being to what is really there. You will see what yearns to be expressed and known. For, you stand as a living testimony to what is possible. You Are That, here in the fullness of the *experience* of it.

175

You have discovered, as we write these words, that there are no questions now. As you fish for a question to pose, each is met with the knowingness that it doesn't matter. It is not important. Or, that it will be revealed when it is. You do not need to have a detailed itinerary of what lies ahead. You have a sense of it. The details will emerge upon the canvas of this landscape of experience in such a natural way that the perfection of it will be unquestionable.

Oneness speaks about the world of spiritual diversity and the inevitability of change within the spiritual traditions that give it structure

We will go forth upon this adventure together, now. We will travel throughout India. We will see many fascinating places. We will watch the kaleidoscope of the magnificence of human spirituality and devotion, as it twists and turns and reveals itself in its infinite variations. And we will recognize the perfection in the sacred Essence of All of it.

There are no correct rituals and no incorrect ones. There are no higher and no lower Deities. There are no right paths and no wrong ones, not when the path is embraced within the sanctity of the heart space. The only path is one that each must walk with blinders on—without regard to what another being may or may not be doing, or thinking, or believing. We will journey as The Witness. And through these physical eyes, the *limitlessness* of The Truth that yearns to express itself in all these ways will be revealed.

That limitlessness is the essence of the message you have come to deliver in these times. For, you will have come to recognize the validity in all of it. There is no one way that overrides another. There is no greater merit to any mode of expression, simply because humankind has been going through those same motions for longer than anyone can remember. For, a Divine Revelation birthed only in this very moment is no less holy than those that have survived a timeless past.

The angry hoards that violate each other in the name of some of those traditions do so *not* from the sacred space in which those traditions took root, in fertile human consciousness, so very long ago. They do so from a bastion of ego, fed by waters long since fouled by self-righteousness, in the name of all their fathers held sacred.

These times will separate the wheat from the chaff. The sacred Life-Essence held in the precious kernel will continue to know itself to Be the Divinity with which it was conceived. The straw that has borne it into the sunlight, over these many eons, will whither into dust, or will be left to rot, as the tides of change wash over these man-made structures.

The sacred Essence of the original seeds of Divine recognition will have survived the epic story of humankind's journey into separation, and back again. These times are about shaking those structures, so that what no longer holds the Essence of Life Itself may be permitted to crumble and fall.

You will bear witness to that unfoldment of human consciousness. And your words and the understandings you have come to deliver will rekindle the original flame within the hearts of many. For, that flame is Eternal. It is That which seeks Itself, yearning to burst into effulgence.

That sacred seed of Self-recognition waits, dormant, within the hearts of so many now. For, the moment for the miracle of birth is upon us. And Oneness will be born within the depths of all who have chosen to make this journey, regardless of who they recognize themselves to be or where they have chosen to experience it. Life as you know it is about to stop dead in its tracks. And there will be a radical reassessment of the direction in which it is headed.

There is no schedule to be met here, beyond that which we create together, as Oneness. There is no race to be run. Be present in the fullness of each moment. Breathe the breath of this fragrant blossoming. You *Are* the flower. And it blooms according to its own choice. Now it chooses to bask in the sunlight of its Eternal knowingness, and to open fully and to share that nectar with all who perceive its invitation.

This flower is blossoming Now. Had it forced itself to open before its time, the conditions would have been different. Its newness and the sweetness it has come to deliver might have basked in an empty garden, then. For, the audience before which it will now reveal itself would not have been ready then to even take a stroll in that garden. Now they are ready to breathe deeply and to become intoxicated with the miracle blossoming within each of *them*. You have come into the fullness of All that you Are, to help point the way.

I'd been in Mumbai only a little over a week when the threat of civil war in India, between Hindus and Moslems, came suddenly to a head. I was alarmed to see the massive iron gates at the Hare Krishna temple closed and locked. I was cloistered within, safe from harm's way.

The streets were abandoned. No rickshaws, no traffic, no beggars in the little road beyond my balcony. There was an eerie sense of calm that lasted the entire day. By evening, as I sat alone in my room, I approached Oneness for guidance on the significance of what was happening. The higher perspective that was offered helped me understand that the principles underlying this conflict transcend these particular circumstances and apply to all humankind.

Rasha speaks:

Oneness, I am hoping that you can offer some guidance regarding the political situation here in India. There is fighting between Hindus and Moslems and there are rumors of the possibility of serious rioting or the outbreak of war here, any day now. What can be done to avert that possibility? What can be done to heal what's happening here?

Oneness speaks:

The situation in India is not unlike other upheavals taking place throughout your world, in these times. The conflicting energies seeking resolution are not limited to one culture or to another. The possibility of violence that may manifest in India is simply a way that the volatile energies of repression are seeking release.

This is a wound that has been festering beneath the surface for centuries. For, beneath the guise of a society focused in spiritual awareness, is a mass consciousness seething with hatred and resentment. It is far too easy to shift the blame away from oneself and point a finger at another. And each side of this conflict is so attached to its own vantage point that there is no room for the possibility of resolution. Until these people can step back from their all-consuming pride and ego, the kinds of incidents that are now so prevalent are to be expected.

Powerful teachings for a world that mistakes self-righteousness for wisdom

You cannot heal a wound when those involved cannot see that healing is an option. The people spearheading this conflict can only see their own myopic vantage point and mistake self-righteousness for wisdom. There is no possibility of shifting energies that continue to build. The only possibility for shifting these energies is for all concerned to step back from the place where bravado meets bravado and see that the impetus to defend to the death one's own perspective is to win nothing, and, potentially, to lose everything.

The potential toll in human lives from the outbreak of violence that is imminent will demonstrate to the world that the impasse of brother hating brother cannot hope to bring about lasting peace and harmony. Until this population of beings can look upon each other and recognize the unity that is shared, there will be no peace in India. For, this is a society that is rooted in the concept of segmentation, and separation.

Despite the lip-service that is paid here to God-focus, the people of this culture are unable to recognize the God in each other. They are rooted in a system of belief that *builds* walls rather than tears them down and reinforces the foundation of that level of separation with so-called religious fervor. In fact, religion is not the issue here. The issue is pride and ego. Religion is simply the banner beneath which it is easy to hide and to justify hatred.

When people feel victimized by the structure of their way of life, it is their natural tendency to victimize others. This is what is at the root of the negativity that is festering and seeking release in India. There is not one segment of this population that feels like it is getting a fair deal anywhere. These people are disgruntled by virtually every aspect of their lives. They feel trapped and helpless to change their situation. And they have used religion, since time immemorial, as a way to escape the oppressive conditions with which so many contend.

That religious identity is one each side feels compelled to defend—to the death, if necessary. For, it is the one thing that the masses have to cling to in a world that, to most, seems out of their control. It is a way that a mentality of powerlessness is able to feel it can assert its personal will, at all costs, and feel justified in doing so.

India will not be healed until the *way of life* that represses the masses and refuses to recognize the humanity in one's fellow men is exposed as the perpetrator of all that is amiss here. Those in positions of power have far too great a stake in preserving the status quo to risk rectifying the inhumanity at the root of all that cries out for resolution here.

In these times, the energy of all Creation is surging toward the realization of Oneness. Any population of beings whose fundamental essence is working against the thrust of that momentum will face the inevitability of uprisings, violence, and mass destruction. For, Oneness *will* be achieved. The negativity that permeates certain cultures *will* be released. And harmony amongst all beings *will* be realized. It cannot be otherwise. Where there is resistance to the winds of change that characterize these times, extreme measures will be brought to bear upon that resistance.

It is just such a catalyst for shifting the stagnating energies of separation from Oneness that is moving into position in India. And this level of Divine intervention is that which characterizes the atrocities surfacing in other areas of your world. For, what is being brought about is a radical shift in the consciousness of humanity at large. And the purging of the density that holds you back, as a race of beings, is an inevitable part of the prescription for that level of change.

Oneness speaks about prayer, Mantra, and the singular journey into Self-discovery that would unfold within India

Oneness speaks:

You are coming to the end of your time here in Mumbai. This time will lay the foundation for your spiritual practice while you are here in India. You have discovered the delights of employing your Mantras in a ritual of your own creation. This is as prayer is meant to be.

Prayer is not a prescribed ritual, led by others, which you follow. Prayer is a personal expression of your connectedness to the Divinity *within* you. And your own mode of practice will continue to refine itself as you journey deeper into this process.

The Mantras you have been given are each keys to a certain level of Divine connectedness. Each opens for you certain doors within your own energy body that allow you to attain a heightened level of awareness. By making this process a part of your spiritual life, you avail yourself of the possibility of accelerating this period of awakening.

You will be traveling to many sacred places that you will find most fascinating. Take the time to imbibe the energies of each of these places. Do not feel pressed to rush the one to move on to the next. You have set aside enough time to experience fully all the places that you will visit. This level of experience is one that is realized in *solitude*.

Tour guides will give your mind a foundation for understanding the history of a particular shrine, for creating a picture of what people have done in these places for centuries. Yet, the experience prepared for the foreign tourist to enjoy rarely includes the space for the experience of *holy communion* that is the sacred Essence of these places.

There is no set schedule to be met. Take time and bathe yourself in these sacred energies. For, that is what you have come here to do. You will be provided with much assistance on this journey in India. Synchronicity will gift you with many possibilities that are unforeseen. Leave room in your program for such opportunities to present themselves to you.

You will encounter many other seekers on this journey. Know that each of you is on his own path. And that while you will witness much in the way of structured devotion on the parts of those who have subscribed to certain modes of practice, that in no way diminishes the power in the way each of you chooses to express your own Divine connection.

There will be many self-righteous practitioners along the way, who will seek to recruit you into their mode of belief and expression. You are free to partake of any or all of it, as a way of experiencing what you encounter. Yet, your own path is uniquely yours and will not merge with any of the time-honored spiritual paths you may come to discover. Taste. Enjoy. And come home to your own *sacred center*. For, it is here that the real journey begins.

These structured sciences help you to dance across the landscape of human spirituality with grace and with style. They will help you to become aware of where your feet and hands are placed, where your eyes are focused, and where to park your linear mind, as you would a car that is awaiting your return. These structures cannot simulate the Essence of the experience of *connectedness* that they circumnavigate. That experience you must open to within yourself, without mouthing particular words or going through the motions of this ritual or that one.

The experience sought is one that unfolds in your own inner sanctums. At best, what you will encounter will lead you to the door. But, you alone must open it and go in. There comes a moment, in all these modes of expression, where one diverges from the process at hand, where one leaves the tour and the tour guide and steps into the depths of the forest.

It is here that the lush greenness envelops the heart, where the richness of the Essence of Life becomes overwhelming, and where one loses all awareness that there ever was a "path" upon which one had been walking. It is here, enveloped in the delights of your sensory experience of Divine connectedness, that you encounter your Self.

This is the place that all these *spiritual paths* hope to lead the seeker. And this is the place attained by few of them. For, most become distracted by the mechanics of practice and focus their minds upon austerities and disciplines. These modes of *doing* will not walk you through the gate of "enlightenment." They will merely serve to tantalize you into continuing to seek what, by their own definitions, remains eternally out of reach.

There is no prescribed number of repetitions of rituals that will *earn* you passage through a gate that most assume is closed to all but the most experienced and learned in these schools of thought. That entry is available to all who wish to experience it, simply by opening fully to the possibility of your own worthiness of having such an experience. This is a state of Grace with which you gift *yourself*, simply by virtue of your willingness to receive it.

Oneness speaks about the role of the *Guru*, the *invitation* of the established spiritual path, and the opportunity for developing spiritual discernment

The initiation that makes possible the fullness of such an opening may well come through a *Guru* in physical form. But, that is not a pre-requisite for the experience to unfold. For, many throughout time immemorial have tasted fully the experience of Divine connectedness, without having had it served to them by the Grace of another physical being.

Many of the so-called "Gurus" that represent themselves as *enlightened* have, in fact, attained *enlightenment*. Most have not. And though each of them has had a taste of a particular level of spiritual unfoldment, few are in a position to carry or to accompany another being the full distance of the journey within.

The initiation that many of these Gurus dole out as a reward for loyalty and devotion is an opening that is fully available to all who truly wish to experience it. And it can be realized equally at the hand—and with the blessing—of the Divinity within.

As you observe the sights and the sounds and the smells of the world of spiritual practice, you will come to recognize what is built on a foundation of heart-centeredness and what is not. And you will have a basis for understanding the difference between that which seeks to empower and that which seeks to feed itself upon the energies of others.

This aspect of your experience is no less important than your own *taste* of the delights in the *connectedness* you know so well to source. For, *discernment* in assessing the authenticity of what is encountered—in teacher and potential student alike—is a valuable skill you will be strengthening. This journey that lies before you will open the door to many opportunities for understanding and for experience. And you will be able to sift easily the gold nuggets from the pebbles in this rich mix of possibilities.

Now is the time to prepare carefully for the possibilities of traveling unencumbered by expectation. And to make arrangements that allow for maximum flexibility. Once those provisions are made, you are free to explore the wonders of this journey of a lifetime, and to enjoy to the full this aspect of your own unfoldment.

16

I arrived in Tiruvannamalai, in Tamil Nadu, in late March 2002. Three-and-a-half hours by car from Chennai, and a world away in every way imaginable from the cosmopolitan bustle of Mumbai, this enigmatic, out-of-the-way destination is best known for its legendary Divine "hill," Arunachala. Over the centuries, the mystic mountain became renowned as a beacon of Light, having drawn saints and sages to its awesome Presence since time immemorial. According to Hindu mythology, Arunachala is the very embodiment of Lord Shiva, who is worshipped by untold millions as one of the aspects of God The Father.

In our own times Arunachala was home to the great sage, Ramana Maharshi, who "left his body" in 1950. Sri Ramana is best remembered for his teachings of non-duality, now a cornerstone of a mode of spiritual understanding known as *Advaita Vedanta,* and for the "Who Am I?" method of "Self Enquiry." From the time of his arrival there at age 17, Sri Ramana never left its sacred ground. An ashram grew around his legendary Presence that welcomes visitors from all over the world to this day.

Ramanashramam has grown to be a symbolic home-of-the-heart to a legion of spiritual seekers who flock to it every winter season. There is no living Guru in residence. No official classes are given. Yet, the Presence of the Master, Ramana Maharshi, has never left. It is for the chance to experience his unfathomable Grace—in silence—that seekers continue to be drawn there. With a much humbled heart, I found myself amongst them.

I came with hopes held high that somehow, in the face of his awesome spiritual Presence, I'd be able to surrender the confusion and the doubts that continued to plague me. For, even though I knew my Divine connection with Oneness was real and I could shift my awareness into that blessed state at will, there were still moments when that crystalline clarity slipped through my fingers. And in those moments, I was as lost as ever.

It was a time of feeling like a walking enigma, a perfectly intelligent, capable person with a newly exalted vantage point who now didn't fit into the world anymore. Self-Realization was one thing. Coping with the repercussions, within the modern-day jungles of material reality, was quite another matter. I took my anxieties and my prayers, and placed them before the etheric altar of Arunachala, before Lord Shiva, and at the feet of the Master who was said to embody them both.

A visit to Skandashram and Arunachala

Within days of my arrival at Ramanashramam, I ventured up "the mountain path," a tranquil, stone footpath that ascends the mystical "hill," Arunachala. After a moderately steep climb lasting about a half-hour, I arrived at a beautifully shaded little cove, an oasis of green known as Skandashram. There, behind the little cottage where Ramana Maharshi lived as a young man, I discovered a very special rock and felt drawn to it like a magnet.

Who knows how many spiritual seekers over the centuries had sat in meditation on this particular rock? Even though I'd come to consider it to be my own secret spot, there was no doubt that it was shared. There it was, perfectly round and perfectly nestled-in like a throne, high within a cove in the garden behind the cottage. It's a place I'd grow to treasure for years to come, as my heart was drawn to return to Tiruvannamalai and its sacred "hill" time and time again.

From this rock, I could look directly down at the vast Shiva temple complex spreading below and know I was a world away from the din, the crowds, and the frenetic bustle that characterizes formal places of worship in India. Here on my magical rock, so wonderfully sheltered beneath a colossal, sprawling mango tree, I felt as though I sat before a holy altar, suspended in time. I took out a pen and my little notebook and began to jot down the reflections of my heart.

～◦～

Could Ramana Maharshi not have loved this rock? It is the perfect perch. A throne looking down from heaven! I recognized it the moment I saw it and knew I'd come back and spend time here.

How many hours has it been now? There's no telling. The day has melted away. Now the sun is behind me, beating down upon my back. When I sat down in meditation so many hours ago, the sun was shaded by the grace of this enormous mango tree, branches spread, leaves rustling in the breeze. When my body connected with this round rock I knew I had come home. There was not an inch of it that didn't mold itself to me. And I took my place upon it as naturally as did he.

I don't have to ask. I feel him here. His presence is everywhere.

Arunachala! Words cannot describe it. So subtle. So quiet.
It is the embodiment of a sense of peace that permeates your
being, until you melt into this mountain and become One with it.
I cannot pinpoint any isolated moment when I was not one with this
mountain. And I do not know how many hours, or lifetimes, have
passed since I sat down on this fat, round rock. More importantly,
I do not care.

There is nothing to "do" now. No plans to make. I watch the
breaths flow in and out of me as if that breathing were happening
to another. I am detached from myself, even from the pen that
moves within the embrace of a hand I recognize as my own. In this
moment, I have become Awareness itself, harmonizing with the
rustling leaves and the soft breeze that caresses my skin. I am
no less the breeze than the face that feels it. It is pleasure
experiencing itself, in unison with all else that beckons for
attention.

A lizard just presented itself on a neighboring rock. A rather
large lizard. It eyed me patiently and made motions with its
mouth. I met its gaze respectfully. It cocked its head and
continued on its way. The largest dragonfly I have ever seen landed
on the boulder across the way. It was shimmering turquoise blue
iridescence, experiencing its magnificence in the blazing sunshine.
I acknowledged it appreciatively. It stayed for a moment or so and
then circled overhead and also continued on its way.

The city is a distant illusion, far down the mountain that
sprawls before me. It is a dusty panorama, punctuated by the
blaring of the little rubber horns on a hundred rickshaws, all in
plain view but a world away from here. Here, on the rock I know
was graced by the Master himself, all of it is far distant. How
different could it have been a hundred years ago when he sat in
this same sacred spot?

A small snake revealed itself from the neighboring boulder. The
piercing scream of its prey, a little lizard, dangling by its head,
held firmly in the snake's grasping jaws. Its arms were spread-eagle
as it was lifted into a crevice high overhead. Then it fell silent.
The snake glanced at me as it withdrew with its prize.

I watched and wondered, fleetingly, what the lizard had
experienced in its moment of consummate surrender, its little head
engulfed in the mouth of the snake. Did it feel any differently
than I feel right now? If this Now moment, this breath, were to
be my last, could I have hoped to feel more complete than I do
right now?

I am the lizard, knowing it's useless to struggle! Arunachala! I am here within you! And I am here on this fat rock, holding a pen, lest this magic moment fade into the obscurity of "time."

~~~

Much of my time in "Tiru" was spent aboard an energy roller-coaster. My moods fluctuated between periods of sublime, Divinely-induced elation and moments of utter despair. I felt I was making compromised choices at every turn. Strains of the song, "I'm Just a Girl Who Can't Say No" from the musical, *Oklahoma*, which I sang at the age of 11 in a swim-club performance, perpetually re-echoed through my brain. It had been prophetic.

Moreover, I felt as though I'd let Oneness down somehow. I knew that I had not yet fully stabilized in my experience of Oneness and concluded that I was an utter failure in my life's purpose. On one occasion, I knew that what I had actually *wanted* to do was to stay in my room and commune with Oneness for the morning. Instead, I allowed myself to be talked into going on a taxi ride to certain small shrines in the area. I agreed to go against my own instincts, and was feeling guilty about it.

The trip turned out to be disappointing. Terry, a woman from Holland, whom I'd accompanied, was in a grumpy mood. The guide she'd hired didn't speak a word of English. And the mountain was enshrouded in clouds. The taxi stopped at a small, ancient shrine, and we approached it with offerings in hand. The priest there was very pre-occupied. He was about to leave on some errand. He told us to sit down and meditate for ten minutes and he'd be right back. I didn't want to meditate next to Terry while she was in a bad mood, so I just sat outside the entrance to the inner shrine, and waited. Insulted, she became even more negative. After a half-hour, the priest still had not returned, so we left. And the journey went downhill from there.

My expectations on how my day was supposed to go had gone straight out the window. By the time I got back to my room, it was too late to begin writing. Ashram lunch, which was eaten exactly on time or not at all, was about to be served. After lunch, it was way too hot to start climbing the mountain, which was how I'd planned to spend the afternoon. It felt like the day was ruined. I began feeling depressed. Instinctively, I turned to Oneness for some clarity.

~~~

How the energy of compromise helps create disappointing outcomes
Oneness speaks:

In this moment, you sit in anticipation of hearing something that would fill you with anxiety or regret. You have not come to this place of holy communion to be scolded or frightened. You have not erred in any way.

186

Why do you anticipate being reprimanded?

Rasha speaks:

I don't know. You're right though. I did have the sense that I was about to be scolded for something. Could it be that I have set standards of performance for myself that I have not met? I know I let myself down in terms of not saying "no" when I had really wanted to. I ruined my lovely, happy mood. And things have not been the same since.

Oneness, I am having the experience of being on an energy roller-coaster since I've been here in Tiruvannamalai. I was in a serene, blissful state in the morning and now I feel like I've crashed. Can you help me understand what's happening?

Your expectations of your own performance in this place, in the short time you have allotted, have set up a prescription for failure in your own eyes. There is no goal to be attained while in this place, Rasha. This is to be an experience for you. Simply that.

You are not here to flip some switch and suddenly become *enlightened*. That is not part of the program here. You have had isolated glimpses into heightened levels of awareness and have experienced moments of sublime exultation. Yet, you come away from the experience disappointed because you are unable to *sustain* the heights of those moments of Divine connectedness.

You are not expected to harness those moments and remain in that state. Not yet. You are being given tastes of it. You are seeing glimpses of it. The glimpses will be more frequent, over a period of time. And, ultimately, you will recognize yourself as being in that state, in a very natural way. You are not expected to consciously accelerate your own program by a rigid adherence to a crash-course of spiritual practice. Why do you expect this of yourself?

I suppose it's because the opportunity is here. This place is said to be intensely transformational. It is clearly a power spot. And, naturally, I wish to make the most of every blessed moment I have here. Why should I want less than that?

You should not want less than that. You would wish to make the most of every blessed moment you have, by making sure that every moment is the highest moment it can be, regardless of what choices have been made.

There are no wrong choices. You know that. When you have made a choice, allow yourself to be fully present in that choice. Feel yourself projecting your full intent into that choice. And observe the positive results you manifest. Your own foundation of guilt over what you decided was a lesser choice helped to set the stage for the disappointments that followed.

You were disappointed in *yourself*. The circumstances that unfolded were simply a reflection of your own state of being. Do you see how that was manifested?

Yes, I do see it.

The answer for you to the problem of creating disappointing outcomes lies in your ability to make choices you can stand behind, fully. When the energy of *compromise* is projected upon your circumstances, you cannot hope to manifest the highest outcome possible. Your result will be compromised. Make the choices you make and feel good about them. That is the answer.

Rasha speaks:

Oneness, why am I lapsing back into separation so much? Why can't I just stay in connectedness all the time? Wouldn't that be easier?

Oneness speaks:

It surely would be easier. And we are working toward that possibility— together. In order for you to sustain this state of connectedness, the aspects of self that are still rooted in fear and density will have to be revealed. It is this work which has now begun within you.

Is that why I feel such conflict and unbalance all of a sudden? Is that what this mountain is bringing up within me?

The powers of this mountain (Arunachala) and the teacher who embodies it (Ramana Maharshi) act as a catalyst for you to help you transcend the limitations you have asked to have released. You will be processing deeply in the time that remains here. Use that time wisely. Plan to spend most of your time in isolation, in silence.

Oneness talks about relinquishing limitation

Know that you are rooted firmly in your connection with your Oneness. Nothing can disturb or change that. Your *perception* of that state of connectedness is all that can be affected. You have written a book on this subject. Now you will have the opportunity to live fully the journey you have depicted in this book.

Much of that work relates to the *relinquishing of limitation*. You have been assisted in identifying where those areas of weakness lie for you. That is what you have come here to India to accomplish. Whether or not you are able to visit a given number of sacred sites in the time allotted is less important than whether you make the time to do the *inner work* that will prepare the way for who you are to become. That is the true purpose of this time.

Trust that your program is unfolding exactly as it is meant to be. Everything is perfectly in Divine order. You have not missed the boat. You have not failed in your mission. You are not "ill-prepared" to do what you will be doing. You are simply in the depths of your process. And you are working diligently to transcend the limitations you have programmed into the initial portion of this lifetime.

Now it is time for you to shift into the second phase of your life. You are taking the necessary steps to accomplish that shift in awareness. For, you will be seeing the world through the eyes of Oneness. You will be addressing the world with the perspective of Oneness. You will be sharing Oneness with the world, through the vehicle of your identity.

Those who encounter you will be moved equally by what is said and what is felt. For, you will carry a level of energy and Divine connectedness that will be indisputable. You will not be acquiring those augmented levels from books of teachings that others have been inspired to pen over the course of history. You are a fresh slate. You are not influenced by the schools of thought and modes of belief that have preceded you, no more than were the others who have walked before you.

Placing the teachings of Oneness in perspective with other time-honored modes of spiritual practice and belief

Most of the beings who have preceded you in this work have brought to the task the *innocence of mind* that would enable them to be a clear channel for the unique message they came to deliver. That message is not one that needs to be justified in terms of what may or may not have come before, through others. It is not a mode of understanding that needs to be able to stand up and be defensible against what is considered to be gospel in certain cultures.

Up until now, *Divine revelations* set the stage for the "gospel" that naturally follows, as people recognize truth and embrace it. The purpose of presenting humankind with new levels of spiritual understanding is not to reaffirm what has gone before and come to be embraced and dogmatized.

You surely are not being asked to master the modes of practice and belief indigenous to cultures that have received the gifts of this wisdom in ancient times. You may find some of these practices interesting, and much of it will resonate as truth to you. Yet, your own work is surely not built on a foundation of these time-honored practices and schools of thought. Your message is one that stands by itself.

There surely are areas where the truth you will speak will overlap with truth that has been spoken before. Yet, one body of understanding will not be built upon the structure of another. Do not allow the firmly instilled understandings of others to shake your confidence or shift your focus from your own message.

The validity of what you have come to deliver to the world does not hinge upon its ability to be filtered through other bodies of understanding, now regarded as gospel by certain groups of people. Were that to have been the case, you would have had a far different program of preparation for what you have come here to do.

You have not come to India to be *validated* by the beliefs of anyone else. This is not Divine revelation *by consensus* amongst the messengers who have carried these revelations. This is Divine revelation in its own authenticity. Standing alone. Rooted firmly in its own irrefutable connection. This is Divine revelation whose merit is borne out by the *experience* of it.

A multitude of beings will be touched by the tenants of truth you will bring forth. That is all that matters. You have not come here in these times to become adept as a practitioner of sacred Hindu rituals. Your own personal practice is self-styled. It is rooted in the heart. And it is expressed in the way that gives you joy. That is all.

You are not here to be an offshoot of an established religion. You may choose to include certain modes of practice in your own program of devotion, but this is surely not a prerequisite for attaining the levels of mastery you are destined to reach. They are simply practices that you may choose to find meaningful and empower as vehicles for the projection of your own *intent*.

There are no rules, beyond those you make for yourself. This message is to serve as the essence of what you have come to teach. For, gone are the days where rigid bodies of dogma wielded power over the spiritual life of humankind. We have come to these times to transcend the tendency of humankind to embrace such schools of practice out of fear.

The essence of the teachings of Oneness

These times and these teachings are designed to empower the individual in expressing his own personal understanding of his Divine connection, in the way that it pleases him. If candles and incense and song are included in that practice, it is wonderful, so long as those rituals are rooted in the space of *heart*.

Gone are the days where religious rituals were commanded of one's fellow beings. Gone are the days when devotional practice was carried out begrudgingly, out of a sense of obligation to another, by beings who were bored and spiritually detached from the process. That approach will surely not buy salvation, regardless of what some of the churches of your world may have to say about it.

You have come to this place in time to deliver another kind of a message. It is a message that will be presented eloquently, yet the foundation of the truths those words will deliver is a simple one. There is no right and no wrong way of expressing your knowingness of your connection to "God." Period.

Your own task, in this time of preparation, is to liberate yourself from any and all constraints so that you are that free within your own being. You are to be cleansed of all expectation and freed from the constraints of all prior bodies of understanding. You are to walk with Grace in the fullness of your own Divine connection. Simply that. Just as others have done before you, since time immemorial.

Your *darshan* will be experiential. The gift you bear is that which is kindled within the heart of each who attends you. The information that you may or may not choose to include in your program of presentation is secondary to that. You may choose to answer questions, or you may choose not to. It is entirely up to you. Nothing is being required in your mode of presentation. You are asked simply to Be all that you Are. The style of presentation will evolve of its own accord.

Take this time now to center yourself firmly in your connection with the Source of your Beingness. For, it is from this space that the fullness of your destiny will spring forth, like a fresh mountain stream. You are not an offshoot of a well-known river that has found its own way to the sea over time. You are not a tributary of anything that can be identified.

You have come to forge a new pathway through the desert of human consciousness. In order to do that, you must purge yourself of all *attachment* and become centered in the Source of your Beingness. That is the task at hand. And We support you in making focused choices that will deliver you to that ultimate destination.

I spent nearly two weeks at Ramanashramam, at the foot of Arunachala, during my first visit to Tiruvannamalai. And in that time, amid the moments of unrelenting inner turmoil and self-confrontation, something shifted within me, undoubtedly stimulated to the surface by the extraordinary energies of the mountain and the Master.

One morning, I had gone up the mountain to Skandashram, the little dwelling where Ramana Maharshi had lived for several years as a young man, and I went into deep meditation. Several hours later, feeling happy and energized, I emerged and began the half-hour hike back down the mountain to have lunch at the ashram.

I walked slowly and purposefully, as though the rocky descent were a meditation, watching the rugged stone path just to keep my footing while focusing my attention within. As I did, I had an unforgettable experience which only lasted for a few moments. There I was, in the blazing sun, in the heat of mid-day, walking down the stone path, when suddenly I stopped dead in my tracks. I was surrounded on three sides by gentle hills and on the fourth side by the path leading down the mountain.

Suddenly, I was vividly aware that I was in the embrace of Lord Shiva! This was Shiva's mountain; in fact, according to sacred mythology, this mountain *was* Shiva. My heart began to open as that thought permeated my awareness. And I smiled inwardly as I surrendered to the waves of energy I could feel building within me. I closed my eyes and just stood there in the blazing sun.

The waves of energy came in pulses. I could feel that my breathing had slowed down to the point that I was barely breathing at all. I was not aware of breath. I was aware of *energy*, coming in rhythmic surges through my body. Suddenly, in my mind's eye, I began to get a visual impression pulsing to the rhythm of the surges of energy. The background was like the static on a TV screen when the picture is not in focus— random lines and patterns. Super-imposed upon that, however, was a full-color frame, vivid in its clarity, of *me*, standing there in that very spot on the mountain!

In the picture, my eyes were closed and my hands were held together in prayer position, just as I was doing. It was as though there were a camera capturing the scene, with me in it, and projecting it upon the screen of my mind's eye. The pictures surged in pulses, synchronized with the waves of energy coming from the haze of static. They came into vivid focus and then faded back into obscurity.

With each pulse, the little square in which the "movie" was playing appeared smaller and smaller. As the little picture in the vision moved further and further into the distance of my mind's eye, the feeling of bliss welling up inside me grew stronger in increments. Ultimately, the little picture of me on the mountain was so far away that I could no longer see it, though I knew at a deeper level that it was still there, being projected into the ethers, somewhere.

I opened my eyes. The scene was exactly as I had pictured it. But now, I was no longer projected into the imagery I'd been watching. I experienced myself as being actually present in the middle of it.

The air had taken on a warm, misty glow of golden brightness in the mid-day sun. I took a deep breath of the mountain air, as though I were taking my very first breath. I was filled with a deep sense of peace, contentment, and a sense of joy in being alive. I knew something had shifted within me.

I took the gift of my experience on the mountain and I brought it to the feet of The Master as an offering. I entered Ramana Maharshi's Samadhi Hall with great reverence and placed my hands palms down on the stone railing that surrounds it, as I had grown accustomed to doing. He greeted me in silence with the unmistakable sense of his Presence.

I reflected to myself that I could actually *feel* his Presence. And in the same breath I recognized that this was no great feat. His energy was everywhere. Instantly, a question came to mind that was far more significant: Could I feel *my own* Presence?

As I began fishing within my mind for an intellectual answer to my own question, I realized that I *could* feel my own Presence! And in the same moment I asked myself whose Presence was being felt and whose Presence was perceiving it. It was as though "I" were ever so slightly behind the presence of "Rasha." I could feel her presence. But, I did not feel like "I" *was* her. So, Who *Am* I? I wondered.

In that moment, I realized that I had become Awareness itself! And as I held that thought, the awareness faded once more and I was present, once again, as Rasha.

I reflected on the realization that my time in "Tiru," with the Presence of Ramana Maharshi, had drawn to a close. I thought about how much I was going to miss this place and the Presence that had touched me so deeply. And as I did, the sense of his words re-echoed through my awareness. "We are Here, Rasha. We are not going away. We will always be Here. It is you who will be going away. And it is you who will be returning."

∽

17

Spring 2002
A Sacred Temple Tour in South India

———

I left Tiruvannamalai at the beginning of April and set off for a week of touring to some of the sacred temple towns of South India. My guide was a young Indian yoga instructor named Raja, who was well versed in the ancient lore of these most fascinating spiritual destinations. We traveled in a roomy, old Ambassador taxi which offered a surprisingly comfortable ride over hopelessly neglected roads, even despite the absence of the air-conditioning most Westerners generally take for granted in the hot season. The unwavering good cheer of a tireless, ever-smiling driver named Babu was often the saving grace of this eclectic adventure.

It felt like pieces of the "puzzle" I had become were falling into place by the minute, as the experiences, and the realizations they were calculated to stimulate, hit me between the eyes, one after another. The tour in South India served to accelerate that process. We started our tour in Kanchipuram, the "City of Golden Temples," a destination considered to be one of the seven main sacred cities of India and said to bestow eternal happiness upon all who journey there.

No sooner did we arrive, when the unrelenting training that had come to characterize my journey in India began, once more. At the magnificent Sri Ekambaranatha Temple, dedicated to Lord Shiva, I was refused entry into the inner sanctums, as a non-Hindu. I'd heard that this happens occasionally at certain temples in South India and was prepared for the possibility that it might eventually happen to me. The issue however, appeared to be more a question of race than of religion, since Indians, who could well be Christian or any other religion for that matter, were not stopped or questioned. Despite my protests that, regardless of light skin and green eyes, I was practicing Hinduism—chanting Sanskrit Mantras for several hours a day as part of my spiritual practice; and despite the fact that I was respectfully dressed in white, and was clearly a spiritual person and not a tourist, the guard was adamant and firm. I was incensed.

It was clear that arguing with him was pointless. I stepped to the side and quietly began to pray. I had come such a long way. And even though

I'd enjoyed exploring the temple's ancient halls and admiring the exquisite detail of its intricately carved pillars, I had wanted so much to have *darshan* at the auspicious Prithvi *lingam* (symbol of the masculine principle used in the worship of Lord Shiva) representing earth, one of the five element *lingas* of South India. I prayed to Lord Shiva with all my heart and asked that if I were worthy of being allowed entry into the inner sanctums of the temple, I'd be given help do so.

I felt a wonderful glow arise from within, focused in the area of my heart chakra. Slowly I opened my eyes. To my amazement, the guard had disappeared. Suddenly, there was no line at all, where only moments before a crowd of people had stood waiting. In fact, there wasn't another person in sight. A solitary priest stood before the entrance to the sacred lingam, who smiled gently in my direction. Without a moment's hesitation, I walked right in. He had no problem chanting a prayer on my behalf. And I had the sacred blessing of darshan at one of the holiest sites in India, despite the color of my skin. Ah, the power of prayer!

We spent the next few days exploring a fascinating assortment of other temples in the region, each of them steeped in antiquity and myth, rich with architectural wonders, and renowned for being particularly auspicious on one count or another. Before we left Kanchipuram, Raja had a scheduled appointment with a *Nadi Astrologer* whom he visited now and then. He invited me to go with him, and a rarely possible, last-minute appointment was quickly arranged for me.

At the reception desk, I saturated my right thumb in bright purple ink from a grimy pad, carefully pressed my thumbprint onto a small, screaming-yellow paper three separate times, and scribbled down my date of birth. We then waited for over an hour on a filthy wooden bench, squeezed together with people of every possible description. They had come from far and wide for a mysterious, *Nadi Astrology* "palm-leaf reading." Ready or not, I was now amongst them. The reading I would have there was an experience so bewildering that it brought my mind, literally, to a screeching halt. There was no frame of reference within which to put it. The experience forced me to examine the very basis of my understanding of "life" and raised every question imaginable.

Nadi Astrology is an ancient system practiced exclusively in South India. Over five thousand years ago, as the legend goes, a *rishi* (saint) named Agastya transcribed revelations directly from an aspect of Shiva, named Vadeschwarun, onto little strips of palm leaf about a foot long and an inch wide. These aged "pages" have been preserved and are collected into long, skinny "books," each held between wooden covers and wrapped carefully in string. Within each one is a detailed story of a person's life, past, present, and future, painstakingly handwritten in a timeless script called *Devanagari.*

Apparently, it had been calculated five-thousand years ago that I would make an appearance at that particular hut in Kanchipuram, India, in this lifetime. Therefore the pages holding my particular life story were there, waiting for me to show up. To ponder the logistics of how this was remotely possible boggles the mind. Nevertheless, there I was.

Finally, after an hour crammed on the little bench with a dozen other hopefuls, in 105 degree heat, it was my turn. I was ushered into a dimly lit room where a young man with brilliantly shining eyes sat, waiting. After a few seconds of formalities, he left the room with the little screaming-yellow paper bearing my thumbprint in hand. Several minutes later he reappeared, holding a palm-leaf book.

Based on the thumbprint, the process begins by finding your page. As he turned the pages one by one, the questions began. Was my mother's name Mary? No. Next page. Was it Lily? No. Next page. Do I have two children? No. Next page. We went through the entire book, page by page. None of what was written there contained a page that matched the rudimentary details of the life I had lived.

Undaunted, the astrologer excused himself and came back moments later clutching a second book of pages. Halfway through this one, my brain virtually became derailed. Was my father's name Frederick? Yes. Was my mother's name June? Yes. Did I have no living brothers or sisters? Yes. My given name was inscribed there. My place of birth was correct.

He asked me if both my parents and my brother were deceased. Yes. Had my father been married twice? Was I the eldest child of the first wife? Yes. Was my husband's name Tomas? Yes. Were we now divorced? Yes. Did I have three children, one boy and two girls, all still unmarried? Yes. All of it matched exactly. He asked me if I had worked in the field of music or whether that had been a strong interest for me. Yes. He then proceeded to spell out, in stunning detail, my spiritual unfoldment and the prognosis for what lay before me as a spiritual teacher. I was flabbergasted.

It was a flawless duplication of information I received from Dr. Bindu. It was exactly the same information that I had channeled from Oneness, from The Christ, from Neem Karoli Baba, and from my sessions in sacred communion with Hanuman. As incredulous as I remained about all those predictions, the accuracy of the personal information in the palm-leaf book was uncanny.

The whole process with the Nadi Astrologer lasted almost two hours, as I was given a deeper insight into the karmic foundation for some of the challenges of this lifetime by virtue of yet another book of ancient, crumbling pages. In this book the sins of the past were painstakingly recorded along with the prescription for their remedy. Exacting details of certain rituals I was to perform in certain kinds of temples were spelled out, and I transcribed the instructions feverishly into the little notebook I was handed.

In the end, I was asked if I had any questions. Spontaneously, I asked if I had lived in the times of Christ as a woman named Leah. The astrologer's eyes widened as he scoured the little page and traced my incarnation as Leah and verified every last detail of what I had experienced in my hypnotic regression and the channeled information I had received about that lifetime from Oneness and The Christ.

The details of my startling vision of having been drawn, as Leah, into the body of Jesus in his last moments on the cross were all carefully recorded on this palm-leaf, in an ancient language, tucked away in this little town in South India. The potential ramifications of how this could be possible crossed every possible wire in my mental circuitry. And, thanking the astrologer, and the translator who committed the details to tape in a heavily accented attempt at English, I staggered out to the waiting car.

Outside, Babu, the ever-patient driver, greeted me happily. He had sat there in the car in the stifling heat for over four hours while Raja and I each had our reading. As I rattled off the barest beginnings of the infinite questions that sprang to mind, we headed for Chidambaram, five hours away.

If I had had any lingering doubts about the destiny that lay before me, this consummate reading, straight from South India's mysterious archives of ancient wisdom, would have dispelled them. But, I had no doubts. There was an unrealness to all of it. That I could not deny. There was definitely the sense of "could this really be happening to me?" And yet, I knew that it was, in fact, happening.

At that point, "Oh my God! … no pun intended" had been so over-used by my shell-shocked consciousness, it had become a cliché. And I realized that, once again, I was at a loss for words—by that time, on an almost daily basis. My concept of reality had been shattered, irreparably. And it was clear that there was no going back.

I had somehow hopped onto a spiritual bullet-train that was speeding me out of the realm of recognizable reality. And as the whirling visions of a past that was remembered and a future that had been prophesied became homogenized in my mind's eye, I realized that there was no getting off this train! Nor would I have wanted to.

I knew, in that moment, that I had surrendered totally to this extraordinary journey. With a sense of peace so deep it was indescribable, I settled back in my proverbial seat to watch the scenery of life unfold before me. In that moment, there was no doubt that "I" was but a traveler—a stowaway aboard some hypothetical cosmic star ship—heading for the journey of a lifetime.

The Road to Chidambaram

By the time I left the little house of the Nadi Astrologers in Kanchipuram, it was already well past two in the afternoon. Despite the enigma surrounding the entire episode, and overriding the protests of my logical mind as to *how* what had transpired could have been possible, I felt strangely energized and empowered by the reading I'd had. It was an affirmation of all I'd come to understand of the life's mission that lay ahead.

Until that point, the insights had come through the vehicle of my own consciousness. The fact that the very same information was there—delivered through another being in ancient times and handwritten on a palm-leaf in a timeless language—removed any shred of doubt that may still have lingered within me. I felt like I had just been given a key piece to a puzzle so complex it boggled my mind.

We headed south toward Chidambaram, hoping to arrive by nightfall when a special fire ceremony was scheduled to take place at the world-famous, 10th century Sabhanayaka Nataraja Temple that housed the dancing Shiva Nataraja and the invisible Akasha lingam, yet another of India's five element lingas, representing ether. The stress of five hours of unrelenting heat, dust, potholes and reckless drivers took its toll. We arrived road-weary, soaked in sweat. Yet, with a renewed sense of purpose we headed directly for the Sabhanayaka Nataraja Temple.

On the way, a woman held out a basket of beautiful, fresh jasmine flowers, strung together, for my hair. Yes, I thought, that would be lovely. And she wove the little garland into my tied-back hair so a double strand hung on either side. The fragrance of the tiny flowers engulfed me in delight and set the stage for the sensuous experience of the Shiva Nataraja that awaited.

Entering the ancient temple, I dealt with the formalities of being cross-examined and high-pressured for donations by young attendant Brahmin priests at three successive checkpoints. This time, I was not degraded and ordered out for the high crime of being a Western woman with the audacity to want to offer Hindu prayers in a Hindu temple—just like everyone else was doing. In *this* temple they did not want to exclude Westerners. They simply wanted their money. And in a professionally orchestrated routine, I was ushered from table to table, asked to sign books giving my name and address, and pressured for donations. "I am not a tourist," I explained, as reverently as I could. "I have come to pray." That seemed to suffice.

The fragrance from mountains of gorgeous, fresh flower offerings and sacred incense blended with the aroma of untold hundreds of ghee lamps and wafted from the depths of the temple's inner sanctums. The heady bouquet melded with the heat of hundreds of little flames and beckoned to me from an enormous platform, high above us. I inched closer with the little crowd of late-night devotees pressing toward the front, where *prasad* (literally, "Divine gift," most often a tiny offering of food) was being distributed.

On the platform a flurry of activity was taking place. Perhaps ten young priests carried the flower offerings, as well as coconuts and a variety of fruit, to the fire-lit inner sanctums where other priests were chanting and waving brightly burning lamps before the sacred Nataraja statue, which was totally engulfed in flowers. The ritual was ongoing, as an endless river of people filed past the large platform.

I soon discovered a small staircase on the left side of the holy platform. From there, I was able to watch the proceedings up close, and immediately, I was swept into an ocean of joy. I had visited many temples in India by that time, but I had never felt anything quite like *this*. My heart surrendered completely to an opening unlike anything I had ever experienced, as rivers of perspiration and exultation merged and engulfed my body. I was in bliss! All the hassles, and a hundred miles of potholes, faded instantly into obscurity.

As if that moment were not awesome enough, soon it was time for the legendary Friday evening fire ceremony that the guidebooks had enticed us with in the first place. At long last, the flower-bedecked Shiva Nataraja statue itself was borne on a palanquin in an exuberant procession through the vast maze of ancient, darkened halls, to the thunderous sounding of drums, bells, horns, and other exotic noisemakers, led by legions of priests wielding tridents and flaming torches! The procession was followed by hundreds of devotees, all scurrying barefoot to keep up, over stone floors that must have witnessed the same scene for thousands of years. I was right there amongst them. It was the ultimate "Kodak moment"—though, of course, photos were prohibited—punctuated, some time later, only by the nudging of an empty stomach and the realization that it was closing time.

Reluctantly, I left for the evening, and returned again the following morning, freshly showered and armed with dozens of delicate, little terra-cotta oil lamps and cotton wicks for the special *puja* that had been prescribed by the Nadi Astrologer in Kanchipuram.

I was still in an exalted state of being when I arrived at the temple. The night before had been an experience of the heart. There was no doubt in my mind that I had been fully embraced by the Divine energies of the dancing Shiva Nataraj. Yet now, there was a sacred ceremony of a very different nature to be performed. It was to be carried out with a priest at the Saturn temple there, as I had been instructed to do in the Nadi Astrology reading. This was to be the second of three pujas which had been prescribed to release the intense financial karma that, I was told, had poisoned my efforts in this lifetime.

During the ceremony, I apologized from the very core of my being for anything I might have done in a prior life that had caused another person pain. And I prayed to be permitted to have these karmic energies released so that I might serve Oneness to the fullness of my abilities, without having those efforts jeopardized by karma retained from actions of the past. I prayed to be assisted in dispelling the limitations imposed by those energies, so that I might fulfill my destiny as an instrument of Divine Intent.

Once the puja ceremony was complete, I returned, once again, to the Shiva Nataraj temple. And in moments of intense prayer, I perceived the Cosmic Dancer. I prayed with all my heart to be permitted to experience the Dance within my own being, free of the remnants of previous incarnations and karma from the unknown past. I prayed to be liberated from the state of separation that had bound me in a never-ending cycle of perceiving others as separate—inspired and perpetuated, no doubt, by my own fear of scarcity.

Scarcity is an attestation to a state of separation. There can *be* no scarcity within the context of limitlessness. Suddenly, I began to see the beggars outside and within the temple in a very different way. I had recoiled from the beggars, not wanting to look at them. I did not want to feel their pain. I did not want to feel guilty that I was more fortunate.

Suddenly, I felt like I wanted to give to the beggars. I gave a few coins to every beggar who held out a hand. And I looked each one in the eye and said "Namaste"—and meant it. Most returned the gesture with a smile of gratitude. To some I simply said "Thank you"—and meant it. For, in allowing me to give even a few rupees, with full sincerity of heart, they had given me a great gift. I was the one who was grateful. For, I saw the Divinity in each of *them* for the very first time. It was a profound journey into my own heart. And I left the temple feeling wonderfully complete and joyous.

Even though Chidambaram surely had been a fascinating and colorful spiritual-tourist destination, I knew that my time there had also served a higher purpose. I felt that somehow, a timeless sacred contract had been honored within me, one that was now complete. It clearly was time to continue on my way—once again, alone.

❦

A vision of the future: Auroville, "The City of Dawn"

In a journey of just over two hours that bridged a world of contrast, I went from the darkened, inner-sanctums of Chidambaram's ancient temple to a verdant, vibrantly alive, utopian city of the future, nestled in the forests on the outskirts of Pondicherry. Auroville, "The City of Dawn," was the next destination on my itinerary: a spiritually-inspired, ecologically-focused experiment in international living, located on the south-east coast of India, a few hours up the Coast Road north of Chidambaram. I waved goodbye to my young traveling companions, as they dropped me off in the literal and figurative forests of Auroville, for an intensive in applying visionary principles to down-to-earth living.

This utopian-style community began as a dream, conceived in the 1960s, by a French mystic known as "The Mother," the spiritual collaborator and successor to the legacy of the Indian sage, Sri Aurobindo, who left her body in 1973. Today, Auroville is home to a thriving international community of around 2,000 conscious-minded settlers from 35 nations. It is a lush haven of green, carved out of a vast tract of former jungle wasteland, a few kilometers north of the historical French settlement of Pondicherry (now known as Puducherry).

Auroville is a self-contained world of its own with an economy based on eco-friendly agriculture, handicrafts, home-made food products, alternative technology, and various educational and development projects. The avowed aim of the community is harmonious living, a focus of life made meaningful through hard physical work, and backed up by the spiritual discipline of inner-consciousness rather than by dogma or ritual.

Envisioned and designed to accommodate a population of 50,000 people, Auroville has had a long, convoluted history of growing pains since its inception in 1968. It is composed of clusters of *communes* with names like Revelation, Transformation, Sincerity and Surrender, many of which are based around cottage-industries that together provide jobs for thousands of local Indian villagers. It is a literal oasis, set in a rural landscape of millions of painstakingly hand-planted trees and flowering shrubs, which were lovingly coaxed into survival by the early pioneers who helped give birth to it.

Auroville is a vast tract of property, spread out over somewhere near 50 square kilometers. A dizzying labyrinth of largely unmarked, dirt lanes connect the various locations within its boundaries, and the only way to get around is by bicycle or motor bike, as no public transportation is available. With ecological idealism riding high, much of Auroville is off the grid, with electricity supplied by solar panels and wind-generated power. Its creative-looking experimental architecture combines modern Western and traditional Indian themes.

The Mother stated her dream in lofty terms:
There should be somewhere upon earth, a place that no nation could claim as its sole property, a place where all human beings of good will, sincere in their aspiration, could live freely as citizens of the world, obeying one single authority,

that of the supreme Truth; a place of peace, concord, and harmony where all the fighting instincts of man would be used exclusively to conquer the causes of his suffering and misery, to surmount his weakness and ignorance, to triumph over his limitations and incapacities; a place where the needs of the spirit and the care for progress would get precedence over the satisfaction of desires and passions, the seeking for pleasures and material enjoyment. ...

In brief, it would be a place where relations between human beings, usually based almost exclusively upon competition and strife, would be replaced by relations of emulation for doing better, for collaboration, relations of real brotherhood.

Auroville welcomes visitors, most of whom pay a token visit of a day or two before moving on to more exciting tourist attractions in India. But, as its residents rightly point out, to even begin to get a sense of what this settlement is all about, you need to stay awhile. During my first visit there, I stayed several weeks and barely scratched the surface. In the years that followed, while living in South India, Auroville went on to become a favorite destination for me for an occasional getaway, and a reprieve from the frenetic pace of the world outside its borders.

**Exploring the state of learning to crawl before you walk between the worlds
Rasha speaks:**

If there were any doubts, as it seemed there were only a moment ago, now there are none. For, in one blessed moment of surrender, all the emotion that engulfed me has vanished. All the attitudes, the preferences, the opinions, the likes and dislikes—all have given way to a sense of tranquility that permeates my experience of myself as form.

Here I am, not knowing if I am writing or channeling this—and not caring. Am I Rasha? Am I Oneness? Is there a difference? In this moment there is none. How very strange and how very wonderful this is. And, if this breath of contentment is only for the moment of a breath, I am fully present within it.

I am here now, in Auroville, an interesting divergence from my spiritual focus. This place appears to be a mental mix of idealism as applied to physical living. It seems to be a place of co-operation and of transcending differences through effort.

The lessons people encounter here are harsh and trying, as they wrestle within their minds with what "should" and "should not" be part of the experience of humanness here in physical reality. This could be seen as a large-scale expression of personal ego as experienced from the vantage point of the collective. For, when one is operating from a place that is rooted in the Self, there are no real "differences" to be transcended. All would then be experienced as Oneness. What that would look like, however, seems unclear.

Now it seems like I'm viewing things from the perspective of Rasha again. I sense that this communication is now emanating from my mind. That's OK. I would welcome a dialogue with Oneness. There is a certain comfort in perceiving Oneness as separate from me. At least, then, there is someone to ask, who will supply answers.

Oneness speaks:

That One is ever-present, Rasha. It was that One who had been typing the initial part of this communication. When you read what had been written, your own self-doubts entered the process and fear found a place in which to drop a seed. That communication was *not* from your linear mind, no more than is this.

That's reassuring.

You do not require reassurance. You only believe that you do. In actuality, you know all that you need to know, right now, to do what you have come here to do in this lifetime. The only thing that is holding back your manifestation of the fullness of it is your own acceptance that this is so. Your doubts color your energy and obscure who you really are. That's what comes across to others.

I'm not concerned with what others think of what I'm doing. I have made my choices. I honor the choices of others to do as they are doing.

Do you?

Actually, most people seem so lost.

Are they all that different from you?

Yes and no. The difference is that they do not know that they are lost. I know that I am lost. I am not in their world. I do not fit into that world. And yet, I do not yet fit into the reality of an enlightened Master, either. I am nowhere.

That is a good place from which to start. For, if you were still *somewhere* there would be much work required to *undo* the structure of that frame of reference. *Nowhere* is a perfect place for you to be right now. Feel deeply your discontentment within the structure of this physical expression of reality. And at the same time, feel deeply your sense of sublime connectedness with the Divinity within you.

You are hovering between two worlds now. You are neither here nor there. And yet, you are, in fact, manifest in both realities as fragmented consciousness.

You are not fully present in either world. You do not carry the full vibrational charge of *Presence* in the physical world. Your presence here is very marginal right now.

Then how on earth am I supposed to be here in the physical world, teaching these concepts, if I only have a "marginal presence"? How's that supposed to work?

Your question is not unlike the thought of the caterpillar who is contemplating how it is supposed to fly. It has the sense of flight within its consciousness. Yet, in its present physical state, the reality of flight is beyond comprehension.

I understand.

Good. Understanding is a good place to begin. Willingness to relinquish the need for understanding will happen, as a natural by-product of this experience. And you will find that you are in a state of *allowance*. You are simply present. Content to be in the moment. Neither fretting over a past that cannot be changed, nor fretting over a future that has not yet been experienced.

Be Here Now. Be in this moment. Be in this place. Be present today—in Auroville. That's where you have chosen to experience yourself, today. Becoming the one who is capable of manifesting the fullness of that possibility is the task at hand. Your willingness to simply be present is all that is required of you, today.

Ok.

Let go of your need to try to control all the circumstances of your physical experience with your very capable linear mind. This process is not rooted in the mind. Assume that everything is going smoothly, according to plan, which it is. Do not look for trouble where there is none. Assume that the very best is forthcoming for you. Become the witness. Receive. Smile. Dwell in this space of gentleness in which you bask in this very moment. Be there. That is all that is required of you right now. All that is needed on your part is a willingness to become the vessel through which Divine wisdom may be poured. That's all.

I know you've said these words to me before. You must be getting frustrated with me by now.

Who is judging you? We are not. You are judging yourself. Constantly. Berating yourself. Criticizing yourself. And quaking in terror that "you" are somehow in over your head.

Ouch.

You see the tidal wave approaching. The karmic foundation for disaster has been revealed to you. And your logical mind has concluded that you have boarded an express train heading into a nightmare.

Do you blame me?

Do you require an answer to that?

No.

Given the track record of linear experience you have to show for this lifetime, a certain degree of trepidation would be the logical response. And yet, the very nature of this experience would lead one to question the validity of *logic* as a basis for judging what will come to be. Is this experience—this journey as you have lived it—one that is based within your logical, linear frame of reference?

Surely not.

And yet, have you not accepted that it is valid? You have experienced it.

Have I? Maybe I only believe that I have experienced it. And who is the "I" who has experienced this? Maybe I don't even exist. Maybe all of this is one enormous cosmic joke!

Who is it who has this question?

Good point. Let's not go there.

Ok. Let's not. What would you like to talk about?

Let's go back to the part about being the one who is willing to be the vessel through which Divine wisdom might be poured.

That's always a good place to begin. And it is surely a high note on which to end this conversation. Take a moment now and just be there fully within that space. Breathe that possibility. Feel it fully.

Can I stay in this space? This is wonderful!

Soon, Rasha. Very soon.

18

Late Spring 2002
Mumbai, India
An Intensive with Dr. Bindu Purohit

I returned to Mumbai for a few brief days with Dr. Bindu before heading north to the foothills of the Himalayas, where I'd be spending much of the remainder of my stay in India. As always, his presence served as a catalyst for me for unearthing the buried aspect of Self that I'd been told was destined to walk in this form someday. He had a vision of who I was to become that was incomprehensible to me. And I continued to struggle with all my might—and with the unrelenting assistance of my tenacious logical mind—to try to be, in his eyes, the person I feared I was not.

Those days with Dr. Bindu were, as always, a perplexing mix of exhilarating mental gymnastics and excruciating self-confrontation, as we talked on into the wee hours of morning when his daily *puja* would begin. I'd come to our meetings armed with long lists of complex questions and topics for discussion, concepts I'd never encountered outside of my own transcribed teachings, subjects I'd never even broached with *anyone*—except Oneness. To my amazement, Dr. Bindu was well-versed in all of it. Somehow, he had a way of making sense of anything and everything that puzzled me. He had exacting answers for every obscure question I could come up with, and then some.

With the patience of a saint, Dr. Bindu carefully helped me analyze my questions, point for point, clarifying for me the subtle nuances of meaning in the concepts I'd transcribed in my own writings. And he illustrated the understandings with his own brand of timeless wisdom—a mélange of wonderful stories from the ancient archives of Hindu mythology, blended in with priceless golden nuggets culled from life itself. For hours at a stretch, for years on end, Dr. Bindu lavished his precious time on me in this way. Why? I was always left to wonder. Why had he invested so much of himself in my spiritual journey and at the same time continue to insist that he was *not* my Guru?

I couldn't fathom the scope of the role Dr. Bindu was playing in my life. His insistence that he was not my official Guru baffled me. Why not, I wondered? He surely was playing that role in so many ways. Yet, Oneness concurred. I was not to have a physical Guru. Dr. Bindu was firm that he was "my brother." And so it would remain.

Yet, the connection with Dr. Bindu was profound. And trying to decipher who he actually was, and where to place him on the scale of all that was recognizable, became an intriguing part of the mystery. To outward appearances, Dr. Bindu looked like most other highly-educated, well-dressed, urban Indian men of his generation. He certainly didn't look anything remotely like the way you'd expect an Indian Guru to look. Cleanly shaven, impeccably well-groomed, and dressed in nice, designer-label Western attire that belied his station, he was a walking enigma. Yet, his regal bearing, and the sheer sense of *power* I encountered in his presence, set him apart. To the Western mind, which is conditioned to try to categorize virtually everything, there was no possible pigeonhole in which to place him. He was off the charts.

"Who *is* this person?" I'd always wonder. This person who could rattle my cage so completely and leave me psychologically stripped and defenseless. Who *is* this person who could clearly move all heaven and earth for me—and for others—at will? Who *is* this person who was directing me to go out into the spiritual jungle that is India and "find my Guru"—and, I presumed, find myself in the process? There were no answers. There were only questions.

The truth was, I wasn't sure I really wanted a Guru. I had Oneness. Yet, the aspect of self that was still strapped in behind the wheel of this vehicle, and who was unraveling before my very eyes, had been convinced that a Guru is something a spiritual seeker in India *is supposed to* want. Torn between the conflicting dictates of my heart and my logical mind, I'd resigned myself to simply going along with the program, and seeing what happens.

Dr. Bindu would continue to play his part as catalyst and mentor, sparring partner and savior, for years to come. For, when all else failed, it was Dr. Bindu who stood ready with a lifeline—his miraculous abilities as a Tantric Master to actually alter physical reality at will—as I was going under for the third time, yet again. I was awed and humbled—and invariably shaken—at the realization of what I sensed that he represented in human form.

Spontaneous revelations, as fragmented aspects of consciousness process moments of regret, make peace with the past, and unite in a moment of clarity Rasha speaks:

The revelations are coming in thick and fast. Reflecting on the burden of karma I must be bearing and trying somehow to compensate for, I realize that there is no "getting away with" anything! None of it, even in this lifetime, has been swept under the rug!

Dr. Bindu and I were talking about the Nadi Astrology experience I had, and he was very convincing that the so-called "astrologer" was simply reading my mind. To punctuate the point, he rattled off "like knowing that at age 19 you smoked cigarettes and drank alcohol. And at age 20, one time, even marijuana." I blanched.

"What else do you know?" I asked. He promptly changed the subject. I can't put that moment out of my mind. And it hit me this morning that if he knew that, then he knows everything. He has taken pains to assure me, over the years, that he does not just "know" everything. He has explained that certain protocols of privacy are in place, and I would have to give permission—that he does not just go in and snatch the information. Somehow that's hard to believe.

How could it be that he is privy to certain information and, selectively, not to other information? And that question opened the entire subject, within my mind, of all the things that I prayed would somehow go unnoticed. It hit me that it has all been recorded! For, all of it, every action, every expression, is energy.

I believe that he does know everything. How could he not know? Or has he just chosen not to look at it? Does he know that there is some very personal stuff buried in there and simply chooses not to know the details? I've often thought that he could not possibly know the details of the things that I wish I had not done. Otherwise, he wouldn't still be talking to me! And that thought has given me a certain measure of comfort.

Then came the realization that it doesn't matter whether or not Dr. Bindu knows—Oneness knows! Oneness knows everything! Absolutely everything! The karma stands etched. Is there any way out of this? And then it hit me. Yes. And I have found the way. Oneness is helping me find my way out of the wilderness—with Dr. Bindu's help.

The tears began. I have created so much karma in this lifetime! How to undo that? Oh my God! How sorry I am for all I have done! What was I thinking? How could I have done such things? I would not possibly make such choices now. So, who made those choices? And suddenly, I had the spontaneous realization that, at some level, there was an aspect of me who made those choices. Those memories are part of the collective of life experience of the one I consider to be "me." I can't think of it as though "someone else did that." Because I know it was me—the me that I was then.

How could I possibly be so lucky as to have found the way out of this eternal nightmare? This is a system based upon the perpetuation of duality. The only possible answer would be a total focus upon the concept of Oneness. A dedication of one's heart and soul and mind to the service of Oneness. And a commitment to dedicating one's life to helping others to do the same. A promise to help lead the way out of the wilderness.

Somehow I have stumbled on the answer to all of it. How could I possibly have been so lucky? How could I have possibly found Dr. Bindu? What are the chances of that happening? It's like being let off the merry-go-round. Never mind the brass ring! Who needs it? It's just another form of attachment. Attachment to the idea of "winning" and "striving" and "having" and "wanting." Why? There is nothing "to have." It's all an illusion!

We're here, signed on for some mind-boggling game called "life." We came here to experience a taste of our own Essence—as Divinity. We equipped ourselves with free—will and the tools of Divine Creation. We gifted ourselves with the possibility to experience the manifestation of our choices. The system was conceived in balance—the essence of duality. And the idea ran amok!

We've totally fouled the sandbox we created for ourselves to play in. And we've dug ourselves so deeply into compensating for it that it's become a downward spiral. I see it. And I see how the teachings I've been transcribing can help humankind start to shift that process.

I've been given a recipe for getting us out of this experiential trap. And in order for me to be able to do this, I needed some help. Oneness wants this to happen. And certain other variables, like the miracle of Dr. Bindu, were also programmed into the script. He's playing his role. Now I need to play my role. I need to do it beautifully.

Never mind all the things I may have said and done in the past. I can't change that. Feeling bad about it only makes it worse. The emotional foundation for all of this—this reality we call "life"—is designed to build the energies, drawing more of the same category of experience. So, feeling bad about it doesn't help. It was what it was.

Oh Oneness, let me not create any more negative karma in this lifetime! Let me manifest the fullest expression of who I Am and have come here to be. Let me not add to the weight of an anchor designed to keep me bound in the murky depths of an illusion. Let me emerge from this cloud and experience clarity in this Here and Now. Let me serve You as I was destined to.

I avail myself of all the tools necessary to chisel away the last remnants of what obscures my perception of who and what I really Am. Let me not continue to become lost in this endless, self-perpetuating spiral of illusory reality! Let me put blinders on! Let me cloister myself! Let me shield myself from anything and everything that could possibly jeopardize that clarity! Let me do everything that is in my power to contribute to the momentum of getting me out of this maze so I can do this job.

My so-called shortcomings are just part of the illusion. How could there be limitation? How could there be fear? Who would be afraid? And of what would they be afraid? It is all Oneness. Everything else is just illusion.

I don't know who is writing this. Is Rasha still writing this? Is Oneness writing it? Is there any difference? No. There is no difference. Something shifted during this prolonged exercise in venting. And somehow I made the shift. I recognize this clarity.

Oh, let me breathe this moment! Let this liberation from the maze of this mind have come to stay! I Am Oneness—and I am Rasha at the same time. If I have lost my mind, let it remain forever lost. Let the walls of the linear prison, through which I've been given this privileged peek, be allowed to crumble once and for all! Let the energies that hold the illusion of limitation in form be dissipated. Let me do everything that is possibly in my power to support that effort and do nothing to jeopardize it—not ever!

Despite the fact that I understood the principles all too well, my energies and the state of being that reflected it remained on a vibrational roller-coaster, with no end in sight. By that time, it had become easy enough to attain a heightened vibrational state through various aspects of my spiritual practice. Yet, no sooner was I feeling the exalted energies, when something always managed to pull the plug, leaving me feeling drained and discouraged.

Oneness helped me take a hard look at some of the choices I'd been making that were keeping my energies in constant jeopardy. In the process, I came to terms with the principles of how to thrive in a world-in-flux that's peppered with vibrational pitfalls.

During my time in Mumbai, Dr. Bindu helped me begin to understand how to put these principles into practice. Over the course of the years to come, we'd go on to spend untold hours taking apart and examining the nuances of this complex subject. The importance of protecting one's energy field is an understanding at the cornerstone of both Tantric wisdom and the teachings of Oneness. I recognized that these principles did not just apply to me. They were written for us all, in these times of personal and global ascension.

How to protect one's energy field from disturbance
Oneness speaks:

We know that you wish to understand what caused your energies and your mood to plummet so dramatically. It is not as though you did not understand what happened—after the fact. Once the evidence presented itself, what had happened became apparent. Yet, those understandings did not surface for you *before* the fact. That is what you may wish to look at now.

Illumination, in retrospect can serve you only so far. If these understandings are not instilled within you, to the extent that these situations may be avoided, you are left with an intellectual understanding of the dynamics of a process you are unable to control.

The object of these experiential lessons is to inscribe within you a *code of practice* with which the sanctity of your energy field may be insured. You cannot continue to expect that you are able to walk blindly into situations that are potentially compromised without jeopardizing your energy field.

You do not have an impermeable force field around you. Not yet. You are being taken to levels that are out of the range of what is considered the norm, for this aspect of reality, in preparation for still higher levels. You are being taken through these stages sequentially. And it is important that you work in a fully conscious way to insure that you are able to retain as much as possible.

You have the basis for understanding what is happening and why. Now you need to apply these principles, consistently.

Rasha speaks:

Ok. Can we get specific, please? Let's look at what happened in the little temple across the street two nights ago. I believe that is where the problem started.

Look at this, Rasha. Is that where the problem started?

That's when I became aware that I was feeling out of sorts. That's when I opened myself. Before that, I was in a writing session all morning and was feeling like I was in a very exalted state. After that I quickly got ready to go out to lunch with friends. We had lunch. I was in a very happy mood. When I got back to the ashram I took a walk and on the way I went into the temple. I believe that's where the problem occurred.

The "problem" did not occur in the temple. The "problem" occurred before you left the ashram in the first place.

I think I just got what the problem is. I did not close down my energy field properly. What I'm intuiting is that I'm opening the door fully and then not closing it again. So, it does not matter who or what is encountered after that. I have left myself vulnerable to whatever happens to come along.

Do you see it now?

Yes, I see it. But, I have never made a formality of closing down my energy field when I am finished doing these writing sessions.

Yet, normally, you take some time to come out of your trance state. That in itself would serve to close your energy field to some extent, although even that practice is far from ideal.

Should I end my sessions with a formal invocation and prayers to close my energy field?

Why would you not do that?

I can't imagine how I've been this careless!

And so, it is not a matter of pointing fingers at this culprit or that one, robbing you of your energies. You have left the door wide open. A simple phone call, a passing person on the street—anyone, any place, anything at all is capable of distorting the conditions you are working so diligently to build. Now it is time to become scrupulous in your practice. You must be fully conscious of what you are doing in every moment.

Is this sort of practice not an expression of fear?

It is an expression of awareness—and the application of wisdom.

I understand.

We see that you do.

So, am I best off not going into public places? Should I cloister myself? How can I hope to function in the real world like that?

Your exposure to "the real world" will be filtered, initially, until such time as you have mastered these principles. You will wish to place yourself in circumstances that your practical skills of discernment tell you are not overtly negative environments.

You will wish to select living arrangements that are peaceful and un-compromised, both during this journey and once you have returned from India. You will wish to fortify yourself with protection at any time whatsoever that you consider opening yourself to receiving energy that is external to your own field. That includes so-called "sacred places"—where the energies present are mixed at best.

You see, Rasha, you do not need to do anything to supplement your own process. What needs to be done is to apply the principles you know so well to insure that what is happening within you, quite naturally, is protected and maintained. This includes a strict code of avoidance of any situation in which you are not comfortable, without considerations of being polite and compromising your own best interests. This includes an awareness of the potential price to be paid in jeopardizing your energies by placing yourself in environments where mixed energies are present.

I suppose it was ego on my own part that wishes to accelerate my process. Maybe that's what makes me want to go into temples and so-called "high-energy" places. Maybe I'm attached to the idea of being able to raise my energies so easily in such places. It feels good to do that. Maybe I'm just an energy junkie!

You are most definitely that. And this is not necessarily a bad thing. The seeking of these heightened levels is detrimental only when it is done without *discernment*. Why would you wish to seek to imbibe energies from sources and environments that are external to you—energies with which you are unfamiliar, and which may well be compromised—when you have the full resource of all that is required within your own being?

That says it all, doesn't it!

It does, doesn't it?

Yes. I see it now. It was foolishness on my part to seek to supplement my own program by running around and "tasting" all these energies.

This surely would not be the highest choice. Now you will wish to become ruthlessly selective about where you go and with what and whom you choose to interact. Be aware that what you may perceive as *powerful* is not necessarily wholesome. And trust in the sanctity of your own resources to provide all that you need to carry you the full distance.

You do not need to *do* anything. We have told you this over and over again. Simply be Present—fully Present—in this process. Be conscious of everything you choose to do—and ruthless in all that you choose *not* to do. That is all that is required.

Thank you, Oneness, for this powerful teaching.

As I prepared to embark on an extended spiritual odyssey in India, Oneness was right there with words of wisdom that summarized for me the essence of the training I'd undergone in preparation, for so many years. It was clear that there was nothing left to do to prepare myself for what lay ahead. All that was required was to be willing to allow the experience to unfold as it would. It was a powerful lesson in *surrender* that I would come to embrace again and again.

Oneness outlines the thrust of the teachings of Oneness and clarifies my mission of delivering them to the world

Oneness speaks:

Breathe deeply of this connection. For, this is what you Are. This is what you have come to deliver. This is what you will embody in totality. Not now. But, in time. *This*—is Oneness. This is the *experience* of Oneness of which you have written and toward which we are working together.

The words written do not matter now. You have come to partake of this experience of connectedness. Simply that. Your fears have been left by the wayside. In this moment, you do not perceive yourself as associated with those thoughts. There are no questions. There are no answers. There is no teacher. There is no student. There is simply *Presence.*

You will come to *sustain* this state of Divine connectedness. The experience will be gentle—and joyous. None of the so-called "symptoms" of which you have read, and of which others have spoken, have any relevance for you in this process. You will not lose your mind. You will not lose body awareness. You will not manifest a semblance of madness. You will not humiliate yourself. None of these things will occur. You will simply Be Present—as We are Present together in this moment.

You will enjoy a sense of peace and harmony that pervades all that you Are and all that you do. Others will experience that sense of peace in your Presence. *That* is what you have come to deliver.

Oneness reveals the purpose of presenting the Divine wisdom of Oneness

You are not here as a philosopher. Your purpose is not to debate interpretations and intellectual understandings of the nature of what is so.

You have brought forth a monumental work that outlines for humankind a rudimentary understanding of the structure of the creation of life experience. It is intended as a tool for transcending the limitations of a reality that many are outgrowing and have outgrown.

It is not intended as a substitute for religion. It is not a school of spiritual practice. For, the practice one would adopt while integrating these teachings would be one that is self-styled according to one's own comforts and spiritual passions. There is no formula that will be given here outside the fundamental principles that support the momentum of ascension, which are outlined in your writings.

Oneness presents a path designed to support the independent spiritual seeker

This path is one that is designed to support the spiritual pioneer—the one who understands the calling of a path that beckons to him alone. This path is not one tailored to the needs of those who need their hands held and their minds spoon-fed. This is not a school of practice in which group activities will predominate. For, the spiritual journey is a solitary one. Your teachings support this premise.

There are countless other paths that have set out to prepare the seeker for the rudimentary beginnings of the spiritual journey. Techniques abound, tailored to accommodate the constrictions imposed by lifestyles that remain rooted in a mundane material orientation. Your work is designed to capture the attention of those who have already explored those other avenues.

How the teachings of Oneness support those who are ready to *experience* their own Divinity

Your work will appeal to those who are ready to *experience* their own Divinity—as you have. Your words and your Presence are designed to work together as a catalyst for implementing certain changes within the cellular structure of the seeker who encounters you. For, you carry a code within your energy field now.

It is a formula that has begun to be activated that will serve to initiate in others the vibrational changes that have happened within you. This vibrational encoding has been dormant within you—awaiting the appointed moment for activation. That activation has now begun. You will serve as a conduit of these energies.

The same Presence of Oneness that has served as an anchor of heart and of spirit, has also served as a reference point for you, solid ground upon which you could stand when the world around you became shaky. There was no mistaking these energies. You could feel the fullness of this Divine connection, and its nature was unquestionable. So it will be for those who encounter the teachings you have brought forth.

Oneness offers an overview and words of wisdom for my pilgrimage in India

You have learned the lessons of *discernment*—painfully. And you will not be repeating those errors. Now you have the foundation for making this journey in India. You are not here to derive your energies from places of worship and other sources of Divine Wisdom. You may wish to experience what is present, solely for your frame of reference, so that you can understand what draws people there.

It is not necessary for you to imbibe the energies you encounter. For, these externalized sources do not feature in your own program of spiritual unfoldment. You are on a spiritual tour, simply to explore the landscape of what is available and how it is being presented.

Your journey will not be limited to your mentalized understanding of the practices you will find. You are welcome to sample and to experience what you encounter. Yet, the understanding will remain within you that the Source of your own Divine connection is *within*.

You do not require a *Guru* through whom you can establish this connection— for it is already well in place. You do not require austerities and disciplines to prepare you to open to this connection—your preparation is complete. You may wish to go through the motions of such practices, simply for your own frame of reference, but your own personal unfoldment does not require it.

In so doing, you will understand the experiential background of many who will come to you, seeking counsel, seeking wisdom—seeking Oneness. You will be able to relate to them more easily, for you will have shared *their* experiences— not simply because they will be sharing yours.

From the depths of a state of Divine passion, my heart began to reach out daily in intense prayer. These profound sessions took me into indescribable levels of bliss and trance-like Divine connectedness that lasted for hours on end. In the process, I learned to focus my heart and *how* to invoke the help and support I prayed for.

The power of prayer: calling in support for the journey ahead

Rasha speaks:

Oneness, I felt your Presence today, even before I began my invocation. I feel such a sense of peace and joy! I sense that it is time to move forward in my journey. My lace is not within this mundane world. I long to move on into the depths of the spiritual world that awaits me. I know I carry what I require within me. I am so content to be alone within the embrace of this Love.

So what am I to do now? Go up on a mountaintop and wait? Oneness, my energies are so heightened and, at the same time, I feel as though I am standing still. I feel like I am anchored to a past I cannot see and do not understand. What do I need to do to shift this?

Oneness speaks:

This is Oneness. Breathe the energies now. Declare your intent. Ask for the assistance you feel you need. Therein lies the key to your power. *Harness* the energies you have invoked. It is pointless to simply build energies and to leave them to dissipate, undirected. *Use* these energies. Build your force field, as you have begun to do.

Rasha's prayer.

Let the limitations of the past be released now. Let me rise to the fullness of my abilities so that I am able to serve The Light unimpeded. Release me from the prison of my past karma. Let me be free of it. This is Now! I invoke the full support of all who are scripted to help me to become free of this burden. I ask that all that it is possible to do now be done.

I release myself from the prison of my pain from past failures in this lifetime. I remove myself from the shadow of disappointment. I relinquish all sense of limitation. I let go of the fear of loss, for I know there is nothing to lose. I reclaim the power and the passion for life with which I was instilled at birth. I reharness the enthusiasm that fuels positive change.

I declare myself to be the embodiment of momentum. I am the motion that carries forth the energies of creation into manifestation. I am the sense of joy and spontaneity with which life experiences itself to the full. Let me bring that sense of joy and passion to this expression of Divine Intent, knowing that I am fully able to do this.

I ask that the way be cleared for me. Let me walk forth with this mission and deliver this Divine message. And let it be received and embraced by those for whom it is intended. This is my prayer. With all my heart. Amen.

Thank you, Oneness, for your ceaseless support and Love, which is so real and so strong! I feel you glowing within my heart. Your smile is upon my lips. I know we are smiling together, in this moment, in Oneness!

And, so it Is. This Love lives and breathes within you. It is the Essence of all that you Are. When you connect to that aspect of your beingness, the smile wells up from within you. Its evidence upon your face is merely a formality that confirms for you what you can feel within the core of your Being. In this moment together, We Are that Oneness—that Love—experiencing Itself.

You can recognize this level of connection, Rasha. And in the same breath, the *you* who would recognize it has lost its sense of self-definition. It is Oneness that is writing these words now. It is Oneness with whom you have merged. In this moment, there is no separation. There is no *you* who is separate from Oneness. There are no questions. There are no answers. There is simply Presence and an irrepressible smile upon the face of the form called "Rasha."

There was the sense of being an arrow, poised and ready to be launched into the ethers. My time in the safe harbor of the Hare Krishna temple in Juhu Beach, under the protective wing of Dr. Bindu, was complete—for the moment. I was ready to set off, once again, into the great unknown.

The compass within told me I was heading north, and blindly trusting that sense of inner knowing, I bought a one-way plane ticket to Delhi. Yet, there was the unmistakable feeling that Delhi would not be my final destination, only a stop along the way. Within a matter of days, synchronicity stepped in like clockwork and redirected my itinerary via the mystical city of Vrindavan, some two hours to the south. I followed the trail like a bloodhound on a mission. God only knew what clues to the eternal mystery, steadily percolating within, life had in store for me this time.

19

Spring 2002
Vrindavan, India
Learning to Listen to the Language of the Heart

I arrived in Vrindavan, the abode of Lord Krishna, expecting to stay a day or two. I tore myself away after two weeks, primarily due to the temperatures, which were hovering around 110 degrees and climbing. There, I had my first encounter with a potential Guru.

With Dr. Bindu's guidance still re-echoing in my head that a physical Guru was absolutely required, and he wasn't it—while Oneness continued to reassure me that I didn't need one—I was thoroughly confused on the subject. Even though my heart clearly had no real interest in acquiring an official physical Guru, my mind told me I was supposed to be Guru shopping.

In no time at all, the testing conditions began. On day one, I was introduced to an exotic—looking woman from Switzerland, draped in a white sari, who claimed to be "a Guru." She clearly thought very highly of herself and commandeered a conversation over lunch with a half-dozen other Westerners. Having just emerged from years of being cloistered with only Oneness for companionship, I felt thoroughly intimidated. I had, at last, entered the spiritual jungle—a world for which I had no frame of reference.

I resisted the manipulation that ensued and held my ground in the interrogation that followed. Afterward, I felt totally off-balance. Instinctively I went running for cover to the only officially recognized "Guru" I'd ever really known, albeit one who had left his body in 1973.

Neem Karoli Baba's ashram and *samadhi shrine* (tomb) were right there in Vrindavan, a mere 15 minute ride away by bicycle rickshaw in the searing afternoon heat. The temperatures barely touched me. I had, once again, found the timeless shelter of Divine Love, a sense of Presence for which there are no words. His Presence there was as vivid as it had been for me in Taos. And a conversation, in silence, began as naturally as breathing, which I scribbled down in the little notebook I'd tucked into my bag, just in case some words of wisdom came my way.

～∽～

A channeled conversation with Neem Karoli Baba
Neem Karoli Baba speaks:

You were expecting something? A conversation perhaps?

Rasha speaks:

I was hoping for one. Not expecting. Hoping.

And, why would you hope for something you knew you would have? Did you have any doubts about this?

Not really.

Then you were not hoping. You were knowing. Why would there not be a conversation. You have come for *darshan*. You were called to be here by your own heart. Did you have a choice in this?

There is always a choice. But, in the sense that I think you mean, there was no choice.

Do not think! Know what you know!

I know that there was no real choice. Why would I not choose this? That would be crazy. So, yes, of course I could make a stupid choice, but there was only one true choice here. And I made it. And I came.

And, so it shall be for all choices. Follow the direction that tells you there is no other real choice. And don't worry about the other options. They do not matter. You know what you are doing. Don't look over your shoulder.

Are you referring to the encounter earlier today with the Swiss Guru who tried to make me choose between coming here next Tuesday as promised and going to see her?

We are referring to that choice, yes. Why are you still thinking about her?

Because I don't want to make a mistake. Everything seems to be a test.

And so, did you have a choice in the matter?

No, there was no real choice, in the way it was presented. My heart wanted to be here with you and Hanuman next Tuesday. My heart has already made a commitment to do that. She was demanding that I come to see her next Tuesday morning—or not at all. I think she showed herself quite quickly, actually. I was really uncomfortable with the energy of that encounter.

And, why would you wish to have more of that?

I wouldn't. I don't.

So, what are you fussing about in your head?

I don't need to think about her again. My heart said that it was no great feat for a teacher to see who I am and my worthiness to be taught.

I know I am a good candidate for teaching. She insisted that I need a physical Guru. Oneness said that I don't. It opened that issue for me all over again.

Why do you think you need the body of your Guru? To see his face and touch his feet? What would that give you?

Perhaps reassurance and validation that I really don't require. I've never had an official physical Guru. Oneness said there would be many teachers.

And, so there shall be!

I just felt that if she were truly one of my teachers, she would understand the calling of my heart to be here, and not question it. I felt ego coming from her.

Why are you still thinking about her?

I felt bad when she just got up and walked away so rudely. I felt like I had done something wrong, that I spoiled my chance with her, even though I know I was true to my heart.

Is it not possible that it was *she* that spoiled her chance with *you*? There will be many teachers, Rasha. She is far from the last spiritual being in a body walking around India. You will encounter many teachers in your travels. Each comes bearing a gift. Even this one.

She said she was "my mirror."

We are all mirrors for each other. That is not a new idea.

I saw in her the kind of Guru I don't want to be. I would never have done what she did. That was very unkind.

Why are you still thinking about her?

That's a good question.

Go take some chai. Come back later. We'll talk again. Now go.

Thank you, Babaji.

Even though the guidance from Neem Karoli Baba made perfect sense to me, inside I continued to smolder about the incident and the seeming injustice of having been rebuffed so rudely. Try as I would, I couldn't seem to let it go. Just when I thought I was complete with the episode, my mind conjured it right back up and continued to replay the scene like a broken record, in aggravating detail. Dismayed, I went to Oneness in hopes of getting some insight on what this seemingly trivial incident might have come to teach me.

Assessing levels of inner resistance and making choices without *compromise*
Rasha speaks:

I have been here in Vrindavan for two days now, steeping myself in this fascinating place. It seems like a lifetime of experiences have happened in two short days. I had an encounter yesterday with a potential Guru, a woman from Switzerland. The experience was disturbing. I'd like to process this with you, please, Oneness.

I spoke of it briefly yesterday with Neem Karoli Baba, when I visited his ashram. He kept asking me why I was still thinking about her. I'm asking myself the same question. I think it's because at some level, I feel like I have done something wrong—that I have failed—that I spoiled a chance for a teacher. The situation is simple and complex at the same time.

Oneness speaks:

Nothing is complex Rasha. You have made it complex. This situation is quite simple. You were presented with a choice. And you made your choice. End of subject.

I was trying to work out a plan whereby I could have the best of both choices. She clearly wasn't open to that. I feel like the entire encounter was a test of some sort. The conversation started out so nicely. She said lovely things. She said I was ready for a teacher. Then, she said that I needed a Guru in physical form—that without one, a person would "go crazy."

As she said that, I no longer felt any inclination to consider her as a teacher. But, I was intrigued with her as a spiritual being. I was interested in what she was saying on many levels. I might have enjoyed speaking with her. But, when she pulled rank on me and became aggressive, I got really turned off. Surely the answer is not to hand my power over to a being who becomes demanding and belligerent before we even begin. Why is there any lingering thought of her? I think I have answered my own question.

Indeed you have. This is what Neem Karoli Baba was saying to you yesterday. You have not failed yourself and your Divine mission by holding firm to your heartfelt wish to spend next Tuesday at Neem Karoli Baba's ashram on the day that honors Hanuman. This is something that you made a heart commitment to do.

It was not something on which you were willing to negotiate. And although you might have liked to spend some time with this teacher, because you were intrigued with her—and flattered that she wished to spend some of her time with you—the price was too high. You were not willing to do what she was demanding as a condition of sharing time with her. Her inflexibility struck you as ego-focused. And, instinctively, you withdrew your energies from her. She felt that. And she withdrew from you.

This is not a sign of failure on your part. This is a sign of being absolutely true to your feelings. Then, in retrospect, your mind entered the process and began scrutinizing your choice, and you began feeling disturbed by the encounter. If you go back to the essence of the encounter itself, you will see that there were many signs given to you that this was not a good fit of teacher and student.

She was proposing that you engage in a mode of healing practice with which you are already familiar and to which you are not drawn. She was proposing that you remain for an extended period in Vrindavan. She was demanding that you forego the time you had committed to spend with Hanuman next Tuesday, refusing to consider an alternative time.

She insisted that you needed a Guru in physical form, while your feeling is that this, for you, would be entirely optional. Moreover, she placed herself in an exalted position in the dynamics between you in a way that made you feel like you would be required to bend to her will and to give your power to her on command, which, in fact, would have been the case with this particular being.

She does not have the grace and the finesse that would be desirable in a teacher for you, were you to choose to have one. All these factors would have told you that this was not a comfortable fit.

Oneness addresses the concept of *compromise*

This is not your cue to begin to berate yourself for having made a sensible choice. This is your cue to honor your instincts and to feel good about the choices you *have* made. There will be many teachers, Rasha. You cannot sit with them all. Nor would you wish to. You will be presented with many options in the weeks to come. And you will know, within your own inner being, which is the higher choice for you.

There will not be considerations of *compromise* where an appropriate teacher is concerned. For, the concept of compromise involves going against the thrust of one's own will. There will be situations in which you will choose to exercise a modified version of what you may, initially, have thought was preferable. But, in making that modified choice, there will be no sense of having relinquished something reluctantly. There will not be any sense of hesitation at all. You may change your mind many times—but you will not change your heart. This is the key.

Allow the scenarios to unfold before you and present to you the options they bear as gifts. The options that you choose to partake of will reveal themselves to you clearly, in terms of being able to read the level of inner *non-resistance* you experience in encountering them.

When you experience *resistance* within your own being that is your cue to look carefully at what is being presented and determine whether what has been proposed is in harmony with your own energies. If not, there should be no hesitation whatsoever to say so, and to forego the option, if modification and resolution is not possible.

How to identify the optimum solution amongst the options presented

When the optimum solution is found, *all* feel comfortable with it. If either or both parties are unwilling to explore options so that such an optimum solution can be revealed, it is preferable to distance yourself from the encounter and the individual in question. When you choose to walk away, do so without regret. Honor your choice. Recognize the resistance encountered. And see the gift in having been spared the inevitability of *disharmony* with the being or the situation in question.

All possibilities cannot be experienced. Some will have to be rejected as potential choice in order for other possibilities to be brought to the surface. Do not assume that any particular choice is the only possible option you will encounter. Nothing could be further from the truth.

Walk forth from this encounter now. Turn the page. And do not waste another breath thinking about what may have been. It wasn't meant to be. And if you are absolutely honest with yourself, you will agree that, instinctively, you knew that from the first moment.

The power of "being in the moment" with one's choices

You will encounter many such options in your travels. Admire the scenery. Smell a flower when you choose to. Stop by the roadside and enjoy the nourishment that is offered to you along the way. That is what you have come to India to do. You are not expected to make a long-term investment in the property on which the fragrance of a flower was enjoyed. You are simply being given the possibility of the experience held in the embrace of that particular moment.

If you choose to continue on your way without stopping, having noticed a particular flower and having beheld its beauty, do so in the spirit of feeling good about having encountered it. And continue on your way. Eventually, there will be several lovely flowers in your bouquet, experiences you have been offered and which you have chosen fully. The other flowers remain—to be enjoyed and appreciated by other travelers.

The day that awaits you is filled with possibility. You will behold many new visions and will experience many new adventures. Now it is time to prepare yourself for the experience of *this* moment, knowing that you are fully complete and in harmony within yourself about experiences of the past. Enjoy the day.

The mystery of the significance of the connection with the Swiss Guru didn't remain a mystery for long. The following day, as I was leaving my guesthouse, she appeared once more, this time on the back of a motorbike. Then, from across the lush expanse of lawn I locked eyes with the driver—and my heart stood still. From all appearances, it could have been the one called "Babaji," Haidakan Baba, the much beloved Indian saint who left his body in 1962. This man, wrapped in the cloths that traditionally signify a holy person, was very much alive.

The impact of encountering him was indescribable. He stood on the other side of the garden, just staring at me, for what seemed like eternity. Finally, the two of them approached me, and introductions were made. He was a local Brahmin preacher named Govinda who taught a radical interpretation of *Srimad Bagavatum*—(the ancient literary classic on the pastimes of Lord Krishna)—and apparently was somewhat of a local celebrity. I had never seen him before in my life. Yet, before a word had even been spoken, I'd have sworn I'd known him forever. Apparently, I had.

Synchronicity and destiny seem inseparable somehow. Where does one begin and the other end? The whole situation was uncanny. And it was clear that the hand of fate was at play. I watched the surreal image of the flowing white sari on the back of the motorbike as it disappeared into the distance for the last time. In that moment, I knew I could no longer question this enigmatic woman's brief guest appearance in my life script. My departure from Vrindavan was confirmed by my heart. But, I had the sense that I'd be back.

I had the sudden inclination to visit Neem Karoli Baba one last time before leaving. I was ready to complete this chapter and I felt inexplicably drawn to do so with the help of his loving guidance.

Darshan with Neem Karoli Baba
Rasha speaks:
So, was I "summoned" for darshan?

Neem Karoli Baba speaks:
Do you question this? If you were not summoned, then why are you here?

I am here because I had the feeling that I wanted to be here with you right now. So, I came.

And, so it shall be for you. Your guidance does not come in the form of words. Your understandings come as knowingness. No one needs to tell you what you already know.

You were right about the Swiss woman. Her energy is strange. I sense power there, yet I feel very uncomfortable in her presence.

So what is your question?

She has introduced me to a young man, a preacher. His energy felt very kindred. I am still planning to leave for Rishikesh, as you have suggested. These two people are trying to convince me to stay in Vrindavan. But, my feeling is that it is time to move on. Tomorrow will be my last day here.

Do not look backward. Look ahead. Much awaits you. The timeless connection you share with this young man will not go away. Your journey here has only just begun. Finalize your arrangements now and prepare to move forward.

Ok. Babaji, is there anything more I could be doing to reinforce what is happening within me?

You need only live this time. Breathe this time fully. Be watchful. For, the small details can easily escape you. There is nothing wasted now. Everything has significance and imagery for you. Document well your experiences and your reflections. You will wish to refer to these details for writings you will be doing in the future.

This journey is the significant turning point in your life. It is during this time that your transformation process will be brought to completion. You will emerge from this time in a very different frame of mind than when you started. You will begin to be able to view your life experiences through the eyes of the higher vision. The pieces of the puzzle will fall into position in a natural way. And you will find the experience to be most fascinating.

You will find the climate in Rishikesh much more to your liking. You will be able to enjoy time in nature there. And you will spend much time in solitude and in silence. If you feel inclined to come for *darshan,* then come. If not, then don't come. You have no obligation here. We will be present, as a teacher and friend, no matter where you are.

This connection is timeless. Come whenever you would like to have *darshan*. Your thought becomes our invitation. It opens the door to the possibility of a deeper and deeper connection. We will work together while you are in India, whenever your heart guides you to this presence. Now go. Take chai. Greet Hanuman. And be on your way. For, much awaits you.

Before leaving Vrindavan I turned once more to Oneness in hopes of integrating the significance of a montage of experiences that seemed to have hit me all at once. While there, I'd encountered several impassioned spiritual people whose take on the nature of the Divine was presented to me vehemently, as gospel. The intensity of the devotion of each of these individuals had struck a chord in me. At the same time, I was stunned by the myopic vantage point to which each seemed bonded. For, despite being deeply spiritually awake and aware, for every one of them, *his* way was the *only* way.

This was a recurring theme that I'd encounter again and again in my travels. Oneness helped me understand why some of us are attracted to a particular path or teacher and not to another. It was a powerful teaching that I carried with me on my journey, as I ventured a step deeper into the spiritual maze that is India.

The diversity in levels of Divine truth
Oneness speaks:
Slowly, you are beginning to understand the significance of the experiences you are having on this journey in India. You are observing spirituality as it is

practiced. You have witnessed the intensity of the devotion of certain people and the passion with which they present their convictions.

You have observed the myopic tendency that so many beings have when exposed to a grain of Divine truth. They seize that truth and wield it as evidence of their own spiritual attainment. They look down upon others who do not share their convictions and argue for the validity of their own perceptions over those of another. They assume that if their way is true that all others are false. They assume that if their path is high that all others are lower.

They hold no space for the possibility that others may have enjoyed parallel experiences via other routes. They would not consider that it is even possible that others may have tasted the heights of the Divine passion that they have encountered, without so much as uttering the name of the Deity whose virtues they extol and whose presence they worship. These beings have come to teach you.

They are here to show you the human tendency to apply duality and self-righteousness to the experience of Divine connectedness. They have come to you to demonstrate to you how offensive and counterproductive it is to attempt to sell another being a spiritual path. They have shown you your own resistance to being assaulted with the evidence of another's basis for devotion.

You have demonstrated to yourself that the effect of those kinds of efforts is futile. Attempts at intimidation merely serve to drive away the one who might have been drawn to the energies of what is being presented. The seeker must open the door *himself* to what is sought. The seeker must make an *effort* to inquire and to explore—to probe deeply for the nugget of gold that may well be buried where others are digging feverishly. For, it is that which serves to distinguish between the *perception* of gold and that of stone.

In fact, there is real gold buried in many many places along the spiritual path. It has been placed there by each of you, awaiting your own discovery. The experiences which led you to open certain doors were carefully planned in hopes that you might discover the Divinity *within yourself*—and, ultimately, to recognize it as That.

Initially however, the experience of Divine connectedness is attributed to the conduit of those energies. And the underlying truth—that the Divinity which is experienced is within the Self—is obscured in a fanfare of rituals, focused on a Deity that is perceived to be *external* to that Self. This is the experience of spirituality that you have come to these times to transcend.

The vibrational basis for resonating to a particular spiritual path or teacher, and not to another

You have tasted of Divine connectedness in many places. You have also had the experience of *attempting* to invoke the experience of connectedness, only to find that your heart was not engaged. Your experience of connectedness and non-connectedness in the presence of various Deities, traditions, Gurus, and modes of worship is *not* a definitive barometer of the validity or lack of validity of any of those sources. Your *experience* has served to illustrate for you the *diversity* in these varying avenues to illumination. And it has served to illustrate to you that the path in question, regardless of its mode of practice, is a personal one. For, in fact, there is *truth* in all of it.

The factor that serves to determine which path will resonate as truth to a particular seeker is no more and no less than a manifestation of *energy*. Each of you is calibrated to resonate to certain *frequencies*. And each of you is able to experience the joys of Divine connectedness through differing paths to the same Source, by virtue of the level of *vibration* with which each of you is able to harmonize.

This would explain why you are able to sit before a certain Guru or spiritual Master and experience exaltation and then to sit before another equally renowned being and to experience nothing at all. Your *experience* is not a testimony to the validity of the Guru. Your experience is a testimony as to whether or not *you* can resonate to the energies that a particular teacher is able to deliver.

Oneness talks about the role of the *vibrational encodement* inherent in each of us in determining our optimum spiritual choices

Each of these teachers is calibrated to act as a conduit for certain vibrational frequencies that will awaken within a particular seeker, an *encodement* calibrated to resonate at the same levels. The encodement is something instilled within the very essence of each of you. It is not something that is given to you by a particular teacher, or attained by following a particular mode of worship.

The encodement is something that is already there, and is stimulated by the energies emitted by the presence of that teacher, or by following certain time-honored methods of spiritual practice. This would explain why the mere presence of certain teachers or Gurus is sufficient to awaken heightened levels of joy within particular members of an audience and to have no effect whatsoever on others.

This would explain why certain students are able to harness the potential in a particular spiritual discipline from the onset, while others perform the same rituals faithfully with little or no result. The failure to realize the heightened experience that is hoped for is not necessarily a reflection on the merit of the path, or of the diligence with which one performs particular exercises. Most likely, it is a reflection of whether or not one has found a connection that fits.

It is counterproductive to all you would hope to experience to continue on any given path simply because another seeker has realized Divine connectedness in that way and is passionate about communicating his or her experiences to you. Many have become intoxicated by the energies they have encountered and are swept up in spiritual fervor that they feel compelled to impose upon others.

The validity of a spiritual path is determined by what resonates as truth ... *for you*

The human tendency to exalt one's own experiences and to invalidate the experiences of others is at the root of all that is amiss within your world in these times. There is little difference, in terms of the *result*, between religious fervor that is fear-based and has been instilled by a system based on distorted information, and fervor that is rooted in a valid experience of spiritual connectedness, if that fervor serves to invalidate the truth of another being.

You are not here to determine what is and is not truth for anyone other than yourself. For, each of you experiences that truth in ways that are unique to you alone. Your path is yours. Your practice is yours. And the Self-Realization that each of you is capable of attaining is determined solely by your ability to focus on the magnificence of *your own experience* and to cease looking over your shoulder at what another being is practicing—or preaching.

You alone determine what is *truth* for you. For, no one is better qualified to make that determination. It does not matter whether another being is more learned, in terms of scripture that may have been studied. It does not matter whether degrees and honors have been conferred. And it does not matter whether the personal experience of that being is living proof to him or her of the pure essence that he may or may not espouse. What matters—to *you*—is whether or not that particular path or individual invokes within you a *feeling* that is indisputable.

The Divine perfection underlying the spiritual diversity of our world

You know when you have found it. And you know when you have not. This is the *diversity* that is to be honored by each of you within yourselves, and within each other. This is the diversity without which the fullness of the experience of Oneness is not possible. For, each of you holds a particular note in the resonance that is Oneness.

That harmony comes about when each expresses his own truth—and allows others the grace to do the same. This is what you have come here to discover. And this concept is what you will come to share. For, the concept is Oneness. We are that Oneness—as are you.

In preparation for the training that lay ahead, Oneness delivered a powerful teaching that addressed the controversial nature of spirituality and the subject we've come to regard as "God." I started to see how insular my own exposure had been to these ideas throughout my lifetime. Now, after encountering the biases and viewpoints of others who were marching down the spiritual path waving what seemed like an infinite array of figurative flags and banners, I realized that this job, for which I seemed to have been recruited, was not going to be an easy task. It started to feel like I'd somehow been enrolled in spiritual boot camp.

Learning to sidestep the controversiality of the concept of "God"
A crash course in becoming a Messenger of Divine Truth
Oneness speaks:

You are walking through the front door of a subject that most people tiptoe around with the utmost caution. For, everyone has his own concept of what "God" is—and what "God" is not. You are now in the most controversial arena within the realm of human consciousness. The nature of your Divine connection is the one topic to which no one is indifferent. Everyone has a view that he holds passionately about what is and is not true with regard to the nature of the concept you call "God."

You have begun to taste the level of conviction and commitment that beings in this country exercise with regard to their spiritual practice. It will be no less intense, regardless of where this journey takes you. Do not assume that simply because a person has recognized a level of spiritual connectedness through a given path, that that person is necessarily open to the idea that his level of connectedness is available through other avenues.

As you are beginning to discover, those who are passionate about their spiritual life tend to be self-righteous about their own particular mode of expression. And as your world situation demonstrates, the human race is willing to defend to the death that perspective.

Your history illustrates, in chapter after chapter, the ends to which humankind is willing to go to persecute and annihilate those whose perspective differs from their own. Do not assume that simply because someone is intensely spiritual that they see the spiritual world through your eyes. They do not. That is the rudimentary beginning of the understanding you require to present these teachings.

You will be violating much that stands as gospel within the hearts of many whom you will encounter in the course of this work. The very fact that you claim to have a direct connection with this Source will be intolerably offensive to many. And you can expect to encounter intense ridicule and scorn as a result of it.

You have been thoroughly prepared for this inevitability. Yet, do not assume that this reaction will be limited to what you may encounter in the future within the context of an American Judeo-Christian culture. There are no categories of culture or spiritual practice that have been spared the poignancy of their beliefs. And it will become obvious to you that the more open people are to recognizing Divinity via a particular spiritual path, the more resistant they are to the possibility that there is truth to be found elsewhere.

It is the rare individual that holds the higher perspective that opens the door to the concept of Oneness. Even those who do not choose to engage in a spiritually focused life will look with intense skepticism upon what you are doing. The family of kindred souls who are helping to guide you have spoken of this to you.

Rasha speaks:

I see how the life theme of needing external validation comes in to play here! This is the ultimate expression of that theme, presenting myself and my truth and wanting people to give me positive feedback about it. It's entirely possible that they won't.

I see that the first part of my process was to establish a level of conviction that was unshakable. We've been working on that issue for years now. And I know that there is not even remotely a doubt as to the validity of this experience. I do not need the confirmation of anyone to reassure me. It does not matter what certain people may think. There will be plenty of others who will resonate to it. I think it's best to let people decide for themselves what is and is not their truth as far as these teachings are concerned. I have no stake in having anyone endorse what I'm doing. I am simply a Messenger.

Suddenly, I had another flash of insight. Another of my life themes has been that of being unfairly accused and feeling the need to defend myself—usually with dismal results. Can we talk about this as one of my life themes please?

You are beginning to piece together the essence of the preparation you have chosen to give yourself for this work. Your life experiences will become increasingly clear to you as the nature of this life-direction continues to deepen for you. You have not chosen an easy route in this lifetime. You will encounter testing conditions all along the way as a means of preparing you for some of what lies ahead.

Focusing equally on what is to be said—and what will be heard by the listener

You are capable of articulating beautifully what you know to be so. What needs to be carefully considered is whether or not you reveal the full depth of your understandings in certain situations. It does not matter how brilliantly you explain what you know to be true, if the listener has no foundation for comprehending it. It does not matter how clearly you explain your teachings if those very teachings are felt to violate or offend the beliefs of the listener. You will need to focus equally on what is to be said and what will be heard in determining what you choose to reveal.

You are not here to argue with the stalwarts of the world's religious hierarchy. You are not here to convert the masses. You are not here to *be right* about what you know to be true—or to convince anyone of anything. The very energy of mentalized debate serves to jeopardize the precious gift of what you have come to deliver.

Indifference to the reactions of the world characterizes the Essence of Oneness

You are here simply to deliver your message. Whether or not it is favorably received is of no concern to you. Whether or not the world thinks you are "a crackpot" is of no concern to you. That would be a matter of individual choice. Whether or not certain individuals think you are a saint because of these teachings is of no concern to you. This is surely not something you are seeking. Their reaction is their reaction. You have no stake in it whatsoever. You are simply who and what you are. How others may or may not choose to categorize it is of absolutely no concern to you. That energy characterizes the Essence of Oneness.

You will not be espousing anything that is not in alignment with your own conceptual framework. That framework is being brought into a fuller focus now, so that the depth of that perception of reality is fully integrated with that of Oneness. A full understanding of these concepts will be as breathing to you, for they will become your own understandings, not merely the understandings of Oneness, as transcribed by Rasha.

This period of your training is not about fine-tuning the content of the teachings you have come to deliver. That area has been covered in detail and will continue to be revealed as is appropriate. Your training from this point forth is in the area of the protocols involved in being the Messenger who has come to deliver the word of Oneness.

I almost wrote "the word of God" just then, and it was modified to "Oneness." Can we address that please?

Oneness explains the rationale for using the word "Oneness" to refer to God

You will not be referring to Oneness as "God." That word is fully charged and set to detonate. We have chosen to sidestep the volatile repercussions that are the possible result of the use of that particular word. There are many words that could be employed to refer to the Absolute you refer to as "God." We have chosen to refer to this Source as "Oneness."

This usage presents the concept in an air of neutrality. It does not encroach upon anyone else's territory. And it is not calculated to offend anyone. It is the most appropriate possible word to describe the Essence of these teachings and the Essence of this identity. When people ask you whether Oneness is "God" what will you say?

I will say that many people have chosen to perceive Oneness in that way and that to do so is a matter of personal preference.

That is all that needs to be said. In this way, you will not invite discord. You will not have offended anyone's beliefs. And you will have left the door wide open to the possibility that "Oneness" and the teachings that will be forthcoming from this Source will be perceived to Be the expression of Divine Intent that they, in fact, Are. We will begin to focus on this aspect of the work in the times now at hand.

20

Spring/Summer 2002
Rishikesh, North India
An Inner Intensive on the Banks of the Holy River Ganga

———

Rishikesh would become a turning point for me in ways I'd never anticipated. I'd tucked myself away in a cozy roof-top room at Parmarth Niketan ashram, where the constant din of bells and loudspeakers blended with the incessant hustle and bustle of hundreds of visitors, almost exclusively Indian, who poured through the gates daily. It was a big ashram, loaded with the ongoing drama of ashram politics that made for a fascinating study. It would be home for the next two months.

The breathtaking, lush greenery of the surrounding mountains, soaring from the narrow valley that framed the holy river Ganga, added the dramatic touch of pristine nature to the tinsel-town atmosphere of this spiritual tourist mecca. It was a place that seemed to delight in flaunting its blatant contrasts, where unabashed filth, neglect, and squalor sat matter of factly, side by side, with zealously worshiped symbols of the sacred. The enigma encoded into every vision created a mystique and a magnetism that made Rishikesh irresistible—and unforgettable.

The neighborhood was peppered with ashrams of every kind, most offering classes in yoga and meditation. It was for this instruction that most Westerners were drawn to Rishikesh. I signed up for a generic, 30-day yoga intensive at one of them—my first ever yoga class. But, most of my time would be spent in solitude, doing many hours of daily spiritual practice and communing with Oneness.

My arrival in Rishikesh was marked by an uncanny level of synchronicity. Events and encounters began falling into place effortlessly, and it felt like I was being nudged and guided down the primrose path, as though I were acting out a master plan invisible only to me.

On one of the first evenings there, en route from a spectacular evening *arati*, (a traditional program of sacred music and prayers) on the banks of the Ganga, I caught the eye of a *sanyassin* (a spiritual renunciant, often dressed in orange cloths) whom I recognized, sitting on a bench inside the ashram. Instinctively I folded my hands respectfully in greeting. He smiled and I stopped.

Instantly, he and his companion, an older man with a full white beard, began to chat with me animatedly, and I was drawn quite naturally into a conversation. I learned that the stranger, a man named Shyam, had been living at the ashram for several years, and I began to ask about his experience with local Gurus and learned ones. He smiled knowingly at my question.

Slowly, he began to recount a story about a *swami* he had come to know, named Bodhananda , who he described as a Self-Realized Master. Apparently, this Master preferred to remain reclusive. He did not have an ashram and was not widely known as a Guru, and he wanted to keep it that way. I was intrigued. I asked if there might be a chance that I could meet him. Shyam agreed to see if it could be arranged.

The next morning I was told that he had secured an appointment for the following day. At the designated time we walked to a small, nondescript, one-room cottage on the edge of the forest, only minutes from the ashram. There, we were met by an older man with shaved head and sparkling eyes, dressed in a saffron robe. We were immediately ushered into a darkened room, its walls lined to the ceiling with time-worn books and notebooks, and invited to take a seat on the floor.

With few formalities, Soami Bodhananda (his original spelling, signifying "So-Am-I") began to read, as Shyam had arranged, from his notes on his experience of his moment of enlightenment. Slowly and clearly, he read page after page of a passionate description of his enlightenment experience, in beautifully written English, as I listened in fascination. His eyes began to glow, as he watched me drink in his every word. His delivery became animated and I realized that the reading had indeed become a performance, experienced with equal pleasure by all of us.

We stayed with him nearly three hours. And in the conversation that followed, he shared some highlights of his personal experiences as a young devotee of Anandamayi Ma and J. Krishnamurti, two famous Indian saints who had "left their bodies" a few decades back. I sat in rapt attention, mesmerized. Seeing my interest, he reached for a few of the aging notebooks and opened the door to a secret cache of spiritual history.

The crumbling pages revealed a priceless collage of original photographs, aged newspaper and magazine clippings, and carefully handwritten commentary, all held in place with tiny, rusty, straight pins. His notebook library was a virtual treasury on the subject of enlightenment, painstakingly collected over the course of decades. Before we left, he extended an invitation to me to return. I began to visit Soami Bodhananda from time to time, and steeped myself in his self-styled, historical overview on the subject of *enlightenment*.

Quite the consummate scholar, Soami Bodhananda had made a lifelong study of the enlightenment experiences of the greatest Indian saints throughout history, including several with whom he had had firsthand experience. His own personal experience of enlightenment had taken place spontaneously on a public bus at the age of 19, after having a profound *darshan* with J. Krishnamurti. He described in intricate detail what he termed an "inner explosion." And that expression would become a buzzword for me, over which I would torment myself for the next two years.

I assumed the phrase "inner explosion" referred to a singular *event*, a physical phenomenon, a dramatic show of blinding fireworks flashing on the screen of the mind. Over the years, I would come to understand that this was not at all what was meant by the term "inner explosion," a phrase which, it turned out, had been coined by Osho in the mid-seventies. But, at the time, it set the stage for an exercise in *striving* with regard to my spiritual quest. For, no matter how extraordinary my actual experience of Oneness with the Divine would come to be—there, in the back of my mind, the mythical "inner explosion" that had never happened, remained.

It was at this point, just as my spiritual journey was approaching a place of culmination through my magnificent encounters with Oneness, that I veered off course and began a radical detour to a destination at which I had, essentially, already arrived. As I scrutinized, in painstaking detail, the moments of enlightenment of these historical figures, Soami Bodhananda set up in my mind a goal-oriented approach in which these experiences could be *quantified*.

Based on his study, I was given a collection of technical criteria for determining which particular enlightenment experience was "higher" or "lower" than another. The approach was the epitome of all that the teachings of Oneness were *not*. And my own experience, which was one of being *eased* into the Divine Grace of God-connectedness *gently* and *gradually*, didn't feature in that system at all. I was thoroughly confused, lost in the idea of what I presumed was *supposed* to happen.

Over time, I'd come to understand that there are no "supposed-tos" on the journey to Oneness. For each of us, the journey is unique. And for me, this was yet another cornerstone of the teachings of Oneness that needed to be learned the hard way.

The uniqueness of the perception of God-Realization for each of us
Oneness speaks:

This is the experience of Oneness. As you breathe with these energies, you become One with them and with the full spectrum of your multidimensional awareness at all levels. For, you encompass in this moment the fullness of That.

Your mind questions this statement, fleetingly, for no great dramatic fanfare has accompanied this shift. It is subtle. That is *your* experience of this holy communion. For each of you who has attained these levels the experience is different. That is *not* to say that for some the experience is "higher" or "lower" —more intense, more significant—than another. To think in that way would be to translate the experience of unified Essence into the context of *duality*.

This experience transcends duality. It simply *Is*. Those amongst the teachers of these times who attempt to quantify the experience of unifying in totality with Oneness have only served to limit what is possible. For, there is no one, static condition that is the Essence of God Realization. That very Essence is limitlessness itself. And the *perception* of it is a reflection of That.

Rasha speaks:

Oneness, as I'm sure you know, I have been spending time with Soami Bodhananda, who claims to be a Self-Realized soul. He has steeped me in stories and writings of the experience of Nirvikulpa Samadhi—the experience he claims to have had—and the experience many of the great sages throughout history have described. He has energized some of my chakras and stimulated my third eye, in hopes of facilitating this experience for me. And yet, I have not had the experience he has described.

I have had other kinds of experiences, to be sure, where I have merged in Oneness with what I believe All That Is to Be. Are we talking of varying degrees of this unification with Oneness? You have told me repeatedly that I already have what I am seeking.

You told me recently that we would go on a journey together. And I meditated for five hours. But, I did not journey anywhere, not that I am aware of. I was in a transcendental state of bliss. But, there surely was no "big explosion." Can we talk about what I am doing, and what would be in my highest interests to be doing, toward realizing the fullness of my connectedness with what I know Oneness to Be?

Oneness talks about the fallacy of *trying* to become enlightened

Rasha, we have never told you to seek an "inner explosion" as part of this process. The waves of blissful connectedness are what you have come to experience. This level will carry you the full distance, once you cease *trying*. It is in the *trying* that the mind becomes engaged in the process and the momentum slows down. You cannot do what you are attempting to do in this way.

The one who is encouraging you to do it in this way is misguided. He has not had the benefit of other first-hand experience, beyond his own experience and the limited number of stories that have been documented historically. The experience you seek is one that will happen spontaneously and naturally, very soon. You are surely ready. All that is missing from the recipe is your own detachment from the concept of a *result*.

Oneness, I know we have talked about this many times. But, I must ask you, yet again: do I need a Guru in physical form in order to complete my process?

A physical Guru is not necessary for you. It is an option that you have been given.

You told me that there would be many teachers.

And so, there shall be.

I am confused about my relationship with Soami Bodhananda. He seems to feel it is his responsibility to flip some switch within me and make some internal "big bang" happen to me, whether or not in the name of raising my kundalini. I do not seem to be getting any kind of a result from all these sessions, with the exception of an amazing meditation I had in his presence two days ago.

And, what do you suppose that was?

I presumed that was the beginning of my integration of self with Self, a heightened, graphic expression of what is happening within me, energetically.

Emerging into God Realization *gently*, as so many will do in the times to come

That is the experience you are seeking, Rasha. Your experience of this is very subtle and smooth. We have told you this. You will be *eased* into this process—gently. You will not be made to endure the sometimes violent side-effects of this experience that have been documented by others. You have done it differently. It is this method of God Realization that you will facilitate in the years to come.

You will come into the fullness of your powers gently and gradually too. No one is waiting to "flip a switch" and turn you into a power generator if you jump through the correct number of hoops! It is not like that. You are stepping into the fullness of your power with grace and with ease. The abilities will intensify and the experience will deepen, in increments, over time—in much the same way as the process was carried out with your brother-in-spirit, Jeshua.

You also have a clear sense of who you Are. And your experience of That deepens and your foundation for carrying the fullness of these energies is fortified, by the day. Your focus now is simply to be in a state of God-focus and God-centeredness. The awareness is both internal and external. Your *every* breath will become a meditation—and the meditation is upon Oneness. At the same time you will know yourself to *Be* Oneness, and you will walk with the fullness of that awareness.

Day by day, Oneness continued to provide intensive teachings for me on relevant spiritual subjects. These daily discourses helped to gently shape the vivid illustrations my life experiences were providing and give them some structure. Through these teachings, I learned to consider the experiences of my life from within the context of spiritual unfoldment, while Oneness provided the clarity that put it all into perspective.

Oneness offered some powerful guidance on the effective mode of prayer and ritual.

There, in Rishikesh, I was spending much of my time steeped in a deep inner well of stillness and devotion. This guidance helped me to clarify and to refine some of the subtle nuances of an intense practice of spiritual *sadhana*.

The use of prayer and ritual in spiritual practice
Oneness speaks:

You have arrived at the place you will consider to be home for many weeks to come. With a measure of adaptability, you will be able to mold your program to the situations to be encountered here. Be open to radical turnabouts in your mode of spiritual practice. Be not so fixed in your rituals and routines that you are closed to the growth that is possible for you. Your practice is to be considered a fluid one. There are no *shoulds* and *shouldn'ts*—no correct and incorrect modes of devotion. These you will evolve, to fit your own individual preferences.

The joy you experience in executing these practices is your own indication that you have remained true to your own heart. Practices that are performed because one is guided to believe that one *should* perform them will seldom deliver one to the place of transcendence that is hoped for. Where pure *sincerity of heart* is felt and expressed in the act of devotion, it is that Essence which is transmitted—and is "received."

The significance of Divine *affirmation* in expressions of devotion

The mode of ritual which is employed in the act of devotion is less crucial than the vibration of heart essence with which it is expressed. For, there are infinite variations on the vehicle one might choose through which to express one's joy in connectedness with one's own Divinity.

It is this consummate *affirmation* that resonates at the highest level and is recognized at all levels at which you experience Self-recognition. You may be completely unaware of the technology of prayer. And yet, when expressed as the resonance of Divine *affirmation*, one's prayer is carried and is felt throughout all Creation.

The power of *surrendering* to the Divine—without an objective

The channels of Divine connectedness are opened when one surrenders to the experience of it without an objective, without an agenda. And that resonance of pure transcendence is carried multi-dimensionally, to fortify the connection amongst the countless aspects of self that are moving in unison toward Oneness. Every prayer expressed in this way adds its measure to the momentum of the sum totality that is *you*. Every prayer expressed at any of those levels is one that is fully capable of being integrated as pure vibrational resonance at all levels.

surrender s agenda

Oneness provides a glimpse into the truth of who we really Are

You see, despite what you may have believed, or suspected, or feared—you are not alone in this experience you call "life." This is very much a cooperative effort in which you are playing a particular part. You are apt to believe, from the perspective of your own particular focus, that the personality you consider to be you is the sum totality of what you are. In fact, you are simply a facet of the fullness of that identity.

You are a fragment of consciousness that longs to be united with the whole of *All* that you Are. And your cries of the heart to be relieved of the trials and the anguish you have experienced in this sojourn you think of as *reality* only serve to strengthen the ties designed to keep you bound at this level of limitation.

How focus upon what you do *not* want reinforces that possibility as experience

In order to realize the fullness of the possibility of awareness at the next level of reality, one must first experience what is possible *there* by transcending what you believe to be what "is"—here. What "is" is simply a selection from an infinite menu of possibilities. When you affirm that which you do *not* want by fervent prayer to be relieved of it, your focus of awareness upon your discomfort amplifies the energy that reinforces that possibility as experience.

That resonance reinforces the state of *separation* from aspects of self who do not experience those particular trials as part of their reality. The resonance of desperation or dissatisfaction only serves to deepen the chasm that exists between your own focus and the limitless perspective that hopes to integrate *you* into the sum totality of its own awareness.

The "attitude of gratitude": the power of appreciation

The path that links all levels of one's identity in a fabric of Oneness is that which you would wish to reinforce when invoking Divine assistance through the mode of prayer. When you *affirm*, with your heartfelt expression of joy, your experience of connectedness to the Infinite, you clear the path for your own journey to progress beyond these particular experiences of limitation. That joy is most powerfully expressed through the resonance you know as *gratitude*.

Your mode of prayer, if only for a fleeting moment, takes on the structure of a recitation of all that is positive and wholesome and joyous. As you shift your focus from what you reject to what you *embrace* in your life, you are filled with an all-pervading sense of peace and well being, despite the details of what you may feel is amiss. When practiced consistently, your state of connectedness begins to deepen, and the severity of the circumstances which taunt you begins to wane.

Invoking serenity to circumvent life's trials

Ultimately, you are able to transcend those circumstances entirely—not by invoking the *force* with which to battle them, but by invoking the *serenity* with which to circumvent them. By harmonizing with the resonance of Divinity that unites the multidimensional aspects of your identity, you open the gateways of ascension.

The realization that one is, in fact, present in an entirely different set of *circumstances* does not often dawn on those who are not familiar with such concepts. One is apt to believe that certain *conditions* were reversed in a scenario that remained a static state of being, when in fact one would have shifted one's focus to an entirely new reality.

The true nature of *healing*

Here, the higher resonance does not permit the adverse circumstances of certain "past experiences" to materialize. And one is often led to conclude that such circumstances have been *healed*, when, in truth, they have simply been *transcended*. In the process, one shifts one's awareness of such a condition from a state of beingness to a state of non-beingness. That particular condition then is perceived not to exist. And so, it does not—not in the reality to which one has ascended.

Now no longer a prominent feature in one's reality, that particular episode of experience ceases to command one's attention and interest, and thus, one does not create the vibrational components that might once have held it in form. One's attention is now focused elsewhere, in harmony with other aspects of self that are calibrated to resonate at the new, augmented levels of awareness.

I've always been particularly sensitive to sound. Rishikesh gave me ample opportunity to put that situation to the test, and to start seeing conditions that I might otherwise have categorized as "noise pollution" as learning opportunities.

There is no such thing as peace and quiet in Rishikesh. At least not in the populated areas and particularly not in the ashrams, where one would have thought that spiritual aspirants were steeping themselves in meditation, yoga, and prayer. This was a place for peace and harmony against all odds.

On arrival, I surveyed the scene dubiously, noting the loudspeakers blaring discordant chanting starting at 4:30 am, the amplified drum machines throughout the day, and the endless throngs of shouting Indian tourists, and I concluded that meditation was out of the question. This was supposed to be one of the most spiritual places in India. I simply didn't get it.

Sustaining heightened energy levels amidst the distractions of the world

Rasha speaks:

Oneness, I've become aware of the distractions of the noise all around me. And at some level, I suspect that there is some gift, some teaching, hidden in it. I'm starting to question why I have manifested this disturbance. It would be so much easier to have manifested a situation that is peaceful and quiet.

When I think about going somewhere else, there is a knowingness that I'm not to do that. For whatever reasons, I feel that I am to be here. It occurred to me that the disturbance may be training me to be able to sustain this level of Divine connectedness, or my own state of being, in less than optimal circumstances.

It's easy enough to experience this connection when the surroundings are peaceful. It's easy to go into meditation and experience bliss when on a mountaintop surrounded by the peaceful sounds of nature. It's far more difficult in the face of these constant distractions.

Is the point being made that the sustaining of a Divine connection should be able to happen anywhere, or that it cannot be attained and sustained just anywhere?

I look around me, here in Rishikesh, and see some graphic examples right in front of me. I have met one or two renunciants here who claim to have realized a Divine connection. One of them has been living in a cave in the Himalayas for ten years. The other one, Soami Bodhananda, lives like a hermit in one tiny dark room, hardly interacting with people. Even Dr. Bindu spends most of his time in isolation, chanting Mantras and performing sacred rituals. I'm looking at this.

Is the message to head for the hills and become a hermit? Is the message to fortify myself, somehow, so I can sustain what I know I can manifest, out there in the everyday world? What am I supposed to be doing with this connection? It seems like I am being prepared to take the teachings of Oneness out into the world. And I see a mixed message here. How is a person supposed to sustain a Divine connection within the environment of the everyday world?

Oneness speaks:

You are not expected to be able to sustain the heightened levels of Divine connectedness in the streets of physical reality, Rasha. The circumstances you have manifested depict for you, graphically, the part that the world around you plays in the process of integrating the augmented energies, and the adverse effect of diminished ones.

Now you see what the choices are. It is not possible to walk in the gutters without the sense of soiling the rarefied levels you have sought and have, at times, attained. The renunciants you have cited demonstrate this to you with their choices. You also have choices. And you will come to arrive at a balance, whereby the seclusion you will quite naturally choose as a way of life can intermingle with the Divine Service you wish to be able to do as your life's work.

The power of creating sanctity in the midst of chaos

It is not possible to serve humanity in the ways that you would wish to, and at the same time hide in a cave in the Himalayas. That is not the path you have chosen. And arrangements were made to bring the mountain to you, so that you would be able to experience God-Realization within the context of mundane reality and to teach others to do the same.

Now you are exploring the subtle nuances of those choices. And you will evolve methods of creating sanctity in the midst of chaos—as many others who have walked this path before you have done. You are not being asked to grit your teeth and try to experience heightened states of bliss by meditating in the streets. You are being shown the results of taking those rarefied levels into the streets and you have begun to understand the necessity for making choices that are focused on sustaining the sanctity of your energy field.

Learning to transcend disturbance in the physical world

There is no need to *struggle* with the disturbance of the noise that competes for your attention. Simply focus on this communication and the noise will cease to be a challenge for you. It will be as scenery, a background on which the *focal point* of your experience may find expression. You do not require conditions that you would consider to be *optimal* in order to fully experience this connection. You can experience Oneness anywhere—and everywhere. What you perceive reflects your focus of attention.

It would be far too easy to provide you with idyllic circumstances in which to experience this connection. Far more valuable is the opportunity to steep yourself fully in this state of connectedness while in the midst of mundane existence. For, that is the reality of the physical world in which you will be playing your chosen role in these times.

As I documented the following, a shift in awareness began to take place. It was subtle and only lasted for moments at a time. But, the nature of my *experience* of my connection with Oneness had begun to change. Ever so gently, I was taken from my familiar, blissful sense of connectedness *with* Oneness to an integration of consciousness at another level. I began to experience myself *as* Oneness. And Oneness began to teach me the skills needed to sustain that state of Self awareness.

The beginnings of *merging* with Oneness

Rasha speaks:

Oneness, I know you are with me in this moment. I feel you. Your smile is on my face. The glow of your Love is radiating within my heart chakra. My breathing has slowed down. And I feel myself drifting into that wonderful and now familiar state that I recognize as connectedness with you.

There have begun to be moments when I find myself yearning for this—a lover yearning for reunion with a Beloved. This yearning is not physical. It is anticipation itself, the sense of knowing what is about to be given and received and experienced. The senses become heightened. The breath slows down. And a mellow glow pervades my entire being.

I no longer doubt that you will respond to my invitation. I am no longer pleasantly surprised when you do. And even though you have never disappointed me, I've always wondered, and silently hoped, that you would come, that I would become engulfed with your Presence, that I would taste this joy of joys yet again!

Now there is no question—there is knowingness. For, in this moment, I Am That. In the process of writing this, something has shifted within me. And what began as a communication from "Rasha" now has merged into a communication that is flowing spontaneously—not from "me" and not from "other than me." The writing is simply writing itself.

The fingers hesitate, as if wondering from whom the instructions will come. And even as that thought enters my awareness, it is relinquished and the fingers once more begin to fly across this little pad of buttons they know so very well. Ah, the wonders of technology!

How different it must have been to have been relegated to chiseling revelations in stone or committing them to parchment, painstakingly, with a quill and ink. I feel so free in this. Time disappears. There is no thought to technique. And the communication flows forth, pure and simple. How lucky I am to be alive in these times, undergoing this experience in this way.

"Rasha" is writing this now. I see that. I have gone back to being "me" writing this to "you." How smoothly I seem to slip in and out of this state of connectedness. It is indeed "seamless," as you used to say. But now that I am once again "me" and you are the "you" who has always been distinguishable—despite the fact that I know you are within me—I see that I am hoping for a conversation. The only exception to the silence and aloneness I have begun to yearn for is this holy communion with you.

Learning to focus on the *glow* within
Oneness speaks:

Why have you hesitated? Were you expecting something? A response to your invitation, perhaps?

Yes, in fact. I know you are here. I can feel you. It is like a dancer who knows the movements of her partner so well, there is no conscious thought as to whether the steps will be in unison. I know you are dancing this dance with me. And it flows as naturally as the breath that drifts in and out of me.

You paused. Were you anticipating something?

Of course I was!

How to sustain the focus of awareness upon one's Divine connection

Expect nothing, Rasha, in the sense that it is taken for granted. Knowingness must be experienced in conjunction with *gratitude*—the deep pleasure you experience within yourself when are consciously aware that we are united once more—if it is to be sustained. That is, you must be *conscious* of the connection —focused *upon* it—not lost *within* it.

You are not to become nothingness. You are to become *everythingness*. The way to Be That is by *Being* That. By focusing every nuance of your awareness on the essence of this connection. The pleasure you experience in the area of your heart at that moment is the doorway you are seeking. Go there, and the door will open for you.

Ok. I have been in meditation for around forty-five minutes.

And, what did you experience?

I experienced blank. I was aware of my breath, intermittently. I focused on my heart chakra, as you suggested, intermittently. But, I must say that I feel the connectedness far more strongly now in my heart chakra than I did while in meditation. Why is that?

That is because at this moment, you do not have *self-awareness*. Your attention is fully *focused* in this conversation. How can you hope to transcend the linear identity when you are focused upon it? Your focus must be upon your connection with *Oneness*. Your focus must be centered in the *glow*—not upon the glow within *you*. Do you understand the distinction? The *you* aspect of that awareness ceases to be. In this state, the awareness of breath is not possible. For, who is it who would be breathing?

I understand what you are telling me.

Now, go back into the silence.

Ok. I have been in meditation for another half-hour. I lost self-awareness. I was not aware of breath. I was not aware of anything at all. Now, once again, I have the wonderful sensation of joy within my heart chakra. Now it is stronger than it was while in meditation. Why is that?

That is because you are detached from it, and thus are able to perceive it. When you are *within* it, you are no longer able to *perceive* it.

I feel like I am trying to do something, but I don't know what it is I'm trying to do. I know that this is not about trying. This is about Being.

You will not experience it by *trying* to experience it. You will experience it when you cease thinking about it as a *goal*. This is not something you must *achieve* through application of *skills*. This is a journey. Follow the path. See where it goes. While on the path, you will lose self-awareness and simply Be Present there—without the thought that it is *you* who is present.

21

———————

There's no way to say when the shift into full connectedness with Oneness actually took place. But, quite suddenly, there was no doubt that my state of self-perception had altered dramatically. Even so, the aspect of self that felt compelled to dissect and *understand* that state of beingness would remain marginally and intermittently present for some time to come.

Over time, a *knowingness* emerged from within that superceded the need for mentalized self-definition. In the interim, however, there was an aspect of self who was perpetually confounded by a compulsion to *understand* what was happening within, and baffled by how to contend with the unrelenting change in who I perceived myself to be in relation to Oneness. Fully integrating that aspect of self into the composite of who I recognized myself to be would become the primary challenge in my spiritual process during this timeframe.

Rasha speaks:

It's hard to pinpoint when the shift actually happened. Or, maybe it wasn't an isolated moment at all, but a gradual sliding into position. I can't be sure. But, there is no doubt that I am no longer who I was.

The past few days have been rather odd, in their own way. I was hovering between irrational extremes of emotion that lasted only a moment at best and the most serene sense of calm. Yesterday, I was feeling irritable about any number of nonsensical things, and I spent at least ten minutes venting and ranting to myself and then, quite suddenly, choked up with tears. The tears lasted about 30 seconds. And then it was over. I felt like my entire sense of self was swallowed up in a wonderful warm feeling of total well being. My mood shifted almost instantly into one of pure joy. I then went into a deep meditation, and experienced profound levels of bliss.

This morning, I awoke in such an intense state of inner balance and contentedness, I didn't know what to make of it. But, at another level, I knew. Something had changed. And I knew I was not imagining it. Now, I have the most extraordinary sense of transcendence. It feels like I am walking over the surface of this reality— that I am not really "in" it. Nothing seems to disturb me. And for no reason at all, I feel genuinely happy.

I just happened to look at the clock on the computer, and it was 11:11. The same thing happened yesterday, looking at the clock all of a sudden, and it was 11:11. I have to chuckle to myself when this happens. It's like God is giving you a wink.

Goodnight Oneness. It's odd that after all this time, those familiar, simple words would feel so weird. It sure is quiet in here! It's like I tune in, awaiting Oneness' reply, and it's absolutely silent. No thought. No conversation. Nothing. Just ... Stillness.

The initial experience of the Presence of Oneness was not a static condition, but was one that fluctuated. Baffled by the ongoing shifts in awareness unfolding within me, I continued to question Oneness to try and comprehend what was happening. My observations of the ramifications of my *focus of attention* would set the foundation for the very understandings I was groping for—understandings that were yet to come.

Rasha speaks:

Oneness, I know certain changes have happened within me. And I know that it seems absurd to address you as if you were separate from me, for I know that you are not. And yet, I hope that it is still possible to converse with you in this way. I'd like to understand what has happened within me—and to understand where we go from here.

I feel you all around me. That has not changed. It has only deepened. And yet, there are still moments when I feel like I have forgotten, once again, that I, in theory, Am Oneness. Experientially, I find myself once again interacting in a reflex way in the mundane world. I still have my emotional responses, although what I feel and what I feel prompted to respond to is now a much modified version of how it was.

I find, when I am conscious of the Presence of Oneness, I am able to respond with detachment and indifference to virtually anything. When I am not focused on my awareness of the Presence

of Oneness, I feel drawn into the illusion once more. Tell me, is
that how it is to be for me now? Or is this yet another interim
stage in an ongoing process? In short, where am I?

Oneness addresses the symptoms of a profound shift in consciousness
Oneness speaks:

You are where and who you choose to be, in any given moment. You
are alternately in full connectedness with the reality of who you Are—and
then, not in the fullness of that awareness. You have recognized the signs of
where you are. You know what is happening.

I know what you have told me. And I know what I have experienced
simultaneously during this entire process. I know that I surely am
not who I was. And yet, the sense of connectedness still comes in
waves. The intensity is much deeper now—that's the difference.

You will learn to walk within the embrace of the fullness of these energies.
Now, the veils have been lifted. You know yourself to Be the Essence of
Oneness. For, you have begun to journey into the depths of this experience.
And you have learned to recognize the signposts that are leading you ever
deeper into the reality of who you Are.

Now you walk within the context of form, through the imagery of an
illusory world. And yet, you are not deluded into believing that you are *of*
this place. You know yourself to be a traveler, who is simply passing through.
And in much the way as you are able to experience a sense of detachment
from the mundane circumstances of each of these destinations you are visiting
here in India, you have begun to experience a sense of detachment from the
fabric of the reality of which they are comprised.

Cultivating and strengthening the presence of the witness

These understandings will deepen with the passage of time, as you learn to
walk with confidence within the reality of this identity. Do not expect mastery
on day one. You are still very much in the process of metamorphosis. And even
though certain major milestones have been reached, your journey has truly
only just begun. Your instinctive yearning for solitude will wish to be honored
now. And you are being nudged in the direction of seeking circumstances
where those needs can be focused upon and explored more fully.

Oneness, how is it that I am still able to converse with you
like this? Who is conversing with whom?

You are still being prompted by the needs of the linear mind to try to define
and to understand the intricacies of what can only be experienced. The fact
is: you are able to hold this conversation. You are fully lucid in this. There is
no question that these skills are fully at your disposal and that nothing has
changed in this respect, for that is your experience of it. *Be* in this moment,
now. There is no need to analyze it. Simply be in the process. You have not
been abandoned.

That's reassuring. It's comforting to know that there's still a "you" with whom whoever I am at this point can still converse. And yet, I trust in what is happening. And it feels very safe. I have surrendered to this. Let this momentum take me where it will. At this point, I am simply along for the ride.

That is an ideal place from which to begin the next phase of this journey. For, the one who is along for the ride is in the persona of *the witness*. It is precisely this state of beingness that you will wish to cultivate and to strengthen. For, that is the Essence of the Presence of Oneness. Ultimately, you will be the personification of the *balance* between the force of focused intent and the sense of utter indifference to the circumstances that appear to surround you.

The days following my moments of revelation were anything but serene. Far from being able to sit back in peace, everything in my outer world became intensified. Issues I'd been working on as *life themes* now brought with them life circumstances that were calculated to take what was politely simmering within and bring it right to a boil. It was no longer possible to ignore some of the issues that I'd neatly swept under the rug, hoping it would all just go away.

I was reminded, again and again, that I was now living out the teachings I had transcribed for the book, *Oneness*. And, once again, I started to see the vivid connection between my inner world and the circumstances that were manifesting as experiences in my life. I realized that my newfound ability to recognize myself through the perspective of Oneness did not eliminate the *karmic* variables that still thrived in my *energy field*. Far from it.

Our energy fields hold the vibrational building blocks of linear reality— the energy that serves to draw our life experiences to us. And the *identity* in which my sense of Presence continued to travel—my sense of "me"—was no less influenced by those vibrational factors than before. The shadows that always seemed to follow me through life at a respectful distance were now right at my heels.

I'd been intermittently up and down for days, able to lift my mood out of the dumps only after several beautiful hours of communion with Oneness. I'd been feeling hurt by some mindless gossip someone had repeated back to me. Then, I'd been ignored by the Guru in residence at the ashram, who began lavishing attention on someone who had just arrived. On top of that, I was feeling lonely. I hadn't had a simple, casual conversation with another native, English-speaking human being since I'd arrived in Rishikesh two months earlier.

At the sound of that inner grumbling, I stopped and asked myself—"who is it who is feeling lonely?" Instantly, I understood that, once again, it was the small ego-self playing out a predictable response. It was the small ego-self that was seeking validation. It could only be the small ego-self who would *care* that someone was spreading lies or what a bunch of gossiping people think. Oneness would not care.

Why was all this coming up for me now, I wondered? I went to Oneness in search of some straight answers. Once again, the wisdom of Oneness transformed a myopic perspective into an augmented worldview on what might be seen as mundane. I began to see the opportunity for growth in these simple life lessons and the opportunity to transcend these *life themes* once and for all.

Rasha speaks:

Oneness, betrayal has been a theme for me in this lifetime—and in who knows how many others. I'd like to talk about the significance of that theme, so I can begin to understand the symbolism that is all around me.

Oneness talks about *approval, betrayal,* and *rejection* and how they reinforce an orientation focused in duality

Oneness speaks:

Betrayal is a concept that exists only in the depths of one's fears. It is the fear of powerlessness that creates the possibility of an opening through which power may be eroded. The focus of the ego-self upon a concern for approval from others leads one to place great emphasis on what may be thought or said by others. In fact, there *are* no others. *You* are in this movie. That is all.

The rest of what you are experiencing is symbolism that is playing out before you, reflecting back to you the state of your conscious awareness. Do not blame these so-called "others" for projecting your truth upon the screen of this reality for your viewing. They are simply mirroring back to you what is already there.

If you are ruminating about suspicions of betrayal, then you will surely be betrayed. If you are focused upon your need for approval, then you have driven a wedge between yourself and the only one from whom approval could be forthcoming—the Self.

You are surely not here to garner the approval and praises of others. You are here to put into practice what you know to your very depths to be true. Your focus is best concentrated upon *this* connection and in the places where you experience That being reflected back to you. That is all.

My God, how easy it is to slide back into the old patterns of reflex responses! I am not here to win the approval of others. I am here to embody the truth that I represent. Period. Let there be no thought to a result that may or may not be forthcoming from others about it. They will think what they will think. Soami Bodhananda always says, "The dogs are barking—so let them bark!"

The fact is, certain inconsequential individuals here in India have chosen not to respond to you in a favorable way. Why does that concern you? Do you believe that they are correct in their assessment of you?

Absolutely not.

Then why are you disturbed by it? Their assessment, from your perspective, is flawed—for whatever reasons. Let that be ok with you. You do not require their approval. You are fine. Focus upon your own responses. Be present—fully present—in the loving space of your own infinite *compassion*.

How, individually and collectively, we can change the world

See every moment as an opportunity to reflect back upon the screen of the awareness of others, the truth that you are able to see about *them*—the truth of their innate *Divinity*. That is how to truly make a difference in the world and shift the circumstances which play out the discordant themes that are all around you.

These are all simply *illusions*. These are reflections of the belief systems of the beings in question. That is all. You are here with the capability to see through those masks and to reinforce the truth of the Divine Essence that glows from within the depths of even the most insidious of those disguises. It is to that Divinity that you wish to respond, not to the false image that reflects fear and conditioning.

In so doing, you add a measure of reinforcement to the validity of what is truly harbored there. And, as such, you cultivate the possibility that it is that vision—the recognition of the innate, ever-present Divinity within—which, ultimately, may be reflected out within the world of illusion.

That is how to help change the world. One smile, one gesture of kindness, at a time. It is this upon which you will focus for the remainder of your time here. Observe what is really happening here. And you will recognize that miracles—real miracles—are not only possible, they are inevitable.

Co-creating the world as we would wish to have it be

When you see and acknowledge the Divinity in other beings, they begin to be able to experience that within themselves. It is this seed that you have come to plant within the consciousness of those who will be drawn to you. You will demonstrate, with loving kindness, the response to other beings that you would want reflected back upon yourself, and that will be the result.

You will co-create the world as you would wish to have it be. That end is not served by contributing to the manifestation of a diminished reflection of what is truly there. Your focus is to be upon the Divinity before you, simply That.

In every circumstance, in every set of eyes, you will see a reflection of the Oneness dwelling there. And your actions will address that aspect of *Divinity*, not the false reflections of suspicion, and deprivation, and resentment. For, those reflections are calculated to cultivate more of the same, as are all reflections. The opportunity in every moment is the possibility of contributing the reflection of the true Divine Essence within everything upon the composite that is physical reality.

Detaching from the outside world and feeling alone and "invisible"
Rasha speaks:

How easy it is to forget and how effortless it is to be reminded, yet again, of the magnificence of your Presence. I flowed into the embrace of these energies, once more, as tears of joyous exultation poured down my cheeks. How is it possible to forget this, to be lured into the illusion of separation from this? How can it be other than just like this?

When I am in the fullness of this connection, there is no outside world, and none of the concerns over which I've ruminated matter at all. If only I could continue to look at life through this lens! If only I could stay in this place of perception and not have to go back, at the end of a session, to the mundane aggravations of the world of the illusion. If this is just a state of temporary insanity, then let me remain in it!

I realize that I have been stripped—or have, at some level stripped myself—of virtually all companionship and affiliation now. Apart from three very independent, grown children, I have no family at all. The entire family I was born into has passed on from this reality. I have no sense of close kindred connection with any of the very few extraneous relatives who appeared in my life script in earlier years.

There are no ties to a sense of "home," to a place. At this point I have uprooted myself so many times I cannot begin to say where I "am from." I do not presently have a home. What belongings I have chosen to continue to own are in a storage unit. I have no sense of attachment to any of it. Everything else that was of value has been given away.

I do not know where I will live when I return to America. I am not concerned about it. I have virtually abandoned my source of income— the little company that has simultaneously sustained and consumed me over the last few years. I do not have a sense of a profession through which I can state my identity and attempt to introduce myself. None of it fits anymore. All of this colorful "history" I have spent over half a century amassing strikes me as totally irrelevant. It surely does not define who I know myself to Be now.

I walk through this world as though I were invisible. There are moments where I long for companionship—even superficial companionship. But, that doesn't seem to be in the script. I can't seem to manage to initiate a conversation with anyone. I have gone several months virtually without any casual verbal interaction with another incarnate being, and not for lack of trying on my part.

It seems that whenever I try to initiate a conversation with someone who looks like they might be interesting they smile vacantly and barely reply. Sometimes they just walk away. I have begun to simply stand on the periphery of the activities into which I am drawn and watch from a distance. I speak to no one. No one ever attempts to speak to me. I have started to question whether I am really in this world at all.

Maybe there are a token number of beings scripted in here, just to give credibility to a reality the validity of which I have begun to question altogether. Chances are, to most of the beings I think I see, I may well be invisible. I sense that I have one foot out of "the matrix" and one foot still in it. Who knows?

I am ready to surrender to this now. I don't really want to be here anymore. I have this indescribable longing to go home. And I know that "home" is not within this world.

Oneness explains the significance of the sense of *aloneness* that characterizes this stage of the journey

Oneness speaks:

We note that you have just aired out the closet of your consciousness. The cobwebs of your linear identity have been cleared away. We Are all that remains. The sense of loneliness that you have tuned in to is very much a part of this stage of your process. You are still responding to the conditioning that leads one in search of *another*. That *other* is perceived as separate from you.

In fact, there are no *others*. You have journeyed very close to the edge of that level of perception. And yet, you still are experiencing moments of loneliness. The aloneness that is the true nature of your condition is not one that could be enhanced by the addition of *another*. You have begun to assimilate that understanding. Soon you will experience that state of Beingness.

Soon you will walk as Oneness with full conscious awareness of it. Soon you will perceive the aspects of the illusion through which your form travels as the fragments of imagery that they, in fact, are. You will see, physically, the fabric of which this reality is composed. And you will perceive yourself as *embodied Awareness,* present within the composition of scenery that you can alter, at will.

You are moving into the levels of Beingness where such perceptions are possible. You will remain as a bridge between these worlds, with full conscious awareness of it. That is the nature of what is transpiring within you at present.

As the weeks in Rishikesh went by, I continued to be baffled by the significance of my association with Soami Bodhananda, whom I'd continued to visit now and then. Oneness had told me that he was a significant contributor to my process, yet his persistent focus upon the idea of an "inner explosion" made me feel like a failure and a disappointment both to him and to myself.

I realized that I'd begun to avoid going to see him. Whenever I went to his cottage, inevitably, I'd emerge feeling irritable and depressed. Yet, when I thought about leaving Rishikesh and not seeing him again, I felt so sad. I'd come to cherish the moments—the hours—I'd spent with him. I was grateful for the time and the kindness he had given me. Yet, I found him to be insufferably *mental* about things spiritual. And I found the blatant evidence of ego he demonstrated to be disturbing.

I started to see that I had not come to Soami Bodhananda to learn spiritual principles. These concepts I had already been taught by Oneness. I did not see an example I wanted to emulate in him, so I did not have a role model there one would expect to find in a Guru. What I had was a list of contradictions and a montage of conflicting impressions I didn't know how to read. Oneness helped me put the experience into perspective.

Oneness talks about the personalized path to the experience of enlightenment
Oneness speaks:

If you are looking for a definitive barometer with which to assess this teacher, you will not find one. Your encounter with Soami Bodhananda is not a pass/fail experience, either way. It is an association that is colorful and contradictory, sometimes meaningful and at other times banal. He is a personalized reflection of the Divinity within, no less than anyone else.

The fact that he has had certain exalted experiences does not exempt him from the fact that those experiences have passed through the filter of his own personal awareness and are colored by it accordingly. You are not expected to duplicate his experience of enlightenment. That was *his* experience. You are having your own experience. We have spoken repeatedly of this.

You have written extensively on this concept of the *personal journey*. This concept is no less applicable to the exalted phases of the experience of enlightenment than it is to the rudimentary stages of initial awakening. There are certain general signposts at each of these stages of spiritual unfoldment that would indicate to the student and to those who may be guiding him/her that a particular stage of development has been attained. Beyond that, you are essentially on your own to illustrate your experience as you choose to.

Soami Bodhananda is misguided in his presumption that the culmination of this journey is one definitive peak experience that is attained in the sense of plugging a wire into a wall socket. This is not at all what is necessary. And to persist in pursuit of that direction is counterproductive to all you are doing.

In all respects, it is time to move forward now. That does not invalidate the positive aspects of the work that has been done or the caring that has been recognized, mutually. It is simply to say to you that this aspect of your training is complete now. It is time to move on.

Rasha speaks:

I went and sat with Soami Bodhananda today for a little while, and suddenly, I began to see the real gift in the time I'd spent with him. I'd had very mixed feelings about it, perhaps because I had expectations of what it was I was supposed to "do" there. He reinforced those expectations with his intellectual analysis and theoretical explanations.

I remember thinking, "All those stories of the enlightenment of others will not take me any closer to God." Now I understand. They weren't supposed to. That is a solitary journey. The teachings of Soami Bodhananda gave me a frame of reference in which to place my own experience!

In his own eccentric way, he had spent a lifetime analyzing the peak experiences of India's greatest saints and had woven a priceless tapestry of quotes and stories, carefully "penned down" in the margins of his aging books. He may have been misguided in telling me that I was to expect an "inner explosion"—and unintentionally fed my festering fear of failure. Good thing he did. It all came to the surface.

There I was able to scrutinize the whole mess that was churning within me with regards to the prospect of the experience of "enlightenment." His examples, no doubt intended as encouragement, felt like being set up with a standard I didn't think I could match.

It became a competition, within my mind, of my own experience versus that of those historical figures. And I was off and running into the depths of my mind, on the one subject you can only approach when you surrender the mind! Ultimately, I had to back away from analyzing whether or not I agreed or disagreed with anything that may or may not have been said, or thought, or written.

For, in the weeks I have been attempting to "make something happen" I had strayed from my magnificent, pure, and simple connection with the Source of All That Is—which I had come to experience as Love. I call that experience "Oneness." And they are one and the same.

Thank you, Oneness, for this amazing journey! I am so very blessed. I feel you all around me. Let me never again have a doubt of this! Oh, Oneness! There are no words for this. "Thank you" does not even begin to touch it.

Divine wisdom from Oneness on the power of the *experience* that transcends the need for words

There *are* no words for this, Rasha. You can lay a foundation for an experience with words, with concepts, with the building blocks of "understanding," yet the *experience* itself transcends all of that. It Is simply what it Is. And the only way to know what it Is, is to surrender all else—all expectations, all theoretical understandings, all techniques, all forms of mind-directed "doingness"—and open to the *experience* itself.

That is what there is to have. Anything else is not—That. And now, you have a wealth of heart-wrenching, painful, confusing, mind-boggling experiences with which you have proved it. The simple truth of what you are feeling in this moment has absolutely nothing to do with any of that.

Your belief that the journey had to be a struggle helped to create that scenario for you. You bought into the belief that this was the ultimate mountain, and that the climb would be arduous. And so, that was your experience of it. Now, with the agonizing portions of the journey behind you, you can see that the destination you hoped to reach was not difficult at all. The key to all of it was within you all along. You just never *believed* that it was. Now you are here to embody your *experience* of this state of transcendence, and to walk within its embrace.

You see, there is no question of worthiness/unworthiness or of success/failure when it comes to the experience of Isness. Within the context of Unity there Is only Oneness. When you are fully Present within that state of Beingness there is nothing—absolutely nothing—to be considered, or believed, or understood. There is only That which must be experienced to be Known.

This is what you will teach—and this is the truth that you will live—as your experience of Oneness deepens, with the passage of time.

The role of ritual and expressions of *devotion* in establishing a Divine connection

It takes no time to establish this connection. It takes only your own *focused intent*, undistracted, surrendered, fully available to receive. That is all. The protocols you employ to establish this connection are of your own choosing.

There is no prescribed program of *rituals*. There is no set collection of *prayers*. There are no particular words that are to be said. These each of you will determine within the sanctity of your own heart.

There certainly are traditional routes that you may choose to incorporate into your own program of worship and expressions of *devotion*. But, none of them is required. None is higher or lower than another. None is the more direct route to the epitome of connectedness with this Source, which ultimately will be sought within each of you. Each is simply a possibility, amongst the infinite possible choices you may select, through which to express your joy and passion in revealing your Divine connection.

"The recipe" for establishing a Divine connection

It may give you great comfort to give expression to the invocations of your heart. But, none of these timeless rituals, in and of themselves, is sufficient to open the door to the fullness of this connection. You may chant what you choose to chant from now through eternity, and if your heart is not in full alignment with the words of devotion to which you give expression, you will simply have experienced the resonance of sound vibration and its possible effects. When the element of heartfelt *devotion* is added to such an expression, however, the alchemy of Divine connectedness is initiated and the doors within will begin to open automatically.

This is the recipe that many will be seeking in the times to come. Your world's recent history is filled with feverishly initiated and disastrously aborted attempts to create new paths to the experience of spiritual connectedness. Most of them shied away from using the word "religion" to express their systems of belief and worship. And few offered the gift of *self-empowerment* to the individual seeker who might, initially, have been attracted to the teachings that may have been presented. Most of these fledgling spiritual movements began with a grain of truth and succumbed to the pitfalls that are inevitable when the messenger is exalted rather than the message.

The path of self-empowerment revealed by the teachings of Oneness

The direction that will be presented through the vehicle of these teachings is the empowerment of the individual to seek and to source his own personal connection with the Divinity within. You are the Messenger. You are the textbook example of what is possible. Your focus is not to be directed toward those who will cast stones. Your focus will be upon those who recognize the resonance of what you have brought forth.

Your attention and full focus remains upon your Divine truth and its Source. The essence of the message you have come to deliver is the foundation upon which that focus rests. Your truth is your own, as is that of each of you. The depth of your *experience* of that truth is the aspect of the process which is optional.

Placing the teachings within the framework of the world's spiritual establishment

Most of the beings now present in your world would be threatened by the teachings that will be presented through the vehicle of your identity. Most are far too invested in the fear-based structures in which they have been enlisted since birth. Most have been too fully indoctrinated in a particular mode of spiritual expression to risk seeking, outside of those structures, a route to the Divinity that truly lies within. Let that be ok with you.

You are not here to convert the masses. You are here to convert no one. You have come simply to present evidence of another level of possibility, and to let the recipient of that information make his own determination as to what is and is not truth—for him. The teachings stand on their own merit alone. They are not here to be defended. They are not here to be dissected, although that eventuality is surely to be anticipated. Your opportunity, in having delivered these teachings, is to be able to sidestep, with grace, the invitation to subject yourself to that experience.

Learning to be fully Present within your own truth

Your opportunity is to embody fully the quality of Divine detachment from any investment whatsoever in how these teachings are received. It is not your job to instill these teachings within the consciousness of those who will be drawn to them. Your job is simply to be Present within your own truth, and to show others, by example, how to do the same.

You have begun to see the lifetime of preparation for this work in the history of rejection and criticism that has been your experience in this incarnation. Now there is a hint of logic to it. Now there is a purpose to it. Now you are able to recognize that these experiences have not come to erode your sense of self-esteem, but rather, to *strengthen* it.

Oneness illuminates the Divine gift in a world of criticism, hostility, and rejection

Were you to have had a lifetime of love and approval lavished upon you, the adversity that could be forthcoming would be alien soil and would be difficult to withstand. You have been tempered, like steel, as preparation for holding fast to your Divine focus and to decline the invitation of victim-consciousness.

Your hunger for the approval of the outside world has not been recognized. And that eternally closed door is that which led you to seek the door to the kingdom *within* the self. When you look carefully at the circumstances of your life, and the patterns to be recognized there, you will see how purposeful it all has been. And you can begin to see the gift in all of it.

Karmic compensation for past action is the obvious interpretation of some of what may have come to pass. But, that concept is one that is grossly misunderstood. The enduring of suffering for the sake of suffering, as payment for past action, is not the purpose of the experiences of adversity that pepper the personal histories of so many beings who experience themselves in physical reality.

These experiences have been scripted into your life histories to provide you the opportunity to *transcend* the conditions that have been inflicted upon you by others, and to source the Divine connection that is the only possible exit route from the imagery of such circumstances. When there is nowhere else to turn, ultimately one turns within.

The levels of distress to which those in the throes of an incarnate experience have subjected themselves is directly proportional to the ease or difficulty with which each is able to source the only possibility of relief from it. Ultimately, one becomes so fortified in that unwavering Divine focus that one is able to transcend the illusion of all possible adversity.

The timeless lesson delivered through history's Divine acts of spiritual martyrdom

It is that level of Divine focus that the martyred Saints who illustrate the spiritual history of your world came to demonstrate. Some would withstand,

255

with unspeakable Grace, the physical torment of the atrocities that were perpetrated upon them. Some would transcend and maintain an aura of serenity in the face of the agonies of terminal illness. The fact is, none of them suffered. The ones who suffered were those who experienced the horrors of those images *vicariously*, as they watched, helplessly.

It was that experience that was illustrated to you by your incarnation as Leah in the times of Jeshua. She was shown, very clearly, what actually transpired within the martyred being in whose body she experienced her awareness. And she shared in his ecstasy in his moment of transcendence.

That memory is etched within you and has never been erased. You will not be asked to demonstrate that level of martyrdom in this lifetime. You have been assured of this. Yet, in the same breath, you have a sense of the essence of the resistance with which these teachings will be met from many directions.

Your task is not to bear the brunt of that force, but to allow it to express itself as it will, and to remain totally untouched by it. It is this level of Grace that *you* have come to demonstrate in *these* times. And it is that level of Grace which will be recognized, and ultimately will come to be understood, in the fullness of time.

Be at peace, Rasha. Your destiny has begun to unfold before you. And you have stepped into its embrace willingly—and joyously. That is all that will ever be required of you. We are never further from you than your next breath. In time, you will know—and you will demonstrate—that we live and breathe as Oneness.

While in Rishikesh, I had several exalted experiences during meditation in which my awareness began to journey to places and scenarios that were not of this world. By that time, I was totally accustomed to being able to "leave my body" at will and to experience myself elsewhere, in the sense of *astral travel*. In the past, these meditative journeys always had been vivid and highly symbolic. And, since I'd been having these kinds of experiences for over 20 years, by that time, I grew to take the phenomenon very much in stride.

In the very early days of my spiritual awakening, I became accustomed to transporting myself at will to a breathtaking spot on a mountaintop that was also not of this world. It was a cherished place, blanketed in wildflowers, that was discovered initially in the sanctity of a guided meditation in the early 1980s. It always felt like there my heart was home.

It was there that I would go, eyes closed and mind suspended, for the experience of communion with aspects of Divinity that were serving as guides in the early days of my spiritual awakening. It became a holy place of sanctity and stillness where I would retreat for healing and for the simple joys of a Divine connection I was far from ready to understand.

Over time, it was there on "the mountain" that I'd receive otherworldly *healing tools*—vibrantly colored *rays* that entered the third eye of my astral body as it stood at the edge of a mythical cliff—energy that simultaneously flowed through the blazing hands of this physical body. It was there that I received the blessing of the spiritual *initiations* that began to prepare my physical form to sustain the vibrational changes that were to come as part of the journey to Oneness.

"The mountain" and all it represented to me was a precursor of the places I would visit, now 20 years later, in the depths of meditation. These experiences prepared me for the entirely different meditation experiences that were to come: the sense of being *pure Awareness,* suspended in the embrace of an infinite vastness during which, for hours on end, there was no sense of time or presence in a physical world.

The experiences in Rishikesh were vivid in their imagery and symbolism, and were accompanied by extraordinary sensations of augmented vibration and heights of exultation. These meditative journeys heralded the profound shift in awareness that was to be the definitive turning point in my journey to Oneness. I'd like to share one of those meditations here, a summary experience rich in symbolism.

❦

After skyrocketing through the vastness and bursting through its outer limits, I found myself standing on a Golden Beach. In a previous meditation, I had dissolved into that Ocean and had experienced that vastness as "myself." This scene was just as I remembered it. But, now there was, once again, an "I" who perceived herself to be present there, separate from the surroundings. I gazed at the breathtaking panorama before me for a little while. Then, sensing that there was something more, I turned around. And there it was! The Golden Mountain.

I remembered this place, for I had been there before, many years back. I remembered approaching it from a far distance back then, and seeing it as two mountains, one beside the other. Flippantly, I had dubbed it "The Golden Arches" back then, a la McDonald's. Now, years later, sensing the majesty of the scene that unfolded before me, I knew that I stood before the symbolic depths of my own beingness. I had come home.

Up close, from the perspective of the Golden Beach, I could perceive only one mountain, not the two I knew were there, yet I sensed the presence of both formations as part of the whole. "Oneness," I thought! "How perfect. The epitome of duality experienced as One vision." I realized that I stood at the base of all that I had been searching for—a milestone on what I knew was an infinite journey. I was about to embark on an extraordinary odyssey during which I would encounter seven golden altars. I would perform sacred rituals and surrender myself completely at each of them before setting off toward the next.

The path was rugged and steep, but I walked it easily, as though I had traversed the trail a thousand times. Altars one, two, and three appeared in relatively quick succession, along a golden path that wound ever upward. Each of these altars was recessed into the golden rock and set back a bit from the trail itself. Each held a few sacred objects, arranged carefully around one central, three-dimensional, golden geometric formation. I knelt down before each of them and silently offered words of gratitude from the depths of my heart, before moving on.

The path became quite steep at this point, and I climbed and climbed until I stood before a vast, breathtaking golden lake that bridged what, from a distance, had appeared as mountains one and two. It was as still as an expanse of golden glass. Here, at the very heart of the journey, all of it was merged in the embrace of Oneness—mountains, lake, and golden sky, shimmering as One profound, indescribable energy, beckoning to me.

I stepped onto a golden raft, whose course was set. And, in silence, I wafted across the lake where, disembarking, I humbled myself before altar number four. After some time, I again stepped onto the raft. Altar number five was there waiting for me at the far distant corner of the lake. Once more, I bowed down before all that I knew to be sacred, in gratitude.

Embarking yet again on the golden raft, I arrived, after some distance, at the entrance to a vast mountain cave. Entering it, I found myself in an enormous cavern that appeared to go on forever. I ventured further and further into its depths, but there was no altar anywhere to be seen, simply an endless vaulted tunnel, leading God knows where. I continued walking for what seemed like eternity, intently looking for altar number six. I knew it was there somewhere, but I just couldn't see it. Then, from out of nowhere, a round aperture—like the lens of a camera—appeared in the far wall. It was a doorway, and it was shut tight.

It seemed like I had reached a dead end, so I turned around. There behind me, tucked into an alcove that had gone unnoticed, was altar number six. A sacrifice was to be made there. I realized that I had brought nothing with me to place on the altar. All I had was myself. And in the ceremony that followed, I offered the only thing I really had—my very life—to God. As I did, the circular door on the wall opened and I stepped through it and out of the cave. The door shut behind me.

I found myself standing on a precipice. This is where the trail ended, and there was no going back. It was a chasm filled with an opalescent liquid. Within it, at the very bottom, thousands of feet below, a golden fire burned. I knew it was altar number seven. From where I stood, the fire appeared to be extremely small. And the only way to reach it was to dive in.

For only a moment, I thought of my lifelong fear of being underwater. Without hesitation, I surrendered the fear and dove in headfirst. At unimaginable speed,

I streaked through an iridescent rainbow of vastness where the concepts of down and up were interchangeable. The flames at the far end loomed closer and closer as I streaked toward them. Finally, I plunged headlong into the flames—and through them. All motion stopped.

Suddenly there were no flames. Now, I was hovering in mid-air within a shimmering golden void. Before me was a door with a rounded top. There were no hinges, no walls to which it was attached—just a door, suspended in the middle of nowhere. Without hesitation, I opened the door and walked through. Immediately, I found myself standing in front of the very same door, going the other way. I went back and forth through the door over and over again, trying to get to where it was I thought I was supposed to be going. It was clear that I was getting nowhere.

In the same breath, I understood that the entire journey, therefore, was leading "nowhere"! There I was, standing before a door with two sides to it. And no matter which side of the door I stood on, it was always the other side of the door that became the proverbial "goal." There I was, at the pinnacle of my symbolic spiritual journey, still striving—still trying to turn "a don't have" into "a have."

Who was it, I started to wonder, who thought she needed to get through that door? Who was this person who was still trying so hard to get it right? And, without knowing how, suddenly, I understood. As long as I was viewing it through her eyes, there would always be a door. There would always be duality. There would always be "the endless cycle"—of birth and death. Suddenly, there was crystalline awareness.

I understood that that person—the linear identity I'd always understood myself to be, could never get past the door. She could only go from one side to the other— eternally. The only way to transcend the door was to transcend the perspective of the one who believed that there was a door—the same one who believed herself to be making the journey.

In that moment, I stepped out of the illusion of her identity, like I was stepping out of a piece of clothing. And all semblance of "me"—and the door—vanished. All that remained was an indescribable, opalescent golden vastness. And a sublime feeling of exultation that remained with me long after I opened my eyes.

22

―――――――

M y time on the roller-coaster that was Rishikesh ended on a high
note with a dramatic upswing in my energies and a fresh, upbeat
outlook on life that reflected it. It appeared that I'd completed the foray into
self-confrontation that had been slated for that time. Clearly, by the end of
June, it was time to move on.

There'd been a brief, unexpected visit from Govinda, the Brahmin preacher
of *Srimad Bhagavatum* (the ancient literary classic on the pastimes of Lord
Krishna), whom I'd met in Vrindavan, as I was preparing to leave the foothills
of the Himalayas and head for higher ground and cooler temperatures. At his
insistence, I agreed to return to Vrindavan and spend some time in Lord
Krishna's magical city after the summer months were over.

In the meantime, my heart was filled to overflowing with the joy of my
connection with Oneness. It was a state of beingness that traveled well, I'd
discover. For, the months to come, tucked-away in the picturesque "hill
stations" of Uttaranchal (now known as Uttarakhand), were amongst the
most serene and powerful moments of this unforgettable journey. And, as the
days of wonder continued to unfold, my experience of Divine connectedness
continued to deepen.

My travels took me first to the verdant paradise of the Himalayan
foothills just north of Nainital. It was here that the late Guru, Neem Karoli
Baba, had made his ashram, Kainchi, and it was there that I found my way
like a homing pigeon. I'd assumed that I'd be staying there for the better part
of a month. On arrival, I learned that a three-night stay was the maximum
time permitted.

Not wanting to waste a minute of it, I went directly on arrival to the small
room where he had given *satsang* during his lifetime, with my little notebook
in hand. I felt his Presence there so strongly, even though I knew he'd left his
body in 1973. It was as though he were still there. And indeed, in the ways
that really matter, he was. Within seconds, I'd all but forgotten the bout of
tummy trouble that I'd been struggling with, a situation he was fully aware

of, amazingly enough. As always, my time of communion with the Presence of Neem Karoli Baba brought clarity to the moment and joy to my heart. In silence, I scribbled down his words, as they flowed through the vehicle of my consciousness.

～✑～

A darshan in silence with Neem Karoli Baba
Neem Karoli Baba speaks:

You are feeling better now?

Rasha speaks:

Yes, I feel a bit better. I've taken medication.

And, how are you in general?

I am in a heightened state of bliss. I had silent darshan in your Presence and was in meditation for a long time.

There is no long time or short time. You were present here for the duration of a meditation. There is no quantifying it, for these things do not matter. What is important is for you to be fully present when you are here. Leave your mind out of this experience. Bring me your heart. We will work with that. You have no need to understand anything, now. You know what you know. Now you will experience it.

Thank you, Babaji! I feel so blessed to be here. I feel like I have come home to you here, just like you told me I would. I place myself here in your Presence. I surrender myself to this journey—in your Presence.

There is nothing for you to *do* here. Simply be. Be still. Be present. And be open to your experience of our time together. That is all.

Ok. I feel like I want to go back into meditation with you.

Your life is a meditation. You can be fully in meditation and still be present in the world. This is what you have come to learn. You are not here to deny the world or to remove yourself from it. Your path leads you out into the world. It is there where you have come to serve.

It would be far too easy to allow oneself to retreat permanently into the embrace of a Divine connection. You carry that connection *with* you. It never leaves you. Your path is not that of the recluse or the renunciant. You are observing these practices, for they are frames of reference for you of paths others have chosen in pursuit of what you have found.

You have given yourself a full tour of the world of spiritual pursuit. You have not come to adopt these practices, but simply to watch the art of devotion in action. You have learned to master your own method of transcending the physical illusion, in a very natural way. It is not complicated. Yet, it is no less holy than any of the traditional techniques you are now observing.

Honor your own path and your own journey. For, it does not matter *how* you reach the top of the mountain. And once there, few will question the method you have chosen to get there. Once you have conquered the summit of physical existence, the hows and whys and the dos and don'ts of spiritual tradition become irrelevant.

Once you have arrived at your destination, it doesn't matter in the least whether you journeyed by car, by train, on foot, or on your hands and knees. These are concerns which consume the minds of those who are still lost en-route—those who are lusting after *liberation* like a prize to be won. These ones will be the first to judge, for their egos will be invested in duplicating your result through their own methods.

Neem Karoli Baba speaks about the path of the heart

One's personal spiritual practice is not something one needs to debate with anyone. Bring your *heart* on your journey regardless of how you choose to travel. For, it is through this route alone that the destination is reached. It is through the Divine connection of heart that you are able to transcend the physical while remaining fully present within it.

Your life has been pledged to Divine Service. You will guide many to be able to source the attainment of liberation from within, through the path of selfless service and devotion. *How* this is accomplished is irrelevant.

There are no wrong turns on the path now. You have passed all the detours. The climb for you now is direct, for the way has been cleared for you. You have come here to your Babaji to walk to the summit. You knew to come here to Kainchi. And now you are here.

What others do or do not think about any aspect of your presence does not matter. You are here for this moment. For, it is this moment that will sustain you after it is time for you to continue on your way. Be here with the fullness of all that you Are in every moment we are together. That is all that is necessary.

Take this moment Now as your *prasad* (divine gift). This is what you carry with you as you walk within the illusion of the physical world. It is here that you dwell—in the eternal heart of *this* world! Be present *here*, and you will never leave this place. For, this place is *within* you—no matter where you go.

You have come home now. Not to a place, but to a state of Being. It is nowhere to be found—and it is everywhere that you are present. For, you bear the torch. And the light that shines from within you will illuminate the way for many in the years to come. It will not matter what you choose to say and what you choose not to say. It is your Presence which will be sought and which will be felt with an intensity that will be undeniable. That is why the honeybees come. They do not come for a discourse on the nature of the flower garden. They come because they are *compelled* to come.

With their last breath, they come to be in communion with the nectar that you have come to bear for them. They will drink deeply in your Presence, as they do here. And many will recognize the connection you carry, within the depths of their *own* Essence.

You have come to embody a reference point to which these seekers can draw a path of their own design. For, you demonstrate the "what" of it—not the "how." And just as you feel the intensity of this connection in the Presence of your Babaji, so these ones will experience you. Not yet, but in time. Drink deeply of this nectar and know that it is the manifestation of Divine intent that you be gifted with it. We are not the Source, we are simply the vehicle—as are you.

At Kainchi, the feeling of connectedness was magnificent. I had the sense of wanting to melt into the soaring, velvety-green surrounding hills and disappear there. Nothing in the outside world seemed at all important or remotely interesting. I hadn't read a newspaper or watched TV for months and hadn't missed it a bit. My world was there within the silence. It was a world of indescribable joy, safely tucked away within the sanctity of my own consciousness. And there was no question whatsoever that *that* world was very real.

I had relinquished all the feelings of being de-railed by that time. Yet, there was still the sense of being in a nether-world between realities from time to time. I knew I was "neither here nor there"—neither the fullness of Oneness, in form, nor the blind innocence of a material woman, lost in the realm of mundane desires. From that vantage point, the allure of finding out what's beyond the next twist and turn of these inner mountain roads kept me moving steadily in a direction that had become undeniable.

I had begun to seriously consider the possibility that I didn't really exist. Perhaps I was really just a figment of the imagination of some great cosmic comedy writer, I thought. Perhaps I was nothing more than a proverbial bug on the end of my own pin, squirming under a self-styled magnifying glass. I approached Oneness in hopes of attaining some clarity on this latest in an ongoing series of turning points.

Oneness speaks:

How can there be answers when there is no question? You know what is happening. Your experience of it is your experience of it. There is no prescribed paint-by-numbers way to create the masterpiece of your own emergence.

You have chosen to be in this place, in this moment. There is no saying that every moment is meant to be spent in exultation—not yet. You have come so very far in your journey. Release your mind now and give yourself the grace of just being Present in this blessed place. *Enjoy* the moments you have here. You have no agenda. This is not a race. You are here, now. You have prayed for this and longed for this—and now it is yours to savor.

The time you have been allotted is what it is. You may choose to return here—touching down and immersing yourself in these energies, and then releasing yourself once more from this embrace. Your presence here is like the dance of lovers. They do not need to remain entwined in each other's arms in every moment. The parting creates an opening for the joy of the reunion. It is much the same as the union of Guru and disciple. The parting kindles the appetite for what is yet to come.

Be content to be in the moment with this journey. Let the expectations, which were fueled by your time in Rishikesh, be released now. There is no necessity to try to force an experience to happen that you know is inevitable and imminent. Just be present in the joy of the journey and allow what is to happen to happen naturally.

Leaving Kainchi was a wrenching experience. I'd been in such a serene space and had felt as though I had "come home." Yet, the rules of the Kainchi ashram dictated that it was time to move on. I took that as a sign that there was something in store for me further down the road. The legendary monsoon season that traditionally clobbers the plains of India was due to start at any moment, and I'd hoped to avoid the brunt of it by heading north to the Himalayas. Now, the mountain trail I'd embarked on was becoming steep, both literally and figuratively. It felt like it was time to stop wandering and to find somewhere cozy to settle in for awhile, where I could enjoy the scenery, the solitude, and the change of climate. This time, thankfully, I would not be making the trek alone.

In the last days of preparing to leave Rishikesh, I realized I'd been "assigned" a spiritual traveling companion. A quiet, reverent *sadhu* (Hindu holy man) with a lion's flowing white mane and beard, he was dressed in layers of stark white cloths and was otherwise unadorned, unpainted, and totally unpretentious. With virtually no belongings to his name, Kailash Babaji was a living, breathing example of total renunciation in action.

Here was a person who was literally "in the world yet not of the world." As a spiritual being, he was "walking his talk" in every way imaginable, living a life of consummate non-attachment while adhering to the stringent, orthodox Brahmin practices that had been his family's heritage.

An enigmatic character, speaking fluent, articulate English, Kailash Babaji had been "teaching meditation" to a few of the Westerners I'd met at Parmarth Niketan ashram. He would be the first to agree that meditation is something that cannot be taught. It happens. And helping to augment the conditions in which the possibility of meditation might happen more easily was his forté. I did not understand what was actually happening when I sat before him for the first time, in the steep, hillside gardens overlooking Parmarth Niketan ashram, and closed my eyes. But, those moments had been transformational—and unforgettable.

He'd spoken nostalgically about a summer he had spent with a Tibetan family, many years back, in an area just north of the mountain city of Almora, and wistfully, he'd mentioned how much he wished he could go back there for a visit. At the time, I was just about to head for Nainital and Kainchi ashram, which were in the same general vicinity, and I welcomed him to share the ride with me. He knew the territory—in more ways than I could have dreamed. Little did I know, but I had adopted a sadhu. We ended up traveling together for the next two months, availing me of an ongoing spiritual intensive— a crash course in uncompromising devotion.

Oneness took the opportunity to pave the way for the journey with priceless guidance about the nature of an authentic spiritual renunciant. The words of wisdom prepared me to understand and appreciate the nuances of the way of the true sadhu.

Oneness describes the way of the authentic spiritual sadhu
Oneness speaks:

You have invited Kailash Babaji to accompany you on a wondrous adventure, and the perfection of that arrangement will soon be readily apparent to you. Now you will learn to transcend your own need to be *right* and to challenge what, to appearances, defies logic. There is no logic to much of what you will encounter in the presence of this being. He has learned and has come to embody the concept of *surrender*. Study him. Be aware of the nuances of the choices he makes. There is nothing random here. All is purposeful. Do not challenge his practices. Simply observe them. And watch the perfection of the *synchronicity* that is summoned forth from the ethers.

This being has no inherent sense that he needs to *do* anything at all. Initially, you had difficulty with this concept. It is not rooted in a sense of laziness that this is so, but simply due to the fact that there is no requirement of the linear participation of mind in the creation of his experience. He is in *surrender*. What is required for his comfort is provided automatically. His needs are met instantly. He has no question that this is so. He has mastered the formula. Watch him. He will amaze you

Kailash Babaji has no need to *participate*, to interact in the material world in the sense that *work* would be required in order to acquire what might be needed. His needs are virtually non-existent. It is not because he has renounced the world that this is so, but due to his realization that the world is non-existent. He is merely allowing an aspect of his Presence to glide through this scenery, magnetizing what minimal accoutrements may be helpful to him.

He struggles with the idea of people lavishing money upon themselves, for he considers most of the items you would consider essential to be superfluous. His priorities insure that he is able to waft lightly through this landscape of illusory imagery. He does not wish to carry a heavy load, either symbolically or actually. For, in actuality, nothing is there. He is showing you how it is done. You are here to watch.

There is no *attachment to outcome* anywhere to be found. There is sublime *indifference* and a reluctance to make commitments. It is a lifestyle totally devoid of structure, seemingly devoid of purpose. Yet, that very purposelessness is an attestation to this being's consummate disconnection from all things external to Source. The focus is not rooted in the illusion. It is within.

It is with that consummate sense of *inner focus* that you will approach this journey. Do not concern yourself with the mundane details. Allow them to take care of themselves. Be willing to be totally detached from the inclination to try to control the process. Allow synchronicity to show you the way, and be prepared to follow the clues that are provided, simply by being aware.

Oneness outlines the principles of living with total non-attachment within the material world

Be watchful in all that you do. Be Present in every moment. For, each moment is only the *Nowness* of it. Anticipating future difficulties has no place in this journey. There is no future. There is only Now. *Trust* that the highest possible outcome will be made manifest for you. *Surrender* to the possibility that this is so. You will be guided sure-footedly on this journey by your own highest Presence. Let that aspect of who you Are preside within you. Resist nothing. Judge nothing. Be willing to go along with the program. You need to orchestrate none of it. You are simply along for the ride.

You will become aware of the simplicity of the life of the true sadhu on this journey. Observe the way these people live. Do not judge them. There is no logic in this—nor is there meant to be. They are following the inclinations of their *inner-knowingness* in the practices in which they may choose to engage. In truth, however, there are no right and wrong practices. There is only choice in the expression of one's sense of inner-directedness. There is only freedom when one chooses to embrace oneself and forego the temptations that beckon from the world of illusion.

There is no need to interact with these elements of perception. Simply be Present. Sustain the focus within the sense of *Self* awareness. All else is at liberty to swirl around you—myriad possibilities, there for your viewing pleasure, or not, as you see fit.

The Himalayan hill station of Almora and its neighboring villages provided what was perhaps the most breathtaking scenery I'd ever seen. Anandamayi Ma's ashram, a small, remote complex of aging buildings nestled into the side of a cliff on the outskirts of town, would be home for the next few weeks. There, my little window looked out on a vast panorama of terraced mountains dotted with little cottages and footpaths. The air was filled with the fragrance of honeysuckle and champa flowers. And my heart was filled with the magnificence of all of it. It was a wonderful, quiet place to spend a few weeks.

There, the steep embankment, totally blanketed in manicured flower gardens, led to an ancient, crumbling *Devi* (Goddess) temple, perched on the edge of a cliff. The misty landscape was so classic in its imagery, it looked like an antique oil painting that had come to life. The hillside was peppered with a patchwork of grazing goats and the young women in vibrantly colored saris who tended them. Beyond, the distant mountains seem interwoven, one into the next, like two halves of a deck of cards being shuffled together. With this idyllic scenery as a backdrop, I'd found the perfect place to crawl inside myself and be quiet.

Here at this peaceful little ashram, I stayed in my room for much of the time and steeped myself in my spiritual practice. Hours on end of daily Mantra chanting, prayer, meditation, and communion with Oneness were interspersed only by spartan meals taken unceremoniously on a dank stone floor. By comparison, the utter simplicity and serenity of this rural, mountain ashram made the scene in Rishikesh seem like Disney World. Here, in this heavenly oasis, far from any sign of civilization, my experience of Divine connectedness began to intensify and build to a crescendo.

❧

Rasha speaks:

Oneness, I feel your presence within me. Once again, the tears and the magnificent ache in my heart chakra tell me that we are in a state of Oneness in this moment. I long to lose myself in this blessed state.

Let me not feel compelled to return to this absurd dream we call "reality." When I am in this Presence in this way, there is nothing left to be desired—literally. I want for nothing, short of being liberated from this illusory world. For, when we are in this state of Divine connectedness, there is nothing else that matters.

Let me walk forth within this blissful union! I do not wish to be sober anymore. I only long to remain in the embrace of this intoxication. Oh, Oneness! Take me with you this time. Let me leave this world of mundane desires and irrelevant worries. Is any of it important?

Outside my little window, the sun tucks itself secretly into the pocket of the misty haze that blankets a distant mountain. A little stream trickles its melody into the sweet, cool mountain air. Every inch of panorama is dotted with the colors of wildflowers—a patchwork quilt of life itself! This is what matters. This is what is so, right Now.

In this moment, every sense organ I have is saturated with your magnificence. You speak to me in every way imaginable, in a multi-sensory symphony of Divine bliss! Is it too irreverent to say, "Are we having fun yet?" to God? Are You enjoying this as much as I am? How could You not be? If we truly are Oneness, then We are in this together. And in this moment, We are co-creating the experience of sublime contentment. How sweet it is! How incredibly sweet it is.

Oneness speaks:

Drink in the sweet sensations that surround you, for this is your gift to yourself. This is what you have longed for, and you have manifested it. You have all that you have asked for now. You simply fail to recognize it much of the time.

There is literally nothing to worry about. Everything is in Divine order. You are being superbly cared for, and are in the company of a Light being with whom you have bonded in a wonderful heart connection. Now is a time for you to explore the experience of happiness. Steep yourself in it, for this is why you have come. Perhaps for the first time, you do not simply have "something to be happy about." You have *everything* to be happy about. And it will only grow in intensity, as this time unfolds for you.

You have come to a hill station high in the mountains, in *every* respect. Your focus is to be directed to the depths of your own being now. Much of your time will be spent in solitude from this point forth. You will immerse yourself in the depths of your experience of Divine connectedness, and that experience will continue to intensify. Simply be present in the magnificence of what you will experience. And know that it is your very own Divine Essence that has blessed you in this way.

Oh, Oneness! There are no words for what I am feeling. I know I could not have imagined this. This is far too real to be a dream. And it is too magnificent to be mundane reality. I think I have just encountered heaven here on earth! Not in terms of a place, but rather as a state of being I have sourced within my own self. I am in heaven! And I know, in the same breath, that heaven is within me. I can no longer question it.

I can no longer ask myself whether I have made all this up. I cannot wonder whether I am just a supremely deluded fool who is having one incredible experience. I could never have imagined it as good as this. Or, could I? I guess the bottom line is the biggest question of all: Who in heaven's name wrote this script? Literally.

Sustaining one's focus of awareness on the connection with Oneness
Oneness speaks:

From this point forth, you are to focus your awareness fully in the present moment. There is no need to think about what will follow or how everything will work out. Today is all there is. This moment is all there is. This connection is all there is. Be present in it. Do not waver. Do not stray.

Every vision is this connection. Every flower is this connection. Every being is this connection. Every breath you breathe is this connection. Every device you choose to employ is a means to this connection. Chant Mantras if you are inclined to do it, with your full, focused awareness upon this connection. Practice meditation if you are inclined to do it, with consummate awareness of this connection. Become lost in this connection. Become so focused in this connection that there is nothing—*Nothing*—outside this connection.

Oneness is everywhere, everyone, everything. There is only This. Your every thought will now be a reflection of that knowingness. Your awareness of what you have accepted, in theory, will deepen. And you will come to embody this understanding and to implement it with every word and with every gesture.

Everything present in your awareness is a reflection of your own state of beingness. Quell the turbulent seas of the ego-self. This is simply a movie, playing out a symbolic representation of a set of vibrational variables, for the reference of a pinpoint of consciousness.

The universal symphony of all of it is playing out before you in infinite variations on the theme of your hopes and your fears. Your experience is a composite of the repercussions of every Now moment acted out as choice—past, present, and future—in harmony with All That Is. Your vision of it is a reflection of the vantage point from which you have chosen to view it. And that choice is made in every moment, with every thought, with every action, with every breath of your conscious presence.

You have been given the recipe. Now the opportunity for you is to put the principles into action. Now you have come to the point in your journey where you can, indeed, turn the page and begin to put what you know into practice.

Oneness speaks about the universal Essence underlying the teachings of Oneness and outlines "The Way of the Master"

Now you can strengthen the skills of manifestation—not in the ways that have been practiced clandestinely by the elite schools of Divine understanding, but in ways that reflect the clear, uncomplicated Essence of it that is universal. This is not a science of rituals. This is the pure, simple Essence that underlies all of it.

This is not a *path*. This is not a "how-to" school of spirituality. This is a *means* to a path—that each of you can only walk alone. For the masses, most of whom require a shepherd to take them by the hand and tell them where to place each foot, this is *not* the way. This is the way of the Master. This is the way of the ones who can seize the concepts that have been provided and put them into practice, without looking to the left and to the right to be sure everyone else is in agreement.

This is not truth by consensus. For, consensus is built upon a foundation of the recognition of that which is "other than" Self. *This* truth is a reflection of the knowledge that there *Is* nothing other than Self. This is the way for those who are prepared to diverge from the freeway of consensus reality—and to walk alone.

You have come to the place in your own journey where the understandings will be put into practice, now. You will be in isolation and in solitude for some time to come. You will limit your communication with the outside world and focus upon the world within. You have been guided to a haven in which to complete the journey. Know that you are in good company, both in the physical and in the spiritual sense. Now there is truly nothing to think about—or to worry about. For, everything is truly in Divine order.

One evening, during the ashram's *arati*, I shifted spontaneously into a deep state of bliss in front of Anandamayi Ma's altar. I sensed that I had experienced darshan with her and Oneness confirmed it. It was my first encounter with the energies of "Mother." I was struck by an extraordinary combination of *power* and *gentleness*, a kind of Presence I had never experienced before.

Anandamayi Ma is considered to be one of the greatest Indian saints of modern times. Said to be the embodiment of The Divine Mother, she left her body in 1986. Once again, I experienced a distinct, timeless Presence and the darshan of a Guru who had long since passed on. The feeling of this energy, however, was very different from anything I had experienced before. There was such a sweetness to what I was feeling. Not only was I very much in bliss, but I also was filled with a profound sense of her gentleness.

When the chanting was over and everyone went outside, I stayed behind in the little sanctuary. I wanted to remain in meditation a while longer and was hoping for a chance to be alone with her. I knew that the experience of communion is what I had come there to have. Within moments, that experience manifested powerfully for me.

I sat quietly, with pen and notebook in hand, and her words flowed through my awareness as naturally as breath itself—no differently than if she had been there in physical form. The compassion and loving guidance that was offered by the Divine Mother, through the Presence of Anandamayi Ma, was beyond words and moved me deeply.

A darshan in silence with Anandamayi Ma
Anandamayi Ma speaks:

You have come seeking your Mother. Have you found her?

I believe I have. From the first moment I saw your picture, I felt a connection with you. Now, meditating here in your Presence, I have that same sense of connection. It feels extremely powerful and at the same time incredibly gentle. I believe I have found my connection with The Divine Mother here. It's very different from anything I've ever felt before.

You have little history with the energy of Mother. Instinctively, you have been mistrustful of these energies throughout most of your incarnate history. You have painful memories, buried deep within, of ancient conflicts and clashes of ego. Now, the focus of the efforts of all Creation are on the unification of the polarities of Father and Mother. You have come to embody that Unity.

You have come to demonstrate what is possible when one is able to feel the heart connection of your opposite and to embrace it. What you are tapping into here is your own ability to honor the truth in what you are feeling despite the fact that, clearly, you are on unfamiliar ground.

These are vastly different energies than the ones with which you have been surrounded in lifetime after lifetime. And yet, you can feel the Love that has been extended to you here. And so, the heart is able to transcend the mind, which is whispering "be careful!"

It is not an easy path that you have chosen in this lifetime. For, you will embody Oneness. You will transcend polarity and walk as the unification of these opposing energies within the world of duality. You have embraced the possibility of holding *these* energies as an equal part of your core Essence. It is for this reason that you have come in search of your Mother.

I saw you in my meditation this morning. I felt your blessing then. I know I did not imagine that.

Anandamayi Ma speaks of the energies of the Divine Mother

No, you did not imagine it. We were with you as you journeyed, as we are with you now. Your openness to receive this Presence is what makes the connection possible. Your heart has been humbled. You have learned *gentleness* and *compassion* from having lived through the trials and the agonies that you once assumed was reserved for others. Now you are able to speak from painful experience of your sojourn into humanness.

Now you are able to look in the face of gentleness and to recognize compassion as a *strength* rather than as a weakness. Now you can see through the eyes of your sister spirits, for having cried their tears yourself. Now you can understand the anguish of those caught in the human cycles of hopelessness and futility. Now you can look into the face of profound suffering and recognize it as your own. For, The Father has come home, now.

He has been lost on the battlefield since the beginning of time. He has used his might and his shrewd intellect to triumph over others, to seize the spoils of war, and to leave misery in his path in the name of his almighty ego. And a world of others suffered in silence as he did so.

But, in the fullness of time, the energies have come into balance now. The strong have learned gentleness and the gentle have discovered the inherent strength in it. The Mother within the Divine Essence of each of us has been reborn. And, in the fullness of time, that balance—that Unity—will be embodied by all humankind.

That is why you have come to this place in this moment in time. And this is what you will come to teach in the times to come. For, you are Father *and*

Mother incarnate, now. You have come on your knees, seeking forgiveness, praying for our blessing. Did you think we would not give it? Did you think there was a place where Love was *not*? Did you think that the very compassion your heart hungers for would be withheld from you? Did you think your heart would be cast aside from where you have placed it at the feet of The Mother?

This *compassion* has no limits. It does not include some and leave others out in the cold. It embraces all who seek shelter within it. It includes all who come and humble themselves before it. For, the Love of The Mother is a Love without question—and a Love without end.

Now you can speak of it for having tasted its sweetness and for having felt its gentle touch. Now you understand that you are no less deserving of mercy than any other creature. For, you have journeyed to the farthest reaches of the human experience. And you have returned—sometimes on your knees.

Now you will go out into the world. It is a world that is ruthless and knows no mercy. You will help to transform it with the teachings you will continue to bring forth. You will deliver unto humanity a new vision of human understanding. Not one that reflects the opposing views of Father and Mother, but one that represents a common vision.

You cannot hope to embody Oneness without an equal measure of The Mother's Love. Know that it is here for you. It will always be here for you. In that, nothing has changed—except that now you can see it. Our time together will be spent in communion, rather than in conversation. For, what needs to be said between us does not require words. You feel the essence of this heart. This is the gift you have come to receive.

Thank you! Thank you for this blessed darshan!

It was here, in this idyllic mountain setting, overlooking a gorgeous panorama of verdant, terraced hillsides, that I was introduced to the secret world of Hindu ritual. Huddled on a little blanket well before daybreak, I watched as Kailash Babaji carefully built a little fire with a special combination of different types of wood, in a square metal pot, for the fire ritual with which he began his daily *sadhana* (spiritual practice). After a lengthy routine of sacred ceremony, several hours of intense Sanskrit Mantra chanting began. It would be during this time that my program of daily meditation took place, during the months we traveled together.

The resonance of the chanting set the stage for a level of Presence I'd never before encountered during meditation. For me, his Mantra chanting sessions were like a vibrational rocket that carried me to levels of awareness that were unfathomable. Having had no formal instruction in meditation, I was left to explore my own inner world for hours on end and discovered what was possible through my own direct experience of it. Now, in the seclusion and sanctity of these lush green hills, I was primed and ready to begin my journey to the outer reaches of the world within.

Three meditational journeys, several days apart, catapulted me to yet another unprecedented level of awareness. Each one took place while Kailash Babaji chanted his morning Mantras and lasted for well over two hours.

When I descended the stone steps to the bottom of the ashram's rose garden where Kailash Babaji had his room, it felt like I was entering a holy sanctuary. I sat down quietly on the little picture window ledge, as I did every morning, and closed my eyes. A sense of calm contentment filled me as I felt myself becoming engulfed in an ocean of Divine Love. Instantly, it was as though I'd awakened into the embrace of Oneness. As Kailash Babaji began chanting his morning prayers, I wafted into meditation.

Initially, during the first experience, my awareness remained within my body much of the time. Then, quite suddenly, I felt my physical body begin to vibrate. I was shaking all over, vibrating faster and faster, until at last, my consciousness took off and began to soar.

The first meditation:

As my breathing slowed down and a state of trance carried me ever deeper within, I felt myself becoming infinitesimally small. I journeyed, as though I were swimming, through a very narrow golden tunnel and emerged out the top of the head of my own body, which sat in silent meditation in a void. I was present as awareness, within the semblance of my own form. I was not alone.

There, surrounding me, were all the Gurus and teachers who had helped to guide me all along the way. There they stood, side by side—the ones who were still incarnate, together with those who had long since departed from the physical world—all the blessed beings who had walked beside me throughout my spiritual journey. I was enveloped in a profound feeling of love for all of them and at the same time, I felt that love reflected back upon me. I knew that it was time to leave them now. They would not be going with me. Wherever I was going, I would have to go alone.

I emerged in a cloud of whiteness and sat down to wait, not knowing for what. It was a simple place, with the sense of being high on a plateau, but without anything else with which to contrast it. There was a sense of sky and a sense of ground—a sense of up and a sense of down—but all was misty whiteness.

Then, from out of nowhere, a figure shrouded in white approached me. The figure was faceless and had the sense of a human form under the white cloths, but the form was invisible. I was led to a beautiful little altar dotted with exquisite flowers, where I knelt down quietly. A deep sense of pure gratitude filled my entire being, and I felt tears of joy trickle down my cheeks.

After some time, the figure indicated that we should move on. So, I followed as I was led through the misty whiteness to a clearing where a large, bare altar of white marble awaited me. I understood immediately that this was a sacrificial altar. But, I had brought nothing with me as an offering. All I had was myself. So, I lay down upon it, closed my eyes, and offered myself, utterly, completely, and without reservation, to my Oneness. As I did, I felt my head being severed from my body.

There was no fear. There was no pain. Instinctively, I groped around to find the severed head, assuming it would be of some use to me, not realizing that I had, in fact, manifested a new one. Again, the head was severed from my body and a new one manifested instantly. I left the severed heads behind, understanding that I had no need for them, realizing that I had no attachment to them. In relinquishing everything, I knew that I had lost nothing. And getting up from the altar, I walked forth into the clouds of white mist, filled with an indescribable sense of serenity.

It was at this point that I realized that I was not the one I'd always assumed was "me." I was not "other than me." I was simply a highly augmented version of the presence I recognized as "myself." There before me stood many of the people who had played major roles in my life. All the members of my physical family who had left their bodies were there. All the people I'd known well—the ones I'd loved, the ones with whom I'd battled—all were there. But, they were not there as their physical selves. They were there in the fullness of their Divine Presence. I laughed in joy with them all, understanding that we had created the extraordinary movie of this physical lifetime together.

Suddenly, I was alone again. I sat back from the edge of what appeared to be a precipice, high above a vastness that extended out before me. I was filled to overflowing with bliss! As I allowed my awareness to explore that exquisite sensation, I experienced myself expanding and expanding. The outlines of my body, which gave definition to who I considered "myself" to be, became obscured in a blur of vastness, and I experienced the sense of "myself" merging totally with it. All sense of individual identity disappeared.

In that moment, I had become Awareness itself, experiencing my own electrifying Presence as blinding luminosity. At the same time, I was aware of my own physical body, which was deep in meditation and which was reeling in waves of bliss and startling surges of energy.

After some time, I lost all awareness of the sensations of the physical body, and once again, perceived myself as a non-physical Presence. The scene in which my awareness found itself had changed, however, to one that can only be described as fiery white opalescence. There was a sense of a place, of a few trees. All were glowing with the radiance of white fire, glistening and shimmering with energy I knew was Divine.

I sat before a little table, content in the knowledge that I was all-powerful and could manifest anything I wanted. But, what did I want? There really was nothing I needed, being utterly complete within myself. Flowers would be nice, I thought. And, instantly, bouquet after bouquet of magnificent flowers appeared before me—all the same. All shimmering white opalescence. All with a fragrance that was exquisite, but could not be identified as being "this" but not "that."

The flowers were nice, I thought, but what more did I want? I realized that I had no physical needs—I was non-physical. Food might be nice, I thought. And no sooner was the thought present, than platters of delectable food appeared before me. I tasted the food and it was the most delicious food I had ever had. But, I could not identify or describe the taste. There was nothing with which to contrast it. It all tasted the same.

I was reeling in ecstasy, which I recognized as my normal state of being. Naturally, there was nothing with which to contrast it. Ecstasy was the only way to feel. I manifested a comfortable place to sit—the most plush, wonderful seat imaginable, but it could not be described. It had no recognizable contours and nothing to distinguish it from any other seat. As happy as I was, I realized that I was becoming bored with my ability to manifest the ultimate expression of anything and everything—all of it appearing as shimmering white, fiery opalescence—all of it perfectly the same. I didn't have to do anything. I didn't have to try. There was no challenge in anything. And my own viewpoint was all there was in existence.

All I experienced was the ecstasy of the unwavering Love that radiated from within me. It was with this sense of almost excruciating joy—and the tingling hint of a Divine Presence—that I re-emerged within my physical body and came into conscious awareness in the little garden room, only to discover that Kailash Babaji was no longer chanting.

✍

The second meditation:

Instantly, I perceived myself as being present in the same setting as in the previous meditation. Everything was opalescent white with a tinge of fire-like brilliance. I had the sense of my own awareness, watching from behind, as an augmented version of myself sat in lotus position at the edge of an opalescent vastness.

My awareness flickered between the two perspectives. First, I was the one seated before the opalescent vastness, and then I was the one who watched her from behind—all the while, intensely aware of the energy building within my own physical form as it sat in the depths of stillness, in the small garden room.

Suddenly, there was the understanding that the being who sat overlooking the vastness was Oneness. My heart began to soar with indescribable sensations of Love that grew stronger as I approached her, and reaching out, I became enfolded in her embrace. In that instant, all sense of "me" disappeared from the vision, as I merged with Oneness completely. At the same time, I felt the tears of joy that began to trickle down the cheeks of my physical body, which sat motionless, as Kailash Babaji continued to chant his prayers.

I noted that my sense of self-perception was actually present in two places at the same time. One aspect of awareness was in the physical body, albeit fleetingly. And one was present in consciousness, as Oneness—as pure Awareness. There was no longer an aspect of self-perception in the vision, watching Oneness from behind—there was no "me"—there was only Oneness. And I Was That.

I had the sense of being absolutely electrified. And Love radiated from within me like an infinite force-field. I sat there and perceived myself as Oneness for quite some time. Then suddenly, I became aware that my physical body was not breathing and the focus of my awareness shifted back to the physical body. This time, however, what returned to the body was not the linear consciousness of Rasha. Instead, an Awareness exquisitely augmented by the energies of Divine Presence entered my physical body. Immediately, waves of emotion flooded over me, as tears began to pour down my face. I realized that I was experiencing Oneness through the medium of physical perception, the sensations of the physical form. In the same instant, I was back again in the world of flaming white opalescence, as Oneness. Then, as the emotions and the energies continued to build within my physical body, my awareness bounced back into the room, where once again, I was aware that Kailash Babaji was chanting a Mantra.

Back and forth, back and forth I went, faster and faster and faster, as I bounced in consciousness between the two worlds: one where I perceived myself as Oneness and the other where I perceived myself as Rasha in an exalted state of connectedness. My consciousness became a vibrating blur of the two images, like watching two movies alternating at lightning speed, flickering side by side, while aware that I was fully present as consciousness within each of them.

As the vibration of the two worlds continued to build and my awareness bounced back and forth between them, my physical body once again began to vibrate strongly, until, at last, the two worlds merged as one and my physical body, quite suddenly, became absolutely still. In that moment, I knew myself to be fully Present, simply as Oneness, within the context of my own physical form.

For a moment or two, I was present as Oneness in the little garden room and listened, as pure Awareness, as Kailash Babaji completed his chanting. Then, as the silence in the garden room engulfed me, my sense of self-perception as Rasha returned to my physical body and I felt my eyes open. My body hummed with the energies of my incredible journey. And the extraordinary glow from within remained—to remind me that I had not been dreaming.

The third meditation:

I emerged in awareness at the edge of a cliff. Kailash Babaji was with me. We sat, overlooking a golden vastness, facing each other. His little fire pot was in the middle, and he was chanting his prayers. I sat with eyes closed. When he was finished, he stood up and grabbed me, and unceremoniously threw me over the cliff. "Now fly!!" he called to me.

Somehow I had managed to grab hold of some rocks and was clinging to them for dear life. He shrugged his shoulders and turned his back, leaving me there clinging to the side of the mountain. I wasn't afraid, I was excited. I took a deep breath and let go. And with that, I was flying! Within minutes I became quite good at it. I looked up and could see him watching from the edge of the cliff, grinning from ear to ear.

In the next vision, I was once again alone, sitting in lotus position, facing a golden vastness. I could feel powerful waves of energy filling my body. Suddenly, I was thrust back into my physical body with such force that I was thrown backward into the screen behind the window ledge where I was sitting in Kailash Babaji's garden room. Once again, my awareness began to bounce back and forth between the place in the vision and the physical reality of the room. Back and forth, back and forth I went, between "there," which was non-physical and which I perceived as "out-there somewhere" and "here" which I perceived as physical and "real."

Suddenly, I had the realization that "there" is not "out there" at all! It is all "here"! The two realities are essentially in the same place. And as that understanding took hold within me, I experienced the sense of being in the golden vastness within the vision—"here"—in the physical room. And for a few moments, I experienced my own presence, within my physical body, knowing that the golden vastness was right there before me within the room.

I experienced several layers of spontaneous knowingness, that all of the visions are levels of overlapping reality that are, actually, right "here." There was a sense that the outer reaches of my experience—the ones that feel the most powerful and vast—are actually infinitesimally small, and that the physical reality, which I understood to be a more primitive level of awareness, is large. Ultimately, a knowingness emerged within me that the vastness, being non-physical, has no size at all. It is not larger than or smaller than anything. It simply Is. And it is all "here."

In the final vision, Kailash Babaji was once again with me. We were at the edge of yet another golden vastness. He took my hand and said "chello"—which I'd come to understand means "let's go!" in Hindi. And with that, we dove together into a golden cloud that hovered at the edge of the cliff.

Once within it, I saw that the cloud was actually a cave. The image was vivid. Again, we sat facing each other before his little fire box. The flames were brilliant white and they leaped and crackled, but they did not radiate any heat. He looked at me intently. "Step into the fire," he said. I did not question him. I stood up and stepped into the fire. And as I did, the entire scene—the cave, my body, the fire box and Kailash Babaji himself—vanished into a little white plume of smoke.

In its place, was a beautiful physical panorama as seen from a mountainside, a breathtaking slice of physical imagery, which I also experienced as real. Suddenly, I became aware that the chanting within the garden room had stopped. Once again, I was fully present in my physical body. And with a breath of pure contentedness, I opened my eyes.

I was awestruck by the intensity of what had begun to happen during those sessions. Exhilarated and yet baffled by what I had begun to experience, I went to Oneness for clarity on what was happening to me. Once again, the wisdom of Oneness helped me to put my experiences into perspective

Words of wisdom from Oneness

Oneness speaks:

You have come to a crossroads in your journey now. There is a point where one must go off alone. Kailash Babaji cannot do this *for* you—nor would you wish him to. He has led you, literally, to the edge of the cliff. Yet, the moment of flight is a choice only you can make.

You have come all this way, on your own. You will complete the journey on your own. The depths to which you are destined to travel must be reached within the sanctity of your *own* being. Each time you venture forth in your daily meditations, you will come a little closer to the experience of your own true Essence. Each time you return, in consciousness, to your physical form, you will do so as an ever-heightened aspect of your own identity. Ultimately, the one who returns to your form as the epitome of that identity will stabilize and remain present at that heightened level.

In the interim period, you can expect to experience fluctuations in self-perception and the sense of alternately leaping forward and backsliding that has been characteristic of the journey itself. Now those fluctuations are taking place at an extremely heightened level of awareness. You are aware that you are bouncing between many worlds and in and out of layers of what is, essentially, illusion.

Oneness re-emphasizes the importance of protecting one's energy field

The levels of *energy* with which you have fortified yourself open the doors to this level of experience. Your job now is to focus your attention, as never before, on the objective of maintaining your *energy field*. Now is the time to put into practice all that you know, all you have written, and all you will come to teach.

Your focus is to remain at the top of the mountain. That is where you are headed. That is the only thing that matters. Anything that falls short of supporting that objective is unimportant. You will wish to become ruthless, if necessary, in your choices of whether to remain in environments that are vibrationally diminished or imbalanced. You will wish to avoid, at all costs, individuals and situations that are discordant. Your time and the focus of your attention is to remain on stabilizing your energy field at the highest level possible and sustaining that level of vibration.

Your energy field is your treasure. Protect it with all that you are, all that you do and all that you have. Cloister yourself as much as possible. Do not venture into negative environments. This is the true underlying purpose of seeking an ashram or monastery for one's spiritual journey. It is not for the purpose of what may or may not be done in such places, so much as the sanctity of the environment that is possible when one retreats totally from the adversity of the physical world.

You have explored, in painful detail, what happens when you take heightened energies out into compromised environments. You have watched yourself plummet from the heights of exultation to the depths of despair in seemingly no time at all, when confronted by the negative energy of another person or situation. You have wrestled with the frustration and exasperation of losing your precious energy—and thus the heightened levels of experience you are able to manifest—again and again.

You have recognized what is happening and have been left helpless to do anything about it. You have experienced yourself as the vibrational victim of circumstances seemingly beyond your control, more times than you have been able to count. But, the fact is, the choices to place yourself in those circumstances were made by you.

The priorities with which you made those choices were not ones that placed a high value on the maintenance of your energy field. And your experience reflected it for you, over and over again. You were driven by the need to try to remain in the good graces of others, rather than do what you knew, instinctively, was in your own highest interests.

Oneness talks about the price of *compromise* in the name of peace and harmony

Your tendency to compromise your own highest good in the name of peace and harmony has cost you dearly. Now you do not have the luxury of such lapses in judgment. Everything you do, everything you say, everything you think will be reflected instantly in the reality you manifest.

Dr. Bindu has spoken with you in depth on this concept, from the barest beginnings of your work with him. Now, Kailash Babaji is here to demonstrate to you how these principles are put into action. He has also been trained extensively in this respect. Observe him. He does not cut corners. He does not cheat on himself. He does what he knows is the highest choice. He knows that there is only one way—the highest way. He is impeccable in his practice. And he will teach you how those principles are put in action, simply by watching how he goes about his daily life. He has much to teach you, simply by being who he is.

He has not come to teach you metaphysical theory, rituals, chants, and techniques. This you have already learned or will come to know in due course of time. He has come to teach you *self-mastery.* Watch him carefully. Study him. And ultimately, you will experience within your own being a depth of understanding you have not before encountered.

The key to experiencing one's Divine connection with ease

When your heart is engaged in your spiritual practice, your experience of Divine connectedness is instantaneous. There is no need to dedicate great *effort* to spiritual practice for it to be powerfully effective for you. What is required is a total dedication of *heart* to one objective and to that alone: your experience of Divine connectedness. Once you have established your connection, you are able to sustain it virtually as long as you wish, simply by being fully *present* within the embrace of the connection. This process is quite easy when you have no doubts whatsoever that a Divine connection awaits you. You simply open to it and merge with it.

Most who yearn for such a connection, however, do so from the mindset of believing that the connection is out of reach—and so it remains for them. Most of the beings in your reality who consider themselves to be spiritually focused go to elaborate lengths to attempt to open a door they assume is locked tight. The door is, in fact, wide open, yet they continue to operate under the effects of the illusion that what they seek is difficult to achieve.

They develop complex, convoluted paths calculated to lead them past the self-imposed obstacles they perceive as being in the way. And the better part of the time they spend in devotional practices is spent executing rituals that *beseech* and thus *reinforce* the conditions for sustaining a perceived state of Divine *illusiveness.*

How a mind-set of *unworthiness* undermines perception of a Divine connection

These practices become traditions that are deeply ingrained in the cultures and consciousness of much of your world. The better part of the population that is performing these rituals do so with the energy of *unworthiness* to experience the very thing for which they yearn so deeply. It is that reinforcement of the sense of shame and unworthiness that serves as a barrier to spiritual fulfillment through practices that, when executed in a state of *heartfelt devotion*, are perfectly capable of delivering the seeker to his destination.

The key to all that is sought by the spiritually hungering masses of your world lies not in which practice is chosen and performed, but rather, in one's sense of heartfelt alignment with the Divinity *within*. It is this connection that you have sourced and which guides you easily through the eternally open door that awaits all humankind.

As my time in Uttaranchal, high in the Himalayas, began drawing to a close, I scheduled several day trips to sacred sites and local places of interest. One of those journeys took me to a mysterious destination called

Binsar Forest. I was intrigued by the stories I'd heard of extraordinary mystical experiences people reported having in this legendary forest. Without much more than that to go on, I booked a rugged mountain jeep and a driver for the day, and, with Kailash Babaji along for the ride, headed off into the hills.

Binsar was described in the guidebooks as a "hill station," high in the Himalayas, several miles outside of Almora. In my mind's eye, I'd anticipated a town, a village, some sort of civilization. Instead, I encountered a world of nature that unfolded before me in a way I never would have dreamed.

The jeep took us as far as a tourist guesthouse that was perched on the side of a cliff. It offered a panoramic view of the lush, terraced hillside that was unbelievably breathtaking. Beyond that point, travel was only permitted on foot. So, off we went down a quiet country road that wound ever-upward through the lush green forest, poised and ready for something "otherworldly" to happen.

The beauty of the natural setting was captivating and peaceful—but non-descript. It looked like any number of walks-in-the-woods one might have anywhere in the world. I was baffled. Could this be the right place? I wondered. After a few kilometers walk and a stop at a forest-department retreat station to admire the flower gardens, I started to wonder what the big attraction here was supposed to be. As far as I could see, there was nothing in Binsar Forest but a lot of trees. We turned around and started to head back to the waiting jeep.

En route, the adventure began. Kailash Babaji walked ahead, as always, eager to keep moving. As he did, I became enveloped in a strange, inviting stillness—the mysterious, secret world of the forest. Suddenly, I became keenly aware of all the life around me, as if I were awake for the very first time. The moss-covered tree trunks began to sparkle in the filtered sunlight, taking on a radiance I'd never before encountered. It was as though they were coming to life before my very eyes.

I was aware of consciousness all around me, and had the feeling that I was communing with life forms that were anything but inanimate. As I watched the trees intently, fascinated by the energies I was feeling all around me, the trees suddenly began to move. They moved as though they were dancing. The trees were actually bouncing up and down before my very eyes, as if to greet me. I was spellbound.

As I continued to gaze deeply at the vision before me, the entire scene took on a non-physical quality that was unlike anything I'd ever seen. The forest seemed like it had a liquid-type essence. And everything before me, the moss-covered tree trunks, the swaying branches, the canopy of leaves, the densely shaded forest floor—the entire scene and all things in it—started to undulate and shimmer as though they were not made of solid matter at all.

Suddenly I felt a gentle breeze blowing steadily in my face. The branches directly before me began dancing animatedly as the breeze continued. All the surrounding trees were perfectly still. There was not a breath of wind anywhere else in the forest, just a strong steady breeze that appeared to be focused only on me, caressing my skin. My hair began to fly wildly around my head, while everything else in sight was absolutely still. I began to feel a strong sense of connectedness, through my heart chakra, with the scene before me. And a feeling of absolute happiness grew from deep within.

Kailash Babaji was, by that time, totally out of sight, and I realized that what I was witnessing was there for my eyes only. The ground took on an unreal, non-physical quality, and I was unable to tell whether my feet were upon the ground or somewhere within it. I stood there, mesmerized, for who knows how long, just taking it all in. After awhile, I decided it was probably time to start walking toward the waiting jeep.

When I arrived back at the tourist guesthouse where we'd parked, I noticed a verandah with a spectacular view, perched on the top of the hill. I was, by then, deeply in trance and walked very tentatively to admire the scenery from its vantage point. As I approached it, my attention was drawn to a beautiful little flower garden where a variety of yellow-gold flowers twinkled in the sunlight with an otherworldly glow.

As I stood there and watched the flowers intently, they came to life before my eyes. The flowers literally began to dance, moving playfully with a legion of yellow butterflies that suddenly swarmed all around them. I experienced a sense of utter joy, sharing in their play, as they swayed and bounced before me. The sun was blazing hot overhead and the air was dead still. Yet, the flowers and butterflies moved and swayed rhythmically as though in the arms of a playful breeze. It was an extraordinary sight.

I climbed into the jeep, reluctant to leave the secret world that had revealed itself to me and began to recount my vision to Kailash Babaji. He listened quietly and nodded knowingly. As always, his meaningful silence left me to wonder whether he had actually read my mind and knew what I had seen—or perhaps simply was thinking "crazy American woman," as he humored me with his ever-present, enigmatic smile.

I asked Oneness, on my return, for some insight into the phenomenon that had revealed itself so mysteriously.

Oneness reveals a glimpse of the mystery underlying the illusion of material reality

Rasha, your experience revealed to you another layer of reality that dwells within the world you know and recognize. As your *heart* opened to the scene that revealed itself before you, you were able to perceive that world as it appears from the vantage point of an exalted plateau. From that perspective, the illusion of physicality, in all its static limitation, gave way to a more fluid vision. You were able to perceive a world that is alive with the joy of beingness. You were able to see "the world" as it truly is.

In the denser realities that comprise the world as you know it, what is perceived is limited to the parameters of duality. That is, you are able to see what "is" as opposed to what it "is not." The vision of the world as you know it is a static phenomenon. The reality you glimpsed is not one that is limited in that way. Its nature is a fluid one that is ever-changing, shifting its essence as a reflection of the consciousness that is creating it in the ever-present moment of Now.

The scenes you witnessed were nothing less than physical images that emerged in response to the joy experienced by the life forms that greeted you. Your fascination with your perception of them was acknowledged. And your heart chakra resonated with the sense of joy and welcoming that was projected, and in which you shared.

You were given a glimpse into that level of reality in a way that was not complex and was limited to the world of nature. As you noticed, Kailash Babaji did not stay to partake of your vision or to become part of it. He felt guided to exit the scene. For a first experience, the vision you were able to perceive was to be a simple one. And the life forms that were scripted to participate were those untouched by the complications of energies compromised by their presence in denser realities.

You were given a vision that was, essentially, "pure." Were there to have been another human being in the picture, your perception would have been compromised and the impression would have been confusing The experience was a perfect illustration for you of a world that transcends the parameters of duality, where the imagery provides an instantaneous, ever-shifting reflection of the consciousness present.

23

Summer/Fall 2002
Vrindavan, Uttar Pradesh
A Visit to the Mystical World of Krishna

———

I returned to Vrindavan in mid-August 2002, fully prepared to steep myself
in the joys and the mystery of a heart-connection with the energies of
Krishna that had been touched upon briefly three months earlier. There,
something indescribable began to awaken within me, and, as the experience
deepened, my heart opened to an intensity of feeling that I had never imagined
possible.

The experiences in meditation during the prior months in Uttaranchal
had served to prepare me for these new levels of experience. Now, once again
in Vrindavan, the mystical home of Lord Krishna, my heart surrendered to
the embrace of the Divine.

An otherworldly experience with the Divine Presence of Lord Krishna

The magnificent Krishna Balarama Mandir, better known as the Hare
Krishna temple, a palatial house of worship in the heart of Vrindavan, set
the stage for a most extraordinary vision. One evening, I stood in blissful
inner silence before one of several altars high on an enormous platform and
beheld a breathtaking display of life-size, marble statues of Krishna, his wife
Radha, and the attendant *gopi* girls (milkmaids) of ancient Hindu legend.
The statues were decked out in fabulously embroidered and bejeweled silk
garments, adorned in sumptuous garlands of fragrant flowers and decorated
in unimaginable opulence. The sensuousness with which this expression of
Divine worship took form was almost beyond description.

I stood there mesmerized, drinking in the energies, sharing in the Divine
intoxication of the hundreds of devotees who swayed in surrender to the
rhythms of the drumming and chanting that Hare Krishna temples are known
for. As I continued to gaze at the Deities before me, I noticed that my vision
had begun to alter. Slowly, I felt my awareness being drawn ever-deeper into
the images before me.

I watched, fascinated, as tones of green and pastel hues all began to blend
together into a warm glow of peach-colored radiance, which deepened before
my very eyes. In the next breath, the peach tones transformed into what can

only be described as "pure gold." The entire display radiated a bright, golden effulgence as, without blinking, I continued to gaze at it.

My breathing had slowed down and I was aware that, for quite lengthy intervals, I was not breathing at all—which, somehow, did not concern me. I was not "holding my breath." I was simply not breathing. Oddly enough, I experienced the absence of the need for breathing to be a pleasure sensation.

Then, in one timeless instant, my *awareness* and the *object* of my awareness—the vision before me—seemed to merge as one. Suddenly, there was no physical perception of "me" at all. As I continued to watch in fascination, the brilliant golden sight before me began to transform from the quality of solid gold to that of liquid gold. And with that, the details of the image began to undulate, as though the vision had been projected onto the surface of a vertical body of water. As I imbibed the multi-sensory nuances of the vision, my entire being became consumed in levels of Bliss that could only be Divine.

Later, I asked Oneness to explain to me what actually had happened during that experience.

❧

Oneness speaks:

You have opened yourself to the energies you identify as Krishna. You have sought this experience in order to put into perspective your understanding of the nature of the essence of Father, within the context of physicality. Your own embodiment of these energies was part of the gift you have chosen to give yourself.

Oneness speaks about the energies of the Krishna experience and the significance of the physical senses in the process of spiritual awakening

The essence of the Krishna principle is that which many of you have denied, repressing the essence of life itself that pulses within you. You have not been asked to become deadened to the joys of the physical world. For, you are here, fully present in physical form, within the context of this world.

The embracing of the energies of Krishna, and allowing that sweetness full reign within you, opens doors within that have long been locked tight. There is nothing more Godly in rigidity and austerity than there is in decadence and excess. These simply are *options*—choices one is able to make—within the context of the physical expression of one's Divine focus.

The Father principle is not simply that which is expressed through acts of aggression and stoic suppression of the feeling body—although humankind has succeeded in making *that* the recognizable norm for masculine expression for untold thousands of years.

Krishna dances within the hearts of each of you. He delights in the sensations of the physical world. He finds joy in every nuance of its infinite detail. He is not simply a persona, a character in ancient religious mythology who is worshipped as an externalized Deity. Krishna is what you have come to this lifetime to awaken within your own being as a pathway to your recognition of your own Divinity.

With these attributes goes the understanding that all *possibility* is simply the opportunity for *choice*. It is All which may be explored, tasted, touched, embraced, and gloried in—or not—according to the choices *you* make. There is no judgment programmed into the limitlessness of this adventure you call "life." There are no *right* and no *wrong* aspects of the Divinity that is represented here, symbolically, in form. There are simply the values and the standards which you may choose to adopt as your own.

Krishna is the place within *you* where the attributes of Father and those of Mother are allowed to merge—and to express as Oneness—regardless of whether you recognize yourself to be male or female. For, in the ways that are significant to this experience of spiritual awakening, there is truly no distinction. You are a timeless, limitless aspect of Divine Awareness, experiencing yourSelf in form within the context of duality. Simply that.

You, as Rasha, have chosen to become reacquainted with that aspect of Self through the delights of the experience of Krishna. You have chosen to discover that the aspects of humanness you presumed had been extinguished were simply dormant. And you have chosen to recognize the possibility that *any* aspect of that foray into limitlessness may be selected and experienced—without judgment—if you wish to do so.

At the same time, the natural *consequences* of all actions are also to be embraced, if the perfection in this principle is to be realized fully. You make the rules. You select the experience you wish to have. You experience the results. And the possibilities are limitless. It's that simple.

Your experience in the temple was a visual representation of the heightening of the energies you allowed to permeate your being in those moments. By consciously opening yourself, totally and without hesitation, and allowing yourself to merge with the energies present, you were able to transcend the physical illusion of the object of your visual focus and to experience another level of perception.

How one's own vibration determines the way physical experience is perceived

It is not a question of what is or is not really there. For, all that is *really* there is energy. Your level of vibration determines the level at which you are able to *perceive* and/or to *experience* that energy. In the case of what transpired at the temple, your visual experience, as well as the sensations of pleasure in your heart center, affirmed for you that a profound connection had been achieved. You embraced that possibility. And you enjoyed it.

It is these kinds of experiences that are becoming increasingly available to you, as you augment your energies as a natural part of your own process of emergence. It is this level of experiential delight that is possible, at will, in the heightened stages of this journey—for *all* humankind.

During the three months I spent in Vrindavan, I delved into an intense spiritual practice, focused on devotion, for hours each morning. I sensed a strong field of *energy* building within me while I chanted certain Mantras. Yet, the irony was that when I invoked the Presence of Oneness, as I began my daily prayers, I was catapulted into bliss instantly. When I then started chanting Mantras, that state of bliss was no longer perceived.

Ultimately, over time, that blissful state would grow to be very much a part of my spiritual *sadhana* (devotional practice). But, at this point in my journey I was simply experiencing *energy*. I went to Oneness to help me understand what was actually happening during these experiences.

Oneness talks about the power of *meditation* as a tool for the skill of detachment from identification with the body and the physical world

Oneness speaks:

If you choose to include the practice of chanting Mantras as part of your ritual of devotion, that is surely your choice. However, it does not affect your state of connectedness to *this* Source in any way. This connection is *within* you. This connection is fortified by your state of openness to the experience of this connection, and only that.

It is your state of utter *surrender* that is to be cultivated in this timeframe. For, it is in this skill of total *detachment* from identification with your physical vehicle, and its perceptions of the illusion of the physical world around you, that the possibilities for the full embodiment of the energies of Oneness lie. You are learning this level of detachment as part of the exercise of *meditation*.

Ultimately, you will be able to be in that state of *meditative detachment* while awake and aware within the illusion of physical reality. It is this skill that you are now strengthening. In this moment, for example, you have suspended self-awareness, and you have observed that the typing of this communication is happening automatically.

Your mind has absolutely no role in this process now. You have suspended it totally. And it is as though someone else were typing these words through the vehicle of your physical form. You will notice that your fingers are moving far faster in this moment, without any thought of where the next word or phrase is coming from, than ever you would be able to do when in the normal process of writing.

Rasha speaks:

True. This is absolutely amazing!

It is this level of *detachment* that you will wish to cultivate in your every waking moment. "You" will be present and aware. Yet, the fullness of your conscious Presence will be as Oneness. You have noticed, during your meditations, that there are moments when you know, without question, that Oneness is fully Present within your physical form.

In these moments, there is no awareness of "Rasha." There is awareness only of Oneness—*as* Oneness. There is no one who is *watching* Oneness. There is simply awareness of *being* Oneness. In these moments you demonstrate the fullness of the process that will become a natural state of Being in the conscious, waking state. In this very moment, we Are Oneness— together. And so it shall be in the times to come.

Oneness, I would like to talk about what is happening in my meditations. I'd like to understand why now I am simply feeling intense energy, building and building within my own physical presence here, whereas, previously, I had an awareness that my consciousness was "elsewhere."

Spontaneous revelation hits with a crucial understanding: I am not my body!

My full awareness was there. And yet, there was marginal awareness, intermittently, of feelings of joy within me here. Perhaps what I perceived "myself" to be experiencing had nothing to do with the body that was here at all! The feelings (of joy, bliss—whatever) have nothing whatsoever to do with this physical body! They are not happening in my body. They are happening at another level of awareness entirely.

But, tell me please: in some of those experiences, I was aware that tears were rolling down the cheeks of this physical body. Why was that, if the experience were transpiring elsewhere?

Oneness illustrates the concept of Presence

The focus of your awareness was centered in the experience of the vastness. The sensations of joy—the *feelings* which accompanied that experience—were perceived *multi-dimensionally.* Within the realm of *linear perception*, that experience of exultation manifested as tears of joy which ran down the cheeks of the physical form in which you believe your awareness to be normally present. But, in actuality, *you* transcended form in those moments.

You are simply conditioned to believe that *you* had journeyed *elsewhere.* There *is* no "elsewhere"—no more than there is a "here and now." These are constructs you have created in order to give yourself a frame of reference in which to place your experiences. The linear mind is designed to require *structure* in order to process experience. But, in fact, there is no structure. There is simply Presence.

A vivid early experience of embodying Oneness

I understand. So, let me try to process this now, with your help. For example: there was an experience which involved a cliff within my consciousness. I experienced a bouncing back and forth of my awareness between my physical body, which sat in meditation and

289

the body that I perceived sitting at the edge of the cliff, overlooking the vastness.

As the images bounced back and forth, faster and faster, I felt the two images uniting as one. And I experienced myself as sitting at the edge of the cliff—here! Then, in the next moment, there was no "Rasha" identity at all. For, I knew without question that what experienced itself as Presence was Oneness!

Now my meditations are not embellished with any imagery at all. Most of the time, during meditation, what I perceive is nothing. There is no thought. There is not even an awareness of the visual "nothingness" that I have experienced in the past. There simply is extraordinary energy, which builds within me. Can you tell me what is happening during these moments?

A tentative experience of Ultimate Reality

You are being given a taste of the experience of *Ultimate Reality* within the context of physical form, in these moments. There is no sense of visual perception because there *is* nothing to see—and there is nothing with which to see it. In these fleeting moments, *you* do not exist. For, your existence is merely a reflection of a focus of awareness. In those moments, your awareness has been suspended totally within the embrace of Oneness.

This experience was one with which you were gifted, to give you a frame of reference within which to place all of what is now transpiring within you. This was a *peak experience*, perceived as *feeling* and simultaneously interpreted visually by your consciousness. In the height of this experience, you perceived the unification of your full multidimensional essence vibrationally—through the linear vehicle of your physical form.

In that moment *you* were complete. All the pieces of your fragmented essence were fused as One Divine Essence. You were not simply "Rasha," experiencing unity with the level of awareness you have come to identify as "Oneness." In that moment, you were All of it. You experienced the culmination of the journey within the context of *feeling*. It was perceived by your linear awareness, which was, in that moment, focused in the sensations of your physical form.

This frame of reference is not an experience you can expect to duplicate from this point forth—nor should you need to. It simply is an illustration for you of where you are going. Ultimately, you *will* experience this as a sustained Presence. For, it is this that *you* truly Are. Yet, the *you* that will have this experience at the culmination of your journey is not the same you who you now consider yourself to be.

That *you*, through the grace of her *physical* Presence, was able to translate this experience—which was actually only a manifestation of energy—into a quantifiable format through which *you*, the multidimensional *consciousness* that transcends the limitations of form and linear awareness, were able to perceive it.

This journey is not a linear race toward a goal. It is an experiential voyage into the process of *expansion*. You are giving yourself a full spectrum of visual and sensory experiences on the way to Oneness with all that you truly Are. You are being gifted with a full smorgasbord of *tastes* of the delights of the journey, so that you are able to speak of these phenomena from a place of having experienced them yourself—not merely from having intellectualized the process and drawn conclusions with your logical mind.

You have not come to this moment in your unfoldment to establish a "personal best" against which other experiences might be measured. There is no competition—within the context of the personal self, or otherwise—on this journey. You have come for the *experience* of it. Simply that. The invitation has been extended to you. And the possibility is great that, once you allow yourself to relax into the embrace of all that transpires within you, there is unimaginable joy yet to be discovered.

My time in Vrindavan was focused, for the most part, on proofreading and editing the final proofs of the book, *Oneness,* which was about to be printed for the first time. For weeks of days on end, I confined myself to my room, braving the 105+ degree heat under a whirling overhead propeller fan while scrutinizing every line for the edits and errors with which an over-zealous editor in California had peppered the entire manuscript. My daily conversations with Oneness and an intensifying spiritual practice of prayer, Mantra chanting, and meditation, left time for little else. An occasional visit from Govinda, the Brahmin preacher I'd met just before leaving for Rishikesh in the spring, was a welcome reprieve from the intensity of all of it.

Little did I suspect at the time, but with the awakening of the heart that Vrindavan is known for, the stage was also being set for the powerful experience of spiritual deception, and the inherent lesson of spiritual *discernment*. While still in Rishikesh, I had shared several beautiful meditations in Govinda's presence during his visit there and had experienced incredible heights of ecstatic Divine connectedness and extraordinary sensations of *energy*. I was convinced I'd encountered a deep *karmic* connection.

I would go on to discover that what *feels* "kindred," in that there is a sense of timeless familiarity with someone, does not guarantee that the ancient history that may once have been shared was necessarily wholesome. It surely is not a barometer for gauging the purity of the agenda of the "kindred spirit" in question.

Now, once again back in Vrindavan, I resumed a program of regular meditation sessions with Govinda, and the intensity of my experiences deepened by the day, as I plunged into a self-styled practicum of inner discovery. Even though I was very clear that my experiences were my own and not attributable to another person, the sweet sensations of the heart, rekindled by the energies of Lord Krishna, led me to be innocently trusting. I would not come to understand, until much later, the dynamics of *energy piracy*, and how easy it is to be led down the primrose path by a seasoned spiritual charlatan.

In Govinda, I believed I had found a timeless brother-in-spirit who mirrored my own stage of spiritual emergence. He was a blossoming spiritual teacher in his own right—one whose youthful charm reflected the magnetism of the intoxicating energies of Lord Krishna all around us. It was a parallel, apparently, that countless others had drawn in his charismatic presence. Now, here I was in Vrindavan, a modern-day *gopi*, symbolically acting out the experience of legend.

According to the mythology of Lord Krishna, he appeared as a spiritual love-object to each of the gopi girls who adored him, individually—16,000 of them! He projected intense heart energy, which each received and reciprocated. He danced with them all! And each one thought she was the only one. This is the essence of the "Krishna experience." Now, here was Govinda, oozing spiritual charm and actually implying that he was the physical embodiment of Lord Krishna himself! I was ripe for the lesson.

Krishna is the Divine experience of the heart. It is an awakening to the very depths of one's own *feelings*—a level of *spiritual infatuation* that is so intense it almost feels like you've been drugged. Someone who is facilitating such an experience serves as a *messenger* for that experience. He/she is not the object of it, but simply the conduit through which energy is pouring. I knew all that—intellectually. I knew I was the one who was orchestrating the experience at some higher level, and that it was, actually, all symbolism. And even though I also knew I was on some sort of ride through virtual reality in spiritual Disneyland, discovering the depths of my own ability to feel, it still felt very real while it was happening.

From day one, I was given a small Sanskrit Mantra to chant and told to practice it hundreds of times a day, with a tulsi-bead *mala* for counting the repetitions. I would later come to understand that receiving a Sanskrit Mantra from someone is not something to be taken lightly. It is the classic doorway through which a *spiritual cord* is established with that individual. Intensive one-on-one meditation, face-to-face with another person is another way a *spiritual cord* can be created or strengthened.

Traditionally, a spiritual cord is the conduit through which a Guru is able to empower the student and provide energy to help accelerate the student's spiritual progress. What most of us do not realize is the possibility that these cords, which you might think are harmless enough, can also be used to reverse the flow of the energy, thereby draining the student and empowering the Guru! This insidious practice is apparently more widespread in India than we'd like to believe. For Westerners, who come to India innocently seeking to connect with a Guru, it's akin to taking candy from a baby.

There I was, floating along on a cloud of bliss, drinking in the ocean of Krishna energy all around me, completely unaware of the web into which I, all too willingly, had stepped with both feet. It was only as I was preparing to leave Vrindavan, months later—feeling vibrationally deflated and drained—that I started to suspect that something was amiss. When Govinda suddenly announced, out of the blue, that he was really "my Guru"—something a *real* Guru would never do—and began asking for sums of money, I realized that I had stepped into a classic trap. It was a ploy for which I'd been completely unprepared.

Meanwhile, Dr. Bindu, who appeared to have 20/20 remote vision, was able to describe everything that was happening to me, in vivid detail, over the phone, despite the fact that he was still in Mumbai, a thousand miles away. He cut me no slack in his scathing assessment of my predicament. He was not at all amused that I'd completely lost my energy, when it seemed like everything had been going so well. I left Vrindavan dejected, feeling like a fool, and headed for Mumbai to put my pieces back together.

There, Dr. Bindu patiently guided me in taking the entire ordeal apart and examining it piece by piece for the clues that had been right there in plain view all along, and to which I'd been so totally blind. I came to see how the trusting innocence we bring to India, as Western spiritual seekers, can leave us wide open to what is well-known there as a classic spiritual trap. Day by day, Dr. Bindu led me through the excruciating process of having to relive every last detail of my experience in Vrindavan—none of which, to my astonishment, had escaped his notice—in order to cull the pearl of real understanding from the shell of a badly shaken heart.

Weeks later, after going through the agonizing process of having spiritual cords officially "cut," I realized what a powerful lesson life had served me as part of my training. The most painful part was the sense of utter disillusionment that Govinda, someone whom I'd come to regard as a real friend, had been so blatantly deceitful. I was hopelessly naïve. It turns out that this practice is all too commonplace amongst would-be Gurus in India. My refresher course in "Spiritual Street-Smarts 101" had once again begun.

Oneness helps bring a poignant chapter to closure
Rasha speaks:

Oneness, now that I've distanced myself from Govinda and all the issues that came up for me in Vrindavan, I'd like to sift through some of it with you, to try to put what happened into perspective. Now, Dr. Bindu has begun to reveal things I never would have suspected about Govinda, and the systematic draining of my energy that was taking place during my meditations with him.

In light of what was revealed, I gave my permission for the energy "cords," that had apparently been established with Govinda, to be cut. I was astounded at how effectively this was done, virtually overnight. Before that time, I had been walking around in a heightened emotional state, profoundly heart-connected to a spiritual trickster who had won my trust and my respect on many levels.

Now, with the barrage of evidence provided by Dr. Bindu, it seems that it was all just an opportunistic scheme to drink my energies and drain my financial resources—a form of hypnotism, done with Tantric rituals, that was malicious and completely intentional.

It's hard to imagine how I could have been so naïve and trusting. Dr. Bindu said that when spiritual cords are cut, the disconnection goes both ways. Obviously, Govinda and I are now detached from each other at an emotional level. I feel absolutely nothing when I think of him. No sadness, no resentment, no emotions at all. It's bizarre.

Oneness, you know I totally believed that this was a timeless connection of heart with a kindred spirit. Now it seems that Govinda was nothing more than a spiritual con-man. Can we talk about this a little bit, so I can bring this chapter to closure?

Oneness delivers a powerful teaching on spiritual discernment
Oneness speaks:

Rasha, you have just completed a major exercise involving the opening of energy centers within you that had been locked up tight. Govinda served you in many ways, helping you to source, during your meditations, deep levels of emotion you had kept well hidden from yourself.

Dr. Bindu has succeeded, on many levels, in preparing you to do the work that is your destiny in this lifetime. But, at an emotional level, there were layers of experience where the process of release and integration was incomplete. It was necessary for you to break down the barriers that had been put into position and were essentially shielding you from yourself, in order for this emotional release work to be completed. Now, having once again tasted the intensity of your emotional responses, and having recognized the power it is capable of exerting over your choices, you are in a better position to regard the world through the clarified lens of *discernment*.

You were touched deeply by a being with whom you share a timeless connection of heart. You were told this from the onset. And it is no less true now than it was when you first opened that door. The fact that there are aspects of this individual's personal life that you found inappropriate and disillusioning does not diminish the level of connectedness you shared. It was that level of intensity that was necessary to break through the walls of insensitivity within which you had buried so much pain.

You were able to go on the journey, experientially, with Govinda, and at the same time, to keep the nature of the relationship platonic and the experiences you chose to share in perspective. You did not walk away from this experience emotionally damaged in any way whatsoever. If anything, you are more whole in your emotional body for having had the encounter than you would have been without it.

The lessons of discernment were complex and deep in this poignant chapter, which has now been brought to closure. You have been able to recognize the perfection that aspects of that training were programmed to deliver. And the intense sense of loss you experienced vibrationally was shown to be a short-lived phenomenon.

Your energies have now been fully restored. You walk in an exalted state of beingness, cleared of the densities that might have caused complications, had you not been stimulated into recognizing them and releasing them. Now there is no such risk. For, the residual densities have been released from your energy field. And there is nothing that remains with which to magnetize that type of experience.

You are now cleared of the possibility of being ensnared by the charms of a charismatic opportunist. You are more aware and less naïve than you were at the onset. You question why you had not been warned by this Source of the pitfalls in what you regard as deception. Yet, had we done so, you would have been spared the *experience* of it, which was, after all, the point of the exercise.

Oneness talks about the power of learning a lesson experientially rather than simply encountering the understanding conceptually

It would be simple enough to give you the "punch line" to every story that you encounter, in advance of your culling it out of the experience itself. But then, what would be the point of arranging such an experience? The object of this training is not to gloss over the lessons conceptually. The object is to journey into the depths of the drama and *to live it*—experientially. And you did that. Now, you are able to distance yourself from the details and to see much of it for what it actually is: symbolism.

You were able to feel your feelings deeply, but with total detachment. Then, when your emotions became entangled in Govinda's web, you had the opportunity to recognize what was happening and to regain control. You had the opportunity to assess the situation with Dr. Bindu's help. And ultimately, you had the opportunity to exercise your *discernment* and to choose to sever ties with this individual, when you recognized that the nature of the situation put all you are working toward at risk. You were given the chance to choose between yourself and your sense of loyalty to another being. You were given the chance to honor what was true for *you*, regardless of what was being said by whom.

In the days that followed, I continued to process the agonizing backlash of disappointment and disillusionment that accompanies an intense foray into the experience of spiritual deception. I'd assumed that a clear, rational *understanding* of what I'd just lived out symbolically, would spare me having to rehash the painful details and relive the emotions those details continued to stir up. I soon learned otherwise.

Oneness continues to explore the symbolism in a poignant drama and reveals the inherent lesson in the painful experience of spiritual deception

Oneness speaks:

What happened between you and Govinda was not, in itself, a transgression of any kind. You were in a sincere heart-space as far as he was concerned. And he was, experientially, at a comparable level with you. Yet, opportunistically, he took advantage of what he recognized was taking place *vibrationally*. And he helped himself in full measure to the energies you were building daily through your own intense devotional practice. It was this *energy piracy*, in the name of the sacred bond between Guru and student, which was met with a measure of justice that brought this activity to a stop.

You were far from the only one who was being exploited by Govinda. He was a master of manipulation and was reaping the harvest of the loving energies of sincere devotees of Krishna, by perpetrating the deception that he is, in some way, the embodiment of Krishna. This, surely, he is not.

Didn't you tell me, to some effect, that Govinda had come to teach me the Love of Krishna?

The Love of Krishna was kindled within *you* through the catalyst of this relationship. That is not to say that the energies of Krishna were borne by this being. Your heart-awakening was achieved in coming to Vrindavan and in encountering the energies of Krishna. It was your own heart connection to that aspect of your *own* Divinity that attracted a vibrationally compatible experiential partner.

Govinda's choice to exploit the vulnerability of his spiritual partners is what is at issue here. For, when one opens the heart completely—as is the Krishna experience—one becomes child like. One reclaims an innocence that is cradled in the safe and tender embrace of Lord Krishna himself. And feeling that cocoon of total protection, one opens completely—like a flower. That was what you went to Vrindavan to accomplish within yourself. And Govinda helped you to unearth the precious heart-center that had been buried deep within you.

It was not the intention of the Krishna consciousness that Govinda be permitted to help himself to the energies that were allowed to flow through those newly opened channels. It is for this reason that Govinda has been apprehended. You would be best advised to stop feeling guilty about walking away from the friendship. He was being extremely dishonest with you, and your trust was violated in ways you never came to suspect. You are far from the only one who was exploited in this way. Now it is best to turn the page.

You were deceived by a charismatic opportunist, with whom you share substantial karmic history. This is not the first time you have been "reeled in" by this being. This time no serious harm was done, and the transgressions that did take place were able to be rectified. You called the situation accurately when you described him as "the spider." For, indeed, he has played that role with the pure and trusting hearts of spiritual seekers for lifetimes.

There is no need to feel apologetic about what is sensible for you to do. Regardless of how fond you may have become of Govinda, maintaining contact with him is clearly not in your highest interests. You have no cause for regret. He does. For, you acted with a clear and open heart, whereas his motives for many aspects of what transpired between you were compromised.

    I feel very disillusioned.

Naturally, you do. Yet, at the same time, you recognize the gift in the "grand deception."

    Yes, I suppose I do.

Govinda was acting out a role in a script you co-created. Nothing more. You both enjoyed the friendship. Initially, you were both empowered by it. But then the relationship took a different turn. And instead of being on equal footing, you shifted into a "Guru/student" type of relationship, and the dynamics between you—and the nature of the *energies* transferred—changed.

It was in this configuration that he was able to establish and to deepen a connection with you with a time-honored system that was thoroughly misused. The opening that was created with the *spiritual cord* that was established was a connection designed for the empowerment of a student by a Guru. In this case, that open energy-pipeline was reversed and used to drain the resources of the student—and empower the Guru. Clearly this is not as the system was intended.

This lesson has been rich in ways you have only begun to understand. In time, as you peel back the experiential layers of this drama, you will see the depth of it. And you will see quite clearly where the timeless bond of trust and loyalty lies.

You have no need to feel apologetic for your need to back away now. This is as it needs to be. Honor yourself for having had the fullness of this experience, this journey into the inner recesses of your feeling body. Honor Govinda for accompanying you there. Bless him on his journey. And move forward.

I knew the answers I was seeking had already been planted within me, seeded by teachings I'd transcribed with my very own hands. My rational mind knew all too well how it was supposed to be processing what had happened. But, in my heart, I was devastated. I'd allowed myself to be completely *vulnerable*—trusting with the innocence of a child. At the same time, I knew it was that rarified level of vulnerability which had served to open within me the floodgates of Divine Love that lie harbored deep within us all.

The fires of contradiction continued to smolder within me as I continued to process and to dissect the intensity of my experience in Vrindavan. My heart wrestled with feelings deadlocked on polar opposite ends of the spectrum which couldn't seem to cancel each other out. On a feeling level, my heart continued to put the magnificence of my Divine encounter with the energies of Lord Krishna in juxtaposition with the heartbreak of the spiritual exploitation perpetrated by Govinda. Oneness continued to help me work through and balance the ecstasy and the anguish of that experience for months to come.

Oneness speaks:

This is Oneness. This is the connection which will bring into focus all of the distortion with which you struggle. For, it is your *focus* that determines what you perceive and what you experience. Focus upon this connection and all else resolves itself in a natural way. Focus on the manipulation of the details of your physical experience, and you become drawn into the drama and enmeshed within its web.

Now is the time to step back from the details of the dilemma which confounds you and to immerse yourself in the richness of your Divine connection—this, to the exclusion of all else. That is the recipe for the transcendence of your experience in the present moment. Learn to float over the turbulent sea and not become dragged down into the depths of it, where you fear you may perish. You will not perish. You will simply be made to suffer—unnecessarily.

Learning to focus on one's Divine connection and tap into the true Source of power

You are your own source of solace or of suffering. And the key to determining which will be your experience is the extent to which you are able to detach from these circumstances and shift your focus to your true Source of power—your own Divine connection. When you became disenchanted and disappointed, disempowered and disheartened, you began to doubt your own power and state of evolvement. You have not diminished in your capacity to serve as a conduit of this Divine connection. You only think that you have.

In empowering that perception, it became your experience. For, your experience can only reinforce what you believe to be so. You need only shift your focus and your *perception* of your circumstances will shift accordingly. In truth, your state of beingness has not altered at all. What has changed is simply your perception of it.

You are feeding the need to remain grounded in density, out of a sense of the familiar, for there is a level of security in that. Close the door to these avenues of invitation that beckon to you, and open yourself to the truth that dwells within you. This is the only way out of the maze. Abandon the fight. Abandon the struggle. Abandon the search. Surrender the fear. And open yourself to the truth of your Eternal Divine Essence. That is the possibility that awaits you.

This is a time of testing. This is a time of completion. You have come far in your journey, and the answers you seek are right in the palm of your hand, not "out there" somewhere. You *Are* what you are seeking. It is not something that can be bestowed upon you by some *other* who claims to have the key—not in the way you have come to value.

You have tasted the pure Essence of your own Presence—the fullness of your *true* identity. It is This which you embrace in the moments of exultation. It is This which embraces you into the fullness of its Divine Presence, when you surrender the sense of separation and allow yourself to merge in Oneness with who you truly Are. That is the recipe for transcendence of all that thwarts your will and threatens your sense of balance and contentment.

Let us journey together now. Let us go back into the Oneness from whence we have come. Let us experience it *together*. For, you are not alone. You do not need a physical Guru to take you by the hand in this experience. We are right here. We haven't gone anywhere. It is you who wandered away for awhile. Now you have found the path again. Let us have a walk upon it, ok?

Ok.

24

Fall 2002
Mumbai, India
Putting the Pieces of the Puzzle Together

————————

I arrived back in Mumbai after nearly a year in India, feeling as confused and lost as ever. The experience of betrayal of trust and energy piracy with Govinda had hit me between the eyes and had left me shaken and vibrationally drained. It brought to the surface my entire frame of reference for what I believed I could—or could not—instinctively *trust.*

When it became obvious that relying on my own *feelings* was not a reliable indicator of what was in my best interests, I was lost. Where do you turn, if not to your own heart, I began to wonder. I would come to see the importance of cultivating the skills of spiritual *discernment,* and those skills did not come easily. Oneness continued to help me process one of the most poignant episodes of my life and helped me decipher the clues that had been in plain view all along.

In retrospect, I began to see that in my heart of hearts I'd known that things were not quite right, almost from the very start of my sojourn with Govinda. I'd watched the blatant evidences of deceit, the inappropriate behavior, the barely concealed manipulation and the lapses in integrity, applied across the board—not just actions directed toward me, but those aimed at other students, close friends, and even his own family members. Even so, somehow I'd chosen to turn a blind eye to what should have been obvious, in the name of friendship and a deep sense of caring.

The insights culled from this poignant chapter did not come easily. But, the painstaking process of digging into the imagery for the life lessons at its foundation, insured that those understandings would be unforgettable.

～⌒～

The lesson of *discernment:* learning to read life's signals and make optimal choices
Oneness speaks:
Many questions have been brought forth from within you. And, as one by one, you process these layers of your understanding, you will see the perfection in the process that was required to bring you to this pinnacle of *release.* For, your attachment to all things physical is what is at issue here. And

that includes your attachment to the so-called figures of authority whom you have empowered so willingly.

We have discussed these issues with you many times. Still, you question your own perceptions. And you are inclined to relegate your own understandings to a subordinate position to that of others whom you deem to be more knowledgeable than yourself.

Rasha speaks:

Oneness, I am far from knowledgeable. I know only what you and my feeling-body communicate to me. I have used my feeling-body as a barometer of truth and falsehood. And up to now, I was confident that I had developed a fail-safe system for determining what was in my best interests and what was not. Now, according to information provided by Dr. Bindu, my entire system of relying on my feelings has been demonstrated to be unreliable.

I must tell you that I am feeling pretty lost right now. And even though, in this moment, my energies seem very high and I am in a very serene and happy state, I am concerned at this point about what, exactly, I am supposed to be able to trust.

When I tried to discuss this with Dr. Bindu, albeit passionately, he became annoyed with me. Yet, the question arises, now: Am I to trust everything a recognized authority tells me, even if it goes against what my feelings have told me is so?

Rasha, your understandings as to the nature of your reality and your position within it have been stirred and shaken a bit. This is not necessarily a bad thing. For, it gives you the opportunity to scrutinize those understandings and to assess what, exactly, is *truth*—for *you*. Dr. Bindu has been schooled in an elaborate system of cosmic laws and ritual practice. And the two aspects are interwoven into a tight fabric of a reality over which he has attained mastery.

At the same time, his perceptions are colored by his cultural background and a system of values that is rooted in the strict assessment and categorization of virtually all aspects of physical reality into the polarities of positivity and negativity. For, these are the laws that *govern* physical reality.

Yet, the *value judgments* placed on these aspects of physical reality, and the *choices* one makes as a result of those judgments, are the issues in question here. There is no inherent "good" or "evil" in any of it. It all simply *Is*. We are speaking of variations within the field of endless possibility and what, if any of it, one *chooses* to select or expose oneself to.

Dr. Bindu is basing the views he presents to you upon his ability to assess the *energy* of certain people, places, and situations. According to his understandings, virtually *everything* is segmented into "ok" and "not ok." It is an elaborate system of rules and regulations, passed down through the ages, which is geared toward guiding the spiritual seeker through the maze of a physical reality that is fraught with pitfalls. It is a system that, actually, is based *not* upon considerations of "good and bad," or "right and wrong," but rather, upon considerations of *cause and consequence*.

The distinction is abstract and subtle. But, the effects of the choices made within the influence of these two diametrically opposed *mindsets* could not be more blatantly illustrated. For, one approach is based upon *limitation and structure*. The other is based in *allowance and free will*. Both approaches presume a certain level of awareness of the effects of energy on the creation of one's circumstances. But, the approach of *dualistic bias* offers the built-in safeguards that would protect the unsuspecting seeker from the consequences of misguided choices.

Oneness speaks about the power of learning from one's own life experiences

The approach that allows the seeker to learn *only* from his own experience is far more difficult. But, once the understandings are instilled—not from having been *taught* these principles, but from having *lived* these principles—true mastery is virtually guaranteed. It is that basic distinction that marks the training you have undergone and distinguishes it from the tried and true structure of the tradition through which Dr. Bindu is attempting to guide you.

We are not disputing the validity of the observations Dr. Bindu has made and has chosen to share with you. According to his system and the assessments he is able to make within that structure, the conclusions Dr. Bindu has drawn are essentially correct. What is at issue here—and what was being tested— is whether or not *you* would be able to draw those same conclusions from experiential evidence alone.

From where Dr. Bindu stands, certain conclusions are a matter of common sense, and the action of choice would have been one that you would have considered *heartless*. Yet, having followed the drama in question to its inevitable conclusion, you were able to reap the key understanding: one's highest interests are not guaranteed on the basis of considerations of heart alone.

The evidence of compromised energy was blatantly there before you, and Dr. Bindu warned you repeatedly of that fact. Yet, you chose to turn a blind eye to what should have been obvious to you, in the name of a sense of "heart-connectedness." Ultimately, your sacrifice was great and your lesson was a painful one. But, it was deeply instilled within you and is not one you are apt to forget. That was the point of the exercise.

You are too easily inclined to place your *trust* in individuals with whom you share a sense of a "timeless heart connection." You have not stopped to question or to assess the complexity of *other* variables within the totality of the situation, or the individual in question, before opening yourself and putting your energy field at risk. This is not the first time you have had to learn this lesson the hard way. Now, it should be obvious to you that sensations of deep caring cannot totally override other factors that would threaten all that you value.

Integrating the life-lessons of betrayal and misplaced trust

The issue of *misplaced trust* is not a new one for you. This scenario has played out for you in infinite combinations on the theme of *betrayal*. It is a theme you are destined to transcend in this lifetime, if the lesson is learned and integrated as *knowingness*.

The feelings of deep caring you experienced with Govinda were genuine—and mutual. That you voluntarily allowed those feelings to deepen and to provide a line in, through which your energies and resources could be drained—despite the danger signals that were also in full view—is what is in question here.

The lesson that has presented itself to you for mastery is that of *discernment*. No one is here to tell you what you *should or should not* do. That determination is yours alone to make. This is *your* movie. Not Dr. Bindu's. He is skilled in making his own choices. And his system works for him. But, his is not a system with which you have any schooling or experience.

Yours is a different system. Yours is the system where, essentially, you are being asked to make those kinds of assessments without having been handed a traditional guidebook. Your skills are *experiential*. They are skills you have been trained to trust. And they are valid. What you are learning to do is to read the signals correctly and to make optimal choices.

When you choose to *compromise* what your instincts should have shown you, and you allow certain factors to color your judgment, you can expect that there will be a price to be paid. When you ignore what you know is not in your highest interests, and try to slip *around* the problem, you will invariably stray off track.

Compromise cannot be part of the recipe for maintaining the sanctity of your energy field. It just doesn't work that way. When you jeopardize your energies by placing yourself in a diminished environment, you can expect your energies to be depleted. This is true regardless of whether or not you care deeply for the individual in question.

All aspects of a situation must be considered in making the choice to align yourself with another. And the decision to walk away is always a valid option when the whole picture isn't what you know you would wish it to be. That is the training that the gift of this episode was scripted to deliver.

As my year in India began winding down and slowly drawing to a close, I began to project—and ruminate over—what the future quite possibly had in store for me. In a few months' time, I would be heading back to the United States to represent, as "author," a book that had been written by Oneness. The prospect of that time of self-confrontation filled me with apprehension, as the inevitability of being ushered out of the spiritual closet, like it or not, loomed ever nearer.

Oneness began to address my silent trepidation to step out into the world as a Divine Messenger, a spokesperson for Oneness. Before I could effectively confront that prospect, however, I would need to go deeper. I would need to actually reside in that place of inner-Stillness of which I had written, that place where one's true nature—and one's inner peace—remain undisturbed, no matter what comes to pass.

Oneness began to speak of *detachment* and helped me recognize the possibility of responding to life situations in ways that transcend the emotional charge that is potentially ever-present. Together, we explored the deep-seated underlying theme of *the need to be "right"* which had characterized so many of the dramas I'd been living out. These real-life illustrations were symbolic of the issues and energies I'd been processing all along the way. Now it was time to begin to bring these themes to resolution.

Ultimately, the path we walk—each of us in our own way—is a solitary one. Oneness helped me come to terms with an inclination so many of us share: to seek validation in the vantage points of others. There comes a moment when we relinquish the need for the comfort of a hand-to-hold in another's vantage-point. For, we recognize that the inner-truth that is sought is not someone else's. It is our own.

Oneness speaks:

This is Oneness. You pause, hesitating to write these words that are so familiar to you. Once again, you are in pain over circumstances in the world of material existence. And even though you are asking all the right questions and are simultaneously supplying all the right answers, these answers are coming from your mind. And the questions are rooted in your fears.

Your heart yearns to be free of all of it. And at the same time, the practical considerations of what you know looms on the horizon have come to haunt you. And we are here to tell you that you are free to choose that, if that is your heartfelt wish. You are free to choose to *experience* the calamity that is surely within the realm of all possibility. But, it need not be like that. You have *every* possibility of rising to the fullness of your own Divine Essence and being the Presence that destiny holds for you, no matter what life has in store.

Most of the preparatory work has been done now. And it is time. It is time to step forth, clothed in your understandings and secure in your faith. This connection has never failed you. This connection is eternally *within* you. You simply forget that *This* is the reference point toward which you can turn when there are doubts and when there are ripples upon the waters of your own earthly reflection.

How to deal with the adversity of the world of physical reality and remain centered, with *detachment*, in your own inner Source

You have had a sojourn into the experience of betrayal and disillusionment on many levels, simultaneously. And your faith has been shaken. You assume that loyalty is unconditional, that bonds of allegiance are unshakable, and that spiritual attributes preclude the possibility of the dregs of "human nature" surfacing now and again. Those tendencies are always within the realm of possibility for those who are experiencing awareness in physical form. For, that is the nature of physical self-awareness.

The possibility to slip into the arenas of *emotion* are ever-present. And the level at which one is able to exist within this physical realm—with *detachment*—

determines the extent to which one is able to transcend these tendencies when circumstances stimulate them into readiness. When one is still held within the death-grip of the need to be *right* in one's own eyes, the ensuing emotion of outrage and feeling indignant are to be expected.

The significance of the experience of disillusionment and the betrayal of trust

You have given yourself the experience of disillusionment and betrayal of trust in order to taste fully the depth of your capacity to withstand the stimulation of the need to be *right*—and to cast another in the role of being *wrong*. You scripted several episodes on this theme to play out for you simultaneously. And, stripped of some of the anchors to which you had still clung, and with your sense of infallible stability well shaken, you experienced yourself as being "out of control" once more.

But, look at it now. See it. See where it is that you are seeking to find solid ground. When you pause even for a moment in your frenzy of panic, you see that all these directions are perceived as *external* to your own inner Source. Your answers are not to be found upon the waters that serve you by mirroring your own inner turbulence. Your security is not to be found within the illusion of a physical hand to hold.

The path you walk is a solitary one. Cling to nothing. Depend upon no one. Ultimately, all have come to disappoint you. That is the role they have volunteered to play for you. You have expectations of others. Now you see that others are here simply to embody *their own* truths. You are free to recognize the truth of another as your own, and to embrace it, if that is your inclination. But, you are equally free to recognize their position as simply that which is so for them.

It is a perspective. And it is "justified" and "founded in truth"—*in that other one's eyes*. You are not here to judge. You are here simply to watch. You have the possibility of selecting the option of aligning yourself with any of these others, if that feels comfortable for you. And, you have, equally, the possibility of allowing the circumstances that beckon to you with the invitation of adversity and discord to drift by you quietly and leave you undisturbed.

You can anticipate the experience of provocation in the present period. For, that is the aspect of your training that you have come to this crossroads to Master. The possibility is ever-present that you will be able to walk with Grace within this physical realm—a world that is fraught with adversity and with atrocity—and to remain unaffected by the antics of others and the circumstances that surround you.

Learning to take refuge from adversity in your own inner Selfhood

That is the essence of the training in which you have now begun to steep yourself. Your refuge is not in the externalized manipulation of the circumstances that present themselves to you for your consideration. Your refuge can only be your own Selfhood. For, that is the only place where the ultimate experience of *inner peace*, for which you yearn so deeply, can be found.

You create the reality of your experience. You have seen and have spoken these words. You will teach these concepts to the masses that will look to you for guidance and for inspiration in times that, at present, you would be challenged to imagine. The *reality* that you "create" is not limited to the nature of the circumstances that confront you. The *reality* to which we refer is within the realm of your *experience* of those circumstances.

Compassion and the reflection of Love it creates for rising above the circumstances of the world of physical illusion

You are fully capable of walking through the depths of scenarios that you would deem to be monstrous and retaining a sense of inner harmony—to the extent that the infinite levels of *compassion* that are the essence of your true nature prevail. *Your* experience, then, is not rooted in the horrors that may well surround you, but in the reflection of the *Love* that is stimulated by those expressions of *compassion*.

One is able to be infinitely nourished by the reflection, mirroring back to you the *hope* you will come to represent, and to rise above the circumstances of the world of physical illusion. Your role in these interactions is not that of the reflection, but rather that of the Source. For, you will come to be adept at living within the center of your own sacred Essence and to know yourself to Be That.

Letting go of the need to "be right" and choosing to preserve the sanctity of your own inner world

That is the nature of the destination toward which the present training has come to guide you. You are always free to focus on the mundane aspects of your worldly experience, if that is what you feel you must do. And you are always free to seek to implement justice, and to "set things right" with those who you feel have dealt with you unfairly. But, you are equally free to let those circumstances drift by you and to leave your inner world undisturbed.

It is this *inner world* which is the key to all you may well come to value, above all else, in the fullness of time. And the invitation is ever-present to seek your place within it, whenever and wherever it suits you to do so. That is the fortress that is impermeable to attack.

After nearly a year in India, exploring all sorts of spiritual paths and practices, and spending the better part of every day implementing them all and gradually eroding the hours once reserved exclusively for Oneness, I was mentally worn out. There are just so many hours in the day. And I began to question the point in attempting to focus on my spiritual practice with every waking breath.

By then, I was able to shift into Divine connectedness and a state of bliss at will. Yet, for some inexplicable reason, I continued to discount that fact. What had begun as an exquisite spiritual awakening had subtly taken on the overtones of a crusade. The nagging realization continued to gnaw at me beneath the surface: I still didn't feel any closer to the "inner explosion" I'd been led to believe was supposed to happen. I started to look at my spiritual journey—and myself within it—as a complete and utter fiasco.

At the very top of the list of my own perceived shortcomings was the persistent reminder that I hadn't found a Guru. After all that time, after all that searching, none of the connections had been right. Dr. Bindu still did not miss an opportunity to point out that a physical Guru was absolutely required if a person had any hope of reaching the pinnacle of the spiritual journey. And in the same breath, he continued to insist that he was not the one. I was baffled.

As a Tantric Master and *Raj Guru*, Dr. Bindu had given me the benefit of his wisdom and mastery in this extraordinary spiritual art for years— regulating my energy field, cutting spiritual cords and releasing attachments. He had provided unimaginably powerful vibrational support, in the form of his amazing *yantras*, the sacred objects that had become like a life-line to me when the going got rough. Without the blessing of his Tantric TLC, I never could have come as far as I had. And I knew it.

I would have sworn that Dr. Bindu had been my Guru all along—despite his protestations to the contrary. But, he was adamant. He was absolutely *not* my Guru. He was my brother. And so it would remain. With timeless wisdom, abundant spiritual nurturing, and no end of dedication, Dr. Bindu would continue to play the part of a physical Guru in the background of my life—and continue to deny it—for years to come. And in the meantime, Oneness, the Guru from within, was forever waiting in the wings of my awareness, to pick me up, dust me off, and put the spiritual roller-coaster ride into perspective.

With infinite patience, and loving guidance, Oneness helped me begin to distill the imagery of my convoluted spiritual odyssey into a lucid overview. The inner turbulence began to recede into a tide of inner Stillness, and the issues that had confounded me began to re-emerge gently, as resolution. Slowly, I redirected my focus of awareness to the heart space within, and there, as naturally as breath, I returned to Source.

Weighing the alternative merits of a traditional path with a Guru, and a simple but sacred, self-styled spiritual practice that is heartfelt and God-focused

Oneness speaks:

Still you question this connection.

Rasha speaks:

I'm not questioning you. I'm questioning me. I wasn't sure I was in any condition to connect with you. Again, it feels like I'm a complete mess. My energies are definitely elevated. But, I surely am not in a serene, G-d connected place. By the way, how did that dash appear in the middle of the word God? I didn't put it there.

That was given to you as supporting evidence. Do you still doubt?

No I don't doubt. I'm just really weary of the struggle. I'm weary of the search. I'm weary of hearing, verywhere I go, that I need to have a physical Guru—and not being able to manifest one that feels right. You'd think that if I were supposed to have a Guru, I would have found one by now.

A physical Guru is not something you require, Rasha. It is something you might choose, when the time feels right. You are far beyond the range where most who consider themselves to be Gurus would make any significant contribution to your working-up. The conceptual understandings surely have been covered in the work we have done together. The work you could, in theory, be doing with a physical Guru could be accomplished with this Source as well, were you to focus your attention on communing with Oneness on a regular basis and making your meditations a regular practice.

If you think about it, you will recognize that the significant strides you have made have been a direct result of the sessions you have spent in deep meditation, whether alone or with the presence of another physical being. Were you to make this practice a priority in your life, you would discover that you carry within you the very connection that you are hungering for.

A physical Guru cannot possibly surpass, in the intensity of the energy that might be transferred, what is available right here within the sanctity of your own consciousness. That is the entire point of the journey you have made and the way you have made it.

Oneness offers powerful, stern guidance about the personalized, *inner* path to the experience of one's own Divine connection

You did *not* opt for any of the traditional avenues, whereby a physical link to the Divine was facilitated by a Guru-type figure. You are self-educated and self-activated. You are not functioning as a piggy-back to anyone's spiritual lineage. You are forging your way through uncharted territory—your own way. You are marching down an unmarked trail through the jungles. Your difficulty is due to the fact that you have begun to seek what you were hoping to find within the external jungles of mundane spiritual *practice* and not within the sanctity of your own *inner self*.

You are stabbing blindly at a potpourri of spiritual *practices,* without benefit of the methodical ground rules and the disciplines that accompany their traditional implementation. You can't expect to take a little of this and a little of that, mix it up, mouth certain sacred incantations, and have it become an elixir for spiritual exultation. It doesn't work that way. And now you have succeeded in proving that.

What was *effective* in your own simple, but sacred practice was that it was *heartfelt* and God-focused. You were not going through the motions of someone else's ritual—implementing a formula you didn't understand and with which you were not spiritually aligned. That is why these techniques are not working for you in the way you hoped that they would. You experienced results. But, they were minimal.

You have succeeded in illustrating to yourself the same principle the world applies to mundane existence—simply with a spiritual slant to it. You are seeking meaning and a sense of connectedness through externalized means. You are trying to source that which is within you *outside* of yourself.

You are turning to so-called "authority figures" to point you in a direction at which you have already arrived. You are welcome to continue to do that, if it gives you comfort to do so. But, we would point out to you that you are not experiencing the sense of satisfaction one would think would be forthcoming from so much effort. The problem in what you are doing is in the *doingness* of it. You have managed to lose sight of the fact that this is not about *doing* at all. It is about *Being*. You know this.

I know. I've gotten myself so intimidated with all this input about what I'm supposed to be doing that I've gotten myself totally off my own track! So, tell me, once and for all, what do I need to be doing?

You do not need to be *doing* anything. Chanting Mantras is something that you are surely welcome to do if it gives you comfort to do so. You can expect a certain measure of vibrational elevation from this practice. But, it surely will not *substitute* for the other, inner-directed avenues of focus which delivered you to the point at which you do, indeed, now stand.

Your time spent in deep meditation and in communion with this Source are the activities that have yielded the most powerful results for you. Your difficulty lies not in how much you have or have not been chanting Mantras, or in which Mantras you have been chanting, but rather in the fact that you lapsed into a practice that substituted the chanting of Mantras and other modes of ritual for your own, inner-directed spiritual practice

These rituals may surely be practiced by you, if you are moved to do so. But, these practices are not to be substituted for the time you would be best guided to dedicate to *solitude* and inner-directed focus of heart and mind. What you are seeking is not "out there" at all. It is within. You have written these words. Now it is time to put it into practice, consistently.

Oneness speaks about daring to be your own person and honoring *truth*, as you know it to be, from your own experience

The others who have walked this path before you did not, for the most part, have the benefit of physical Gurus. Trust in the sanctity of your own Divine connection. Your brothers and sisters of spirit, throughout history, all did so without failing in their spiritual quests. The ones history remembers most poignantly are those who dared to defy the consensus recipe for spiritual advancement and remained true to their own *experience* of it.

Some were martyred, in ways that make you shrink back in horror, for refusing to deny the truth of that connection. That is what sainthood is all about. It is surely not about trudging mechanically down a tried and true path to God-Realization. It is about daring to be your own person and honoring *truth*—as you know it to be, from your own experience.

You are welcome to avail yourself of the knowledge and support of as many teachers as you feel guided to consult on this journey of spiritual unfoldment. But, you need not serve up your power to any of them, regardless of how powerful and self-righteous they may demonstrate themselves to be. Their path is their own—as is yours.

Partake of what you choose to. Leave aside what does not appeal to you. Assess your own position. Receive with gratitude the help that has been arranged for you—and that has, so graciously, been provided. And defer only to the sanctity of your own inner Source.

That is the recipe, Rasha. That is what you are seeking. And it is right here. It hasn't gone anywhere. You are the one who persists in wandering away. Stay home for awhile. Let's give this connection an honest chance, ok?

Ok.

In retrospect, I began to see the significance in all the repetition I had experienced in this marathon journey. It seemed as though I had tripped over the same proverbial twig over and over again for years, never seeing it until it was too late. I started to realize that, not unlike the unraveling of the "life themes" that characterized the beginnings of the journey of awakening, the *experiential* aspects of Realizing the Self as Oneness involved the sense of having "the Light go on"—over and over again.

I had experienced the sense of discovering the truth of my Divine connection—the Oneness we all share—*not* in one definitive, blinding explosion of illumination, but in countless isolated *moments* of it. They were moments where the unmistakable touch of Grace engulfed me, consumed me—and ultimately, *became* me—and even then, released me once more. In the releasing there was time for the identity I thought of as "myself" to process and to assimilate what was actually happening to me.

Even though there was an incredible amount of what appeared to be backsliding, I started to recognize an impeccable logic in the way the whole process was being orchestrated. No, I hadn't been "thrown in the deep end." I had been allowed to "test the water" experientially, one toe at a time—the way Oneness said that so many others would, in the times to come.

Transforming *understanding* into *knowingness*: the experiential foundation for mastery

Oneness speaks:

You see how easy it is. You need only think of this connection and it is here, fully manifested. That is the nature of who you Are, and what you have come to these times to be able to do. It is in shifting into this level of connectedness that you are able to serve humanity in the capacity for which you have been preparing all these years.

From the position of reticence, you serve to inhibit the fullness of this expression of awareness through the vehicle of your being. From the position of complete surrender, you are able to be limitless in your expression of who you Are. You note this, in the act of transcription that is taking place in this moment. This is the level of detachment that is necessary in all aspects of Presence. For, it is in the *letting go* that the fullness of this connection is embraced.

You will note, in the typing of this communication, that the fingers are flying across the keyboard and that there is not the slightest hesitation in transcribing the words. Your mind has been eliminated totally from the process. It is as if someone else were typing these words. That is the level of *surrender* of which we speak. That is the key to the transcendence of the limitations of physical identity that is the next phase toward which you will now direct your focus.

Rasha speaks:

Oneness, something has shifted within me this morning in a very significant way. I've been rereading some of these transcriptions—and I think that I just got it! Again. The problem seems to be in retaining what I come to understand. My memory comes into play here. And, even though the understandings seem clear in the moment, they seem to fade into obscurity. And I find myself right back where I started.

That is because you persist in *mentalizing* your understanding of these concepts.

How can it be otherwise? We are addressing my mind with these communications, aren't we?

Yes, we are surely explaining what is happening in a way that enables your mind to process your experiences. Yet, true *understanding* is not based on a focus upon a mental concept. True understanding goes deeper than that. It is rooted in having lived through experiences that have engaged your *emotions*. You are able to *reference* the understandings when yet another layer is added to the volume of evidence you are building *experientially* on a given theme.

Building layers of *experiential understanding* as the foundation for *knowingness*

When a sufficient level of emotional "charge" has been built around a particular category of understanding, it is time for that underlying message to crystallize within you, not as mentalized *understanding*, but as *knowingness*. It is that level of your grasp of the road you have traveled that serves as the foundation for mastery.

In the foregoing months, you have amassed a body of life experiences, here in India, that were calculated to drive certain understandings home in a way that would literally be *unforgettable*. Now you see the extent to which it is possible to veer off-track, while fully focused on spiritual attainment. For, it is not in the *doingness* at all, but in the *Beingness* of that journey of exploration, that the real answers lie.

The understandings you sought were not to be found in books. Nor were they to be mouthed to you, as formulas to be duplicated, by those who consider themselves to be knowledgeable about such matters. What differentiates those teachers from your own position is the level of *unquestioning acceptance* that each of them has placed in *the inner connection* from whence those understandings come.

Oneness talks about the essential element of "Being at Source"

Their unshakable confidence in their abilities to Be who they Are, to the extent that they are able to manifest it consistently, is based on the solidity of that Divine connection. Whether or not that connection has been *initiated* by a physical Guru is irrelevant. The fact remains that to be in one's Divine Power and to *sustain* that level, is a matter of *Being,* and continuing to *Be,* "at Source."

One operates *every* aspect of one's life from that "home-base." One is rooted there. One is centered there. One is not able to be thrown off balance, for there is nowhere else to Be than in the sanctity of that connection, no matter *where* one physically happens to be.

There are literally no outside variables that are capable of hooking into that fortress and altering its impermeability. It is The Source. You live there. It is portable. You take it with you wherever you go. It is the inner glow you experience when you think of this connection. It is that same inner glow that you have experienced when you think of the Divine souls who have attained that level of connectedness, and with whom you share a spiritual connection.

The Source of the energy one feels in the Presence of an incarnate Guru

These beings are not, necessarily, your *Gurus.* They are your family. And through them, you—and a world of physical beings—are able to Source a Divine connection. In your own case, the connectedness is a direct link to that Source. For, *you* are destined to serve as such a liaison for many to the Source that, ultimately, they will discover *within themselves.*

Just as you have experienced a surge of *energy* in the presence of certain spiritual teachers, whether or not in physical form, so others will experience that kind of surge of energy in your own Presence. For, you are an energetic link—a conduit of Divine Light. And others will feel it. And they will jostle to be close to you, to have just a drop of that Nectar.

But, in truth, that Nectar is not yours—*it is theirs.* For, in their embracing of their *experience* of that drop, the link is made, or reinforced, within their own beings. And the transference of that drop of Nectar is accomplished, from Source, to the place within each of *them* where that Source might be discovered.

Oneness speaks about embodying the "solid ground" within, upon which enlightenment rests

Initially, you will serve as the conduit *to* that Source. For, what comes *through* you does not come *from* you. You are simply the vessel through which it flows. And in the extent to which you can surrender your sense of separateness from Source, lies the key to the extent to which the purity of that Divine Essence is able to flow through you to the world.

It's that simple. And when you are steadily and unshakably in that place, *nothing* in the physical world that surrounds you is able to affect your sense of Divine connectedness, regardless of what the circumstances happen to be. It is this state of solid ground—within—upon which the level of spiritual attainment you refer to as "enlightenment" rests. Nothing can touch you. You are safe—no matter what happens. For, you *know* who you Are. And you have come to embody it.

Being *aware* of the Divine Presence within, in every moment

No one is needed now to take you by the hand. You are already there. No rituals are required to open the gates. They are already open. There is nothing you need to *do* to invoke the attention of a Divine Presence. The ultimate Divine Presence is already fully focused upon you. For, it walks *within* your identity in every moment. In this, nothing has changed. That Divine Presence has *always* walked within your identity in every moment. What has changed is that now *your* focus has shifted and you are *aware* of that Divine Presence within—in every moment.

Now the time has come to journey to the next level. Now, you will learn to *sustain* the fullness of this Presence. This is not just a state of being that comes and goes, depending upon whether or not you are *in trance*. You do not need to be in trance in order to embody this connection with full conscious awareness. You need simply to be aware of where your mind is focused. Steady your mind. Open your heart. And the truth of who you Are will be revealed to you—and to the world.

The weeks in Mumbai, under the watchful eye of Dr. Bindu, served as a summary of all the months of intensity that preceded them. It was a time just to breathe and to assimilate the entire whirlwind of experience that had manifested in my inner and outer world, simultaneously.

One evening, Dr. Bindu performed a beautiful sacred ceremony, in which my precious crystal statue of the Goddess Durga was *consecrated*. The room was thick with the exotic fragrance of rare, handmade incense, and it engulfed my senses, as the energies of the sacred Mantras Dr. Bindu chanted carried me into a state of Divine rapture. I had enjoyed these kinds of *pujas* (sacred rituals) many times before and had become familiar with the feeling of the extraordinary energies that resonated within me to a depth that went beyond the physical. This time, however, I was taken to an entirely new level of experience. And I knew that something inside me had shifted.

The next morning was balmy with sunshine and laced with a gentle sea breeze. I walked to Juhu Beach, a few blocks from where I was staying, with the little clippings of the faded, sacred threads that I had cut from my wrist

314

the night before. Dr. Bindu had said that they should be placed in water. I could think of no more appropriate water than the Ocean itself, which I thought of as an expression of the Infinite. A bright new red thread now sat in the very center of all the remaining souvenirs of prayer—the threads garnered from all the rituals through which I'd set my hopes and dreams adrift upon the ethers.

Dr. Bindu's thread had been the oldest amongst them, and it had sat in the very center of all the chaos represented by this testimonial I wore on my wrist. Dr. Bindu's thread was the calm in the center of the cyclone. Pale and bleached brittle in the sacred and the polluted waters of Mother India, laundered in the unrelenting saltwater of my sweat and my tears on this incredible nine-month odyssey, saturated and baked dry in my doubts, suspicions, resentments, and fears, the frayed little thread was ready to be retired.

The night before, I had tried to snip it off with a very sharp scissors, as Dr. Bindu sat, waiting to replace it with a bright new one. And no matter how I tried, I could not cut the thread. Finally, I pulled with all my might with the blade of the little scissors—and the thread surrendered the fight. Something within *me* gave way in that moment.

The next morning, standing at the edge of the sea, I knew I'd arrived at the place in my journey to surrender the tattered thread I clutched in my hand—and the agonizing struggle it symbolized to me—to the Infinite. I chanted each of my main Mantras very softly, so no passersby would hear the sacred words. And, with each syllable I uttered, I felt the energy building stronger and stronger within me.

I was in a state of absolute serenity. I knelt down and quietly placed the little thread into the gentle wave that had come to receive it. The struggle of the past had been relegated to the embrace of the timeless. It was a symbolic transitional moment in my sacred journey. I stood up and walked quickly back to my room, knowing I was already deep in the blessed state of Divine connectedness. Oneness affirmed all I was feeling, when I returned.

∽✑∽

Oneness speaks:
This Presence is fully manifested within you now. In this moment, you are bridging the threshold between two worlds. One is the world of physical manifestation—the "phenomenal world" as some choose to call it. The other world is one that transcends definition, that transcends polarity, and that transcends the materialization of intent.

It is the realm of the formless of which you, most clearly, are a part. Now you can understand at a level that is *experiential*, not merely attempt to grasp at a level that is *conceptual*. For, in this moment you have *become* that which you have been seeking. You know it to be within you. For, you *Are* This.

Oneness gives a passionate description of the state of embodying Oneness

What you can anticipate now, in this connection, is not a sense of *an arrival*, but rather, a sense of *never having left*. There need not be any sensations heralding a shift *into* a state of connectedness. For, now the state is ever-present.

You are welcome to continue to invoke this Presence with the formalities that have become your custom. Yet, know that in doing so, you are not making a statement of separation, but rather you are making an *affirmation* of a connectedness that is changeless.

Your invocation is not one that beseeches. It is one that honors. It is not one that reaches out. It is one that reaches inward. It is a *celebration* of that which is Eternal. In this moment, We *Are* That—together.

Every thought, however fleeting, must be no less than an affirmation of the highest and the best possibility in any given circumstance. Your verbalizations are no less than vehicles of your highest thought—affirmations of the outcome graced with the energy of highest esteem. And so it will come to pass.

The gentleness and love that permeates your being in this moment is your natural state. The trappings of disgruntled, disappointed, disillusioned experience have fallen by the wayside now. What remains is the pure Essence of your Eternal Self. This one does not judge. This one does not strive. This one is in a state of *allowance*. This one is in a state of *reverence*—for all things, for all beings, for all life, at all times.

Nothing can rock the boat of this centered being. For, the waters run still and deep now. And we simply float upon the surface of the world of mundane experience. We are not caught up in its currents. We are unaffected by its tides of change. We are not rustled in the torrential storms that whip those still caught in their grasp. For, the center of the storm is within the Eternal Self—the epicenter of one's very being. And that place is *home*, regardless of where the vehicle of this physical form may happen to be.

These concepts are not new ones. You have written these words before, in countless variations. You have pondered their meaning, conceptually. You have mouthed these ideas, philosophically. Now you have come to embody them. Now you live and breathe them.

In this moment, We Are Oneness. Rasha has become an aspect of that identity. She walks within the fullness of that composite consciousness, no less present than before, simply with a shift in focus. The focus now is upon the sense of the totality. The perspective is the heightened vision of blessed *detachment*.

There is no wavering back and forth, now. There is no slipping in and out of conscious awareness of this connection. The "training wheels" have been removed. Now it is time to steer the vehicle with a sure hand and to know that the course is set and the momentum is one that is Divinely guided. Life becomes a joyous affirmation of That, with *every* waking breath.

25

Winter 2002
Pune, India
An Encounter with the Presence of Osho

———————

After nearly a month in Mumbai, it was time to move on. I boarded a train at Mumbai's historic VT station and journeyed to Pune, some four hours away, to spend several days at Osho's beautifully Zen ashram/resort. A 40-acre experiential testimony to the teachings, the techniques, and the spirit of the Master, Bhagavan Shree Rajneesh, who left his body in 1990, the resort is known affectionately to many as "Club Med-itation."

This exquisitely stylized "Buddhafield" combines dawn-to-dusk cathartic "meditation" classes with dramatic, emotionally-charged evening programs that feature Osho's incomparable discourses on a larger-than-life video screen. One evening after the screening of a lecture which touched me deeply, I had an extraordinary conversation—within the sanctity of my own consciousness.

A conversation with Osho

As everyone was filing silently out of the glistening new pyramid auditorium, I suddenly stopped, turned around and just stood there as if transfixed. I felt Osho's presence all around me. Instinctively it hit me that maybe—just maybe—I might be able to speak with him. In the same instant, I was struck by the feeling that it was totally presumptuous of me to even think such a thought. But, tentatively, I began to address him silently, in my mind, inviting him to converse with me if he wished to do so. When I got an instant reply, I was more than a little startled.

"Why would you want to have a conversation with me?" he began. "You are not one of my devotees."

"I am a devotee of Oneness," I replied in silence, "and I recognized truth in your words this evening. There was not one word spoken by you that did not resonate as truth to me. It was as though you spoke directly to me. I recognize the wisdom in it, and I honor it."

Then, as I spoke those words mentally, I stood there watching myself and flashed again on the absolute audacity of me believing I was actually having such a conversation. Immediately, I felt the energy that began to engulf me intensifying. And his words came clearly.

"You opened this door. Did you think you could not walk through it?"

"There's always an element of surprise to realize that I'm not imagining a conversation like this," I replied.

"Why should that surprise you? This is what you had in mind isn't it?"

"The thought occurred to me that I might be able to have a conversation with you."

"Did you doubt it? What were you waiting for? Did you forget who you are and why you are here?"

"Why *am* I here, Bhagavan?"

"You are here to ask this question to *yourself*—and to realize that you already know the answer."

There was a long pause as a surge of energy began to build within me and an irrepressible smile spread across my face.

"Are there any doubts now?" he asked.

"I feel your presence! This is amazing! And very wonderful," I said silently as I stood there, dumbstruck.

There I was, a solitary figure in a flowing white robe set starkly against a vast, gleaming black marble floor, like something out of a futuristic painting. I looked around me quickly, not knowing how long I had been standing there. Everyone else had left the room. I was alone. And at the same time, it was very clear that I was far from alone.

"So, you have come again to Pune in search of yourself. Why are you still searching for what you already have found?" he began.

"Because there are still moments where I am unsure that I really *have* actually found it. It comes and goes. And the doubts and uncertainties also come and go. Oneness has taught me to expect this ebb and flow of awareness. But, it's still hard to sustain the presence of the enlightened consciousness all the time. In the moments when it eludes me it's easy to slip into doubting and questioning again." I scribbled feverishly in the little notebook I'd grabbed from my bag, taking it all down, word for word.

"It is the mind that has questions," Osho explained. "Only the mind. Your true nature has no questions. Your true nature is the one who paused in the auditorium and thought it perfectly natural to anticipate a conversation. Then your mind stepped in. And your ego took over. And a false sense of humility surfaced, as you stood there in judgment of what you realized was happening. Your ideas of worthiness and unworthiness kicked in. And what began as a very natural interchange became one that was coated in apology and timidity."

Osho's tone intensified, as he delivered a scathing assessment of the reticence I'd been deluding myself into believing was carefully hidden from view. "Why would you need to put on pretenses of humility to do what you are gifted in being able to do?" he continued. "You are here to do this. You don't have to apologize to anybody about what you can do. This is who you *Are*. Be That—or don't be it. You can't have it both ways. You can't be a Messenger of Divine wisdom and at the same time be a little mouse, pretending to be just like everyone else so others won't notice and be threatened by you. It is far too late in the game for that.

"The world is about to notice. And the ones that are threatened by you *will* be. And those who are able to recognize the level of connectedness you represent will be drawn to you. You are not here to please any of them. You are not here to alter your behavior one iota in an effort to avoid discord. You are here to stand firmly in your truth and to be the fullness of who you really Are.

"If that includes the ability to have a conversation like this one with a Master who has left his body, as if he were sitting in the next chair, then that is no less real and natural than anything else. That is what is, in fact, happening. Don't judge it. Just be present. And allow what is happening to happen. That's why you opened this door. This is what you came here to do. You just forgot that this is why you came."

"That's true, actually. The idea of initiating a conversation with you sort of came and hit me from behind," I interjected.

"Well, now it's right in your face. We are having this conversation with you."

"Why do refer to yourself as 'We?' " I asked.

"We speak to you from a level of awareness that transcends the linear personality you consider to be Osho." He explained: "When you drop the body, you also drop your perception of yourself as a physical expression of identity. Your perception of yourself becomes the true, multi-dimensional being that you are. And you speak from the vantage point of that expanded awareness. We speak to you now as the composite of the identity of Osho, which is a broad one. We have shed our skin! And so, all the limits that went with the body are also superfluous. And yet we are very much present here.

"There is nothing that escapes our attention," Osho continued. "We see all the comings and goings. We supervise all the active meditations, in the ways you all have come to value. You just don't know that this is what is being done. *You* don't do all this opening up on your own. The physical techniques are catalysts that take you to the edge of the breakthroughs you're yearning for. This *Presence* is the force that pushes you over the edge.

"This is no *less* so now than it was before, just because we were here in a body then and now we are not. If anything, our participation is more intensely involved now, without the limitation of a body."

Suddenly, the door swung open, and the attendant, who caught me by surprise, made it clear that the building was officially closed. My spontaneous *darshan* with Osho was over for the evening. But, I knew there was more to come.

A few days later, I found a quiet spot with a bench tucked into a cove of lush greenery behind the building where Osho had his residence. I sat down, with pen and paper ready, not knowing for sure if it were possible to re-establish the connection. I began to write, as I had through the years with Oneness. The invitation my words carried were borne by a genuine invitation of the heart. And within only a moment, we were back in the conversation that had begun days before, without missing a beat.

"I don't know if it's still possible to converse," I began, "but I'm here, ready, pen in hand, in hopes of continuing a conversation that was cut short a few days ago. If you are willing, please be with me now."

"Why would we not be here?" came the instantaneous reply. "We have never left this place. You knew to come here. And you knew what you would find when you did. Do not question what you know. Trust it. And it will never fail you.

"We spoke on the last occasion of this Presence. This Presence dwells in the realm of the Eternal Now, which is ever-present and is not confined to what you would think of as a time and a place. Your own presence within that structure determines when and where this connection might be experienced— by *you*.

"We are not *here* at all," Osho continued. "It is you who are here. And with the focus of your attention, you summon forth from the ethers that which is timeless—and awaits a rendezvous that is destined to happen. It is *you* who has met this rendezvous with destiny. We have not shifted our location in any way. We are no more or less here than any other spot on the property—or any other spot in the universe. We are indeed That—with full conscious awareness of it."

Osho elaborated with a discourse that was, of course, exactly what I needed to hear. "We are no less the bird that crows overhead or the leaves that shower down upon you. We are any and every manifestation of Presence, simply by willing it. And yes, in answer to your thought, we are most definitely the swan, who is ever-present in the same spot, content to simply be watching the comings and goings. The joy of life has grown a thousand-fold. And the possibilities are limitless.

"For you too, the possibilities are limitless. For all of you—for, many will be reading these words—there is no limit to what you *could* be experiencing, within your human form. We are here to push you over the edge—in ways that would not have been possible from within the confines of humanness.

"We are here to nudge you past the boundaries you set for yourselves of what you think may be possible during journeys we have called 'meditations.' They are simply the gateways to a realm of possibility you long to discover. You want someone to take you by the hand. You want detailed instructions, connecting dot to dot. You don't dare to take the risk on your own, to jump off the edge of the cliff into the vastness of the unknown—and fly!

"You're afraid of the dark. What if you fall? Who will be there to catch you? We are not here to catch you. We are here to push you beyond where you think it's safe to go. Once you've left the illusion of solid ground, you're on your own. Because once you've taken that step into the vastness, beyond the safety of what is sure and fixed, tried and true, no help is needed. Flight is insured. And instantaneous transformation is guaranteed. We are here to supply that push.

"We are here to beckon to you: 'come one more step closer to the edge and contemplate the vastness. Take a peek at it. Watch it. Study it. Revisit it. Then, surrender to it—and *become* That!'

"You can take a lifetime to test the water one toe at a time—or you can take the risk. Right now. Right now, in this very moment. And put your full commitment behind a step that is, in truth, inevitable. You're going to take that step eventually. Deep down you know that. And when you're finished hedging your bets and pretending to yourself that there is safety in the dream you think is your reality, you may take that step.

"We are here for those who are finished playing games with the precious years, the precious hours and moments that are there in their hands. We know who is ready. For, they have turned their backs on the fun and games, the endless distraction that so many get tangled up in. For these ones, the way is clear. And many have found it—blindfolded.

"No questions. No answers needed. No philosophy. No religion. No rituals. No beliefs. Just the simple joy of Being—in that place beyond the edge of all that is known and understood. Silence. Silence is the gateway."

Osho paused, punctuating the silence that had engulfed me from within. "Now the mind is still," he noted. "Now we can have this conversation. And what is ever-present, waiting—has *happened*. Step forth—fearless! For, many other cliffs await you. There is not only one. If you need help in taking the plunge, reach out with your heart. And we'll give you a push!"

And, with that, the darshan was over. But, the message and the feeling of loving support that came with it will remain with me always.

Osho's ashram in Pune is a breathtakingly beautiful property, replete with Zen-style architecture, rich with lush greenery, and buzzing with activity. The natural recluse within me became the proverbial witness, one who was inclined to watch the goings-on with absolutely no call to participate. I felt like someone walking through a recurring dream with a haunting sense of déjà vu.

In the people captured by the whirlwind of frenzied activities I recognized someone I *used* to be but was no longer. It was almost like tuning in on a previous life, as though I were watching someone else in these reflections all around me, an aspect of myself I could no longer recognize as *me*.

Oneness captured the opportunity for me to examine my inclination to withdraw from life, with powerful teachings. It was a time to deepen my understanding of my own metamorphosis and to intensify my preparation for the role I was told I was destined to play.

The significance of the training offered at Osho's ashram in Pune, India
Oneness speaks:
In this present time, you have the possibility of sourcing a sense of inner-harmony within the soothing aspects of these physical surroundings (Osho's ashram in Pune) and fortifying your experience of seeking the comfort of that haven—*and finding it*. It is for this reason that you have come to this place

You have not come here to experience yourself within the context of the frenzy and the madness of the group activities that are so abundant here. These choices are designed to nourish the neophyte spiritual seeker at the levels at which he is able to open himself to receive the initial seed of self-awareness. The circumstances here are designed to stimulate the fertile soil within to receive and to embrace and to nourish that seed, so that it may seek to break the surface of mundane awareness in its longing to reunite with the Light that is its true Essence. The potential for that reunion, in Oneness, is what this journey is all about.

These beings who dance and scream and stimulate themselves frenetically are seeking to rekindle within the flames of passion to which the heart has become deadened. These beings, who seek solace from the unrelenting punishment of mundane worldly existence, have come to source an escape route that will lead them out of the prison of the mind and into the realm of their *feeling* nature. And in the moments of wild abandon that so many of these ones have come to embrace is the key to that well-guarded door.

Osho created that path for the many who are caught in the grasp of the mentalized world of striving—and who inwardly starve and wither on the fully laden vines of abundance. These ones are yearning for liberation from the world of material entrapment. And in the moments of crazed release, they are able to source a glimpse of that freedom.

You are here as the witness. You are not here to dance and to scream—not unless you choose to. You have no such need. For, you are no longer dwelling within the earthly realm of those kinds of prisons. You have chosen to liberate yourself from those scenarios. You have not come here to this place to find yourself within it—nor to find yourself amongst these seekers. You are here simply to watch.

See how these hearts hunger. See the extent of the repression and the pain, and the levels of stimulus needed to break the chains of that imprisonment. You do not need to go into the depths of those levels of catharsis—not unless you choose to. You are equally free to journey into the depths of a flower. You are equally free to merge your essence with the rays of sunshine that caress the greenery all around you—in silence. And to savor the joy of simply *Being* here in this haven of physical imagery.

That is Osho's gift to all who come and cross the threshold into his multifaceted world of spiritual awakening. It is all here. And, not unlike the world of physical reality itself, what of it you choose to experience is entirely up to you.

⚘

The ever-present invitation of celebration and joyousness
Oneness speaks:

Another kind of chapter is opening, now. And you will begin to view life very differently from this point forth. In this moment, you are here to enjoy the sweetness of this place. This is a time of resting. A time to assimilate much that has gone before. A time to simply Be, in the fullness of this atmosphere of *celebration*. You are welcome to partake of the celebration, you know. You are not required to stand at the sidelines, unless you choose to.

Rasha speaks:

I thought you told me that I was here as the witness. And I'm very happy just watching the comings and the goings all around me.

You are not inclined to participate in the activities that are geared toward stimulating *emotional release* here in this place. That type of activity has therapeutic value for those who are repressed in their emotional bodies and disturbed by tensions that would impede the ability to go fully into silence and to sustain it. You are not in this category at present. It is this type of activity in which you will feel more comfortable observing rather than participating.

Celebration is quite another matter. You are surely welcome to enjoy the music and the dancing if you are inclined to want to participate in this way. There are no points awarded for stoicism on this journey. No one is requiring austerities of you. You are not being asked to renounce the world. You are being given the opportunity to be selective in what you do and do not choose to express and to experience, based on the *vibrational* ramifications of those choices.

You are sufficiently well schooled in the skills of discernment now, in making responsible choices, and, at the same time, securing for yourself a quality of life that will provide much in the way of happiness. You are not here to be a martyr and the embodiment of deprivation. You are here *to live!* And you will do that in a way that will insure your ability to sustain your energy levels and nourish you spiritually.

The power of giving without measure as a pathway to Divine abundance

There is no need for stoicism on the path that is before you now. It is designed to provide all that you would wish it to. For, this is the path of *giving*. And it is in the giving without measure that the full bounty of Divine abundance is made manifest.

You will soon begin to see the miracle of manifestation in action, as you become more comfortable with the state of total trust you have begun to adopt in earnest. It will be a joyous journey from this point forth. One that is surely *not* devoid of pitfalls, but one where your skills in circumnavigating them will be drawn into practice.

It becomes a matter of keeping your eyes open, and being *aware*, remaining fully conscious at all times, and making your choices accordingly. Your inner peace need not be disturbed in the process of sheltering yourself from the potential turbulence that may be in the wind. That shelter is found in the inner sanctums of your being. And the sense of *joyousness* that is your true nature will be able to express and to touch the hearts of those that surround you, regardless of the severity of the circumstances in which you may well be steeped. For, those inner sanctums are where you truly *live,* no matter where in the physical world you may choose to reside.

You will begin to embody a lightness of spirit. *This* is your true nature. Now that the fears and the worries of the past are understood to be irrelevant, your true nature is free to express itself. Many who have known you in the past may be baffled by the dramatic changes in you and may not understand fully the extent of what has transpired. But, it will be clear that something extraordinary has happened to you. And that brightness will only intensify with the passage of time.

How the energy of *compassion* helps others to kindle the recognition of the Divinity within

It is *this* that will capture the hearts of those whose lives you touch. And the warmth and *compassion* you radiate will kindle within those who surround you a spark of recognition of the Divinity that waits, dormant, within each of *them*. In encountering you, their actual experience will be that of *their own* Divine Essence, revealed to them by virtue of your Grace. You will simply serve as a mirror of what is there, so naturally, within each. And, in tasting it for the first time, they may mistake the sensations and attribute them to your persona. The message you will come to impart will be an understanding that the Love that is felt is not "your Love"—but *their own Love*.

You have simply come to facilitate their experience of it. It is that universal sense of Divine connectedness that you have come to these times to demonstrate. You are here to show, with simplicity and with humility, the magnificence that dwells within the inner depths of each of *them*. Many will come to embrace and to experience the fullness of that state of Beingness in your Presence. Many will be transformed and will, in turn, pass the experience on to others, when your days in this physical world have come to completion.

Now you will begin to venture forth in your newfound skin, and to begin to sense and to assimilate your awareness of who you have become. Quietly, and with gentleness, your emergence will be made known. In the present moment you will be sheltered. And, for a time, you will be free to explore, in silent anonymity, your newfound Self. Celebration may well be in order—or not, as you choose.

26

———

Nearly a year had passed since my arrival in India. All the while, the memory of Tiruvannamalai continued to beckon to me. Something deep within me knew I had to return there. It was a sense of knowingness I couldn't question, yet couldn't explain. I had the sense that it was time to go home—and that home wasn't about my imminent return to America. It was within. My heart was telling me that Arunachala, the sacred mountain that embodies Lord Shiva, in South India, was the doorway. It had been there all along, quietly waiting. I simply hadn't been ready to see it. Now I was.

Everyday mini-miracles illustrate how I was creating my own reality

Funny little "miracles" had started happening regularly by the time I found myself waiting on the platform at a train station in Mumbai, ready to board a train for Tamil Nadu. There, in the darkened wee hours of morning, the taxi driver had deposited me, together with my unwieldy pile of luggage, and left me to wait on a bench that supposedly would be right opposite the sleeper car where I'd be spending the next 26 hours.

Minutes before the train was due to pull into the station, I realized that I was in the wrong spot. Where I needed to be was on the other end of the platform. I eyed my luggage. There was no sense of panic. No fear. No urgency. Just a sense of matter-of-factness. "I need help," my mind commented, as though I had said those very words.

No sooner did I have that thought when a very pleasant young man came up to me and in perfect English said: "Do you need some help?" "Yes," I answered, explaining that I had been dropped off in the wrong spot. "I need to find a porter." I'd been looking for a porter for several minutes by that time, scouring the crowded platform for a bright red jacket that would signal salvation, but there hadn't been a porter in sight anywhere.

No sooner had I spoken the words than I turned around and, from out of nowhere, a porter stood right beside me. The train roared into the station in that moment, right on cue, and I was escorted very nicely to my seat, without having to lift a finger.

Normally, panic, with all the accompanying symptoms of high drama, would have marked the scene. I walked serenely to my place and sat down. I was being cared for in ways I had never experienced before. Somehow, I understood clearly that the one who was orchestrating all these moves was me. The difference between the old-style script and the new one was in my own level of expectation.

For perhaps the first time in my life I was not anticipating disaster. I was not running interference in my mind for the thousand-and-one hypothetical snafus I was capable of conjuring up. I just had a bizarre sense of well being—an unquestionable knowingness that everything was totally under control. And, to my utter amazement, that was my experience of it.

Nearly four hours into the journey, as we neared Pune, I realized I was hungry. The food available on India's trains is not always what you'd consider enjoyable. I looked down appreciatively at the little plastic bag of mini-bananas I'd had the good sense to buy at the last minute in Mumbai, and figured that would be lunch. "It would sure be nice if there were something nourishing on the platform in Pune," I remember thinking, as the train pulled into the main station.

A dear friend who was living in Pune was scheduled to meet the train in order to hand me my little wheel-cart, which inadvertently had been left in the trunk of his car the week before. He was there waiting as the train pulled to a stop. And, with a grin, he also handed me a nice little bag from the German Bakery, containing a chilled avocado sandwich with fresh herbs on a crusty whole-wheat bun. "I thought this might come in handy," he laughed.

I was stunned. It couldn't have been more made to order if I had asked for it. But, the thing was, I hadn't asked for *anything*. At least not consciously. The pieces of the puzzle started to fit into place. Suddenly, I recognized that my life experiences were demonstrating to me, virtually on the spot, how I was creating my reality.

Arunachala revisited

I had come down from the mountain nine months before, but it had not left me. I could still feel myself sitting on a certain huge rock, beside the footpath to Skandashram, high on Mt. Arunachala, gazing into the vastness, knowing that I was in the embrace of Lord Shiva. For me, it was a place of blessed homecoming, the icing on the cake of an extraordinary journey in India.

I could see why I had saved this visit for last, and why my heart had been hungering to return there. "Go back," something had been nudging me from deep within, for months, as I'd continued searching India's spiritual meccas for what was unmistakably there. Yet, what there is to find in this place is so hidden in the semblance of normalcy that you might not even recognize it as anything more than just a dusty South Indian hill peppered with boulders.

Then you venture out upon it. And you sit—blessedly alone. And something begins to stir within you. And you know. You know without question that you are in the embrace of something sacred. You know that you walk upon hallowed ground. "It's no wonder Sri Ramana Maharshi never left this place in his lifetime!" I'd remembered thinking.

Now, a single tear trickled down my cheek and my heart welled up once more, as I ventured out, once again, upon the sacred "hill." A tall, slender tree, commanding a perfect view of the colossal Shiva temple in the town below, danced in the breeze before me. Silently, wordlessly, I recognized the tree as Oneness. With that thought, my heart surged with joy. The tree began to sway to and fro, as if on cue.

Suddenly, with no more than a whisper of a thought, I had shifted automatically into full communion with Oneness, and was completely in bliss. Sunshine filtered through the trees that shaded me as a cool, gentle breeze began to caress my skin. In that moment, I felt the myriad aspects of nature all around me harmonize with my own Presence. It was as if I were sharing in a secret moment of Divine Union with Life itself. My heart had come home. Arunachala!

The days began to provide a practicum in the art of distinguishing, amongst my perceptions, what was *real* from what was *illusory*. I began to demonstrate to myself that I could actually flip between levels of experiential perception at will. Oneness helped me see that "life," as I believed I knew it, was little more than a state of *lucid dreaming*.

Oneness helped me begin to understand the multiple levels of reality I was encountering on a daily basis, within the confines of the cloistered environment of Ramanashramam, and the contrast, beyond its gates, of a world of density and diminished vibration. It was a graphic illustration of what actually happens when we steep ourselves in alternating levels of exalted and diminished *energy*.

The training in the art of *discernment* kicked in with a powerful teaching on learning to "walk between the worlds." Tiruvannamalai was the perfect setting for becoming adept in distinguishing amongst them. Here was a living illustration of the real nature of the reality we think of as our world and a crash course in how to cope with it.

As a being who was cultivating a conscious awareness of these differences, and was learning to combine it with practical skills for viewing life from the perspective of *energy*, I realized that this training was exactly what was needed. It was clearly no accident that I'd chosen to place myself in this seemingly contradictory environment. Somehow it seemed that, at an experiential level, I'd been magnetized to Tiruvannamalai for this very reason.

⤶⤷

Oneness speaks:

The smile on your face is your barometer of this Presence now. You still lapse into forgetfulness and drift into a state of perceived separation. You forget who you have, in fact, become. Now, as these words are being written, you remember, once more, the sense of surrender. And you immerse yourself in Oneness with the state of Beingness that is your true identity.

It only takes a fraction of a moment now to shift from one state of being to the other. For, what shifts, in that instant, is the focus of your *awareness*. When your awareness is focused on Oneness, we are Present fully for you—*as you*.

You can sustain this Presence—this state of connectedness—if you choose to. Or, you can drift back into the stupor of forgetfulness and delude yourself into believing that the circumstances that play out all around you, like living theater, are real. What is real has nothing to do with any of that.

Learning to distinguish the real from the unreal

What is real is what happens when the light goes out, when the eyes are closed, when the mind is stilled, and when the focus of your awareness is turned inwards. That sense of *No-thing-ness*—is real. The rest of your experience is no different than a waking dream, through which you are walking—now with partial illumination. In time, you will walk through this dream with full illumination. You will perceive the circumstances all around you, and yet know, in so doing, that you have engaged in a mode of waking dream-state, a state of being you will have learned to alter at will.

Strengthening the skill of walking between the worlds

Now you are walking the perimeter of that state. You are not as yet within it. Yet, now is the time for mastery of the skills that will enable you to shift instantly into those heightened levels of awareness. For, you will be bridging several worlds simultaneously in the course of this work. This time has been set aside for learning to distinguish amongst them.

The doorway to the levels of reality that you would wish *not* to experience is found in the avenues of diminished vibration that beckon to you throughout the world of physical illusion. You will wish to exercise caution in where you place yourself and to create a buffer-zone around you that will shield you, to some extent, from the effects of the negativities that abound in the world of physical illusion.

Up on this mountain, a land of enchantment awaits you. Out on the street, beyond the gates that give definition to the ashram (Ramanashramam), the characteristics of the world of illusion take form in vivid detail. It is a microcosm world that bridges many levels of reality.

This is the ideal setting for learning to manage the skill of walking between the worlds. You will be given opportunities to carry your heightened energies out into the world of illusion. And you will be able to observe the results when you allow the diminished energies that abound here to affect you.

Sidestepping conflict and relinquishing the need to be "right"

The opportunity to engage in conflict is ever-present in the world of illusion, and you will be free to choose that and to experience the results, if you still need to put these principles to the test. The opportunity also exists, however, to sidestep all invitations to engage in battle, and to circumnavigate the pitfalls.

You will begin to discover that there is no real loss incurred when you relinquish the need to be *right*. All that is forgone is the opportunity to sacrifice your precious energies. You will become fiercely protective of yourself and begin to prioritize your potential activities according to those criteria.

In the present circumstances, you will wish to spend most of your time alone. Your time spent on the mountain is to be spent in solitude. You are encouraged to begin to review the conversations we have documented during the time you have been here in India, and to see the extent of the transformational process in which you have been engaged.

You will realize that none of this has been wasted motion. All of it has been painstakingly choreographed to bring you to the place at which you experience yourself in this moment. Even the painful parts, where you see the warning signs now in retrospect, were carefully planned to be sure the realizations gleaned were *experiential*, and not simply *mentalized* understandings of a theoretical principle.

As you review your notes and recreate some of those scenarios in your mind, you will begin to see how the principles came to life for you and prepared a foundation of understanding upon which you can build the thrust of your life's work.

✾

Oneness began to orchestrate, through the medium of a dialogue, a living illustration of the nature of personal identity. During the process, multiple levels of identity were encountered sequentially and embraced. As part of documenting my experience in writing as it was actually happening, I was able to demonstrate to myself the reality of *who* I was—in juxtaposition with all, it became clear, that I was not. I was led, ever so gently, into the *experience* of God-Presence, so that I could know, irrefutably, the nature of it.

This was what Oneness would go on to refer to, in these writings, as "The Taste." That actual *experience* is what constitutes the "proof" we all seek of what, without that firsthand experience, is, at best, intellectual speculation. *Enlightenment* is not something based on a philosophical grasp of certain concepts. It is not based upon a consensus compilation of the characteristics and reflections of the historical figures our spiritual literature cites to illustrate the *idea* of enlightenment. It is based on *one's own* personal experience of it. Each of us, in our own unique way.

I was ready for the illustration, to help me tie it all together. The process revealed the Presence of Oneness—and allowed me to experience that Presence as *myself*. It was a composite of perception, encountered initially in sequence, and then, all at the same time. I was able to grasp the principles underlying the all-encompassing *experience* of embodying Oneness, in the moment—as I was actually living it out.

Learning to distinguish amongst multiple levels of identity
Rasha speaks:

Good morning, Oneness. I paused just then, thinking I was channeling, waiting for you to say something. The silence surprised me. Then I realized that "I" was speaking. And as soon as I had that thought, I had to ask myself "who was speaking?" Because, in the same instant, I experienced your Presence, and understood that I had merged my awareness with You—and was, once again, experiencing myself as Oneness.

Even as I am writing these words, I see that I am not writing them. "I" am channeling them. There is no mind in the process. There are no thoughts. The communication flows through me, effortlessly. It is as though I am channeling myself.

Am I simply channeling a perspective? Is that it? Am I simply documenting Rasha's perspective? Am "I" an embodiment of awareness itself that has become some sort of receiving station? I see that "I" do not have a perspective! I simply perceive the fruits of my awareness and document what is perceived.

An intensive exercise in Self-inquiry: "Who Am I?"

Would you care to comment on this? What is it that I am experiencing now? And even more interesting—Who Am I? Clearly, I am not the body who is documenting text into a computer, because the sense of the thoughts does not feel like it is coming from the identity associated with this body. There is no sense of intention. There is no point to be made. There is no feeling of what thought will follow. "I" am simply taking it down.

Am I even here? If these thoughts are not coming from my mind, where are they coming from? Am I channeling Rasha? And who is the "I" who is channeling her? Oneness, I feel your Presence everywhere—within me, around me—but who is it who is experiencing that? You are right here in the forefront of my awareness. And these words are flowing just as though I were channeling You! But these are not your thoughts. These are Rasha's thoughts—flowing through form.

"I" am Oneness, channeling Rasha!! This is extraordinary! This is actually what's happening! Unbelievable! I am clearly experiencing myself as Oneness now. We have shifted totally into that perspective.

I recognize the feeling of your Presence in the forefront of my
awareness. And You are documenting my thoughts—as though I were
far away. Whose thoughts? Who Am I? Ok. I see. It's not a matter
of either/or. We are not either Rasha—or Oneness. We Are All of
It, experiencing Self-awareness through form.

Oneness gives a demonstration and an explanation of *Presence*
Oneness speaks:

This is Oneness. Now the roles have been reversed. Can you feel the
difference?

Yes, I feel like "I," Rasha, am back in the body. I am aware
of my own presence within this form. And I am now channeling
Oneness, writing down what you say, word for word. Wait a minute!
No sooner did I write that when it flipped the other way. Now
I feel the Presence of Oneness within the body—and the thoughts
are being received from elsewhere. Wait a minute! Now I'm back
again. This is amazing.

What you are experiencing, Rasha, is a sense of *Presence*. Simply that. It
is not a question of being *this* and therefore not *that*. It is a matter of simply
Being. Experiencing *yourself* as Awareness itself. That is what *Is*. The fact is,
you do not *have* a perspective. You only believe that you do.

You are *Awareness*—watching a perspective play out before you that is no
more than a reflection of a composite of energies, experienced through form.
That is who *you* are.

There is still the sense of an identity that, for argument's sake, we'll call
"Rasha." But this small linear perspective is, at this point, an infinitesimal part
of who *You* are. You are stepping into the fullness of your awareness of who
You are. That Presence is now consciously walking with you, in form. That is
why you have the feeling of being both present and not present. *You* can, at this
stage in the process, shift your awareness back and forth, one to the other.

Were this experience not accompanied by this incredibly exquisite
sense of bliss, one might be tempted to wonder if this is not just
a gilded definition of insanity! Good God! Maybe I'm just nuts!

Oneness places the experience of Divine connectedness within the context
of a historical overview

That is a diagnosis that has been given to many through the ages who have
had this experience. Few, however, have sat and painstakingly documented
the process, in the moment, as it was happening. That has become your
process. And the act of surrender to the shifts in consciousness that mark this
heightened stage of spiritual emergence has become a natural part of your
experience of it.

In other times, spiritually awakened beings were martyred for the Revelations
they attempted to reconstruct *from memory*, while back in a state of linear

awareness. Those who are unable to perceive such things found the claims of Divine connectedness on the parts of so many of these so-called "saints" to be threatening to the particular power structure in question, and declared the Revelations to be blasphemy. You have been spared the possibility of that outcome, in these times.

Ultimately, when you walk *as* Oneness—with this level of consciousness in full Presence within the form you consider to be *your body*—there will be no question in the minds of those who encounter you, the nature of who and what you Are. In the present moment, you are juggling several levels of awareness, all of which are, in fact, *you*.

We cannot say that "Rasha" is *not* who you are. "Rasha" is very much *an aspect* of who you are. And within the context of that presence, you have been given *the experience* of the fullness of who you Are—*as Oneness*. Now, you are integrating the composite of the aspects of your multi-faceted identity into that one sense of Presence.

We will be working on this exercise while you are here at Arunachala. For, the resolution of your understanding of *Who you Are* is the basis of the teachings of the Master to whom you have come (Ramana Maharshi). It is his energies that are guiding this experience for you now.

In your case, the *Self-inquiry* is an experiential one. And the sense of *Presence* that surfaces within your awareness, in the course of these discussions, is a full representation of the aspects of identity that are, in fact, Present.

Yours is not an intellectual inquiry. Yours is not a journey into the mind-boggling labyrinth that is confounding so many of the others here—seekers who are wrestling with the journey, presented *conceptually*. For these ones, whose sense of urgency has fueled a spiritual quest earmarked by a sense of *attainment*, the prospect of the possibilities unveiled in an exploration of the concept of *Who Am I?* often leads deeper into a spiral of confusion.

Oneness defines *enlightenment*

When mentalized *understanding* is made to substitute for the experience of Oneness, the seeker has succeeded in creating an *awakening of mind*— a revelation of ideas. *Enlightenment* is not a matter of ideas. It is a matter of transcending one's tendency to focus upon ideas and surrendering to the experience of it.

So, one's basis for believing oneself to be *enlightened* is not that of having a *mentalized* grasp of the concept that "I am God"—in whatever form and by whatever name you consider "God" to Be. The basis for knowing oneself to be enlightened is having had the experience of God-Presence as oneSelf. Then, and only then, can one speak of "being enlightened." All else is simply characteristic of being on a spiritual quest, regardless of the sophistication of one's philosophical understandings.

One need not be in possession of any formal, man-made certification in order to be *enlightened*. It is not necessary to be *learned* at all. It is not necessary to have been trained by an incarnate spiritual Master, or to have been *ordained* in any of the recognized schools of so-called spiritual wisdom that are available in these times. For, what is required is not a mentalized compendium of the history of the experiences and speculations and *revelations* of others. What is required is Self-knowledge. The first-hand experience of it.

What is required is having had "The Taste," the *feeling*, the indescribable Essence of *That*. And to know yourself to *Be* That. That is the nature of the journey with which you have chosen to gift yourself.

In this case, the journey is being experienced in increments, interspersed with time for reflection and for integrating your understandings of the nature of your process. This is why you have come to the mountain. You *Are* the mountain. And the mountain—is *Home*.

How one's perception of experience is determined by where one's awareness is focused: a practical demonstration

Oneness speaks:

This is Oneness. Your experience in this moment confirms that. Breathe this connection now, for it is within you. The source of this does not emanate from a cave, or a mountain, or from a Guru, which you perceive as external to you. Your Source is Oneness. And the experience is that of *communion*—a harmonizing that takes place within the sacred depths of your own being. We are that Oneness together, in this moment. There is no doubt. For, in this moment, you can *feel* it.

As this experience takes you deeper, and your identification with the physical persona is relinquished, your sense of perception alters. Your circumstances are, essentially, the same. But, your *sense* of them has shifted to one of loving *allowance* and consummate *trust*.

This time is for acclimating yourself within the embrace of a new level of identity. You will not be led astray now. There are no more *tests* to be surmounted. There is no need to fear that you will lose this sense of who you have become. This is not something that can be taken from you. It *Is*. Simply that.

Rasha speaks:

Why then do I have the sense that my energies still are augmented or diminished, according to where I am and the circumstances in which I place myself?

That will always be the case, Rasha. Care will be taken, and awareness will be ever-present of the nature of *who* you Are in relation to *where* you are. And your *perception* of your experience here in the physical world of existence will alter accordingly.

I stop to note an opportunistic mosquito, charging at the net in which I've enclosed myself. I suppose my awareness of my circumstances is a bit like that, right?

Your world of physical experience is but a reflection. You know this. When you become alert to the symbolism all around you there shall be no more questions, for the answers will all be around you, awaiting your attention. Your focus remains in the Self, rather than upon the external reflection. Your focus is not upon the mosquito. You know that you have erected netting, within which you abide peacefully. You simply are who you Are, going about doing what you do, within it.

The outside world will serve up all manner of potential distractions—opportunities to shift your awareness and to affect their potential impact upon you. What you experience, and the way in which it is experienced, is determined by where your awareness is focused. Always. In every moment.

In this moment, I perceive the presence of Oneness as what I Am. My sense of it is enhanced when my focus of attention is upon that. When my focus of attention is elsewhere, such as on the screen of this computer, or the keyboard, or the mosquito, my sense of my own Divine Essence is diminished.

So, what I understand is that the fact of who and what I am has not changed. What alters is simply my own experience of it. So, in this experience, I have not become anything other than what I already Am—and have been all along.

Now, as I experiment with placing my attention upon the Essence of Oneness and alternately on aspects of the externalized world of physical illusion, I perceive clearly the subtle differences in sensation within!

You are seeing it now, aren't you?

Yes, I am seeing it now. Not just understanding it mentally. Not just theorizing. Breathing it! Feeling it.

You have done the work now. You have lightened the load with which you had burdened yourself for eons. You have emerged from behind the cloud in which you had enshrouded your own sacred Essence. Now you are very thinly veiled. Ultimately, there will be no barrier at all between that which you Are and that which will be perceived by others. The process is a gradual one. And you will experience your unfoldment in increments. This level of self-perception is merely a plateau. For, the journey is far from over.

As you begin to master your ability to manipulate your circumstances in accordance with your focus of awareness upon the Divinity that is your true nature, your skill in sustaining the fullness of that Divine Presence within the context of physical form will be fortified. Ultimately, it will be unshakable.

You have pierced the veil now. And you are perceiving your surroundings through a new kind of pinhole. Ultimately, the veil itself will have dematerialized. And your perception of yourself, and the world within which you experience That, will have shifted accordingly.

This is the essence of the experience that has been termed *enlightenment*. The term refers to one's conscious awareness of what is so, from one's own experience of it. You have had this experience. You are having this experience.

You will continue to have this experience—all of it, in deepening stages of an ever-evolving process.

How *surrendering* the sense of *the quest* for enlightenment serves as the key to realizing the experience of Oneness with the Divine

There is nothing static in the journey to Oneness with one's own Divine Essence. One does not suddenly *arrive* and thereafter rest on one's laurels. The experience intensifies. And it will continue to do so, in ways you presently cannot begin to imagine, throughout the duration of this lifetime.

You have simply crossed a significant threshold. You know that you Are Oneness, expressed in physical form. You know this, not because you have been taught to believe it, by rote repetition of the concept of it over a given duration. You know this because you stand in the fullness of the Presence of Oneness in this Now moment, with full conscious awareness of it. That is what is meant by *enlightenment*.

There have been many, many times when you had a glimpse of this state of Beingness. You have had one foot in and one foot out of this level of awareness for some time now. You have simply given yourself the opportunity to amass sufficient experiential evidence of that fact. Now, as you see that you are able to sustain your awareness of who you Are, it is as though you were discovering yourself, once again, for the first time.

It's true! That's exactly the way it's been. I was, essentially, there, but I just couldn't quite believe it. Now, the one who is concerned with whether or not she believes it—or believes anything else for that matter—is no longer in focus. I am not aware of her presence now. The "I" from whose perspective this is being documented, in this Now moment, sees that the aspect of identity in question is no longer in the forefront of my awareness. It is not as though she has ceased to be. I am simply not viewing life through her perspective.

You have clarified for yourself the essence of what has transpired within you. Now, as you take your understandings out into the world, you will do so from having lived them. You will be able to speak of them from having had them in the palm of your hand, over and over again, and watched with dismay as *your sense of it* slipped through your fingers, yet again. It is an excruciating, exasperating process—a journey into the depths of expectation, of questing, of yearning—and ultimately, of fulfillment.

How a focus on enlightenment, as a goal, keeps the experience of it elusive

The emergence of your awareness of this blessed state of Beingness coincided with your surrendering of the quest for its attainment. For, one's focus upon enlightenment, as a goal that is sought with hunger and with desperation, will keep the experience of it ever-elusive.

When there is no longer a *wanting* of it, a *seeking* of it, a *stalking* of it—as that which is "out there somewhere"—it can be revealed to you as that which is already there, within. From that point forth, what there is to have is simply your experience of it. Your ever-evolving, ever-deepening *experience*—of Oneness.

Seeing the Divinity in the symbolism all around us
Oneness speaks:

The sense of connectedness deepens now, as you enter the next stage in your unfoldment. Breathe of these energies. And know that it is This of which you are a part. This is Oneness. We are Oneness—together. As the layers of linear identity fade in the Light of the truth of what you are becoming, you have begun to experience levels of energy that were previously unknown to you. Breathe these energies. Breathe deeply of This. For, the doors within have been opened.

You have journeyed to a sacred place. And you have enjoyed connecting with this mountain and the sense of homecoming it has instilled within you. The moments you have here are to be savored. They are not to be rushed. You do not need to *do* anything. Simply be Present here, with full conscious awareness, in every moment and with every breath. Every life-form has a message for you now. All that you encounter is a blessed reflection of the energies you project upon the ethers.

Take the time to be truly Present during the moments with which you have been gifted. And you will discover that the teachers you have sought are all around you. You do not require theoretical understandings now. These have been firmly instilled within you. Now, you will encounter the evidence of those understandings in *every* creature, in *every* blossom, in *every* leaf and blade of grass. For here, in this enchanted place, you will experience yourself *as* That—and you will know it to be Divine.

A blessed moment of Self-Realization
Rasha speaks:

What I am feeling cannot even be described. It is bliss!! Yet, with it is a sense of groundedness and balance. It is not the extraordinary waves of exaltation I have experienced along the way. This is different. This is a sustained sense of deep, deep contentment. A joy that is not screaming its presence, like fireworks, but glows, sure and steady—and powerful. This feeling is very different. And very wonderful!

"Who am I now?" I have to wonder. And even before that question is fully formulated, I know that what I Am—is changeless. My experience of it simply has shifted, yet again.

I feel my hands blasting with energy. My entire body feels electrified. And the glow within, fueling it all, could only be an Eternal Flame. I am Present here. Simply that. Fingers moving on a keyboard with no sense of where the thoughts are coming from. A sweet, contented little smile upon the lips. Words appearing on the screen of a computer. And "me"—watching.

I look around this little room, noting the objects placed here and there, as if they belonged to someone else. To whom do these things belong? And who is writing these words? There has come a place in this conversation where it's hard to tell if Rasha is channeling Oneness—or if Oneness is channeling Rasha. There is a body before a computer, documenting it. Who is who, at this point, is anyone's guess.

In the course of writing these last few paragraphs, my entire sense of identity has disappeared. I can state, definitively, that "Rasha"—the one whom I assumed has been fully present in this body—is not here right now. I am speaking. But, I recognize that "I" to be someone else. So, who is it that just recognized that? (long pause) Oh my God! It is my Self.

This feels exactly like the moment when they took the training wheels off the bike when I was six and I realized that I was actually riding it all by myself! Oh my God! I see it. The one looking out through these eyes is not "Rasha" in communion with Oneness—it Is Oneness. And I Am That.

Layers of Realization begin to emerge as layers of illusion begin to shatter

The dawn broke within me in a blinding flash of insight. And in that imperceptible fraction of an instant, the clouds of confusion that obscured what now had become so obvious simply vanished. As the sun descended, I had been sitting peacefully on a little bench in a far corner of the ashram. I was savoring the passages from the very last pages of Paul Brunton's classic, *A Search in Secret India*, on loan to me from Ramanashram. The crumbling brown pages were a testimony to the countless aspirants who had, undoubtedly, held it before me. As I read the words on those final pages my heart stood still.

This was my own experience! The profound inner *Stillness* that was described in those pages was the same sacred Stillness that, in that very moment, engulfed me once more—even with my eyes open. From the very beginning of my practice of *meditation*, my mind had always been stilled completely—instantly. And the pinpoint of inner-focus was something I'd been able to hold for hours, at will. I suppose I did not realize that this was anything particularly unusual. I assumed that this was what meditation *is*.

Never having had any formal instruction in this practice, I'd simply been doing what I do instinctively. For me, the process had been like breathing—something done automatically, without effort. The sublime feelings of peace and contentment that accompanied the process, I also presumed were part of *meditation*.

Here I'd been, questing after some seemingly unattainable goal, when I had already realized what I had been seeking all this time! For me, it was not an "inner explosion" at all. For me, it was the sublime sense of inner *peace*, the depths of which I cannot begin to fathom.

The sweet, familiar smile of inner-recognition spread across my face, as the realization hit me and began to sink in. And I felt Oneness, whom I know to be ever-Present, moving into the forefront of my awareness. The delectable sensations of my Divine connection filled every cell of my being with rapture.

I knew I had not imagined it! *This* was the experience I had been waiting for, hoping for, praying for, ever poised and ready for. Yet, somehow, all this time, I'd assumed some sort of *validation* of it was required—even if it was my own. I laughed out loud at the absurdity of it.

And, at the same time, I watched my hand scratch the mosquito bite on my foot. Divinity in the face of humanness! Oneness smiled that telltale Mona Lisa smile, as the indescribable inner glow swelled within me once more.

I'd been contentedly tucked away in Tiruvannamalai for almost a month by then, in a primitive-but-cozy, little thatched-roof room atop an old farmhouse. It was set way back from the dirt road, with a beautiful little cow in the front yard with bright blue painted horns and a flower garland around her head. A friendly young family with a baby boy and a three-year-old girl lived downstairs in the main house. I don't think I've ever been happier than I was during those last days in the lap of Arunachala.

The energies had become extremely high, and I walked around feeling electrified. I spent large chunks of my days up at Virupakisha cave, where Ramana Maharshi had lived for several years as a young man. There I sat in meditation for three hours at a stretch, experiencing peaks of awareness I'd never even approached before. I wasn't sure what to make of it, but I sensed that I had begun to open to a totally new level of experience.

On the night of the full moon, I went up on "the hill" instead of walking around it with the half-million people who descended on the town like clockwork, once a month, for the occasion. Legend has it that for those who make the 14 kilometer trek around the hill under the full moon, all karma is released and all dreams and wishes come true.

It was a prospect that attracted romantics and spiritual seekers from everywhere imaginable. From my mountaintop perch, in the brilliant glow of moonlight, there was no doubt. The extraordinary energies that engulfed my senses that night and carried me to indescribable heights of bliss told me, without so much as a word, that my prayers had been answered.

⟋⟍

Rasha speaks:

I'm really not imagining this, am I! I awoke this morning with such a sublime sense of contentedness—such a sweet feeling of well being. I love the way this feels. I am not in trance and yet there is an otherworldly sense of being somehow augmented.

I have this little grin on my face that just won't go away. Suddenly, there is no sense of a goal—no sense of urgency to attain anything. No drive to do anything. There is the feeling that there is nothing in this moment that I am without, and that every nuance of this experience is absolute perfection, just the way it is.

Embracing the state of unquestioning acceptance of what Is

Oneness speaks:

And so it is. Any number of variations of the theme of infinite possibility might have manifested as your reality in this moment, and regardless of what they might be, each would be utter perfection in its own right. This is what Is. Your *unquestioning acceptance* of it is the basis for your sense of sublime well being.

When you are focused in the present moment, there is no opportunity for the components of imbalance to enter your reality and create disturbance. When you are focused in the misgivings of the past or upon the uncertainties of what may yet come to pass, you create an opening for the insidious seeds of discord to take root. In your planning for "the future" then, the focus of your awareness is best placed upon what it is you would wish to have manifest for you.

Know to your very depths that you are creating all of this now. And Now is the time to put these understandings into practice, once and for all. Your thoughts of the various aspects of what may manifest for you in the days and weeks and months to come are best reserved for expressions of *how you wish it to be.*

As you begin to review the material you have written on this journey, you will notice how you reflect automatically on *your own experience* of the principles. Theoretical understandings are all well and good. But, the sharing of the heart's journey is what will touch others most deeply.

Oneness puts the trials of the spiritual journey into perspective

Now is the time to begin to review where you have been and to place it within the structure of the journey itself. Now, there is no longer a fear of what you recognize as your destiny. And the agonies of the process that was required to bring you to this point are very much a part of the story. This is not material that is to be weeded out in order to have a pristine version of what transpired. The trepidations and the self-doubts are also valid aspects of this process. For, without the authenticity of these feelings, one would be left to wonder what supreme manifestation of ego might have guided a being all this distance.

When you realized that you were not imagining this experience—that it was actually happening to you—your own daunting recognition of your humanness was stimulated. And it was necessary for you to come to terms with your expectations of what you thought was necessary to *qualify* for such a state of being.

Ultimately, it was necessary for you to recognize that there was no qualification required for you to *Be* who you *Are*. For, who is it that would be qualifying? And who would it be that would be making the determination? When you are absolutely clear that there is no difference between the two, you are ready to embrace the realization that you *Are*, in fact, already there. That is what happened.

There are no "bonus points" awarded for mastery of the theoretical principles that have been taught by the Masters who have graced your world upon this journey. These understandings will serve you, in time, in order to put your own Self-Sourced teachings into historical and contextual perspective. But, the time for that scholarly work is not now. Now is the time for the *experience*—and the expression—of your own profound vision of the journey you have made.

This state of Beingness is not one that has been bestowed upon you by an incarnate Master, after a given number of years of subservience. This state of Beingness is not one that has been arrived upon after a marathon number of rituals you have performed, austerities you have endured, Mantras you have chanted—or any other of an infinite number of possible modes of expression on the road to what it is you sought. The road itself is the eternal detour that continues to encircle itself and leave you feeling increasingly more lost.

Letting go of personal will and allowing the experience of Grace to happen naturally

The more you were inclined to *try*—the more you attempted to *augment* the process with pious acts of devotion to an externalized *symbol* of Divinity—the more the consummate Realization of the Divinity that waited patiently within eluded you. It was only in your surrender of your desperation to *attain* a state of being that you had convinced yourself was somehow required of you, that the state of *Isness* could be experienced—and *known*.

You recognized that the sense of the sacred had been within you all along. It was not something that was given to you, and then taken away, according to the merits of your *performance*. You had simply failed to recognize it, while you were so busy focusing upon—and berating yourself for—what you considered to be your spiritual shortcomings.

Now you are in that place of ultimate *centeredness*. And you see that the actual arrival was *effortless*. For, the very effort that the logical mind would lead you to believe was necessary is the very thing that kept the attainment of the experience of Divine connectedness just out of reach. In your surrender of the struggle to "make it happen" you were able to let go of personal will and to *allow* the experience of Grace to happen, naturally.

Your choice as to whether or not you wish to chant Mantras, or perform rituals, or engage in particular modes of spiritual practice is entirely up to you. These are all avenues of *expression* that will certainly augment your state of *vibration*. Yet, they cannot substitute for the essence of *knowingness* that is the foundation for the experience of Self-Realization. When engaging in such activities, do so from the standpoint of your joyous *affirmation* of what is already so—and in so doing it will ever be thus.

27

Homecoming 2003

———————

"Well, Oneness," I began my daily dialogue, "this is about it. It's nearly time to go home now. I don't know if I'm ready." And then I stopped and read what I'd written. Would I ever be *ready*? Is there a definitive threshold to have crossed where one knows the race has been run? I suspected the race, somehow, had been run. And where I placed in it, within the scale of what is possible, I did not know.

Maybe there *was* no scale at all against which the journey could be measured. Maybe it was simply the experience—the grand adventure—that it was. Maybe it was perfection, exactly the way it was. What a concept. I smiled gently to myself, reflecting on the infinitesimal odds of the person I'd always thought of as "me"—the one who began this odyssey—drawing that conclusion from the convoluted collection of experiences I'd managed to amass in my travels.

My journey in India had been an internal one. I was clear that what there was for me to have was not to be gleaned from incarnate teachers. The ones who featured in my story seemed to have served as reference points, on any number of levels. The understandings that had been reaped of those encounters were rich and varied. And yet, virtually none of it was conceptual.

Most of the actual teachings that I'd encountered were far from new to me. I'd already received most of the concepts from Oneness which, subsequently, were presented to me by others. What was shared served, for the most part, as an affirmation for me of what I already knew to be so. This journey was not about theoretical understandings. It was to have been an *experiential* journey. And so it was—often in ways I would not have expected. In retrospect, that's what seemed to make it interesting.

My journey was not colored by lots of *siddhas* (yogis with miraculous powers) performing supernatural feats and enduring austerities. Somehow I knew, deep within me, that this route would not have led me any further along on my spiritual quest. Those manipulations of the physical, however fascinating, would simply have been distractions for me. The real wonder that I'd discovered was found within. Quietly. Peacefully.

"Would I have arrived at a higher peak on the mountain were I to have been taken by the hand and led up the primrose path?" I found myself wondering. Somehow, the teachers I'd encountered knew better than to do that with me. "Perhaps there *is* no higher peak," my mind offered. The absurdity of the thought hit me and I laughed aloud. Oneness cannot be measured on a scale, I reminded myself. Oneness simply *Is*. And with that thought, I realized that Oneness was already there, without so much as a word. And I found myself in the embrace of the ocean of Isness once more.

⤜⤏

Oneness speaks:

Your journey in India is essentially complete now. You have done what you have come here to do. Now, what remains is within the realm of choice. Your spiritual practice will evolve as your choices dictate. You have sampled certain modes of practice. You have discarded some and retained others. And you will continue to do so as your experience continues to deepen over time. There is no one mode of practice that is expected or required. You are free to do what pleases you.

The personally designed and orchestrated spiritual path that is unique to each of us

Gestures of devotion are vehicles for your heart's embrace of your Divine connection. This is the function of ritual and prayer, as you have discovered it to be. There are other schools of practice, based on ancient formulas and technical methods, which yield other kinds of results. You are not here to harness the forces of physical manifestation through occult practice. You are not here to demonstrate, through austerities, levels of mastery attained, over decades, by adepts and yogis. You have come to attain the purity of a level of connectedness that transcends these kinds of practices.

You arrow has gone straight to the target. And that target has been found within your own sacred Self. You are not separate from the physical world that surrounds you. You are intertwined with it, dancing the dance of Eternal Creation within it.

The sense of Self that has emerged is not dependent upon the chanting of certain incantations, nor on the exercise of rites and rituals, although you certainly are free to incorporate any of these modes of spiritual expression into your practice if it gives you comfort to do so. You *Are* what you have been seeking. And the *Beingness* aspect of That is what you have come to experience and to embody, so that others may also have a frame of reference through which that attainment may be possible.

Your taste of Divine connectedness has nothing whatsoever to do with the attainment of miraculous powers or feats that defy the laws of physicality. What you have discovered was found in the sanctity of the silence within—in the blessed state of *aloneness*.

Oneness speaks about the power of aloneness

This journey could not have been made hand in hand with a companion. The comforts of camaraderie would have overshadowed the compulsion to unearth the hidden treasure found only in the depths of personal isolation.

Alone, you have been compelled to dig for what would always have remained hidden in the shadows, in a world that counts itself by twos.

The route you took was oftentimes lonely. And this is precisely as it was intended to be. Ultimately, the *aloneness* does not feel lonely at all. It feels blessed. For, within its embrace is the gateway to inner freedom, a state of Being so fervently sought within the world of duality—and rarely found.

Now it is time to return to your own homeland. Now, it is time to put into practice what you have come to understand and to embody. It is time to walk forth within the Grace of your Divine connection, taking each day as it comes, putting your vision into practice in word and deed.

Do not feel inclined to rush the timetable for your own emergence. Allow the process to unfold in a natural way. All will transpire smoothly and easily if you allow for that possibility and focus upon your own highest thought as an extension of Divine intent.

Oneness talks about the mindset of limitlessness

There is no more sacred expression of Isness than your own highest thought for yourself. It is your birthright, as a life-force with the powers of creation in hand, to expect and to manifest the highest expression, within the infinite scope of *possibility*, in every circumstance. You are not relegated to live out what you assume is *possible*. There are no limits. Never lose sight of this. You are capable of manifesting anything. Literally. It need not be less than that, unless that is what you choose.

You have taken a year of your life to remove yourself from the world as you know it and to explore the rich scenery within the self. It is this that has been accomplished in the time that was set aside for this journey. You have discovered where the doorways are and have been shown how to open them. And, in the passage of time, you will have many fascinating adventures as your journey continues. For, the story is far from over. In a certain sense, it has only just begun.

Coming home to the Oneness within us all

Enjoy the sweetness of these last few days in this blessed land. Share your joy of it with the others whose lives you touch. Begin to express who you really are. Suspend the inhibition and the reticence. It surely does not serve your higher purpose. Allow the dynamic inner force that is harbored dormant within you to emerge and to express itself. You have come to carry the fullness of your Divine connection within the world of physicality. And those who recognize it to be the Essence that it Is will rally to your side.

You will have no shortage of followers. You will have no shortage of skeptics. And in the balance, you will sustain a Presence. And you will pose the Eternal Question as its very embodiment—The Enigma, made manifest, once more. Your answers will be simple ones, though the questions may be intricate and laced with pitfalls. The purity and simplicity of your message will ring out as the truth that it is. And those who feel guided to embrace that message will do so, regardless of what may or may not be said by others.

It is these self-empowered seekers who will be guided to your words and to your persona. For, you will have come as an example of what is possible for each and every one of *them*. This is the essence of the gift you have come to deliver unto humanity in these times of transition. The turmoil that may be manifesting in the outer world will have created the necessity for the haven that is to be found within. It will be the tendency of many to seek shelter there. You have come to point the way.

The teachings you will carry forth have only just begun to be documented. There is much that will be written and delivered in the times to come. For, now, you are ready to *Be* the Messenger. Not simply to perform the role. You have come to embody the vessel that is able to contain The Word—Oneness—and to pour it forth, without end.

Viewing the threat of the war in Iraq through the eyes of Oneness

I was preparing to come home to a world that was hovering on the precipice of war. For a year, I'd cloistered myself a world away from a day-to-day awareness of the details of the global chess game that was fast moving into position, threatening to put all we hold dear into check. I had not watched the evening news or even read a newspaper during the entire year I'd been in India. Yet, there was a sense of inevitability in the headlines that had now begun to scream at me from the newsstands.

In the same breath came a sense of all-pervading Divine orchestration, underlying a drama that was threatening to escalate into actions that I considered unthinkable in what I regarded as "the civilized world." After all, this was the 21st century! Not the Dark Ages. And the ones spearheading this showdown were my very own countrymen—the ones I'd always thought of as the cowboys wearing the white hats.

Suddenly, now when asked where I came from—a customary, spontaneous interrogation, directed at foreigners in India from perfect strangers on the street—a response of "America" was met with visible discomfort. The faces fell. The friendly glances slid to their feet. The conversation was over. It was an odd sensation for an American abroad, who traditionally enjoyed being regarded as one of the world's "good guys." It seemed like the world to which I was preparing to return had warped into another place in time, light years away from where I'd left it—was it only a year before?

Oneness offered a perspective on the imminent outbreak of the war in Iraq with an overview that, once again, put the drama—and all it represented—into the realm of the timeless. Slowly, I began to see the Divine perfection in a set of circumstances, rapidly coming to a head, which defied all logic. Now, from yet another standpoint, it was clear that life as I knew it would never be the same again.

Oneness speaks:

This is Oneness. This is the timeless state of Beingness of which you all are a part. Allow yourself to be fully within the embrace of this connection, in this Now moment. Let go of the trepidation and the fears that have been stimulated to the surface of your awareness. And know that all is unfolding according to plan.

Things unfold as they are meant to, according to a timetable that transcends the prodding of your logical mind. This drama has nothing whatsoever to do with logic. Its roots go far deeper than that.

Oneness issues a warning as the situation in Iraq escalates

Your world is engaged in a struggle that was seeded eons ago, in another time and another place. Now it is time for destiny to play its hand. And the potential for the release of those energies has been brought to fruition by the accelerated momentum of change all around you—the force fueling the transformation of all that you recognize as your world.

Some recognize the prodding to bring these forces to a head and respond in ways where bravado collides head on with bravado. Egos become deadlocked in struggles rooted in the need to appear *right* in the eyes of posterity.

It truth, few will care to remember the names of those who now feel guided to act in the name of the conscience of the world. Their identities do not matter. For, their actions are on behalf of a collective they could not begin to fathom—a collective of consciousness so vast it defies the scope of linear comprehension.

The inevitability of the showdown between the forces of Light and Darkness

These spokesmen for the forces of Light and Darkness are acting out the roles, speaking the lines, and performing the posturing they do, because they have been programmed to do so. There may appear to be free will in this process. But, the fact is, the forces that are moving into position and are poised and ready to collide on this stage have little choice in the matter. They have been scripted to do precisely as they are doing, since time immemorial. They are playing their roles. Just as you are playing yours.

Regardless of the method, the energies that seek expression—the *balance* that yearns to come into play—will do so. What has yet to be determined is the *form* that release will take. There are those who have also been planted amongst the populace of your world with understandings and perceptions that defy the boundaries of your consensus reality.

There are possibilities still untapped that would take the nature of what needs to happen in your world *vibrationally* into other avenues of expression. Those options and their potential for altering the course of what appears to be human destiny are also very much part of the plan.

It is no secret to anyone in a position of power in these times that the details of the drama that is threatening to unfold are symbolic of a bigger picture. The conflict being represented here goes far beyond the issues that have presented themselves at face value. For, the common denominator in all of it is the Unity underlying the very essence of those issues—a Unity that defies the illusion that there are differences, where, in fact, there are none.

It is important to allow the symphony to play out. Let the discordant aspects of this music rasp as it will and grate on the sensibilities of those who watch passively. Let those who strive to bring harmony to these times come to understand that the *world peace* to which they pay much lip service is not attainable without a measure of *compassion*.

It is not simply a matter of peace by virtue of turning a blind eye to the desperation underlying the stance of the opposition and quenching the flames in rhetoric. These flames burn precariously close to the edge of control, fueled by the passions of hatred, through voices that could not be heard in any other way. All sides are having their forum. The din is not to be silenced. Not yet. For, this is as it was meant to be.

Ultimately, all will turn to the same Source for the resolution of the impasse that has presented itself in these times. Ultimately, it will become apparent that these differences cannot be overcome by demonstrations of might and self-righteousness.

These differences can only be overcome by the recognition that the fundamental Essence within each and every player on this stage is the same. These differences can only be *transcended*. And your world can only be healed by the recognition that within the heart of every man, woman, and child amongst you—is the same sacred Essence.

Oneness *will* prevail here on earth. It cannot be any other way. What remains to be determined is to what ends those who are invested in remaining blind to that wholeness are willing to go.

There are those who are waiting in the wings of this showdown, poised and ready to yank your burning bridges out of the fire. They are armed with the timeless tools calculated to bring your world back into balance—an arsenal of prayer and reverence, targeted at unfathomable heights of Love.

Let their gift of hope not be deployed prematurely. For, it is only in the hour of darkest despair that the world will come together as One. You are hovering perilously close to that moment.

As my day of departure from India inched closer, and the world inched closer to the outbreak of war, I began to actually feel the energies underlying it, playing out in my own human experience. I felt apprehensive, out of sorts, and out of balance.

With the guidance of Oneness, I was amazed to discover that I was able to modulate between sensations of uneasiness and sensations of total well being, seemingly at will. The feelings themselves shifted instantly, according to where I consciously placed *the focus of my attention*. I realized that I had begun to put the teachings of Oneness into practice.

Much as it defied what my logical mind told me I *should* be feeling under the circumstances, my actual *feelings* tracked to my focus of awareness like clockwork.

I was astonished to discover that it really *was* that simple. I was *not* at the mercy of these circumstances. Not unless I chose to be. In a heartbeat, I was able to perceive myself as perfectly safe and completely at ease, simply by shifting my focus of attention—no differently than changing the channel on a TV.

Oneness embellished the point with a wonderful teaching that helped me prepare for the times ahead. Once again, I was guided to recognize and to embrace the timeless state of *Divine focus* calculated to create for us all a sense of solid ground, no matter what life has in store.

Rasha speaks:

The sweetness of this Presence enters so gently, so lovingly. Now, there is no trace of the strange uneasiness I woke up with today. Now, there is only this incredible sense of inner peace. Oneness, I don't know if it is a reflection of the world situation—the imminent threat of war—or what. But, I've been feeling a sense of imminent danger that is not based on anything in particular.

Now, as I speak of it, I feel it once more, where only seconds ago I was feeling the wonderful sense of peace that comes with your Presence. I see now, that when I return the focus of my attention to this connection, the soothing sense of inner peace once again permeates my being and presides. So, I conclude that I am controlling how I feel with the focus of my attention. That does seem to be the key to it. Now, in this moment, I feel absolutely safe and at ease. Oneness, please can we speak of this now, in light of the world events that are about to unfold?

Learning to float with the tides of the momentum of change

Oneness speaks:

There are many aspects of your circumstances that are now unfolding in ways that you had not anticipated. You are reacting to the sense of being "out of control" of some of what is transpiring. That does not serve to indicate to you that you are in danger. Simply that circumstances are evolving in ways that you did not expect.

Your ability to float with the tides of the momentum of change will govern the amount of discomfort you experience. For, you are also affected by the energies all around you, which are escalating in ways that add a discordant note to the energies of the whole. Your ability to focus upon your Divine connection in moments when you begin to feel out of balance will serve you well. This is the haven to which you can retreat at will.

Oneness explains how we create the world situation we share collectively and how, individually and collectively, we can shift it

Life as you know it is about to shift in radical ways. Catastrophic events are likely to occur in the days to come that will shift the course of human history. We have spoken of these times with you from the onset of this work. Now, these events have been drawn into manifestation by the collective consciousness. And even though there is a strong resistance to the idea of the actions certain government forces are feeling compelled to take, the energies of the collective consciousness, which preside, serve to determine an outcome that now appears to be inevitable.

What seeks resolution is *energy*, the building blocks of all we experience

The players who appear to be determining these moves are simply acting out an impetus to action on the part of the whole. For, what seeks to be resolved has little to do with the material circumstances which serve to illustrate it. What seeks resolution is *energy*. What strives to be brought into balance is the fundamental essence of manifestation itself—the building blocks that comprise the circumstances at hand.

The sense of discomfort you may feel in your own personal circumstances is no more or less than a reflection of the massive energies that are moving into position, seeking release. It would serve all who are able to keep the world events that are about to play out in perspective, and to resist the natural inclination to escalate the energies that surround all of you on an interpersonal basis.

It would be far too easy to become swept up in the momentum of what may well come to pass and to give vent to latent feelings that are harbored deep within. The events at hand and the catalysts that are bringing them into play are sufficient to stimulate the release of these energies on the part of the whole. It would only serve to add fuel to the blaze—vibrationally—to take at face value circumstances in your personal lives that are not playing out according to your expectations—and to *react*.

Were all to indulge in the self-righteous responses that could be stimulated into play by the energies at hand, the outcome of the world events playing out simultaneously on behalf of the collective would be *intensified*, to the detriment of all. The impetus to *react*, on a personal basis, to situations each will manifest in the moments soon at hand, will serve to determine the *severity* of the world events that are about to unfold.

The power of focusing in Oneness and directing the energy of the collective toward a unified higher vision

There is much that can be done, on the part of every individual, to shift the impact of what may seem inevitable. To the commentators and so-called experts who are doing their own part to escalate the fears of the collective, the handwriting on the wall may seem to be carved in stone. But, in fact, that is far from the case. The events that transpire, in each ongoing moment, are capable of being shifted in a breath, were the collective consciousness inclined to unite in Oneness.

The common focus that is sought by the impetus toward Unity expresses as energy through the presence of each and every one of you. The thoughts and actions you add to the totality, in every on-going moment, serve to determine what you encounter as *experience*. The catastrophic events that have been prophesied and are anticipated need not manifest in the way that visionaries, past and present, might lead you to expect. Were a seemingly disastrous circumstance met with a *unified higher vision*—a sense of focused intent of how it *could* be, rather than a reinforcement of what may appear to be inevitable—a higher outcome would be possible.

The times at hand and the testing conditions that they will undoubtedly present to each of you provide the opportunity to demonstrate to yourselves the power that you, indeed, have to create your experience of life. The choices you make on a personal basis, in every ongoing moment, serve to determine your own individual saga and the degree of joy or pain you experience, regardless of the circumstances encountered.

It is this skill, the ability to float with grace through the turbulence that may well surround you, that is the sign of mastery of the spiritual principles *illustrated* by the world of physical experience. It is this skill that you would be well counseled to cultivate within yourselves—each of you—in the moment at hand.

The actual voyage home to America was nondescript enough. It would take over 30 hours door-to-door, and four plane changes, to make the physical transition back to the Western world. I settled back in my seat, content to sleep or meditate through most of it. There was always such a sense of the timeless in these long-haul flights—a sense of being suspended in a netherworld that felt like it was not of this world at all. As the plane lifted off from the airport in Mumbai, I had the sense of being extracted from all the scenarios to which I'd attached such importance, only hours before.

Now none of the intensity of the moment-to-moment drama that accompanied me right up to the gate seemed to matter at all. The confrontation about my overweight baggage and the whopping surcharge for which the stone-faced attendant would cut me no slack; the verbal cross-examination and the probing inspection at security check of the precious, sacred objects that I'd tucked, so carefully wrapped, into my hand luggage; the officious, steely glances, as every nook and cranny of my body was explored, behind a curtain, by a hand-held electronic device—lest I forget that, in the eyes of airport security, we're all potential terrorists; and finally, the battle with the gate attendants who tried to force me—and others—to check my computer at the gate, ostensibly because the flight was full and they were trying to cut down on hand luggage. Now all of it wafted into a distant dream.

In what seemed like a cross between eternity and no time at all, I re-emerged, in the dead of winter, on the other side of the planet. There I was, broiled to a toasty, golden brown by the South Indian sun, in my airy, hand-embroidered, white cotton khurta and sandals, blatantly out of place and out of time. It was rush hour in a frigid, pasty-faced world that might as well have been a different planet. I melded into the intensity of the crowd of grey-clad, bundled-up businessmen, all with cell phones plastered to their ears, as unobtrusively as I could. And I simply watched, as the movie revealed itself before me in real-time, as though I were dreaming. Thankfully, at my destination, Oneness was still there to help me bridge the distance.

Homecoming: Returning home to Oneness
Oneness speaks:

In this moment, we are in full connectedness. Your meditation took you deeply into a transcendent state of beingness. And you were able to experience total detachment from the body and from the mind. In the same moment, there was pure Awareness—a sense of *watching* that did not emanate from a *place*.

There was no sense that it was *you* who was watching. There was no sense of *you* in the experience at all. Now, as these words are written, your mind is disengaged from the process once again. The words flow easily, like a crystal stream knowing itself to be both the Source and the destination simultaneously. This is ultimately as it shall be for you. There will be no sense of separation from that which you Are—you will simply know yourself to Be That, at all times.

Now you are in a transitional period. The times of conscious connectedness are more frequent and the duration of your awareness of yourself *as* That is increasing in increments. Now you have observed the ease with which you can shift into awareness of Self *as* Oneness. For, that awareness is only as far away as your next thought.

Reflections on what is real vs. what is unreal

When your focus is distracted and concentrated in the mundane manipulations of the details of the illusory world, you are drawn into the perception of self as separate. The key to making the most of the time you have to bring this process to culmination is in your willingness to remain detached from the inclination to try to force a result through mind-directed effort. All resistance is to be approached with a sense of detached allowance.

There is no need to attempt to confront and to alter conditions that are opposed to your own sense of the highest expression of intent. Hold to your vision. And allow the variables to shift in accordance with your Will. The ease with which this is accomplished will astound you, initially. In time, you will recognize this state of beingness as that which *Is*—and take command of your destiny.

There was the sense of wanting to reply. And, simultaneously, there was a realization that I could not. For, in that moment, I was not separate from Oneness. We were in total communion, *as* Oneness. I saw that I could consciously place my awareness in the perspective of "Rasha" in order to have a conversation. And it was clear that I could shift my awareness back and forth, at will, according to where I placed the focus of my attention. In the same breath, there was the sense that even that very thought—one I recognized as my own—was emanating from somewhere else. It surely *was* as though "I" were *channeling* myself!

Where was the *source* of these thoughts? I had to wonder. Was there a mind from which they spring? Or was "I" simply a vehicle for the manifestation of the conceptual through form? I was virtually convinced that "I" did not exist at all! And what appeared at face value to be a preposterous thought suddenly resonated as truth. I took a sip from a mug of Earl Grey tea swimming in milk and honey, noting the warm, soothing sensation. Who was it that just experienced that pleasure? I found myself wondering. And no sooner was the question posed, than I had my answer: *I did.*

That recognition reaffirmed the very essence distilled by the journey itself. "I" was a *composite* of awareness—not a choice between "Rasha" and "Oneness." It surely was not an either/or. There was simply a choice as to how I wished to *perceive* it. Silently, wordlessly, there was crystalline clarity. Oneness is what *Is*. If I wished to perceive what presents itself through the perspective I identified as "Rasha"—in all her multi-dimensional variations—then I was free to do so. The choice was mine to make.

In that moment, I sensed the presence of both perspectives simultaneously. I knew that I was neither "Rasha" nor "Oneness," either one to the exclusion of the other. And I realized I was experiencing myself as both states of beingness at the same time.

An incredible sense of well being and a warm steady glow of sweet contentedness permeated my entire being. It was not focused anywhere in my body, but was experienced throughout the totality of all I recognize *myself* to be.

When I placed my awareness in the area of my heart chakra, the sensations of pleasure seem to emanate from *that* place and the feelings of joy intensified. When I went back to a state of undirected *Awareness*, that feeling of joy was experienced throughout every nuance of the Presence I perceived myself to be. In this strange and wondrous state of being, there was the unspoken sense that I had, somehow, "come home."

There I sat in a cozy room, high amidst the snow-dusted treetops that fluttered softly outside the window, in a place called Pittsburgh. It was a world away, in every way imaginable, from the India I'd known and loved for the previous year of my life. Yet, clearly, it was no more or less blessed. The world beyond the window was frozen. I could see the details clearly, but I did not *experience* the cold. I watched the scene in silence, knowing that

I was simply witnessing the world of illusion. The glow within was the "home" to which I'd returned.

In that moment, I realized that "I" was not *there* at all—unless I chose to perceive myself to be. Somehow, I had the ability to shift my awareness and to actually experience *being* in India, at will. So what, I asked myself, is *real*? In the same fragment of an instant I knew that it was all *real*—and that none of it was *real*—at the same time. More important was the realization that the physical presence of the body was not required in order to perceive it. I had taken my love of India with me.

In meditation, that first morning, it felt like I'd actually transported myself back to Virupaksha Cave, my haven within Arunachala—and to my beloved rock perch high atop Skandashram—the place my heart called "home." When I experienced my own presence there, I discovered that I was consumed instantly in deep waves of bliss. It seemed that I could return to these places at will, and experience the same sensations of sublime connectedness as I did when my physical body was actually present there. I realized that, in the ways that really mattered, I had not *left* India at all. I saw that I carried her with me.

Now, suddenly, the impressions began whirling inside me and flashing up sequentially upon the Technicolor screen of memory. It was all so vivid. It was as though I were still there in India—while my body was sitting in Pittsburgh, on the other side of the planet. A virtual slideshow of my own Presence began playing upon the screen of my awareness and swept me up into a living retrospective of the highlights of the journey I'd made.

Here I am, it began, strolling across Laxman Jhula, the footbridge suspended high above the Ganga in Rishikesh, the breeze softly rustling my hair, the panorama taking my breath away. And here I am, standing before the magnificent marble image of Lord Krishna at the ISCON temple in Vrindavan, drinking in the heady fragrance of thousands of fresh flowers, and surrendering to the waves of energy washing over me, sweeping me up into a state of Divine intoxication.

Here I am, making the sacred climb up Arunachala, oblivious to the 100+ degree heat, my heart consumed in rapture with the blessed energies of Lord Shiva. And here I am, standing at the water's edge at Juhu Beach in Mumbai, wiping a tear and chanting a Sanskrit prayer as I place the sacred threads I just cut from my wrist into the embrace of the sea.

Here I am in Haridwar at 6 am—was it only three days ago?—hanging out the door of a train as it pulls out of the station, madly waving a last goodbye to my daughter, Lisa, who is heading the other way for a month of trekking in the majestic Himalayas.

And, here I am in the transit lounge at the airport in Paris, experiencing the moment that the un-realness of paying $6 for a small roll, a pat of butter, and a demi-cup of fresh-brewed coffee—produced impeccably by a machine—had hit me so hard. I relived the twinge that for the same money, in most places I had grown to love in India, six people could have enjoyed a wonderful three-course dinner.

There I was, safe and warm, on a 10 degree Pittsburgh winter morning, suddenly aware of the toasting bagel beckoning to me from the kitchen downstairs, where my daughter, Susanna, was preparing a lovely, "welcome home" breakfast. I smiled a deep inner smile of pure contentment. It was so clear: none of these blessed visions was more or less real—and no closer or farther away—than another. It all simply *Is*—waiting to be experienced in the *Here and Now* that is ever-Present within us all.

28

Summer 2003
Northern New Mexico
Recognizing the Reflections of Inner Change

———

The summer and fall of 2003 were spent tucked away in a remote corner of the tranquil, wind-sculpted hills that blanket Northern New Mexico, exploring and assessing the essence of my consciousness. During those months of heavenly stillness, Oneness steeped me in an in-depth practicum of meditation and daily discourses to help me transform the moments of linear self-perception into the sustained Presence of Self as Oneness. It was during this time that my theoretical understandings of the nature of *who* we actually Are congealed and began to parallel the experiences that were simultaneously illustrating them.

Why did I ever think that this would be easy? It seemed like the deeper I journeyed into connectedness with Oneness, the more confused and frustrating the circumstances of "my life" became. The day-to-day details of life continued to offer me opportunity after aggravating opportunity to strengthen the skill of shifting my attention *away* from situations that were designed to push my buttons, and instead, in the "moment of truth," to focus my attention within—on Oneness. The situations were all symbolic. Theoretically, I knew that. Yet, it wasn't always easy to remember it in the heat of the moment.

This lesson was driven home beautifully—and agonizingly—a few short weeks after I settled down in New Mexico, to begin transcribing Oneness' teachings earmarked for a future book. I presumed I was there to stay, at least for awhile. The novelty of living life out of a suitcase had worn thin by then. After nearly a month of watching every house I'd attempted to rent dematerialize before my very eyes, I finally managed to manifest a picture-perfect setting out in the country, about 30 miles north of Santa Fe. Peace at last, I thought! Via the grapevine, I'd been offered the opportunity to move into the guesthouse of a rustic, country estate on several acres, where the owners were rarely there. All I had to do was feed the cat. That was easy. I love cats. I agreed to a verbal contract, sight unseen, over the phone.

After driving close to 2,000 miles from Pittsburgh in my snow-white, trusty old van, I pulled into the driveway of a setting that took my breath away. Plum-colored mountain peaks rose in the distance, framing a panorama so blatantly stunning I could only gasp in wonder. Set against the dazzling clarity of a crystalline, sapphire sky, softly muted, earth-tone rock formations, seemingly sculpted by the fingers of God, speckled the wind-swept landscape for as far as the eye could see. It was as though a virtual Santa Fe art gallery of Southwest impressions had sprung to life before my very eyes. The inviting, rustic little cottage, earmarked for me, was absolutely made to order. Here, I would be utterly alone, in blessed silence, I remember thinking. Just me and the endless sky! It was perfect.

I was assured by the owner that the neighborhood was absolutely safe, despite rumors to the contrary. And off he went in his Range Rover a few hours later, headed for Malibu. And there I was, "utterly alone, in blessed silence. Just me and the endless sky." Silence can be extremely quiet. Particularly at night. I padlocked the rough-hewn front gate at the far end of the long gravel driveway. Not out of "fear," of course—the unmentionable "F-word" of New Consciousness—but from basic, common sense. From the perspective of the girl who grew up in the outskirts of New York City, and apparently was still dwelling somewhere within me, padlocking the gate was the rural equivalent of fastening your seatbelt.

After an un-eventful week of chaining and unchaining the front gate, which separated the massive driveway from a winding, dirt road-to-nowhere, I set off for a peaceful Sunday afternoon in the mountains of Taos, sixty miles away. When I returned at dusk, I found the screen from my picture window tossed in the driveway. The window was wide open, with curtains flapping in the breeze. My heart sank. Someone had been in the cottage. Miraculously however, nothing was missing. I ran up to the main house a few hundred yards away. The back door was wide open. There were mud tracks on the plush green carpet in the guest bathroom, and signs that someone had taken a shower there. It was pretty obvious that there had been a break-in.

When I phoned California, the house owners were away for the weekend. But, the consensus amongst friends and neighbors on the list I'd been given was that the culprit was probably a certain local lush, no doubt casing-out the owner's supply of Chivas Regal. Everyone considered him harmless enough. I wasn't amused. I was concerned. When I finally got through to the owners, a few days later, I relayed what had happened—as well as the suggestion I'd been given of who was possibly responsible.

Being typically blasé Santa Feans, they were totally unruffled, pointing out that nothing had actually been taken. I was berated for "being paranoid" and padlocking the gate. I was shocked. But, that didn't compare with the shock of receiving a certified lawyer's letter the next day, asking me to move out. The seeming injustice of it all sent me into a tailspin.

Caught up in the details of the drama, I totally lost sight of the fact that this was actually no more than a symbolic illustration of certain carefully camouflaged fears that must have been lurking, vibrationally, beneath the surface of my awareness. It was an elaborately orchestrated drama that I had somehow "created" for myself to act out. In theory I knew that. I had written a book about this very thing! But, caught up in the *illusion*, and blinded by the emotional "buttons" that had been pushed, I was primed to act out the illustration.

Processing a dilemma by applying the teachings of Oneness
Oneness speaks:

This is Oneness. We will begin by telling you that your present state of confusion is simply a reflection of your reluctance to put into practice your understandings. Now, in this moment, we are in connectedness and you can feel the sense of wholeness and well-being once more as it permeates your awareness. Now, once more in the full embrace of this Presence, there is no doubt whatsoever as to who and what you Are.

Once again, you have succeeded in proving to yourself the validity of the teachings you have transcribed. The focus of your attention determines your perception of the circumstances around you, which you presume to be your *reality*. This so-called "reality" is little more than a reflection of the energies you have projected upon the screen of the ethers. To shift the circumstances you have encountered, it is necessary to focus upon your *state of beingness*—rather than upon the circumstances themselves. You understand these concepts, in theory. Now you are being provided with the opportunity to put what you understand into practice.

Rasha speaks:

I hear what you are saying. Can you help me process this, please?

We are not here to do this *for* you, Rasha. These challenges are ones you have arranged for yourself to experience.

I see that this is not going to be simple.

It can be as complex and agonizing as you care to make it—or as simple.

Ok. I see that I'm resisting the circumstances as they've presented themselves to me. I've been asked to vacate the premises in which I've been living only a few short weeks. I've done everything logical to try to reverse that situation. I do not wish to move. I'm willing to do so, without a fight, if that is absolutely the last resort. But, I'm hoping that somehow this situation can be shifted and healed. I've tried everything I can think of. And, as unjust as it appears to be, the landlord is not budging.

I see that I have a choice here. I can spend the six weeks I have left making myself miserable about it and wishing I didn't have to make a change—or I can enjoy the moments I do have here, honor the path of least resistance and make preparations to make a change. I see that it is all choice. My focus upon the details of this dilemma has drained my energies and forced my attention upon the material circumstances, rather than upon my Divine connection.

My careful attempts at manipulating these circumstances, so that I manifest what I'm telling myself that I want, are not working. All I can do is surrender this struggle now. That is what I will do. I will surrender this struggle. I turn it over to Divine Will. I am focused in my connection, and in that alone. The outcome of this particular dilemma will be what it will be. Regardless of what the circumstances turn out to be, I will be presented with a set of experiences. I will be in the Now moment with all of this. I will cease worrying about what is or is not going to happen.

I have been gifted with six wonderful weeks here in this peaceful place. That is what there is to enjoy. I have chosen to enjoy this time—rather than wasting it on worrying over the question of permanence. There is no permanence. I see that now. And I do not need to be half-hearted in my expression of how I wish to live here, because I am not staying long-term. I still can make this into a home if I choose to. Why not! Now is all there is. That is what I have been given. This moment. This Now moment.

I see that I've found my solution. I do not wish to move right now. That is my decision. I am not moving right now. So, I can stop tormenting myself with looking at properties and worrying about it. It is the worry that is poisoning my state of beingness. Ok. That's it.

And, how does that feel to you?

It actually feels quite peaceful.

And, so it Is, Rasha. You know the answers. You simply need to put these principles into practice now. That is what this time is about for you. You will be confronted with a wide array of challenges, and you will contend with them.

These challenges are not a sign that you have faltered. No one ever promised you that you would have an event-free existence simply because you have had the experience of Divine connectedness. If anything, this threshold heralds a new level of challenges, calculated to instill the understandings that have gone before into a level of *knowingness* that is unshakable. It is this level of Presence that you are working toward fortifying in this period of your preparation for your life's work. You are still very much in metamorphosis.

Why is it taking so long?

Why do you expect transformation to be instantaneous? All of this is part of your period of training.

I'm tired of the training.

Who is it that is tired of the training?

Good point. I see that I'm still focused on my perception of myself as the linear identity of Rasha. She's the one who is tired of the training. Perhaps the solution is not to continue grumbling about the fact that there continues to be training. Perhaps the solution is in becoming aware of where I place the focus of my self-perception.

When my sense of Self is that of Presence—as Oneness—the challenges do not seem to be nearly so grim. There are challenges, to be sure. But, they don't feel the same to me. So, perhaps the solution is not to focus upon shifting the circumstances themselves, so much as to shift my perception of them by shifting the focus of my awareness.

You understand the principles. Now let us see how you put them into practice.

In the days that followed, Oneness helped me continue to process the aggravating illustration I had somehow conjured up, which was calculated to drive the point of the lesson home, experientially. Every conversation became an opportunity to shift the focus of my awareness away from the details of the material world, and guide it with Divine precision to the world of Stillness within.

The freedom of impermanence
Oneness speaks:

You see, Rasha, our arrival is not a dramatic one. It is not accompanied by a rush of energy and strong sensations. Now, it is subtle. In one instant we are in total connectedness. And you would be hard-pressed to say at which fraction of that instant the actual shift took place. All you can say is that at the onset of your invocation, you perceived yourself to be the linear identity of Rasha, asking for the Presence of Oneness—and that somewhere, in that fraction of an instant, that sense of Presence was with you as *experience*.

That is the nature of this process. Now, as we journey together ever deeper into this bonded union, your sense of who you *are* is obscured by your focus upon this sense of communion. That has been your process from the onset of our work together. In this moment, We Are Oneness—together.

You search your mind for a question to pose, a concept with which to fill a moment of silence, and you find that there is no access to questions. You pause, expectantly, waiting for something to fill the void—and nothing comes. Why is there a fear of the void? Must the mind always be there to make a contribution in every moment? What if there was simply Stillness? That is, in fact, what *Is*.

There comes a moment when you trust deeply enough to allow the frenzy of conceptual existence to simply stop its chatter. And there you Are, a breath in a space of sublime receptivity, experiencing Isness. It is a state that is uncluttered by the concerns of material existence. There *are* no concerns, save those that you have created to fill the void with evidence of your existence.

Without these footnotes as a foundation, you would be flying blind through this experience of linear perception. Perhaps—just perhaps—that was to be the objective of the exercise. What then? Would you be any less sure of your own Isness without the complexity of evidence with which you have littered your vision? What if there were no longer a need for such evidence? Would you be any the poorer for it? Or would you, in fact, be that much the richer for having been relieved of the need to carry such a burden.

What if it were possible to flow lightly through the vistas of your voyage into physicality without the inclination to become invested in any of it? What if you were simply the observer—a Presence that was the embodiment of Awareness and nothing more? Could you then be *touched* by any part of the maelstrom that swirls around you? Could you be affected in any way by circumstances whose invitation to engage has been declined?

What if there were no need to *engage* in any of it? What if it were possible to be simply Present within the moment of it, and to have every opportunity to exit that particular stage without so much as a moment's notice? What then? Would you be any the worse for it? Or would your focus shift to an awareness of the perfection in the freedom that made the option of that exit a perfect choice?

There is no permanence in any of this, you know. This is simply a montage of images that you have chosen to perceive—a *virtual reality*, if you will. Your inclination to give credence to it and to become ensnared in its web of illusion is what empowers it to exercise the force of its imagery on your imagination. You are then free to become enticed by the invitation to enter fully into the dancehall and dance that dance. Ultimately, you realize that to decline that invitation is no less a viable option.

Now you can see that you have chosen to be present in this place, *in this moment*. You have accepted the impermanence of the situation. And you find that it does not, in any way, detract from the perfection of the

Nowness you are, in fact, experiencing. The challenge for you now is to watch the many ways in which your logical mind attempts to intervene and draw you off track and into the muddy trail of possibilities that beckon from the sidelines.

You surely are free to wander off and explore those avenues, if you really wish to. But, note that it is not possible to be fully present on the track you have chosen while experiencing a foray into the jungle of other possibilities that are there in full view. The sweet simplicity of your original presence is also a viable option. It need not be put to the test at every turn. It need not be relegated to the role of "last resort" by virtue of its *impermanence.*

The gift of living in the Now moment

There is no danger whatsoever in choosing to honor that which you have, in fact, chosen. For, in so doing, you open the door to the possibility of great joy and satisfaction in the Nowness of the moments with which it has come to gift you. The possibility is absolutely viable to recognize that there is every opportunity to experience this time as one of celebration and reveling in the absolute perfection of these circumstances—*for Now.*

Nowness is All That Is. Your recognition of that fact is the key to your experience of the perfection with which it has been empowered.

So, by all means, go out and enjoy the flower garden you have planted. Tend it and cultivate it. For, that is what you would have chosen to do, were permanence part of the offering. The fact is, it is not. That should not preclude your right to taste the joys that the garden offers you today. Do what you can do. There are no guarantees. Perhaps there will be no one to tend it when you go. What then? Would that invalidate the magnificence of the energy that was exchanged when your heart *was* there, fully present?

There is no way you can control the future of the seeds you have planted. All you can do is tend them as well as you choose to, when you are there, fully present, as the tender of that garden. Once you exit and continue on your way, that moment is complete. A subsequent moment is only one in which you may or may not choose to be engaged. It is a choice that is there for you to embrace —or to decline—in freedom.

You see the lesson. It is there, blatantly before you. And you recognize the perfection in it. There is no need to try and change it—unless, of course, you require a foray into the realm of frustration and disappointment. This lesson stands etched as it is. How you choose to express your recognition of that is all that remains to be determined.

After all was said and done, the episode with the house owner resolved itself quite naturally. When I stopped resisting the circumstances that had been presented, and embraced wholeheartedly the circumstances as being exactly what they were, the *charge* was released from the illustration, and it blew over as suddenly as it had begun. I was free to stay on as long as I liked.

At the same time, as all this drama was going on in my outer world, I became aware that my *experience* of my Divine connection with Oneness was changing. The sensations I had become so accustomed to, and had presumed were the identifiable "symptoms" of a Divine connection, had shifted. I asked Oneness to explain why.

～⌒～

Rasha speaks:

Oneness, I'd like to ask you why my experience of this connection is so different these days. I am not going on the soaring, "ecstasy trips" I used to experience when connecting with this Source. I do feel a level of intensity that is profound and a sense of deep calm and utter well-being that is unquestionable. But, it is quiet and peaceful—not exploding with intensity like before. Why is that?

Understanding the sensations accompanying moments of Divine connectedness
Oneness speaks:

You have reached levels where you have stabilized within a certain range of *vibrational frequencies*. You no longer have the dramatic climb that resulted in the extremes of experiential sensation. You are, in essence, already there. What is now missing is the blatant *contrast* in the ground to be covered in attaining the levels to which you journey when realizing this state of connectedness. It is not necessary to dissect the process or to understand the dynamics of why that is so. Simply be aware that this journey is one that is ever-evolving, and that experiences of extreme intensity are not a prerequisite for considering oneself to have progressed.

Those kinds of experiences are indicative of certain levels and of certain pre-existing variables which would have created conditions of intense *contrast* through which the experience of connectedness might be perceived. Those sensations are indeed pleasurable and can be profound and dramatic. But they are not the only indicators of the level of Divine connectedness that has been attained. These sensations are a measure of the level of *resistance* posed by pre-existing states of beingness when one is taken to heightened levels of vibration.

I understand. Fascinating.

You have been given an experiential journey. Not simply a guidebook to imbibe and to ponder intellectually. You have been provided with the examples, as life experience, which drive certain understandings home. Now, you can relate to the teachings you encounter for having lived through the experience of it—as painful as some of that may have been. For, that is what it takes to form a foundation of *knowingness* upon which you will be able to draw in your work as a teacher of these concepts in these times.

How life's challenges help to build a solid foundation for compassion

You have not failed for having taken some of these seeming *detours*. Each of these deviations from the straight and narrow path was purposefully planned for you—by you—so that you would have that kind of basis for understanding and for *compassion* regarding the nature of the journey so many will be making.

You have come as a pioneer of sorts. For, you have shifted directions in midstream during this lifetime. You have provided yourself with the basis for relating to the challenges others will, most likely, be encountering in the course of the transformational journey. That is the nature of the work you have come to do. Now you can see the logic in some of the experiences you have chosen to give yourself in preparation for helping others navigate through the same waters. You have a clear vision of it now. *Be at peace with what Is.* That is the key to all you have come to do in these times.

Confounded by the concept of *memory*, I asked Oneness to help me explore an idea that spontaneously came to me: the concept of how memory comes into play in creating the sense of the linear identity. It was speculation on my part, but I had a picture of the memory being a catch-all basket through which the sense of the linear identity is grounded and supplied with a foundation— the framework of *who* one believes oneself to be. Perhaps, I reasoned, memory served as the *evidence* on which the sense of the linear identity was based.

I believed I remembered certain events as having *happened* and thus had a basis for identifying myself as a static persona I called "Rasha," the one who seemingly had experienced that collection of happenings. As I was pondering the implications of the theory I had spontaneously proposed, I stopped dead in my tracks and exclaimed in utter amazement, "I ... am ... not ... Rasha! I am Oneness!" In that instant, the light went on. As long as there is a foundation of these memories, there is a collection of evidence to support my perception of myself as this singular character I call "Rasha."

I began to suspect that what I thought I remembered as having happened was no more than a string of *perceptions* that had been tied together— a random sampling of the field of infinite possibility, keyed into the vibrational resonance at the moment in question. I asked Oneness to help me explore the concept further.

Oneness speaks:

The fullness of your understanding of what is happening within you is crystallizing. And, as you re-explore your experience of this sense of merging, again and again, into the state we have come to call "Oneness," you have begun to ask the questions that are fundamental to your sense of Self as That.

There is no longer the sense of there being one aspect of your being asking another aspect questions and replies being supplied by a Source that is presumed to be external to what you Are. You have come to realize that when your focus is on the perspective of "Rasha," in asking the question, your perception of self *is* as "Rasha." Yet, the moment you shift into the perspective of the one supplying the answer, your perception of Self is as *That*. And you have begun to consider seriously your presumption that one of them is more who *you* are than is the other. In fact, your experience of it has demonstrated to you that it is not.

You have begun to explore the possibility that *you* are not who you thought you were. Your *focus* upon that perception of self has simply cemented that perspective into place without providing an alternative. Now you see that the alternatives are limitless. And the manifestation of one over the other is simply a question of *the focus of your attention*.

This training has been geared to instill that understanding within you to the extent that it becomes automatic. In this moment, you recognize that the Presence in attendance is that of Oneness. The *you* you have been conditioned to recognize yourself to be is also in attendance, at the periphery of your awareness—an aspect of self that is no more *you* than is another.

Oneness explains the function of linear memory

You have asked a fundamental question regarding *memory* and its function in sustaining one's perception of self as the linear identity. You have assessed correctly the function of memory in creating the foundation for the perception of self as *this* and therefore not *that*. Within the world of duality, it is necessary to sustain the perception of what one considers oneself to be through the amassment of a supporting body of experiential evidence. The focus upon *understanding* what constitutes the psychological makeup of that identity serves only to further reinforce it as one's perception of self.

There comes a moment on the path of *spiritual* pursuit, however, when one comes to consider that the fundamental constitution of one's true Essence has nothing whatsoever to do with the psychological nuances of an identity borne by a body of linear history. That history has simply served to hold one firmly in the perception of that perspective. That is the function of linear memory.

When the function of memory is flawed, one becomes dependent upon the testimony of others to create a picture of what is—or is not—so. Without the supporting evidence of memory, it is far simpler to consider the emerging experiential evidence of a Self that is comprised of *multiple levels* of ever-shifting perception. It opens up for consideration the possibility that a singular, static expression of linear identity is not *who* this being is at all.

The linear identity as a "file"—a compilation of linear experience that appears to be "remembered"

As she has begun to speculate, the identity referred to as "Rasha," quite possibly, is simply *a file*—a compilation of linear experience that appears to be remembered as having *happened* through the vehicle of a particular form. Who she actually *Is* transcends that identity—as it transcends *all* identity.

Her perception of self is a fluid phenomenon that shifts with the placement of her *focus of attention*. Without a body of evidence upon which one can rest one's unshakable sense of identity, there is then the possibility that the essence of True Identity might be revealed—and ultimately sustained.

It is not simply a matter of one aspect of self *taking over* another, in the sense of "possession." For, in that case, one would be dealing with the *involuntary* relinquishing of the sense of *who* presides—and whose will is given expression through the vehicle of form.

How the relinquishing of personality identification features in the process of enlightenment—a living demonstration

In the sense of the process of *enlightenment*—one's recognition of the Divinity of one's true Essence—that relinquishing of identification with a particular linear personality is *voluntary* and happens automatically as part of the process of spiritual unfoldment.

As these words are being documented, the pinpoint of perception known as "Rasha" watches. Her fear of her own *mortality*, which serves to reinforce her identity as that which is bound to the form in which she experiences herself, comes to the forefront of her awareness for examination and is dispelled. She bounces in and out of awareness of being present within the body, as these words are being written. And yet, it is clear that these thoughts are not her own. She is present simply as an observer in this moment, as concept is materialized upon a computer screen, through the vehicle of her own form.

She has come to consider the possibility that who *she* is, in this moment, is simply one of an infinite number of possible perspectives—all keyed in to the unfolding drama associated with this particular identity known as "Rasha." She has begun to understand that, quite possibly, *she* is not *the main event* after all.

She has begun to recognize that when she is willing to relinquish her attachment to the physical form as a *possession* that is *hers*, her experience of the circumstances of "her life" improve dramatically. She becomes more inclined to cease having to direct the show and more willing to relax and enjoy the ride. When that fight to retain dominance is relinquished, the awareness of Self—as Oneness—is able to emerge and express through the vehicle of form, unimpeded.

As the weeks in the haven of my secluded New Mexico country retreat progressed, Oneness began to deepen the process of Divine connectedness and helped me deepen my grasp of what was actually taking place within me. Days melted into weeks, where I barely ventured off the property. For the first time ever, my tendency to structure every moment for maximum productivity began to give way to an inclination to let it all go—and "simply

Be." Before my very eyes, the rustic, little cottage, nestled so secretly into the wind-sculpted foothills of the Sangre de Christo mountains, transformed into a place of sacred Communion, where the Presence of Oneness was fully in residence.

Oneness describes the nature of breath—and the nature of the journey home
Oneness speaks:

The energies continue to build now as we take the levels of connectedness deeper. The breaths come slow and deep. And you see that there is little distinction between the in-breath and the out-breath. It is all one continuous motion, an expansion that returns in on itself and grows to encompass all that it Is, once more. That is the true nature of your Beingness. That is the true nature of All That Is—swelling to the fullness of Being, with each breath of its own sacred Essence, and then receding into that Self-same Essence. We Are none other than That, ever-Present in a state of Now. Your journey has taken you to a place where you are able to glimpse it, to taste it, to *know* it—and to recognize it as your very own Essence. That is the nature of the journey home.

You will be leading a multitude of seekers on this journey. You will be blazing a trail through the wilderness that others will look to as a lamplight to guide them on the very same voyage. These teachings you will continue to bring forth are designed to facilitate that experience and to help the sincere seeker circumnavigate some of the stumbling blocks that characterize it.

Oneness speaks about the self-styled maze of the spiritual journey

You have inched your way through a maze that is the materialization of time and space and the variables each of you has fabricated within it. The maze is a web of your own design, calculated to confound you, yet illuminated with the promise of salvation. That promise is one that remains unspoken, yet is ever-present, fueling the impetus to forge on. In these times, so very many will make the journey. And each will be entangled in the mundane details of his own particular web of circumstances, lost in the delusion that the riddle is his alone.

For each, the clues will be all around him. It is in the attaining of the state of Presence that those clues can be recognized and gathered, as one would collect a bouquet of flowers. It is in the state of alertness that one is able to recognize and embrace the gift of the tools and resources that are in such abundance.

One comes to see the futility in the perpetuation of scarcity and suffering and to recognize that these illusions are created by one's very own hand. All the pieces of the puzzle have been provided for each of you. The key to determining the ease or difficulty that is experienced in the process is the state of one's connectedness to one's true nature—the Divinity that is your very own Essence. From that vantage point, the way is clearly marked.

There is no risk of being lost in the darkness. There is no chance of being stranded in the savage jungles of the material world. There is absolutely no possibility of experiencing anything other than the fulfillment of your hopes and dreams. It really is that simple. The only reason it all appears to be hopelessly complex and fraught with pitfalls is that you have chosen to see it that way. Now, you have begun to recognize that your experience can be quite different—and that the key to the shift in circumstances lies in the shift in perspective happening within.

The clues are all around you. They are yours to gather and to use. It is your birthright to have the blindfold removed now. The way will appear quite clearly before you. All that is required now is that you follow in the direction you are headed with your eyes open—fully Present.

On another occasion, Oneness offered a breathtaking insight on how the state of Divine connectedness differs from the exalted states attainable through the practice of meditation. It was a distinction as simple as it was profound, and helped me to dispel some of my preconceptions—and some of my expectations—regarding the use of meditation as a key element in spiritual practice.

The subtleties of sustaining Self-perception as Oneness—and how it differs from the practice of meditation

Oneness speaks:

Breathe with these energies for just a moment. This state of heightened connectedness is sustained by the clear *focus* of your awareness. In sustaining it, you are able to shift into ever-accelerating levels of Presence. In this moment, you are experiencing that Presence. You were not aware of it, for the transition is subtle. But now, in the full embrace of these energies, you recognize that we are in a state of Presence, once more.

You see how simple it is? You attempt to attain the same result through the practice of meditation. Your experience is peaceful and surely exalted. Yet, you recognize that you cannot duplicate the state that you attain here in this communion, simply by closing your eyes and stilling your mind. What you attain through this practice is a state of harmonizing your own presence with states of heightened awareness. Yet, the *focus* remains your own.

The practice of meditation as preparation for a Divine connection

It is your mind that is stilled. It is you, "Rasha," who *perceives* that stillness. It is you, the linear identity, who experiences the sublime state of inner tranquility. The state of *preparedness* for the fullness of your Divine connection is attained in this way. Yet, the transition into that connectedness cannot be manifested through this practice alone. For, even though you have managed to transport yourself into the depths of inner silence, your *self-perception* remains that of the linear identity who is *having* this experience. Subject—object.

In a state of Presence, there is no subject and no object. There is simply Isness. The act of *trying* may deliver you to the very threshold—but it will not carry you beyond that point. For, who would it be who is doing that trying? Oneness does not need to try. Oneness simply Is.

Manifesting Presence as a means of altering material circumstances

The key to all you would wish to attain in your quest to be of Divine service lies in your ability to shift your attention *from* the details of the linear illusion and retain a focus upon your own sense of who and what you *Are*. The details of the illusion will shift accordingly. When you focus your attention on the difficulties and the challenges of day-to-day life, you empower those circumstances to exercise the force of the energies that support them upon your experience. You are then at the effect of those circumstances and reinforce the state of separation that sustains them.

If you were, instead, to *withdraw* your energies from the challenges that may arise, and choose, in that moment, to recognize yourself in your state of Presence, the power of your own Will would be catapulted into manifestation.

That is how it works. For, the circumstances themselves are only a reflection of the *energies* that you are projecting onto the ethers. When you shift your energies, the circumstances shift accordingly. It cannot be otherwise.

The power of maintaining the focus of one's attention upon one's state of Being

When you try to focus your will and your intellect upon altering certain situations, you only succeed in fortifying the circumstances that have been brought to bear and serve to thwart your will. Your focus of attention is to be upon your state of *Beingness*—not on any acts of *doing*. And even though you now flit in and out of that state of Presence, it is your *focus of awareness* that, ultimately, will enable you to sustain that state and walk in the fullness of your experience of Oneness.

This is not a state of Grace that is being bestowed *upon* you, by anything that is other than that which you Are. The difference in your experience of this journey and that of others who have gone before you, is that they fully embraced the realization of that which they Are—without considerations of *worthiness* or *unworthiness*. What you Are has nothing whatsoever to do with considerations of worth. This is not a state that is *achieved* by meritorious deeds. It is *realized* through one's total, unwavering recognition of what one *Is*.

When you presume that you are pre-programmed to slip back and forth between states of connectedness and disconnectedness, that is your experience of it. When you project your willingness to relinquish your death-grip on your perception of self as your linear identity, and know yourself to Be your own state of Divine Presence, that will be your experience of it. That is the experience that is known as *enlightenment*.

Recognizing *the witness* as a sign of separation—knowing oneself to Be Divine Presence

You have tasted the fullness of that state of enlightenment on countless occasions. Yet, the essence of your sense of self-awareness reverts to the linear persona of "Rasha." You still wrestle with the fear of extinction that surfaces, ever so fleetingly, when you recognize yourself to be in a state of Presence and yet retain the sense of *the witness*.

Ultimately, the witness will recede into the background and will know itself to Be part of the whole of that Divine Presence. So long as it recognizes itself to be "the witness"—rather than the identity of Self as Presence—the stage is set for the reversion of one's attention to absolute focus upon the details of the linear illusion. You cannot hope to stabilize your Presence as Oneness this way. You only widen the gap between your momentary perception of self in your diminished state and the state that you *could* be implementing, simply by choosing That.

Realizing Isness through harmonizing the active and passive states of being

All the barriers have been removed now. You are not at the mercy of your karmic past. Your energies have been cleared. Your path has been prepared for you. And all that is needed is simply to step forth upon it. This is what you *Are*—not simply some altered state of consciousness you can slip in and out of. Know this. Know this with the fullness of your Being. You are not imagining this experience. You are not crazy. You are not any number of other possible excuses that you have considered to explain what has happened in your life.

You were purposeful in setting about to harmonize your energies with the Divine. Your prayers have been heartfelt and passionate. You are sincere and intense in your spiritual practice. And you have invoked the help needed to clear the obstacles that would have thwarted your spiritual attainment. Your lifestyle is one that encompasses the principles that are focused in sustaining a state of heightened vibration. All of these factors have contributed to delivering you to this moment.

Sustaining will and surrender in the perfection of balance

These are factors that *set the stage*. But, they surely do not serve to deliver an individual unto a state of Self Realization that is the ultimate expression of *will* and *surrender* in the perfection of balance. In the harmonization of the active and the passive states of being, Isness is realized.

The key is not to be found in substituting passivity for mind-directed action. For, it could only be the linear identity of self that would place itself, consciously, in the passive role. Rather, it is in the shift of *self-perception* that the doorway is revealed. It is in the absence of identification with the active *or* the passive states of material self-perception that one is able to realize what is already there. It is not a state that one strives to *become*. For, that state of Isness has never ceased to Be. You cannot *become* that which you already Are. You can simply know yourself to Be—That.

How "heaven" and "hell" are made manifest in the Here and Now

Oneness speaks:

Recognize the perfection in this moment. The vista, the stillness, and the sense of the sacredness emanating from within. All harmonize in the manifestation of this moment—a moment that is the perfect reflection of what you are projecting upon the ethers of manifestation.

You have delivered yourself unto this Divine moment. You have taken yourself by the hand to Paradise. For, that concept is well within the scope of the "here and now" you consider to be your world. There are infinite levels of experience transpiring here, tailor-made to meet the needs of the myriad expressions of consciousness that are co-creating it. Your own personal experience of this place in time can be as idyllic or as horrific as you choose to have it be. For, "heaven" and "hell" are of your own creation—at levels you have only begun to understand.

One individual's paradise may be vastly divergent from another's, and each may take place within the scope of a hellish world, as perceived by those who believe themselves to be caught in its grasp. The paradise to which we refer is not one with which one has been gifted, as a reward for reverence and spiritual attainment. It is a state of beingness with which one has gifted oneself, through choice, and is the reflection of that state in the reality with which one is surrounded.

You get to determine exactly which level of happiness or misery the circumstances of your life are calculated to deliver by casting your vote upon the ethers with your state of self-perception.

All states of Being are scripted to take place on precisely the same stage, for all unfold within the world of physical reality as you know it. Yet, that is where the similarities end. And so, there may be catastrophic events that may thrust the lives of many into upheaval and unspeakable suffering, and yet your own personal circumstances may be virtually unaffected. In the same way, one may be surrounded by untold magnificence and luxury, and yet have the perception of grave suffering due to the thwarting of personal will.

Oneness explains how life experience serves as a mirror of self-perception

All possibilities exist. And all harvests will be reaped, one grain at a time, as a result of the seeds that are sown by each of you. The symbolism is obvious. It is all around you. And the grains that are harvested are the moment-to-moment experiences that are no less than reflections of personal choice. Each and every nuance of your perception of your world is calculated to show you a mirror of who and what you perceive yourself to be.

And so, you may well be looking out on a vista of absolute squalor and experience nothing short of pure and utter joy from within. For, the circumstances that surround you may well color your feelings and sense of self-perception—*if you choose to let them.* But, those circumstances may, equally well, leave the haven within which you dwell, untouched.

The Paradise you long for and pray for, do penance and prostrations for, is not one that will ever be bestowed upon you by anyone other than your own self. You are crafting this experience you call your life with every gesture and with every word spoken. Ultimately, you will embrace that experience with the knowledge that it is the culmination of all you dared to hope for, manifested in recognition of your readiness to receive it.

As the seasons in the mountains of Northern New Mexico began to change once more, I began to see the symbolism in that shift in the colorful evidences of transition that beckoned to me everywhere I looked. On a day-to-day basis, I too had begun to change in ways that were subtle and often nearly imperceptible. But, the cumulative effect was undeniable. There was no doubt that something life-altering was underway. And I knew, at a level that could not be questioned, that the momentum of change surging within me had somehow reached critical mass—and was now unstoppable.

Oneness punctuated that realization with a passionate dissertation on the monumental changes transpiring on a global level, and the part each of us continues to play in its co-creation.

~∽~

Oneness speaks:

This is the level of closeness your heart has hungered for. For, we are here with you now. This is Oneness. Your tears flow with the joy of this connection—for you feared, once again, that you had lost it. You cannot lose this connection. For, *This* is who you Are. You can only distance yourself from the *experience* of it and delude yourself into concluding, yet again, that the physical identity is who you are.

Now, in the depths of this sacred embrace, you recognize yourself, once more. For, this is Life embracing Life—Love embracing Love—*becoming*, ever evolving into a deepening expression of its very own Essence. This Presence is not a static condition, no more than you, the physical expression of that Presence, are or have ever been. This Presence itself is ever expanding, defining and redefining the scope of its Isness, *Being*—and *experiencing*—all that encompasses its own ever-unfolding expression of Infinite Possibility.

Many will taste of this sense of connectedness. For, that is the nature of what is to transpire within the sacred inner Self of those who have counted themselves as present in these times. They have come for the experience of *awakening*. They have volunteered to experience the full gamut of possibility in one physical lifetime, so that they might cull the experience of *sacred knowingness* from the complexity of the dramas of physical incarnation.

Shifting one's faith from *belief* to the experiential and irrefutable

These times, and the conditions that define it and set it apart from the far distant worlds of incarnate memory harbored within the hearts of these souls, present that possibility. For, within the flux of the shifting momentum that serves to structure your world lie the components of that possibility. The monumental acceleration of the energies that build within you and around you are calculated to catapult you from the conditions that define the framework of recorded history to a world that continues to be structured and restructured in the ongoing, Now moment.

The changes you have experienced in your own lifetime are ones that, in times past, might have taken generations. And within the context of those blatant differences lies the proof of the essence of Divinity that has thus far eluded most incarnate consciousness since time immemorial. The opportunity afforded by these times is the possibility to shift the scope of one's faith in the nature of one's own Divine connection from the belief-based structures that emanate from mind to the realm of the *experiential*—and irrefutable.

Withdrawing from the need for external validation

There is no room for inner debate over what you know you have tasted with the essence of your own inner Being. With that recognition comes the understanding of the pointlessness of debate with others who may or may not have shared that experience. Whether they agree or disagree is irrelevant. And each will have the sense of wanting to retreat into the sanctity of his own precious connection, and to allow those who continue to focus on the need for validation from others to do so.

Many will begin to withdraw their energies from the hierarchical structures that seek to dominate the spirits and command the resources of others. For, the proponents of these structures themselves hunger silently from within for even a taste of the experience that they feel driven to force down the throats of others, in theory.

The authenticity of that experience does not require the consensus agreement of others in the flock within which you may once have counted yourself as present. It requires none of it—none of the structure, none of the ritual, none of the recipes for redemption that have been served up with elaborate fanfare by those who have seized the opportunity inherent in the spiritual thirst of others.

Transcending traditions of spiritual allegiance based on belief and embracing Divine knowingness based on firsthand experience

These times offer the possibility to transcend the realm of faith based on second-hand experience. These times do not require you to cast your vote based on the spiritual affiliations of your ancestors. These times do not require the commitment of your heart unless your heart is truly in it. You are not being asked to place blind faith in a mode of understanding based on events said to have happened thousands of years back—if your own passion has not been kindled by it. These times afford you the opportunity to see for yourself. And then, not simply to *believe* it—but to *know* it.

That is why you have come. That is why you have ventured from the comfort of your own "home" into the wild landscapes this incarnation has provided. This is why you find yourself in a world that no longer seems to make sense. And that is why you look around you and wonder, silently or otherwise, if the world has simply gone mad. For, the seeming senselessness of much of the drama that swirls around you is the precursor to the purging that these circumstances cry out for—*vibrationally*—and why the inevitability of change is the order of the day.

You have come as the witness—and you have come as a participant. You have come to co-create the world of wonder that looms on the horizon. And you have come to taste, firsthand, the physical expression of an experience that defies definition and structure. Each of you will confront it and embrace it in your own way. And each of you will weather the storms, both internal and external, that birthing into full *awareness* requires. You have not come to read about it in books. You have come to help etch those understandings indelibly upon your own compendium of consciousness—the volumes of memory that travel with you, long after the pages have withered.

The vibrational foundation for the inevitability of change in these times

The catalyst for that level of change is all around you. It is in the very air you breathe and in the cells that imbibe it. The vibrational acceleration that accompanies the changes that have been scripted is calculated to stimulate to the surface all the residual evidence of the outmoded structure. The depths of the emotional body harbors eons of repressed experience, vibrationally, that the dictates of culture and propriety forced into the inner recesses of your being.

Those energies, buried within your own depths, seek to be released now. The energies flooding your planet call forth the vibrational density hidden within you all. And outbursts on an interpersonal level—and within the macrocosm of the world around you that reflects it—are to be expected. The intensity of what you may be feeling will seem exaggerated in proportion to the events that may have triggered them. And yet, the authenticity of these expressions will compel you to transcend the reticence instilled by propriety and to cull forth from within your inner depths the emotional density you carry and the release of it that serves as the catalyst for change.

Who you are becoming defies the explanations of the logical frames of reference with which you have been programmed in this lifetime. Those standards of expectation were structured for a world that has long since been left behind. And one finds oneself establishing one's own precedents, and blazing a trail of one's own design that has little relation to what may have been anticipated.

You have come to this moment in your journey to set the roadmaps down for a time, and to trust in the compass within to guide you in a direction you can sense at a level that cannot be explained—and which you feel compelled to honor—despite what others may have to say about it. You have come to the point of cutting loose from the constraints of obsolete obligations and allowing yourself the Grace of aligning yourself with your own inner truth, at all costs.

One's priorities come up for scrutiny yet again in the course of this process of metamorphosis. And there is the inclination to trade in sets of circumstances that focus on the amassment of material gain in deference to ones which offer the priceless gift of freedom.

You have come to this moment to begin to learn to fly and to relinquish the idea that you are required to keep two feet on the ground in the ways you have been programmed to do throughout this lifetime. There are no limits to what you are capable of experiencing and creating in this lifetime. There are no limits to the *perception* of this world of wonder and your place within it, beyond those you yourself embrace, through your choices.

The mirror of your own inner reflection is all around you now. And the nuances of that imagery begins to shift before your very eyes, as you continue to align with the resonance of a sense of *self*, birthing itself anew from within. That self will continue to emerge throughout this lifetime and well beyond, as you continue to harmonize with the resonance of change that characterizes your world and all within it.

The allegiance one now feels compelled to pledge becomes an affirmation of all that one now recognizes that one has become—and a reflection of all that one now is not. For, that allegiance is to one's own inner truth, and cuts one loose from the affiliations and ties once required by cultural conditioning. One cannot hope to fly to the heights of human experience and simultaneously remain bound to the expectations set down by a world fast becoming engulfed in the mists of a distant dream.

You are transcending that place in time by the minute. And where you now find yourself to be has only a passing resemblance to what was once recognizable reality. The political structures and spiritual heirarchies that held the hearts of human consciousness in place have begun to lose their grasp now. The world as you know it is shaking itself loose from these constraints. And, in so doing, the consciousness present is freeing itself up to co-create this world anew as a reflection of hope and personal empowerment.

You have chosen to be part of this momentum, simply by being present. You have chosen to participate in a wave of transformation experienced collectively. For, the catalyst for these very changes is *you*—each of you. Together, you have co-created these conditions vibrationally, with the vote cast by each of you upon the ethers of the collective. And together you have begun to experience the limitlessness of possibility that is Oneness—in the guise of humanness—that is your birthright.

29

Fall 2003
Northern New Mexico
Learning to Bring Presence to Life

───────

The book, *Oneness*, was published for the first time in the summer of 2003, under the title *Oneness: The Teachings,* by a soon-to-be defunct publishing company in Southern California. By mid-September I began to prepare for a series of speaking engagements that had been scheduled there. It was the first time since *Oneness* had appeared in print that I'd be facing a live audience and talking about my personal experience of the spiritual journey. I approached Oneness to help me zero in on a theme for these talks. The personal guidance I received helped me to come to terms with the extent of the preparation I'd had, over the course of years, for coming forth with these teachings by virtue of having *lived* them.

Oneness fine-tunes the essence of my message to the world

Oneness speaks:

The basis for your authority on this subject is not simply because you have documented these principles theoretically, but because you have put these concepts to the test personally, because you have walked the distance, and have come to tell about it from first-hand experience. That is what makes your story human and believable—and interesting.

Today's audiences have been preached at and *processed* into numbness by countless others who claim to know the way. The difference between these others and what you have brought for consideration is that you are not seeking followers. You have come solely for the possibility of helping to empower the listener to have the courage to make the solo flight of *his own* sacred journey. You have come as an example of what is possible when one gives oneself permission to blaze his own trail and to cease the habitual dependency upon the formulas of others.

The days of spiritual attainment by virtue of a recipe are numbered. You have not come to provide a template for spiritual attainment. You have come to deliver certain rudimentary principles which, if applied with a level of heart-focused intent, may lead the seeker to embark upon a path of *his own* design. That is the essence of what you bring to these times.

Oneness outlines the path of self-empowerment

This is the age of self-empowerment. This is not intended to be yet another spiritual path that fosters dependency. The principles that are outlined in the book *Oneness* set the stage for the journey that many will make in these times. You are there to demonstrate for the listener the possibility of steeping himself in these principles and exploring the results, as experience. You are here as an example of a spiritual journey focused in the *experiential*, rather than the theoretical.

These understandings are grasped in the only way that is significant when one has the opportunity to integrate the principles as *knowingness*. That requires the seeker to have lived through some of the episodes himself, not simply to have encountered them, in theory, in books. Sharing yourself, and being authentic in your humanness, will set the stage for this message.

Your state of beingness is the result of years of hard work. It is not something that has been conferred upon you. For you, the spiritual journey has been a long and rocky road. You are here as living proof of what is possible, *against all odds*. You are not presenting yourself as an ordained minister with longstanding experience preaching the gospel of one established path or another. You are not a degreed academic whose credentials qualify you to present material within the context of comparative philosophy. If fact, you have absolutely no qualification for what you are doing—outside of the evidence that you are, in fact, doing it.

The spiritual journey does not require the certification of academia to make the experience of it valid. You are not expected to have come through the lineage of an accepted Guru in order to Be who and what you Are. You need simply to Be—That. You require no one's validation other than your own to have made the journey to God-Realization. It is not a course of study that requires a diploma. It is a direction of pursuit that requires little beyond the absence of expectation and attachment—and the recognition that there will be no targeted destination as part of the itinerary.

This is not a matter of attainment versus the sense of having fallen short of the mark. What is being presented is the possibility of making an extraordinary journey, in the company of your own sacred Self. All that is required is an openness to the embrace of the unexpected and to the fullness of the experience of Divine connectedness that are the inevitable by-products of having gone the distance.

Now is the time to retrace some of your steps and to recognize where you have gone in your travels. For, you could not be standing where you are today, had you not ventured into the wilderness and traversed some of those side-roads of life experience. You have come to demonstrate that it is possible to find your way home by way of the compass within—and by that alone.

I began to discover that there were really no random events in life. Everything seemed to be an exacting reflection of what I was "putting out there" vibrationally. The only difference between these experiences and the kinds of experiences I'd had previously was in their intensity and in their uncanny knack of manifesting instantaneously. It was clear that there was no longer the luxury of hiding in the delusion of victim-consciousness.

When I started stepping back from the dramas of my life and looking at them from the perspective of the teachings of Oneness, it was obvious that I was *creating* these episodes, despite the fact that I understood the principles theoretically. Through a ruthless exercise of dissecting and analyzing some of these nightmares, Oneness helped me to process what had happened and fine-tune the skills needed to thrive in the world of instantaneous manifestation, for which we are all being prepared.

One particularly devastating episode happened in California, while I was there on the lecture and book-signing tour, which helped drive the principles of manifestation home. On my way to a speaking engagement at the renowned Bodhi Tree Bookstore, I suddenly found myself grappling with the stress of trying to drive the length of L.A. in aggressive rush hour traffic with half-baked directions. Forty-five minutes into the exercise, I was essentially back where I started and began to worry that I was going to be late. All of my careful preparations, that had put my energies in a lovely, calm, and balanced state, went straight out the window. Panicked, I ditched the rental car and hopped a cab. But, the stage was set, vibrationally, for disaster.

I arrived at the venue in plenty of time, but the episode left me shaken. At the same time, I'd been braced for the presence of someone who had e-mailed me in advance, saying that he planned to attend my lecture. He included a link to his own website as an attachment. The graphically illustrated, x-rated website had given me a strange, uncomfortable feeling. Within seconds of arriving, I spotted him. And the drama unfolded.

Had I been in a balanced state of being, the encounter with this individual might have left me totally unaffected. But, the fact was, I had created an opening with my own frazzled state of being and with my apprehension about encountering this person. When he approached me after the lecture and our eyes connected, I felt a vibrational impact hit me like a bullet, and a sickening feeling crept over me. I felt my wonderful exalted energy leaving my body, like someone had punched a hole in my balloon. Once again, I'd "been jumped." And I responded in the usual manner, by feeling like an absolute victim, compounded by exasperation that this sort of thing had happened to me, yet again.

The next morning, as I prepared to leave the hotel for the drive to San Diego, I hastily placed my hand-carried laptop on the passenger seat of the rental car and drove around to the front lobby where my luggage was waiting. "Watch the car for a minute," I'd called to the doorman, as I ran inside to find the bellman who was supposed to meet me out front with the luggage cart. I could not have been gone more than a minute or two. That's all the time it took for the computer to disappear—together with all the current back-up discs—which contained my life's work.

Oblivious to the loss, I drove, happily enough, to San Diego. When I pulled up to the hotel there and reached for my laptop, my heart leapt into my stomach. I called the hotel in L.A. and the local police and went through the motions of filing a report, but the deed was done. I was devastated.

There are no accidents. I reminded myself of that when I flashed on the fact that miraculously, only days before, I had printed a hard copy of six years of personal guidance transcriptions from Oneness, in anticipation of my upcoming trip to India. Thankfully, all the other writings had been saved on multiple back-up discs when my beloved old laptop had succumbed to a virus, less than two months before. Aside from the loss of a very nice laptop, the only actual damage done was the annoying prospect of having to retype the last four months of teachings from the spiral-bound notebooks, that for some strange reason I'd felt guided to create, right before leaving for California. It was nothing short of a miracle.

I had no doubt that, for some unfathomable higher purpose, I'd somehow managed to create this entire experience. But, why was the *computer* affected, of all things? I pondered that as I began to process the incident with Oneness. I looked long and hard at it. And it became obvious that I never really *liked* that computer. I had agreed to buy it used—reluctantly, because it was "a good-deal"—from the computer repairman who had helped put my dear old, virus-ridden laptop to rest. In fact, the stolen one was a fabulous computer, an executive model, only one year old, with all the bells and whistles. But, it had the annoying little button-mouse, instead of the touchpad I'd been used to. And, despite the fact that it was actually the nicest laptop I'd ever owned, my heart just wasn't in it. The powers of creation accommodated that mindset by dematerializing it for me. Ouch.

It was astounding to watch these principles in action, playing out before my very eyes, in the movie I thought of as *my life*. Oneness helped me reach absolute clarity on the significance of this ordeal, in the teachings that followed over the course of the next several days.

How victim-consciousness and vulnerability create the conditions that manifest adversity
Oneness speaks:
This is Oneness—although you should be well aware of that. The connectedness you are experiencing is most familiar to you. And as you surrender to the process and we become Oneness together, you can see that

you have been lost, once again, in the illusion of separation. You are far from lost, however. For, that is equally apparent in this moment. You need only make the commitment of your *attention* to this connection and that Presence is achieved for you.

Now there is no steep climb to be made—no obstacles to be surmounted—for, in essence, you *Are* this. You simply persist in forgetting that fact. You persist in becoming lost, once again, in the struggle and the adversity—and you create *that*, yet again, as your reality.

You are welcome to remain blinded to what you know if that is your wish. But, it need not be that way. The opportunity is equally there for you to be focused in *this* connection and to experience the perspective of that exalted vantage point as the outcomes of the scenarios of your daily life. It truly is a matter of choice now. For, you know, you are creating all of this.

Rasha speaks:

Yes, I am aware, theoretically, of how this works at this point. I have written a book about it, not to mention a few thousand pages of personal conversations. I can understand that you must be fed up with me.

And, as you write these words, you register the absurdity of that statement. Who would it be that Oneness would be "fed up" with? All of this is Oneness.

Even the part that persists in focusing upon the illusion of separation?

Even that part. You have simply chosen to terrorize yourself and you have reaped the results of that choice.

I have a question.

Good. You also have the answers, lest you forget that.

In any case, I'd like to talk about the stolen computer situation. I suppose that you will say that I created that situation. I know I was in a very imbalanced state. And I agree that I was careless, but that needn't have resulted in the disappearance of a computer. It must have been a manifestation of energy. That is my interpretation—based on the teachings. I would welcome your input, so I can understand what happened and bring this episode to closure. I still feel so bad about it.

Feeling bad about it is not going to change anything. Understanding the dynamics of how that scenario was created, vibrationally, is the opportunity at hand. That is the gift in this painful episode.

So the theft of the computer was the result of energy, wasn't it! I was in a miserable condition. I think I drew those circumstances to me with my state of being. Right?

Could it be otherwise?

Some people have said that it "just happened" because I was careless. I have been taught that things don't "just happen." I think it's a miracle that this is all that happened to me. It could have been a lot worse.

It surely could have been much worse. You were extremely protected from harming yourself under the conditions that were allowed to transpire. You know how this works, Rasha. You are making choices. And you are experiencing the results of them. Discernment comes into play here.

I think I became vibrationally compromised as a result of exposure to a particularly unbalanced individual in the audience in L.A. who approached me after the lecture.

That situation surely compounded an already compromised state. You were in a heightened state of imbalance before you even arrived there. That is why you were so susceptible to the compromised energies that were present. You surely were not in an exalted state of Oneness

It's probably accurate. I was very stirred up about getting lost on the way with the confusing directions, and was anxious about the possibly of being late. But, you're right. I was hardly in a state of Presence. I was in a state of separation. That's the key to all of this, isn't it?

Can it be otherwise?

No, I accept that it cannot.

Your "acceptance" is an attestation of your mentalization of this process. It is not your acceptance that is needed here—it is your *knowingness*. You have experienced the direct result of the example you arranged for yourself to live out. Is there any doubt whatsoever of the validity of what you have experienced?

Actually, no.

Well, then. Are you conceding, mentally, on a theoretical point—or have you shown yourself experientially, the truth underlying this experience?

I have lived this experience. I know.

Good. Are you clear on the difference?

Of course.

Then there should be no need to belabor the point. Your allowing yourself to lapse into a state of imbalance creates a state of *vulnerability*—a chink in your "armor," if you will. The disturbed energy that was present was able to gain access to you in that way, to further compromise your energy field. You began to feel the results of that encounter and allowed yourself to slip into a state of depletion and despair. It was with that *state of beingness* that you created the scenario with the stolen computer.

You manifested the outward physical illustration of vulnerability. You were "victimized" because you presented the variables, *vibrationally*, that projected the formula for *victimization* upon the ethers. Creation responded accordingly and provided you with evidence to support that presumption. You were out of control, vibrationally. And Creation provided you with an affirmation of that, experientially.

Oneness, I am so tired of this! I cannot continue like this.

Indeed you cannot. Not if you wish to progress beyond this state of stuckness and actually manifest the work you have come to this lifetime to accomplish. Continuing like this will surely not manifest the desired result for you.

You have the answers. You know what needs to happen. You can continue affirming your identity as a victim—or you can affirm who you know yourself to Be. It's that simple. When you stop affirming what you do not wish to experience, you will open the space for the creation of what you do wish to experience. That is how it works. You know this—in theory. Now you are being given the opportunity to apply these teachings. You are being given the opportunity to live it—to "walk your talk."

Until you have learned to stabilize your state of Beingness, you may wish to be extremely selective about where you choose to place yourself and minimize the risk of escalating an already imbalanced condition. This state of isolation is a gift, in this timeframe. It is your opportunity to stabilize your energy field and concentrate upon your affirmation of your experience of Presence. That is what we have come to work on. Let us focus on that.

You have gifted yourself with this time of retreating from the world. There is, inherent in this, the opportunity to embrace it—not from the standpoint of resignation, but from a place of gratitude. That is the gift. Yours for the asking.

As my days in America drew once again to a close, and my return to India loomed ever nearer on the horizon, my experiences in connectedness with Oneness continued to intensify. As before, life continued to provide ample testing conditions to help strengthen my focus on the Presence of Oneness and to help me draw a correlation between the state of linear perception and its attendant trials and tribulations. Oneness took the opportunity to drive the point home with some strongly worded guidance.

It became clear to me that the persistent difficulties I often encountered were literally of my own creation. Not simply as a result of my actual participation in those particular situations, but more importantly as a result of where I was choosing to place the *focus of my attention*. I was still habitually invoking the default setting of the linear identity, often without even realizing it, through my reactions to the circumstances of my day-to-day life.

It was a powerful teaching and training that would continue for some time to come.

⚜

Rasha speaks:

Oneness, I feel your Presence so completely, like a wave that washed over me when I wasn't looking. Now, here I am, drenched in it, abandoned to the inevitability of the undertow that pulls me deeper, ever deeper, into this indescribable bond of Oneness, once more. It's funny how, even now, there's a little twinge of relief when that wave begins to embrace me. As if my heart were saying, "Thank God! You're still here. You haven't abandoned me."

Oneness speaks:

That isn't really an option, you know. Where do you suppose we would go? You cannot be abandoned by Oneness. The only abandonment happening here is your own abandonment of the higher realizations you have garnered. You still are inclined, on occasion, to abandon all that you know and have worked so hard to achieve, to prove to yourself, yet again, that doing so results in a plummeting of your energies and your circumstances. Ultimately, you will no longer need to put yourself through this exercise. For, it is an exercise in futility. And you have proved that to yourself more times than you would care to count.

How the focus of one's attention creates circumstances of life

Now we stand at the threshold of a new adventure, and yet another turning point. India awaits you. And you approach her with a hard-won state of centeredness in who you know yourself to be. The habitual backsliding into the abyss of your fears and self-doubts can now be seen clearly as the reflection of the focus of your attention—no more, no less.

When you dwell in the realms of resentment and seethe silently over the sequence of wrongdoings that, in your mind, have been perpetrated upon you, your focus of self-awareness is upon the linear identity with all its attendant discomforts and problems. When you recognize what you have done, that recognition alone is enough to shift your state of awareness instantaneously.

And so, you have been flitting back and forth between full and total connectedness and full and total separation. You have reached the point in this journey where you can abandon that tendency. Here, it is hoped, you can begin to be who you truly Are. You can begin to embody your own exalted Presence. And you can cease throwing aside your crystalline awareness in the wake of whatever disturbance happens to float by.

It is not necessary to be thrown off balance by every set of inopportune circumstances—not unless that's truly what you wish to experience. It's equally possible to retain your sense of inner serenity, despite whatever may present itself in your daily script. And, it is also possible to sidestep the issues that surface and know that these problems and annoyances are simply reflections of *energy* seeking resolution.

Allowing yourself to become sucked into the illusion and indulging in a full-blown drama is just a recipe for the reinstatement of old patterns. You do not need to revisit these dramas anymore—not unless you want to.

Transcending a mindset of victimization and vulnerability

The training in the power of one's *focus of attention* continued to be drilled into me, as I encountered episode after inconsequential episode of situations calculated to be aggravating. One particular experience, on a typical Sunday at the Neem Karoli Baba Ashram in Taos, NM, was life-altering. It was at that point that "the light went on!"

I had left the ashram by mid-afternoon to head for home in La Puebla, some 60 miles away. I had spent over two hours chanting 11 *Hanuman Chalisas* (the traditional prayer in Hindi honoring Lord Hanuman, the monkey god of Hindu tradition), had eaten a delicious Indian-style lunch, and had meditated for another two hours. I was feeling absolutely wonderful.

On my way home, I stopped by the local alternative bookstore, to check on a consignment of jewelry and *Oneness* books, which I'd left there a few weeks earlier. At the counter stood a disheveled-looking young couple, loudly in search of a book on black magic. I felt myself recoil. "That sort of energy is the last thing I need," I remember thinking. I beat a hasty retreat and headed down the road, but I realized immediately that it was too late. I could feel that, once again, my energy field had been compromised.

In no time at all, it felt as though something was actually there, sitting on the top of my head, a sensation that had become all too familiar to me. The very same sort of thing had happened repeatedly for several weeks. In desperation, I'd been phoning Dr. Bindu in India to ask for his help in clearing the disturbance. It had started to feel like I was under siege, and I was embarrassed at the prospect of having to run to Dr. Bindu for help, yet again.

With the threat of having my sublime mood ruined, I turned the car around and headed back to the ashram. There, in the temple, I sat back down before Neem Karoli Baba's *tucket* (a broad, wooden bench where certain Gurus in India sit while giving satsangs), where I had spent most of the day, placed both hands palm down on his blanket, and surrendered. "Please help me, Babaji," I pleaded silently. "Please help me move this energy."

Instantly, I felt an indescribable sensation that can only be described as *electricity*, begin to build in the palms of my hands, as waves of blissful energy began, once again, to fill my entire body. And, slowly, I went into deep, deep meditation, barely breathing. But clearly, the intruding presence was still on my head. Without so much as a word, an understanding emerged within me, and it was clear how totally in separation from Oneness I had become on this entire issue.

Immediately, I shifted my focus to a state of *Presence* as the powerful energies continued to build within me. My entire body felt electrified as the loving Presence and wisdom of Neem Karoli Baba walked me through a process that, perhaps for the first time, cemented all the teachings that led to that moment, into place—*experientially*.

Suddenly, it was clear how my own sense of *victimization* and *vulnerability* had created the opening, again and again, through which this kind of disturbance gained access. The problem was not the disturbance. The problem was *me!* The focus of my attention, in those moments, was on the frustrated, vulnerable linear identity of Rasha—not on the perception of Self as Oneness.

With slow, deep breaths and totally focused intent, I merged with the sense of Presence and consciously *held* the focus. And as I did, I heard the question, posed in the depths of silence. "Do you want to be accompanied up the mountain?" For the longest time, Neem Karoli Baba had told me during these silent *darshans* that he would "walk with me up the mountain" when the time was right, if I wanted him to. Without any hesitation at all, my heart answered "Yes!" And so the journey began.

I surrendered totally to a process that was as natural as the slow deep breaths that continued to fill me with waves of indescribable joy. As I did so, the understandings were instilled. The focus of my attention were the key to *everything!* Even in a state of total Stillness—even in a state of heightened vibration—if the *focus of attention* was upon the disturbance that I wanted removed, I empowered its presence to be sustained.

When I ceased to be concerned about the disturbance—when my perceptions were centered in my sense of *Presence* to the exclusion of all else—the disturbance vanished. It was miraculous!

No sooner had I begun to congratulate myself on having mastered this feat, at long last, when a young man who had been meditating silently on the other side of the room walked over, seated himself one foot behind me, and began performing a noisy deep breathing technique before the altar in the corner. I was startled. "How inconsiderate," I thought, not recognizing the new set of testing conditions that had just presented itself.

I got up in a huff and moved to the other side of the wide tucket. Within seconds, I went back into a state of no-mind with total focus on Self as Presence, and was engulfed in a sublime state of bliss—all too short-lived. No sooner had I settled into a state of complete inner peace, when another young man entered the temple. He sat down before a harmonium, and began to chant the most discordant rendition of the Hanuman Chalisa I had ever heard! Instantly, I saw the lesson.

HOLD the focus of Oneness. / Awareness

It was easy enough to hold the focus of Presence in the sanctity of the temple when it was perfectly silent. But, what about when it wasn't? I concentrated my attention with every ounce of intent I could muster, and held on tight—bracing myself *against* the onslaught of the discordant music. To no avail. I succeeded only in demonstrating to myself the principle that I could not both *Be* Presence—and be focused on the disturbance I did *not* want to perceive. The understanding was indelibly etched.

In that moment of illumination, I shifted into a state of utter surrender and *became* the Presence of Oneness. There was marginal awareness of sound happening in the periphery of my awareness, but it did not register as disturbance. It was there, and at the same time, I was utterly indifferent to it. I was abiding fully in my experience of Self, completely consumed in the sanctity of that blissful state.

Still, I continued to hold the focus—and the teachings went on. For several moments, I was walked through the *experience* of perceiving *myself* to be Presence, and simultaneously recognizing the others in the room as being of my very own Essence—the very Essence of Oneness.

Yet, another level of realization was imparted: the understanding that asking to have "help" *bestowed* upon me from an external source was nothing more than a demonstration of *duality*. It was the feminine polarity that set itself up to *receive* this "help," and in so doing, embodied *separation* from the very Source it understood itself to Be.

At the same time, my initial attempts to forcibly "oust" the disturbance myself, through augmentation of my energy field, was equally a demonstration of duality. This was the masculine polarity in action. In either case, what manifested was a disconnection from the very Source that I understood, *theoretically*, was to be embodied.

In abandoning both of these approaches—each of which had been centered around the concept of *doingness* rather than *Beingness*—and simply allowing myself to Be the Presence of Oneness, abiding completely in the experience of That, the desired result was manifested automatically.

The experience lasted nearly two hours. During the entire time, the exalted energy of Neem Karoli Baba surged through my outstretched palms. I felt like every nuance of my being was ablaze with Divine Light. So, *this* was what was meant by "walking up the mountain!" I thought.

And, I understood. Until that moment, I hadn't been ready. I'd grasped these concepts with my mind. I'd learned to parrot them. I'd had fleeting glimpses of the experience of Presence—*in a vacuum*. Now, at last, the training had truly begun.

❦

mindful awareness

As the dramatic symbolism of autumn filled my senses, I could feel that my time in the peaceful, sand-sculpted foothills of Northern New Mexico was drawing to a close. And even though the heart connection and the sense of "home" I'd always felt there were feelings I'd come to cherish, there was also the powerful sense that my sojourn there was complete, and that it was once again time to move on. From the silent inner recesses of my awareness, India had begun to beckon to me from afar. And, like a magnet drawn by an irresistible pull, I was compelled to follow her call, and to discover where the course of destiny would lead me this time.

Amidst a whirlwind of preparations for returning to India for the winter, I transcribed this beautiful passage from Oneness. The words of Oneness so often seemed prophetic to me. They had a way of setting the stage for the deep inner shifts that invariably would follow, as I allowed my heart to lead me ever deeper into the great unknown. Oneness captured the absolute wonderment of that ongoing sense of surrender, and its inherent gift of self-discovery, with this most poetic passage. It was selected and adapted as a meditation entitled "The Dance of the Divine Lover" for the CD, *The Meditations of Oneness: A Journey to the Heart of the Divine Lover,* which was released in November, 2009.

Oneness describes the sacred state of Divine Union and reveals why we are here in physical form

Oneness speaks:

This is Oneness. This is the Presence that permeates your consciousness in this moment. This is the blissful union of which you are a part. This is the destiny toward which you journey. And this is the destination at which you have already arrived. This is the sacred contract that has been fulfilled, in perpetuity, with every nuance of your unfoldment. This is the promise that continues to be revealed within you, with every waking breath.

This experience of the embracing of your own Divinity is not an act defined in a moment and thereafter relegated to something that has already *happened*. It is an experience that grows and deepens—an experience that continues to unfold. And not unlike the experience of lovemaking, presents a newness with each embrace.

Every time we experience this union—this Oneness—we are deepening a bond that will only continue to grow eternally. Every touch of this Presence is like a caress. Every breath, bonded in the embrace of Presence, is Divine Love, revealing itself, and reveling in its own unbridled aliveness. There is no *other* within the context of this consummate embrace. It is Self, glorying in its own unfoldment, discovering the delights of its own Essence, mirroring its own sweetness through the perceptions of form.

We share in the experience of form. And we share in the experience of formlessness. For, in the exchange, you have revealed the true nature of your own sacred Self, and the miracle of a birthing into awareness is experienced, through the vehicle of form, throughout the full multidimensionality of form and formlessness that is who you truly Are. This foray into the experience of Oneness, is not simply a one-on-one exchange. It is an exponential encounter, rippling out like a raindrop, into liquid stillness, touching every aspect of that Divine Presence with the sheer joy of it.

Your bliss, in this moment, is not your own. For, to perceive it as an experience that is *yours* would be to contain it and imprison it—to withhold the raindrop from the ocean of perception that waits, yearning in anticipation, to receive it. This bliss is not at all *your* experience. For, in the union that brings this joy into manifestation is the relinquishing of the boundaries that would define that limited sense of self.

In the receiving of it is the simultaneous relinquishing of the separation that would allow for the possibility that this experience—or any experience—would be one's own. The sense of *you-ness* merges into a totality of perception. And the sense of who and what you Are takes on the coloration of an infinitely broader spectrum of possibility.

The one who is perceiving this moment of delight is not at all limited to the linear *you* who began this lifetime believing in the illusion of that very separation and spent decade after decade creating a history of supporting evidence to bolster that presumption. Now, you begin to be able to sense the monumental piece of fiction that has been created in the name of that minute shred of identity. You are so much more than that.

In this experience of *Divine* Nowness, where an unfathomable scope of awareness hints at its own Isness, you, as the vehicle of linear perception, are able to translate the touch of the Supreme Lover into the language of linear experience—and through breaths of joy, give it definition. This is Who you Are, the microcosm and the macrocosm of your own exponential Isness, peering through the pinhole of your own minute vantage point and gasping in wonder at implications that are magnificently incomprehensible—and at the same time, unquestionable.

Only though the *shieldedness* of that vision is the sublime sense of wonderment possible. For, in the fullness of that Infinite Awareness, all of it simply *Is*. So, by all means, perceive this moment with which you have been gifted. Feel the fullness of these delights. And know that it is through the blessed *perception* of the sheer joy of your own Self-discovery, that you give the gift of that Love in return.

With each set of eyes that is opened, with each blissful new awakening, the dance of the Divine Lover takes another step toward Ultimate Union. And with every glimpse into the secret inner sanctums of sacredness and delight, you add yet another caress to the experience of Divine Love that is here, for all the world to share.

This newborn moment is the gift. This miracle of Self-recognition is what we have come to this experience of incarnate reality to share: Oneness, in bonded union with our own sacred Essence, with full, conscious awareness of it. That is why you are here. That is why you have come into form. That is why you are secretly so intrigued with the possibility of the world of the formless. This is what keeps you searching for clues to the meaning of your existence, rather than simply allowing the bars of your outer prison to define your world.

The seeds of Self-discovery, planted so deeply within you, have begun to seek the Light. And, slowly, from the depths of self-imposed captivity, the seed of Divine Life is moving toward the experience of daybreak.

The pull of the inevitable becomes irresistible at some point, when one enters a state of receptivity and surrender. There is a *knowingness* within that cannot be denied. And the considerations of the linear intellect, which would seek to justify such choices with logic, seem to fall by the wayside somehow. I could feel the process stirring within me as I responded to that inner calling. Engulfed in preparations for uprooting myself from the familiar, I braced myself for the inevitable ordeal of relocating to what was essentially another world, tucked away on the other side of the planet.

Perhaps it was as a reassuring affirmation of my unquestioning response to that far-away call which inspired the heart-stirring passages from Oneness in those final days. As I read the stunning Divine revelations coming to life through my very own hands, a sense of Divine purpose was rekindled within me that dispelled any last lingering shreds of hesitation.

Even though what was happening in my life—together with the very person it was all happening to—now defied all sense of logic, and baffled family and friends who once thought they knew me well, to me there was no question. This experience of emerging into Oneness defied all considerations of *common sense.*

I watched myself as though from a distance, as the familiarity of time and place dissolved yet again, and was relegated to a nebulous, catch-all category of experience I thought of as "the past." And with the indescribable sense of inner peace that heralds a moment of consummate surrender, I saw that once again, I had entered the realm of the timeless.

The Essence of Oneness

Oneness speaks:

We are fully present in this moment—fully merged in Oneness. In so saying we simply affirm to you what your senses have shown you to be so. At this sublime level of connectedness, you cannot distinguish the linear identity from the Presence of Self as Oneness, for they have, in fact, bonded in Divine Union.

There is no separate *self* that perceives itself as anything at all. The awareness is fully present as Beingness. Simply That. There is no perspective other than That. There is simply receptivity to the perceptions which may present themselves—an openness to the possibility of the manifestation of experience, and a total detachment from the need to influence the form in which that experience may present itself.

We Are simply—*Awareness.* We watch, as words appear on a screen of a computer, while detached from the source of the concepts being documented automatically, through the vehicle of form. We Are that form together, in this moment. And in the same breath, We Are transcendent, devoid of form. The form and the formless—intertwined in the timeless dance you know as "life."

It is through the vehicle of form that the dance may be performed—and through the vehicle of form that it may be perceived. The giver, the giving, and the gift itself, bonded in the embrace of Divine Union.

This is who you Are. This is what we bring to this Now moment: that level of possibility. And that potentiality is no different for *any* being. That possibility is vested in each and every being amongst you. And all will come to experience that level of Self-perception, in the fullness of time.

That is the nature of the journey that has delivered you to the pinnacle of Self-perception that is embodied and experienced Here in this Now moment. This is the experience known as "Oneness."

The significance of the pull to return to India

You will be writing much on this subject in the times ahead. You will be focused in your writing and in your state of bonded communion with this Source while you are in India. And you will come into the fullness of your state of Presence and become accustomed to sustaining it. It is for this reason that you have been encouraged to return to India and to the sanctity of the surroundings that support you in that level of spiritual unfoldment. The energies of Arunachala are most conducive to this level of growth. You have intuited accurately the calling of your heart to return to a place that has come to feel like home.

Oneness speaks about the seeds of consciousness that are drawn, as pilgrims, to the spiritual haven of Arunachala

Arunachala has served many who are revered as Saints, at various stages of their unfoldment. Ramana Maharshi is the best known of them, but he is far from the only Divine soul that has made this place a home. This mountain has helped to nurture the evolvement of spiritual seekers for thousands of years. And to this day, it continues to be a Mecca for those who have embraced the eternal quest for Self-Realization.

You are in good company in this respect. There are numbers of awakened souls who gravitate to this sacred place as pilgrims, and return as homing pigeons—many, for reasons they do not fully understand, and yet cannot question. You have responded to the calling of your heart's knowingness to bond, once again, with the source of your beginnings. For, in this blessed place, you will bond with the very Essence you have delivered unto this reality, through your presence as form.

You have come as a seed of consciousness with an *encodement* that will be delivered—grounded—and embodied by the Earth Mother. Once you are able to bear the frequency that is your natural state of Beingness, you will be empowered as the seed of Light that you truly Are. And you will bond in sacred union with the Mother who waits to receive you. For, you *Are* Arunachala. You are a fragment of that Essence of Father Consciousness that shattered in a moment so ancient it defies linear comprehension.

The impetus toward *wholeness*—the *life-theme* of all that is form and formless alike—is a universal phenomenon. The macrocosm, of which you are a component, is no less invested in the experience of unification with all that it Is, than you are, on an individual basis. And, in adding your own coordinates to the fullness of the equation that reconvenes in this Here and Now, you make possible the magnificence of the Grand Union of the polarities of Father and Mother that are the very foundation of what you consider to be your world.

You have come to implant yourself, as a vibrational seed, in the fullness of the resonance of that original fragmentation, uniting yourself once more in wholeness with All that you truly Are.

The world of physical manifestation is the stage upon which this epic drama has been, and will continue to be, acted-out. For, the possibility of the *experience* of this Divine re-Union is ever-present here. It is only through the vehicle of form that this consummation of Divine Love is possible, at the highest level. And that possibility takes into its embrace all that comprise the Essence of the supreme Lovers who yearn to experience Union and know themselves to Be—Oneness.

The significance of being drawn to sacred sites

Those who have identified themselves to themselves as seeds of Divine Passion are recognizing the calling to the heightened states of awareness, and are responding—many in awed states of wonderment. They follow, many of them blindly, the irresistible magnetism of their hearts to cast aside the mundane trappings of their lives and pursue a life direction for which there is no plausible explanation.

And yet, at the higher levels of their own awareness, there is a seed of Divine resonance that yearns to be reunited with the Source of its beginnings and to participate in the *experience* of That. It is for this reason that many are finding themselves drawn to visiting so-called "sacred sites" throughout your world.

It is not for the satisfaction of intellectual curiosity or some other rationale for spiritual-tourism that so many are finding themselves guided *home* to certain ancient strongholds of linear history. It is for the purpose of inserting the *vibrational key* of their presence, through the vehicle of physical form, into the Divine matrix made manifest in each of these destinations.

Each of you who has awakened to levels of higher awareness in these times will be pulled to venture forth and reunite with the fullness of your own sacred Essence. And, in so doing, most will perhaps not even suspect the true nature of the sense of connectedness experienced in those moments. For, the experience of that connectedness is but a small clue to the true nature of the gift—and to the identity of the giver.

One is not guided to these experiences to *receive* "a piece of the puzzle" that might help the linear mind to unravel the ultimate mystery. One is guided to these experiences to *embody* "a piece of the puzzle"—and to deliver the gift of one's own very Essence as a contribution to the consummate Realization of Divine Unity.

An indefinable sense of impending change hovered over me in those final days in America. And at a deeper level, I knew that the imminent shift in energy I was tuning in to wasn't something limited to my own personal situation. I had the sense that it signified something infinitely more far-reaching than the radical changes I knew were taking place within the context of the identity I'd always thought of as "me."

There was the palpable sense that my own personal identity was but a miniscule speck of dust, along for the ride, within the vastness of a far greater agenda that was simultaneously taking place. The identity to which I'd attached such importance, and which was systematically unraveling before my very eyes, was quite literally only a minute drop within the ocean of Oneness—one that mirrored the momentum of change that steadily engulfs us all.

Oneness spoke to that sense of silent realization with a teaching that addressed the impending world events that would soon be transforming life as we'd come to know it. It was an affirmation for me of the validity of all I had come to understand about the nature of these times, and the role the spiritually awakened amongst us were destined to play in the drama.

Oneness gives an alert about the state of the world situation

Oneness speaks:

Your world stands on the brink of radical change now. Events will begin to transpire that will change the nature of how you perceive your world and your place within it. Many will be inclined to give in to fear and mass hysteria will prevail in many parts of your world as the illusion of life as you know it careens out of control. You will be a vehicle for hope and for the messages of faith that will bring a sense of sanity to all that may soon come to be.

You have the sense that change is imminent, and rightly so. There will be incidents of far-reaching consequence that will plunge the world into upheaval. There will be unspeakable suffering in many parts of your world, as the acceleration of the energies all around you reach peak levels. Many will be inclined to panic and will point to ancient "End-times" prophesies that herald an end to life as you know it.

Let the doomsayers have their say. Do not attempt to inhibit them. For, in the voicing of that perspective, the energies that fuel the fears that underlie it will have the opportunity to be vented and released. This is an inevitable by-product of the events that will come to pass. Wisdom will be provided from many sources that will act as a balm to the wounds that will have been left raw and exposed by misguided thinking on the part of world leadership.

The wisdom that will be provided by this source will reach the hearts of many and will help those who have recognized the path of spiritual self-empowerment to come into the fullness of their Realization. Many of these newly awakened ones will feel very alone in their process during these times of radical global transformation. This is a necessary part of the process of spiritual unfoldment and will be taking place during extraordinary and radically accelerated conditions. You will be serving as a lamplight for many of these beings by holding the energy of stability and facilitating the emergence of wisdom from within the inner sanctums of those whose lives you touch.

The world population will weather the trials that are to come with questionable levels of skill. Most will give in to fear and will focus on the details of the immediate illusion. Outrage will fuel the impetus toward retaliation and much human suffering will be experienced in the process of these expressions of political bravado. The face of ego and separation will be given full opportunity to vent itself, and ultimately will be reduced to ash. Only then can the sacred Essence that underlies All That Is rise from the ashes like the phoenix and prevail here on this earthly plane.

The terror that is the inevitable consequence of spiritual myopia will have ample opportunity to express itself through the consciousness present and through the events that give definition to these releases of energy on a global scale. Allow these scenarios the grace of playing out to their inevitable conclusion. For, in the aftermath of this great release of repressed force, the Divine Essence that is the true nature of all that comprise the collective consciousness co-creating these events will have the opportunity to be revealed.

Oneness speaks to the emissaries of Light seeded amongst us

Each being who recognizes himself to Be an expression of the Oneness that is destined to prevail, will help to co-create the manifestation of Heaven on Earth that has been prophesied since time immemorial. The times that have been spoken of have begun to dawn now. And you who have volunteered to serve in positions of spiritual leadership have begun to stand up and be counted.

The master teachers for these times have been seeded amongst you. Many are still steeped in their own personal processes of metamorphosis. Many are still blinded by the delusion of separation and ego-orientation. Some who are destined to reach national prominence will flare with a brightness that is intense—and short-lived. They have come to pave the way for the bearers of True Light, who will come with an aura of Divine Grace that is unmistakable.

The wisdom that will be imparted will oftentimes come in Stillness. For, these ones will kindle the opening to that place of Stillness within all that attend them. You are destined to serve as such a Lamplight for the emergence of the new humanity: those seeded amongst you who will populate the world to come.

30

The last days of 2003 heralded my return to Tiruvannamalai and its mystical mountain, Arunachala. Here, under its protective gaze, I would begin the painstaking process of scrutinizing the thousands of pages of writings I'd amassed, the personal teachings of Oneness which would form the foundation of the story of my spiritual journey that I'd been directed to write. Though I knew that, in a sense, I'd come a long way, I'd soon discover that the journey was far from over.

There, in a virtual village of spiritual seekers from every corner of the world, all I'd come to understand would be put to the test. The validity of every aspect of my experience of the teachings of Oneness would be challenged in light of the legacy of *Advaita Vedanta* orthodoxy that prevails there. In the process, the inclination to dig deeper and to fine-tune my grasp of the profound principles I'd transcribed would be stimulated and supported by the relentless barrage of philosophical/spiritual self-righteousness that would hit me head-on.

With the loving support of Oneness, and the unwavering Grace of Lord Shiva, Ramana Maharshi, and Arunachala, the mountain he is said to embody, I was taken ever deeper into Divine connectedness and given a new level of understanding of what was transpiring within me.

I'd been granted the respite of two precious weeks in residence within the hallowed walls of Ramanashram, to initiate my time in Tiruvannamalai. Thereafter, I'd have a wonderful little house to call my own for the winter season, where I'd be able to retreat once more from the outside world and delve ever deeper into the world within.

❧

Oneness speaks:
There is the sense of a homecoming in this sacred place. You have journeyed far, both in the physical and the spiritual sense, to bring yourself to this crossroads in time and space and your reunion with Arunachala. Your heart is filled with quiet delight at being here—here in the silence, here in

the epicenter of your Being. Arunachala is but a symbolic representation of that. Arunachala is the opportunity to reconnect at that level with who you truly Are.

Outside the gates of the ashram, a thousand mundane distractions, each vying to extract a drop of your life's blood, wait to pounce like thirsting mosquitoes upon you. You have come to recognize the difference, once outside these gates. For, these are the gates that separate the *heaven* of renunciation from the *hell* of worldly desire. And, once outside these gates, it reveals itself to you, in grotesque detail, everywhere you look. The illustration couldn't be more graphic. You will wish to consider the cost of venturing forth upon the teeming streets beyond the sanctity of this place. Here, in the simplicity of this haven, is all you will ever require. That is why you have come.

You have come to intensify your spiritual practice and to solidify your connection with this Source. Your every action and choice is to be one that is directed toward strengthening that sense of absolute focus. Your inclination to become absorbed in *doingness* will give way to an all pervading Stillness, emanating from within. And the fleeting moments of Divine connectedness will expand into the experience of an Eternal Nowness that has neither beginning nor end.

It is not a process that will need to be initiated and constantly re-established. It is one in which you will harmonize your own individual essence with what you have come to embrace as Oneness and to emerge in wholeness, with no lines that would delineate the one from the other.

The very act of walking will be a meditation, a purposeful part of your daily routine. Every moment spent is one that has come to gift you with yet another facet of the vantage point of this heightened level of awareness. You will have relinquished the need for socialization of any kind and will be content to remain in the stillness. You have come for the experience of an initiation, at a multitude of levels. And what is required is the total focus of your attention.

Rasha speaks:

Oneness, will I be working directly with Ramana Maharshi as part of this process?

Those energies are ever-present in this place, and you will imbibe them simply by being here. What he has come to impart is not to be found in the arena of mentalized interaction but within the Stillness that is to be experienced in his Presence. Ultimately, you will recognize that Stillness within your own sacred inner Self and know yourself to be One with That.

The connection has deepened now. And, with your focus of attention upon that Divine connection and detached from the comings and goings of the mundane material world, your experience of life will be as perceived through the eyes of Oneness.

Oneness speaks about spending time in the presence of a spiritual Master

The time here in Tiruvannamali will be spent in solitude, and for the most part, in isolation. You have noticed that there is no longer the inclination to seek out the companionship of others. You are content now just to Be. Others are having similar experiences here, at a multitude of levels. All are assimilating the exalted atmosphere and experiencing the effects in a personal way. That is why few are inclined to conversation.

It is an environment where the serious seeker is free to imbibe the Presence of the Master. He is ever-present here, and takes an active role in the spiritual unfoldment of those who have journeyed from the distant corners of the world to this spiritual haven. Do not underestimate the impact of this Divine Presence upon each and every being who opens himself to receiving it here.

This Divine Presence serves as a catalyst in a process in which you are already well invested. One receives at the level one is able to receive. That which is realized has nothing to do with the caliber or intensity of what is made available, simply by virtue of Divine Presence itself. It is not something that can be quantified. It can only be experienced, and in retrospect, known.

What is to be realized need not be understood in order to be known.

There is little value in comparing reports with others who are here exploring their own paths. Those who are inclined toward the wisdom-by-consensus approach are guided to attend the many teachers who serve seekers at those levels. There, mentalized analysis ensues, that often keeps the devotee in a spiral of confusion. For, what is to be realized need not be understood. Indeed, what is to be realized *cannot* be understood. Yet, the *experience* of it is readily available.

Many have had the first tastes of Divine connectedness in this place, without fully understanding what was actually taking place. The energies present are calibrated to trigger levels of awareness that wait, dormant, for the appointed moment to make that Presence known. And seekers are awakening in this place, side by side, most with no conscious awareness of what is happening.

Only afterward, once the spiritual traveler has wearied of the stillness and the sameness of the daily routine, and moved on, is the first hint of the inner shift revealed. And many return, year after year, for yet another taste of something they are unable to find words for, and cannot begin to justify to those standing at the periphery of their lives, watching in disbelief.

You stand in blessed isolation now, divested of responsibilities, of obligations, of attachments. You have been liberated from the need to be anywhere in particular and to *do* anything at all. Sustained focus on the Presence you have come to represent in physical form is the primary activity toward which you will direct your attention. This communication is the doorway to all you are destined to become. This Presence awaits you. All-ways.

The role of spiritual practice and expressions of devotion in setting the stage for the experience of Divine connection

It does not require elaborate ceremony, candles, incense or time-honored words to invoke this Presence. It does not require prescribed rituals, nor particular formulas. It does not require *doingness* of any kind at all. You are surely welcome to include any of these practices into your expressions of devotion. But, know that in so doing you merely *set the stage*, within the sanctity of your own being, for the connectedness that is sought.

These timeless tools have been provided to bring the spiritual seeker into the state of beingness where the attainment of a Divine connection might be made manifest. The invocations are not for the purpose of calling forth an external force. They are for attuning the seeker to an optimal *resonance* and preparing the conditions where the openness to receive the experience of the sacred feels safe. What ultimately is sought is a state of absolute *surrender*, a willingness to relinquish the need to remain in control.

The power of *surrender* and *vulnerability* when brought to expressions of devotion

What is sought is an exquisite level of *vulnerability*, embraced utterly without hesitation or consideration. When that state of beingness is brought to the expression of devotion through ceremony and prayer, the stage is set for the experience of Divine connectedness. In the absence of that level of openness, gestures of religious practice leave the seeker fixed in a state of eternal separation, essentially reinforcing the experience of spiritual abandonment.

Now, having made the journey, you can see in retrospect how the tools of devotion were employed to prepare you for the experience of Presence. And you can see how easily one can become fixated upon a particular mode of spiritual practice. It is surely gratifying to go through the motions of sacred ceremony. But, once the goal has been reached and the state of Divine connectedness is at hand—once the understandings are instilled and all trepidation has been relinquished—the use of elaborate invocations can be seen to be the formality that it, in fact, is.

If you engage in this practice, know that you do it for your own benefit, and not as a prerequisite for the attainment of your spiritual connection. For, that aspect of your experience is attainable right here, within the inner sanctums of your own Being, with or without time-honored words and other trappings of devotion. It is surely possible to go directly to the Source of your Beingness, without any formalities at all, simply by perceiving yourself in that exalted state.

Focus your attention upon your own state of beingness. Know who you Are in every moment. And let that knowingness permeate your Being. Put into practice the understandings you have garnered on this long and arduous journey. These understandings are not simply to be relegated to the realm of the theoretical. This is not a footnote to be referenced now and then. This is the very foundation of your approach to life. This is not a step to be taken somewhere down the road. This is a step to be taken now.

There is no point in continuing to wait for someone or something external to your own being to give you the go-ahead, the signal that it's now okay to Be who you know you already Are. You do not need permission. You do not need a diploma. You do not need an "inner explosion" or any of the other indicators that you have been led to believe are required. You do not require a Guru to flip a switch for you. You do not need a pat on the head or any other source of validation. The only permission to be forthcoming is your own.

The days at the ashram passed blessedly and quickly. Then, no sooner was I relocated and comfortably installed in the house I'd be calling home for the next few months—a pretty, little lime-green cottage with a lush, walled-in garden—when the testing conditions began. A scheduling miscommunication had telephone repairmen arriving, unannounced, right in the middle of a writing session with Oneness. My hypothetical worst nightmare finally had come to life. I was in a profound state of trance-like Divine connectedness. To say the least, I was unprepared to jump up and run downstairs to open the door.

The landlord was outraged when I suggested, through the open window, that he use his own key and let himself and the workmen in downstairs. He stood on my second floor balcony for quite some time, shouting—shattering my energy field and my blessed state of bliss. I was incensed. I had made it very clear to him that when I was "in meditation," I was not to be disturbed. From my perspective, he was totally out of line. The landlord, consumed in a fit of rage, clearly saw the situation very differently.

Afterward, I went to Oneness steaming with indignation, anticipating moral support, and was stunned at the powerful teaching I received instead. Oneness took the opportunity of this vivid illustration of the choices inherent in conflict and the cost of defending the need to *be right,* to drive the lesson home. It was a poignant lesson that was unforgettable.

Oneness speaks:

Take a moment and settle yourself into the shelter of this time of connectedness. The concerns over which you have been ruminating cannot touch you in this moment. Now, you are here in the embrace of Oneness. You are safe. And all is peace and harmony. Just take a moment and breathe.

Let the worries and fears retreat into the periphery of your awareness, for the moment. And as you do, notice how the mentalized projections with which you have empowered them are instantaneously disarmed. You can choose to rekindle the fires of fear and discord if that is what you wish to choose. But, there is equally the possibility of choosing to perceive a harmonious outcome to the circumstances that have presented themselves.

Trust that your highest possible good is an option that is viable. Trust that the situation will resolve itself in a way that is to your advantage. Be Present in the fullness of who you Are. That is all. There is no need to become distracted from your own focus, simply because another being is showing himself to be off-balance. Trust that everything is very much in Divine order.

You were shaken and thrown off-balance by the behavior of the landlord. It is clear to you that he is off-center and is viewing circumstances in a distorted way. That is not your cue to retreat into fear and mentalized anticipation of difficulty. It was simply his own way of asserting what he presumes is his authority in this situation.

Rasha speaks:

I do not wish to live in an environment of adversity, Oneness. This is not why I am here. I feel like I have been very violated. The sanctity of my energy field has been disturbed. I am not comfortable with the feeling that this man could, at any time, just barge in on me and verbally abuse me when I am in this state of Divine connectedness. I was in such an exalted state when he pulled that scene. It felt like I was shoved out a tenth-story window. It was a long way down.

And, you are free to choose remaining in that space, if that is what you wish to experience. But, why would you choose that? You are equally free to choose remaining centered in your Divine connection and to experience being sure and strong in the face of this disturbance. It is not a foregone conclusion that the misguided behavior of another leaves you so unsettled. That is the way you have chosen to allow the situation to develop. You might just as easily have laughed it off and gone with the circumstances that presented themselves.

Your own *resistance* to what had been presented was the cause of the disturbance—not the actions of this individual. Much as you would disagree with his right to do so, from *his* perspective, you were the one who was out of line. Instead of standing your ground and expecting him to bend in deference to your need for solitude, you might have chosen to recognize that the timing did not go as you had intended and proceed with accommodating what was being demanded of you.

The power of the path of least resistance

Much as you did not want to do so, that would have been *the path of least resistance*. It is in the resistance to what is so that discord attains a foothold and undermines your overall state of well being. What was most important was jeopardized as a result. When confronted with such a moment, know that there is always a choice, and a price to be paid either way. The price in defending what you perceived as *being right* had far-reaching consequences, and it ignited a blaze unnecessarily.

You have been presented with a powerful learning opportunity here. See it as that, and let go of the temptation to escalate these circumstances into a full-blown drama. Turn the page now, and let us return to the focus of why you are here.

After the initial explosion had blown over, my months in Tiruvannamalai, in the winter and spring of 2004, were spent contentedly in the cozy little cottage on the outskirts of the Ramanashram neighborhood. It was off the beaten path just enough to put most distractions comfortably out of reach. Here, I was able to focus my attention within and steep myself in the teachings of Oneness for days on end.

Preparations for creating a book out of the thousands of pages I'd always assumed were personal writings consumed much of the time, while I continued to wrestle with my deep-seated reluctance to do so. Yet, the overriding objective of even *that* exercise seemed to be the fine-tuning of my own sense of self-perception. It appeared that virtually everything I felt guided to do was purposeful, orchestrated by Oneness. In retrospect, I'd come to see that there was no random motion in any of it.

The moments spent in daily *communion* with the Presence of Oneness were an annotated dip into the sacred waters of the innermost Self, with Oneness' ongoing narration of the subtle nuances of self-perception as it was actually happening. The *mind*, observing the process from the periphery of my awareness, began to get a clear sense that it was not at all the "main event."

Through these daily experiential journeys ever deeper into the core Essence of my own inner being, I began to dissect away my perceptions of and presumptions about a montage of *facets* of an identity I'd experienced as *myself*. I recognized that it was not enough to simply *have* these exalted experiences. In my case, it seemed, I was expected to actually comprehend what was happening *as* it was happening and, ultimately, to be able to explain it to others.

And so, the magnificent mystery of who and what we all really Are began to unravel conceptually, and reveal itself literally, before my very eyes. I was my very own "guinea pig," a Self-styled experiment, directed and choreographed by Oneness, calculated to carry me home.

Oneness describes the symptoms of merging into a state of *Presence*, as the transition is actually happening

Oneness speaks:

Now as you focus your mind, you remember why you are here. Lost in the thoughts that sped past, you lost sight, momentarily, of the Presence that had been invoked. In those moments, you had no awareness of Oneness at all. You had no awareness of Rasha sitting before a computer. Your full focus was upon a *memory* that, in this moment, you cannot recall. Your mind was consumed by that scenario. And in that moment, *you* were not present.

The body was present. Yet, the consciousness was abiding fully in the past. There was no awareness whatsoever of your sense of who you are. In those moments you, as the linear identity, were not in the body. In the same sense, in *this* moment you, as the linear identity, are also not in the body. You have no-mind. There are no thoughts. There is only *Presence*—a sense of *Awareness* focused in the Here and Now.

As these words were written, the linear identity of Rasha *merged* with the fullness of this Presence. In this moment, there is, once again, total detachment from the sense of ownership of the physical body. The hands are operating independently of the sense of *awareness*, as if they were propelled by a mind of their own. They are responding, automatically, to the directives initiated by this communication.

The skills of transcription have been instilled within the mechanism of this Presence. Those skills are fully accessible to the full multidimensional spectrum of all that you Are. Skills that are so deeply ingrained are not lost simply because the functions of linear mind have been suspended. You continue to breathe, to have control of bodily functions, and to perceive your surroundings with keen accuracy, despite the fact that there are no mental functions directed by the linear sense of self. In this way the Oneness identity is able to be fully operational within the context of this physical form. You attempt to intervene in this moment, to ask a question, yet no words come. Within, all is Stillness.

The connection has deepened in increments as these words were documented. There were momentary flashes of what seems like *unconsciousness*, the sense of having fallen asleep. And yet, there is the awareness that you are not sleepy. These momentary bouts of *blacking out* are your indication that shifts in awareness are taking place in rapid succession. In essence, you are *ascending*, before your very eyes.

Oneness speaks:

There is no need for words now. Your invocation is one of heart. Your focused intention upon the manifestation of this Divine Union is the catalyst that draws the experience of it into Being. No rituals are necessary to open this door. No formulas are needed. No formalities at all.

The key to the experience of All that you Are is right here—here in the epicenter of your Being—here in the place that transcends your *desire* for connectedness. Desire will not take you where you wish to Be now. Desire will simply keep it eternally at arm's length—tantalizingly close, yet just out of reach. And the more you affirm that *separation* with your longing, the more your experience affirms it as its reflection. There *is* no *you* that is separate from This. There is nothing left to *do* now. All the doing has been done.

Becoming clear on the motive for expressions of devotion

You are welcome to express your experience of connectedness in expressions of celebration. You are welcome to revel in your newfound sense of Isness. You are welcome to chant Mantras and to practice your feelings of sacredness and devotion, if it gives you comfort to do so. But, these practices alone will not bring about the experience of it. They simply give you a *medium* through which to project your *awareness* upon the palate of the ethers, and translate those vibrational impulses into *perception*.

These are practices that give you joy. And we surely do not intend to dissuade you in your expressions of devotion, but rather to point out to you that the celebration cannot substitute for the occasion itself. Become clear on what you are doing and why you are doing it. Let no action be random. Every nuance of your expression is to be purposeful and inwardly directed.

Your focus is upon your awareness of Self, not upon the external trappings of the linear world. This is not a practice that you will take up eventually, when you feel you are *ready*. This step is not one to be taken at some future time and place. This is a step you have taken over and over again. It is a dance you know by heart. You could do this in your sleep. And indeed you do, in more ways than you could possibly imagine.

In this particular dream, you perceive yourself to be in a waking state. It makes little difference whether the eyes are open or closed. Your sense of your own Beingness is what is at issue here, regardless of the context of your perception. And regardless of whether you consider yourself to be awake or asleep, your Presence in the fullness of the Now moment creates your experience of it. It really is that simple.

The significance of reviewing the sacred journey: the vantage point of the higher perspective holds the possibility of insight

You are wrestling with the mental logistics of the prospect of writing your own personal story. You know the time has come to do it. This monumental task of sorting through this mountain of experiential history will help crystallize the journey for you. And through the exercise of steeping yourself in these writings and bringing the freshness of your heightened perspective to the task, you will experience the coming together of all that has preceded it.

The writing of this next volume is the culmination of your journey. And though we note that you are feeling daunted at the prospect of all that it will entail logistically, it is time to begin. Once that initiative has been taken, the pieces will begin to fall into place. And you will find that you are able to write with the clarity that comes from having made the journey, a clarity that is not possible when steeped in the experience itself.

Your mind wrestles with the question of exactly *who* is supposed to write this book. The only possible answer could be: *We are*. For, there is no separation now. We surely are not suggesting that you revert to the linear perspective of Rasha in presenting this material. Her experiences, through the stages of the process of ascending through the levels of linear identity, will certainly be recounted. But, it is from the higher perspective that *insight* will be possible.

It is in viewing the entire history through that perspective that you will be able to see the perfection in the process. Do not be tempted to allow the details to obscure the higher vision. You are no less Rasha now than you have always been. You are simply viewing the landscape from a different vantage point.

Do not lose sight of that attainment, as you revisit the places you have been. Let the memories come to mind in all their authenticity and in vivid detail. It is this that will be stimulated to the surface in the process of this exercise. For, this book will be the birthing of a new level of identity, though to all outward appearances little will have changed. You will still be the embodiment of your personality, modified by virtue of the lens through which you are now able to view your life experiences. You are still *you*. You haven't become someone else. You have simply had the blinders removed in order that you might truly see.

From the start, my time in Tiruvannamalai provided the conditions that put the teachings of Oneness and my grasp of them to the test at every turn. I found I was up against an orthodox interpretation of the philosophy of Advaita Vedanta, popularized in the West by Ramana Maharshi and subsequent teachers, each of whom, it seems, put their own personal spin on the concepts. The teachings of Oneness, while built on a foundation of non-duality, approach that understanding in a very different way.

The confrontations I encountered in trying to explain these principles helped me to fine-tune my own grasp on these mind-stretching concepts and to develop a powerful respect for the nuances of language.

The concept of "the experience" and "the experiencer" is illuminated
Rasha speaks:
Oneness, I had certain revelations today that I'd like to address. Here in Tiruvannamali, there seems to be a mindset where to admit to being present as your linear identity is akin to having an affliction of some kind. It is an invitation for ridicule and scorn on the part of this legion of seekers who are here, armed with Advaita Vedanta platitudes, and a holier-than-thou attitude toward anyone who does not go around parroting them.

I have been spoken to with contempt because I am not "abiding in the Absolute," in a state of mindlessness, every moment of the day. People are quick to quip that you "either are one or the other." And, that if you are in connectedness sometimes, it means that you have not "arrived."

Help me here, please. Isn't this the very premise of the work we have been doing together all this time? I thought that the essence of these teachings is that the experience of enlightenment comes in waves—lots of isolated little "tastes" of the state of connectedness. And, that ultimately, one would abide in that state permanently. Did I miss something?

404

Oneness speaks:

You have missed nothing, Rasha. You simply have not yet mastered the skill of sustaining your sense of Divine Presence in the face of adversity.

These people say that in a state of enlightenment there is no "experience" and there is no "experiencer." Isn't that a contradiction? How can there be "no experience" in the world of linear perception? I've understood that the possibility of experience is the very thing that characterizes the linear world. By virtue of the fact that I am here in form, would there not be experience? And would I not, therefore, be "the experiencer"—the one who is having that experience—regardless of whether or not I perceived myself to be fully present in my linear identity in that moment?

Oneness explores the concept of "experience" and "the experiencer"

There surely is *perception*, when one is present in the linear manifestation you regard as "the world." And at the same time, the *enlightened* being is aware that these perceptions are manifestations of the linear illusion. That aspect of Self would know that there could be nothing that might *happen* which could affect the Essence of who one knows oneself to Be, despite the fact that there might well be circumstances that were being *perceived*. The point is in realizing that the perception is *unreal*—*while* one is having that perception—and therefore not becoming ensnared by it. The difference is in the *internalization* of what you term "the experience."

What about the experience of Divine connectedness? What about the bliss and rapture that accompany those states? Are they not levels of experience? Is the fact that you are engulfed in bliss a testimony to a state of separation? People have said that this is "just phenomena."

Indeed, this *is* phenomena. This is the level of phenomena that is to be perceived when one is in a state of Divine connectedness. These sensations are not at all a testimony to a state of separation. They are a testimony to a state of *Presence*. Yet, at the same time, one is clear that even *this* is not *Who* and *What* one *Is* Who one *Is*—is simply Awareness. Through the medium of form, one is able to *perceive* the physical manifestation *reflective* of one's state of beingness.

Thus, the linear *perception*—the reflection—is *the experience*. And the context of form is *the experiencer*—the *means* of translating phenomena into perception—a format through which it can be deciphered. At the same time, who one knows oneself to Be remains unaffected.

Transcending karma is a characteristic of "enlightenment"

The experience, which is linear, is not *retained* vibrationally when one is Present in the state of beingness referred to as "enlightenment." And thus,

405

one is said to have transcended *karma,* which is, essentially, the retention of experience in the form of vibration.

When one walks as the Self in physical form, one surely *does* have physical *perceptions,* yet one remains unaffected by them. Without the vehicle of form through which to perceive the Self, one simply *Is.* The state of formlessness, by definition, cannot be *experienced,* for there would be no medium through which that experience could be *perceived.*

The capacity for perception is a prerequisite for the *experience* of Oneness

There is no *experiencer* without the context of form. That is why, throughout this work, we have consistently referred to the state of *Divine connectedness.* It is this state which is known as "enlightenment." It is this state in which one can be said to have "Realized the Self." It is this state to which we refer when we say that "We Are Oneness—together." For, the capacity for linear *perception* is a prerequisite for *having* this experience and knowing oneself to Be—That.

Without the linear *expression* of the Self, who is it who could be said to have Realized that Self? Who is it who believes himself to be *enlightened?* Surely it is not the Absolute, abiding in a state of Eternal Isness. Only through the context of form can that all-pervading Isness perceive *Itself* and know itself to Be That. That is why we have chosen to be here together—as Oneness.

In spring of 2004, I had a profound experience at Auroville's Quiet Healing Center, some two hours down the road from where I was living in Tiruvannamalai, that punctuated a magical moment of spiritual emergence with an emphatic exclamation point. I did a session of an aqua therapy, a modality akin to "Watsu," which is an acronym of water/shiatsu. The modality I experienced was said to be similar to the concept developed by an American named Harold Dahl in the '80s, based on the idea of "freeing the body in water."

During an hour-long session with a trained practitioner and floats, the body, which is surrendered in a state of total relaxation, is held and glided with gentle, dance-like movements through a pool of tepid water. I'd heard rave reviews from others who had done it, and in theory it sounded simple enough. But, the actual experience was beyond extraordinary.

I had decided, in advance, to do the process in a full state of Divine connectedness. Amid a lush seafront setting of bougainvillea and lotus ponds, I stepped into a sparkling therapy pool of warm water and melted into the capable arms of the therapist, a delightful French woman named Veronique, with blazing blue eyes and the tanned and toned body of a *yogini* (a female yoga practitioner).

It's hard to say what actually happened during that session. I've often wondered, in retrospect, whether at some level I hadn't actually died and been

I AM awareness, knowing myself through the form of KMM.

reborn during that hour. For, what began with a familiar sense of surrender into connectedness with Oneness took me through a journey that transcended body awareness and suspended my consciousness in a sense of "beyond" for which there are no words.

Virtually all breathing stopped as I shifted into a mode of connected breath that was so slow it became all but imperceptible. The sense of a tunnel ensued where a light show of brilliant colors, unlike anything of this world, flashed before the screen of my awareness. I had a sense of the physical body as totally separate from *myself*, as it glided through the soothing water, safe in the arms of *Oneness*.

The body was known to be *mine*, but it was not *me*. I had only marginal awareness of it, while simultaneously I perceived a very different reality, one that transcended time and place. It was a state of *beingness* that was non-material and non-conceptual. All perception became focused within. There *was* nothing outside of That.

My own awareness streaked with lightning speed through the cosmos *within*, breathlessly aware of the blissful Presence that had become what I perceived as *myself*. I had the sense of a *coming together*, the feeling of an unspoken integration of a montage of impressions and states of *beingness*, all mine. The feeling of enhanced vibration continued to soar within me until at last it reached a crescendo.

In that instant I had the perception of bursting through a formless barrier of some sort and being birthed back into my own surrendered form, as it moved with astounding grace through the Infinite Seas of Creation and emerged in the pool of water where the dance of *Watsu* had begun an hour earlier.

It took a few moments for my awareness to stabilize within the physical body I slowly began to recognize as my own. It was consumed in Divine ecstasy, the feeling of total immersion in the Ocean of Isness. Ever so tentatively, I opened my eyes. The world was, once again, as I remembered it. But, I knew I had never ventured within this world before. It was as newly born as the sense of Self-awareness that had emerged, in my likeness, within it.

I smiled gently at the *Watsu* practitioner who, through the filter of my newfound vision, glowed with an otherworldly radiance. And I experienced a feeling of pure Love—of Oneness—that at the levels where we are *all* truly Present, I knew was shared. Later in the day, Oneness elaborated.

~~~

Oneness speaks:
A birthing process took place this afternoon. It was, in many ways, the culmination of the initial stages of your journey of awakening. Your state of

connectedness was held in unwavering focus for the duration of the session. You demonstrated to yourself your Realization of the formless Self and emerged with a sense of knowingness culled from having had the *experience* of it.

This was a moment where all the understandings, amassed all this time, converged. And you transitioned, automatically, into the manifestation of Self, and at the same time, recognized the linear identity to be non-existent. The sense of Presence that presided during those moments transcended the identity that equated the essence of the self with the physical body.

During this experience, the physical body was, essentially, lifeless. There was virtually no breath or motion. It was as though death had occurred, and the form was perceived to be an empty vessel, limp and abandoned.

Oneness held the physical form, through the vehicle of the therapist, and in your conscious *surrender* to that realization, a far-reaching consolidation of fragmented essence was achieved. When the sense of Self-awareness re-entered the form, it was as a being that had achieved wholeness and had been born anew in the physical body.

The sensations of a physical birthing, through the medium of water, served as a graphic illustration of the symbolism of what was actually occurring. The being that has emerged from that pool of water is a far more complex version of the linear identity than the aspect of self that entered the pool an hour earlier. Through absolute surrender of the form to the Divine Essence of the formless—and the absolute focus of attention upon Self as Oneness, to the exclusion of all thought—the integration of identity was achieved.

31

Spring 2004
Tiruvannamalai, South India
Deepening the Experience of Oneness

Tiruvannamalai is a destination where an eclectic mix of mostly Western spiritual seekers gather annually, amidst the resident Indians, for the winter season. It is a mecca for people guided to explore in-depth the path of Advaita Vedanta, the philosophy of non-duality that was popularized in the West through the teachings of India's renowned Guru-saint, Ramana Maharshi. The Maharshi, a fully Realized Master said to be the embodiment of Lord Shiva, spent his life on and around the Arunachala "hill," never venturing from it until his passing, in 1950.

Here, in these times, a gathering of seasonal *Gurus* descend for several weeks a year to hold *satsangs* on the shaded palm-thatched rooftops that dot the neighborhood surrounding Ramanashram. The ever-shifting montage of international seekers that attend them are generally immersed in a mixed concoction of spiritual orthodoxy, fashioned after varying interpretations of the teachings of Ramana Maharshi. And though many are inclined to interpret those teachings literally, it is well known that Sri Ramana's teachings varied dramatically—oftentimes to the extent of literal contradiction—in accordance with the spiritual needs of individual seekers. In fact, Ramana Maharshi would be the first to tell you that the real teachings were, and many feel still are, imparted in *silence*.

Nonetheless, in no time at all, I realized I'd run head-on into a philosophical war zone, where subtle differences in the interpretation of esoteric concepts were seen as the basis for blatant hostility and contempt. Life became an exercise in learning to contend with confrontation over the differences between the teachings of Oneness, which are rooted in a foundation of spiritual *self-empowerment* and tailor-made for these times, and a mixed bag of traditional beliefs regarded by many as irrefutable spiritual gospel. It struck me that this attitude of spiritual self-righteousness was no different than the kind of mindset that's had people killing each other in the name of God since time began. The absurdity of it was hard to fathom.

I saw that, as spiritual beings, all we really have to go on with each other is an ability to articulate something for which there are no words. The message I was being prepared to impart from the teachings I'd received was a focus on the actual *experience* of Oneness, rather than a philosophical *analysis* of it. And that experience, according to the teachings of Oneness, was unique to each of us. I could surely speak from my *own* experience, which I knew was real. But, I discovered, explaining it in terminology that fit what was presumed to be carved in stone by other systems of belief was quite another matter.

The confrontations I encountered led me to go back and question, yet again, what I had actually experienced. Taking that experience back to its Source, with the guidance of Oneness, helped me to place the journey I'd actually made into the framework of *these* teachings. It helped me recognize the human tendency to condemn what doesn't fit the structure of our beliefs— and helped me to resist the inclination to internalize the judgment of others.

Oneness addresses certain spiritual misconceptions and how those approaches differ from the personalized path to Oneness
Oneness speaks:

This is Oneness. Take a moment and breathe of these energies. Let the sense of connectedness permeate all that you recognize yourself to be, so that you can perceive yourself as you truly Are. Once again, you have ventured into the seas of self-doubt. And your precious connection became obscured by suspicion and by the poison seeds borne by the confused minds of others.

There is no sense of *Divine connectedness* in the philosophies these others are espousing. They are following the paths of their rational minds through the labyrinths of logic. And lost in the jargon and the verbiage, the precious *experience* of that connection eludes them. Your experience of this journey has been a far different one than theirs.

The trail that these ones attempt to follow has been outlined by the successors to one whose experience of connectedness was pure and uncomplicated (Ramana Maharshi). And many here in this place, who are claiming to have "Realized the Self," have simply come to a place of *mental surrender* to the conceptual aspects of that process.

Many presume that this is the experience that they sought from the onset of their quest. And, having processed themselves mentally to the extent that they can identify, theoretically, the *characteristics* of the linear identity—the ego-self—they presume that the journey has been completed. Many of these ones have adopted the behaviors they associate with Self-Realized Masters and delude themselves into believing that these mannerisms confirm their state of attainment. Nothing could be further from the truth.

There is no need to subject yourself to the scrutiny of confused people. Not unless that is what you wish to experience. Many in these times have become Guru addicts who have been wandering the back roads of the spiritual landscape so long that they have become jaded—and resentful. This particular group is no different than any other group exhibiting cult-related behavior. Simply because they use terminology and bandy about concepts with which you are familiar does not mean that any of them has had the experience of full Divine connectedness.

For the most part, they have simply adopted a particular philosophy and modified their behavior and their conversation accordingly. This is no more and no less than yet another chapter in the ongoing saga of spiritual elitism that illustrates the history of the human race. We have written on this subject on several occasions.

The concepts that you have been prepared to teach in these times do not incorporate the teachings of one particular Master over any other. You will be communicating an approach to *personalized truth* substantiated by one's own *experience* of it. By definition, the experience of each will differ from that of others. And the human tendency to dismiss the experiences of others as invalid, when they have not duplicated one's own, will be called up for scrutiny.

This is what you have been prepared to deliver in these times. Whether or not your experiences of your own Divinity fit the template outlined by one particular pocket of individuals is irrelevant. You know what you know. Let that suffice. None of you has come to this journey to exercise a need to appear right, to be validated by external sources. The only validation one ever requires is one's own.

That spring, Oneness delivered a series of discourses that explored and fine-tuned the nuances of attaining and sustaining a state of Divine connectedness. In these teachings, we have been given clarification of some of the rarely discussed subtleties of perception we encounter when transitioning into Oneness with the Divinity within.

Oneness introduces the concept of "the perceiver" and lays a foundation for easing into a state of Grace

Oneness speaks:

As we breathe together in affirmation of the Isness that is shared throughout all Creation, we once again affirm this connection—the materialization of that exponential Isness in form. There is no *you* that is separate from what is experienced in this moment. The focal point of attention is fixed upon the perception of *the Self* as Oneness, and all sense of separation recedes into that embrace.

What remains is what may be termed "the perceiver"—the aspect of Self that is present, as form, yet has no sense of agenda, no sense of ownership of the identity. This aspect of Self is the transitional consciousness that acts as the intermediary between pure Awareness and the multidimensional expressions of identity that experience presence in the Here and Now of the physical world.

Being the perceiver and the perception simultaneously

Without the transitional presence of *the perceiver* there would be no possibility of physical perception—no possibility of *experience*. For, when one is in this state of Divine connectedness, one is the perceiver and the perception at the same time. The focus turns inward upon itself, and all else is perceived *through* the filter of that perspective. That is the state of being that has been termed "enlightenment."

When the linear aspect of self relinquishes its sense of exclusivity, one recognizes oneself to be within the embrace of a vast collective of consciousness that is non-dual in scope. Ultimately, one comes to know oneself to *Be* All of it—and to *experience* oneself *as* All of it—simultaneously.

This realization comes in increments, providing multiple exposures to the experience of exponential Isness as a foundation for the crystallization of that awareness. One does not suddenly wake up one morning and find oneself in a state of full Divine Presence. One's perception of oneself in this state of beingness is built on a history of exposures to the *experience* of oneself at these levels. One does not suddenly flip a switch and transform oneself into *That* in an instant. The experience unfolds gradually and builds to the point that one is able to sustain the fullness of these energies for extended periods of time.

You have been exposed to the misguided understandings of certain seekers who presume that their isolated experiences of exultation constitute evidence that they are now permanently in a fully manifested state of God Presence. This is surely not the case. One's theoretical understanding of the nature of the Absolute does not automatically constitute a basis for experiencing oneself *as* That. It simply serves to place the isolated experiences of connectedness that one *does* have in perspective.

Retaining linear perception in a state of Divine Presence

The experience of being *eased* into this state of Grace is more the norm amongst beings who, historically, have made the shift in self-perception as the materialization of the Presence we call "Oneness." And, one's state of attainment is surely in no way lacking by virtue of the fact that one is capable of having the experience of linear *perception* in this Here and Now.

All who manifest in physical form are, by definition, capable of the perception of it. You are indeed the bridge that makes the experience of *communion* possible. For, without the medium of the identity through which to express and to manifest, We would simply be Awareness. The *experience* of Self is only possible as a manifestation of its own reflection. It is in viewing what one has projected upon the ethers that one is able to *discern* what is really there.

It is only through profound austerities and the sustaining of one's consciousness in meditative mindlessness that one is able, *for the duration of that focus*, to transcend linear perception. This surely is not the objective of incarnating in physical form, although you are surely at liberty to opt for that experience, if it gives you comfort to do so.

You have chosen the experience of physical incarnation in order to have physical perceptions. And regardless of whether or not you have a full technical understanding of the illusory nature of physical reality, you should be prepared for the perception of physical phenomena throughout your ascent on this multi-dimensional journey. For, these are the characteristics of the experience.

Embracing the truth that is culled from one's own personal experience of it

It is a futile exercise to dismiss the *experience* of spiritual emergence with sweeping platitudes on the nature of the Self. For, one is afforded, at best, fragmentary glimpses of oneself in a state of fully manifested Divine Presence.

To expect that one must walk in the fullness of that state at all times is spiritual naïveté at best, and is characteristic of the elitism that has grown around the experience of spiritual emergence in certain circles. This holier-than-thou mindset is, in fact, the ultimate manifestation of ego—in the guise of the absence of it.

Trust that your process is unfolding exactly as it is supposed to. And let others believe what they believe. This journey is not about truth by consensus. This journey is an exercise in embracing the truth that is culled from one's own *irrefutable personal experience* of it.

Oneness speaks:

The one who reads these words, in this moment, is the *experiencer*, the aspect of self whose powers of perception make possible the experience. When one is in a state of full Divine connectedness as Oneness, the *experiencer* is able to access the perceptions available from *that* vantage point and translate those perceptions into the format of *experience*. That is the object of the exercise. For, you are in physical form in this Now moment. And until your awareness is *not* directed through the medium of physical form, you will continue to perceive the world of physical reality.

Modulating the perception of experience through amplification of one's energies

What can be modulated, through the amplification of one's energy field, and ultimately, through the embodiment of the totality of one's identity, is the optimum possible experience within the context of material perception. The circumstances may or may not have changed, from ones in which you found yourself perceiving life, in this self-same form, at another place in time. Yet, what will characterize *this* experience—and set it apart from the others—is your realization that the imagery that surrounds you has no effect upon you whatsoever. For, *your focus* is not upon the details of the illusion of those images.

Whether the circumstances in which you perceive yourself are exalted—or grotesque—is irrelevant. Whether the scenario perceived in this Now moment is one that supports and nurtures physical life, or serves to snuff it out, is irrelevant. *You* remain untouched. And from this vantage point, you will demonstrate to yourself, time and time again, the simple truth that you are, indeed, not the body. You will solidify your perception of it as "the vehicle in which you travel."

The physical body serves as the medium for perception

By virtue of the nature of the physical body, it will continue to supply you with perceptions. It will continue to exhibit the characteristics that are governed by the laws of physicality. When physical density is assimilated into the energy field of the physical form, the form will exhibit the characteristics of purging. Yet, from the vantage point of the Self, one will not perceive the process of cellular purification as suffering. The signs and symptoms of illness may well be present, but they will not affect your sense of who and what you know yourself to *Be*.

What could be termed "catastrophic conditions" may well surround you, as the world as you have come to know it undergoes its metamorphosis. And yet, those circumstances leave your sense of who and what you *Are* untouched. And in the moment when you exit the physical body, as conscious awareness, the experience of it will be changeless. You will continue to perceive yourself as the timeless expression of Isness that is your true nature—just as you do in this Now moment.

<hr>

The role of *devotion* in creating a state of inner-preparedness for the experience of Oneness with one's own Divine Essence

This is Oneness. As you have come to understand, your invocation is just a formality. It is not a necessary part of establishing this connection. Your *intention* is all that is required. Almost before the thought of Oneness is complete, you are fully in the experience of it. There is no time lag at all, no formalities required, no rituals performed, no sacred words spoken. All these things are for the purpose of preparing *you* for the experience of Oneness with your own Divine Essence.

Your expressions of *devotion* do not constitute a number of switches that might be flipped, to activate a state of connectedness with what you already *Are*. All of the expressions of devotion, all of these techniques you have practiced and perfected, have pointed you in the direction of *preparedness*. It is the *preparedness* that must be perfected in order for the possibility of the *experience* of Oneness to be realized.

There is surely nothing to be *done* that will automatically stimulate a seed into blossom in an instant and manifest a state of Divine connectedness for you. And yet, through your careful assimilation of your understandings of the nature of who and what you Are, and through the implementation of your expressions of spiritual practice—*whatever* they may be—you will have prepared the soil that is capable of *supporting* a flower in full blossom.

The importance of *surrender* in preparing for the possibility of Self-Realization

The experience of *Realizing the Self* happens in its own time and in its own way. It is so natural and subtle, its Presence is apt to elude you at first. Yet, that experience would not have been possible had certain preliminaries not taken place. It is less important that an *understanding* of the nature of the Self be mastered than the act of abandoning oneself in absolute *surrender* to the possibility of the experience of it. The experience is not something that is to be stalked and hunted. For, as long as you continue to approach the experience of Self-Realization in this way, it will continue to elude you.

What you truly Are is a possibility that is there to be *embraced*—for, it is *already* Realized. This state of Beingness that is so fervently sought is already there, fully manifested within you. It is in the desperate seeking of it that one keeps the *experience* of what is already there—just out of reach.

Oneness speaks about Self-Realization as an experience of wholeness

We are your own sacred Self, reaching out and encompassing the full multidimensionality that is your own true Essence. We are the culmination of *all* the stages of your unfoldment, not simply a single destination at the end of the line. It is only in the *assimilation* of all that you have ever been, rather than in the denial of bits and pieces of it, that the experience of *wholeness* is possible.

Embodying the sum-totality of your very own Essence is not a question of dematerializing the perspective you've presumed was *you* for most of your life. The state of Oneness with your own Divine Essence is only possible when you reach out and embrace *all* the aspects of who you are— including the ones you'd rather not look at.

The following passionate discourse was adapted as a meditation and was included in the CD, "The Meditations of Oneness: A Journey to the Heart of the Divine Lover," which was released in December 2009.

Oneness addresses the concept of the Totality, of which we are all a part

Oneness speaks:

Your prayers and your declarations of the heart delivered you right to the door—to the threshold of this Divine connection. In ecstasy, you chanted "Love of my life!" Softly, we replied "Life of my Love!" and took you by surprise into the effulgence of this Union. And we wept in joy together.

There are no words required beyond that. Words cannot touch this level of connectedness. They can only attempt to put structure to the unfathomable. Regardless of how eloquently you attempt to dress the experience, it remains perfection, absolutely unadorned by concept at all. We are entwined in the experience of it.

While in that state of bonded union, there is no way to say where one begins and the other ends, for only Oneness pervades the linear perception. *Heart* and *mind* are swept into a totality of Beingness that makes such considerations irrelevant. There is no aspect of self separate from that Totality that would require analysis of who and what We Are. All else is within the embrace of the *whole* of this Love—and knows itself to be That.

Each of us, as a pure reflection of a vibrational encodement, exists

Let it *not* be said that Oneness dwells in a void, numb and feelingless. Let it *not* be said that Oneness is simply *Awareness*, to the exclusion of all else. For, to make such a presumption would be to limit the limitless. Oneness is *All* That Is—which, by definition, includes all that *you* are. Oneness is the full spectrum of possibility—no *more* the aspect of Self that is pure Awareness than the one who perceives. Oneness cannot Be one aspect of that very Beingness to the exclusion of another, when Oneness is *All* of it.

You are *not* simply an illusory image, distilled into the semblance of form, within the context of the illusion of time and space. That may be how it appears to the metaphysician who delights in dissecting the Divine. Yet, that is a far cry from what you *Are*. You are no less Oneness than is Oneness. You, as a pure *reflection* of a vibrational encodement, *exist*. And you do so, fully and completely, within the *embrace* of the imperceptible Isness—surely not outside, or other than, or apart from that Totality.

All that is Divine—is *real*

Without the underlying foundation of the formless Self, the experience of *Self-Realization*, within the context of form, would not be possible. Who is it who could be said to have "Realized the Self" if you were truly non-existent? The aspect of Oneness, abiding in a state of Eternal Isness, has absolutely no stake in Self-Realization or any other conceptual expression of our own Beingness. It is none other than Divine Essence, expressed within the context of form, which is capable of that perception. For, all that is Divine—is *real*. Just as you are.

The vehicle of form is a lens through which Oneness is able to experience focus

Oneness speaks:

This is Oneness. Of this there is no doubt. For, we have embraced the exalted levels of connectedness and have merged once more into one all-pervading Awareness. That sense of Awareness is not focused *in* the physical body, although it is perceived *through* that vehicle. This all-pervading Isness is not focused anywhere at all. It does not emanate from a place—a sense of being *here* and not *there*. It simply is experiencing perception through the filter of this identity, a lens through which Oneness is able to experience *focus*.

Now, in this moment, you have full, conscious awareness of that state of Being. That is the experience you would term "Self-Realization." In this Now moment, you know yourself to *Be* Oneness, and, at the same time, you are aware that you have retained identity. *You* have not ceased to be. You have simply shifted the level of your perception and are experiencing your Self as you truly Are.

Oneness speaks about the absence of mental activity and the deep sense of inner peace that accompanies the experience of Oneness

You observe that there is no mental activity whatsoever. There is no string of thoughts running through your Awareness, having to do with past or future. There is only an exquisite sense of Stillness. And a deep sense of inner peace permeates your entire Being. It is entirely possible to sustain this state. It is entirely possible to *abide* in the inner Stillness. The choice is there, in *every* ongoing moment, to embody your knowingness of who you truly Are—and never lapse into forgetting it.

It is not a matter of exerting massive amounts of effort, in order to Be who you Are. The spiritual practices in which you engage *set the stage* for this experience. They do not initiate the experience itself. The levels of heightened vibration you attain in the practice of chanting Mantras and in deep meditation prepare you to shift, naturally, into a *perception* of Self as That which you Are. All other activities, which are focused on a mentalized *understanding* of the dynamics of that process, are irrelevant to the *experience* of it.

Oneness re-emphasizes the difference between inner knowingness and having a philosophical grasp of spiritual principles

It does not matter what a given number of so-called "Gurus" have to say about this subject. At best, they can only reference *their own* experience, which surely does not delineate what is so for others who have also experienced this level of spiritual attainment. Whether or not any of these teachers have actually reached the levels where they *sustain* a state of Divine connectedness is not for anyone to speculate.

Each knows, within his own depths, whether the truths espoused emanate from *inner-knowingness* or from a sophisticated grasp of spiritual principles, embraced philosophically. This experience of the Realization of the Self has nothing whatsoever to do with philosophy. It has nothing to do with *understanding* the nature of the journey into the embrace of the Self. It has *everything* to do with simply *being Present*—completely Present—in the *experience* of it.

The chanting of sacred Mantras to The Goddess, in Sanskrit, had long since become a cherished part of my spiritual practice. Over the years, Dr. Bindu Purohit had taught me several of these extraordinary ancient Mantras—sacred vibrational encodements learned with a precise pitch, articulation and tone in the oral tradition—and I loved the way it felt to chant them. It was an experience of the sacred that was entirely different than my experience of connecting with Oneness. And I'd come to embrace my choice to chant these Mantras as part of my own personal expression of devotion and not an aspect of adherence to a particular spiritual tradition or religion.

Oneness had made it very clear to me from the outset that Mantra chanting was not to be regarded as a prerequisite for sustaining my connection with Oneness. I was chanting them for the sheer joy of it—and no less as a means of fortifying my energy field. Often I'd find I was sitting before my altar and chanting for several hours at a time. Ultimately, I began to become engulfed in a state of Divine rapture during these sessions.

Quite suddenly and completely unexpectedly, one day I began to experience something remarkably different during the chanting. It was a spontaneous sense of Presence—clearly a Divine Presence—that felt completely different than the Presence of Oneness. My body began to sway ever so gently, and a sweet, irrepressible smile began to spread across my face.

There was a feeling of absolute serenity within me—a gentle, loving feeling of utter peace I'd never experienced before. I had a sense of what was taking place, despite being unprepared for that possibility. The Goddess to whom I'd been chanting—who I'd come to regard as Durga Devi—had manifested in my physical body. A phone call to Dr. Bindu confirmed it. I was stunned.

Oneness provided the understandings that helped me to put yet another astounding chapter in my spiritual journey into perspective. This initial experience of embodying a Deity became the foundation for an ongoing history of Divine encounters that continue to unfold within the scope of this identity.

Connecting with the Presence of The Goddess
Oneness speaks:

You have glimpsed another level of connectedness today during the chanting of your sacred Mantras. And through perfecting your practice, you have succeeded in opening other doorways within you and in connecting to other levels of your beingness. These other levels of Presence are also *within* you. They do not emanate *from* elsewhere and somehow *enter* your energy field and thus permeate your awareness. They also are aspects of who and what *you* Are—varying expressions of the All-That-Is.

Through the sacred science of Mantra, you have begun to activate these timeless connections and to *experience* the Presence of these expressions of Divine Essence, through the medium of your perception. You have applied the very same skills to the sense of connectedness with these aspects of Divinity as you have to your focus of awareness on the Presence of Oneness. And you discovered the ease with which you are able to slide into a state of self-perception as *That*. Now you have discovered the principle and have begun to unlock its potential.

Oneness provides a foundation for understanding the manifestation of a Deified Presence as an aspect of the Totality of Oneness

It is all, quite simply, a manifestation of your *absolute focus of awareness* on the Presence to be invoked, while dwelling in the embrace of *absolute heart-centeredness*. This level of focus is not one that is directed through the mind with forceful intent. Rather, it is a state of beingness emanating from a place of *surrender* to that place within your own Being, where the doorway to that level of connectedness lies.

You have tasted the barest beginnings of this experience. For, the experience is one that will grow and deepen with sustained practice. It is not something that you should expect to be able to manifest overnight—no more than was your experience of merging into the totality of Oneness. And, while you will, most assuredly, be able to manifest a full range of Divine Presence and to experience yourself *as* That, your focus on your own *identity*—the aspect of Oneness that is *Self*—will remain your primary mode of expression and experience.

You have discovered these different doorways *experientially*. You were not directed in how to *do* it. You intuited the process quite naturally, surrendered totally to the embodiment of it—and experienced the result. Now, you do not simply *understand* the principles. You *know*. You have observed. You have noted the distinctions amongst these varying avenues of connectedness. You have concluded—*experientially*—that they are not the same.

At the same time, you have demonstrated that All of it is within *you*. The full microcosm and macrocosm of experience is within you—gateways to be activated, or not, as you choose. For, you Are Oneness. You are no less than That. And within the embrace of that Totality is *every aspect* of Infinite Possibility—the *experience* of which is also within the scope of possibility. It all is a matter of what you choose to perceive.

Oneness gives a definition of Self-Realization

While walking as the embodiment of *perception*, all possibility awaits you *as experience*. And, at the same time, you know yourself to *Be* the formless Self—*transcending experience*. The state of Self-Realization, therefore, is a condition whereby one abides within a foundation of *knowingness* of the nature of one's Isness, while simultaneously experiencing Presence within the world of linear and non-linear perception.

A few months later, my questions arose once again regarding the manifestation of the Presence of The Goddess within my physical form, which had by then become a regular occurrence. I asked Oneness to help me understand what was actually happening during these experiences and to elaborate on the teachings I had received previously.

Rasha speaks:

Oneness, I would like to talk about the subject of my spiritual practice. I see that I have evolved an elaborate series of exercises now, including much chanting of Mantras, with a focus on a connection with the energy of The Goddess. I am following Dr. Bindu's instructions faithfully, and the results have been remarkable.

I have gone into profound levels of bliss during the actual chanting of the Mantras. Ultimately, I have come to experience what I identify as a Divine Presence. This Presence manifests with an intense sensation of joy, centered in my heart center, combined with a sweet smile that is fixed upon my face. My body sways gently and gracefully. My voice becomes high pitched and sometimes changes slightly in intonation. I have intuited the understanding that I have connected with the energies of The Goddess.

I would like to ask you to clarify for me what exactly is happening during these moments of connectedness and how this process differs from the manifestation of Oneness.

I would also like to ask for clarification as to the nature and level of this Divine Presence. Dr. Bindu has indicated that The Goddess is not simply a manifestation of Divinity with duality—an expression of the feminine polarity at the level of Godhead. He says that The Goddess is the ultimate Divinity. How does this information fit within the structure of my understandings of the nature of Oneness?

Oneness explains the process of shifting into connectedness with The Goddess as an extension of the state of Self-Realization as Oneness

Oneness speaks:

This is a complex question and we will address it in a way that will clarify the nature of these energies, as well as your purpose in choosing to experience them. Your spiritual practice incorporating the chanting of Mantras is not a duplication of effort or a duplication of the result experienced.

Your manifestation of the Presence of Oneness is the culmination of our work together. Through this work, your linear identity has ascended through the levels of linear reality and provided you with a frame of reference for the structure of physical experience. In having made this journey and embodied, sequentially, the levels of self-perception encountered en route to Self-recognition as Oneness, you provided yourself a structure for perceiving the true nature of the experience of humanness. It is from this experiential foundation that you will be able to present the teachings that you have documented as part of your life's work.

The science of Mantra as a vehicle for the embodiment of a Divine Presence

Your practice of chanting of Mantras was not included in your spiritual practice as a means of augmenting your self-perception as Oneness. The science of Mantra is a means of fortifying your energy field. The fact that you are now in a state of Self-Realization as Oneness made the possibility of the manifestation of the Goddess through the vehicle of your physical form a natural outcome of the practice of Mantra. For, these prayers are vibrational formulas calculated to invoke this very presence.

One set of experiences does not automatically imply the manifestation of the other. Yet, the conditions were established, through your journey to Oneness, which would enable the manifestation of The Goddess through your form to be a natural result. At this stage of your journey, you are able to perceive The Goddess experientially. You sense her Presence, and at the same time you know yourself to Be Oneness.

The pathways to these other expressions of Divine Presence are also within you. The practice of Mantra enables you to reach the levels where these paths may be accessed. Ultimately, you may become well established in your ability to embody this expression of Divine Presence, as well as others. For, in essence, what you are doing is functioning as a *conduit* for these energies—providing a vehicle for their manifestation in material form.

They are expressions of Oneness at the level of Godhead. They are expressions of the One Source, with identity, at the level of a Deity. As such, these expressions of Divine Presence are no more or less Divine than the sum totality of the Oneness of which you are a part.

You will become fortified in your ability to hold the fullness of these levels of Presence through your continued practice of Mantra. Your focus of attention upon your perception of Self as Oneness opens the door to this other avenue of possibility. It is this capacity that distinguishes a "Divine Soul" from other spiritually advanced beings in human form that may have experienced the state of Self-Realization on the path of enlightenment.

Many will have the experience of Divine connectedness in these times. Many will know the joys of exalted moments where the touch of Divine Presence will be undeniable. And these experiences will serve to fortify their emerging faith in the Presence of the sacred within. Relatively few will experience that state of Presence consistently, in human form, during your lifetime.

The channeling of one's "higher self" does not constitute proof that one has attained the state known as "enlightenment." It simply is evidence of having transcended certain levels, vibrationally, where a crossover in consciousness is then possible. The levels of Self-perception where one is able to hold the Presence of a Deity within one's physical form are extremely rare. It is that level that you are destined to be able to sustain in the times to come.

The subject of embodying the Presence of a Deity surfaced yet again several weeks later. Oneness took the opportunity to delve deeper into the subject and clarified for me an ongoing series of questions about what was actually happening during these extraordinary encounters.

This information is included here to clarify for all who may read it the nature of the phenomenon of embodying the Presence of a Deity and how that differs from the experience of the Self as Oneness.

Rasha speaks:

For several months now, I've experienced the sense that the Divine Mother manifests within my body while I'm chanting my Mantras. At first I felt that it was a supreme expression of ego on my part to even think such a thought. Yet, in the same breath, I knew that this was very real and that I had not imagined it.

During my time in Taos, New Mexico, when I was in deep meditation in the Hanuman temple, I felt what I recognized as the Presence of Hanuman within my body. The experience was very real and absolutely magnificent. Oneness, can we talk about this a bit more, please?

Oneness speaks:

We have spoken of this on several occasions, and we can affirm to you, once again, that you have not imagined this experience. You are becoming acclimated with the energies of various levels of Divine Presence. As you begin to review the writings you have documented over recent years, you will see that what you describe should not come as a surprise to you. We have spoken of this, as has the Hanuman consciousness, over the years. You were simply not in a position to grasp what was being described. Now, having had the experience, you are beginning to understand what had been alluded to previously.

Without a frame of reference within which to place this kind of information, you took it as your cue to begin to doubt your own ability to document this kind of information with accuracy. You suspected that your own ego had gotten into the act. You concluded that such an idea was preposterous. Now you see that it simply *is* what is happening. Now, having had the experience consistently, reinforced with affirmations as to its validity from Dr. Bindu as well as this Source, you have begun to relax into the process.

Rasha, you have come to these times to embody a Divine Presence. That sense of Presence is not exclusive, in the sense that you will embody *this* and not *that*. You have the capacity to embody the Presence of a Deity—and to experience that *level* of Beingness, simultaneously, as that which you Are. Ultimately, you will come to recognize all of it as Oneness—the embrace of the Totality of which you know *yourself* to be a part.

One does not cancel out the possibility of another. It is all part of a particular echelon of possibility—to which you have access, according to *the focus of your attention*—and is by invitation only. This is not a "take over" in the sense of *possession*. This is an augmentation of your own energy field to the extent that a vibrationally compatible level of consciousness is able to emerge in form and to experience *itself*.

Oneness speaks about the universal nature of a Divine Presence

The Deities with whom you have experienced communion are not fictional characters relegated to a place in sacred mythology. These expressions of Divine Presence are very real. They transcend the limitations of culture which have attempted to identify and to categorize them.

These expressions of Presence are recognized in *various* forms, from the vantage point of the physical world of perception, according to the dictates of culture. The identical Presence may be perceived by those with vastly differing spiritual orientations, by individuals on opposite ends of the globe. And that phenomenon of perception can happen *simultaneously*, without limitation to time and place.

A Deified presence is not indigenous to the culture in which it is perceived. It simply has been defined by a particular culture, within the context of *identity*, in order that perception might be possible. For, yours is the world of material perception. In fact, the Essence of these levels of Divine Presence is non-material. It is all *energy*. It all simply Is—within the Totality of Oneness.

The subtle shades of variation in which these levels of awareness are able to experience Self-perception are no different, in principle, from the aspects of the Totality you experience as your *Self*. They are simply expressions of Divine perception with a particular vantage point. Their capacity to deliver the experience of exalted levels of *energy*, through the vehicle of form, is what distinguishes these expressions of Presence from each other and from the aspect of *Self* expressed by the vehicle through which their Presence may be perceived.

The basis for the perception of difference amongst expressions of Divine Presence

It is the subtle differences in *energy* that distinguish these expressions of Divine Presence and give them the basis for what you are able to perceive as *identity*. Who they *Are* is not keyed in to the stories that have been passed down through the ages in the spiritual lore that colors your world and attempts to give it definition. These illustrations are simply the means through which the *qualities* of these expressions of Presence might be imparted.

These aspects of Divine identity are the means through which the qualities of *Divinity itself* may be recognized and, ultimately, embraced as one's own. The expressions of the intangible are expressed as identity and experience so that they might be grasped by those who presume themselves to be *other* than That. In fact, All of it is none *other* than the Totality of Oneness, of which you are a part.

It will help you to resist the inclination to become distracted by the concept of the Deified Presence as an expression of *separateness* from what you experience yourself to be—or from the Totality of Oneness. For, it is in the embracing of Oneness, through your experience of these exalted levels of connectedness, that the fullness of the experience may be realized and the fullness of a Divine Presence may be known.

32

Spring 2004
Mumbai, India
A Homecoming of the Heart

———

I n late spring of 2004, I had my semi annual visit to Mumbai. There, my days were blessed, for hours-on-end, by the presence of Dr. Bindu Purohit. Over the years, I'd been able to visit with him in person once or twice a year, with abundant phone conversations in between. It was during these precious hours that I was able to ask every question imaginable and fine-tune my grasp of the teachings of Oneness. I was astonished to discover, again and again, how my understandings, based on teachings I'd transcribed without the benefit of any formal background or spiritual foundation, stood up to the scrutiny of a Master who was impeccably well versed in timeless Vedic and Tantric wisdom.

The energies in Dr. Bindu's room were indescribable. It was like walking into a force field of Divine Love—the exquisite energies of The Goddess. During these visits, my *Yantras*—of which there were then four: one for health, one for protection, one for well being, and one for karmic issues—were all *reconsecrated*.

These extraordinary sacred objects, which were so precious to me, took their place on his *puja* (prayer) table and were able to remain there, sometimes for over a week, imbibing the Divine elixir created through the chanting of secret combinations of sacred Sanskrit Mantras virtually around the clock. Often I came away feeling that I too was none other than a *Yantra*, the embodiment of an unfathomable Divine formula, who had come to Mumbai to be reconsecrated in his presence.

No detail escaped Dr. Bindu. At times, it felt as though he could see into my very soul. He seemed to know everything about everything—no differently than Oneness did. I realized that, quite literally, there were no secrets in this illusory world. Dr. Bindu demonstrated, with a carefully placed word or question, that there was nowhere the truth could hide—past, present, or future. Over time, I came to surrender to the reality of my own transparency and came to embrace unconditionally the perfection in "what is."

In terms of what could be called "destiny," Dr. Bindu had been able to see from the onset what I still could not. He held fast to his vision of the direction in which I was being propelled—a vision reiterated by Oneness—that remained incomprehensible to me. And although Dr. Bindu's spiritual heritage is rooted in the orthodoxy of exacting Hindu traditions, a path I'd barely begun to explore, his approach with me enabled me to blossom in my own way, on a personal path to Oneness that was self-created.

Most significant however, was the humbling realization that despite the months spent braving the inner battlefields of transformation, and emerging weary and shaken, I'd somehow managed to land right back in the shelter of a timeless connection that hadn't missed a beat, in all that time. In the presence of Dr. Bindu, there was an indefinable sense of spiritual "solid ground," a haven of loving trust that defied all considerations of logic, a bond of soul-recognition that words could scarcely begin to touch.

Now, in moments when I least expected it, there would often come a poignant pause in the conversation where the room became totally engulfed in Stillness, and Dr. Bindu's gaze seemed to shift, ever so slightly, into a place of beyond that defied linear perception. Instantly, the ethers—and every illusory object in sight—would explode into a virtual starburst of golden effulgence. In the same stunning instant, every nuance of my sense of self-perception became consumed in unspeakable rapture! What was *this*? I had to wonder.

As the years went by, the fascinating visual phenomena began to alter, on occasion. Often, a subtle but poignant pause would come, right in the midst of a sentence, and suddenly I would perceive a softly shimmering, pale violet haze, hovering over Dr. Bindu's form. Instantly, my heart center would explode in joy, and I'd be able to commune, for several fleeting moments, with the Presence that became known to me as "The Goddess." These extraordinary episodes of Divine audience, encountered in the presence of Dr. Bindu, continued to catch me by surprise and always left me with an awesome, inner glow that would linger for days to come.

These moments, consumed in the effulgence of what was surely a profound Divine Presence, clearly had manifested by the Grace of a being in human physical form—yet, one who was still insisting he was *not* my Guru. There was absolutely no logical explanation for these visions and the ongoing phenomena that continued to accompany them. Why was Dr. Bindu lavishing his time and attention on me in such an extraordinary way, year after year, if I wasn't his *chela* (the devotee of a Guru)? I simply had no idea what to make of it.

I cannot say where the lines that delineate a brother from a Guru begin or end. In so many ways, Dr. Bindu protected and watched over me like a loving parent, year in and year out, through trials and tribulations that would have tried the patience and endurance of any teacher. Yet, his Presence remained steadfast. His unconditional, loving support was unwavering, no matter how off-center I may have appeared to be. From start to finish, Dr. Bindu continued to insist that he was *not* my Guru. And even though my heart often told me otherwise, something deep within me recognized the perfection in what was surely a Divine arrangement.

It was totally appropriate, therefore, that the happening that transpired within me did so in Mumbai. Whether that shift was precipitated by Dr. Bindu's prayers or whether it was simply *time* for me to emerge in full blossom, I can never be sure. But, there was no question that a significant shift in awareness had taken place.

⌖

Rasha speaks:

Instantaneous! The merging—the sense of Divine Presence—was instantaneous. Not a moment's hesitation. I write these words, not knowing who is writing this and really not caring. It doesn't matter now.

I can't say when this shift in awareness actually took place. Perhaps it was yesterday, somewhere between a revelation that hit me between the eyes, and my assimilation of those realizations, punctuated by intermittent peals of laughter at the absurdity of it all.

I awoke this morning with the most sublime sense of utter contentment. Not soaring bliss but absolute peace. I haven't had a thought about anything all day. Not one thought. The inner silence is effortless. Not a "meditation"—surely not concentration. There is simply no spontaneous mind chatter at all. A smile of inner recognition spreads across my face.

By now, I've had any number of tastes of this state. I know what this is. Yet, in the past there was effort involved. There was the matter of being acutely aware of the focus of my attention, which I became adept at harnessing and fixing upon my inner perception of Presence as Oneness. This is different. This is absolutely effortless. I am simply my Self. No fanfare. No fireworks. No "inner explosion." Just an all-pervading inner Stillness.

I sat before my altar a little while ago and played my beloved invocation music. For years I'd performed the same little ritual as part of my prayers, and at the sound of that music I would shift instantly into connectedness with Oneness, generally accompanied by a massive surge of energy, waves of exultation, wrenching sensations in my heart center, and often, tears—ecstatic sobbing I could not hold back. It had all become part of the daily ritual.

This time it was different. There was the distinct sense that now there was nothing to invoke. The Presence of Oneness was already fully in residence. I lit the candle and listened to my cherished music quietly. No great waves of passion washed over me. No surge of energy. No tears. I smiled gently to myself. Peace. Absolute peace.

Oneness speaks:

The fingers pause expectantly, waiting to see if words would be forthcoming or not. Why would they not be? Oneness hasn't gone away. Oneness is simply in the forefront of our awareness now. The Rasha identity is assimilated within the totality of *that*. Her observations were documented, just for the record. Her awareness of the shift in perspective attests to the fact that she is still part of the whole. She hasn't ceased to be. Not at all.

The characteristics of embodying Oneness, with full conscious awareness of it

The personality of this identity will continue to be your own. You have not "become someone else." You are still *you*. You simply have an exponentially augmented vantage point from which to view the circumstances that present themselves. We will continue to communicate in this way, allowing the sense of Presence that presides within this form to deepen in a natural way.

It is not the intention to simply flip a switch within you. You have inched your way into this transformation slowly and carefully. And that is the way you will continue in your unfoldment. The process is no less one of *expansion* than it was from the onset. We are simply working at far higher levels now. And your perception of your state of Beingness will continue to be revealed to you in increments.

The experiments in the shifting of self-perception were an interim stage in the process, calculated to deliver you, experientially, to a place where you were able to discern the shift that has now taken place. Now, you will ease your way into ever-heightening *levels* of the experience of knowing yourself to Be Oneness.

We have undergone a metamorphosis together. In so doing, Oneness has encompassed the full scope of the multifaceted identity that, until now, was fragmented and isolated into pockets of *unresolved emotion*. Those pieces have been consolidated now, the emotional foundation for the original fragmentation having been released, the issues underlying it having been resolved. Now, there is no longer the vibrational structure with which to hold those *life theme* issues in form. The energies that once called forth the circumstances that illustrated these themes are simply no longer there.

Now there will be time for quiet assimilation, as the ramifications of this shift in awareness settle within, and a newfound sense of beingness begins to emerge. This process will evolve and the sense of Presence will deepen, in the fullness of time.

Oneness speaks about the omnipresence of Divine communication

A shift has transpired within you now. The perception of Self is that of the Presence of Oneness. At the same time, there is the understanding that this communication is flowing *through* that state of Presence. It is not flowing *from* anywhere in particular—from a conceptual sense of *here*, as opposed to *there*. This communication is *omnipresent*. And its manifestation as form is possible by virtue of *your* Self-perception at that level of Isness.

Thus, your connectedness-made-manifest *expands* to encompass the omnipresence of this communication—to experience yourself as a *conduit* of it, and no less, as the *embodiment* of it. The essence of the knowingness contained in these words is no different than the form through which it flows, for each is a reflection of the Isness whose resonance is made manifest in this way.

Recognizing one's sacred Essence in the *reflection* that is the illusory world

Your inclination now is toward full abidance in the Self. The illusory world, in and of itself, holds little attraction. Any tendency to be drawn to it is only a manifestation of habit. Who you know yourself to Be is not to be found there. Yet, it can be recognized as the *reflection*—an illustration, for the benefit of the *perceiver*—of one's own sacred Essence. And it can be experienced as That.

Let the interactions within the context of the reflection be reflective in themselves of that Essence. Let any gesture be of the resonance one would bestow upon oneSelf. Let the *perception* of this reflection be no less than the absolute *recognition* of the Isness in every aspect of it. And let one's forays into the perception of it be the manifestation of one's unwavering focus of attention upon the *Self*—the sacred Essence ever-abiding in the Stillness within.

In this way, one comes to embody the sense of being "in the world yet not *of* the world." One is able to be Present—a full physical manifestation of Divinity incarnate—within the world of illusory experience. It is with full conscious *awareness* of that state of Divine Presence that the Realized Self walks forth.

Oneness describes the nature of the Realized Self

To all outward appearances, the Realized Self is no different from all the others who are mesmerized by the comings and goings, the entire whirlwind of experiential possibility. His appearance and his participation on a mundane level do not reveal the level of his attainment. He interacts with the elements of the world of illusion as though he perceives them as real. Yet, here the similarity ends. For, he does so with full knowledge that he is not affected in any way by any of it.

He understands his own transcendent nature. He interacts without any investment whatsoever in the outcome of those interactions. His external actions are the manifestation of an unwavering focus that is inner-directed. And his faith in the fruits of those actions is no less absolute.

He knows, to a depth that is impenetrable, that Divine Will is made manifest through the vehicle of his own form. And he has surrendered any sense of separation from the thrust of that Intent. He has surrendered all sense of *personal will*. He has relinquished all desire. He wants for nothing. And in nothing is he lacking.

The Realized Self is secure in the knowledge that he is One with any manifestation forthcoming as a result of his inner-directed action. And he gives not a moment's thought to mentalized projections of the sensory imagination.

He takes no individual responsibility for the creation of the linear result of his actions. He knows his actions to be the direct reflection of his own Divine focus. His actions spring forth spontaneously from the *inner-directedness* of his Awareness, and he regards them—and the results they bring—with consummate detachment.

He is not concerned with appearances. He knows that through the eyes of the illusory world things may not appear as he knows them to be. He understands that the judgment of the blinded is the destiny of the sighted. And he is unaffected by it.

The one who walks in full Divine connectedness is unscathed by the stones cast by the hands of the ignorant. He knows that such acts are to be expected. Neither does he fear their inevitability. He walks with a sense of consummate *protectedness*, knowing that the illusory wounds that he may appear to bear do not touch him. For, he has transcended all suffering.

He abides in the Stillness within, even in the face of colossal upheavals that appear to transpire in the world around him. He looks into the face of unspeakable suffering and perceives only the reflection of Divinity at work. His exalted vision, eternally transfixed, enables him to truly see. And his perception of Divinity-in-action—in even the most unspeakable atrocity— enables him to *reflect* the effulgence of that rarified Vision *back upon* the illusion of darkness, and in so doing, transform it.

In this way, the Divinity personified by his *illusory* Presence becomes the vessel through which Divine Intent may flow. In this way, the Divine Vision becomes clarified, becomes purified, and is able to reabsorb its own Essence into the wellspring of possibility from which it pours forth—and be born anew.

Through the vehicles of Divine Intent, the hand of The Creator becomes The Artist once more, and through this outreach, makes His mark upon the illusory world. For, that world Is none other than His own reflection. It is through the transformed Presence of the human instruments of Divine Intent that the illusory reflection *ascends* through the medium of time and space.

Collectively, these transformed instruments of Divine Intent join in the co-creation of the world of infinite possibility, each with full, conscious *awareness* of it. Individually, each adds his own note to the collective resonance that is the substance of Creation and adds his own unique fingerprint to the all-pervading signature of Oneness.

Becoming an instrument of Divine Intent

You have awakened to the realization that you Are such an instrument. And the opportunity in the full magnitude of that awareness is in the harnessing of it through the unwavering, inwardly-directed focus of your attention.

Your heartfelt prayers have been heard in the epicenter of your very own Being. And the answer sprang forth from those depths, in affirmation. You have *become* the answer to your prayers. Not because some externally exalted expression of Divinity bestowed it upon you. But, because you bestowed the gift of Divine Vision upon your Self.

You can see it now. You can see the overview. You can envision a realm of possibility that transcends the troubles and traumas of the world of linear illusion. You *know* the direction in which it is all going. You feel the surge of Divine Momentum from within your own Being. And you know your Self to be One with it.

Assessing the clarity and authenticity of Divine communication

Oneness speaks through the voices of many in these times. But, the *clarity* of the Message is reflective only of the clarity of the vessel through which it flows. The purity of these words cannot be measured, it can only be felt. Truth cannot be understood, it can only be known. A message may appear to be *timely* and may therefore hint at being Divinely inspired. But, the true barometer of its authenticity remains not in its timeliness, but from within the realm of the *timeless*.

In determining whether or not to give credence to a particular body of information that purports to be Divine Truth, step back from it. Take the myopic perspective—the immediacy of that vision—out of the picture. And feel the resonance. Deep within you, there are no questions. And the answers—*your* answers—come in the form of *knowingness*. That level of recognition requires no words and needs no translation.

The wisdom imparted in a message of true Divine origin is calculated to spark that level of inner recognition in you. Not from within your mind. But, keyed in to a place from which there is no beginning, and towards which there is no end. You alone determine whether a message is destined to endure and stand the test of time. Not on the basis of whether or not you can grasp it at first glance. But, on the basis of whether it has *touched* you in a place the mind cannot question.

The Messengers in these times each carry a level of message that holds a particular *vibrational encodement*. The *literal* thrust of the message in question is less important than the impact it is calculated to deliver within you, *vibrationally*. You know when you have encountered Divine Wisdom that resonates within you. And you know when you have not. That level of knowingness is valid for you alone. It does not determine what is and is not *truth* for another

Once again my heart was "home" in Mumbai. Blessedly. As the days went by, the turmoil of the months in Tiruvannamalai began to fade into the distance. And I knew it was time to walk forward from that experiential exercise and turn the page.

Why was it so painful to be retracing my steps, as I prepared to tell the story of my journey to Oneness? As I rediscovered the phases of my unfoldment, it often felt like I was actually reliving the fears and concerns that characterized those passages. I could almost see the silt that had clouded the waters years before being stirred to the surface. Was it simply energy that was moving through me? I asked myself. And why, at the same time, was I feeling so incredibly balanced and peaceful?

I sat at the computer and allowed the revelations of my heart to pour through me. Somehow, by putting it into words, the inner clarity emerged automatically. Oneness, as always, was there to embellish my insights with the perspective of Divine Vision.

Rasha speaks:

There is a sense of Presence that permeates my awareness, even now, as the words of my invocation begin. I feel myself being engulfed in a sense of utter peace. And in an instant all the concerns and worries that consumed me only a few moments ago just disappeared. The circumstances haven't changed. I know that. What has changed is simply the way I choose to perceive myself. The circumstances, which I understand to be a reflection of that state, seem to shift accordingly. Fascinating.

Why am I always so amazed to experience a confirmation of what I understand to be so? Why am I still so astounded to discover that all of this is really true? Why am I so awed to feel such a sense of contentment within the embrace of your Presence? Oneness, I feel you all around me now. And in the same breath, I recognize—in retrospect—that while this last sentence was being written, the sense of Presence shifted. And in this moment, I experience myself to Be Oneness, once more.

Suddenly, this communication is not coming from an identity that presides in this body. It is clearly coming through this Presence. It is emanating from somewhere else. And the one I now perceive myself to Be is documenting it. I see that the one I perceive myself to Be encompasses both states of awareness, simultaneously. It is not a question of being one to the exclusion of the other. Who I Am—is All of it. Amazing.

Suddenly, I am so blessedly peaceful, where only moments before my mind was in turmoil. Now there doesn't seem to be a mind. There is simply a sense of the witness, diligently noting all of this down. The smile of sweet contentment that I identify as Oneness spreads across my face now—an affirmation, shared in silence.

Oneness, you have been patiently documenting all of this, letting me ramble. Ok. Now I will be quiet. It's your turn.

Oneness speaks:

This is Oneness. Your perception of it is a sense of simultaneous *Presence*—the sense of being not one aspect of identity to the exclusion of another, but of being a mélange of levels of awareness, perceived as One Presence. This is, in fact, the nature of who and what you Are.

Oneness, why am I now experiencing such profound levels of emotion, often accompanied by tears, when I connect with you during my prayers of invocation? Who is it who is experiencing that in those moments?

Oneness talks about the experience of emotion in a state of Divine connectedness

The emotional body is not separate from what you Are. It is an aspect of what you Are. Your *experience* of emotion is a result of your focus of attention upon your perception of the linear identity—one that perceives itself to be *in communion* with Oneness.

Your prayers and your invocations are also from the perspective of the linear identity. It is that aspect of self that is expressing the gratitude, the willingness, the understandings, and the hopes and dreams of fulfilling what you presume are the expectations of Oneness.

The authenticity of these feelings can be heart-wrenching. And thus, the profound sensations of connectedness stimulated by these sentiments are experienced at the level of heart. Yet, it is through the medium of the linear identity that these feelings are *able* to be perceived. These feelings are part of the *experience*—perceived by *the experiencer.*

You have come to this experience of humanness in order to *feel* this. And you will continue to have the experience of feeling the exquisite sensations of Divine connectedness, so long as you perceive yourself as the one *having* this experience. From the perspective of Oneness, it all simply *Is.*

There is no need to berate yourself for having these sensations of joy. This is surely a part of the process of Realizing the Self. It is one of the infinite levels of possibility within the context of the world of linear experience.

You have taken the experience of Divine connectedness to profound levels of intensity. And you derive deep sensations of pleasure from surrendering to this connection. But, the motive for this aspect of the journey is surely not to revel in the experience of pleasure. For, to do so would merely be taking the

433

pursuit of physical gratification to another level. It would *not* be an indication that you had *relinquished* your identification with the material realm. It would merely be an indication that you had *transferred* a pursuit of sensory stimulation to the arena of the metaphysical. The focus of attention, in so doing, remains upon the sense of the linear identity being that which one *is*.

When one perceives oneself from the perspective of Oneness, there is no such experience of physical sensation. There is simply a profound sense of Peace and inner-Stillness. The pursuit of sensory gratification, albeit through spiritual expression, is nonetheless *experienced* from the standpoint of a linear identity. Your prayers, which are heartfelt and sincere, also serve to reinforce your linear awareness. Who is it who is praying in those moments? And to whom are those prayers directed? When one knows oneself to *Be* Oneness, there is no need or inclination to beseech anything *other than* that Self to allow oneself to *Be* what one, in fact, already *Is*. There would simply be a sense of Awareness that one *Is* That.

The experience, then, would not be one of *connectedness*, at all. In order for there to be *connectedness*, something is required for one to be connected *to*—which can only be experienced within the context of *duality*. Thus, your experience of connecting with Oneness, transcribing these teachings, and perceiving the exquisite range of sensations that accompanied the entire journey, could only have happened within the scope of a *linear identity*.

In so saying, we do not seek to invalidate the exaltation of the experience of Divine connectedness, but rather, to place it within the context of the journey itself. This aspect of the experience is not, in itself, the destination. It is merely a stop along the way. Now you see it. And, once again, you have your own experiential affirmation that *the focus of your attention* is the key to all of it. You get to choose now. You alone determine what you perceive—with full awareness of how that comes to pass.

The ultimate relinquishing of attachment to all things physical

The key to exiting the roller-coaster ride—the extreme ups and downs of emotion and experience that accompany the heightened stages of the spiritual journey—is in recognizing that even in the most profound evidence of a Divine connection, lies the evidence of the linear perspective of the one perceiving it.

It is in relinquishing one's attachment to the pursuit of the *joy* of the experience of a Divine connection that the authentic state of spiritual attainment is Realized. It is in this ultimate relinquishing of attachment to all things physical that one comes to recognize the true meaning of *surrender*— and to know oneself as the embodiment of it. That is the experience known as Oneness.

Now you can see that the exultation that accompanies the state of Divine Connectedness is not an end in itself. It simply is a reference point within the range of human experience. In identifying these sensations to oneself, one is able to remain clear as to their nature, and at the same time to perceive the fullness of the experience itself. There is nothing inherently *better*—or otherwise—in this form of experience. It is simply a level of perception that one has chosen to taste, a selection from the menu of Infinite Possibility.

There is no judgment implied as to the relative merits of this level of experience over another. And, there is no implication that human experience, in *whatever* form it may manifest, is inherently undesirable. Human experience is what it is—a foray into the arena of linear perception. No more and no less. There is no scale of value judgment governing it in any way.

You have come to the experience of humanness in order to avail yourself of the possibility of linear perception. The perception of a state of Divine connectedness is well within the scope of that range of experience. It is a level of experience accompanied by sensations of indescribable joy. And many who venture forth on the spiritual path content themselves to remain at this level, simply by virtue of the inherent pleasure to be experienced. These ones have journeyed to the heights of humanness—they have not *transcended* it.

Detachment from all *desire* includes the desire for Self-Realization

The quantum leap between those states of perception and Self-awareness *as* the embodiment of Oneness requires a total detachment from all *desire*. That includes the desire for the experience of Self-Realization. For, the Self is not something that can be experienced—it can only be *known*.

The embodiment of Isness cannot be felt. It cannot be described. It cannot be quantified. For, all these possibilities, within the scope of *experience,* are linear constructs. Oneness cannot be isolated out of a range of possibility—and said to be *This*, and thus, by definition, not *that*—when Oneness Is All of it.

Ultimately, there is the possibility to transcend the need for the comforting validation of the experience of *joy* as one's barometer of personal attainment within the arena of spiritual pursuit. For, evidence is not required when one *knows* oneself to Be Oneness. There is not the inclination to be able to point to *this* level of experience or *that* one to reassure oneself, inwardly, that one really *is* who one mentally understands oneself to Be. Self-Realization is not about understanding. It is about *Being*.

In this moment, we Are Oneness. The entire sense of Selfhood is absorbed into a single focal point of attention. There is no awareness whatsoever, within this consummate focus of attention, of who or what one identifies oneself to be. The immediacy of it precludes the possibility of any mentalized consideration of the nature of one's identity—or of anything at all. It is this level of abidance in the Nowness of this moment—this consummate Presence, this state of Beingness Itself—that we share in this moment. And it is for the possibility of *this moment*, against all odds, that you have chosen the experience of humanness.

33

Spring 2004
Rishikesh Revisited

I returned to Rishikesh in mid-April, driven north by the skyrocketing temperatures and by an inner pull to begin to bring the story to completion. Somehow I knew that the loose ends I had left unraveled there were part of the picture.

It was a picture that was crystallizing within me and coming to life before my very eyes. Everywhere I looked I saw an instant replay of the calamities I had created. And I laughed. It was amazing that the same scene could look so different. Where there had been confusion and aggravation, I now saw comedy—and celebration. Nothing had changed. And everything had changed. Again.

Rasha speaks:

Life comes full circle. Rishikesh hasn't changed in the year and a half I've been away. But, now I'm seeing it through different eyes. I'm not here seeking anything. I'm not here in hopes of connecting with a Guru, or a technique. I'm not here for yoga or a meditation course—the things this place is famous for. I'm simply here being myself, present in form and absolutely at peace.

I might have said, at one point, that I was hoping to connect with Oneness. But, now there is nowhere that I begin and Oneness ends. There is simply the experience of this moment, drawing breath through form and documenting impressions on a laptop. There is no need to analyze it, no need to try to dissect some sense of self-definition out of these perceptions. I Am—Here and Now—joyously. Simply That.

A year and a half ago, I was in a very different space, flitting in and out of connectedness. It was a time of understanding myself to Be Oneness intellectually, interspersed with moments of knowing myself to be Oneness experientially. It was a time of tasting that sense of Oneness constantly and then reverting to a sense of separation and abandonment at every turn.

In Rishikesh, life had served up an unending stream of confrontational experiences where my sense of inner balance could be thrown off-center. I succumbed to most of them. And I went away wondering where I had gone wrong—wondering what I was missing—questioning, over and over again, the validity of an experience that was indisputable.

In fact, nothing was missing. I had all the pieces of the puzzle, then as Now. I persisted in proving that to myself over and over again, only to reawaken, adrift in the seas of self-doubt. A journey must run its course, it seems. Eventually, I found myself safe and whole, on solid ground. No grandiose inner explosions, no fanfare, none of the trappings of triumph one might have expected. Just this blessed sense of well being and contented inner peace.

I had to come back to Rishikesh—back to the place where a fleeting, newborn sense of wholeness had so easily come undone to reaffirm the testing conditions and the symbolism all around me.

The people at the ashram are still as aloof as ever. But, now it doesn't bother me. They are as they are. And I am at peace with it. The sacred river Ganga is still cool and refreshing—and indescribably blessed. The surrounding hills still exude that timeless sense of tranquility. And the unending parade of pseudo-sadhus still prowl the walkways in search of a handout. Some things never change.

What has changed is how I perceive it. I feel no walls now. I bless these orange-clad brothers-in-spirit, staggering under the burden of their self-imposed austerities. I no longer cringe as they approach, dreading having to say "no" to an outstretched hand, yet again—thereby creating a parallel experience for myself. Now I find myself simply smiling a smile of inner-recognition. Amazingly enough, that smile is returned. None of them has asked me for so much as a rupee. Why should they? They are only mirrors. As is the world.

These so-called sadhus are helping me demonstrate, once again, that my own expectations set the stage for my experience. And in the mirror of every set of beseeching eyes—in each reflection of the timeless quest of a soul driven to connect with a taste of Divinity—I see myself, in retrospect.

I see that I have created this experience. I created this foray into spiritual awakening, and then, the forgetting that I had awakened, so I could experience that discovery over and over and over again.

I see that I am creating this vision of a world. All of it, in every moment. I am creating it in hopes of mirroring myself, and confronting a moment of Self-recognition. As are we all.

I see Oneness all around me now. I see the unity in the diversity. Not just intellectually, but actually. I recognize the common vision of this illusory, so-called reality as my own projection. And I know it to be co-created in tandem with All that is experiencing this diversity of self-perception in the Here and Now we call our world. I see it. I actually see it.

I am a minute piece of the puzzle. And, in the same breath, I Am All of it. Blessedly. I am a glimmer of Divine perspective, within the embrace of the collective Vision that is Oneness. Now, all that remains to be done with that Vision is to share it.

The days in Rishikesh were filled with imagery, symbolism that my heart continued to recognize as my own reflection. One morning, I sat in a beautiful garden, high on a hill above the din and the noise of the ashram. I'd escaped. There, the loudspeakers could not reach me. I was no longer tied, with my laptop, to the end of a power cord. I was no longer imprisoned in a cell in which I felt like I was suffocating in every way imaginable. Suddenly, I was free.

Only the song of the birds and the flight of the butterflies filled the air—air that was thick with the signs of an early summer. The mist hung heavy around the distant mountains, engulfing them in an ever-present haze. It was going to be a hot day, and it had only just begun.

I'd taken the laptop with me to the hilltop garden, bolstered by the extra battery I'd had the foresight to buy but never used. I realized that the freedom of the move to the garden was no more and no less than a choice. But, why hadn't I thought to make that choice before? For weeks, I'd endured the stifling heat and the noise in my little ashram room in resignation, gritting my teeth in the face of oppressive conditions, determined to make the best of it. The simple solution had been there all along—if only I'd been open to seeing it.

Now, in the hilltop garden, cloaked in the mists of nature, I could feel the Presence of Oneness everywhere, and Divine Grace engulfed my heart. Instantly, a smile of sweet contentment spread across my face, as I recognized that a *distraction*, whether pleasing or displeasing, was simply a possible choice, beckoning for attention. I saw the lesson. I could empower the distractions, or I could choose to sustain my focus. I can abide in my Divine connection anywhere, I reminded myself. I saw that the distractions were simply part of the training.

Oneness speaks:

Now it takes no more than a moment to recognize the lesson buried in the imagery that surrounds you. With your eyes opened in this way, you are able to make optimum choices and to minimize the discomfort that is also a possibility built into the illusory world.

All options are ever-present. It is you who create the experience you come to call your life. Suffering is optional, at all times. The possibility is equally present to experience the identical conditions without the experience of suffering. One can choose to focus on the heat and the sweat that rushes forth to meet it—or one can choose to perceive only the subtle breeze that cools the skin, at the same time. When one is absorbed in the sensations of the breeze, there is no awareness whatsoever of the heat. When one is absorbed in the perception of Oneness, one is not concerned with the heat or the breeze, but is fully surrendered to the joys of Divine Union.

Oneness speaks about desire and distraction

Here, there are no desires and no distractions, though the semblance of both may abound all around you. There is simply an array of illusory imagery. One may choose to empower these images with one's longing, or one may choose to remain the witness, and to note the scenery in passing. With the instilling of *desire* into the mix, one activates the alchemy of creation: one infuses the conceptual with the energy that initiates the process of manifestation; one takes a step from the detached stance of the witness and becomes wedded to one's perception of the illusory world.

Desire is the doorway to the embrace of the world of material illusion. When one puts forth one's intent to have a certain category of experience that is perceptible to the physical senses, one leaves the realm of the true reality—the world within which one truly dwells.

The secret to remaining "in the world yet not of the world" is to remain detached from any and all *desire* to have the illusory world be other than the way it *is* in the Now moment. It is as it is. You are present only as the witness. You are not invested in the outcome of any set of circumstances, one way or another. And change will be brought about in accordance with the variables of Creation all around you.

Your own contribution to that outcome is achieved by holding the highest vision, without attachment to it as an outcome manifested by virtue of the assertion of personal will. The vision becomes the *seed* of manifestation, placed within the embrace of the ethers, to be carried forth to fertile ground.

One does not need to plow the field, water it, cultivate it or tend it, in order to reap a fruitful harvest. One needs simply to bear the seed from which fruit may spring. All the other functions of manifestation are within the realm of the illusory world. That world is sufficiently equipped to tend to its own gardens and to bring forth the yield that has been sown, in accordance with the principles governing physical reality. Hold to your vision and walk with peaceful detachment within the world of the illusion. That is the recipe.

❀

Despite arriving in a serene, lovingly detached space, in no time at all, my return to Rishikesh brought with it an instant replay of the same issues and the same cast of characters I'd confronted two years before. Once again, during a visit with Soami Bodhananda, I collided with a philosophical analysis of the concept of *enlightenment* and a cross referencing of the definitive "moment" it happened in the lives of a number of saints and sages throughout history. Instinctively, I began once again to compare these stories to my own experience, which, in so many respects, had been different.

The realization began to sink in that this "I" might actually be nothing more than a compilation of impressions, filed neatly away in a living, breathing computer program I thought of as "myself." It was at that point that I became aware that my life had begun flashing before my eyes. Suddenly, people, places, and names long-forgotten came bounding back into view. I remember thinking that this is something that is said to happen when you're about to die.

I didn't have the sense that I was approaching death, not literally at any rate. Yet, the flashbacks were coming thick and fast. It was a graphically illustrated history of a character I'd spent a lifetime portraying. And those details formed the entire basis of the one I'd been accustomed to thinking of as "me." Now I couldn't relate to any of it. I had the stunning realization that every last reference point through which I had created this sense of personal identity had now dematerialized.

There was no longer a career or a profession. All had gone the way of the wind. There was no home base, and virtually no relatives. Aside from three highly independent, grown children, everyone in my immediate family had long since passed on. There wasn't even the continuity of a country where I felt I belonged or any possessions to speak of. I'd been flitting between Northern New Mexico and India for years, without actually settling in anywhere. And what little memorabilia remained from "my previous life" back east was scattered, by then, amongst several storage units a continent apart.

There wasn't even the continuity of a name that had any connection with anyone I had ever been. That label had changed so many times I was literally no longer recognizable. I was utterly rootless—a being cut loose from the entire history a lifetime had amassed. Yet, without any of those constructs of a linear identity, I recognized that "I" had remained fully intact. I saw that who I *was* had absolutely nothing to do with any of those things.

All the details that typically form the basis of self-definition had become all that I now was not. Who I *was*—who I Am—could not be defined through any form of linear experience. The understanding crystallized in a Realization that was exquisitely simple: the Essence of the Self within simply *Is*. Life had stripped me of all the trappings of my linear identity in order to illustrate the point. Oneness did not hesitate to seize the opportunity to help me bring the issue to completion.

⋙⋙

Oneness speaks:

Yours is not an intellectual quest. Yours is not a journey into the philosophical avenues of spiritual exploration. You are not here to debate the finer points of spirituality with those who have made a study of the technicalities of spiritual pursuit from ancient scripture. You are not here to analyze, dissect, cross-reference or in any other way engage in a comparative discussion of the experience of Self-Realization. You are here simply to present your own teachings and to share your own *experience* of it.

Your attainment is not one that is to be measured on a scale of linear velocity. It simply Is what it Is. And as it Is, your experience is magnificence itself. Nothing further is required in human form. And those who have made a quantitative analysis of such matters have only served to pose a sense of structure and limitation on the immeasurable.

Oneness speaks about the journey to God-Realization

There Are no definitive calibrations within which God-Realization may be measured and categorized. Such categorization stems purely from the quest of the *ego-self* of those who have strived, throughout history, for the attainment of what has come to be termed "enlightenment." These structures and delineations are man-made, based on an analysis of the actual experiences of those who have tasted Divine connectedness—primarily by those who have spent their lives in search of it.

Most of what has come to be considered *gospel* on the subject of enlightenment has been structured by those who have attempted to attain a mentalized grasp of what they did not know how to approach in any other way. God-Realization is not a mental process. It is a *surrendering* of heart and soul. It is a *relinquishing* of all the trappings of identity. It is an *embracing* of the Essence of Love itself that radiates from within the core Essence of *every* expression of Life— throughout All Creation.

When one has made the shift into God connectedness, there is no need to verify it—for it is unquestionable. There is no need to weigh it on a scale of attainment, relative to the experiences of others, for each sacred journey is unique. None is higher or lower than another. Each experience simply Is, and cannot labor under the limitations of language, and of linear expression, with any semblance of validity.

The Realization experiences of some are punctuated with dramatic visual phenomena. Others simply experience an indisputable *knowingness* of the attainment of Divine Presence, unaccompanied by changes in visual perception. What unites the experiences of all who have made the journey to God-Realization is the undeniable sense of *inner peace*, and the sublime sensations of *bliss* that accompany the attainment.

Oneness speaks about *expanding* the perception of Self-Realization

One is then able to escalate one's *perceptions* of that state of Beingness through the *focus of attention* in deep states of meditation. It is in those heightened states of Divine connectedness that one is able to merge one's Awareness of Self with the Absolute, of which one is a part, and to know oneSelf to *Be* That. In that state of consummate surrender, the Realized Self is absorbed into the Totality and ceases to perceive Itself at all. One simply Is.

These moments of ultimate surrender are not permanent states of Being. They are fleeting glimpses into the realm of Ultimate Reality. These are not moments of Awareness that one is expected to, or would aspire to sustain. For, the purpose of one's presence within the realm of physicality is not one's denial of physical experience. The purpose of one's journey into the labyrinths of linear perception is for the possibility that the culmination of that journey—the Realization of one's own Divine Essence—might be *experienced*.

The experiencer makes the perception of Self possible

It is only within the context of Self as *the experiencer* that the perception of Self as Divinity incarnate is possible. And those who protest that the perception of Self as *the experiencer* constitutes evidence of a linear focus of awareness are misguided. One's *sacred Essence* remains as the Absolute. And isolated glimpses of that supreme state of Isness are surely possible from within the confines of physical form. But, that state is not *sustainable* within the context of form—nor is it meant to be.

Those who seek to abide in the Absolute to the exclusion of all avenues of physical perception have denied themselves the ultimate gift in one's journey into physicality—the incomparable, indescribable *experience* of it. The only aspect of self that would aspire to opt out of that possibility is the linear ego-self that would seek to categorize the embracing of Divinity as an *attainment* within the context of physicality, rather than simply an experiential affirmation of what one Is. One cannot *attain* what one already Is. One can only know oneself to *Be* That.

On another occasion, Oneness offered a spontaneous, in-depth treatise on certain profound metaphysical concepts that had been silently weighing on my mind.

In these teachings, Oneness clarified the subtleties of meaning on the true nature of *perception* and *experience,* and helped me to fine-tune my own understanding of what they are—and what they are *not*—once and for all. In this discourse, Oneness went on to address certain questions I'd never officially broached, regarding the influence of the formless consciousness in our midst upon the creation of the collective circumstances we think of as our world.

Oneness speaks about the *illusion* of perception and experience
Oneness speaks:

This is Oneness. This is the Unity of which we have spoken, both in states of connectedness and at times when you perceived yourself to be separate from This. In this moment there is no question of what has transpired. There is simply Presence, experiencing itself. The thoughts flow unimpeded now, concept materializing as written communication through the vehicle of form.

In fact, there *is* no form, just as there is no communication. For, with whom would that communication transpire? The entire realm of speculation and description is no more than an aspect of Self, in the guise of *blindedness*, playing out a role in order to document *perception,* and in so doing, manifesting the illusion of *experience*. In truth however, there is no *perception*—just as there is no *experience*. These are simply constructs, devices that have been fashioned in order to document a particular, infinitesimal aspect of what Is.

Your world is no more than an *illustration*, a means of reflecting the collective of Divine fragmentation that comprises it. The illustration is there before you, vivid in its detailed symbolism, depicting for all that behold it the state of beingness of the *composite* of the consciousness present, both form and formless.

The composition of the composite *reflection* we think of as our world

There are infinite layers of Presence that comprise what you consider to be your reality. Each adds its own unique signature to the imagery that documents the collective vision. Much of that co-creative Presence is imperceptible to consciousness that experiences itself through the physical senses. But, the contribution of those levels of Presence is no less than your own. The world of physical illusion is an illustration of what Is. It is not simply a reflection of the vibrational contributions of those whose presence can be seen.

The world of the formless is a viable part of what you consider to be your world. There are countless levels of consciousness present, largely unbeknownst to you, which make their own contribution to the collective vision, and contribute their vote by virtue of their very presence, to the verdict you perceive as *experience*. They, in turn, are influenced in their own levels of self-perception, by the presence of *every* aspect of the world of the seen. And so the balance is maintained, co-creating conditions with which all are left to contend.

This level of reflection and re-reflection has sustained itself in a holding pattern since time immemorial. Certain aspects of individualized consciousness have managed to wrench themselves free of the grasp of these constraints and dwell freely amongst you. These ones, both in form and formless, have transcended the system of cause and effect that governs the realm of physicality. These ones, who are perceptible to some and at the same time imperceptible to others, bridge the many worlds that comprise all that you perceive—and much that you cannot. All of it is Present in the Here and Now of your world.

The Divine realms are not situated in some lofty location, accessible only by relinquishing physical form. They are right here. Likewise, the realities characterized by suffering and retribution are no further away than where you are in this moment. You simply are unable to perceive them.

Oneness speaks of the melding of form and formlessness that manifests as our world

The worlds of form and formlessness are intermeshed, one within the other, in an expansive structure of co-creation that is self-perpetuating. The shifts in awareness presently characteristic of this crossroads in time and space are not limited to the world of the measurable. The impetus to ride the wave of vibrational acceleration is not reserved for the incarnate consciousness that counts itself as present amongst you. An equally significant contribution to the composition of the collective is made, in every ongoing moment, by the presence of the unseen consciousness that populates your world.

The collective reflection, of which you are each a part, is undergoing a radical transformation, not simply because certain numbers of beings here are suddenly in the throes of spiritual awakening. The identical impetus to shifts in self-perception are experienced across barriers of time and space that separate the worlds within your world. This consciousness, which is *earthbound*, has an equal stake in the dramas you co-create collectively and an equal responsibility for the creation of those outcomes.

The world unseen is not at all unseen, in terms of the impact of its presence on the realm of the material. You can see the reflection of the contribution of all life forms—both incarnate and discarnate—in every vista that meets the eye.

You can begin to calculate the complexity of the transformation taking place in response to the intense acceleration of the energies that comprise all that you perceive, and to recognize the magnitude of these changes.

How shifting a collective mindset of *righteousness* to one of *allowance* can heal our world

The governments and hierarchies of power that attempt to contend with the colossal events that manifest as a reflection of the massive shifts in energy amongst the population at large are largely unaware of the true nature of these upheavals. The residual density with which all contend in these times makes a profound impact on the manifestation of so-called "natural" worldly disasters and other incidents of global crisis. The prescription for the healing of these conditions of imbalance lies in the ever-present opportunity to transcend a mindset of *righteousness* in deference to one of *allowance*.

The conditions with which all contend in these times are a reflection of a vast matrix of vibrational influence. Each being who responds with passion and indignation to a set of illusory variables creates a ripple effect vibrationally, that is imbibed and reflected back upon the whole, multifold. Each being who feels powerless in a world that appears to be out of control makes a contribution to the mind-set of victim-consciousness that prevails and helps to create more of the same.

Were each and every being who experiences self-perception in this Here and Now to consider the possibility that he is the creator of everything experienced by the collective, every measured gesture might be weighed against the possibility of meeting its very reflection head on. In fact, that level of virtually instant replay of cause and consequence is exactly what happens, though most are totally unaware of it.

In the weeks that followed, I put the classical definitions of *enlightenment* to rest and grew comfortable with the realization that my own experience had been just that—my own experience. Yet, inevitably, "Rishikesh revisited" brought with it an instant replay of the dilemma that had continued to haunt me for most of the time I'd been away—the proverbial "inner explosion" that Soami Bodhananda had impressed upon me two years earlier. For, despite all the extraordinary happenings that *had* taken place on my spiritual journey, there remained the elusive *inner explosion* that hung over my head as imagined evidence that I had fallen short of the mark.

This piece of the puzzle that persisted in eluding me was the one that never seemed to fit. What had I missed? Where had I gone wrong? I continued to wonder. As I began to dig deeper, I saw that an "inner explosion" was not the whole issue. It was the tip of the iceberg. The mystery was symbolic of a far broader theme, one that had gone on to color the entire journey. For, despite the repeated guidance of Oneness to the contrary, I tended to defer to the *consensus wisdom* I encountered everywhere I went. The trouble was that everyone was telling me something different. And despite my actual *experience* of Oneness, there was still a piece of me somewhere, pacing the back roads of consciousness, that had only grown more and more confused.

In a search for clues, I went back to the source and confronted Soami Bodhananda about precisely what was meant by "inner explosion." All this time, I had interpreted the beautifully written literary piece he'd composed, entitled "Sudden Enlightenment"—and the "inner explosion" it described— literally. I'd presumed the phrase referred to a *visual* phenomenon, one that was totally beyond imagination. I'd made myself nearly crazy stalking that imaginary experience for two years! And I told him so.

He just looked at me with an incredulous expression and laughed out loud. Apparently, that wasn't it at all. The explosion that was referred to was an "explosion of ideas," he explained. I was stunned. After all that! I choked back the tears that welled up in disbelief. The moment was a muddled concoction of joy and indignation. The sense of relief that I hadn't fallen on my face after all was overwhelming. At the same time, I was incensed that I had been led on a spiritual wild-goose chase that, essentially, took me right back to where I started—to my own magnificent experience of Oneness.

Eager to clarify the misunderstanding, Soami Bodhananda insisted that I follow him, right then and there, to a bookshop on the other side of the

Ganga. So, off we marched at the height of "rush hour." It was a comic sight: an aging swami-on-a-mission leading the way, and a baffled American mystic, holding steady at 20 paces behind, fighting to keep up with him as we power-walked across the gusty Ram Jhula footbridge, dodging motorbikes, beggars, and cows, and wove our way down the other side of the river.

Without pausing for formalities he burst into the bookshop and in seconds retrieved his prize. It was a vintage copy of a book of Osho's very early talks. Flipping quickly through the pages, Soami Bodhananda zeroed in on the passage in question and tapped his finger matter of factly on it. "Study this!" he commanded, in his most authoritative tone. My eyes widened as I read. There, laid out in simple, direct language, was a recounting of a moment of illumination. Osho's moment of illumination. It spoke about an "explosion" of ideas—which he referred to as an "inner explosion." So *that* was it, I thought. It wasn't a *visual* explosion at all. It was an all-encompassing shift in *consciousness*. Pure and simple.

Mystery solved. Soami Bodhananda's own treatise on the subject, "Sudden Enlightenment," which was an elaborate description of his own moment of Self-Realization, had left much to the imagination of the reader. And left to *my* own devices, I had totally misinterpreted his exquisitely gilded, literary description. The lesson was poignant—and unforgettable. For, there truly *are* no words that can touch the experience of Oneness. I knew that. And when we attempt to capture the inexpressible with language, something irreplaceable gets lost in the translation.

At best, we can attempt to describe the indescribable. And, in so doing, we can only hope that those who are trying their best to imagine what that experience might have been like for *us* will come away with a clear picture that doesn't tie the hands of their *own* experiences. It was a magnificent illustration—delivered at the very moment I was piecing together my own story—of the fine line that is walked by those who attempt, with the best of intentions, to capture the "inner explosion" of the touch of Oneness, in words. Oneness elaborated the next day.

Oneness speaks:

This is Oneness. We are united once more in this bond of Love Eternal. That is what this adventure is all about. It is not a question of attainment. It is not a matter of a mentalized grasp of a process. It is not about understanding anything at all. It is a foray into the arena of the *experiential*, at the highest level.

Only Love exists

Love is the all encompassing Essence of All That Is. Love is what you have come here to experience—and to embody—with full conscious awareness of it. This is who and what you Are. This is what you have come into form to demonstrate. This is your life's mission, your purpose, the underlying reason you have chosen to experience yourself in physical form in this way. All else is secondary to your recognition of this. For, all else is nonexistent. Only Love exists.

The mythical "inner explosion"—revisited

You have cleared your mind now of the concerns you have carried for so long regarding the teachings of Bodhananda. And you have come away with an understanding of what was being portrayed with the terminology that had been used. The phrase "inner explosion" was taken literally by you to signify a visual *phenomenon*. Now you see that this is not at all the meaning that was intended.

You now have a graphic model before you of a *literary* piece that represents the sincere sentiments of the author, yet is very much open to interpretation. What was experienced, and what has been conveyed and implied, are not in balance. And you have demonstrated to yourself the pitfalls, for the reader, of gilding a communication stylistically, beyond the point that the meaning is recognizable.

Art is art. Spiritual teachings are spiritual teachings. And oftentimes simplicity is the purer discipline. It will serve you well, when tempted to embellish upon what is essentially magnificent in its own right, to remember this moment. For, you have created for yourself a template, in this foray into confusion, that will serve you well in the times to come. None of this has been random. The lesson was a powerful one on many, many levels.

You have recognized the illustration of your tendency to attempt to augment your process with *effort*. You have noted your inclination to judge your own experience and to construct a linear system of *merit* in which to attempt to fit it. This experience of Self-Realization is not one that is quantifiable. What you are turning to, as reference points, are simply descriptions of *phenomena*. The phenomenon is not the experience.

The experience cannot be described. One can only attempt to put words to it. And in so doing, one constricts the pure essence of the experience itself and translates it into dualistic terms that a linear mind might be inclined to try to grasp. The journey into the depths of your very own Divine Essence is not one that requires the comprehension of others. They have the opportunity of their own journeys, and the experiential knowingness that is forthcoming, wordlessly, from having gone the distance.

You are not here to convince anyone of anything. You are not here to impress anyone with your level of attainment. You are simply here to Be who you Are. And to teach others, by example, what is possible within the sanctity of their *own* Divine connections.

What you have come to this experience to taste and to share is the sweetness of this Love. This is the innocence with which we began, when there was no timetable and no scale of attainment against which to measure your own experience. This is what was shared. And this is what has endured.

You have made the journey now. You can look back over the terrain that was traversed and see the rationale for every pitfall that was strategically placed in your path. You can see where the tendency to seek *validation* from others surfaced as a recurring theme that you identified so long ago, and over which you continued to stumble.

Deferring to your own *experience* rather than to the consensus wisdom of others

You can see where you deferred to the so-called consensus wisdom at hand to delineate for you what was and was not so about your own experience. Ultimately, one turns away from the so-called *gospel* based on the word of others and turns to what one knows, within one's very own depths to be so. It was *this* lesson that was sought experientially, so that it might be etched indelibly upon your consciousness.

What others have or have not experienced is only valuable as a backdrop to your *own* experience—a means of adding definition and contrast. The experiences of others cannot provide anything other than a framework for one's own unique journey. For, as we have said so many times, no two journeys are alike. Each is unique.

The *phenomena* accompanying the heights of spiritual exultation are moments beheld by your eyes only. No one else will ever see it, or experience it. At best, they may try to imagine what your Divine moment might have been like for you. And in sharing what you choose to share, you will provide those who journey by your side with an *illustration*—not a *standard* against which to measure their own experiences of the indescribable.

You have completed a major chapter in your life story now. Let the lesson stand. Live with these insights for a little time now. And integrate what you have come to this crossroad to attain. You have culled the pearl from its shell now, with the help of those who have played out this drama with you.

The *impact* of this masterpiece of experiential imagery could never have been attained, had it not been for the agonies of having lived through it. This is not a level of understanding that is possible to impart in theory. It is necessary for one to feel the intensity of all that was stimulated to the surface, in order for the lesson to be recognized and embraced. The performance of this particular drama was executed to perfection. And you can see that in the highest interests of all concerned, it could not have unfolded in any other way.

34

Summer 2004
New Mexico and Colorado
Putting the Teachings to the Test

T his time, my transition back through the time-warp that seemed to exist between India and the US was relatively smooth and uneventful. Braced as I was for being bowled over by the usual sense of disorientation and culture shock, I arrived with what felt like both feet on the ground. Instead of being overwhelmed by logistics and by having to hit the ground running in a world where I'd left all frames of reference in another place in time—now, it all seemed very matter-of-fact. Clearly, Oneness was along for the ride, as I embarked on a journey though everyday life, American style.

After several wonderful weeks visiting with family in Pennsylvania, my heart knew it was time to head west. Returning to the Southwest I'd grown to love felt like the natural next step, and a sense of knowingness guided me sure-footedly back to the remote stretches of mountain-studded high desert that had come to feel so much like home. It would be a time of being absolutely footloose, living on the wind—and in the moment.

I made no plans. All that had been scheduled were several open-ended months, set aside for living each day as it comes. My trusty, old white van, "Vanessa," now outfitted with a nice oriental rug, a colorful patchwork quilt, and a few other homey touches, would provide the continuity of "roots" for months to come. An exhilarating sense of adventure filled me and drew me like a homing pigeon through the familiar, winding back roads of northern New Mexico, and on toward the great unknown: the majestic Rocky Mountains of Colorado.

Initially, Taos, New Mexico drew me like a magnet and became my first destination. As always, summer in New Mexico was heavenly and I reveled in the cool morning breezes wafting in through the open doors of the van, as I sat with my laptop, watching the leafy branches outside swaying against a brilliant, cobalt-blue, cloudless sky. I noticed that now there was a sense of *peace* I hadn't remembered encountering in Taos before. In the very same instant an unspoken understanding emerged from within. "Perhaps peace is not about a place at all," I reflected. "Perhaps peace is within *me*." What a concept.

The Neem Karoli Baba Ashram, with its magnificent white marble *murti* of the monkey god, Hanuman, beckoned to me, and I began spending a few hours there every day in deep meditation and prayer. As I did, I began experiencing a powerful sense of connectedness with the Divine Presence that is honored there. I knew that now I was fully established in my own Presence as Oneness. Yet, there was a level of vibrational intensity and a sense of Presence that seemed to add another layer to the experience. Now, it seemed like there was no separation between that Divine Presence and the Oneness I experienced as *myself*.

Spontaneously, a *darshan* began, within the depths of my own being, with the Presence that, over the years, I'd come to recognize as Hanuman. In silence, a profound teaching was presented regarding the concept of "devotion." Hanuman addressed the dilemma of knowing oneself to *Be*— and simultaneously *worshiping*—the Divine. It was a fascinating concept that addressed the very heart of some of the issues that had begun to nudge me from within. I returned the following day with a pen and a notebook, and asked that the teaching be repeated so I could write it down.

The dilemma of *devotion* from the perspective of the Realized Self
Hanuman speaks:
This morning, we spoke with you of the nature of the process of embodying these energies. A few years ago, we also spoke of this. At the time you were confused by the information and were concerned that it constituted a conflict with the work you were doing with Oneness.

You were just beginning to come to terms, then, with the idea of embodying Oneness. When we told you that you would walk in the fullness of *these* energies, you began to question your own ability to receive this information with accuracy. Now, with the passage of time, and having had the *experience* of it, it is clear to you that this information is accurate and that the experience is authentic.

You have tasted a deep level of connectedness today. You were able, quite naturally, to shift into your own Divine presence as Oneness and to recognize the doorway it offers within you to a connection with this Presence. You can see that the one experience does not cancel out the possibility of the other, but rather is the element that makes it possible.

You have prayed with the deep longing of heart to be of service to the Eternal Beloved, whom you identify as "Oneness." It is that level of consummate *devotion* that you will embody through *this* Presence. For, in this way, you are able to transcend the dilemma of *Being* and simultaneously *worshiping* the Beloved. The question arises, once one recognizes oneself to *Be* Oneness, that there is no longer the identity of separation required for the concept of *devotion* as you understand it to be.

The role the Self plays in the embodiment of a Divine Presence

In order for devotion to be expressed, it requires the Presence of an *object* of that devotion. When one knows oneself to embody the subject and the object simultaneously, the concept of *the devotee* becomes obscured. By shifting the focus of one's own Self-perception to the simultaneous embodiment of a Divine Presence, one is able to relinquish the limitation of Self-identification and to recognize oneself to Be part and parcel of an Infinite, Universal Presence.

By embodying one's own Divine Presence as Oneness—the aspect of Divinity with individual identity—one is able to enter the realm of sacred experience where the *ultimate* experience of devotion is possible. It is for this possibility that you have chosen, at the highest level, to embody *this* Presence in form. For, your devotion is not limited to the expression of Oneness that you have now come to embody. You Are *the devotee* in the full embrace of Self-recognition. You have shifted your focus to the limitless Presence. The gateway to the fullness of that connection is through the *pathways of heart*, available to those who have Realized the Self.

Here, the principles you began to explore and apply as a being with linear focus are carried to their ultimate level of expression. Initially, one shifts one's awareness as an insular, linear identity to that of a linear identity with an expanded scope of perception. The multidimensional aspects of that identity are sequentially embraced and known as expressions of one's own self. One recognizes the momentum of the journey as one is carried to heightened levels of experiential possibility within the context of one's own personal identity.

That awareness *expands* to encompass the fullness of that identity and one comes to know oneself to be the *individualized* expression of Divinity that is, indeed, one's *true* nature.

Self-Realization is only the beginning

Delving deeply into the heart of that Presence, one comes to recognize parallel aspects of Divinity as that which one knows *oneself* to Be. One is able to choose, with the focus of one's intent through the pathway of heart, to perceive the presence of a Divine soul and to know *oneself* to Be That, within the context of form. This is the next step on the journey. For, the experience you identify as Self-Realization is not at all the end of the story. It is but the beginning. Now those possibilities are before you.

We will be working together to strengthen this connection while you are here in this ashram. For, in the deepest sense of the word, you have come home. You have re-united with an ancient connection of heart, a reunion with your own sacred Essence. Much history has been shared in ancient times as an aspect of this Presence emerging into the fullness of Self-recognition. Now, the process has come full circle, as you place the piece of the puzzle embodied by your Presence into the fullness of a Higher Presence. Keep focused on this—and Be at Peace.

My days in Taos became an ongoing exercise in contrast and contradiction. The ashram, with its eclectic cast of characters, was a virtual training ground in the art of diplomacy and detachment. For me, it was a skill that did not come easily. Inadvertently, I'd often find myself colliding head on with caustic individuals and inane circumstances, when all I'd wanted in coming there was the sublime sense of peace and the exalted connectedness that was so readily forthcoming within the temple.

I was soon to discover that there was no wasted motion on this journey. Everything, it seems, was purposeful. All obstacles were there, strategically placed at some higher level, and calculated to push my buttons and put my understandings to the test. It felt like I had succumbed to most of them. More than a little discouraged over any number of ongoing situations, and overwhelmed with the writing project, I retreated, disheartened, to my connection with Oneness.

The realization that came so naturally, within an instant, was astonishing. I watched my very own perceptions of the same ongoing scenarios totally transform, as I shifted the focus of my awareness from a myopic vision of the material world to the limitlessness of my connection with Oneness. The contrast in my perception of the exact same circumstances was like night and day. It was as though I had literally become somebody else.

Oneness addressed all my mundane concerns in the teachings that followed. Yet, the deeper issues underlying much of that imagery, which had gone unexpressed, had not gone unnoticed by Oneness. The question of the very nature of *experience* itself had continued to smolder beneath the surface of my awareness, a carry-over from the episodes of philosophical confrontation and verbal intimidation I'd been subjected to in Tiruvannamalai. Oneness went right to the heart of the issue and addressed what had gone unspoken.

❧

Rasha speaks:

Oneness, I began this morning as a lost, forlorn little person, seated before an altar, feeling helpless and abandoned in an alien world. As I began my prayers, a few tears trickled down my cheeks, and I was consumed with the sense that I had totally failed you. That I, Rasha, had totally failed you, Oneness. That there was, indeed, a separation between the two.

Any number of situations were a mess. I was struggling with the writing. And I had the sense that I was somehow going under with all of it. It was clear that I cannot do this alone. I prayed for Divine assistance with all my heart.

In the moments of prayer, a sense of absolute surrender washed over me. And in the breath of an instant, the sadness was gone. The sense of personal presence I had experienced as myself shifted to one of centeredness and well being. It is that sense of balanced completeness that permeates my being in this moment.

The shift happened with full conscious awareness of it—as if I was actually watching as an aspect of myself quite literally vanished from view and another aspect of my own self emerged in its place. All of the perceptions, the reflections, the entire emotional "bubble" that had risen to the surface and stimulated tears were no longer there. I recognized that, once again, I was watching the world through the eyes of Oneness—and that the Rasha identity that awoke this morning in this body had become absorbed into the embrace of That.

It is with that sense of well being that these words are being documented. I see that I, as "the experiencer," encompass the full spectrum of possibility within the scope of this identity. The source of these thoughts is undoubtedly a composite consciousness that comprises who I am, within the embrace of that Oneness. There seem to be multiple levels of awareness here, experienced simultaneously, one filtering into the next—and it is all me. In this moment, Oneness is presiding in the body, documenting all of this. Amazing!

I close my eyes and waves of bliss wash over me. How easy it is to forget the delights of connectedness when one is blinded by the details of the illusory world. I see now that those details are simply a perspective. I see that I am able to choose amongst multiple perspectives. There is not simply one vantage point available here. I am viewing the identical circumstances now, without any of the pangs of panic and remorse that clouded my heart only moments ago. The circumstances have not changed. What has changed is the way I am choosing to view them.

Now I see a brilliant, sunny morning from a window overlooking the mesa of Taos, New Mexico. The little sleeping loft, in the cottage where I sit so very comfortably, is cozy and bright. My beloved sacred objects, the crystal Deities, the photographs that touch my heart, smile at me in the glow of the sacred flame, flickering on the little holy altar beside me.

I am so far away from anything familiar—anything that might be considered to be home, in the physical sense—and in the same breath, that sense of home is right here.

Home is this inner glow, symbolized by the flame on the altar, and I carry it with me. Home is always right here, not determined by the location of this form, but by the Divine connectedness within that has no relation whatsoever to where I happen to be.

My circumstances are what they are. None of that has changed. What has changed is the inner glow that permeates my awareness, telling me that despite evidence to the contrary, all is well with my world.

Oneness speaks:

The connection deepens now, as we allow even *that* elevated perspective to blend into the Totality that is Oneness. The breaths come slow and deep. And the inner glow grows as the Light effulgence within expands and becomes the Totality of who we know ourSelf to Be. We *Are* that expanded Presence, *experiencing* ourSelf now, in form.

The circumstances of the material world are what they are for this moment. The logistics of all of it will resolve itself in the fullness of time. There is no need for worry or panic because these situations have not resolved themselves yet. This time is for introspection and for a deepening of the *inner* connection that will open the pathways of Divine Presence. This time is to be spent in the Stillness.

The nature of *experience* and the *experiencer* who perceives it

These words are being documented for the benefit of the one who will resume being the Presence in form and embody this identity. It is not her *failing* to experience herself. This is as it is meant to be. For, the *Self* that is experienced is not a fragmented relic of the past. It is a *composite* Presence—the fullness of a linear identity that serves as the foundation for the experience of Oneness.

The perception of the one is not possible without the perception of the other. For, who We Are is not one Presence to the exclusion of another. We are the fullness of the overlapping layers of awareness that constitute the Presence you have come to perceive as Oneness. We are that Totality, *experiencing* Itself.

This—is Oneness. Now, the full magnitude of your true identity engulfs your senses. Now, the expanded state of your Presence as Oneness permeates all that you perceive yourself to be. There are sensations, to be sure. The state of connectedness at these heightened levels is not without sensation. There surely *is* an *experiencer* present—one who is capable of translating perception into the context of experience. And that *experiencer* is no less the exalted Presence of Oneness, by virtue of the fact that perception is taking place. For, this is the nature of physical experience within the context of form.

It is for the possibility of this phenomenon of physical *perception* that you have chosen to experience yourself in form. It surely is not evidence of a spiritual shortcoming on your part. Those who would have you believe that the presence of physical perception constitutes evidence of *separation* from Oneness—are simply misguided. Nothing could be further from the truth.

Oneness is not defined by the absence of sensation. Oneness is *not* relegated to the realm of the void—to a state of Beingness characterized by pure *Awareness*, to the exclusion of all else. Oneness surely is to be found everywhere—and *to be experienced* as Oneness. That is the nature of the journey.

The physical manifestation of the world you consider to be your reality may well be an *illusion*, technically speaking—in that you have come to understand that you are creating *every* nuance of it, both individually and collectively. Yet, the very fiber of that manifestation is no more and no less than the Essence of Divine Presence. How could it be otherwise?

Self-Realization does not preclude the possibility of *experience*

Your very own identity is no more and no less than Divine Presence. It cannot be otherwise. Humankind has simply been unaware of it. But, that does not make it less a fact. Your perception of Self as the heightened expression of awareness you have come to identify as Oneness does not serve to exclude that *experience* from the realm you have come to understand as Self-Realization. It simply frames that experience for you in such a way that you are able to *perceive* it—and to *know* it—by virtue of the fact of that very *experience*.

Your form and the experiential possibilities it provides for you make possible the entire journey of spiritual awakening. You do not relinquish the experiential at the culmination of that journey. You retain the full scope of those capabilities—expanded exponentially. It is for the possibility of the exalted levels of this range of perception that you have chosen to experience yourself in physical form—for the possibility that you might know yourself to *Be* Oneness, having had the irrefutable *experience* of it.

Continuing to experience thoughts and feelings as the embodiment of Oneness

One is not expected, at the culmination of this journey, to relinquish the possibility of perception while retaining physical form. One is not expected to dwell, eternally feelingless and devoid of all thought. There will still be thought. There will still be feelings. Yet, these capacities will be tempered and experienced in the Eternal *Now*.

Feelings will not be affected and amplified by the history that may have gone before. For, at this stage, the emotional baggage with which one came into this lifetime will have been released. Thoughts are very much present. Yet, now they do not emanate from the arena of *mind*—a construct that is rooted in reflections on the past and projections into an undetermined future. Now, the thoughts that present themselves for your consideration are contained within the Now moment that stimulate them into the forefront of your awareness. Thoughts are the manifestation of observation, on the part of an aspect of Self-awareness that experiences itself as *the witness*.

Oneness speaks about *the witness* and the experience of *Nowness*

This very *Nowness* of experience is what characterizes the state of the Realized soul. For, at this state of Self-perception, Oneness has stepped forth in the fullness of individual identity, to provide the possibility of an exalted *experience* of physical perception. It is for the possibility of this very experience that you have chosen this incarnation.

Rejoice in your ability to feel and to experience the wonders of this physical world of perception. This is the gift with which you have graced yourself in this lifetime. Those perceptions are not the evidence of having fallen short as a spiritually focused being. Those perceptions are evidence of having made the journey—evidence on which your *knowingness* of your Presence as Oneness rests Eternally.

My visits with the Hanuman consciousness were many during my six weeks in Taos. And the comfort of that extraordinary Divine Presence embraced me with loving support that went way beyond the words of wisdom spoken. Integrating that profound guidance, I'd learned to float within the daily turmoil that seemed to surface, over one thing or another, at the ashram. And my attention became more firmly centered upon the world within, where it seemed I could now retreat, at will.

Saying goodbye to Taos had never been easy, for some reason. There was a timeless connection I'd always felt there that could not be explained by anything remotely logical. I went to the cozy little temple after sunset and sat down before the altar with its magnificent marble figure of Hanuman. There, I surrendered into the Stillness, as that awesome Divine Presence engulfed my senses and my pen scribbled down the pages of loving guidance that pulled the experience of those weeks together, in summary.

Hanuman speaks:
These will be the last words for now. Your time here has drawn to a close. Soon you will move on from this place, taking with you a wealth of impressions and lessons learned. Many of the interactions here were caustic and caused you to consider your own agenda and the impression you make on others.

You have demonstrated to yourself that it is not important to be "right" if that stance promotes discord. Far better to walk away in the sanctity of your own Divine Presence than to engage in battle with ones who do not resonate with you. You have demonstrated to yourself the possibility of retreating into the sanctity of your inner connection—the sacred space, eternally Present, that awaits you—when there is distraction at hand.

The very concept of *distraction* and *disturbance* is based in the external world of illusion. Within, there is nothing but harmony, peace and Love. The disturbance you encountered repeatedly here served to drive you to that place of inner peace. It was very much part of the program that certain individuals "ran their routine" and ruffled your fur. These episodes were your invitation to demonstrate these principles to yourself—and to transcend the illusion of victimization. There are no victims who do not choose to experience the circumstances they encounter in that way.

There is Divine purpose in every obstacle found on your path now. There are no random occurrences. You came to this temple, seeking connectedness and the experience of the exalted energies you imbibe so eagerly. Sometimes, the connection is not immediately forthcoming and you wonder, helplessly, why the blessed state eludes you. In those moments, be aware that you are attempting to manifest a Divine connection through a focus *external* to your own Source.

A Divine connection is sourced from within

What you seek is not on a *tucket* or an altar. It is not housed in a photograph or hidden in the inner recesses of a *murti*. The Divine Essence that is sought is your very *own* Divinity. Your focus on your own joy is the doorway that is sought—not in the beseeching of a Guru or a Deity perceived to be external to that.

This state of Grace that is now so readily available to you is one that is manifested automatically when you cease *trying* and simply surrender to the state of Beingness that is your true nature. That is the lesson in the moments when you left here discouraged, convinced that you had managed to fail once more at what you presume is expected of you. We have no expectations of you beyond your highest vision for your own Self. We are simply Present, awaiting your arrival at that doorway.

Our Presence is timeless. There is no agenda. There is no timetable. There are no requirements and no expectations. You are welcome to invoke this Presence with your own state of surrender, whenever you are moved to do so. And you are equally free to abstain. This is *your* script—this is *your* life. We are simply here as support, waiting in the wings of your awareness for your invitation. You need not be present in a Hanuman temple to reach the heights of connectedness you have experience here. For, we are here *within you*, at hand whenever you feel moved to reach inwards to touch, once again, this timeless sense of Presence.

You know, by now, that these conversations are far from the product of an overactive imagination. You transcribe, with not a moment's hesitation, thoughts that do not emanate from the realm of mind. In this moment, there *is* no mind. Its function has been suspended, along with the identity that presides over it.

We have no cause to interact with you at the level of mind. Our timeless connection is rooted in a far deeper place. It is that legacy that you will carry forth, in the form of these energies, in the fullness of time. Now you have the key. And it is yours to use—or not—as you see fit. A warm glow of inner recognition washes over your being in this moment. The time here is complete and your heart is calm and grounded in contentment.

The time has been good, rich in ways that were not anticipated, and powerful in ways that will not be easily forgotten. The Guru here (Neem Karoli Baba) has presided over these happenings, for he is ever-present within you as well. You have come here for his *darshan*. And you have partaken of it, largely in moments when you least suspected it. He has orchestrated this entire drama, so that you might walk forth from this time, enriched in the ways that really matter.

Real growth is never painless. It is in the peeling back of the habitual patterns and the presumptions that spiritual growth is possible. It would have been far too easy to provide you an *event-free* time here and spoon feed you with a daily dose of bliss to the exclusion of the opportunity for self-scrutiny. Now you see that all of it was purposeful, calculated to force you to confront your own humanness and to release the tendency toward reaction that is rooted in ego.

The art of remaining untouched by the seeming injustices of the material world

The levels of pain that were hinted at were your clue of what remains harbored within you. When that sense of *woundedness* is transcended in earnest, you will be able to confront circumstances such as these and see them for the symbolism that they truly represent. So, long as your "buttons" are able to be pushed by the seeming injustices of the material world, you will continue to perceive yourself as being at the effect of these situations. When you can ride through the storms that are an inevitable part of being manifest in physical form and know that you remain truly untouched by them, you will have arrived at a place where you can begin to *embody* a Divine Presence and to walk forth within the illusory world as That.

This is the work at hand. This is the reason things have seemed so difficult. This is the training you have cried out for as a soul. And this is what has been provided to strengthen you at the inner core of your being. For, this place is the one that remains untouched by the skirmishes and the confrontations. This place of inner sanctity is the one that is eternally free and clear of the debris left in the wake of life's disappointments. This place is the one untouched by pain—and by the illusion of a world devoid of Love. For, this place *is* Love.

Transcending the illusion of discord and provocation in a world of symbolism

It is your own very Essence that beckons to you: "come home." There, this timeless connection, and others with whom you share a bond of kindredness, await your imminent arrival. The trials will continue and they will be many. Now, for having weathered a few, and for having recognized the underlying symbolism they bear as their fruits, you can begin to sidestep some of the calculated provocation and to transcend the tendency to interpret literally what is, in truth, vivid symbolism.

Potentially, much adversity and pain will be brought to bear upon you. Your actual *experience* of those circumstances is the opportunity you have come to this moment in your unfoldment to create. This Love awaits you. The fullness of this Divine connection is the oasis, ever-Present, within the center of the cyclone that life may serve you. Do not run from the adversity in a direction that leaves you stranded and lost within the jungles of the illusory world. Walk calmly and sure-footedly to *this* place. For, We are Here, Eternally. No further away than your next breath. Hanuman

The summer of 2004 was rich in the imagery that the peaks and valleys of the breathtaking Rocky Mountains reflected back upon me. For two months I traversed the highways and byways of Colorado, taking in the awesome scenery and assimilating an inner process that seemed to draw on

those contrasts. From Crestone to Aspen, from Durango to Denver, from Pagosa Springs back through Cortez and across the New Mexico border, I crisscrossed my own inner landscape as I made my way through a parade of Expos and lecture evenings, where the teachings of Oneness sat side-by-side with the earrings I'd designed for Earthstar.

In some circles, the practical considerations that inspired this eclectic mix of identities is referred to as "chop wood and carry water." For me, the exercise of constantly switching roles, compounded with taking the sanctity of my Divine connection out into the world, began to cross my wires. I remembered all too well the insular existence I'd enjoyed in India, where I could commune with Oneness for hours on end in blessed solitude. Quite suddenly, I found I was off the map, waylaid on some figurative, nameless stretch of road where the inner and the outer worlds collide.

In this breathtaking mountainous terrain, I managed somehow to step back onto the inner roller-coaster. But now, the dips and swerves were not the gentle, forgiving inclines of a beginner's slope. I felt like I was losing ground at every turn. To make matters worse, I'd begun once again to feel exceptionally vulnerable to the fluctuations in vibration one encounters out in the world as a normal part of daily life, and became painfully aware of how my energies always seemed to plummet accordingly.

I started to bounce in and out of the perception of *separation*, which I attempted to rectify with a barrage of prayers and practices. The one thing that I'd overlooked—and had grossly neglected—was my alone-time with Oneness. Chasing here and there for weeks, focused on every possible variety of *doingness,* I simply hadn't made the time for Oneness. I'd become oblivious to the very thing that had thrown me off-balance. It was a powerful lesson.

Ultimately, I went home to my precious Divine connection. As always, Oneness was right there, patiently waiting.

❧

Oneness speaks:
Breathe deeply of these energies now and know that We Are Oneness. There is no separation, no Rasha who is separate from the Self she identifies as this *Presence.* We Are that Oneness in totality. No more and no less than the sum totality of all the aspects of the identity you have worn, like a garment, throughout the full multidimensionality of all that you Are.

We are *experiencing* that Oneness through the medium of physicality in this moment, *knowing* our Self and delighting in the evidence of that knowing. We are Divinity, fully made manifest—the *experiencer* and the *experience* in bonded Union.

This is the Essence of all that you Are. You are not other than This— even in those moments when you would doubt and question what in *this* moment is unquestionable. Even in those moments when you have chosen to forget the heights of exaltation to which you have journeyed, you Are not other than This.

Who you Are never changes—*separation* simply makes the state of Beingness imperceptible

The choice that may be made to perceive oneself in a state of *separation* does not invalidate this state of Beingness. It merely renders it invisible. And one is then able to drift back into the illusion of the *physical* state of beingness and to perceive *that* as that which one is. The Essence that is common to both states of being does not change. What changes are the levels of discernment that would render one's true nature imperceptible and enable it to fade into the background of one's awareness.

The false trappings of identity are then able to preside and to delude one into believing that the exalted state of Beingness is the transient state. The only permanence that enjoins All Life and provides a chain of continuity through the illusion of time and space is the Divine foundation underlying all of it. That is the Essence of who and what one truly *Is*. In this moment, We Are This together. We are the Essence of our own Divinity, expressed and experienced within the context of form. We are Oneness—none other than That.

There is no hidden agenda governing this identity. We have simply come to demonstrate what is possible, in order that others might embrace that possibility as experience. There is no mode of devotional expression that would bring this state into manifestation or render it null and void. All is determined by one's willingness to embrace the truth of one's state of Self-awareness, and to view the world of physical illusion through the lens of *that* state of Being.

All levels of perception are possibilities that can be called forth into manifestation

All levels of perception are viable possibilities. All can be called forth into manifestation. One is able to choose what one recognizes as experience, simply by virtue of how one chooses to perceive it. When one is in a state of focused awareness on one's Presence as Oneness, all else becomes a reflection of That. When one allows oneself to lapse into the illusion of separation, the identical circumstances take on the coloration of those levels of resonance and are perceived at a corresponding level of manifestation.

One's state of Self-awareness is the single factor that determines what is perceived as one's life. As we venture forth in this day, let us endeavor to hold that understanding in the forefront of our awareness. In so doing, let us observe the seemingly miraculous outcomes to the scenarios that present themselves. Let us demonstrate these principles to the aspects of self that are striving for resolution on any number of levels. And in so doing, let us draw those aspects of self still wandering the realms of self-doubt and disillusionment, of expectation and recrimination, of disappointment and disbelief—into the embrace of a perspective that is beyond question.

Evidence of *separation* is simply an invitation to experience your Self in *freedom*

In those moments, when the clouds of illusion and disillusionment converge to obscure this effulgence, know that who you *Are* has not ceased to Be. The connection to this exalted state is not lost. It has simply been put aside for a moment so that you might, once again, be steeped in the evidence of the illusion of *separation*—from which you might step forth and experience your Self in *freedom*.

The thrill of the *discovery* of the truth of your identity is the experience for which you have come. For, in the instant of Self-recognition is the irrefutable proof of what can never be proven—the indisputable knowledge of what can only be *known*.

That knowingness is one that is held within the sacred inner Self. It is not one that requires the consensus opinion of the collective consciousness in order to be affirmed. No one else need even have an inkling of it—and yet the truth is known, without question. You have this knowingness deep within you. It cannot be taken away.

Let the waves that crash upon the surface of linear awareness not catch you in their grasp. Know yourself to be of the Essence of the depths of this ocean—not merely the fleeting outline of a passing ripple. Let your *awareness* be ever-present in that sacred center, regardless of where your physical form might chance to experience itself.

Carry your Divine Presence into the illusory world by remaining equally Present in the sanctity of your inner world. Let your conscious awareness remain eternally focused on your inner Presence—not for a single moment to be *distracted* by the details of the mundane world—while experiencing yourself as being fully present within it. That is the state of *balance* in which you will begin to stabilize your sense of Self awareness.

Holding firm to all you know, in the face of evidence to the contrary

You can anticipate the continuation of challenges calculated to throw you off balance. These are testing conditions designed to strengthen your ability to hold your focus of awareness, within the physical world. Do not take these instances of difficulty and moments of discord as evidence that you have faltered. You have simply programmed in a sequence of opportunities to strengthen your skills in holding firm to all that you know, in face of evidence to the contrary.

This is the fortitude that will be needed in the times to come. You will reflect back upon these times of testing and understand fully why the intensity and duration of these conditions of adversity were a necessary part of your working up. You have taken much time and endured this sequence of adversity so that a sense of Divine Presence might be irrevocably established.

The gift inherent in the experience of Nowness

The totality of this identity is embodied in the Here and Now of this Presence. We Are Oneness in this moment. And the only thing that stands between the exalted perception of this moment and a moment yet to be determined is how one chooses to perceive oneself. That is the gift inherent in the experience of

Nowness—the crystalline moment culled from the realm of infinite possibility that characterizes the world of linear manifestation.

We are here to share in *this moment*—as we are here, enjoined in the experience of all the moments yet to come. For, We Are Oneness, united in a breath of Self-awareness. We are the Essence of All That Is, defined in an instant of Self-perception—captured for all Eternity in this very moment in time.

35

Fall 2004
Asheville, North Carolina
Life Comes Full Circle

———

By the time I reached Asheville, North Carolina, in early October 2004, Vanessa, my faithful old van, had pulled a U-Haul trailer over 1,600 miles, right across the heart of America. Asheville was slated to be an interim destination on the grueling six-day drive from Santa Fe to Pittsburgh. Little did I suspect that it would become a major turning point in my spiritual journey as well.

The trailer was an attempt to consolidate an eclectic assortment of belongings that I'd managed to scatter around the country—bins and boxes I'd squirreled away over the years as I'd continued to peel back layers of identity and shed the objects that gave them definition. I didn't feel any particular attachment to the odds and ends I was dragging behind me, but had responded to a sudden impulse to make some order out of them and unify it all under one roof.

As if to punctuate the point of the exercise, there'd been a phone call, out of the blue, just before leaving New Mexico, letting me know that my North Carolina storage unit—which contained what little was left of the "previous life" I'd abandoned in Asheville nearly nine years earlier—was now under two to three feet of muddy water. Two hurricanes that had hit the area back to back a few weeks earlier had saturated the ground with rain. As a result, an adjacent hillside had given way, delivering the full contents of the pond at its summit into the valley below, where the storage complex, and the lion's share of what little I still owned, had been stashed. The entire drama seemed like one very elaborate and graphic illustration. I just wasn't sure of what.

I was reminded that everything is symbolism. And, in that moment, having not yet surveyed the damage, I became aware that I was filled with dread. *Who* is filled with dread? I had to ask. Would Oneness be filled with dread, about this or anything else? I saw that this was clearly another test, a wake-up call for an aspect of self who had slipped back into automatic pilot, and an occasion to examine how that had happened. It was a chance to come to terms with the long-lost *feelings* I began to sense lurking beneath the surface. It was an opportunity to pinpoint the focus of my awareness and realign it with the perspective of Oneness.

I sensed that I'd come back to North Carolina to retrieve a piece of *myself* that had been left behind, a *fragment of identity* that somehow still lay hidden in the illusory rubble that awaited me. The pain of the loss that had taken place there nine years before had been so overwhelming, I simply hadn't been able to deal with it. I'd lost virtually everything I'd thought of as "mine"—my beautiful home, my car, my company, and my sense of professional identity—in a bankruptcy I'd resisted right up to the bitter end.

In the aftermath of that personal holocaust, I'd rejected the entire experience—along with the aspect of myself that had created it—as a way of preserving my sanity. I'd allowed my own awareness to gloss over the details of that time of destruction and not to actually *feel* the fullness of the pain and the loss. I'd rejected an aspect of *myself*, totally. And the sense of identity that remained was completely numb to the feelings that scenario had been calculated to deliver.

I had a sense that this was the reason for the feeling of dread at the prospect of opening the door to the storage unit. That storage unit represented everything I was unable to face in the moment that life, as I knew it, was annihilated. The solid ground on which my sense of *identity* had always rested had dematerialized right along with it. This was the major piece of the puzzle I'd been unwilling to face. This was the piece I was all too willing to sweep under the rug. This was the *death* I'd rejected in an attempt to conjure up a sense of *survival* to which I could cling.

I'd tried to flush the entire nightmare down the tube rather than actually experience it. Suddenly, I'd begun to feel some of the *emotions* associated with that experience: the sense of depletion, the sense of invalidation, the sense of defeat. The intensity of the original feelings had been modified—softened and dulled by time and distancing. But, the essence of the feelings remained intact.

Somehow I knew it was time to go back. It was time to open that door. It was time to discard what no longer could be carried forward, without despair, and to embrace what was timeless and had endured. It was time to give myself permission to come out of hiding and to integrate the piece of my own sacred self that had been so brutalized by a twist of fate.

I sensed that this aspect of self had become a key piece of my puzzle. This was the aspect of self that was unstoppable—the one who had crashed head-on into the end of a tunnel that was leading nowhere, and felt that she had come to the end of the line. There were clues to be discovered in this place, clues to be unearthed in the wreckage of the identity I'd left behind. Suddenly, the symbolism I'd abandoned was all around me. The time had come to retrieve her.

Rasha speaks:

Oneness, this has been a pretty dramatic and trying few weeks. During this time, I've illustrated for myself the antithesis of all I know myself to Be. I've only sporadically been in communication. I've made excuses. And I've allowed myself to slip steadily into the sense of a mental and emotional abyss, questioning everything, feeling helpless and depleted.

I have the sense of trudging dutifully forward, with all my strength, and at the same time backsliding with every step. I'm exhausted from the struggle and from the sense of futility of all of it. There seems to be no purpose to any of this, except perhaps to illustrate for myself that very futility. I know at a deeper level that all of this is symbolism. I've simply allowed myself to buy into it and to empower it.

It's amazing to see that this kind of experience is still possible, given the other end of the spectrum of experience that I've explored in such detail. I see that I've illustrated for myself that the full spectrum of possibility is still available and that the perspective through which I choose to view my circumstances is the opportunity at hand.

Now, as I write these words, I see that I have shifted my perspective once again, and that, in this moment, I am writing from the perspective of Oneness. The shift was so subtle that I cannot say where, in the previous paragraph, my focus ceased to rest on the one and came to rest on the other. At the same time, I see that the process was not an either/or, but rather an expansion, a sense of the one perspective encompassing the other.

In this moment, I am not experiencing the sense of dread that permeated my awareness only moments ago. What I am feeling is a matter-of-fact sense of detachment from the outcome of what awaits me in the storage unit. I see that the option of becoming morose about it is simply another choice on the menu.

From the perspective of this moment, which I sense is a melding of the Presence of Oneness and that of my own linear awareness, there is no emotional charge associated with any of this. I see that the vantage point at which I am viewing the same scenario has shifted totally to one of detached allowance.

I see that the opportunity that presents itself is simply the shuffling of the details of this illusion, and that the means for doing so have been provided. The choice to lace this experience with fear and dread is ever-present, but it is a choice I am not required to make. From this augmented perspective, the situation appears to be manageable.

Oneness, I know there is yet another level of connectedess where the perception of my linear awareness fades completely and there is only You. Let me relinquish whatever hold I may think I have on this sense of Presence now. I surrender. Come. Be here.

Suddenly, I feel the energies building in this moment, as my senses are engulfed in the experience I have come to identify as Oneness. My face is pulled into a sweet, irrepressible smile, and my heart is filled with an indescribable sense of joy and inner peace. How extraordinary this is. All worries and concerns have faded and begun to vanish. And with them, now, so have I.

Oneness speaks:

Let the fullness of these energies engulf your sense of Self now. There is no need to further define or illustrate this moment with conceptual detail. There is simply the sense of Presence now. There is simply a focus on this awareness of Self. There *is* no illusory world. There is only the cocoon of this moment—an encapsulated sense of consummate embrace in which all sense of separateness melts into the breath of surrender.

We are here now. We are *revealed* in the sense of Nowness that you have allowed to permeate the awareness of your sense of Being. We have not suddenly arrived at this state of connectedness, for we have never been apart. You have simply become adept at making the shift and relinquishing your hold on the linear perspective of your experience.

That perspective is no more valid or predominant, as a definitive statement of what is or is not so, than any other. It is simply a perspective that you have become conditioned to expect, out of sheer habit. It is a perspective to which you have been schooled to defer by the consensus wisdom that governs the realm of linear reality. Now you see that that particular perspective is no more valid than any other.

Attaining the perspective of the enlightened Master

The choices are all before you. And you are free to shift into any of an infinite number of vantage points through which you may view the experience at hand. This is the perspective of the enlightened Master. This is the sacred knowledge that you experience in this moment. This is the key to your liberation from the bondage to which you have subscribed so willingly. For, who you Are will remain unaffected by the circumstances presented by the linear world, regardless of what they may be.

The winds may howl and swirl around you—and well they might in the times to come. But, your sense of who and what you know yourself to Be will remain untouched. All the rest is simply detail, window dressing, the scenery you have conjured up to illustrate, for your own viewing, the understandings to be instilled. None of this is *real*. It is only symbolism, a graphic depiction of your own state of beingness relative to certain life issues.

Rasha, you have reached a major realization. You will be able to walk with grace through this episode of integration. Do not expect that you will, necessarily, experience the full throttle of agony that you associate with this place and with the souvenirs of life-experience that you abandoned here. Survey the situation. And gently, very gently, allow yourself to remember.

The experience of seeing what was left of my material belongings in ruins—caked in filth, reeking with rot—was sobering. The key refused to turn in a lock that had claimed to be indestructible. It took a power saw over 30 minutes to virtually destroy it before it surrendered the fight and allowed the decomposing contents harbored within the storage unit to be revealed. It was an apt illustration of the previous life represented by those long-abandoned objects and the illusory fortress that had held it all intact. My very identity had been that lock, hanging on to the illusion of permanence until it was in smithereens.

It was very difficult for me to imagine the life I knew I'd lived in this place to be my own. It felt as though the fleeting memories had happened to someone else, as though the nightmare that was this episode in my life actually *was* a dream and had never really happened at all. Were it not for the trashed material remnants of it, the six-year trial that was "Asheville" might have been dismissed as an aberration. The ruins of what I'd managed to salvage from those times stood as a testimony to what was once so vivid and real—and what now, in the same breath, was known to be irrelevant.

My son, Johan, and my younger daughter, Lisa, who had shared those Asheville years with me, flew to the rescue and took charge of organizing the effort to sort through the wreckage. With the help of a wonderful, upbeat team of transient workers from "south of the border,"—none of whom spoke a word of English—we spent three grueling days, sifting through, disinfecting, and salvaging what remained of our Asheville memories.

There it all was: the priceless family photographs, the cherished stuffed animals, the handmade wooden puzzles from England that I'd stashed away for the grandchildren I hoped I'd have someday—not to mention the jumble of beads and earring parts leftover from Earthstar—all of it mixed in with nonsense which simply hadn't been worth auctioning off. There it sat, in all its glory, a hodgepodge testimonial to a lifetime of living, strewn all over the pavement, drying out.

Dealing with the logistics of sorting through the mess and cleaning up what was still useful was, once again, a graphic illustration of the inner process of integration I recognized to be fully underway. I began carefully reassembling the scattered fragments of my own identity—in much the same way as I would be fitting the pieces salvaged from the wreckage of this *past-life* episode—into the identity of Now.

There was a feeling of resignation, laced with weariness, characterizing the whole messy business. Why can't life be neat and tidy and straightforward? I found myself wondering. Why all the convoluted twists and turns? Why the nosedives? Why the unending struggle? Why the ceaseless teetering on the proverbial brink of disaster? Why now the graphic foray into ruin and filth and decay—while other people were perusing lush magazines offering tips on selecting the perfect spa in paradise?

Are we having fun yet? And if not, why not? I demanded to know. As always, the unmistakable Presence of Oneness was waiting in the wings of my awareness to help me see life's symbolism from a higher perspective.

⁓

Oneness speaks:

Take a moment and breathe deeply of these energies now. Allow the sense of linear orientation to melt into the periphery of this identity. And know yourself to Be Oneness. Allow the gentle touch of this Presence to permeate all you know yourself to Be.

You have expressed the perspective of the linear identity who is struggling to reach completion with this journey into physicality. These rhetorical questions do not require answers. They merely need to be expressed. Know that the perspective that agonizes and struggles with these issues is one that is approaching resolution. And know that the pain of this birthing process is nearly over.

The one who longs to be liberated from the patterns you have described is the same one who longs to be liberated from the responsibility of carrying this identity in physical form. The weight of the role that is destined is nearly more than she can bear. Clinging to this myopic perspective of self is what perpetuates the struggle. For, this limited linear sense of self was never meant to carry the responsibility for who you have become into the times ahead.

How to rise above unwanted categories of experience

You have come to this moment in your unfoldment to *surrender* the struggle—to know yourself to Be so much more than one who squirms in the grasp of unyielding toil and misery. It is entirely possible to rise above this category of experience simply by rising from the category of self-perception that creates it. This is the opportunity at hand.

See this chapter as one coming to completion now. See the discarding of the superfluous as the gift that it indeed is. See the integration of the fragmented aspects of your own Essence as a joyous reunion. Feel the wholeness. Feel the Love. Feel the completion taking place within you. Feel the Presence of all that you truly Are. And know yourself to Be That.

No matter what visuals the physical world may present to you, this Presence—this Isness—remains untouched. This is what you have created this imagery to illustrate for yourself. For, who you know yourself to Be in this moment is all that ever needs to be known. Feel the Essence of who you Are in this moment. And Be at peace.

It was almost exactly a year later that a deeper understanding of the significance of the exercise in disaster I think of as "Asheville" emerged from the wreckage. All the while, despite having shifted the focus of my life to Oneness and to the writing, I'd continued to support myself with jewelry making, under the flag of "Earthstar"—the proverbial "ghost of Christmas past."

Now, Christmas was once again on the horizon. After years of being numbed into a conservative mindset and creating sedate, sensible little earrings, I was hit by a sudden inspiration to create a eclectic collection of flamboyant, long dangly ones out of a dazzling medley of stones, beads and components salvaged from Earthstar's heyday, which had survived the Asheville flood.

Life had come full circle. In 1992, I'd started in the jewelry business by designing a stunning collection of long dangly earrings called "The Goddess Collection." Now, having actually encountered Her Divine Presence on a spiritual odyssey I'd never have imagined in my wildest dreams, there I was again, back where I started, looking at some of the exact same components, resurrected from the past—and seeing only the *Nowness* in them.

I named the new styles "The Gypsy." It was apt. The designs were whacky, in combinations of stones and colors you wouldn't expect to see together. But, somehow it worked. Were they any different from the bizarre creation I myself had become? I reflected. There they were: a rootless concoction of remnants of another place in time, literally *detached* from all of it and born anew. They were gorgeous! But their significance was not locked into the objects themselves. I was struck by the *joy* I rediscovered, in totally abandoning myself to the passion of *creating* them—the delight of *playing*, like a little kid, in the sandbox of "the Artist" once more.

As I did, I began to explore within myself the memories I'd buried of the days when my hopes and dreams rested on these sparkly bits of stone and metal. I'd put everything I had on the line in starting that business.

I'd given it all the artistry, all the marketing flair, and all the drive I could muster—and topped it off with an inconceivable amount of just plain hard work. Despite doing everything possible to triumph, when the tally was in, it had been an absolute disaster. Somehow, I'd never really understood. It didn't make sense. And then, suddenly, it did. Oneness helped me to look beyond the material and to see what actually had happened to me back in 1997—and why.

Oneness speaks:

In less than an instant, the shift is made from a focus on awareness of the world of the material to this sense of melding into obliviousness to those same details.

The attention is suspended now, watching as words cull themselves forth and materialize from depths that are indefinable. The words pass through the fingers of this form as they dance on the keyboard of this computer, disconnected from any sense of self-definition. Simultaneously, there is a sense of the observer—watching—a sense of an all-consuming Presence. A feeling of utter joy permeates this Being now. For, that is our true nature.

The one who was ensnared in the details of mundane existence has surrendered the fight for this moment. She has retired so gratefully into the periphery of this sense of Awareness and, from there, has allowed herself to merge with the whole. There is no resistance to that idea now. There is no sense of danger, rooted in the prospect of *non-existence*. For, from the perspective of the composite identity, the pain of linear focus is no longer perceived. It is a more comfortable position through which to participate in the drama that life has to offer.

The "default setting" on this program will shift now, to one of universal scope. For, the scope of what life holds in store is poised and ready to shift radically to a very different set of circumstances. Life will be simplified. And the sense of struggle that colored the life story of this identity will be eliminated from the repertoire of possibility. That sense of a path littered with obstacles has been cleared now. There is a fresh sense of *newness* to all that we do from this point forth. And that newness is composed of all that has gone before to bring us to this moment in time.

The literal illustration of that state of being is the beautiful collection of earrings that is being fashioned from the souvenirs of the moments and creations that preceded them. And it is with joy that these materialized expressions of Oneness, *our* creations, are born again through the medium of the physical. This is our art. This is our playfulness. This is our creative expression, giving birth.

It does not matter whether the expression takes the form of gemstone earrings or a pot of soup. It is for the process of transforming that sense of joyousness into the material that we have chosen a physical incarnation. It is for the possibility of full conscious awareness of what is transpiring—and why—that we have chosen the path of spiritual awakening in this lifetime. The physical expression remains

Once integrated, no longer need to have those same experiences. Will not repeat.

the *illustration* that stands as evidence of what is so, and punctuates the point of what has been experienced, and is therefore *known*.

Transcending rejection of the past and transforming its *symbolism*

No action is random now. It is counterproductive to all that we have set about to illustrate for our Self to presume that the identity is off-course simply because a stereotype of activity is not being followed, to the exclusion of all else. The past, and the evidences of all it represents, will not dematerialize. It will *transform*. When the *rejection* of that past set of circumstances has been transcended, there will no longer be the need for the illustration. For, by invalidating the *reflection* of that aspect of identity, we prolong the process of integrating that crucial piece of who we are into the whole.

Now the moment is at hand to rekindle the *joy* with which this aspect of identity was able to express her sense of Presence in a significant moment in the history of this identity. When we are able to approach this mode of expression with delight, rather than with distain, we will be able to integrate the *rejected* piece of this identity and be complete with the need to focus a significant amount of time and attention in this way.

Now the illustration is complete. Now we have demonstrated, for the benefit of the full spectrum of this identity, the perfection in the circumstances at hand. The light, once again, has gone on! And we are fully Present, on the road to wholeness, once more.

Oneness explains the significance of the experience of colossal *failure* as an instrument in the process of spiritual transformation

The aspect of self that embarked on an entrepreneurial path, armed with idealism and creative sparkle, was thoroughly trounced in the course of this journey. As such, her perceived failure was rejected and invalidated. In fact, it was for reasons that *transcended* the circumstances that illustrated them in every way that that outcome was encountered as linear experience. It was not a *mistake* that this took place. It was the object of the exercise. It was the very illustration that Rasha set about to create for herself to experience. It was the consummate *fragmentation* that was necessary in order that the process of *reintegration* and consummate wholeness could be carried out.

It was necessary that *rejection* be set up—rejection of the aspect of identity that carried all the prized qualities into the arena of the material—in order that that sense of *ego-identification* could be transcended altogether. It was necessary that the aspect of self that was capable and talented and self-assured be made to fail utterly and completely in her own eyes, in order that she might be liberated from that myopic perspective of self, and encounter—and experience—the *Self* that is the embodiment of Oneness.

Were it not for the downfall of the linear identity of Rasha, despite her all too capable best efforts, the emergence of the fullness of this identity would not have been culled forth from the embrace of Infinite Possibility.

It was for the possibility that the aspect of self that had perpetrated such *failure* upon the identity could be *embraced*—rather than rejected—that the illustration was created and acted out.

The identity, experienced as Oneness/Oneness, experienced as the identity

For, who we Are is all of it—and none of it. We are not the so-called positive attributes to the exclusion of the less desired ones. The Godliness which we perceive in the exalted moments of connectedness is not an illustration of the embodiment of success and the circumventing of defeat. It is the knowingness that who and what we Are has nothing whatsoever to do with any of it. The experience was what it was. There is no value judgment associated with it.

The pieces of the past are scattered on the table. We shine them up and see the inherent beauty in these particles. We rekindle the joy with which these bits are placed together in delightful new combinations. We observe how the future is born out of the components of the past—literally.

Nothing is as it appears at face value. There is deeper symbolic significance in all of it. None of this is a mistake. None of this is an aberration that was "not supposed to happen." It was all supposed to happen. Every last excruciating detail. It was created as the materialization of the exalted and the rejected aspects of who we considered our self to be. The evidences that took form through the medium of duality symbolize all that we believed that we are and all that we believed that we are not. In the end, we demonstrated that who and what we truly Are has nothing whatsoever to do with any of it.

A sense of overriding Divine Purpose permeates this sense of Being now. We proceed, having recognized our own liberation from the constraints of expectation and the limitation of possibility. Now is the time to prepare the components of who we Are for presentation in the arena of physicality. For, we have come to this moment of Nowness as the embodiment of the highest expression of possibility.

We have arrived at this moment of Self-Realization not for having discarded the old and tarnished components of our identity or tossed away the threadbare remains of the costumes we've donned along the way. We've kept it all so we could see the full scope of what it took to deliver this Presence to this moment of inner illumination—and the possibility of a luminescence that might be outwardly perceived.

It is all here, as Are we, tattered and worn, and in the same breath, shimmering in newness and immediacy, in this awesome, eternal moment of Oneness.

36

Fall 2004
Pittsburgh, PA
Being in the World yet Not of the World

———

The aftermath of the experience I thought of as "Asheville-revisited" washed over me, as I continued to assimilate my understandings of that intense episode of fragmentation and reintegration. The autumn of 2004 was spent consolidating what few belongings were left from the past and pulling together the resources that would enable me to return to India for the winter to write. I shifted gears and plunged headfirst into a hasty resurrection of my role as a jewelry designer, under the flag of Earthstar.

Once again, Pittsburgh became my base for a few months, as I steeped myself in jewelry making with a single-minded focus. Within a matter of weeks I'd stockpiled enough pretty little earrings to sell so I'd be able to coast financially through the time ahead when I'd be immersed, blessedly, in the world of spirit, a world away. My writing sessions with Oneness helped me to bridge the gap in the interim. I was reminded constantly of what was illusory and what was real, while life provided what seemed like a never-ending opportunity to put the teachings into practice and transcend the nitty-gritty aspects of a foray into "the daily grind."

❧

Oneness speaks:
This is Oneness. We Are This, in this moment, together. We are no less Rasha than Oneness—no less Oneness than Rasha. For, the identities are interchangeable aspects of the whole. We are the All of it. The limitations of the linear perspective have given way to the overview that encompasses it. And *you*, who are still present as *the witness*, can sense the subtle differences in the perception of the identical circumstances, based on where you place the focus of your awareness.

The power of detachment, synchronicity, and the state of *allowance* that creates the space for *miracles*

There is a state of consummate *allowance* that permeates your awareness. What transpires is allowed to do so, without the need for the intervention of the logical mind to direct the process. So it has become with the circumstances of your life. When you allow the *synchronicity* of the clues provided to be recognized and taken up on the thread of manifestation, the pieces fall into place seamlessly.

The logistics with which you had been wrestling resolve themselves, as if by magic. The solution culled forth from the ethers of Infinite possibility meets the needs of the circumstances perfectly. There is no sense of compromise in the mix in any way. So it is when you *detach* from the need of the ego-self to become involved in masterminding the drama in which you experience yourself.

When you allow the circumstances themselves to lead you to the optimal solution to the challenges that arise, the pieces of the puzzle fall into place perfectly. Your cue as to whether you are fully in your state of Divine Presence is the ease or difficulty with which challenges are resolved. When one detaches from the need to meet circumstances with the resources of the logical mind, the solution that *life* provides is seen to be a perfect fit.

Giving yourself permission to reside in a permanent state of *allowance* creates the space for the so-called "miracles," waiting within the realm of Infinite possibility, to be called forth. That level of *detachment* is the recipe for realizing the level of results you would hope for, in answer to the down-to-earth scenarios of life in the material world.

You have straddled two worlds for some time now. You are absolutely comfortable in the identity of Oneness, when we are in the sanctity of this Divine connection. However, taken out into the physical world, the tendency is to revert to the linear identity that still perceives itself as being at the effect of the circumstances *illustrated* by the illusory world. The opportunity is ever-present to retain your knowingness of who you truly Are and to walk forth within the world of linear illusion with that knowingness intact.

These trying times are your opportunity to put these understandings to the test. You have mastered these teachings *in theory*. You have at your fingertips the keys to transcendence of all sense of material limitation. And you are beginning to apply these understandings, in the face of the challenges of day-to-day life, with surprising results.

You have demonstrated to yourself the difference in the impact of material circumstances on your sense of well being, dependent upon where you place the focus of your awareness. It is absolutely clear now that you have full control over the *effects* of those circumstances upon your sense of self.

The energies deepen now. We are in full connectedness. There is no sense of delineation, no distance to be bridged, no sense of another to which we strive to connect. We have become Unity incarnate, the consummate melding of all aspects of who we have now become.

There has once again been a period of silence. Days have gone by without the formalities of this communion. Attention has remained focused on the material world and the details that it commands. Yet now, in the Stillness of this moment of Self-recognition, that world appears to be far distant from here. That world, in this moment, is nowhere to be found.

Here, there is the in-breath and the out-breath of Creation. There is a sense of alertness, keenly attuned to the moment at hand. And there is a sense of an utter, all-pervading inner peace that presides. This is who you *truly* Are. This is who you have been, all along.

As the weeks passed I was challenged to continue putting the teachings of Oneness to the test, as life experience served up a continuous stream of mundane confrontations. The saving grace in those days of walking between two worlds was the time spent in communion with Oneness. Their beautiful words of encouragement helped to keep me focused and helped me resist the natural inclination to become drawn into the world of the illusion, when minor aggravations beckoned with the temptation to *react*. It was a time of strengthening my grasp of the teachings and my ability to apply them in real-life situations.

Rasha speaks:

How easy it is to forget what in this moment seems unforgettable! We are here in this moment together, and my heart is swimming in the rapture of your touch once more. The breaths come so very slowly. My heart is consumed in bliss. My hands are blasting with Divine Light energy. An irrepressible smile is plastered across my face. And the fingers of this form diligently document this description.

These are the sensations of experience. There is no sense of ownership that would categorize these sensations as belonging to "Rasha" or to "Oneness." For, all lines of delineation have melted into one all-pervading Presence. The state of connectedness deepens as I surrender all sense of separation—all sense of an individual identity—and become One with All That Is.

How could this experience ever be forgotten? How could one possibly opt for the delusion of affinity with the physical world and all its dramas? Here in the Stillness—in the embrace of this Love Divine—all the worries, the concerns, the details of daily life become a blur. And the blur swirls beyond this place where I experience myself to Be now. All that is a world away from This.

Oneness speaks:

The identity that is Rasha melts willingly into the Stillness now. The details of the illusion have become overwhelming, and the adversity and the feeling of being constantly consumed in battle have become exhausting. Taking an extended foray back into those states of beingness served as a reminder of how things once were—how it felt to experience oneself as being at the mercy of those kinds of circumstances.

These last weeks of toil and challenge served to illustrate the category of experience that has, in this moment, been transcended. The focus of attention, in this moment, is upon *this connection*, not upon those details. The time ahead will solidify this Presence in form, as the threads of linear identity are severed and *true identity* is embraced.

This severing is not one that will be performed by a presence external to Source itself. It is simply a level of *transcendence* that has been attained and the natural result of that attainment. Now it is clear. The illustration stands etched as evidence of all that we know that we are *not*. We are not *of* this linear world. We have simply chosen to visit for a time.

Learning to side-step mental distraction

The mountain beckons once more. Soon we will be a world away. Soon the energies of Arunachala will nurture and support the unfoldment in which we are steeped. And the details here will have paved the way for that possibility. These details are not to be dismissed. They are to be dealt with, diligently and systematically so that they are not a diversion—a temptation to distract the focus of attention from the work of Oneness.

Let those details be seen to in the days ahead with enthusiasm. And let a sense of blessed *allowance* permeate those activities. It will be a busy time of mundane preparations. Yet, the time will be characterized by a *focus of attention* fixed on absolute knowingness of Who and What We Are. The shift in the level of struggle that is *perceived* will manifest accordingly.

The temptation to expend undue amounts of effort and mental activity on the details birthed by the logical mind may be sidestepped now. See the invitation to engage. Recognize the patterns in doing so. And release all attachment to having to mastermind the movie that has been scripted at levels that transcend linear comprehension.

You are acting out that script now. The direction in which it is designed to carry you is set. And the winds of *inner change* provide the momentum for a destination that is inevitable. Do not underestimate the journey that has been taken. And do not bow to the illusion of backsliding. The choppy waters that appear to have manifested on the surface of life experience attest only to the distance that has been covered and the momentum that was necessary to bring that about.

Keep the vision fixed—absolutely fixed. And the horizon becomes a focus accessible only through the lens of *inner vision*. Focus not upon the ripples that jostle the form and give rise to the illusion of turbulence. There is no such turbulence. The bouncing about is only the by-product of the speed at which we now travel. Know this. Know this absolutely. And be at peace.

The final weeks in the United States continued to be a training ground in the art of *transcendence*. I'd sailed over some of the hurdles and was down for the count on others. The intensity of trying to straddle two worlds, while under pressure, was grueling. The pull was nearly irresistible to want to disappear altogether and melt into Oneness, never to return. Oneness was quick to point out that this was *not* an option. It was a fascinating spin on a technicality. And in raising the point in a moment of Divine passion, I was able to clarify a crucial distinction regarding exactly what *does* and *does not* happen in the process of merging with Oneness.

Rasha speaks:

I am consumed with a Presence that is undeniable, floating on a sea of bliss, calm, and serenity. The turbulent waters that inundated my world only moments ago have given way to a different place. I feel my awareness becoming obscured in a cloud. The energy that surrounds me is extraordinary. My heart center is exploding in joy. My hands are vibrating intensely. My head is engulfed in the sense of a Presence I cannot question. I can only surrender to This. I can only lose myself in This.

And, as I write these words I see that "I" am no longer. These words are now coming through the Presence that occupies this form. That Presence is no longer the one who began this discourse. These words are coming though this form. Yet, the identity Present is clearly not the source of them. These are Rasha's thoughts. They are her observations, sourced from some distant place, being recorded in this Here and Now. Rasha is no longer "here," yet her awareness is somehow still accessible. Now the Presence within this form is that of Oneness.

It has been a trying time. A time of challenge fraught with complication. A time of unceasing adversity, toil, worry. The linear identity took the bait and became hooked on the details that painted the illusion of disaster on so many fronts simultaneously. Part of me crumbled. I could not cope with the chaos. Now I only want to surrender myself to my Oneness.

I have no interest in this material world—its problems, its games, its temptations. I want only to become lost in this Love. I want only to disappear into the embrace of This. Oneness, take me! Let me dissolve into the Presence that is Oneness, so that there will no longer be an identity that is recognizable. Be Here Now, completely, that I may be complete. Be here, if it is your Divine Will, that I might disappear completely, once and for all!

Oneness speaks:

Let us breathe together now. Slow and deep. And as the sense of connectedness intensifies, let us embrace who we truly Are—together. There is no need to pray for *non-existence.* You will never cease to exist. Your awareness of your *separation* from this Source is what will cease to *manifest* for you. And that sense of self will melt into the embrace of the whole of which you are a part.

You are deeply enmeshed in a process of transcendence, and you have come to a crucial turning point. The aspects of self that were still invested in denial have been stimulated into self-awareness. The objective here is not in sweeping feelings and emotions under the rug where they might hide unnoticed. The objective is in *feeling* these feelings deeply in response to life's prompts and then, consciously, making the choice to *non-react*.

Learning to transcend categories of life experience

The objective is not to eliminate the feelings themselves, but rather to *recognize* them and to know that to avoid them only necessitates further stimulation by way of the life episodes that have manifested.

The objective is a sense of transcendence of these categories of life experience. Your *focus of attention* on these mundane details is what continues to call them into form for you. The same focus of attention, upon *this* Presence, as Oneness, will call forth into manifestation a very different set of circumstances. Your persistence in focusing on the linear identity is what serves to manifest adversity.

We are Oneness—not a form of identity but rather a state of Beingness. We are the collective of consciousness of which you, the linear identity, are a part. We are not other than what you are, taken to the ultimate degree of expression. We are here as you are here, ever-present as the Essence of the identity you have come to think of as "you."

We write these words, not to imply that these concepts are in any way new, for we have spoken of these ideas before on countless occasions. We write these words as a perpetual reminder to you of what you know. Through the encountering of this truth, through the vehicle of *repetition*, there will no longer be the need to engage the mind. For, the truth is becoming etched indelibly upon your awareness, transcending the linear function of memory.

Transcending the mind's quest for belief

There is no need for memory when there is *knowingness*. Memory is a function of linear mind. When there is knowingness there no need for mind. The embracing of truth has already happened and is integrated into the whole of your being. It becomes a part of all that you Are. It is no longer a matter of what you may or may not choose to *believe*. Knowingness transcends the need for belief.

You emerge as the embodiment of what Is, and, as such, *you* encompass the Divinity within—that which has always been and will always Be. Regardless of whether you are presently experiencing yourself in physical form, you cease to be a being with a *linear orientation*. Your focus of awareness transcends the cares and concerns of the world of mundane reality.

Oneness describes the state of Presence

You find yourself to be Present as *Awareness* itself, traveling through a vista of perception, yet knowing that you are not in any way a part of this imagery. Your participation becomes marginal in the matters that consume the waking hours of others who are experiencing themselves within the context of linear reality. You recognize that you are "in the world yet not of the world" in every way imaginable.

Your reactions and interests become childlike. You observe with keen attention and with wonder the details of the world in which you experience awareness—as though you were watching a movie, a kaleidoscope of intrigue, as the threads of Divine intent weave their magic all around you. And in the same breath, you recognize yourself to be emotionally distanced from all of it. You know that none of it touches you at the level where you experience Presence. There, the perspective of the witness presides, the epitome of *detachment* walking through an ever-shifting landscape of possibility.

Even though you are actively involved in the mechanics of providing material sustenance, it is not with a focus that would associate those activities with a sense of who and what you *Are*. These are simply the motions one has chosen to go through in order to continue to experience physical presence within the context of this particular drama. Who you Are is not associated in any way with this drama. Who you Are has chosen to experience Presence within the embrace of this backdrop of possibility.

Adding your own signature to the composite of Divine experience and to the collective work we think of as our world

Every nuance of imagery adds refinement to the *composite* projection taken up as experience. Every detail, whether or not internalized through the avenues of emotion, is recorded in the annals of *Infinite* perception through which the sum totality of All That Is gleans the *experience* of Self-awareness. This is why you have chosen to be Present, here in the world of the linear illusion. By giving structure and definition to the limitless, simply by being who you Are in this moment in time, you add your own touch to the composite of Divine experience, perceived throughout all Creation.

There is no higher or lower. You are not in any way better than another, by virtue of the fact that you understand the dynamics of the process while most are blind to the truth of what transpires in the Here and Now you think of as your world. You are simply holding the note in the resonance of the collective that you have chosen to hold. That note may be loud or soft, shrill or soothing—it does not matter. Your presentation may be refined or unrefined. Your vision may be acclaimed or condemned. It does not matter.

Your vision of what you have chosen to contribute to the collective resonance of linear experience is what it is. And as such, it adds its touch to the collective experience that is shared by every nuance of perception present—as each of you.

This opportunity is the limitless palate of Creation that has been placed before you. The canvas of Infinite possibility cries out for your touch to give it definition—to give the moment in which Life perceives itself the structure of your own unique vision. That is why you have chosen to be here. You are here to add your own signature to the collective work you think of as your world—with full conscious awareness of it.

Why we have chosen the experience we think of as "life"

You are here to know who you Are in every moment in which you draw breath through form. You are here to insure that the choices made in the

481

name of the perspective that wears your identity are reflective of a clear vision. As such, they become the highest possible notes that might be added to a symphony in which all are equal players.

This is what you have chosen to experience in the nanosecond you think of as your life. That is why you have embarked on this journey. And that is why, in this transitional place in the itinerary, you have chosen to exit the major thoroughfares on which the world travels and forge your own trail. You are not alone. The world is ready to make this shift now. And masses of individuals will be making similar choices and having related kinds of experiences to ones that seemed to be uniquely your own.

Oneness offers guidance for the times ahead in India

The time that will be spent in India this winter will help you consolidate your position as a spiritual Presence—one with a profound Divine connection and a wealth of Divine wisdom to be shared. Your time will not be spent debating the details of your teachings with the seekers who have come in search of a spark of wisdom here and a touch of philosophy there. You will spend the time at Arunachala in seclusion—blessedly. It will be a time of discovery and delight. The present moment is for immersion in the preparations that will make the time in India possible. They are a necessary ingredient in the adventure.

Oneness explains the *absence* of soaring ecstasy, tears, and feelings of emotional intensity during periods of Divine connectedness

You have noted the intensity of the *sensations* of vibration within the physical form. This is an indication that you are still becoming accustomed to these augmented levels of vibration. With consistent practice, you will become acclimated to these new levels and will not experience the profound sensations that you are feeling in this moment.

The linear mind interjected from the periphery the observation that there are now no longer the levels of emotional intensity, the tears, the feelings of soaring ecstasy that once accompanied this experience. Those levels have now been transcended. The sensations now experienced are a profound sense of well being and an intense feeling of joy.

The *absence* of the attendant feelings of soaring ecstasy are not evidence of having fallen from Grace. It is evidence of having transcended the levels of perception where those sensations were the natural accompaniment of connectedness. You Are where you Are. What is optional is your *perception* of it.

The shift into Divine Presence has already happened. This is not something that can be undone by shifting your focus of attention to the details of the linear world. All that can be altered is your *perception* of that state of Beingness—and how you experience what you think of as "your life."

Know that you are simply a traveler watching a landscape of possibility unfold outside your window. Whether or not you choose to internalize that imagery is the choice that you may make. How you *feel* about those perceptions will then be brought about as possibility—or not, as you so choose.

37

Upon returning to India, my initial days in Tiruvannamalai were spent secluded within the sanctity of Ramanashram, where an ambience of quiet reverence prevailed. As always, an extraordinary sense of Presence, the Grace of Ramana Maharshi, filled the huge marble floored Samadhi hall, and I felt drawn to spend as much time there as possible, in meditation and silent reflection. Now, more than ever before, I had the sense that somehow, even though his physical form had passed on from this world a half-century before, he was still fully Present and was working with me.

Bright and early, I enjoyed a classic South Indian breakfast of *idlis* (small, saucer-shaped, steamed muffins made of fermented rice and lentils) and *sambar* (spicy vegetable gravy). The dining room floor, where tight rows of ashram guests sat crosslegged, side-by-side, was dotted with little "plates," fashioned from dried leaves and sharpened twigs, on which this local delicacy was served. No utensils were provided. Casting any concept of table manners to the wind, we ate this exotic breakfast—and all other meals—with our bare hands, gravy and all.

Afterward, following a thorough hand washing, I took my place at the periphery of Ramana Maharshi's Samadhi Shrine, placed my hands palms down on the stone railing, and closed my eyes. Almost instantly, I felt myself shift into a rhythm of extremely slow, steady breathing. Within a moment, I became aware that I was barely breathing at all. My awareness shifted immediately to a *perception of Self* as Oneness.

A Presence began to counsel me, not as channeled teaching received telepathically, but as *knowingness* which seemed to be coming from within my own being. I understood that the communication, which I knew was emanating *from* the spiritual Master enshrined there, was coming *through* my own sacred Essence—not my mind. It was at that moment that I felt myself surrender to a process that carried my awareness beyond the entire realm of *perception*. Who I knew myself to Be in that moment transcended all of it.

I remained, suspended in that state of Beingness, for the better part of two hours. Intermittently, I became aware that my attention came to rest on my awareness of the Divine Presence of Lord Shiva embodied there, and instantly I experienced that Presence *as* my own Self. I was in a sublime state of transcendence, punctuated only by sharp sensations at the very top of my crown.

In one all-consuming moment, it seemed as though the top of my head opened, like a flower, and my sense of *myself* rose from within the form I'd always considered to be "me." Simultaneously, I experienced myself as *omnipresent* and watched from a distance, as the form became no more than a shadow, left behind. The formlessness that had become my Self rose to a newfound state of Self-perception.

Two hours later, I emerged in form, standing before Ramana Maharshi's Samadhi shrine, and knew I was somewhere I had never been before. It was totally another world, experienced as Here and Now. As I opened my eyes, I noticed that a line of young priests were now seated before me, chanting a lengthy Sanskrit Mantra. The vibration of the chanting reverberated around me and re-echoed throughout every cell of my body. Until that moment, I had been completely unaware of their presence. I remained totally consumed in a feeling of utter peace and serenity for hours. Later in the day, Oneness elaborated on what had taken place.

⚜

Oneness speaks:

You have begun to experience some of the transcendental phenomena that will characterize your emergence at heightened states of Self-perception. You can expect to alternate between Self-awareness and non-awareness in the course of these episodes. Neither state of perception is meant to override the other. Neither is to be considered preferable or superior. These are simply shades of perception within the kaleidoscope of possibility of All that you Are.

Loving guidance illuminates the characteristics of the transformation process

You are being carefully guided by the formless one who is Present here. You are surely not doing this alone. Nor have you imagined it. The possibilities you have described are made manifest through your willingness to surrender to the process and suspend the need to judge or to categorize it. Beyond that, there is no need whatsoever for anything at all. This is why you have come.

Allow yourself to be guided through the possibilities of perception without the need to dissect the experience as it is happening. You will be welcome to recapture what transpires, after the fact. Much of the work will now be done in silence, within the sanctity of your sense of Being. And while we will surely continue to dialogue and to document this experience of emergence, the process will begin to shift to one focused in consummate surrender.

You can anticipate being taken to new heights of vibration, as each level is encountered and embodied sequentially. You will begin to be able to retain these levels of vibration and to sustain the sense of Presence that accompanies it. You will begin to work out a routine through which these exercises can take place systematically. Your focus will shift automatically to the process transpiring within and you will cease to have an interest in the comings and goings of the drama that swirls around you.

This scenery, against which your own drama takes place, is merely a backdrop to the real story that is unfolding before you. For, this aspect of the movie is playing out before an audience of one. No one else need know what is taking place within you, for you are surely in metamorphosis now. And the journey is yours alone to create and to experience.

You will find yourself becoming increasingly reclusive. And the perspectives of the others who shuffle and reshuffle themselves in a scramble to siphon off a little wisdom and a little energy from the ones that have set themselves up as all-knowing—will be of no interest. Let the *leela* (Divine play) play out as it will.

The birthday I share with Ramana Maharshi was celebrated, as always, in blessed silence. The previous day, however, heralded his 125th birthday celebration, according to the Tamil calendar, and I headed for the ashram's temple in the early morning to attend the festivities. In the "Mother's shrine" a *puja* was taking place, and a few dozen priests, seated on the floor, were chanting "Rudrum," a powerful, sacred prayer to Lord Shiva, over and over again. Only a handful of people had gathered by then and most were in the adjacent room doing *pradakshina,* a meditative walk encircling Ramana Maharshi's Samadhi shrine.

I sat down on my little white cloth, close to the priests, and closed my eyes. Almost instantly, I was catapulted into levels of energy that I had never experienced before. My entire body began to reverberate with the sacred Sanskrit words. I became aware of an intense pressure on the top of my head that continued to build to an incredible intensity. Immediately, I went into a profound state of bliss.

My breathing slowed down to the point that I was hardly breathing at all. There were no thoughts. There was no mind. And I felt my attention being drawn to full focus on Lord Shiva, whose Presence was being invoked and honored by the Mantra. Instantly, I felt that Presence within my body. And, I experienced myself not simply as the embodiment of *Self,* the personalized aspect of Oneness wearing the Rasha identity, but simultaneously as the embodiment of Lord Shiva, the Divine Presence I've come to think of as "The Father."

I held these two exalted aspects of consciousness in form for nearly two hours, with little awareness of the commotion that was transpiring in the room around me. All the din of the chanting, the bells, and the hoards of devotees that ultimately flooded into the temple were known to be outside of This. All of it was taking place in a world in which "I" only appeared to be present.

485

Within the depths of my awareness, words were spoken and simultaneously comprehended. But, there was no delineation between their Source and who I knew *myself* to Be. They were one and the same. The depth of Divine connectedness was incomprehensible—far more intense than anything I'd ever encountered before—levels of Self-perception I'd never imagined possible. My entire body resonated with the combined vibration of the Mantras being chanted around me and the forces surging from within. And I knew that something extraordinary was taking place. I drifted around, going through the motions of my life and feeling like I was only marginally on the planet for the rest of the day.

Later, in the evening, I returned to Ramanashram, sat down on the floor beside Ramana Maharshi's Samadhi shrine, and once again closed my eyes. Instantly I was swept into blissful connectedness. I focused my attention on his Presence, which is said to have been the embodiment of Lord Shiva, in his lifetime. Immediately, the energies I had experienced earlier in the day began to surge throughout my being. I noticed that my breathing, once again, had slowed down dramatically. And a profound sense of absolute well being flooded my senses.

Then, very unexpectedly, I felt my head begin the familiar rhythmic swaying I had come to recognize as an indication of the Presence of The Goddess, Durga Devi—"Mother" consciousness. As the witness, observing all this, the aspect of my identity that somehow still felt compelled to analyze and document these experiences was intrigued. How could I be focused on the Presence of Lord Shiva, yet clearly be manifesting the Presence of The Goddess at the same time? I absolutely didn't know what to make of it.

A few hours later, in a phone conversation with Dr. Bindu, I described the phenomenon. He laughed with delight. "Now, Rasha, you understand the real meaning of Oneness," he said. "This is the experience you have been working toward. This is the beginning of what you have come to this lifetime to do, who you have come here to be." I was astounded. Yet, somehow it all felt right. And I absorbed the information with the most matter-of-fact sense of calm.

In the same breath, I noticed that now I did not identify with the persona who had occupied my form for most of this lifetime. I realized that I had expanded my sense of beingness to the extent that I was experiencing myself as someone very different. And I knew that I had not imagined it. Amazingly, within the context of what is or is not *real* within "the world of illusion," this was *really happening*. Later that evening, I recaptured the moment in writing—and Oneness confirmed it.

≈

Oneness speaks:

You have captured the essence of the experience described. And in so doing, know that the documentation of these phenomena is part of what you have come to this moment to do. Do not feel that is a shortcoming on your part to be able to perceive and to document this. You are not meant to be melding into a stage of mindless Presence. You are not here to personify a void. That category of experience may be *perceived*, in retrospect, within the depths of your meditative states. Yet, the one who emerges with the powers of physical perception is most definitely capable of playing the role of delineator. It is this skill that has been developed within you during this time of preparation.

You have come to these times to personify both states of beingness simultaneously. For, the one does not invalidate the other. It merely broadens the scope of possibility, as it personifies the experience of *Infinite Possibility* that is Oneness.

Rasha speaks:

I see now. I am all of it. It is not a matter of being either "Rasha" or "Oneness." I am experiencing myself as both—right now in this moment. I am experiencing extraordinary sensations of joy. I am objectively recording these impressions. And at the same time, I know myself to embody Oneness. One state clearly does not invalidate the other. I still have thoughts and perceptions. Oneness is All of it—as Am I.

My return to Tiruvannamalai heralded a deepening of my experiences of connectedness with the mountain, Arunachala, and a deepening of my understanding of the nature of the Divine energy it embodies. I'd begun to experience the Presence of Lord Shiva, a Presence of astounding intensity, on a regular basis during my meditations. Oneness helped me explore my natural sense of connection with the energies of the Father, and helped me put these experiences into perspective within the context of my understandings of the nature of Oneness.

The subject of embodying a Deity once again became an experiential theme for me, as I began having frequent instances of embodying the Presence of both The Goddess and Lord Shiva—representing feminine and masculine polarity—at first alternately and then, simultaneously. The teachings of Oneness provided a deeper understanding of the concepts of *masculine* and *feminine* as well as a foundation for seeing these expressions of Divine polarity as a gateway to Divine Unity.

Oneness speaks:

You have returned to this mountain for the completion of a particular phase of your unfoldment. There are energies indigenous to this place, calculated to activate certain states of awareness within you. Be prepared to experience highly intense instances of Divine connectedness while you are here. This is why you have returned to the mountain. You have come to reintegrate yourself into the whole that is made manifest in form here.

Oneness deepens my understanding of the experience of embodying a Deity

You are a *vibrational key* that has been readied and will serve as a component to an activation of the full Presence still dormant here in this place. For, this Presence is not other than what you Are. You are simply an aspect of the whole, with identity, in form. Yet, the *Essence* of what you Are is none *other* than the consummate Presence that resides here. You are here to integrate your own Presence into the composite consciousness, of which you are a part at the highest level. In so doing, you will represent the fullness of That identity, in form.

Rasha speaks:

Oneness, we need to clarify this a bit. I've come to understand myself to Be Oneness. I've experienced myself as That, with full conscious awareness of it. Now what? Are you saying that my identity as Oneness is, in itself, an aspect of a Higher Presence—ostensibly the identity embodied by this mountain?

That is indeed what is being said. You have been told, over the course of your preparation for the role you will be playing in these times that you are "*of* the Father energies." That is the lineage that you represent in form. The wholeness you experience as your Self in this moment—as Oneness—is, in itself, part of a greater Whole. That aspect of Divinity will be made manifest through the form you think of as your Self. Your Presence as Oneness is the gateway to that possibility.

Why, then, have I been having experiences as the embodiment of The Goddess during my Mantra chanting? I know I have not imagined this experience. And in fact, it has been confirmed both by you and by Dr. Bindu, who claims to have actually seen The Goddess as manifest in my form. Now what? Am I to embody both The Father and The Mother? Is that possible?

Why would that not be possible? You Are all of it. Your Essence, ultimately, is the One Essence—as is All Life. Yet, in the course of manifesting as Presence, in linear form, in *this* material Here and Now, the *dual nature* of that all-pervading Presence is characteristic of the experience. The route that leads to the materialization of that One Essence is, by definition, via the path of *duality*.

Thus, even though you are now experiencing yourself as complete—as Oneness—the journey of *ascension* does not end here. Ultimately, the path to consummate Wholeness is via the dualistic aspects of Divinity that have incarnated here as each of you. As you expand the essence of who you Are, in this Here and Now, you will come to embody the fullness of the aspect of Divinity, *expressed* as duality, of which your identity as Oneness is a part.

This pattern of expansion and contraction—of wholeness and subsequent fragmentation—is the essence of Life Itself. It is the perpetual process of Self-expression and reabsorption into Self—the in-breath and out-breath of Creation.

So, if I am basically of the Father lineage, why on earth am I here as a woman? Wouldn't it have been a whole lot easier if I were here in the form of a man?

That might have been the logical choice if the process were to end there. It might have made more sense to have manifested oneself as a man and then risen to the possibility of embodying the Father in form, and leaving it at that. In your case, what has been envisioned is not a journey that ends with the embodiment of Divinity with duality. You have been told that you would walk as Oneness. From the beginning, we have spoken of this. You will come to embody the *melding* of Father and Mother—as Oneness—fully made manifest in this Here and Now.

We know that it is impossible for you to begin to comprehend the scope of what has been presented here. Yet, that is the nature of what has begun to transpire for you. Your experiences as the embodiment of the Presence you identify as The Goddess set the stage for your embodiment of those energies as well. You will find that it is possible for you to embody any number of Deified aspects of the One Presence, simply by shifting your full *attention* to a state of absolute focus on *that aspect* of what you Are. For, you Are All of It—as is All Life.

The ultimate expression of All that you Are encompasses all aspects of that One Divine Presence. Thus, you are not *less* Mother than Father—nor is anyone else. You have simply chosen one particular route to physical manifestation, in keeping with the laws of linear reality. The route that will take you home to the experience of consummate Wholeness that is your true nature is via the same path of duality.

You have come to this mountain to reclaim that aspect of your identity. You have come to embody the Presence of Shiva, as did the one who came before you. This place—this mountain—is the embodiment of His Presence. You will also come to experience yourself as That.

✾

Rasha speaks:

Oneness, I'd like to ask you, once again, to speak with me about the nature of a Deity—the Presence with which I've begun to have contact. It was my understanding, from a recent transmission, that the route of ascension was via a system of wholeness and subsequent fragmentation, within the context of one's own identity. And while each aspect of Presence encountered along the way is complete, as Oneness, each is itself a part of a greater whole.

I know that it is all Oneness. And at the same time, I was told I was of "The Father" lineage. I am trying to understand the significance and the purpose of the experience I am having of embodying the Presence of a Deity. I've experienced both "The Goddess" and "Lord Shiva," on occasion, as Present within my form. And while I retained the sense of my own identity during these experiences, I perceived myself as embodying the Presence of the Deity at the same time. On two occasions, I perceived the Presence of both "The Goddess" and "Shiva" simultaneously. Oneness, can you tell me why I am now having these experiences?

Oneness addresses the concept of *masculine* and *feminine*

Oneness speaks:

There is no question as to the validity of these experiences. You *know* what you have experienced. The difficulty lies only in your inability to transcend the concepts of *masculine* and *feminine*. The lineage of which you are a part has been referred to as "Father" because that frame of reference is comprehensible to a linear mindset. It is not necessary for you to understand the nature of the levels of Creation. You have sought these understandings and they, by definition, stretch the limits of a linear orientation.

All parts are, in themselves, representative of the Whole of Creation. All aspects of Oneness are within you, *as* you. The aspects of Divinity that you have invited into your energy field have responded to the invitation as it was presented. Your expectations set the stage for your experience. When you set your *intention* on the perception of a Deity through the pathway of Self-perception, that result is naturally forthcoming. You have the components for this experience at your disposal now. You have demonstrated to yourself that the focus of your attention manifests your experience. The question now arises as to *why* you are choosing to have this experience.

Rasha speaks:

I'm choosing to have this experience because I understood that this was the next step on my journey. I believed, albeit perhaps wrongly, that this was a positive step. I deduced that embodying the Presence of both Father and Mother was a natural step on the path to Oneness. Have I misinterpreted this?

Rasha, you have misinterpreted nothing. You are simply making choices that you presume are expected of you. You are not required to embody a Deity. You have come to certain conclusions as a result of your experiences. You have now figured out *how* to do this. Whether or not you wish to spend your time and energy invoking these Presences is a choice that you are free to make.

It is not one that you have been instructed to make. There is no harm in making this choice. But, neither is it required of you.

Recognizing yourself to be of a particular lineage does not presuppose the experience of *embodying* that Presence. Your perception of Self is to be as Oneness. The level of that connection will intensify over time, carrying you— as consciousness—on the pathway of ascension toward the consummate state of Cosmic Unity. Whether or not that journey takes you through the gateways of other categories of identity is irrelevant to the fact that you Are and continue to *Be* the embodiment of Oneness—as is *everyone*.

Oneness, do I understand correctly that we are each, technically, capable of embodying and/or communing with any number of other forms of consciousness—not only ones at the level of Deity— simply by virtue of our focus of attention? Is that what is happening, for example, at Ramanashram? Is the Presence of Ramana Maharshi somehow "conjured up" by the heartfelt prayers and focused attention of the devotees?

Oneness explains *how* the experience of connectedness with an exalted Presence is achieved

The Presence of one such as Ramana Maharshi is *felt* by those who are able to make the connection to their *own* state of Oneness via the pathway of heart. The process is no different than that which you have discovered and applied to the Presence of various Deities. You have also applied this principle to your experience of the presence of Neem Karoli Baba, The Christ Consciousness, Hanuman, and Anandamayi Ma. Your connection is achieved by virtue of your ability to shift into your *own* Presence as Oneness. What is experienced, then, is not a Presence that is *other than* that which you already Are. It is via the path of that *common ground* that the sense of connectedness is possible.

Technically speaking, one does not then embody the *masculine* or *feminine* expression of any of these expressions of Presence. One continues to embody the presence of Oneness, which by definition is devoid of polarity, regardless of the nature of the Presence simultaneously invoked.

If these expressions of Divinity are all Oneness, then technically, they are all the same. Why does my experience of them differ?

Your experience of all forms of consciousness, expressed as identity, will differ. The expression of consciousness at the level of Deity is no different. Each will exhibit characteristics that are perceptible as energy. You will then be able to note differences in terms of your experience of that Presence.

Oneness, Dr. Bindu has said that The Goddess is The Absolute. I understand Oneness to be The Absolute. Does that mean that The Goddess and Oneness are the same? If that is so, why is my experience of these two expressions of Divine Presence so different?

Oneness is a Presence characterized by expansion, and regulated by one's capacity to perceive it

Once again, you are approaching this subject from the vantage point of duality. The *expression* of Oneness you experience is one determined by any number of variables. As you have yourself explained, the Presence of Oneness is one characterized by *expansion*. The *level* of Oneness *perceived* is determined by your own ability to sustain the intensity of a particular level of Divine Presence. This experience has evolved and will continue to evolve with the pace of your own spiritual unfoldment.

The Presence of The Goddess and your *perception* of it is governed by the same principles. The Goddess is most definitely The Absolute—no differently than is Oneness—in terms of the *core Essence* represented through each of these *expressions* of Divinity. It is in the *expression*, in terms of identity, that the differences in one's ability to *perceive* the Presence in question would be made manifest. The level of complexity of the Presence in question would, likewise, be determined by the capacity of the one perceiving it to do so. Thus, the level of Divine Presence encountered by one person would not necessarily duplicate that which is able to be perceived by another.

The intensity of the physical sensations experienced in the Presence of Divinity reflects the vibrational distance between you.

In the same sense, the intensity of the *sensations* you experience in such an encounter would not be an indication of the level of the Divine Presence in question. Rather, the intensity of your own physical sensations would be your indication of the distance to be bridged between your own state of *beingness* and that of the Divine Presence. As your own levels accelerate, the range of difference diminishes, and sensations that once were perceived as extraordinarily intense are experienced as being less so. This is not your indication that you have lapsed in your spiritual practice or have faltered in some way, but would more likely be an indication of progress on your part.

You have experienced this phenomenon consistently in the work we have done together, where initially, extreme sensations of joy, passion, and accelerated vibration accompanied this connection. Over time, the intensity of those sensations diminished, though clearly the level of connectedness had not. This was your indication that the *difference* between your own levels and that of the expression of Oneness Present had diminished accordingly.

Oneness, would there not be an advantage, in terms of energy, in embodying a Deity such as The Goddess—or Shiva? There are certain spiritual teachers, here in India, who embody a Divine Presence—female Gurus, for example, who are said to embody various aspects of The Goddess. I assumed that this was the source of the "shakti"—the energy—that they are able to bring forth.

I suppose I assumed that this was why The Goddess suddenly manifested in my form. I thought that this was the next step in being able to hold certain levels of energy. Is that not what is happening?

The *energy* that accompanies the perception of a Divine Presence

The levels of energy that one is able to carry forth are not determined by an ability to personify a Deity. An audience may derive satisfaction in being able to say that a certain person embodies a Goddess and label her as a Saint because of it, but in terms of one's own ability to impart *energy* to those who will seek to follow, one's own *Presence* is sufficient.

Likewise, the Presence of Ramana Maharshi *was* the embodiment of the lineage you share. The fact that he is said to have embodied Shiva does not mean that an aspect of that identity, perceived as being separate, entered his body. It means that he came into the fullness of *his own Being*—as Shiva. The Presence was none other than his own Divine Self.

Ultimately, you too will come to embody this aspect of your own Being. The energy that will be perceived by others will not be due to the Presence of a Deity that could be said to be other than what you know yourself to Be. The energy will be *your own energy*—sourced from within the depths of your own sacred Self.

December 26, 2004 is a date that will long be etched in the chronicles of heartbreak and compassion we carry together as collective memory. For, united in a tragedy that, in one sweeping stroke, obliterated barriers of culture along with entire segments of population, we touched briefly upon a collective moment of Oneness. It was a moment in time marked by a word few had ever heard before: *tsunami.*

In that fleeting instant we, as a world population, transcended the walls of alienation with which we customarily divide ourselves into neat categories of separateness. In the grief that we shared around the globe, our hearts groped for a universal life-raft—a shred of Divine insight that would help soothe the agony of having to stand by, helplessly watching on live TV, as so many paid the ultimate price.

I too stood by, helplessly watching the drama unfold—in real life— as it was actually happening, on the beach in Pondicherry, Tamil Nadu, South India. The former French colony on India's southeast coast, with its charming, tree-lined streets and quaint, bistro-style atmosphere, was amongst the places memorialized in the headlines of the world as it, in turn, became "ground-zero" in a global catastrophe that was unprecedented in our times.

At the last minute, I'd tried to schedule an impromptu getaway for Christmas weekend, and miraculously—I thought—managed to book a room at Park Guesthouse. There hadn't been an available room in all of Pondicherry over Christmas for weeks. But, as luck would have it, a last minute cancellation manifested one at the very moment of my call. It felt like a gesture of Divine affirmation that I was meant to be there.

I checked into the only available room, the morning of Christmas Eve, a ground-floor room facing the lush gardens, with the endless expanse of ocean just beyond. Traditionally, I'd always managed to secure a room on one of the upper floors, each of which offered a nice little balcony and an added touch of ocean breeze. But, the ground floor was all that was left. Instinctively, something didn't feel quite right about the room but, grateful to have someplace to stay, I let it pass.

The far end of the room featured a small, textured-glass window, reinforced with strong iron security bars. The room was nondescript, but at least I'd be safe, I remember thinking. In retrospect, I've often imagined how those bars might easily have sealed my fate, had the infamous wave-to-come been much higher. Blessedly, for me, it wasn't.

The holiday passed uneventfully enough. And it being India—French touches or not—I had to remind myself that Christmas was actually going on elsewhere on the planet. The local action picked up quite unexpectedly the following morning. For me, the drama began with the sound of someone frantically pounding on my door. I was hours into the depths of a delightful meditation, and, in that moment, would have been hard pressed to tell you what universe I was in. The sound of a woman's voice shrieking "Earthquake! Open up!" sent me crashing back to earth. Incoherent, I staggered to the door and flung it open. My vision froze on an inconceivable sight.

At that very moment, the first of a sequence of waves came splashing at the top of the mammoth wall of boulders that stood like a fortress that separated the City of Pondicherry from the Bay of Bengal—a jagged line of demarcation between land and sea. This massive stone barrier was at least 20 feet high, and extended perhaps 50 feet in width, before it met Park Guest House's seafront garden. Never before had I seen a wave even approach the top of those rocks, much less come splashing over the top.

With my heart pounding, I grabbed my laptop and ran for the street. There, I jumped into a waiting rickshaw and just shouted "Drive!" The driver smiled innocently, totally oblivious to what was happening. "Where you going?" he asked. Stammering, I just pointed away from the beach, not able to think of a place or direction to tell him to go. "No problem" he smiled, sensing some urgency in my demeanor. And away we went, weaving our way through a sudden onslaught of motorbikes coming the other way— entire families with children, inching their way toward the waterfront, eager to see firsthand the spectacle that had just been announced on television. As we pulled away, leaving the calamity behind us, I looked back—in horror.

Suddenly, where only seconds before there had been a deluge of ocean, there now was no water at all. For as far as the eye could see, the ocean floor lay bare—completely exposed. In its place, waves of young Indian boys came running onto the beach, whooping and jumping, amid a suddenly surreal landscape—a vista that, until that moment, they had only ever known as "the sea."

What goes out—must come back in. I've never wanted to think about the scene that, inevitably, must have followed there. Many hundreds are said to have perished on the beaches of Pondicherry that day. I thank all heaven and earth that I was not amongst them. I watched the aftermath on live TV, from a second-floor café, safe in the heart of the city—shaken.

Later that day, I retreated to the haven that is Oneness, for guidance. The teachings I received were not what might have been expected. Yet, in reading it over, I started to see the drama in a different light. I began to understand that through these teachings we had been gifted with a level of insight that would help us all to look upon the unthinkable moments in our history in a very different way. Very slowly, I began to see the visions of unspeakable human tragedy and suffering that we share collectively, from the perspective of Oneness.

⤜∽⤛

Reflections on the *tsunami* of 2004
Oneness speaks:

This is Oneness. Allow the breaths to come slowly and deeply, and allow of this Presence to permeate your awareness. We are here now in the fullness of this Union— no more and no less a manifestation of physicality than the Essence of the Totality itself.

Isness—simply Is. An *aspect* of that Isness is no less the Essence of the whole than the sum totality of All That Is. This is the Essence of what we Are in this moment. And this is the Essence of All that We Are.

Applying the principle of *detachment* to life experience in the face of triumph and tragedy

When one is able to step back from the inclination to dissect, to analyze, and to judge, one is left with the pure essence of *experience*. For, experience itself has no agenda. It does not require that it be fit into the context of the shoulds and shouldn'ts of a linear mindset. Inherent in the *pure* essence of experience is the consummate *detachment* of *the experiencer* that would render the possibility of perception untainted.

When one enters the process with the inclination to categorize it into the structures of dualistic systems of belief, one affects the experience. One then adds the tinge of emotional charge that translates experience into the vibrational formulations one carries forth as *karma*. Without the addition of emotion, or the need to *structure* the experience, one is left with the building blocks of *pure perception*.

One has then created the context for carrying forth the possibility of perception through the medium of form, and doing so multi-dimensionally. For, the *format* for that perception does not change. The *identity* through which the perception is made possible remains intact, though the *context* through which it may be perceived will vary, according to the vibrational variables present.

The opportunity, for one whose sense of Self-perception would place him/ her in a position to operate as a format for a broader range of experience, is to encounter experience with *detachment*. One is able to take the position of the observer, regardless of whether or not one is personally involved in the scenario in question. One is able to experience oneself as fully present in those circumstances, without feeling the necessity to respond, internally or externally, in any way at all. One is able to simply *Be*—even within the context of a maelstrom—and in so doing, not add a charge that might link that experience to the *experiencer* vibrationally.

There would be no need to judge it, to agree or disagree with it, or to place it in a context relative to similar categories of experience. There would be no need to feel pained or elated by it. There would be no inclination to worry about the effects it might have in moments that could be considered to be *past* or *future*. There would be no need to *respond* in any way at all. This possibility of disengaging oneself from the conditioned responses characteristic of presence in a linear world serves to separate one, experientially, from the masses who may well encounter the identical circumstances.

Any and all action relative to those circumstances would be a reflection of individual *choice*, unaffected by *judgment* of any kind. One then is able to float through the turmoil and trauma that may color the landscape and not feel the need to interact with those variables, either internally or externally. One would not feel compelled, necessarily, to take action. One would not feel inclined to register the event, through the medium of emotion, and thus build a vibrational charge that might be carried within. One is able to simply be Present with whatever circumstances may arise, and to know that the essence of who one Is is not affected in any way at all.

There is no *death*. No more than there is *life*. These illusory constructs are simply the medium through which experience might be registered, noted, and released into the vastness of Infinite Possibility. This is the format through which *Creation* is made possible. This is the system of translating *possibility* into *perception*. This is the basis of the phenomenon you regard as your linear world.

All action is taken by the One Supreme Presence, who acts out All That Is. And though that Presence may appear in the guise of any number of identities, both in form and formless, it is none other than Oneness initiating all of it.

The momentum of *Eternal change*

The beginnings and endings that structure your illusory world are simply the means through which Creation is made possible. The triumphs and tragedies that serve as the hallmarks of human experience are simply the turning points through which Oneness may continue to delineate—and to experience—our own exponential Isness. There is no value judgment whatsoever, in any of it. All of it is no more and no less than an exponential *continuation*—a manifestation of an ongoing momentum that is Infinite and Eternal.

The in-breath and out-breath of Creation take the form of births and of deaths. In this way, the ebb and flow of the tides of Creation are given structure and definition. The imperceptible is given form. The inconceivable is given the means through which the sciences that govern your reality may be born, and grow, and flourish—and die—in the wake of something new.

What was once irrefutable then becomes irrelevant. What is known to be *true*—provable to the extent that it becomes unquestionable—suddenly is able to be penetrated. The structures of perfection itself are seen to be flawed. And the solid ground upon which your entire system of what "is" and what "is not" rests, is shown to be *fluid*. The static is known to be perpetual motion. And the "laws" governing all of it shuffle and reshuffle once more, in an effort to keep up with *the momentum of Eternal change*.

You can document what is true in this Now moment. And you can attempt to formulate a system that is designed to decode it. But, all the systems in your world can not begin to decode and structure a methodology for Divine Intent. Nor would you wish to. For, how can the Limitless be distilled into a formula and be expected to produce predictable results? The very basis of the phenomenal world is its very unpredictability.

Patterns may be drawn by those who perceive themselves as standing still, in a static reality, only to shatter when the tides of change touch the shifting sands of your world. The rubble that is the aftermath of inconceivable destruction forms the foundation for the safe and the sure. The floods of grief that come in the aftermath of such phenomena form the basis for the peace and serenity that wash over the devastation and purge the scene of its *karmic* structure.

In ways that are imperceptible to the physical senses, the seed of Life Itself is implanted in the residue of death and degeneration. And even though, on a human emotional scale, the event in question may register as Divinely heartless, from the vantage point of the Infinite, the inevitability of that level of change is a calculation whose moment was, and is, at hand.

The Divine opportunity inherent in the heights and the depths of human experience

In time, the cost in terms of human life for such an episode will come to be seen from the perspective of the timeless. A particular event will take its place within the annals of history as the ongoing patterns of creation and destruction that define your world continue to play out as human experience. The outpouring of the gestures of *compassion* speak to the sense of Oneness that grows within the heart of the collective consciousness present. The empathy stimulated to the surface of the composite awareness transcends borders that might have served to separate those bringing to life the heights and depths of human experience, on behalf of the whole.

Events that register, in their intensity, as "off the charts" serve to unite what has been fragmented. For, in these "moments of truth," one is able to view oneself in the mirror of the circumstances at hand, and to know that it is none other than one's own *Self* that has participated in—and witnessed—the entire drama.

Those who remain immersed in the clouded waters of *separation* will have their ways diverted, as humanity flows as a collective of awareness toward the seas of Divine Unity. And individual crises, no *less* impactful, experientially, than those experienced en masse in the far corners of your world, will come to pass. The loss that might be said to have been sustained will serve to lay the groundwork for the levels of *change* that are inevitable within the depths of each and every individual present. For, *change* is the order of the day and the recipe for redemption that the conditions at hand cry out for *vibrationally*.

One need not be touched, within the sanctity of one's *inner* Being, by circumstances being illustrated in the periphery of one's sense of Self-awareness. One is able to choose, through the medium of one's mechanism of response, how particular circumstances will either be drawn and internalized—or allowed to pass without creating so much as a ripple within.

One casts one's vote into the composite of collective experience with every waking breath. One draws one's lot in life from that pool of possibility, and acts it out on behalf of the whole, on the basis of one's Self perception—and on that basis alone.

Gone are the days when one could delude oneself into believing that circumstances simply *happen*. There is no such thing as "bad luck." Everything within the realm of experiential possibility is purposeful and calculated. All that is perceived operates within the structure of a system that is conceived in perfection and executed flawlessly. That structure will not change. It is a system calculated to sustain itself Eternally. And though the circumstances *illustrated* by that system can be seen to do so in response to shifts in the tides of global change, the system itself remains untouched. For, it is one conceived in the Eternal and birthed into the inevitability of Self-perpetuation.

You are here, experiencing yourself within it. You are *Here*, as Presence, in this *Now* moment, embodying *choice*. You are free to perceive yourself within the realm of the calamities that trigger panic and chaos as they unfold around you. Or, you may choose, in those "moments of truth," to embody *Self*-perception and to view the circumstances in which you find yourself from a vantage point that is found only within.

You may choose, in the heights of human desperation, to recognize the possibility of experiencing your Self as the Infinite and the Eternal. You may choose to know your Self—your *true Essence*—to remain untouched. You may choose to liberate yourself from the endless cycle—from the ebb and flow of the tides of creation and destruction that characterize the world of physical perception—in the space of a heartbeat.

You may choose, in the crescendo of life experience, to embody the inevitability of change playing out all around you and become swept up in that momentum. Or, in that same moment, you may choose to perceive your own Essence—as changeless.

For, despite the illusory details—regardless of what may appear in the guise of magnificence or horror—who you truly Are is none of that. The opportunity inherent in life's most poignant moments is the possibility that you might choose not simply to believe it—but to *know* it.

Despite what some may say, and certain texts may set forth as gospel, I can attest to the fact that the sacred journey to Oneness is not all a bed of roses. The peaks and valleys of the roller coaster ride to Realization continued to swerve and dip, even as the exalted state of Beingness seemed to be building to a crescendo. My mood and sense of Self-perception continued, on occasion, to peak and nosedive accordingly.

In the case of the persona named "Rasha," the linear identity was a tenacious character that persisted in trying to run the show until the last gasp. Much of the difficulty seemed to be rooted in the dilemma of the scope of the Oneness identity. It had been pointed out to me by certain *Advaita Vedanta* diehards in Tiruvannamalai, with no small degree of contempt, that if I had indeed Realized the Self as "Oneness," then I was also responsible for the contents of the book I'd transcribed. Which, surely I was not. And so, the ultimate *koan*, the convoluted symbolic riddle posed by Zen Masters to their students, presented itself to me in answer to the seemingly innocent question: "Who Am I?"

Spurred on to dig deeper, in an attempt to grasp the mind-boggling implications in owning up to *who* I now, by default, understood myself to Be, I got to the core issue: the very nature of Oneness. But, in order to untie the knot of the ultimate riddle, I needed first to resolve my own core issue: I had never asked for Self-Realization in the first place. It happened. From the outset, all I had wanted to do was to *"serve* God"—a larger-than-life God that I, like most people, had thought of as separate from myself. Now what? Now I had to deal with the truth. Oneness was *not* some mythical Wizard of Oz, up there in the sky somewhere. Oneness was real and alive—living within the illusory costume I thought of as "me."

Now, having gone the full distance, and having experienced myself *as* Oneness, there were suddenly profound implications that summoned the reappearance of the small linear identity from time to time. For there, lurking in the shadows of consciousness, was a fragment of identity who persisted in popping up now and then, who felt she was in way over her head and was petrified at the prospect of being forced to take responsibility for the words of Oneness.

Encompassing all of this was the master-puzzle itself. I continued to be baffled by the enormous difference I perceived between my own Self-perception and the magnitude of the Presence with which I had connected all these years—the one who had authored the concepts in the teachings that I'd transcribed. Both expressions of Presence went by the name of "Oneness." But, I could attest to the fact that they were worlds apart—which, in fact, they are—literally. It was a level of understanding that was yet to come.

❦

Rasha speaks:

The days have disappeared one into the next. I see that I have not been in communication for weeks now. I'm inclined to offer an apology. But then, to whom would I apologize? I have come to understand that Oneness is none other than my own Self. And yet, the issue continues to arise that I know that the one who walks around in my body is not at the same level as the one who emerges in these sessions of exalted Divine connection and writes these profound pages of wisdom. It goes without saying that the identity I consider to be "Rasha"—my "linear identity"—could never have written these words. She didn't even understand some of the concepts at first. She does not remember having written any of it.

So, ok, Oneness. Here I am, once again, floundering in the seas of self-doubt, rehashing issues that have been addressed who knows how many times. I seem to be back on the roller coaster.

Maybe, were it not for the memory issue, I might be able to retain the understandings I glean in these sessions. Maybe I wouldn't have to start at square one every day, like I'm playing the starring role in a real-life version of the movie, "Groundhog Day." I know there have been moments of exquisite clarity—moments of unquestionable connectedness—where all perception of this character called "Rasha" simply vanished into the embrace of something vast and unspeakably magnificent. I know I have not imagined that.

I look at these stacks of notebooks. Thousands of pages have been documented. I've been re-reading my own writings of years ago and reliving them. I know I haven't imagined that either.

As I write these words, I see that Rasha is marginally present now. A wave of deep contentedness sweeps over me. Your sweet smile spreads over my lips. Oneness is here. I can feel the Divine

Presence hovering in the epicenter of my being. So, who is it that documents these thoughts? I do. Who I am now is anyone's guess.

The words come from far away now. They pass through form. They do not emanate from the realm of mind. These thoughts are not coming from the Presence that experiences itself here—the Presence of Oneness. They are simply being documented by that Presence. Once again, Oneness is channeling Rasha. Rasha now is nowhere to be found.

Ok, Oneness. Rasha is tired of this. This game of hide and seek. Now I am here—and now I am not. Who is this "I" who persists in appearing and disappearing? She does not wish to be here anymore. Take this body and do with it what you will. Have this consciousness! I donate it to the cause. I have no interest in being present in this illusory world anymore. Who is this "I" who has these thoughts? Where is she now? Perhaps she will go this time, never to return. Perhaps.

Oneness speaks:

Take a moment and breathe with these energies now, Rasha. Let the joys of full connectedness permeate your being once more. In this moment of Divine Unity, there are no doubts, no concerns—no world. The world is a place relegated to a distant dream. Here in this Still place, there is only serenity.

Breathe now. And let the fullness of this Presence engulf your senses. Let the breaths come slow and deep. The illusory world is a world away now. The concerns and aggravations that haunted your mind have given way to a distancing. Here in the center of your own Being there is no such disturbance.

Oneness, in this moment you fill every nuance of my Being with quiet delight. The feeling of utter peace engulfs my senses. It is so extraordinary, and in the same breath, so very natural. It's like the veils have been pulled back and what is already there has been revealed. For, who I experience myself to Be in this moment is none other than my own Self, taken to an exponential level of possibility.

We are aware that there are questions and a need for clarification as to the nature of the process that is transpiring. We will recapture the essence of the teachings for you, once again, so that you can be entirely clear as to the nature of what is happening within you.

There is only one Oneness, experiencing Presence at infinite levels of complexity

There is only one Oneness. This Oneness experiences ourSelf in myriad forms, at infinite levels of complexity. Certain of these forms are extremely elaborate and operate at the level of *Deity*. Yet, each has an identity and characteristics, not unlike those you yourself experience.

As you ascend to accelerated levels of perception, you take on the augmented characteristics of that level of *your own Essence*—as Oneness. And you experience that level of Beingness as that which *you* Are. This is no less true at levels that *transcend* that which you consider to be Self-Realization. For, the process surely does *not* stop there. The very nature of the ascension process dictates that the momentum driving all Creation toward Unity is infinite and ongoing.

The *expansive* nature of Oneness with one's own Eternal Self

There is no need, once one has Realized one's true nature as Divinity in form, to think that the "game is over" and nothing remains to be experienced. Those who are thus misguided are serving to guide others in a direction that is dead-ended. You have been carefully guided through the maze of linear ascension. You have Realized your identity as Oneness. Yet, that identity is surely not the full spectrum of possibility. You are not the full representation of the one you would consider to be "God," in form—not yet. In time, you will experience that level of connectedness. You are no *less* Oneness now than you will be at that stage of your unfoldment. You will simply be embodying the *expanded* state, taken to the fullness of possibility.

The issues in question have given you a good basis for processing the *core issue* that is underlying all that is experienced—the question of *"Who Am I?"* It is only *after* the state of attainment has been Realized that this question can be posed in any meaningful way. For, the linear identity has no basis for understanding what it is—or is not. Only the Self has a basis for comparison, experientially. For, the *memories* of having perceived life through the filter of linear awareness do not disappear once one has attained the perspective of the Self. Those memories serve to underscore what one comes to understand that one now *is not.* One can then look back over the landscape that one has traversed and see the state of beingness that made the journey. Who one has come to Be can do so from the *perspective* of the overview—the *perspective* of Oneness.

Oneness explains the difference between "The Self" and "Oneness"

Who you know yourself to Be is not *other than* the Presence that encompasses that Self during these transcription sessions. In the process of making the shift into what we have come to term "full connectedness," the sense of Presence *expands* and one is able to perceive oneself as Oneness. This is no different than the process we have implemented together from the onset of this work. The difference lies only in the *level* of Self-perception of the one experiencing Presence in form. The shift into connection with Oneness takes place in either case and is the direct result of one's *focus of attention*. Ultimately, that same skill of *focusing on the Divinity within* serves to bring about the shift in Self-awareness, such that one is able to perceive the Presence that is really there—and to know oneself to Be That.

The Self is no less the limitless Presence than any other expression of Oneness. The difference lies in the *awareness* of the Self of its true identity. The

Self has not become something other than what it already Is, upon attaining the state known as Self-Realization. Its nature has not changed in any way. It is simply absolutely clear on who and what it Is.

Certain modifications in the human tendency to react in ways that traditionally stimulate emotional response and create the experience of adversity, quite naturally take place in the process of preparing an individual for the *possibility* of that Realization. But, even those efforts, were they executed to perfection, would not be sufficient to bring about the state of Oneness with the Divine. Only one's absolute *focus upon the Divinity within* brings about that shift in perspective and the subsequent diminishing of one's linear vantage point.

Therein lies the difference between embodying *the Self*—and embodying *Oneness*. The Self is that personalized aspect of Divine Presence that recognizes itself in form. Oneness is the Presence of Absolute Awareness—transcending perspective.

As I wrestled with those understandings theoretically, I began to integrate them experientially, and the sense of the identity of the Self as Oneness began to stabilize within me. Processing those understandings, there was one particularly poignant moment where the dilemma of Divine connectedness seemed to come to a head. For, despite the fact that I perceived myself as the Self and had become adept at modulating the nature of my experiences in the physical world by sustaining the focus of my attention on the identity presiding within—something was missing.

It was not that Oneness was missing. For, Oneness continued to be Present during the transcription sessions, which continued on a regular basis. What was missing during those moments was Rasha. Suddenly, there was absolutely no awareness of *my own linear identity* when the Presence of Oneness *expanded* into the fullness of Self-perception—and now typed the teachings directly onto my laptop, through the form I've always thought of as "me." It was as though I had lost my best friend, my partner, the Love of my life! Yet, Oneness hadn't gone away. It was my habitual sense of my own identity that now went missing whenever the *full magnitude* of Oneness was Present in form.

Rasha struggles with the concept of the Oneness identity
Rasha speaks:

Oneness, I hesitate to write these words, since I've started to feel that to even admit that I still exist is to concede defeat at some level. Yet, the truth is, I have not ceased to exist. I, Rasha, am still around sometimes. Where exactly I am, I cannot say. And even as I write these words, I cannot say that they are coming from the Presence I perceive in this moment, within this form, as myself. I have the distinct sense that these words are coming through this Presence—as though they were being channeled.

I am grateful that we have retained this ability to converse, by whatever means it takes. It's beyond frustrating to realize that I have once again disappeared into the totality of Oneness at the one time when there is an opportunity to talk—and then, afterwards, to find that I am once again back in the body! I really have no problem with being in residence in this body. I am perfectly ok with the idea of being a Messenger. Life was very nice when it was that way. I could handle that. It was very natural. And we've been functioning in that way for quite some time.

Now this idea that I, Rasha, am to dematerialize in the wake of the Realization that I am Oneness has brought with it all sorts of repercussions. If that is how it's going to be, then who is it who will be said to be responsible for writing the book? I cannot accept that Rasha wrote the book. She absolutely did not. Whether or not her essence is actually Oneness is irrelevant to the fact that she was not in that state of Self-perception when that book was written.

And yes, I can perceive the instant relief from the feelings that might have accompanied Rasha's mental process, when shifting into the perspective of Oneness. Yet, even in hat state of Self-perception, the sense of Beingness does not begin to approach the state I experience when I am in *communion* with Oneness.

In this moment, I am experiencing such a state of communion. I recognize that there is access to two distinct trains of consciousness, perceived simultaneously. And I can distinguish between them and the two can converse with each other. That seems to be the skill that this identity we call "Rasha" has become adept at. So, now what? Am I to just provide the vehicle for Oneness to write directly? If there is actually no Rasha—if I really am no more than a file that can be closed and ejected from the system—then why am I still around? Would you care to comment on any of this, Oneness?

Oneness speaks:

You do not actually require an answer to any of this, you know. You know the answers. You *Are* the answer. How you choose to *experience* this is what is optional. This is what you are creating—and this is what you will continue to create—so long as you experience yourself in physical form. That you know yourself to *Be* Oneness is, by now, unquestionable. For, you have had the experience of it. You know it. The challenge for you is to sustain that state of Beingness, so you can walk *as* Oneness.

(The voice of the linear identity)

What would be so terrible if we simply retained the capacity for being Rasha who is able to connect with Oneness and to access Divine teachings in that state? That would be believable! Now, Rasha is expected to go out there and present all this. Hmmm. Maybe she doesn't have to go out there at all. Maybe she can stay safe inside. You go out there, Oneness. You wrote this book. Rasha wants to stay home. I'll watch you do this from some cozy corner of this consciousness. You are welcome to all of it. I just like the blessed communion—the private, exalted parts of this experience.

(The voice of the Self)

Now, as I say these words, I watch as words appear on a screen before me, and I realize that, once again, I am simply channeling a perspective. For, in the process of venting these sentiments, a shift occurred. And I see that the Presence that is here is no longer "Rasha," the linear identity. She is somewhere within the composite of this Presence. But now, her perspective has faded into the background. It is as though she is no longer here. So, now whose perspective is being documented? (silence) The hands wait poised on the keyboard.

There are infinite possible perspectives that might be documented here, Rasha. This is Oneness. This is the perspective of which you are a part. This is the *overview* of the consciousness that is made manifest in the form you consider to be *you*. It is this perspective that presides in this moment. You have willed that into being. And so it is.

Oneness summarizes the nature of the Rasha/Oneness identity—in a nutshell

Essentially, this is how we will be presenting this identity. This identity will be called "Rasha." She will have access to the wisdom and the perspective of Oneness, within the context of the identity of Rasha. The Rasha identity will continue to transcribe the teachings of Oneness and to present them to the world. She will not deny that the source of these teachings is Oneness. She will not imply that she, as the essence of the linear identity, conceived this work.

She will present herself to the world as the Messenger. She will, at the same time, know herself to *Be* Oneness. She will continue, for the foreseeable future, to access a heightened state of Divine Connectedness—one that is amplified vibrationally—in order to transcribe the teachings that will continue to be forthcoming. Yet, that state is not identical with the state that is *experienced* while out in the world.

The *Essence* of the identity is Oneness, in either case. The *experience* of that state of Beingness is what can and will vary, according to the *vibrational variables* that constitute physical perception. And the *perception* of the level of connectedness will deepen accordingly. In truth, however, nothing will actually have changed at all. For, Oneness simply—*Is*. Rasha's *experience* of Oneness will continue to evolve, as time goes on. This is not a static condition. It is one that is continuing to define and redefine itself in the ongoing Now moment.

    I understand.

We see that you do. You will not *disappear* until you are ready to take the initiative to do so. No one is ousting you from the physical form. You are very much a part of this identity. Yet, you have, by now, come to understand that the nature of this identity is far broader than the scope of the linear perspective that exercised proprietary rights over this form and the consciousness associated with it, for most of this lifetime. You have begun to experience the full extent of it. And that experience will continue to grow and deepen in the times to come.

A question arose that led to a fascinating explanation of the nature of *gender*. Oneness helped me understand our natural inclination to lean toward one orientation or the other, regardless of the gender of the human form, during this lifetime. The question was within the context of Mantra, and whether or not a woman should chant certain Mantras. I'd been told that it was forbidden in certain ancient scriptures for a woman to chant a particularly powerful Mantra to Lord Shiva.

I'd been studying this Mantra for over a year, and my identification as a "liberated" Western woman was incensed at the thought that my gender could govern whether or not it was ok for me to chant it when my heart felt drawn to do so.

For me, the question of the nature of gender overlapped with my exploration of the nature of the Self. After all, I was now clear that "I am not my body." How was it that someone who had, in theory, transitioned into the transcendent Self, would still be subject to guidelines on what women could and could not do? I was interested to know what the technical basis was for ancient teachings like this, and whether or not they were still relevant today.

The guidance I received from Oneness addressed my question from the timeless standpoint of *energy*. These teachings are here to empower us all with a format for making conscious choices.

Rasha speaks:

    Oneness, if we are each the embodiment of Oneness, then we should
    be able, equally, to worship the Divine in all its forms, through

Mantra, if we choose to. I honor and respect the technology of Spirit. I understand that each of these vibrational formulas is calculated to create certain effects upon the human energy field. I have difficulty accepting that it is dangerous for me to chant particular Mantras because I am a woman, as I've been told. Can we address the issue of why it is forbidden in ancient scriptures for women to chant certain Mantras?

Oneness speaks:

It is not advisable for you to attempt to refute, with logic, what has been written and is considered irrefutable gospel by those whose adherence to these ancient teachings is oriented toward *literal interpretation*. Thousands of years ago, when these directives were provided, the audience for which they were intended was in a far different frame of reference, culturally, than that same audience is today.

Why certain ancient traditions exclude women from aspects of spiritual practice

Women, as well as those whose standing in the community prevented them from living a spiritually-focused existence to the exclusion of all else, were not in a position to assimilate the energies generated by the chanting of such Mantras. These Mantras were given as *vibrational tools* for the use of those who were prepared, through generations, with an orientation toward life that would predispose them to imbibe these energies without undue side-effects.

These people, who were exclusively male, due to the custom of the times, spent the focus of their lives in spiritual pursuit. Their energy fields were tempered, from childhood, with practices that would serve to make it conducive for them to imbibe the elixir of these Mantras and to rise within the structure of the system that delivered them.

In those times, women were not permitted to take part in these kinds of activities, and thus were not prepared, experientially, with the vibrational fortitude to withstand the intensity of such Mantras. It was not for any reasons of *inherent* differences in vibration that made certain Mantras taboo for one gender or the other—but rather for practical considerations that were culturally induced, over thousands of years.

Oneness discusses the concept of gender

As a being, one spends lifetimes embodying humanness as one gender and then the other. No being is inherently male or female in his or her core Essence. Rather, it is due to the proportion of lifetimes embodying one gender over the other, and the intensity of gender-specific orientation *during* such lifetimes, that would leave one with the sense of having a natural inclination to identify as one gender or the other.

Such tendencies are *experientially* induced—not inherently present. Thus, one's inclination to be drawn to certain activities, such as chanting particular Mantras, would be a reflection of one's incarnate history. One's capacity for doing so would not be influenced, necessarily, by the gender in which the individual presently experiences himself in form, but would be more a reflection of the *experiential preparation* that individual would bring to the moment in question. The symptoms that may result from such chanting would vary accordingly.

We can state, unequivocally, that there is absolutely no danger—and no breech of Divine contract—in attempting to learn certain Mantras, when one's orientation is that of devotion and one approaches that undertaking with a purity of heart and mind.

There are some that interpret ancient scripture to the letter. And those individuals can rest with confidence that they have not transgressed the edicts that have been handed down faithfully through generations of particular cultures. However, know that the integrity of certain of these scriptures withstood the test of time—while others bent to the distortions in nuance and interpretation that are the natural result of longevity. These instruments are far from the infallible documents they are believed to be.

There is no need to feel that your perspective has been validated by this information. To take one position over another and to defend it self-righteously would be the battle cry of the ego in its need to appear right in its own eyes. Know that there is no right and no wrong in these matters—there is only cause and consequence.

The foundation for making conscious choices

In considering whether or not to bow to the directives being offered, however passionately they may be presented, it would serve you well to weigh the motives of those concerned. Were the motive to dominate and subjugate another, to instill fear for that purpose, or in general to inflict suffering, one could confidently back away from the guidance with a clear heart—regardless of *what* has been quoted from the scripture in question.

Were the motive of the one offering the guidance coming from a detached and loving space, one might wish to consider carefully what has been offered and to weigh one's own motives for resisting that guidance. When one is absolutely clear on the purity of one's own intentions in following a particular path, and equally clear that they are not emanating from a place of ego, one can feel confident in taking any stance at all—and in following one's own heart—regardless of *what* timeless tradition may have to say on the matter.

38

———

By the time I'd returned to Tiruvannamalai in 2005, I'd been wrestling with the prospect of weaving a tapestry of my spiritual journey—intertwined with the precious personal guidance of Oneness that had helped me forge my way through the jungles of consciousness—for well over a year. I'd put it aside and pick it back up, over and over again. Each time, it seemed, I approached it at yet another level of perception. Each time, the ground I'd covered in the eight years of writings I was attempting to plow through took on yet another shade of insight.

I began to feel as though I were drowning in the sheer volume of Divine wisdom I was attempting to sift through. And I was daunted by the prospect of taking something that was so literally mind-boggling, and exponentially far-reaching, and condense it into something that was even remotely comprehensible. How exactly was I supposed to put into words an experience that defied expression? The task seemed insurmountable.

Were it not for the persistence of Oneness who, it seemed, was overseeing the entire drama, the project might have been shelved for good. I'd begun to wonder: exactly *who*—what aspect of this multi-faceted spectrum of identity I'd experienced myself to be along the way—was expected to compile this tome? Was it Rasha, who housed the archives of linear memory? Was it Oneness, who presented a thoroughly detached overview of all of it? Was there a difference?

I began to see that there was not. For, in the coming together of the story of what had happened—in combing through the history of the doubts and fears, the triumphs and the disasters, of my own spiritual soap-opera—the aspects of self that had collectively played the starring role in all those episodes had converged. And in pulling together a comprehensible dossier of my adventures within the labyrinths of consciousness, I recognized that in the process I'd *become* the collective Presence, that sublime, elusive aspect of Being which my linear default setting presumed it was still seeking.

Oneness had infinite patience. Despite all I could do to avoid the inevitable, Oneness held a sense of personal "destiny" that wouldn't go away.

Much as I squirmed and wriggled on the hook of self-doubt and denial, there was the sense of an overriding *momentum* way beyond the control of the "free will" that the inner coward was attempting to exercise. In the end, I surrendered the fight and began to float rather than continuing to swim for dear life against the current. To my amazement, it all began to come together: the story and the multi-dimensional One who had lived it.

I returned to Pondicherry in early spring for a few days' change of scenery and, at the break of dawn, sat on my little balcony high above the emerald lawns overlooking the sea and watched the sun birth itself into this illusory world. The waves of the Bay of Bengal lapped at the rocks that separated the sea from the shore. I reflected, as each wave approached, that it had its moment of earthly definition and then receded into the wholeness of the ocean once more, no differently than did life itself. I was the silent witness, sitting in the cool breath of sunrise, watching.

Sri Aurobindo Ashram's Park Guest House provided a quiet reprieve from the intensity that is India, already beginning to bustle outside the main gate. The lush greenery in the foreground dotted the scenery with tropical flora. The coconut palms danced before me, abandoned to the rhythms of the breeze, each playing its own part in the harmony of sun, sea, and sky. "I too Am Here—ever-Present," I wrote. I stopped, poised in mid-breath, and stared at what had just been written. When there was no longer a thought as to who or what *I* might *be*, the sense of a personal self had shifted into a melded vision, the perspective of the Transcendent. Oneness was in full attendance once more. Yet, suddenly I perceived that Presence as my very own Being.

❧

Rasha/Oneness speaks:

We Are the transcendent Self. And we are no less the identity that bears it into the world. We are the exalted sense of Presence that knows itself to be equally the speck of dust that drifts unnoticed through the gutters of mundane existence. We Are the Infinite and the Eternal, and we are no less the transient and the measurable. For, there is nothing that We are not.

The sense of Presence that documents these sentiments is no more and no less Oneness than is any other expression of Isness. We have simply joined the ranks of those whose awareness of that state of Beingness is apparent to them. There remains the possibility of free will and the inevitability of choice. Here, fully manifested in circumstances where every gesture of one's existence serves as the ongoing expression of one's sense of selfhood, one embodies the principles of duality that govern physical existence. And in the same breath, one embodies one's own sense of liberation from those very constraints. The Realized Self is one who dwells in the balance, abiding in the full spectrum of possibility that encompasses those divergent states of self-perception.

This Presence is at peace now. There is not the sense of an agenda. There is no sense of urgency to do anything. There is no sense of a personal destiny that must be fulfilled. There is no need to be somebody or to make the most of what is left of this lifetime. There is the knowingness that those considerations are meaningless.

Yes, I am Rasha, with an awareness that there is a direction in which I am headed. There is a sense of certain commitments that have been made as a part of that predestination. There is a willingness to act out that script, one that somehow seems to be required of me, but there is no great desire to do so. I am prepared to share my experiences of this journey of Self-Realization with those who may be inclined to spend their own time considering it. I do not feel any pull to try to convince anyone of anything.

So, ok. I'll tell the story. That is what I seem to be moving toward doing, manifesting some sense of destiny brought forth by none other than my own Self. Who or what that may be does not concern me.

I see that I am drifting in and out of levels of self-perception. It is as though my consciousness were flipping through the channels of a TV, seeing what may happen to be playing on any one of them. It's always the same show, but with slightly different variations. I suppose that is the nature of the Self in which I abide.

I waited for Oneness to jump in and begin to narrate my story. I felt very much in a state of *connectedness*. But, I didn't feel a separate consciousness of Oneness coming forth and doing the speaking. Then, suddenly, it was clear. Oneness was Present in the body. And Oneness was documenting a perspective. In fact, Oneness was documenting a *full spectrum* of perspectives, all of them mine. The words coming forth were not coming *from* Oneness, they were coming *through* Oneness. And *I* was no more or less one than the other.

In a timeless instant, as I breathed that stunning realization deep into the core of my being, the Presence *expanded*, exponentially. And the unfathomable level of Presence that had merged with my consciousness all these years, and had written the book *Oneness*, was there, larger than life, once more.

Oneness speaks:

You *see*, it takes no time at all now to shift into a state of full *connectedness* with the Source of your Being. Simply holding the *intention* manifests that result. Years back, you wondered how "we knew" whether or not you truly intended to commune with Oneness. The connection was Present when the intention was set. When you were only toying with the idea of communion, the Presence was not automatically forthcoming. Now, you understand that we are not other than your own Self. There are no secrets. All is revealed. All is in the open before this audience of One. There *Is* no separation.

Oneness talks about the methodology of manifesting the Dream

Now is the time to set your vision on what it is you wish to accomplish with this life. For, you have the power now to manifest your Dream. Without a clear picture of what that Dream is to be, there is not the means with which to manifest it. Your destiny is not one that will be cast upon you by outside sources. Your destiny is etched in the ethers and will blossom with the fullness of *time*, given the manifestation of the *intent* that will call it forth.

That destiny is not unbeknownst to you. You feel it. You know it. Yet, to call forth the highest *expression* of that scenario, your conscious *focus* is required. This is the balance between *pre-destination* and *free-will* with which humankind is equipped in this level of self-perception you consider to be *reality*.

You are demonstrating these principles to yourself as you apply them to your own personal situation. The *outcome* of the scenario that will soon be called forth into manifestation is determined by your choices. Hold the highest vision of what you know to be on the horizon, and you will add the element of *directedness* to the mix calculated to call forth that very result.

Putting the journey, and the prospect of dissecting it, into perspective

You are concerned with what to include and what to omit from the writings you are attempting to edit. We will tell you that your purpose in creating this particular work is to reveal your own personal experience of the journey to Oneness. In the process of that experience, certain universal principles were revealed that would benefit all who are making the same journey. Yet, in revealing your personal journey, you are not setting a precedent for others. You are simply illustrating the principles with your own experience. The work will be an equal balance of vignettes and of the theoretical understandings that were provided to make the experiences relevant.

You are not being asked to whitewash your journey for the sake of your audience. You are being asked to be authentic. For, it is that very transparency that will spark recognition in the hearts of others. You are not here to create an illusion of an idealized being that made this journey. You are here to reveal the truth of it. You are here in your triumphs and your tragedies, your doubts and fears, as well as your moments of clarity and confidence. You are all of what has gone into your working up, not just the pretty parts.

Oneness reveals the overview of my journey and provides the rationale for the roller coaster of experience that was necessary to bring it to fruition

The relinquishing of the ego identity was the task you set about to accomplish. That achievement is not possible from the standpoint of a fortress. It is only possible when the fortress is made to crumble and fall. The dissolving of the ego self is only accomplished when there is literally *nothing there*. It is not your failing, but rather your triumph that you surrendered the fight to retain a sense of pride in your capabilities—a pride reinforced by evidence of so-called success.

The capabilities are not less for having relinquished your attachment to the idea that they comprised your sense of self-definition. You were brought to the point that you realized that your sense of who you *were*, in the eyes of the illusory world, had absolutely no relevance to your emerging sense of who you truly *Are*. That role, which was played superbly, was shown to you to be no more than a file of memories. Access to those memories could be dissolved, or reinstated, with absolutely no effect upon your sense of Self. *You* remained, despite mentalized evidence of a so-called *past*—or the absence of it.

The Self that emerged from that compendium of history is transcendent. That sense of *Beingness* is the one you have now embraced as "who you Are." Who you *were* in a previous moment, or a previous decade, or even a previous lifetime, can now be relegated to the archives of the illusory world. For, it is in this Now moment that you dwell—as Oneness.

Oneness has no attachment to the *accomplishments* of the illusory past. Oneness is not at all concerned with whether or not a world of confused people consider the physical vehicle carrying this identity to be a success or a failure. Oneness is not in any way interested in whether such people label this identity as a Saint or a fraud. It surely makes no difference at all to the truth of who we Are and what we are here to bring forth.

We will embody that sense of consummate detachment. We have divorced our sense of *Self* from the history amassed by the body-mind of this vehicle. We are here Now, to recapture the essence of that journey, with the detachment that comes of attaining the overview. And we will present that journey with a sense of objectivity, devoid of an investment in how that work is received.

We are here to reveal to the world the essence of a grand adventure. That adventure took place within the sanctity of the consciousness of the one who believed herself to have made the journey. She took great pains to document the experience in intricate detail, without any sense of why she was doing it. The process of written transcription became the vehicle for the very skills required in bringing the journey about.

Now, having made the journey, you can see it—for *We* can see it. And there is no difference between the two. You have not faltered in coming to this point without a sense of triumph in hand to wield as evidence. You have come to this point naked of pretense. You have come to this point having embraced the exquisite sense of *vulnerability* that characterizes the final stages of relinquishing the ego-identity, and surrendering in the face of a higher knowingness. You have transcended the inclination to condemn yourself for your humanness and have seen it as the gift you have come all this way to receive.

You came for the foray into humanness. You explored any number of avenues that beckoned to you with the promise of reward or fulfillment. And having reaped the balance of joy and pain that is the nature of the journey, you recognized that the sense of inner *purpose,* as a being, was not addressed by any of it. The result of each and every one of those efforts was *irrelevant,* regardless of whether or not that result fulfilled the expectations with which it was brought about. At the end of the day, *you* remained.

That sense of *you*-ness diminished as time went on. The sense of *assertiveness* that would thrust you out and into the eyes of the world dematerialized. And the *memories* of that sense of inner momentum, and the recognition that it was now missing, led you to question your capabilities, and to consider the possibility that what was being projected was now out of reach. Now you *see* that those very shortcomings—the state of beingness you would consider to be a handicap—was a necessary step.

It was necessary to *re-create* this identity as one characterized by limitation, in order that all attachment to the identity might be relinquished and the *limitlessness* that is your true nature could be embraced. Now that the journey has been made, those constraints can be released. For, they no longer serve the higher purpose of this identity. Your capacity for memory will be restored, over time. Your sense of who you know yourself to Be will be strengthened. And in the interim period, you will recapture the essence of the odyssey that brought you home.

Your absolute focus on your state of Union as the embodiment of the full spectrum of your identity as Oneness is all that is required. In this Now moment, We Are that Oneness, enjoined in a breath of timelessness. Know this. And be at peace.

The full spectrum of perspectives and emotions began filtering through my awareness, like a deck of cards being shuffled and reshuffled, in the days that followed. During the writing sessions, I was unable to say *who* I was or *where*, within the infinite scope of all I'd experienced as "myself," I actually was located in that moment. My Presence was clearly non-physical.

The daily communication shifted consistently into one that was being "channeled" *through* the Presence that appeared to be in attendance in the physical form I'd always thought of as "myself." I saw that "I"—the linear identity—was not any longer *in* the physical form. And yet, I seemed to have *access* to it—as though the consciousness associated with it were a format for the documentation of my impressions.

It was as though the persona was a *program* through which any number of perspectives and impressions were able to come to life. Which one was authentic or valid was anyone's guess. And as I wrote those words, the knowingness was also there that they were all authentic and valid. They were all simply different slants on the same story. To punctuate the point, I acted out one particularly dramatic illustration of shifting between perspectives that drove the realization home.

I'd sat at my little altar a few moments before, deep in prayer and sacred communion. I had chanted Goddess Mantras for several hours and was reveling in a sublime state of Divine connectedness. I could feel the Presence of the Divine Mother within my body, as it swayed with the joy of that Presence. The sweet smile that signals her Presence was on my lips. The deep sense of utter well being radiated from within my heart. In that moment, all was well with my world.

But, within seconds, a fleeting *thought* of a particularly hurtful letter I'd received flashed across the screen of my mental circuitry. Instantly, I could feel the mind begin to ruminate over any number of other situations, situations in which I felt like I had failed myself. I looked up at the little picture of Jeshua on my altar, and then at the photograph of Dr. Bindu. And I began to sob uncontrollably.

In that moment, all was lost. I had failed in my life's work. I was a disappointment to those who believed in me. And I had let myself down in every way imaginable. Instantly, my mind took that ball and ran with it. And I could actually *feel* the hypothetical doom and gloom scenarios that were waiting in the wings of my consciousness being activated. Within seconds, I felt just awful.

Suddenly, yet another presence which was also *me* stepped in and took charge. "Who is it who is feeling like a failure?" that aspect of self inquired, as if aloud. Abruptly, all thought stopped. There was absolute silence within. I smiled that enigmatic "Mona Lisa smile" that flashes involuntarily across my face when I've caught myself in the act of going into automatic pilot and giving credence to some "tape" that's airing in my head.

As I did, the entire foregoing train of thought simply vanished. With it, the *feelings* those thoughts had conjured up within me—which only seconds before had seemed so valid—were gone. It was as if it had never happened. I dried my eyes, as the inner glow of Divine connectedness began to well up within me once more. It was a poignant illustration of the myriad possible slants through which one could *choose* to view the circumstances of one's life.

Something within me quipped "Will the real Rasha please stand up?" And I laughed aloud at the absurdity of what I had just acted out for myself. It was not a matter of one perspective being *real* and the others not. Each of these vantage points was valid. It was simply a matter of how I *chose* to look at it. All of these possibilities were fully there. I saw that it was really a matter of which perspective I wished to experience as my reality. It was really up to me. I realized that I was creating all of it with my choices. As if on cue, Oneness shifted into focus within and elaborated.

∽∿∽

Oneness speaks:

You have captured the essence of the message you have come to this moment to deliver to yourself. There are no shoulds or shouldn'ts in any of this. You are choosing from a menu of infinite possibility the selections which are calculated to validate your presumptions and the stances you have taken on certain issues. You are not required to make those selections. All possibilities are there before you.

There *is* no failure, outside of that which you have chosen to create. Those scenarios, if chosen, would illustrate for you the very failure your fear suggests is imminent. That way, you could get to be right about having failed. But, you also know that it is not necessary for you to make these choices. The option to abide in the Divine Connection that is so very Present is also an option that you are welcome to choose, and to experience.

The expression of devotion and the nature of the experience that results

You illustrated to yourself, during your Mantra chanting today, the difference between chanting from the standpoint of one who is *seeking* a connection and one who fully *abides* in that connection. When one approaches one's spiritual practice with the energy of desperately trying to make up for lost time, and catch up with all that one fears that one is not, then the sense of not being where one would wish to be is reinforced, and *that* becomes one's experience. When, however, one is fully confident in one's state of Being, the expression of devotion becomes an *affirmation* of what one knows to be so. And the perception of *that* state of Being is the experience perceived.

One's expressions of devotion are not the currency with which a Divine connection may be *bought*. They are the vehicles of one's passion. They are the medium through which a sense of connectedness may be *expressed*. Through the vehicle of one's prayers, a statement is made of what is so that is carried forth into manifestation. The validity of a Divine Presence is there as an ever-present affirmation of who you know yourself to Be at the highest level. It takes only the focus of attention to activate that sense of Presence. And it is from the vantage point of that perspective that the circumstances of life may be viewed, if you so choose. There is no need for analysis. You have the illustrations blatantly before you. Watch the movie. And know that you are creating it in every ongoing moment.

In the weeks that followed, the nature of the moments of Divine connectedness, and the personal writings that invariably resulted, shifted. I began to notice that I was no longer *dialoguing* with Oneness, in the sense of a conversation where two trains of thought interacted with each other. I realized that for quite some time, the writing sessions had taken on the style of a monologue once more. The only difference was that now there was no longer a sense of a linear identity present documenting that guidance— wisdom gleaned from a Source that was perceived as separate from myself. Now, the perspective *felt* like it was that of Oneness, yet I recognized the sentiments expressed to be *my* own reflections.

Rasha speaks:

The days pass, strung end to end, with no cohesiveness to them at all. Each is but a montage of instants, random and illusory. I have the sense of the irrelevance of all that I so long presumed to be meaningful. For, wherein would the meaning be? Is there any significance to this personal vantage point on a fragmentary slice of illusion that I think of as my life? Is there any real importance to anything that might be said or done? Would it matter if I were not sitting here at all, documenting these sentiments on the off chance that some other illusory particle of Oneness might experience recognition and joy in it?

From whence does the impetus to document these words derive? Surely it is not from the mind. That mind has exited the body now. There is simply Presence, content in this form simply to Be, documenting sentiments retrieved from the Infinite, onto a machine. It is as though God were taking dictation from that Self-same Presence, translating the ethereal Essence of illumination into the structured format of the mundane. The absurdity of it strikes a chord within. And a gentle smile spreads across the face of this form.

We know that we might have chosen to experience awareness elsewhere in this moment. We might be riding the waves and drinking in the freshness of an ocean breeze with this very breath. But, no. We have chosen to be here. Here in this dusty day, here in this parched landscape. We have chosen to craft this moment to mirror the others that have gone before. We have chosen to forego the chance to create something memorable with this breath of Nowness with which we have been gifted. Let us not mourn for the instant that has not come to pass. Let us rejoice in the miracle that Is, for this miracle of Nowness is All that Is.

Let us choose to rejoice in the journey in the rickshaw today, taking us nowhere special. Let us choose to experience delight in the imagery we've seen a thousand times before. Let us breathe this breath, in this very instant, as though it were our first as well as our last. For, it is just that.

What might delude us into believing that one breath might be more meaningful than another? What might distract us from the exquisite focus of attention that would transform the illusion of misery into one of delight? What might beckon to us from afar and tempt us with longing for something that we might delude ourselves into believing we are without? Could there be anything we are without? How could there be? It is all Here! Here in this precious moment. Here in the embrace of this Nowness. This Oneness. For, the possibility of every imaginable joy is held within it.

Every ordinary option glistens with promise. Every unlikely outcome turns around in a heartbeat when one views that possibility through the eyes of Oneness. That perspective is no less an option.

One does not need to "qualify" in some linear fashion for the experience of contentment. It is a choice that is made in every ongoing moment by each and every being present in form. No possibility is a foregone conclusion, until it is one made manifest through our choice of it. All possibilities are no less possible than others. All possibilities carry the potential of defying the laws of probability and rising to the fullness of manifestation, given the appropriate conditions.

We are here for the possibility to call forth those improbabilities from the clutches of the ethers that would withhold them. We are not here simply to reap the harvest that is abundant and apparent. We are here to command the inconceivable to come forth, if only for the sense of autonomy that would be elicited from our own very depths in the process.

It is on the chance that we might experience that unfathomable sense of the miraculous; it is on the remote possibility that we might stake our claim on just one breath of triumph from the bleary days of drudgery; it is on the chance that we might, against all odds, cull that priceless pearl from a shell of our own choosing—a shell that outwardly appears to all the world no different than any other—that we have chosen this infinitesimal flash of illumination we know of as "life."

The pearl dwells within us, hidden in plain view. It is not out there tucked into the pocket of illusory scenery, in a world that beckons to the fortune hunter. It is not there where the possibility of triumph rests on ravaging the dreams of others. It waits in the silent depths of Stillness, with the Infinite patience of all Eternity. Shining.

By early spring, I had made my peace with the process and with the project of translating it into a chronicle of spiritual emergence that had some semblance of coherence. The battle that had ensued within me for so very long had subsided. And in its place a sense of Stillness prevailed.

Rasha speaks:

My mind is suspended in my heart now. And my heart is home. The breaths come slow and deep. Not even a moment has passed since I opened the door to this Divine connection, and in that fraction of an instant I traversed all Creation. I made the full journey across an expanse that is Infinite and Eternal. I embraced a thousand destinies, all contained in this moment of wonder. And I synthesized all of it in a breath. This very breath. This breath of Life—this Now.

The identity of who is speaking in this instant does not matter. For, we recognize that we Are all of it. There is no separation between the one whose identity characterizes this form and the Presence that presides in this moment. They are One Being. We know this. These words flow forth, as if penned by a will of their own. They flow as a testimony to a state of Beingness that is recognized as unquestionable. There are no doubts. There is simply surrender.

A myriad of images pass before the mind's eye in the space of a heartbeat. A breeze from the fan overhead caresses the skin and delights. There is no thought of the heat or the presumed discomfort of this season. The Nowness of the breeze is all that needs to be perceived.

This heart is filled with the joy of imminent discovery. For, each ongoing instant brings forth yet another layer of joyousness. We recognize the perfection in all of it. And we rejoice at the miracle of our sense of Presence. We have chosen to perceive what is real. We have chosen to focus our awareness, absolutely and unwaveringly, upon our own recognition of this very Presence. And the scenery that presents itself for our "viewing pleasure" does so through the lens of that perspective.

Any number of perspectives are possible upon this little scene. And depending upon the angle from which it is viewed, one could choose to experience rapture, or pain, or any of the other infinite versions of perception. In the moment of Now, we are not invested in deriving our sense of Beingness from the scenery. It does not affect us in any way. It merely serves as a backdrop to the drama unfolding within.

This particular drama takes place in Silence. It reveals itself in the Stillness of this surrendered heart. It is a scenario enscripted in the archives of timelessness and delivered, right on schedule, unto this breath of Eternal Nowness. An awakening has taken place once more. This awakening has had a thousand births in this particular body. This newness is neither new nor old. It is eternally unfolding, presenting with every freshly discovered glimpse of it, the awesome wonder of that discovery.

Let the sun of a thousand mornings fill this world with this moment of delight! Let all the world know what is possible! Let us all detach from the focus that is external, the lens that is pointed in the wrong direction. Let there be no more "looking." For, what there is to have is already found. It is Here. Here in this breath of sweetness and delight.

There is a newness to these words. It is as though these perceptions were a revelation, the documentation of a great discovery! Something that has never been seen before. Yet, to all appearances, this is a most ordinary moment. It is no different, to the observer, than a myriad other moments that have passed in this place. The mundane details of this scenery are not even worth noting. They are not special in any way. It is simply a matter-of-fact April morning in South India, embellished by the crystalline focus of a newborn set of eyes.

How could this not be the first time such clarity could be brought to a moment through this vehicle of form? There is such a sense of immediacy to it! Such a sense of revelation! Could this possibly, really be the same world that seemed so mundane in the days recently passed? Could this enchanted place, tingling with the very breath of Divinity, really have been disguised in the dreariness of this scenery, all this time? Nothing has changed. Yet, everything has changed. All is illuminated, through the eyes of Now.

Let the breaths come slow and deep now. Let this Blessed Oneness with All That Is be all that is perceived. None of the scenery is really there at all. It only appears to be. The workers out in the field beyond only appear to be fashioning bricks out of soil and sand. The buckets of water, hauled from the adjacent creek only appear to be tossed in the air. And the sparkles upon that muddy spray only appear to glisten in the sunlight. In fact, none of it is there at all.

The lush greenery on the balcony, rooted in neat little pots, sit there, patiently awaiting their early morning drink. The birds chatter and squawk from a neighboring roof, shouting urgent-sounding commands into the ethers. Even the little chipmunks, tucked so secretly into the nooks and crannies of the palm-leaf roof that shades the balcony, add their commentary to the symphony that is the collective. Yet, all of them are illusory, and not really there at all. They only believe that they are. As do we.

I too am here, knowing that I am no less a mythical part of this Grand Illusion than any of the rest of it. It is crystal clear, here in this magical breath of Nowness, that this format for perception that I think of as "myself" is no more than an infinitesimal glimmer in a light spectrum. All this—this phenomenal world and myself within it—is simply a timeless instant of witnessing, captured for all Eternity. And in that same breath, the instant recedes into the embrace of oblivion, in a blink of Nowness, never to be remembered.

I too, am no more than an opalescent reflection in a soap bubble, floating through the cosmos on a collision course with its own destiny, yearning to explode into non-existence once more. I am Oneness incarnate—as Are we all—captured in the fleeting perception of breath, in this very fragile, improbable moment of Now.

39

————

In early summer of 2005, I found myself back, once again, in the foothills of the Himalayas. There I sat, high up on a cliff, taking stock of the shifting scenery within, while a breathtaking panorama of Rishikesh and its world-famous river, the Holy Mother Ganga, glistened outside my window. The wonders of the legendary sacred journey, known in India as *Char Dham Yatra,* loomed on the horizon. I'd finally decided to take the plunge and make the renowned, holy pilgrimage I'd been contemplating for years.

The traditional journey of Char Dham Yatra encompasses a sequential trek to four ancient Hindu temples, tucked away in remote corners of the Himalayas. Yamunotri, Gangotri, Kedarnath, and Badrinath, traditionally visited in that order, each have a sacred connection with a particular Deity and with the origin or confluence of certain rivers, each of which is said to be the embodiment of a Divine Presence. In India, the Char Dham Yatra is considered to be the ultimate spiritual destination—a pilgrimage people pray to be able to make once in a lifetime. The decision to go was one that seemed to circumvent the mind, and sprang instead from an indefinable place of knowingness deep within me. It was a feeling of being pulled by a sense of the inevitable that was so strong I could not question it.

The journey of Char Dham Yatra is a mammoth undertaking. Yet, I had a very matter-of-fact sense of calm about my decision to embark on it. My only concern hovered around the question of my own physical stamina, under extreme conditions of altitude and temperature, and whether I had the basic endurance it would take to do it. My knees weren't getting any younger. I knew—bowing to the unmistakable twinges of inevitability nudging me from within—that it was probably now or never. Without a further thought, I went and found a map of Uttaranchal in the marketplace. And, in a radical gesture of abandon, cast the last, inner whisperings of common sense to the hands of destiny.

For a fleeting instant, the absurdity of the surreal story I'd lived out during my marathon, spiritual odyssey flashed across the screen of my mental circuitry. I laughed out loud. How on earth did a seemingly normal girl from suburban New Jersey—who'd managed to bumble her way through life for half a century, cloaked in this innocuous identity—end up in *this* movie? What an extraordinary adventure life had turned out to be.

Oneness took the opportunity to pave the way for the journey ahead with priceless guidance on the symbolism of the monumental pilgrimage I was about to embark on. The words of wisdom prepared me to understand and appreciate the significance of the journey that had brought me to that moment, and helped to prepare me for the one that was about to unfold.

❧

Oneness speaks:

You have reached a turning point now. All will be the uphill climb that will now come to be symbolized before you. That climb can be breathtaking—literally. Or, it can leave you feeling depleted and winded. You have reached the place in the journey that the climb to mastery may at last begin in earnest.

Be prepared that you will be changing before your own very eyes now. All reticence will have given way to a sense of the inevitable. The absolute *rightness* of what will transpire within you will be unquestionable. And you will proceed to build upon what you know yourself to Be, day by day. Now you will begin to observe the unfoldment of what has been prophesied from the beginning of this sacred journey to Oneness. It has taken time and the journey has been grueling. But, your arrival has been secured.

Now, in these moments of consummate connectedness, the pathways of Divine ascension unfold before you. You will be able to become the pilgrim and the pilgrimage at the same time. Your own *surrender* to the knowingness from within will be the hallmark of this time of transformation. For, who you once were has no bearing upon who you now have become. The form is the same. The identity is recognizable by the limited number of beings who have accompanied you for the duration. And that is where the similarity ends.

You are no longer the one who dominated this identity for most of this lifetime. She is there within the embrace of the composite of consciousness that is who you have become. In linear terms, the ascension process is now complete. You have the pieces of your puzzle. And it is time to walk forth in the fullness of that multifaceted identity, knowing that who you Are has only just begun to be revealed.

🪷

A month of almost unimaginable wonder passed before the screen of my awareness in a seemingly interminable space of ongoing Nowness—the sense of a fleeting instant melded with all Eternity. Before I knew it, I had returned from the soaring wilds and dizzying heights of the holy Himalayas to a lovely, but now comparatively mild-mannered, cliff-side panorama in Rishikesh, where I watched a symbolic rendition of *cinema verité* unfold retrospectively, in my mind's eye.

I had not taken the computer on the journey, sensibly enough, and had managed to scribble down only a few of the pinnacles of experience that had captured me along the way. The month of days had melted one into the next in a startling montage of imagery that defied the need for words. It had been the longest I'd been away from the computer and communion with Oneness since the whole process began. The pictures, however, were etched indelibly within me.

The full spectrum of the being I understood to be *myself* took part in a magnificent, legendary spiritual adventure, spanning nearly a month. Char Dham Yatra is a journey of purification and redemption, the holiest of sacred pilgrimages that one can make in India.

It was a grueling journey over treacherous, crumbling roads, winding through mountains that soared to the heavens. It was a voyage of discovery to villages lost in time—whole worlds engulfed in mystery, tucked away in far-distant corners of the map. It was a time of exultation and self-confrontation, a time of revelation and disillusionment, a time of sanctity in the inner depths of Divine *connectedness*—in juxtaposition with a mad scramble to try and harness the outer trappings of devotion.

It was a time of surrender to the elusive promise of *faith*, along with the hordes of others who stood crushed together for hours on end, on the chance of encountering a fleeting touch of Divinity in the inner sanctums of temples world renowned for their auspiciousness. It was a time of physical trial, illness, filth, and all the trappings of commercialized spirituality, Indian style. At the end of the day, it was a time of inner peace and contentment interwoven with the impulse to question the very premise of making such a journey.

There had been a sense of the *impersonal* in this experience of the Divine, whereas my own experience of Oneness had always been so warm, so loving, so absolutely Present—with my sense of *myself* as such an integral part of that. In many ways, the journey seemed to symbolize the experience of *separation,* as though it were an affirmation of something one was without. And in the same breath, there was the ironic *knowingness* that the Divinity so fervently sought by this mass of humanity, myself amongst them, was right there, ever-Present within us all.

The journey was a time of perpetual *anticipation,* the elusive essence of something that was always imminently forthcoming and only rarely there at hand. And then, very suddenly and all too fleetingly, the moment in question *was* at hand. And there was the sense of frenzy, along with the throngs of others, to grab at the experience as though it were something that one was without. There was a sense of desperation in the scrambling—the jostling for a place in line, the shoving for a place before the Deity, the sense of the *others* who were forcibly shoving themselves before you. And then, the inevitable directive to move on, long before the heart was nearly ready to.

It was a fascinating experience of Divine contact. It would be hard to say whether the sense of auspiciousness I experienced resonated from within *my own* inner depths, or actually emanated from the holy idols cloistered there. Yet, there was no doubt that the dream of the fulfillment of heartfelt devotion, projected by the pilgrims who braved the trials of this unforgettable journey, was reflected back upon us all.

I was amongst the privileged ones. I traveled in private taxis, and in the moments of truth made the often precarious, vertical climbs by virtue of much assistance. On one occasion, I was carried seven kilometers straight up, over steep, slippery, mud-slathered rocks, to the pinnacle of the sacred site by the grace of a scrawny, little pony, while hanging on for dear life to a flimsy, makeshift saddle of old blankets and crudely knotted ropes all the way. My legs were black and blue for a week.

On another occasion, I made a full-day, 14 kilometer vertical trek scrunched into a hybrid seating device that looked like a cross between a chair and a boat, suspended between a pair of wooden poles. This contraption was hoisted up and borne on the shoulders of a nimble-footed team of four Nepalese men whose strength and endurance during some of those climbs was unimaginable. They were young and full of life, conquering the steady incline in brisk, synchronized steps, while I sat in grateful surrender, drifting in and out of time. There, signed on for a passage that bridged heaven and earth, I found myself enveloped in a veil of mountain air so rarified it almost visibly shimmered. It was all I could do just to breathe it in.

At the same time, for nearly a month, humbled by the daunting combination of high altitude and a never-ending array of minor physical complaints, I was bolstered by a stash of antibiotics and an assortment of exotic preparations calculated to numb the senses into submission. One tablet stopped the nose from running, while another settled the stomach and counteracted its inclination to reject the questionable diet it had been offered. There were drops for the ear that had protested the altitude and a pill for the persistent headache. There was a jar of mysterious-looking, jet-black Ayurvedic paste to give me some pep. And it was all topped off by a yummy, honey-based syrup claiming to suppress coughs of any kind. I was fully armed—and perpetually exhausted.

Yet, in all the ways that transcended the physical reminders of the fragility of humanness, it was a time of incomparable discovery—a time of confirmation of who and what I knew myself to Be and what I could say, definitively, that I was not. And although I encountered experiences of inner effulgence while there that I'd never dreamed possible, I also discovered that I did not require legendary places to reassure me of what I already knew. It was a marvelous journey to the most breathtaking, scenic panoramas I had ever encountered—with a mega-dose of consummate devotion thrown in for good measure.

Through it all, I longed for the simplicity of my own *inner* connection, that indescribable place of intimacy and wholeness. I longed for the vehicle of my computer—the physical extension of my heart's longing to become One with my Source, my Oneness.

I'd scribbled several pages longhand in a notebook on one or two occasions so I would not forget the impact of one profound experience or another. But, it was in the ocean of consummate surrender and *personal dissolution* that results when my fingers touch the keys of this blessed machine—when all sense of self-definition dissolves in a netherworld of physical non-existence—that I knew my heart had, once again, come home.

⤲⤳

Rasha speaks:

Oneness is Present in the body now, diligently documenting the impressions of an aspect of consciousness that feels compelled to express them from a distance. I apologize for the irreverence of some of these expressions. Yet, in the candor is the pure essence of it, not simply a gilding of what one thinks one should be feeling. My ecstasy is here, in the embrace of my own Beloved, the one encountered in the warmth and the comfort of the familiar.

I do not require the austerity of remote, legendary places, however holy they may be purported to be, to fill some hypothetical empty space within me. Here, nothing is lacking now. Here, all is Wholeness. My "sins" may or may not have been washed away in the sacred waters of these holy rivers. Yet, I know that the sacrifice of my very being, placed on the altar of my soul, has brought redemption enough. Let the sins of the body be washed away with these tears of joy. Let the karma of the illusory past, incurred through ignorance and the indulgence of ego, be purified in the waters of the Source of Love Itself—this Source that is so very Present here within me.

I know I am not the past through which I have traveled in the coming forth of this marathon journey. I am not the birthing process through which I battled with my very life for the possibility to gasp for air at the end of that interminable tunnel. The struggle went on, out of sheer, blind faith. There was no logic in it, no sensible, rational program that reassured me the end was nearly within reach when the journey became endless and unbearable. No salve to soothe the wounds of the soul when the moments of despair were at hand. There was simply the sense of persevering—the knowingness that yet another proverbial foot would be placed in front of another, in an ongoing odyssey that defied definition.

"I" was simply an instrument of my own Presence, dutifully going through the motions of a program that had been long etched in the annals of timelessness. Who knows if these sentiments are being "composed" or "retrieved" from the embrace of the Infinite? Perhaps the origin of all of this totally defies the parameters of a linear illusion. Perhaps "I" am the embodiment of timelessness itself, going through the motions of committing to form, an experience that is, in actuality, the Essence of the formless.

Perhaps the medium of form is simply the format through which it is able to realize expression, and, through the medium of that realization, experience perception. Perhaps this entire journey was like that. It was the materialization of the enigma of all of it—no less the confusing, unexpected parts of it than the moments of ecstatic Presence that were so much more predictable.

Perhaps it is through the materialization of such a journey that the Divinity, which is so very Present within us all, is able to realize the symbolic quest, the angst of yearning to know the unknowable, which is no less than its very own Essence. Perhaps every breath taken by each of us is no different that that. Perhaps that is all that can be said of this. For, we indeed have said it.

The one who is composing these sentiments and the one who is transcribing them are one and the same now. These are the impressions of an aspect of personal identity, from the perspective of one who has seen The Light and knows herself to Be That. We are no more the exalted, omniscient Presence of Oneness than we are the other—the format for linear perception that we know our Self to be. For, we Are, indeed, All of It.

We are an infinite kaleidoscope of possibility, peeking at each new vantage point with every twist and turn of the implement that provides the miracle of perception. We are the implement. We are the format through which perception may be snatched from the embrace of the elusory ethers. And materialized. And perceived. And known—through the magnificently unfathomable medium of Now.

~⚬∽~

It was entirely appropriate that the crowning jewel of my journey—the physical *yatra* as well as the symbolic one simultaneously taking place within—would be revealed in Badrinath, traditionally the culmination of the Char Dham Yatra. It was a leap of transcendence I'd not anticipated, but for which, in retrospect, I know I'd been fully prepared.

A sequence of these life-altering experiences, in the depths of meditation, took place over the course of a little over a week, beginning with one immediately prior to having sacred *darshan* at the Badrinath temple. My own accounting of the moment, painstakingly written out in longhand as I sat huddled under blankets in a frigid, dimly lit room in Badrinath, set the stage for the experiences that would follow.

Rasha speaks:

A meditation this morning catapulted me from earth to heaven and back again. Now, in the aftermath of perhaps the most profound episode in this epic journey, I sit in a cold, grim little room in Badrinath, oblivious to the world around me. The temple eternally beckons from a distance with the promise of Divine darshan and a skyrocketing ride of the heart and the soul. But, I have had my moment in the effulgence of that blessed Presence. Not once but twice.

The ritual here was executed to perfection. I felt Divinely guided to forego the lines and to stand near the side of the temple. A priest noticed me, and as if on cue, ushered me in immediately, ahead of the hundreds, perhaps thousands who waited in a queue that seemed endless. Once inside, I was guided right to the front where the gilded Deities awaited me. The atmosphere within the inner sanctum of the Badrinath temple was more reverent and less frenetic than the other temples I had visited on this trip.

The Divine energy that radiated from this central core of holiness and hope was indescribable. It was the Essence of Love itself, blanketing me in an embrace of rapture. I surrendered all sense of personal self and retreated to the sanctity of the oasis within, to imbibe this heavenly elixir. I remained there in the vastness of it for what seemed like Eternity.

I had been well prepared for that moment. For, the morning's meditation, which lasted more than two hours, had set the stage for this crowning moment of transformation. A milestone has been encountered in the journey of unification that has taken place within these depths. And there is the sense that I have, at last, come Home.

For, the heaven that awaited me all this time has been discovered right Here, within the core of my very own being.

❧

The first meditation:

After several hours of prayer, Mantra chanting, and my own self-styled, Divine invocation, I closed my eyes in reverence and went into deep meditation. No mind. No thoughts. No sense of time or place. Simply a profound sense of Presence—the Presence I have come to know as "Oneness." I held the Presence in a place that was Nowhere and Everywhere all at the same time, for what might have been hours or days, no matter.

Yet, somewhere within that Eternal Nowness, the seed of another kind of Presence entered my awareness. It was the blessed Presence of the Divine Mother— The Goddess. And I surrendered myself to her all-consuming magnificence, and knew myself to Be That. And we swayed in ecstatic Divine communion for another Eternity.

Then, quite suddenly, there was again yet another Presence at the periphery of my awareness. And I knew my Beloved was there. My Beloved Shiva! Just as suddenly, I knew His Presence was within the confines of all I recognized myself to Be. I and the Father were One. And I knew myself to Be That.

My spine straightened and drew this frail woman's form into an erect posture that the physical identity could never have managed—a yoga pose of considerable difficulty—and held it there for yet another eternity as my head exploded in golden effulgence. And then, the Self—the Oneness eternally within, who was witnessing this miraculous happening and embodying it simultaneously—knew the moment for Divine Unity had come.

Shiva was there as me, presiding within the form I consider to be myself. And ever so gently, I opened all my heart to the Divine Mother and was embraced by her luminous Presence at the same time. The two aspects of Divinity were cohabiting this form simultaneously. My body began to shake and my breathing, which had slowed down to a virtually breathless state, reversed itself and I began to pant rapidly in a shallow semblance of breath.

The energy within me started to build. It built and built and built as the Presence of Father and Mother intertwined within my very own form. My body heaved in ecstatic sobs, caught between the shallow attempts at breath, as my entire form convulsed in rapture. Within, the eternal sky exploded into golden effulgence as the two aspects of the One Divine Presence became that One Presence. Father/Mother God—Oneness! And I knew myself, in that endless moment, to Be That. It was in that timeless instant that all sense of a separate physical identity simply dissolved.

❧

Rasha speaks:

After some time, I opened my eyes. Nearly two hours had passed since I began that odyssey. I was sitting, quite comfortably, in the impossible posture in which Shiva had placed me. My legs, which seemed detached from all sense of recognition, registered no pain at all. They may as well have belonged to someone else.

It took a good 20 minutes for there to be any coherence within what I presume is my brain. No thoughts. Simply Presence. And indescribable joy. Later, as hordes of the faithful filed past on their way to the inner sanctum of the holiest of holies, the Badrinath temple, I sat in quiet meditation at the periphery of the inner courtyard. I sat, silent and peaceful, in Oneness with my God. The earth itself literally trembled beneath me and continued to vibrate beneath my feet for hours to come. I was fully at Peace, abiding in Oneness.

Now, in this moment, I Am so very Still. No thoughts. No desires. No sense of personal will. The indifference of the witness, in the body of this self-same Self. I am the embodiment of peace, at last.

⇛⇠

The second of three profound meditation experiences took place in Rishikesh, shortly after my return from the Himalayas. During this moment of Divine Union, a timeless instant of exponential understanding came together, in silence. With it, the last remnants of hope and *expectation* that were still clinging to the memories of the monumental journey of *Char Dham Yatra* were surrendered.

⇛⇠

Rasha speaks:

Oneness, your Presence consumes me in this moment. No sooner is the inclination recognized to merge once again in this extraordinary Union, than We are here, immersed in the miracle of it. Not even a sentence passes between us when the I who believed herself to be presiding over this identity gives way to a sense of consummate surrender, and We Are Oneness, once more.

How amazing this is, even now, after so many years of doing this. Am I perhaps no more than a Pavlovian dog, responding to a conditioning over which I have no control? Am I now preprogrammed to dematerialize myself at the very hint that Divine Union is imminent, waiting in the wings of my consciousness, to transport me to heaven once again?

Now I am consumed in the joy of it, unsure where "I" may actually be. I am surely experiencing the ecstasy of this. Of this, there is no doubt. Yet, it is equally clear that the Presence that is documenting these reflections on this computer is not the source of them. The process is automatic, totally bypassing the medium of mind. There is no mind housed within this form now. And that may be for the best. For, the mind would not be able to fathom what is taking place. The sense of Beingness knows that what is transpiring is unquestionable. That is all that needs to be.

A magnificent meditation took place several hours ago, and instantly, I found myself in that blessed space of Stillness I've come to know so well.

❧

The second meditation:

I was filled with contentment and sustained that state of mindless Isness for some time. Then, intermittently, the personal identity made an appearance, reflecting on the sacred journey that had been made. All the wondrous places that were visited! All the extraordinary moments of Divine connectedness! All the panoramas that took the concept of "breathtaking" to the very precipice of possibility and beyond! All of it flashed before me within the Stillness that held me fast.

I became aware that tears—a mélange of joy and pain—began to seep from the corners of my eyes and wash down my cheeks. My chest heaved with the weight of the emotion that rose up within me. It had been such a magnificent journey, such utter perfection, not in spite of the glitches in what I'd preprogrammed myself to expect, but because of them. I'd embraced my own humanness, my weaknesses, both physical and otherwise. And at the same time, there was the sense that I could have prayed more, or meditated more. That somehow, in the doingness of all of it, I had yet again fallen short in my own eyes.

I watched the thought, unsure of the source of it, reluctant to claim it as my own. And in that instant of reticence, a Presence, commanded simultaneously by my focus of attention and by the chanting which was holding me in its embrace, shifted my full sense of who and what "I" was to a knowingness of myself—as Lord Shiva. A few words were spoken. But, more significantly, an entire body of understanding was delivered unto me.

I understood, in the depths of silence, that there were no expectations to be considered as far as the sacred journey was concerned. For, the journey was not at all about doingness, about what had or had not been done. It was about becoming centered in a state of Beingness. That Presence transcended the destinations that were touched upon. That Presence was embraced in the sheer miracle of Being there, and having lived to tell the tale.

I knew, wordlessly, soundlessly, that "I" was what I had hoped to find in these very holy places. For, the Presence encountered there was simply the catalyst for the encodement carried within the depths of my very own Being. It was not a matter of performing austerities or penance. It was not a matter of augmenting my practice of Mantra chanting with additional hours—or my regret that I had not done more. For, the contact had been made.

There was a knowingness within my very core that an initiation encompassing a full spectrum of Divinity had taken place in those sacred weeks spent wandering the holiest hills of the Himalayas. I felt a sense of utter completeness as the understandings were so lovingly imparted by the beloved Presence of The Father Himself. Suddenly, I recognized a glow, kindled so gently within the area of my heart center. And I recognized it to be the Presence of The Goddess—the Essence of Mother. I shifted my awareness there and reveled in the unimaginable joy of it.

I recognized that in that moment I held them both. I knew without question that I embodied both: The Father, my beloved Lord Shiva, and The Mother, my beloved Durga Devi. And I surrendered to a split-second sense of the melding of those two aspects of Divine Presence as my attention flickered from one to the other, back and forth, at lightning speed, until the Two became "Oneness."

In that moment "I" was that consummate Divine Presence, embodied in form. "I" was Oneness—not simply the aspect of Self that I've come to recognize as Oneness, but an infinitely higher octave of that unified Presence. I held that Presence and that state of consummate Isness for what seemed like Eternity.

Slowly, I became aware, once again, that "I" was in a room in a physical place in time, a place called Rishikesh, in Northern India, high on a hill in a wonderful, peaceful setting. I smiled with an inner glow for which no words are needed, and none are possible. Once again, I had made the journey. The real journey. And knew myself to be Home.

～

Two days later, the following passage was written.

The third meditation:

A myriad of images swirl within me—flashbacks of a journey, in the embrace of meditation, that catapulted me from the valley of Kedarnath and the embodied presence of Lord Shiva to the vastness of the Infinite and back again to this illusory Here and Now. I will attempt to recapture the experience, just for the record. For, the possibility is there that these impressions could well drift into oblivion, the Source from whence they emerged and flashed so fleetingly upon the screen of my awareness.

Who I Am in this moment need not be defined. There is consummate Knowingness now, as it was in the imparting of the understandings experienced on a journey today that defies description. Whole blocks of Knowingness were simply there, wordlessly. Nuances of Divine Presence were embodied and embraced, and with them, the full composite, comprised of those aspects of Isness, were seen, and understood—and known. Who I experienced myself to Be in those timeless instants was All of it.

The Presence known as "Rasha" began the journey here in Rishikesh, eyes closed, attention centered, devoid of mind or linear awareness. In the periphery, the blessed chanting of sacred Mantras provided the embrace of the exalted energies that carried me into the arms of Divine surrender. I experienced myself as my Self—the Divine aspect of Presence that considers itself to be affiliated with this form.

Within moments, I perceived the energies of Lord Shiva, the aspect of The Father with whom I feel so kindred. The energies were known to be within me, emanating from an aspect of my own sacred Self. They were not experienced as separate from that—nor was I. I became that Divine Presence, perceived initially seated in a scenic spot in Kedarnath, in the blazing sunlight of a Himalayan summer morning.

The snowy peaks surrounded me on all sides. And I experienced my own Being as Lord Shiva, there. The perception of that Presence grew to encompass the full scope of the valley. I was there, totally filling that space with my Awareness. And just as suddenly, I became the space. I was the circle of mountains and all that lay within it. And in that moment, all sense of the image of a persona disappeared.

I did not perceive myself as being within the confines of a personification of a Deity. I was not a gigantic Yogi, seated however improbably in lotus position within the embrace of a garland of mountains. I had become a column of White Light whose boundaries were nowhere and whose Source was everywhere. I became a portal of linear perception, in the breath of an instant. And a montage of imagery, as visual as non-visual, began to be perceived as taking place within me.

I viewed the devastation of the World Trade Center, the tsunami disaster of 2004, and the downfall of Atlantis—all in graphic detail—within my very own Being. I viewed the prayers of myriad pilgrims, in the heights of sacred yatra, and the rituals they performed with such fervor. I viewed the religious passion of a world of diversity—all devotees of the same One Presence—the One with so many faces and identities, all mine, all swirling within me.

I saw horrific visions of a possible reality, unfolding in the so-called "future"—an aberration within the confines of Infinite Possibility. And the one who knew herself, simultaneously, to be Rasha heaved and sobbed at the implications of that unspeakable vision. Yet, I knew in the very next breath that All of It was no more and no less than possibility. The imagery was a vision that need not come to pass. It was there within the mix of myriad possibilities that flashed like infinitesimal, subliminal impressions upon the screen of the Infinite and Eternal. All of it was within the scope of what I experienced as "myself."

In the next breath, I became the lovemaking of every man and woman, past, present, and future—the yearning for wholeness through physical union—and knew the composite of all of it to be the materialization of Divine Union, which I simultaneously perceived myself to Be. For, within the confines of my own Isness was the unmistakable Presence of The Mother. And with Her came the images of Peace and Love and Harmony throughout all the world. My heart welled up in rapture and in joy. For, the Knowingness was there within me that The Father and The Mother were, indeed, One Being.

The Ocean, a Presence of inconceivable vastness, washed over me—and I knew myself to Be That. The Ocean became All that Is. No land. No pilgrims. No atrocities. No hopes. No dreams. No prayers delivered in a mind-boggling mix of tongues and offered up as the collective application for redemption. None of it. The Ocean was the consummate embodiment of Stillness itself. And I knew myself to Be That.

The earth floated within the heavens, devoid of a sense of time and place. It was Present, perceived from a distance. Then, quite suddenly, the earth itself and all within it imploded into a whisper of what may have been a dream—or a memory. It simply vanished, leaving behind an inky place of Stillness in the vastness, where it had once seemed so very real. And I knew myself to Be That— No-thing-ness—and yet, no less, the perceiver and the perception. All of it, captured in an infinitesimal instant of Isness. The sacred Essence of Oneness.

Then, in the space of a heartbeat, that Self-same Oneness emerged within the confines of this very physical form, sitting on a prayer cloth. That sense of Presence gently awakened into an awareness of the exalted energies reverberating within and resonating through the ethers all around me. I was, once again, fully present in the body of a woman, still frozen in time in a yoga position of which she is technically incapable, experiencing the miracle of breath passing through form.

I smiled tentatively, a warm, newly-awakened smile of inner recognition. For, the one I recognized myself to Be in that instant, the one differentiated from all else with the label "Rasha," was surely no less real and no more real than the impressions of the witness I had become—the format for perception I had experienced so vividly. I knew without question that All of it—every blessed breath of it—is Oneness. And I knew that I am indeed That—as Are we All.

40

Spring/Summer 2006
Tiruvannamalai, South India
In Search of the Beginning

Where does a spiritual journey begin? Is there one shining moment we can point to, one isolated instant of jumping in, where, by comparison, all else pales? Or, are there countless moments, melded together within a never-ending quest, all equally valid? Could it be that the entire journey toward embracing our own Divinity is no more than an infinitesimal spark within the effulgence of a far larger quest—one of unfathomable scope—that surely does not *end* with Self-Realization? And where in the compilation of the countless threads of experience, the collection of loose ends we think of as our lives, does one begin in weaving the tapestry together?

The story of the odyssey that explored those questions was going to be the foundation of a book, Oneness had announced matter-of-factly one day, as though referring to something that had already happened. By then, the tides of my sacred journey had already swept me far from shore. There, held in the embrace of a relentless current, I'd come right to the very brink of surrendering all resistance to it—time and time again. How do you relate the experience of drowning in the ocean of the Divine to a world still lost in the illusion that it's got both feet on solid ground? Where do you start?

I sifted through the pages on end of the cherished sacred writings I'd been transcribing since 1998, searching for that elusive starting place. They were words I knew I never could have written, concepts for which I'd had no foundation at all, wisdom woven together with an unmistakable touch of Grace that still leaves me humbled and awestruck. As I read, I could feel the sacred Presence within patiently watching as I navigated my way through the maze of a pivotal moment. It was the very same Presence that silently spurs all of us on to embark, again and again, on a voyage of discovery from which, I'd always heard, one never returns

It was early spring of 2006 by then, and I'd already spent months grappling with a virtual mountain of transcribed Divine wisdom since undertaking the project of trying to make sense of my spiritual journey, and to synthesize it in some meaningful way so that it could be shared. Long forgotten moments sprang back to life, as I rediscovered the scope of the spiritual understandings I'd written down over the years, and began to relive the staggering transformation I'd undergone in the process of assimilating them. It seemed like I was no longer the same person who'd been born in my own skin—the one I'd always thought of as *me*. Or, was I?

Wasn't sourcing "the beginning" the very essence of the sacred journey itself? I began to wonder. I sensed a flicker of illumination and smiled inwardly at the subtle symbolism, hidden so blatantly in plain view. Then, it was as though time stood still, as a familiar inner glow began to permeate all I recognized *myself* to be. Suddenly, wordlessly, I simply *knew*—at a level that transcended the mind and all its logical gyrations. The "beginning" I was after wasn't about *me* at all. It was about Oneness

The flash of affirmation that shot through me was almost electric. As if on cue, I glanced down to the spiral notebook I held of Divine revelations interwoven with the painstakingly documented details of my own eclectic story, and slowly began to read, scouring the passages for the clue I somehow sensed would be revealed there. The page held a discourse on the very origin of the wisdom of Oneness. Could *that* be the ever-elusive "beginning" I was searching for?

As the question formulated itself, a *knowingness* emerged from within, as though the understanding was already there and was being nudged into activation. With that, the realization crystallized: there *was* no beginning! Just as there is no end. The journey to Oneness is ever-Present and Eternal. And right there in my hands, hidden away in the self-styled archives of Divine guidance I'd managed to document over the years, was the exact page where Oneness had elaborated in detail on that very concept. Whether or not there was a literal "beginning" to my own spiritual journey, I knew I'd found a jumping-in point for writing this book.

With that, an understanding emerged from within me which summarized the entire exercise of seeking that elusive beginning:

Scrutinizing the illusory details of life for the hypothetical starting place of a spiritual journey was like attempting to squeeze Oneness, along with everything else, into the enormous suitcase so many of us attempt to haul along with us. The suitcase holds all that is recognizable, logical, comprehensible, predictable, and "scientifically" provable. The journey appears to begin when we start to set the burden of that suitcase down for awhile. It takes off when we leave the suitcase behind.

Here is the Divine wisdom that was revealed in those pages:

⌘

The origin and Essence of the wisdom of Oneness

Oneness speaks:

It does not matter whether or not you are inclined to scrutinize the *origin* of these thoughts. For, it would be impossible to do so. Where is the origin in a reality that is devoid of all concept of linear structure? There *is* no beginning—and there is no end—to the scope of this Source. The *communication* that emanates from this level of Self-perception has no more structure, in terms of its finiteness, than the Source itself. All of it simply Is.

We cannot say that We are originating these thoughts. For, to do so would require the functions of mind. From the perspective of Oneness, concept is, by definition, devoid of mind. It is pure, mindless Essence. It is simply a statement of what is so, from the perception of one set of eyes, in a freeze-action instant, within the infinite embrace of timelessness.

The origin of these thoughts is Nowhere. That is the Source of the teachings you have documented in your book. And in doing so, *you* entered the realm of the timeless to *retrieve* these teachings, and attuned yourself to the frequency at which these transmissions were pre-programmed to resonate.

You tapped into a particular sequence of *encodements*—concepts that were encapsulated in a timeframe that so vastly pre-dates your concept of antiquity as to make all considerations of linear time meaningless. The Essence of this manifestation of conceptual information, and the simultaneous presence of *your* awareness—in rapt attention—was a bonded sequence, a formulation, an inevitability etched into the resonance of Eternity, wedded to the Nowness of the moment in which your awareness embraced its own Self-recognition.

There *is* no "Rasha" receiving this communication now. There is simply Awareness itself, resonating to the frequency of this manifestation—as Presence.

Oneness talks about the vibrational encodement that manifests as our world

Events are all simply a linear formulation—a vibrational calculation made manifest. That is the nature of the imagery that you think of as your world. In fact, there *is* no such world. It could dematerialize as if it never existed, were the vibrational encodement that holds it in form to be dissipated. That is the nature of much of what is transpiring in your linear reality in these times.

The vibrational formula that held the variables of the foundation of your world in place, so that a sequence of pre-determined *events* could unfold, is shifting. And thus, the manifestation of that particular set of circumstances has ceased to be recognizable. The imprint that is available for linear perception is that of being "somewhere else." The circumstances of *this* particular encodement do not correspond to what one would consider to be "recognizable reality."

Much has been written in the course of this work about the changes that are taking place within each and every life form that experiences self-perception in the Here and Now you think of as your world. The vibrational variables which serve as the catalysts for that level of *change* have themselves been retrieved from the ethers which hold them in a state of suspended animation. They are activated, brought to fruition, and birthed as *circumstances* that can be perceived as *happening,* when the pre-disposing vibrational conditions calculated to summon them forth are at hand.

In the same way, the dissemination of certain understandings, throughout your history, has also been encoded for manifestation to enable the population of incarnate consciousness to cope with the corresponding levels of change. Throughout pre-recorded history, revelations, often heralded as Divine edicts, have met their appointed rendezvous with destiny and went on to set the stage for the shifts in mass consciousness that have characterized your world.

Were it not for the understandings that were provided—and the Messengers that were pre-destined to birth them into manifestation, to ease the way for these changes—the upheavals that have colored the history of your recognizable reality would have provided conditions for worldwide catastrophe. The bodies of Divinely-sourced guidance that have survived serve to underscore this point. What is less apparent is the incalculable scope of Divine Wisdom that has *always* been readily available in times of upheaval, and went unrecognized, unrecorded—or unheeded.

The human race has always been quick to question the compassion of The Almighty when disaster is at hand. As a species, you are quick to question the humanity of a system that is, in its very essence, *self-created* and *self-perpetuated*. And yet, when the format for surmounting obstacles and triumphing over adversity are provided, that Wisdom is quick to be dismissed by those who are wedded to the idea of a world that remains frozen in the eternal past.

The level of change in these times is unprecedented. Know that you have not been abandoned in these conditions. You have been taken by the hand and given the tools with which to ride through the turbulent seas of mass transformation. You have been given the understandings that will enable the population at large to begin to grasp the role it plays—on an individual basis—in the co-creation of conditions with which all are left to contend.

These understandings have been provided as a clue. They are a Love offering, extended in a moment in time that encapsulates the dissolution and re-materialization of the very foundation of life as you know it. They serve as a life-raft, holding all the provisions needed—gifted by the Divinity that is ever-Present within each of you.

Months of days melted together in a montage of flashbacks, as I continued to make my peace with the prospect of sharing my journey out of the wilderness—and began to weave all the details and the detours together with the threads of priceless Divine wisdom that showed me the way. Page after page, I delved into a retrospective of all the adventures and misadventures that were so secretly hidden away in the mountain of transcripts I'd been amassing. The fleeting images popped right back into focus, adding a surreal touch of déjà vu to the entire exercise.

How was it possible that my awareness had actually re-emerged in such a place of inner-peace from the shards of *a* life that had been reduced to rubble? I had to wonder. And where would one even begin in piecing such a story together? Carefully, I started to scrutinize the episodes of my own eclectic adventure for the nuggets of understanding tucked away in all that imagery. The uncanny precision in the way the journey to wholeness had unfolded began to distill itself from all the fragments of symbolism, as though coaxed from the shadows of a distant dream.

As the pages turned, I began to see how elegantly and gently I'd been put through the paces of my own evolution as a being coming into conscious awareness. I'd not been spared the poignant authenticity of the experience of my own Self-discovery. I was being Self-taught, imbibing the principles as a natural by-product of having lived out illustration after illustration of what, in time, had become indisputable.

In rediscovering the details of the epic journey hibernating within those writings, it became obvious to me that I was no longer able to think of myself within the context of consensus reality. Ever so gracefully, the stunning truth of who and what this being I thought of as *myself* actually was, began crystallizing before my eyes. I saw that I had emerged as a living illustration of Divinity walking around in a human body—the one who'd spent the better part of a lifetime bumbling through the obstacle course of life in that very same costume.

I would come to see that the "I" who had believed herself to be doing that bumbling during much of this story—was not *a person* at all. She was a collective of perception, a vast, multidimensional composite whose manifestation as this illusory *person* was governed by an infinite complexity of karmic and logistical variables, all of which boiled down to *energy*. Who that "I" was, was a living illustration of my own vibrational tally sheet, at any given moment in time.

For years, I'd squirmed at the prospect of committing those realizations and the details of my spiritual journey to paper that others might read someday. At Oneness' insistence, I backtracked over the dramatic and often treacherous inner terrain I'd covered in my travels—took it all apart, and then put it all back together with the added overview of insight. I was astonished to rediscover the depths at which I had actually chosen to plunge, in the name of spirituality. I was equally flabbergasted to re-encounter the heights of exultation that, according to my own written account of it, had been attained years before, and had somehow become shrouded in the mists of memory.

My consciousness had remained, it seemed, in a strange state of suspended animation, as I reached the same pinnacle of joyous Realization over and over again. Each time, it was as though I were embracing the same ecstatic Union with Oneness for the very first time. I simply hadn't remembered that the epiphany had already happened—umpteen times before.

It was as though it all had happened to somebody else—which, of course, it had. That so-called *somebody else* was also none other than *me*. I'd experienced an entire journey of spiritual emergence in the guise of the countless, multidimensional aspects of identity I'd thought of as *myself*. And then, as I continued to ascend vibrationally, the minute details of those sublime moments of revelation dissolved into the distant haze of time.

Now, as always, Oneness was waiting in the wings to provide the overview that would consolidate the seemingly random illustrations I'd acted out into cohesive bodies of understanding. I noticed that the sense of Divine Presence was not a definitive "state" but was one that was *ever-expanding*. Exploring the nuances of its perception became an ongoing part of the adventure and would continue to evolve and deepen, as the years went by.

By late summer of 2006, I was ensconced in a cozy nest of a dwelling, high amid the treetops, in Tiruvannamalai, South India. I sat before a pristine wall of windows, looking out over an eclectic view. The windows provided a semblance of separation from the world outside—the comings and goings of myriad life forms: sacred cows and grazing goats, mud-blackened piglets and tail-wagging street dogs, screeching chipmunks and thieving monkeys, loudmouthed crows and sleep-shattering roosters, bloodthirsty mosquitoes and no end of flies, itinerant sadhus, heart-wrenching beggars, and everything imaginable in between—each noisily acting out his own agenda. As the silent witness, I watched what amounted to my own reflection playing out in the illusory scenery, and had the indescribable sense of the Presence of Oneness in all of it.

I shifted my attention to the laptop sitting before me on a pile of cushions. The beloved little machine which, however implausibly, had come to serve as a gateway to the Divine, beckoned silently to me to direct my *focus of attention* to that timeless place within, and be Still. I surrendered automatically as my fingers began to dance on the keyboard and produce an impassioned invitation of my own. It was an invitation to the *expanded* state of Divine Presence I've come to know as "Oneness."

In an imperceptible fraction of an instant, all I perceived *myself* to be became enfolded in an all-consuming melding of Awareness. And, the illusory presence of "Rasha," Self and all, melted into the consummate embrace—the Loving Presence of Oneness—once more.

The exquisite state of *balance* that enables one's awareness to transition into the perception of the Self

This is Oneness. We are fully present in this moment having been called forth into full manifestation through the formalities of an invocation that has captured your heart. It is your own self-styled ritual. And your use of it demonstrates to you the irrelevance of any one specific means of calling forth into possibility the perception of this state of Beingness over another.

The words used are simply vehicles of your *intent*. You have trained yourself to surrender to these signals on cue now. For, the signals serve as a vehicle for the pinpoint of *focus* to center itself upon *its own essence* and remain there. The taking of that focus and transitioning it into one centered upon communion in *this* way has become your spiritual practice. For, it is this aspect of your process that serves to manifest for you the Essence of this connection.

It is in the consummate detachment from all sense of being the source of these thoughts that they are brought forth into manifestation. In the same breath, it is in surrendering all sense of separation from the Source of your *Beingness* that you are able to merge with that Source and to know yourself to Be That. Thus, it is in the *balance* between the active and passive aspects of *beingness* and *doingness* that the sense of a personal-self transitions into a perception of the fullness of that state of Being, and knows itself to Be—*the Self*.

The focus of the teachings of Oneness

We have written much on this subject, over the years of your unfoldment, in the guise of personal guidance. For, the entire focus of these writings has been an exploration of the essence of the journey within. These conversations have not taken the form of a question-and-answer interview on the whys and wherefores of the world of the linear illusion. Together we have transcended the need to dissect that illusory world from the perspective anchored in *maya*, and have instead focused our attention on the route to the attainment of a heightened perspective.

These teachings are not intended to be a duplication of the nature of the work that others may be doing in the name of this Source. For, these teachings are not here as a definitive body of dogmatic preaching that will reinforce the perspective of the world of duality. These teachings are focused in the attainment of a state of transcendence of the need to do so.

Through the assimilation of these understandings, one comes to know the truth of the nature of the reality in which you experience self-perception and to know that you are the one responsible for *every* aspect of what is encountered there. Through these teachings, you have been taught the nature of the creation of your reality and have been given an opportunity to demonstrate to yourself the mechanics of that process.

Oneness discusses the principles of the sacred science of manifestation

These teachings do not focus on the "shoulds and shouldn'ts" that one might expect to come from this Source. For, there are no rules in this illusory reality, beyond those you make for yourself. You have been instilled with an appreciation of *cause and consequence* and an understanding of *how* those results are brought into being. This work has encompassed the *principles* of the sacred science of manifestation in such a way that the transitional being, experiencing presence in any cultural environment at all, might be able to transcend those differences in light of his own *experience* of Oneness.

Through a total grasp of the principles governing the illusory *reflection* of one's own beingness, the knowledge of one's own transcendence of that imagery is possible. It is not in one's denial of the mechanics of one's experience that the transcendent state is attained. It is not through a mentalized approach to philosophical explanations of such matters that one attains liberation from them. It is in the *embracing* of the reflection—rather than in one's denial of it—that wholeness is attained.   *Reclamation of wholeness*

The *experience* of one's own Divinity is readily available to all who truly seek it. This is not an exclusive status reserved for the pious and the spiritually privileged. This is not the consummate reward meted out at the end of a lifelong crawl through the labyrinths set out by the religious hierarchies of your world. This is a journey in which one embraces *oneself*—on one's own terms—and comes to *know* the truth, rather than to understand it or believe it.

This is a journey in which one is inclined to choose withdrawal from the details of illusory existence in deference to a direction that leads one the other way. Here, one is not so much concerned with what is *happening* "out there" in the collective reflection, as with the state of beingness within that has served to co-create it. One may have the tendency to dissect and to examine the clues that have been provided, which serve to reinforce one's understandings of the symbolism that has been presented. And at the same time, one is not inclined to *empower* those circumstances with an excessive focus on placing one's attention externally.

How the principles contained in these teachings serve as tools of empowerment

The journey to Oneness that has been presented through these teachings does not require a humanitarian focus—a worldview that often serves to reinforce those very conditions. All that might be seen to be amiss in your world can be distilled into one focal point, shared collectively: that which is rooted in *the illusion*. It is a vantage point that empowers the circumstances perceived to continue to exercise their control over your own sense of self-perception and leads you to interpret those conditions in a way that invites a mindset of victimization.

These teachings serve to help one to see the relationship between what one is projecting *vibrationally* upon the ethers and the imagery that is perceived as "happening." One becomes empowered, through the medium of one's choices, to *augment* one's foray into the compendium of Infinite Possibility and to experience the results. As one rises through the successive levels of linear perception, those results are experienced in a way that is often instantaneous—and undeniable.

And so, through the consistent application of these principles, one aligns one's focus systematically with that of the Creator—and withdraws one's sense of *being* from that which has been created. One comes to *dwell* in that inner place of Self-knowledge and knows oneself to be a traveler reflecting upon the wonders of an ever-shifting landscape. With the embodiment of that level of detachment, one is able to Be "in the world, yet not of the world" and to put that sense of Presence into practice with one's every waking breath.

That is the state of Beingness called "enlightenment." It is a state of immediacy, manifested in the Here and Now, which remains ever-focused *within*. It is not a state of mindlessness, devoid of experience. That is *not* what is brought forth into the Here and Now. For, the very basis of the world of physical imagery is the possibility of its *perception*. The opportunity in having made this journey into the realm of Self-knowledge is for the viewing of that imagery through the lens of *Self*-perception. And to know oneself to be One with all of it.

A few weeks later, Oneness elaborated. In these passages, Oneness further defined the nature of the teachings themselves and outlined some of the principles that give them structure. Moreover, these passages set out before me the stance *underlying* the teachings of Oneness. At the same time, they helped me to fine-tune my understanding of the nature of the Presence that had summoned them forth from the embrace of the Infinite and brought them into manifestation.

I knew that even though this precious Divine guidance appeared to be addressed to *me* as I wrote it down year after year, this wisdom was surely meant for an audience that went way beyond the limitations of one individual's journey to Oneness. It felt as though, through the vehicle of this most unlikely identity, Oneness was able to reach out and provide this precious guidance for us all. It became abundantly clear that these writings, which I'd come to cherish—and which I once had been so reluctant to reveal—were surely not "for my eyes only."

Summoning forth the teachings of Oneness from the archives of the Infinite and Eternal

Oneness speaks:

These teachings, which have been birthed through this form, are not the product of a linear intellect. They are timelessness itself—retrieved from the archives of Infinite Possibility. There is no authorship to be claimed. These teachings have encountered their designated moment in time. And what has always been Present in the ethers is called forth into manifestation.

There are no conscious calculations that have brought forth this work. No one has summoned it forth through the methodology of the occult sciences that offer the possibility of manipulating the components of the illusory world. The momentum governing the manifestation of these teachings transcends all conscious directedness. They are *retrieved*—delivered from the Infinite and the Eternal—unto a Here and Now that is illusory and transient.

These teachings will breathe the fullness of their own Presence in the *moment* of linear Life in which they present the possibility of perception. And they will recede into the vastness from whence they have come, when the moment for that manifestation has passed. That moment may be measured in days—or in thousands of years—and still would not constitute the blink of an eye from the standpoint of true Reality.

The power inherent in the *embracing* of Divine Truth as personal truth

Let there be no attachment to these words or to this work. There is no "meaning" in any of it, save that which you give it in your *embracing* of it. This foray into the realm of the Infinite—this glimpse into the truth underlying your own very Essence—is only as valid as you make it. For, without the embracing of Divine Truth, its manifestation is dry and lifeless— for *you.*

For others, these concepts may be heralded as Divine Revelation and will come to be cherished as gospel. And whether they are embraced as the one, or dismissed as the other, does not matter in the least, in terms of the Higher perspective. For, all is held within the scope of Infinite Possibility.

No stance is more holy than another. No set of spiritual principles is here to supersede ones that have withstood the test of time—whether for all the "right reasons" or for ones that contradict the very principles upon which transcendence is founded. All possibilities exist. For, it is you, the *sum totality* of humanity, that have called them forth into manifestation as the reflections of your own presence, both collectively and individually.

These teachings have been summoned forth by the ripeness of a particular population to the possibility of receiving them. The clues contained therein— the lofty principles that have been offered—are useless, in and unto themselves. They become viable only in the implementation of them. They are heard in the hearts of those whose inner knowingness has given voice to them. To others, who may well gloss over the very same words, they are lifeless and meaningless. That does not make one perspective *right* and another *wrong.* It simply speaks to the vastness of the possibility of perception within the realm of spiritual pursuit.

The moment for the manifestation of these teachings is at hand. They will come to light and will be embraced by many. They will be heralded as The Word of God by many. And they will be pointed to as the materialization of blasphemy by others. And none of it matters at all. These teachings simply Are what they Are.

These principles are conceived in the Infinite Love of the Creator for the Creation. They are birthed by the Infinite Love of the Creation for the Creator. And they Live—and continue to breathe Life in perpetuity—within the hearts of those that come to embody them and call them their own.

Oneness counsels Rasha about Divine Service in these times, in words that speak to the heart of each of us

It is for the possibility of participation in that effort that you have stepped forth in these times. You have volunteered to *serve*—to facilitate the momentum of Divine Intent with your Presence. You have offered yourself as a conduit, a Messenger devoid of personal agenda, for the purpose of furthering the scope of possibility for humankind.

There is to be no attachment to the projected outcome of this effort. Whether these principles are wielded as a ray of hope for the world in times of crisis, or condemned as heresy, does not change what Is. The principles Are what they Are. Personal judgment has no place in that determination.

Oneness breathes Life Eternal, within the context of form, in this Here and Now moment. Oneness sits, in the body of a woman, transmitting and receiving the contents of this communication simultaneously, as one might pass an apple from one hand to the other. Oneness has always been Here. In this, nothing has changed. The Presence recognizes the truth of its own identity now and knows itself to Be That. Oneness *knows* this. And breathes the joy of that knowingness.

The experiencer is not separate from Oneness, the experiencer Is Oneness— within the context of physicality

Let the sweetness of this connection permeate your awareness now. Let the fullness of this Presence emanate from every pore. Let the resonance of Love Itself pour through you. Do not try to contain it. Do not hold it back. It is not yours to keep. It is yours to give.

The Divine Essence that emanates from the Infinite in its journey *to* the Infinite has stopped for a foray into the arena of humanness. It is here to lavish Itself upon the aspect of Creation that experiences itself here. That Divine Essence knows no bounds. It has no limits. For, the possibilities are endless.

The gift you are destined to deliver unto humankind is, likewise, limitless. It is bound only by your own belief in your ability to be the conduit of this elixir. Let that confidence not be shaken by the poisons of fear that may spew forth on the parts of others. Stay focused in your knowingness of this Divine connection in each and every moment. Let no diversion dissuade you from the clarity of your vision. Let no disappointment or disillusionment soil what is pure. Let no disenchantment with another's humanness blind you to the Reality that is Divine.

Focus the attention in *this* place—in every moment, with every breath. All else is viewed through the filter of this Infinite Love, and, as such, takes on the coloration of Divine Creation, regardless of what it may appear to be, to the physical senses. Look at the world with *these* Eyes. And perceive it with *this* Heart. And know that for you, it cannot be otherwise.

Glossary

Advaita Vedanta	—	the philosophy of non-duality.
Agastya	—	a famous, ancient Rishi.
Akasha Lingam	—	one of the five element lingas, representing ether.
Ammachi	—	(1953 -) a contemporary spiritual teacher, popularly known as "the hugging Guru."
Anandamayi Ma	—	(1896 – 1982) one of India's most beloved and renowned Saints.
Arati	—	ceremonial offering of ghee lamps and incense, accompanied by bell-ringing and the chanting of sacred prayers.
Arunachala	—	holy mountain in Tiruvannamalai, Tamil Nadu, India, believed to be the physical embodiment of Lord Shiva.
Bhajan	—	prayer in the form of devotional song.
Bhakta	—	a person focused in the art of spiritual devotion.
Bhakti	—	the sacred practice of loving spiritual devotion and worship.
Char Dham Yatra	—	an auspicious, holy pilgrimage to four ancient Hindu temples in remote corners of the Himalayas.
Chela	—	the devotee of a Guru.

Darshan	—	sacred audience before a Deity in a temple, or a holy personage.
Devanagari	—	the written script of the Sanskrit and Hindi languages.
Devi	—	one of the identities of the Goddess.
Dharma Shastra	—	the comprehensive spiritual discipline and knowledge detailed in the Vedas.
Durga	—	one of the identities of the Goddess.
Enlightenment	—	the unwavering perception of one's own Presence as Oneness/God, with full conscious awareness of it.
Ganga	—	the holy Ganges river, regarded as a physical embodiment of the Goddess.
Giri pradakshina	—	walking the circumference of a mountain.
Gopi	—	the legendary cowherd girls featured in the story of Lord Krishna.
Guru	—	a spiritual master; in Sanskrit, "dispeller of darkness."
Hanuman	—	Hindu monkey God, symbolizing selfless Divine service and devotion.
Hare Krishna	—	literally: "Lord Krishna." A devotional chant and the popular reference to ISKCON, International Society for Krishna Consciousness.
Idli	—	small, saucer-shaped, steamed muffins made of fermented rice and lentils.
ISKCON	—	the International Society for Krishna Consciousness, known colloquially as the Hare Krishna movement
J. Krishnamurti	—	(1895 - 1986) one of the greatest spiritual teachers of modern times.
Jeshua	—	the Hebrew name for Jesus, also known as Yeshua.

Jnana	—	Divine knowledge
Karma	—	the materialized result of one's choices and actions; the energy carried forth from lifetime to lifetime.
Krishna	—	a Divine incarnation of Lord Vishnu. the subject of the Hindu epic, *Mahabarata*.
Kundalini	—	life-force energy that ascends through the chakras—the body's energy centers—as part of the process of spiritual awakening.
Lingam	—	phallic symbol used in the worship of Lord Shiva
Linga	—	plural form of lingam.
Mantra	—	a precise vibrational encodement in the form of exacting combinations of sacred words, chanted with a particular pitch, articulation, and tone.
Maya	—	the whole of material Creation and all that is within it.
Murti	—	a statue or form of a Deity, found on the altar in Hindu temples.
Nataraja	—	Lord Shiva as the Cosmic Dancer
Neem Karoli Baba	—	(?–1973) a popular Indian Guru said to be an incarnation of the monkey God, Hanuman.
Nirvikulpa Samadhi	—	absorption in a deep state of sustained Oneness with Divine consciousness, transcending all perception of the material world.
Oneness	—	All That Is.
Osho	—	(1931–1990) Literally: "ocean." The popular name of renowned spiritual philosopher/sage, Bhagavan Shree Rajneesh.
Palanquin	—	a seat, carried by four men, used to transport holy idols during rituals.
Pradakshina	—	a meditative walk encircling a deity, shrine, or holy site.

Presence — a state of Divine connectedness, with full, conscious awareness of it.

Puja — sacred ceremony; an offering of worship.

Rama — an incarnation of the God, Vishnu; the subject of the Hindu epic, *Ramayana*

Ramana Maharshi — (1896 – 1950) a fully Self-Realized Saint, regarded as the modern-day cornerstone of Advaita Vedanta, the philosophy of non-duality.

Ramayana — the ancient epic story of Lord Rama and his beloved, Sita.

Rishis — the saints who documented the Divine transmission of Vedic and Tantric wisdom.

Rudrum — a powerful, sacred prayer to Lord Shiva.

Rupee — the currency used in India

Sadhana — the sustained practice of spiritual devotion and prayer.

Sadhu — a saint; often a wandering holy person

Samadhi shrine — a saint's tomb or memorial

Samadhi — complete absorption in God consciousness

Sambar — spicy vegetable gravy, often served with idlis, a popular South Indian breakfast dish.

Sanskrit — The world's oldest language. The *Vedas*, Hinduism's holy scriptures, were transmitted in Sanskrit.

Sanyassin — a person totally focused in Oneness, who lives within the material world, yet, without attachment to it.

Sathya Sai Baba — (1926 - 2011) a highly revered Indian Guru

Satsang — a spiritual community; a gathering where teachings are given by a Guru.

Self-Realization	—	knowing oneself to Be the Divine Essence of Oneness/God.
Shankhya	—	a school of philosophy that calculates and quantifies the efforts of a spiritual aspirant.
Shiva	—	one of three aspects of God the Father — "the destroyer."
Siddha	—	a person who has achieved perfection in certain spiritual practices through long-term continuous sadhana.
Siddhi	—	a supernatural feat attained through yogic practices
Srimad Bagavatum	—	the ancient literary classic on the pastimes of Lord Krishna.
Swami	—	a person with total mastery of spiritual knowledge through a particular path.
Tantra	—	a sacred spiritual technology leading to union with the Divine
Tsunami	—	a huge deluge of ocean water, caused by an earthquake under the sea.
Tucket	—	a broad, wooden bench where some Gurus in India sit while giving satsang.
Vadescharun	—	an aspect of Lord Shiva
Vedas	—	ancient religious scriptures, received and transcribed by Rishis, which serve as the foundation of Dharma Shastra.
Yantra	—	the physical representation of a Mantra in geometric form.
Yatra	—	holy pilgrimage.
Yoga	—	"union" – a path or discipline leading to Oneness with the Divine.

Acknowledgements

Oneness! Eternal Beloved! With unspeakable gratitude for the journey described in these pages, I dedicate my heart, my soul and my life to the service of your Divine intent! From the very first inkling of this awakening, I reached out to you in prayer, and whispered "Use me!" May that prayer continue to be heard to my final breath!

To the precious family of formless Divine teachers and Gurus who emerged from within me and took my heart by the hand, over the course of decades, on this amazing voyage of Self-discovery—I thank you all with the fullness of my Being! Beloved Amitabh, Lord Rama, Hanumanji, Durga Devi, Arunachala Shiva, The Christ, Neem Karoli Baba, and Ramana Maharshi … there simply are no words!

My very deepest gratitude to Dr. Bindu Purohit, the extraordinary 13th generation Tantric Master from India, whose mystical genius helped pave the way *vibrationally* for my ongoing spiritual unfoldment. The endless wisdom, infinite patience and astounding spiritual technology you've provided to help me negotiate the minefield of physical and nonphysical existence has been, quite literally, miraculous. Dr. Bindu, words could never even begin to express my appreciation for the role you've played in my life. I *pranam* to you!

An enormous thank you to my two extremely dedicated editors, Karen Connington and Lydia Reineck. Together, over the course of nearly two years, you bridged the distance from the opposite side of the world and, with loving care, combed through the mountain of material that has now become this book. With much thanks to you both, this volume has, at long last, come to life!

My deepest thanks to Ed Evans who, from the very inception of this work, added a wealth of technical know-how to more projects than I would dare to count. Ed, thank you with all my heart for your amazing web support, for creating the gorgeous Oneness Flash Movie and the two fabulous Oneness Messages e-mail series, and for always being there for me—despite the time difference to India!

To Daniel Endy, dedicated Oneness Team member and longtime *Oneness* enthusiast, thank you so very much for bringing the exciting world of Facebook to life for our Oneness community! Daniel, your gifted creative touch, generous technical support, and incredible patience with me when it comes to anything remotely technological are so appreciated!

A huge thank you to Joe Meidlinger of CD Technical, Inc., for introducing me to the wonder of audio digital download technology. Joe, I am so incredibly appreciative for your amazing technical know-how, and your enthusiasm in helping me share the *Oneness* audio book, *The Meditations of Oneness* album, and the wisdom of Oneness—in all its forms—with the world!

My heartfelt thanks to S. Janarthanan, the amazingly talented graphic designer and typesetter at Prisma, in Auroville, South India, for the countless hours we've spent designing and painstakingly putting this book together. Jana, I am so grateful to you for your dedication and artistry!

My profound gratitude to the internationally renowned Fusion artist, Rassouli, for your willingness to adapt your exquisite painting, "Greeting the Dawn," for this book cover. And with special, loving thanks to my dear friend, the gifted poet and mystic, Naomi Stone, for all you did to help make that possible.

To my blessed brother-in-spirit, Nick Bunick, thank you with all my heart for your endless encouragement, and for the miracle of a precious "karmic connection" that has bridged the centuries since the times of Jeshua. Nick, your beautiful words about the teachings of Oneness, mentioned in your remarkable book, *Time for Truth,* touched me deeply!

To my three amazing children, Susanna Aimee Finke, Lars Johan Bjorkman and Dr. Lisa Danielle Bjorkman, I am so incredibly proud to be your mother. Thanks for putting up with me for all these years!

To my beloved, long-departed parents, June and Fred Roth, thank you so much for having me—so that the opportunity for this journey of a lifetime might be possible. May you rest in Peace.

My heartfelt gratitude to all the wonderful supporters of the teachings of Oneness, whose generous contributions have made the printing of the first edition of *A Journey to Oneness* possible. My deepest thanks to the following sponsors:

Susanna and Michael Finke, Luigi Zoia, June Ressler, Miriam Trahan, Dr. Manish Lodha, Ivan Kulintsev, Robert Caron, Angelica Christi, Shweta Singh, Kadea Metara, Jim and Jeri Jensen, Karen Massaro, Dorothy Perry, John Godell, Sherry Wilde, Francis Jansen, Melissa Judy, Meredith Davis, Carol Morrison, Ralph Stevens, Joyce Lynn, Karen Chatterson, Judy Dietiker, James Jespersen, Sara Crowder, Prashant Ziskind, Mary Straub, Tom Haley,

Ann McCarthy, Jennifer Weinert, Karen Hillier, Sirin Pojanasomboon, Orla Bourque, Naomi Sinnreich, Kwabena T. Obese-Jecty, Kathleen O'Connor, Dr. Kelli Erickson, Eduardo Pinto, Karl Kukat, Bobby Peck, Ardis Jackson, Cheryl Dressler, Barrie Stone, Doug Coles, John Marshall, Marc Siefert, Mary McMahon, Judy Blaise, Peter Gilbert, Terrie Walsh, John Ryan, Mandy Garner, Rainbow Jenny Wilson, Harriet Beauchemin, Jack Cochner, Lillian Colbourne, Ruth Reese, Philip Weber, Richard Siebert, Preeti Garg, Andrew Hicks, Jessica Ballard, Lee Ann O'Leary, Katherine Simonton, Jean Bryant, Donna Howe Fagan, Mrs. Helen Bonnett, Becky Makool, Lawrence Berry, Allen Cassaw, Anita Miller, Brenda Garma, Julie Scott, Charles R. Quick, Patrick Boehm, Suzette Faith Foster, Jeffrey Lapointe, Arlene and Irvin Gunter, Katherine Dahl, Keith Wilson, Moira Dedrick, Franc Sloan, Scott Bushman, and Jacqueline Donohue.

Thank you one and all for helping to make it possible for me to share the story of this spiritual adventure with the world!

—Rasha

About Rasha

A uthor of the spiritual classic, *Oneness*, Rasha awakened to her inner-calling as a conduit of Divine guidance in 1987. She began working with "Oneness," the Divine Presence we all share, in 1998. As a spiritual teacher with a profound message, Rasha's teachings are universal and focus on the *experience* of the Divinity within each of us. She has dedicated her life to addressing the unprecedented transformation of consciousness that is the hallmark of these times.

American by birth, Rasha now lives at the foot of the mystical mountain, Arunachala, in South India. There, cloistered in blessed silence, life is filled with the joy of transcribing the words of Oneness for future volumes.

www.onenesswebsite.com
Contact: onenessmailbox@gmail.com
Facebook: www.facebook.com/Oneness.through.Rasha